S0-BNG-480

THE DAY PAPER

THE STORY OF ONE OF AMERICA'S LAST INDEPENDENT NEWSPAPERS

GREGORY N. STONE

THE DAY PUBLISHING COMPANY
NEW LONDON, CONNECTICUT

The Day Publishing Company
47 Eugene O'Neill Drive
New London, CT 06320

Printed in the United States of America
First Edition

Editorial Director	The Oldham Publishing Service
Design	Karen Ward
Photo Production	Michael Remus
Indexer	Tammy-Jo Ferdula
Production Director	Mel Seeger
Marketing Director	Eileen Koster

Library of Congress Cataloging-in-Publication Data

Stone, Gregory N., 1943-
The Day paper : one of America's last independent newspapers / Gregory N. Stone.
p. cm.
Includes bibliographical references and index.
ISBN 0-9672028-0-9
1. Day (New London, Conn. : 1881)--History. I. Title.

PN4899.N27 S86 2000
071'.465--dc21

00-024109

To Shinny,

Peter, Christian

and Kimberly

Contents

FOREWORD

FOR DECADES, THE MOST familiar drama in the community newspaper business has been the decline and fall of local ownership. After a family has run a newspaper for one, two, or three generations, there may be no more heirs willing or able to carry on, and an institution that has been part of public life for decades is suddenly in peril. Almost always, the next step is either closing, merger with a competitor, or, in recent years, sale to one of the ever-expanding chains that have now absorbed more than three-quarters of all community newspapers. The independent newspaper, for the most part, has gone the way of the family farm.

The Day of New London is the one newspaper in its corner of New England that has so far remained under local ownership and, what's more, may be able to remain independent for the foreseeable future. Its all but unique status is no accident. It rises in the first instance from the foresight of an owner who looked beyond his own demise to the future of his newspaper as "more than a business enterprise" and as an institution with permanent obligations to its community. Theodore Bodenwein's will placed *The Day* in the hands of a perpetual trust that was charged not only with caring for the newspaper and its employees but with returning a share of its profits, through a charitable foundation, to the community.

Casual readers might not notice that these provisions made *The Day*, at least superficially, much different from other newspapers of its modest size. But over the long run the effects have been beneficial. Less subject to the demand for cutting corners than chain-owned newspapers, *The Day* has been staffed more generously than comparable papers; the results are reflected in the sheaf of professional prizes that it collects every year. Certainly, the newspaper has had good and not-so-good times, and has, like any other strong institution, its share of detractors, but it has given the cities and towns that it serves the benefit of a strong and consistent journalistic presence, offering broad news coverage, a robust editorial voice, and a forum for community opinion.

As a frequent resident of nearby Stonington, I have been reading *The Day* for thirty years. As a journalism critic, I wrote a study of the paper for the 1974 New England Daily Newspaper Survey. But not until I read Greg Stone's extraordinary account did I learn in full the fascinating story of the newspaper's ramshackle origins; of the strength of its foresighted owner, Theodore Bodenwein; and of the difficulties Bodenwein's successors faced and overcame in preserving his legacy. Equally important, Stone vividly chronicles the life and times of the newspaper's heart, its news and editorial rooms.

If this were as far as he went, he would have provided merely a solid institutional history. But as a native he knows his city as well as he does its newspaper, and this work contains much of the often melancholy history of New London and its surrounding towns. Stone shows how the fortunes of the city and nearby areas were interwoven with the destiny of the newspaper. Thus his account will be of interest not only to journalists but to many in the sixteen communities now served by *The Day*.

But the book is worth reading on other grounds as well. More than forty years ago, Allan Nevins, a great historian and former newspaperman, complained that American newspapers rarely took the trouble to record their own history, and when they did they often did it badly, falling short in both comprehensiveness and candor. In this full account, Greg Stone has not only made good use of his extraordinary access to the newspaper's own archives, but has uncovered many additional sources of information. The result is a narrative of extraordinary richness, and worthy in my opinion to stand on the short shelf of superior newspaper histories.

James Boylan,
founding editor of the *Columbia Journalism Review*

February 2000

Introduction

THE IDEA FOR THIS book grew from a lifetime of experiences with *The Day*. As I was growing up, the newspaper was deposited on my family's doorstep every weekday at our rural home in Niantic, Connecticut. Its appearance and texture, its early comics characters, its old column logos and type are engraved in my memory. I delivered *The Day* as a young man at 5 pm every weekday and still remember the route of back roads and country streets I followed on my bicycle, the various odors of different houses, the customers' names, and even the tips they gave me. I went to work for "*The Day* Paper," as everyone called it, in 1966 and have worked there for most of the time since then. Twenty years after I delivered the paper, my children were carriers. The same woman in the business office to whom my father delivered my paper route receipts every week, Virginia Bartnicki, counted the collections from my sons' routes. That is how deep my association with the newspaper has been. This pattern was not uncommon. Whether people admitted to liking it or not, *The Day* was a part of the daily lives of the population that inhabited the southeastern corner of Connecticut.

The late Kenneth Grube, the editor who hired me, filled my memory with stories about the newspaper. These dwelled particularly on the intrigue over the ownership of the newspaper after the death of Theodore Bodenwein, the German immigrant son of a shoemaker who took over the newspaper in 1891 and ran it until his death in 1939. The newsroom was filled with oldtimers, for people who went to work for the newspaper tended to stay until they retired. Their tales were steeped in the lore of *The Day* and New London, the old New England city that was its hometown.

But Grube's stories went deeper than the adventures of legendary *Day* reporters. He was the first one to explain to me the unusual arrangement Bodenwein had created to perpetuate his newspaper and his ideals as a publisher. Bodenwein created a trust to take care of his family while they lived, but more important to preserve the newspaper and keep it out of the hands of publishing chains. Grube, who began his newspaper career in New York state, thought Bodenwein belonged in the annals of great American publishers for having found a way to preserve the independence of his newspaper. And he always thought there was more to the story than had been told up to that time about how the employees, and not Bodenwein's family, wound up in control of *The Day*. Over dry martinis and cigarettes, Grube would grow animated and tell me, "Greg, you've got to write a book about this."

In 1984, I wrote a thesis for my master's degree at Boston University on the newspaper. The title was "A Newspaper Without Stockholders: The Story of The Day Trust." It described how The Day Trust was created, how the men who controlled it (they were all men) carried out the plan, and how the arrangement protected the newspaper from predatory chains. It explained how the arrangement concentrated the earnings on building the newspaper and told of another unusual provision in Bodenwein's will that donated dividends to civic and charitable causes.

The thesis routinely was distributed to new directors and trustees of the newspaper to familiarize them with Bodenwein's will and the philosophy of the trust. Three years ago, I suggested to Reid MacCluggage, the editor and publisher, turning it into a book. My intent was to bring it up to date and bind it into something more substantial than a photocopied thesis. MacCluggage and the directors embraced the idea, but we decided to delve more deeply into the story of Theodore Bodenwein, the newspaper, and the little New England city it served.

When *The Day* decided to publish the book, I was instructed to tell the whole story, warts and all, and I have endeavored to do so. The importance of this story has to do with the disappearance of independent local newspapers in towns and cities across America. Theodore Bodenwein was not the only publisher to look to an unconventional form of ownership to prevent his newspaper from being sold to outsiders. He may have gotten the idea from Frank Munsey, one of the giants of his time among newspaper publishers and an acquaintance of Bodenwein. Another major publisher of that same period, Joseph Pulitzer, attempted to preserve his newspaper, the New York *World,* with a trust. Years later, Nelson Poynter set up the St. Petersburg *Times* under the ownership of an educational foundation. The Columbia *Missourian* is owned and run by the Missouri School of Journalism.

But The Day Trust nonetheless was visionary in 1939 and is unique today. Unlike the others, *The Day* is not owned by a nonprofit foundation or institution. The first obligation of The Day Trust has been to sustain a profitable and influential newspaper, one that is more than an ordinary business enterprise, but a "champion and protector of the public interest and defender of the people's rights." It is ruled neither by stockholders nor a nonprofit foundation. As long as it is profitable, it can pour resources into staff and machinery and spend money covering local news to a degree few other newspapers the *Day's* small size could afford.

The newspaper has been healthy and provident. It fought off competition and made substantial profits. It paid taxes. But most important, it has remained under the control of trustees drawn from the newspaper and the community. It is among the country's last independent daily newspapers. When I wrote my master's thesis in 1984, there were more than 500 independent dailies. When I went to work on this book, there were about 300. When I last checked, there were 265, and the figure is still falling.

This is not an attempt to draw comparisons between the performance of locally owned newspapers and group newspapers. Rather, I have concentrated on telling the story of Theodore Bodenwein and *The Day* with honesty and thoroughness, hoping it will shed light on the inner workings of small daily newspapers, their importance, and the unsung contributions of an obscure German immigrant in preserving their values.

Gregory N. Stone
March 2000

ONE

THE LEGACY

Death today ended the brilliant career of Theodore Bodenwein, publisher of The Day *and an important figure in the New England newspaper field, the sphere of local business and Connecticut politics over a long span of years.*

—*The Day,* (Thursday) January 12, 1939

A HEAVY JANUARY SNOWFALL BLANKETED New London, Connecticut, obscuring the lingering wreckage from a catastrophic hurricane that had laid waste to the city four months earlier. The hazardous conditions on the area's roads did not deter the mourners. They arrived from everywhere, representing all walks of life, filling the pews in the cavernous interior of St. Mary Star of the Sea Church that Saturday morning for the funeral of Theodore Bodenwein, age 74. The son of German immigrants, who had brought him to America seventy years earlier, Bodenwein was the publisher of *The Day*, the New London newspaper he had taken over in 1891, when he was 27 years old, and had operated for nearly a half century. He had died early Thursday morning.

The Day ran a four-column photograph of him on the front page of that afternoon's edition. A rambling and adulatory obituary recounted his rise from impoverished German immigrant to publisher of a successful newspaper. The newspaper wrote: "He was aware for some time that his life's work was done and he looked forward to death calm and unafraid." These words would have had several layers of meaning for the executives and directors of *The Day*. For this inner circle of men, the usual concerns about the future of the newspaper—Bodenwein's life's work and legacy—had been put to rest months earlier. They knew already that they and not the publisher's contentious and idiosyncratic family would take charge of *The Day*.

Theodore Bodenwein's survivors included Edna Bodenwein, then 56, his second wife. His first wife, Jane Muir Bodenwein, better known as Jennie, who won custody of the children in the divorce in 1911, had died five years earlier. Gordon, 45, his son by the first marriage, was a teenager when his parents had divorced. Gordon was closest to his mother and was the sibling most noticeably affected by the family breakup. There was no affection between the coarse and flamboyant Edna and her brooding, Yale-bred stepson. Elizabeth Miles, 42, Bodenwein's daughter by his first marriage, had left the city more than two decades before her father's death, and had married a Cleveland artist. She stayed aloof from the broken family as much as possible.

One or more of the three normally would have inherited *The Day*. But in the final months of his life, Bodenwein and his longtime associates on the newspaper chose another course, one unique in the annals of newspapers, that kept *The Day* out of the family's hands and placed the ownership of the profitable newspaper in a public trust.

The Day had survived the battering of the Great Depression and was financially strong. The nearly two thousand shares outstanding of the *Day's* stock were worth nearly $400,000 in 1939 dollars. Bodenwein managed his business affairs well, leaving an estate worth nearly $1 million. The real worth of his legacy, however, greatly exceeded the newspaper's book value. The newspaper, with its strong emphasis on civic and economic development and local politics and its folksy and popular features and promotions commanded enormous loyalty.

Located in the heart of the city, amidst stores, factories, decaying tenements, and waterfront saloons, *The Day* offered something for everyone: children's features, homespun advice, historic writings about the region, a local political gossip column called "The Tattler," and a list of goals for the city's future, referred to as "A Platform for New London," that ran every day on the editorial page. *The Day* used a projector, known as a spectrograph, to flash timely election results on a giant screen on the face of a nearby building for crowds that often numbered in the thousands. The newspaper provided live accounts of baseball World Series games and prize fights to crowds outside. It used a projector to trace the movements of the base runners. It once had published a "beautiful baby" calendar, with pictures of the city's most attractive new arrivals. It was not a crusading newspaper. Bodenwein emphatically opposed muckraking, which he felt was unnecessary and out of character in a small New England city.

Rather, the newspaper was staid, if not stuffy, and Republican. Bodenwein, who started from nothing, had worked hard to earn a place among the city's institutional power elite, the bank presidents and business leaders. It was largely their point of view on public affairs that was reflected in his newspaper. *The Day* was concerned with "good government," land development, business and industrial expansion, and the furtherance of the institutions that had been bequeathed to the city during periods of prosperity. Bodenwein believed his newspaper should champion the civic virtues that were cultivated in New London's boardrooms.

Across New London and the region of rural towns and suburbs that surrounded it, the newspaper was regarded as more than a business. It was rather an establishment, like the banks, hospital, colleges, and public libraries. "The Day Paper," the name newsboys gave it, was part of the local fabric. High school graduates coveted jobs at the newspaper. *The Day*, delivered just before dinnertime each weekday, was part of people's evening routine for generations. It was no wonder Theodore Bodenwein left this earth in the style of a popular statesman.

THE WEEK HE DIED the flags over the state capital and southeastern Connecticut flew at half-staff. The state legislature abruptly adjourned when it learned of his death. Every daily newspaper in the state eulogized him.

The *Hartford Courant* said, "Mr. Bodenwein made himself what he was, and his life affords another example of what one can accomplish in America by making the most of his opportunities."

The New Haven *Register* proclaimed, "The death of Theodore Bodenwein … ends a strong link in a chain of Connecticut journalists that connects it with the days when copy was written in long hand and there was time to pause and consider well the words before it went down."

The Bridgeport *Telegram* spoke of his dramatic ascent from a disadvantaged childhood. "His life was the kind of success story about which Horatio Alger used to write inspirational stories, only in Mr. Bodenwein's case, we are dealing with truth, not fiction."

Charles Clifton Hemenway, editor of the Hartford *Times*, who had worked for *The Day* early in his career as a reporter and who had remained a close friend, described the legacy his former boss left in his newspaper:

> *The most outstanding visible evidence of Theodore Bodenwein's remarkable qualities was furnished by his newspaper.* The New London Day *is*

> *outstanding among papers published in the smaller cities of the country. It was made so because of his substantial qualities and his genius as a publisher and his hard-headed business sense. These qualities enabled Mr. Bodenwein to rise from a humble start to a place of commanding influence in a community which holds him in highest respect.*

New London, Connecticut, where Bodenwein lived most of his life and built up his newspaper and personal fortune, also acknowledged its debt to him. City Manager John W. Sheedy, who owed his job to reforms Bodenwein and his newspaper backed that created a city-manager form of government, noted, "New London lost its foremost advocate of all that was best for New London."

Mayor Alton T. Miner said, "He probably did more than any one man in the city to promote public welfare and in this activity, he had only sincere motives, sought no personal gain, and desired no praise."

Katharine Blunt, president of Connecticut College for Women, observed that Bodenwein had played a pivotal role in establishing the college earlier in the century.

The tributes were not exaggerations. Bodenwein, the son of a Prussian shoemaker, had indeed made his way from rags to riches. It also was accurate to say that he had assisted in bringing important changes to New London, a city that struggled for generations to find a new identity and source of wealth after the decline of its whaling industry in the 1860s. He had a large role in reshaping the city.

Bodenwein's newspaper provided strong civic leadership for almost fifty years. The newspaper was in the forefront of the effort to locate in the New London area a new college, the United States Coast Guard Academy, a $1 million state port facility, and a major naval base. Bodenwein carried on the tradition of a local civic movement that had in a period of decades produced parks, monuments, schools, and even the elegant Cedar Grove Cemetery, where that January in 1939 he was to be buried next to some of the city's most notable citizens. He used his newspaper to remind the city of the importance of its past, while keeping the community's eyes focused on its material progress.

It is also true that he achieved significant political success. He was elected twice as secretary of the state in Connecticut, was an influential voice in the state Republican organization, and had been considered as a candidate for governor.

However, his most significant accomplishment, the one that would rise above the parochial quality of his life's work in New London, was not mentioned in the eulogies at his funeral or in any of the biographical sketches about him. Yet had it not been for that contribution, Theodore Bodenwein's name would quickly have faded from memory. He would have been merely another successful American immigrant, or just one more conscientious, small-town journalist who fought for what was best for his community and then died and left his newspaper to his family.

But before his death, Theodore Bodenwein and his closest associates at *The Day* invented a solution to one of the most challenging problems confronting 20th century American journalism: the trend of chain ownership that continues today to wipe out locally owned independent newspapers by the hundreds. Newspapers like *The Day* that are rooted in the communities they serve are approaching extinction.

IN 1920, FOLLOWING A period of great newspaper expansion, there were 1,650 independent daily newspapers in the United States. By the time Bodenwein died, there were 1,300. The figure dropped to 850 in 1960, 440 in 1986, 340 in 1994, and 265 in 1999. Bodenwein was acutely sensitive to the threat and feared his profitable newspaper would become a victim of the trend after his death.

The personification of this danger for him was Frank A. Munsey, a newspaper and magazine publisher. Munsey is best known for popularizing the pulp magazine. But in the newspaper industry he was also notorious for having made a career out of buying and discarding newspapers. When Munsey died in 1925, William Allen White expressed the sentiment of many when he wrote:

> *Frank Munsey, the great publisher, is dead. Frank Munsey contributed to the journalism of his day the great talent of a meatpacker, the morals of a moneychanger and the manners of an undertaker. He and his kind have about succeeded in transforming a once noble profession into an 8 percent security. May he rest in trust.*

Munsey wanted to publish his *Munsey's Magazine* in New London to escape labor problems in New York. But the typographical union followed him there, so he abandoned the plans and turned the building intended to be a publishing house into a luxury hotel. Bodenwein knew Munsey personally and respected his genius, but he also feared the predatory forces in the newspaper industry for which he stood.

In addition to Munsey, Bodenwein was probably influenced by Joseph Pulitzer, whose will provided for the founding of the School of Journalism at Columbia University as well as the Pulitzer prizes. Pulitzer also tried, unsuccessfully, to ensure his newspaper, the New York *World*, would remain an independent newspaper under the control of his heirs. The careers of the two newspapermen were strangely parallel, albeit on vastly different scales. Both had come to the country in the 1860s as boys. Pulitzer, seventeen years older, took control of the St. Louis *Post-Dispatch* in 1878 and the New York *World* in 1883.

Pulitzer died in 1911 and his will received considerable publicity. In 1931, less than eight years before Bodenwein's death, the Pulitzer will was broken in a famous court case and the *World* was sold to the Scripps-Howard chain and merged into the *World-Telegram*.

Succession was another problem that weighed on Bodenwein's mind—passing the newspaper to the next generation. Federal inheritance taxes were only part of the problem. He did not trust his family to take over his newspaper. He would be more comfortable to see it in the hands of the executives and directors, whom he had known for years. He was confident they could run it as he felt it should be run. They were more of a family to him than his real family was.

Of his three heirs, Gordon, the son, was the only one who was interested in having a role in *The Day*. He returned to the city and went to work for the newspaper as an editorial writer the summer before his father died. His father hoped that someday his only son would run the newspaper.

That was not to be. The managers and directors of the newspaper did not like Gordon and jealously clung to their reins over the newspaper. They viewed him as a threat to their own control. Charles L. Smiddy, the *Day*'s lawyer, had a particular dislike for him. Gordon was brilliant, but he was also reclusive, and the staff at *The Day* thought he was a bit odd. He was even more out of place in the conventional newspaper of that time because it was common knowledge he was homosexual.

Elizabeth, the daughter, displayed the least interest in the newspaper and New London. She made a life for herself far away, in the artistic circles of Cleveland.

Edna, his widow, was headstrong, fun loving, and a social climber. She possessed a mind for organization, however, and in some ways was the best suited in the family to run a business. But her main interest was preserving the comfortable lifestyle she enjoyed from the newspaper's income.

WHEN HIS HEALTH BEGAN to fail in the summer of 1938, Bodenwein and some of the *Day* directors discussed with Edna the prospect of creating a trust fund and asked her to surrender her six hundred shares of stock in The Day

Publishing Company for that purpose. The stock had been providing her an annual income of about $12,000. Smiddy and the other *Day* directors assured her that she would be well cared for under the arrangement.

The hurricane interrupted these deliberations on September 21, 1938. It was the worst disaster in the region's memory, causing loss of life and extensive destruction. It was the biggest story the newspaper ever covered. Fire whipped by hurricane-force winds raged through the downtown business district for hours. One-hundred-twenty-mile-per-hour winds tore off church steeples and sent small buildings flying. A tidal flood swept over the shoreline, hurling large ships across the railroad tracks and obliterating everything along the waterfront, including the remaining piers from the whaling era and Ocean Beach, a colony of homes and businesses fronting on Long Island Sound.

Bodenwein's condition worsened after the storm. He was hospitalized a month after the hurricane on October 22. There was soon a flurry of activity at the newspaper offices and in the elderly patient's hospital room at Lawrence & Memorial Hospital. Smiddy prepared a final will and Bodenwein signed it in an unsteady hand two days after he entered the hospital. The witnesses included George Clapp, the managing editor of *The Day*, whom the executives had summoned into the hospital room; James M. Shay, a dentist and Bodenwein's close friend; and Josephine Gomes, a nurse.

The six-page document that Bodenwein signed in his hospital room arranging for transfer of ownership of the newspaper to future generations is unique in American journalism. The will contained detailed instructions for the future of his newspaper as well as the legal means to ensure that they were carried out. It disinherited his family and turned the newspaper over to the managers and directors through a trust called The Day Trust.

The Trust resolved for *The Day* three problems that have stumped newspaper publishers in the 20th century. One involves the difficulty of succession: passing a newspaper from one generation to the next without encountering backbreaking inheritance taxes and finding capable successors of similar values willing and able to run the newspaper. Another is the difficulty of newspaper managers to remain true to the motive to run a good newspaper while under the critical eyes of stockholders or owners more interested in profits. And the third is the relentless trend toward consolidation; one that continues to this day and threatens the institution of locally owned newspapers with extinction.

The will would face a legal challenge from Gordon in the 1940s. Gordon would claim the employees had manipulated his father into changing his will and disinheriting the family to seize control of the paper. Forty years later, the Internal Revenue Service would mount another challenge in which the arrangement would prevail.

AS THE WINTER OF 1938-9 approached, Bodenwein's health improved, according to *Day* accounts. He began to display an interest in the business again. Orvin G. Andrews, the *Day*'s general manager, and Bodenwein's other executives kept the old publisher up to date on newspaper matters. Several days before the new year, doctors thought he was strong enough for an unspecified type of operation to relieve his condition.

John J. DeGange, the *Day*'s sports editor, visited him that week. Edna Bodenwein was present. They talked about routine matters at the newspaper. DeGange later remembered that it never crossed his mind that Bodenwein, who had hired him right out of high school in the 1920s, would not recover and return to the newspaper. "We thought he would live forever," DeGange recalled. He was the last employee other than Gordon to see Bodenwein.

On January 12, the publisher suffered a fatal stroke. His son and second wife were at his bedside. Before his death, he requested the presence of a Roman Catholic priest. For most of his adult life, he had been a member of St. James Episcopal Church as were many of the city's elite. But facing death, he returned to the faith of his childhood.

The *Day* office closed for the funeral. The employees in the editorial department sent a large wreath with the numeral 30 in the middle, a symbol newspaper telegraphers had used to mark the end of a transmission and which reporters continued to use to mark the end of their stories. The employees marched together out of the building to the church.

The feelings of the *Day* managers and staff were heartfelt. Rather than repeat his professional and community accomplishments, on the day he died, *The Day* published a highly personal tribute to the man they called "Mr. B." The editorial talked about how employees at all levels felt comfortable taking their problems to him. They marveled at his detailed knowledge of all aspects of the newspaper. Seven years before he died, he had supervised the typesetting for the newspaper's 50th anniversary edition. He fully understood the capacity of the press and the demands of distributing the newspaper. He sometimes sat in on the copy desk, and appeared in all the departments regularly.

> *It may seem trite to say so, to an outsider, yet it is a fact that his influence must long be felt about the newspaper that he worked so*

> *valiantly to establish on a firm basis and that he loved so well. For his memory all of* The Day *family will cherish an affection difficult to describe or define, since it amounted to considerably more than a sincere liking for the man. With it went a great deal of respect, an admiration for the civic ideals and a lively appreciation of the power of his personality. Newspaper men and women are not ordinarily very sentimental folk—or they think they aren't—but the* Day *family has something to mourn today, without trying to hide its grief.*

When the service was over, Bodenwein's casket was carried out of the church by several of his closest employees: George Grout, one of his first reporters and editors who was now a director of the company; Alfred Ligourie, the city editor; Walter C. Crighton, the composing room foreman; pressroom foreman George Kent; Charles O'Connor, advertising director; and John M. Mallon, Jr., political reporter. The long funeral column proceeded along the city's snow-packed streets, along Huntington and Broad Streets to Cedar Grove Cemetery. It passed the grave of his first wife, Jennie, whom he married in St. Mary Church in 1887, when he was 23 and just beginning his newspaper career.

He was buried beside the graves of his first son, Theodore R. Bodenwein, who had died as an infant in 1889, and his parents, Anton and Agnes, who had brought him to America from Europe seventy years earlier and eventually introduced him to New London.

TWO

An Act of Courage

Born in Dusseldorf, Prussia, in 1864, he came to this country at the age of five, the child of German parents in humble circumstances.

—Genealogical and Biographical Record of New London County, 1922

THEODORE BODENWEIN MIGHT HAVE died a German shoemaker instead of a New England newspaper publisher had it not been for an act of courage by his mother and father, Agnes and Anton Bodenwein. Anton worked as a shoemaker in Dusseldorf, in northwestern Prussia, where he married Agnes Bommes late in the summer of 1863.

Dusseldorf is north of Cologne and Bonn, near the border with France. The city was beginning to stir as an industrial center, benefiting from the rich deposits of coal and iron in the region where the Ruhr and Rhine Rivers converge. Iron and steel production, which supported the production of armaments for the "new era" in Germany, would bring substantial growth and prosperity to the city in the 1870s. But those aspirations had yet to be realized when Agnes and Anton celebrated their wedding that summer.

Records indicate that the couple went to the town hall to register their intent to marry late in the afternoon on August 28, just before closing time. They were married in a ceremony on September 3. Agnes was 40, Anton 27. Anton's parents, Karl Theodor and Anna Christina Bodenwein, and several friends signed the marriage license as witnesses. Most of the men, including Anton's father, were shoemakers.

The groom was a handsome and exuberant young man. Later in life, he would be a popular figure in German-American social organizations. We know little about the bride, other than that she was 13 years older. Both were born in small towns about fifty miles south of Dusseldorf, Agnes in Niederkassel, Anton in Luderich.

Agnes was the daughter of Clara Bommes, who raised Agnes and a younger sister, Maria Theresa, on her own. Agnes married Andreas Bachler, a shoemaker, in 1853, when she was 30. They had four children before Bachler left her a widow.

On the day of her wedding to Anton, she was several months pregnant with her fifth and their first child. Five months later, on January 25, 1864, she gave birth to a son, Anton Karl Theodor Bodenwein, who later would use his paternal grandfather's name, adding the final "e" to Theodore. The birth was recorded by the parents four days later. Leonard Peters, 39, a shoemaker, and Joseph Pascher, 37, a wheelwright, signed the birth papers as witnesses.

Europe was going through great changes. The Napoleonic wars earlier in the century had shattered traditional ways of thinking and elevated expectations among the people of Europe. Napoleon's iconoclastic influence was especially tangible in Dusseldorf, which had briefly been a regional capital of the Napoleonic Empire.

Such areas curried favor with the French by subscribing to their ideas and government reforms. The local governments relaxed economic restrictions, eliminated feudal servile restrictions, and centralized the government administration. People were freer to move from one place to another and from one station in life to another, at least theoretically.

But in practical terms, the past still regulated the future for the members of this wedding party. Sons routinely followed their fathers into trades generation after generation. The child born out of this particular bond might very well have followed in his father's and grandfather's footsteps had not history and Anton and Agnes willed differently. The political turbulence of the day and the adventurous instincts of the newlyweds produced a destiny for their son nobody at that wedding probably dreamed of. There were many possible reasons for leaving. Prussia was not secure. Under the leadership of Otto von Bismarck, the central European State was advancing an agenda of uniting the German states into a powerful nation. The resulting upheaval had two practical ramifications for young couples like Anton and Agnes.

Living conditions were often difficult and unpleasant. Rural poverty was driving people from the countryside, but the cities filled up faster than they could furnish jobs and decent housing. Real choices were limited, despite all the liberal rhetoric of the time about freedom. On top of that, there was one matter on which young men had no choice whatsoever: compulsory military service.

The solution for many was in America, where people were free and the streets were said to be paved with gold for everyone who was willing to work. The European cities regularly were pamphleted with news about job opportunities in the United States and agents of American companies roamed the continent recruiting men and women to provide labor for the nation's industrial expansion. General dissatisfaction with life in Germany fed a massive migration to America. The Civil War in the United States only momentarily slowed down this flow. Between 1861 and 1870, nearly eight hundred thousand Germans made their way to the United States.

Three years after Anton and Agnes were married, Prussia and Austria went to war. Anton was drafted and served in that conflict, known as the Seven Weeks' War. He was honorably discharged in 1867. A year later, in 1868, Anton and Agnes decided to join the migration to America. Anton went first. He set out sometime in 1868 on a journey from his ancestral homeland that ended in coastal New England, in Groton, Connecticut. Once he found work and a place to live, he summoned Agnes.

In the spring of 1869, Agnes, clutching her five-year-old son with one hand and her luggage with another, set out for the United States aboard the steamship *Smidt*. The ship sailed from Bremen, a port on the North Sea, to New York. The German port was teeming with people from Central Europe bound for America, as well as entrepreneurs and sharks to help, exploit, or swindle them. Ships like the *Smidt*, a 1,672-ton steam-powered schooner, were built mainly to transport the large numbers of emigrants across the North Atlantic. Though there was some improvement in shipboard conditions by 1869, the ships were still hardly more than cargo vessels.

It helped somewhat that Bremen was efficiently organized for this activity. Emigration was one of the city's major enterprises. Travelers were able not only to secure passage to America in the city but also to arrange for railroad and steamship connections for their journey once they arrived in America and even line up work. Agents, some of them more scrupulous than others, helped with the arrangements and vouched for their clients before the German authorities.

Agnes and Theodore traveled by themselves, according to the ship's manifest. Agnes left behind the four children by her first marriage, possibly with her sister or Anton's parents or her mother if she was still alive. Theodore, at any rate, had two half brothers and two half sisters, the children of Agnes and Andreas Bachler: Gertrude Agnes, who would have been 15; Ann Marie, 13; Andreas, 11; and Carl Andreas, 9. What became of them is unknown. In the various archives of public records that trace the progress of the Bodenweins from Europe to New England, they disappear from sight.

Agnes, by now 45, and Theodore viewed the most significant trip of their lifetimes from the contrasting perspectives of a worried and no longer youthful parent of a young child traveling under difficult conditions and a wide-eyed five-year-old with a keen intelligence and an active imagination. The mother left knowing of the hardships and dangers they faced on the voyage, which took twenty days under the best conditions. Atlantic crossings were still perilous despite technological advances and new regulations to protect passengers.

The *Smidt*, one of the first trans-Atlantic steamers built in a German shipyard, had only recently returned from a harrowing crossing in which the ship came close to sinking in a fierce storm with nearly eight hundred passengers aboard. Several cabins were flooded and many died. The ship had then limped into New York harbor nearly a month overdue in March 1869. This was a period of serious competition for trans-Atlantic business, most of it from European immigrants, and the ship's captain and part owner wasted no time in making repairs, which included replacing the bridge that had washed overboard. The ship made three additional round-trip crossings that year, the first of which brought Agnes and Theodore to America.

The personal discomfort and indignities third-class steerage passengers faced were another matter to worry Agnes. Unaccompanied women had to beware of sexual predators in the crowded quarters. Some lines refused to take women without husbands for this reason. Added to that danger were the notoriously overcrowded, filthy, and unhealthy conditions in the ships. The United States government attempted to address this problem by regulating the number of passengers ships could carry. As early as 1819, Congress passed a law requiring that ships arriving in American ports have no more than two passengers for every five tons of the vessel's capacity. Later, it amended this requirement to base the limit on available interior space. For every passenger, there had to be fourteen square feet of horizontal space. The *Smidt* was significantly overcrowded by both standards. But the authorities did not enforce the regulations. The rules were bent or ignored to make way for this huge deluge of people.

Infectious diseases and fire were commonplace threats. Deaths on board were frequent. The corpses were usually thrown overboard because there was no way to store the bodies in a sanitary fashion. One historian observed:

To immigrants, the ships offered only a cellar on the ocean as crowded and foul-smelling as the slums they had come from or passed through on the way to the landing stage. Since international travelers tended to be either very well off or next to destitution, ship owners took the distinction into close account. This meant silken largesse for the hundreds, on board austerity for the thousands. The division between was immutable. The passengers from the first and second class were advised not to throw money or edibles to the steerage passengers, which could create a disturbance or annoyance.

The situation was so grave that a United States commission put agents aboard ships disguised as indigent passengers. One agent, a woman, reported

Disorder and the surroundings offended every sense. Everything is dirty, sticky and disagreeable. No sick pans are furnished and the vomitings of the sick are often allowed to remain for a long time before they are removed. Worse was the general air of immorality on the part of peeping toms.

But Theodore had plenty to keep his mind off such things. The voyage offered more adventure than hardship. The trip was full of action and stunning sights as they crossed the North Atlantic that spring, arrived in New York, and traveled along the Connecticut shoreline to their new home. America was pulsating with raw and unrestrained energy as it emerged from the Civil War. Material progress was visible everywhere. Such dynamism no doubt fired the imagination of a perceptive five-year-old.

The *Smidt*, carrying Agnes and Theodore, steamed into New York harbor May 5, 1869, entering a scene of astonishing activity on the water and along the shore. The ship passed through the Narrows between Brooklyn and Staten Island and anchored off Staten Island, where it was boarded and inspected by health officials. The passengers crowded onto the decks to get their first glimpses of America. The ship then weighed anchor and moved into the upper bay, between Ellis and Governor's Islands. It was a sight no one would easily forget. A Currier and Ives engraving from the period shows dozens of ships of all sizes packed into that section of the harbor offshore from Manhattan.

This was before Ellis Island was opened as a federal point of entry. Instead, the mother and son set foot in the United States for the first time in the Battery area of New York, at Castle Garden, an early 19th century fortress the state government in New York had turned into an immigration center. Before that, the structure had been a concert hall. Jenny Lind, the famous singer of that time, made her American debut here. The center was on the spot where tourists today buy tickets to visit the Statue of Liberty.

The New York legislature opened Castle Garden in an attempt to remedy the chaos caused by thousands of immigrants arriving daily from Europe. The center was cordoned off from the city to isolate the new arrivals until they could be processed. One purpose this served was to protect the newcomers from mobs of waiting con artists and other predators. Another motive was to insulate New Yorkers from the impact of all the foreign "riffraff" disembarking into the city.

The passengers had to wait on deck for a steamboat to ferry them to the shore. They were crowded aboard these smaller boats, taken ashore to be processed and, with luck, sent forth into the United States through a huge portal facing downtown Manhattan.

Castle Garden looked good on paper. Some of the 19th century lithographs of the center show it as a place of supreme orderliness. In the state Immigration Commission's annual report in 1868, an illustration shows an idealized view of the floor of Castle Garden from a balcony. There are no more than several dozen sedate and neatly dressed persons in the picture. The drawing shows booths where immigrants could buy railroad tickets, exchange currency, and register with the immigration authorities. A view of the exterior in the same report is just as fanciful, with the American and state flags waving over the building and a sign displayed showing the way to a labor exchange for new arrivals. A few carriages are exiting the Battery carrying passengers and luggage. The scene is calm and quite beautiful.

But that was not what greeted Theodore Bodenwein and his mother. Illustrations and first-hand accounts in *Harper's New Monthly Magazine* and other publications at the time describe scenes of mass confusion. There were reports of unmanageable crowds, people sleeping on benches and the floor for long periods, and instances of travelers being fleeced by railroad ticket agents, whose business practices were not under the jurisdiction of the immigration authorities. Despite efforts by the government to prevent it, thieves still maintained posts outside the gates of Castle Garden. The abuses that became rampant at the center and in other ports in the United States led to the federalization of immigration.

The center was railed off into different sections and Agnes and Theodore had to negotiate their way in lines from one spot to another. A *Harper's* reporter observed that the Germans were the best behaved and helped one another get through the ordeal. Germans were then the largest group of immigrants passing through Castle Garden. Agnes and Theodore were among 99,605 Germans who entered the United States there that year.

For all the hassle, the requirements to enter the country were still minimal by today's standards. Agnes was asked cursory questions through an interpreter: Did she have any money? Where was she going? Who was meeting her, and how would she be supported? Once she had cleared these hurdles, she and her son were allowed to leave through a large door into a waiting room, where she, in all likelihood, found Anton waiting. That is how Theodore Bodenwein and more than eight million other European immigrants entered the United States in New York before Castle Garden was replaced by Ellis Island in 1892.

THE DAY AGNES AND Theodore arrived in America and the family set out for Connecticut, a robbery occurred aboard the New York-to-New London shoreline train after the train was disabled in an accident with a train from Boston near the town of Old Saybrook. A German passenger was injured when he tried to thwart the robbery. *The Daily Star* of New London declared in an editorial that lynching would be too good a fate for the robbers. Such crimes were commonplace on the busy routes from the port cities of Boston and New York to the communities of New England.

Many of the travelers were immigrants seeking work in the New England mills. But the trains accommodated more important and elegant travelers also. One of their destinations in the summer was Newport, Rhode Island, a popular seasonal home and resort for the well-to-do. Newport was receiving some competition, however. Promoters in New London were touting the advantages of their shoreline city in eastern Connecticut as an alternative to Newport, hoping the trade would ease the pain from the decline of the whaling industry, the city's most recent source of prosperity. Plush resort hotels, like the Pequot House in the city's south end, were gaining a reputation outside the city for fine accommodations. The hotels dispatched porters and carriages to the steamship docks and railroad terminal regularly for the convenience of their customers.

New London occasionally was the destination of powerful visitors. President Ulysses S. Grant and his family were among the guests at the Pequot House during a stop the year after Agnes and Theodore arrived in town. Many more travelers merely passed through, for this was the main route between Boston and New York. And all the trains had to stop in New London to be loaded aboard a ferry to cross the Thames River.

The winter before, the British author Charles Dickens passed through several times on his way back and forth between New York and Boston on lecture engagements. Dickens complained about how much the train accommodations had deteriorated since his last visit twenty-five years earlier. He referred particularly to the jolting impact when the train cars were transferred on and off ferries crossing the Thames River at New London and the Connecticut River at Old Saybrook.

> *Two rivers (the Thames and the Connecticut) have to be crossed, and each time, the whole train is banged aboard a big steamer. The steamer rises and falls with the river, while the railroad doesn't, and the train is either banged uphill or banged downhill. In coming off the steamer at one of these crossings yesterday, we were banged up such a height that the rope broke and one carriage rushed back with a run down-hill into the boat again. I whisked out in a moment, and two or three after me; but nobody else seemed to care about it. The treatment of the luggage is perfectly egregious.*

The railroad that carried passengers to New London was still relatively new. The section between New Haven and New London had been completed in 1852. A bridge across the Thames River would not be built for twenty years, and ferries were still the only means to get from New London to Groton. Steam and not a team of horses powered the Groton ferry by this time, an innovation introduced by its latest operator, Maro M. Comstock. The ferry was leased to private operators, and New London, which had control, was forever seeking operators who would improve upon the service to create a more favorable impression of the city.

The city that greeted Theodore that May was somewhat the worse for wear. New London had slowed down and grown shabby. It was no longer the busy whaling port it had been earlier in the century. There were probably no more than a dozen large ships in the harbor, and only a few of them were engaged in whaling.

The city's whaling fleet had been decimated by a succession of events. A bank panic in 1857 wiped out many investments. Whaling and banking were closely intertwined because of the money needed to outfit the long expeditions. One of the city's leading whaling captains, Franklin Smith, arrived home from an expedition to find that the bank had foreclosed on his house.

During the Civil War, whaling vessels, which had the advantage of being large and bulky, were impressed into military service as transports, further diminishing the business. This was the fate of the *Nile*, which had set out on a whaling voyage in 1858 and did not return to the city until 1870. In that time, the ship was refitted as a merchant vessel, captured by the Confederacy and used during the war as a prison ship, and placed back into peacetime civilian uses in Hawaii after the Union victory.

By the end of the war, the local whaling fleet had declined to a small fraction of its peak strength in 1846, when there were fifteen whaling companies based in New London with twenty-five hundred men at sea and $2.5 million invested. Some of the whaling companies still in business were turning away from their core trade to new endeavors, such as sealing. Another of the more interesting of these was the guano trade. Whaling ships that once returned with thousands of pounds of whale oil were coming home with their holds full of guano, or bird dung, from the South Sea Islands, to be sold as fertilizer. Much of the remaining whaling fleet was lost when ships were frozen in Arctic waters during the winter of 1871.

Yachts of wealthy New Yorkers appeared in the harbor with greater frequency, but they had not arrived for the season when Theodore and his mother arrived. The interest in the city in becoming another Newport conflicted with the interests of business leaders who sought coarser forms of investment, such as in manufacturing. For decades to come, the city would engage in a debate over whether it should try to replace its declining whaling industry with another industry or concentrate on attracting wealthy summer sojourners and retain a sleepy gentility.

Whaling, for all the romanticism that surrounded it, was a dirty industry, and not everyone regretted its gradual disappearance. Sea captains and merchants who had built fortunes at sea were beginning to enjoy a more luxurious style of life and losing their sense of adventure. They were starting to eschew the coarser activities that brought them their wealth. They built big houses and invested in local real estate.

The city's business and political leaders and the local press agonized over New London's declining commercial condition, and were constantly talking about ways, practical and fanciful, for restoring the city to its proper place and condition. Business leaders advertised in the local newspapers for capitalists to invest in the city. The rundown conditions in New London prompted the Norwich *Daily Advertiser* to run a front-page editorial on the subject. The newspaper lamented the decline of New London as a port and described how the docks along the waterfront had fallen into decay. During a local election campaign, the Republican-run *Star* of New London expanded that characterization to the very moral foundation of the city, blaming the then Democratic city administration. The newspaper, in a clear partisan tone, stated:

There are 100 rum holes, many of them of the lowest tone, in full blast every Sunday. A dozen houses of ill repute are in operation within a few rods of the mayor's office. Extemporized prizefights are a frequent occurrence. In short, everything is going to the bad and New London is gaining the reputation of being the worst governed city in the state.

The city was aware enough of its downward slide to be making an effort to improve. Work was under way on improving the railroad depot, and a number of initiatives were under way to restore commerce and vitality, including a community effort to persuade Yale and Harvard colleges to conduct their colorful annual rowing regatta on the Thames River.

The part of the city the newcomers entered was one of the oldest quarters of New London. It looked out upon the Thames River, where sailing ships rested at anchor or were tied up at docks along Bank Street, the street where the whaling companies and the United States Custom House were located. The city's main business thoroughfare was State Street. It ran perpendicular to the river, becoming a wind tunnel in the winter but a pleasant and attractive promenade in warmer seasons. In 1869, the finishing touches were going onto a luxury commercial building called the Bacon Building. It had marble panels on its façade, huge plate-glass windows with brass casements. This activity was a breath of fresh air in a city that had suffered so many years of decline already.

The railroad terminal was at the bottom of this street, surrounded by old wood-frame and brick buildings. One of these housed the *Chronicle*, one of the two daily newspapers. Ferries and steamboats tied up at docks just north of the station. The layout of the area has not changed much in more than a century. Ferries, rail, and surface transportation still converge there.

The terminal looked up State Street across the Parade, a broad, dusty expanse where the city's early Episcopalians had a church and were buried. It had been used as a drill area for troops during the Revolutionary War. Today, a monument stands there, but in 1869 there was only a flagpole, and one of the topics of debate was how the city could improve this area that many considered an eyesore. The Parade served as the Town Square. Local politicians hung out there to discuss the issues of the day, and reporters trolled the area for news.

The streets were still unpaved, though there were plans to spread macadam on them. The area was the scene of activity of all kinds. It was not unusual to see livestock being herded down Bank Street to be loaded aboard a ship. Seamen from all over the world passed through. That is where Theodore embarked with his parents on the ferry for the mile ride to the other side where the Bodenweins spent the next nine years of their lives.

ANTON FOUND WORK AS a shoemaker and settled down with his family in a rented house in the riverfront village of Groton, on the east bank of the Thames not far from the ferry landing. Groton belonged to New London in early colonial times. It began in 1655 when Cary Latham, who operated the original ferry across the river, built a tavern on the east side of the Thames. The ferry was the lifeline for New Londoners who had property holdings there. Additional settlements followed in the Poquonnock area by James Avery, James Morgan, and others.

Shipbuilding took root along Thames Street, the Groton street that runs along the river. The early shipyards stood near where the Electric Boat Company today builds nuclear submarines for the Navy.

The settlement sat on the edge of an embankment, where the early settlers farmed. The spot overlooking the river was of strategic importance during the Revolution as a coastal defensive position to protect against ships entering the harbor. British troops led by the turncoat general Benedict Arnold attacked the defenses there known as Fort Griswold, causing many casualties and burning many houses and buildings. The story of that battle has been told and retold up to the present and was very much a part of the lore of children who grew up and went to school there.

When the Bodenweins moved into the neighborhood, the area was also beginning to develop as a fashionable retirement community for whaling captains and maritime merchants. These colorful men were Theodore's first neighbors in America. Among the better known was Ebenezer A. "Rattler" Morgan, one of the first whaling captains to use steam power on his ship. He occupied a large Greek Revival House in the Bodenweins' neighborhood, where he speculated in real estate and compounded his fortune. He died a millionaire.

Captain William H. Allen, who lived nearby on Thames Street, had recently returned from a three-year whaling voyage in 1866 with one of the most valuable whaling cargoes on record, nearly a half million dollars. He sailed from New Bedford where his luck became a legend. Sailors declared that whales rose to the surface of the sea waiting to be harpooned by his crew.

Captain Horace Manchester Newbury and Captain Charles E. Allen, also neighbors, commanded boats that were part of the North Pacific whaling fleet that was trapped in an ice flow in the Arctic in 1871, resulting in the greatest loss of whaling craft in history. The tragedy was one of the final blows to the New England whaling industry.

The Bodenweins also lived down the street from Christopher L. Avery, a descendant of a Revolutionary War hero killed at Fort Griswold as well as of James Avery, one of the town's first settlers. Avery also was descended from Cary Latham, the ferry operator and tavern keeper whose grandson still lived in the family house near the ferry landing. Christopher Avery, whose wife only recently had died when the Bodenweins moved into the neighborhood, had traveled to China as a young man, and recently retired as a New York merchant to farm his land along the Thames River. He lived with his three children in a spacious mansion that looked out over the river at New London and a wide expanse of farmland surrounding it.

Just as today's immigrant children often learn English from the culture of television, Theodore was immersed in the idiom and tales of a heroic era in stories that were told again and again about heroism in the Revolution and adventures at sea. That history was still alive, for whaling ships still trickled in and out of the port on voyages that took their crews away from home for months at a time. While whaling was a dirty business that offended the finer sensitivities of many of the local Yankee elite, it was also full of romance. When the ships returned after months at sea, displaying the flags of the whaling firms, church bells tolled, and people crowded to the shore to meet them. The retired old salts told the stories of the past to anyone who would listen.

This drama in New England's second biggest whaling port formed the framework of some of the era's most exciting American literature. It also formed the backdrop for Theodore Bodenwein's earliest perspectives on his world. The society in which young Bodenwein was brought up was class-conscious and stratified. Foreigners like the Bodenweins were not embraced as equals. But unlike the case in Europe, there was an understanding that people who worked hard could earn their way into higher stations in life. But the newcomers had to remember one thing. They had to show the proper respect toward the upper crust and be willing to blend in. An Italian immigrant by the name of Guiseppi Lorenzo made a fortune in the whaling business, but to gain a legitimate place in the upper reaches of New London society, he felt it necessary to change his name to the Yankee-sounding Joseph Lawrence.

Bodenwein noted later in life that most of his learning took place out of school, and one of the lessons he learned well was this: to get ahead, he had to bury his identity as an immigrant, strive to please the important people who surrounded him, and work hard.

He also absorbed a strong sense of the area's history, much of this from those who had participated in it. He ran into romantic heroes in his father's shop and on the unpaved streets of Groton. But he saw they were also practical men who knew the value of a dollar.

Progress was another early influence. Progress was visible to the eye and readily measurable, even in Groton, where the pace was slower than in New London. New houses were rising around Theodore. Work was under way on the railroad on both sides of the river. Ships proceeded in and out of the harbor. And the New London skyline across the river was constantly changing.

By the time he reached his 13th birthday in 1877, Theodore had a complete education, one that expanded well beyond the lessons he learned in the grammar school classrooms. His store of knowledge had been stocked by the trip across the ocean, the discovery of a new world from a child's perspective, and nine years of life living among colorful characters with interesting pasts. But a higher education awaited him across the river in New London where his father took the ferry to buy shoemaking supplies, where the family attended German dramatic presentations in drab, drafty halls, and where newspapers chronicled the advances, setbacks, and aspirations of the times.

THREE

Downcast City & Upbeat Newspapers

These papers and their editors wielded an influence that is immeasurable. There was a character and high-minded sincerity attached to them that has been handed down to modern days as a standard not to be disregarded.

—Theodore Bodenwein, 1896

ANTON'S SMALL SHOEMAKING BUSINESS prospered in the liberating environment of post-war America and his ambition led him to the threshold of another strategic move in life. In 1877, he, Agnes, and Theodore, now 13, gathered their belongings, boarded the local ferry, and moved across the river to New London.

The Bodenweins went first to Blackhall Street, in a working class neighborhood on the outskirts of the city, not far from the red light district, but soon settled in a tenement building on the corner of Bradley and Douglas Streets, closer to where Anton worked. Their neighborhood consisted of crowded and decaying back streets in one of the oldest and busiest parts of the city. Douglas Street, which was wiped from the map by an urban renewal program in the 1960s, was just north of the present location of *The Day.* Bradley Street later became North Bank Street, and today is Atlantic Street, where the *Day's* loading docks are located.

Their new home was near the city's docks and the railroad depot and the neighborhood assumed a gritty character from those influences. Although New

London was going through a business decline due to the receding whaling industry, this remained a busy area, albeit a somewhat rundown one.

Ferries berthed on the half-hour. Sound steamers plowed daily paths between New York's East Side and the steamboat wharves on New London's Water Street. Trains pulled into the terminal every thirty minutes.

Whaling was gradually fading from the scene due to the replacement of whale oil by petroleum products after the discovery of oil in Pennsylvania. But the industry was not completely dead. The whalers still set out from the city on long and heroic voyages that took their crews around the southern tip of South America, to the Sandwich Islands where they picked up supplies and gathered new crews and into the frozen seas of the far north.

The only difference from the past was that there were fewer whaling firms. The declining number did not diminish the risk and heroism associated with these expeditions. A similar heroic sense can be felt a century later when the navy submarines based in the region go out to sea and return. Although the end of the Cold War has reduced the submarine fleet to a fraction of its earlier size, the departure and arrival of the submarines on deployments that last many months are also surrounded with drama and romance.

In 1877, the city was still talking about the 1871 *Polaris* expedition and the death of Charles Francis Hall, an Ohio adventurer. Hall had been attempting to solve a 19th century mystery: what had happened to British explorer Sir John Franklin. Franklin and three ships had vanished into the Arctic in 1845. In 1860, Hall had hitched a ride aboard the New London whaler *George Henry* with Sidney O. Budington of Groton as master. Hall failed to find evidence of Franklin on this try, but met Hannah, an Inuit woman who spoke English. Hannah and her husband accompanied him back to Groton. In 1871 Hall tried again, sailing on the steamer *Polaris* with Captain Budington and the Inuit couple. At Thank God Harbor in the Arctic, Hall and the Inuit Joe traveled by sled to a point farther north than any American had been. They did not find evidence of Franklin and on the way back Hall died. Budington was accused of getting drunk and murdering him but a naval inquiry exonerated him. Reporters had swarmed into the city to cover the story.

When the Bodenweins moved to the city, barrels of whale oil could still be seen on the wharves stacked in rows to season, their bungs, or stoppers, left open for an inspector to smell for the proper level of aging. The streets were unpaved, a source of constant carping in the local newspapers. Farmers brought produce and poultry and pork to markets in the city every day. Not far from the Bodenweins' tenement was the city's most well known bakery, the C. B. Boss

Company, which got started baking crackers for the whaling expeditions. The Boss cracker later was nationally distributed to household consumers.

Anton rented a shop at 49 Main Street, today known as Eugene O'Neill Drive. By a coincidence, his son's newspaper, *The Day*, later had the address of 47-53 Main Street, suggesting that the son built his newspaper where his father's shop was located. But there were half as many buildings on the street then, and Anton's shop, on the fringe of the city's expanding commercial district, actually was several blocks north of the present address of the *Day*.

In his new location, Anton enlarged his business to include the sale of shoemaking supplies. He eventually added pet birds and shoe accessories to his merchandise. The likable tradesman became a popular New Londoner, and his handsome teenage son, who bore a strong resemblance to him, was soon a familiar figure in downtown.

Theodore had received an elementary school education in Groton. The move to New London marked the end of his formal education. To help support his family, he went to work as a clerk in a shoe store, whose proprietor did business with Anton. Soon after he moved to the city, Theodore met George E. Starr, who helped him set a new course.

GEORGE EDGAR STARR WAS born in Middletown, Connecticut, and moved to New London in the 1840s, when he was in his 20s. He ran one of the city's earliest commercial printing companies in a third-story plant on the corner of State and Main Streets, over a confectionery shop. He was one of the city's leading commercial printers and when business leaders decided in 1877 to publish a pamphlet to promote the city as a secondary port or "outport" to New York City, they asked Starr to print the important work.

The pamphlet was the brainchild of John R. Bolles, a New London businessman and secretary of the city's board of trade, who had led an earlier, successful campaign to locate a Navy coaling station near the city. That endeavor turned out to be a critical success for the city, for the station later became the site for the major United States Navy submarine base on the East Coast.

The idea of an outport arose because the New York docks were overtaxed by the explosion of commerce after the Civil War. Some of New London's leaders were becoming worried over their city's languishing economy despite the advantages of its deep-water port. They were desperate for investment of some kind and they seized on New York's problem as a solution to their own. The pamphlet extolled the city's commercial advantages, including its convenient, ample, cheap wharf space, deep waters, manufacturing facilities, abundant water supply, and healthy climate. Seventeen advantages were listed. The publication received favorable comment in the Hartford and New York newspapers.

Starr was in his early 50s when he and Theodore met. He had had a career in printing that spanned twenty years, beginning in 1844 when he briefly had a part in the management of the *Daily Star*, one of the city's first daily newspapers. Starr was a jack of all trades on the newspaper, even doing some of the reporting. This versatility was a characteristic that Bodenwein also would acquire. Starr left the newspaper to open a commercial printing business, which provided Bodenwein with his first exposure to a printing press. At the age of 17, he printed a one-page weekly newspaper called *The Thames Budget*, on Starr's press late at night and sold it in his father's shop down the street.

Starr also opened Bodenwein's eyes to the lore of the city's newspapers, which had begun before the American Revolution, when New London's early printers preached against the British government and expounded on theological issues. In the early 18th century, Thomas Short, the first official printer in the colony, had carried out his duties on a hand press in New London. After Short's death, Timothy S. Green, Sr., of Cambridge became the Connecticut printer. The family published *The New London Summary and Weekly Advertiser*, and later *The New London Gazette* from 1758 to 1844. The Green house, where the press originally was located, is still standing on State Street.

In the 1840s the city's first daily newspapers were appearing. The most durable and significant were the *Daily Star*, on which George Starr had worked and which was a direct descendant of the Green family's newspaper, and its competitor, the *Chronicle*. Both papers appeared during the peak of whaling activity, but also when many adventurers in the city traveled west during the California gold rush. The *Chronicle* published the names of all those men who sailed from the city and Mystic to California in 1849. These included James M. Scholfield, one of the founders of the *Star*. The *Chronicle* lamented, "The gold mania will carry off our most enterprising young men."

Scholfield's abrupt flight from the city and Starr's departure left the *Star* in the hands of David H. Ruddock, a cantankerous and independent man with a knack for stirring up controversy. John Dray, who would later be a printer for *The Day* in its early years under Theodore Bodenwein, was a contemporary of Ruddock's. In a historical sketch Dray wrote for *The Day* in 1896, he had to struggle to find kind words for editor Ruddock:

> *Mr. Ruddock, although not considered a popular man, was possessed of many good qualities, and to some of his trusted employees was*

magnanimous and showed a degree of confidence in his relations with them that, behind his outward manifestations of crankiness—caused many times, as he used to put it, by an ugly liver—there was hidden many evidences of his best qualities of humanity.

Ruddock made himself and his newspaper a lightning rod for controversy through his espousal of the cause of the South and slavery during the years leading up to the Civil War. The sympathies with the South were not unusual. New London had strong economic links with the South. It produced, among other things, cotton gins and bought the South's yellow pine for its shipbuilding. Its whaling firms sold guano, bird droppings used for fertilizer, to southern plantation owners. Ruddock's paper was staunchly Democratic, whereas the *Chronicle* began as a Whig publication and gravitated toward the Republican Party at its outset in the city.

The *Chronicle* operated out of a building on the waterfront, in an area known as Holt's Block, just north of the railroad station. The *Star* moved about the city and in 1867 eventually settled at the corner of Bank and State Streets in a building that overlooked the Parade. The structure is still standing. The *Chronicle's* publisher before the Civil War was a legendary character, Colonel William O. Irish. In his 1896 historical sketch, Dray offered a more flattering portrait of Irish than he had of Ruddock, the *Star* editor:

He (Irish) was in 1860 a man of imposing and knightly appearance, perfect physique, had curly black hair and a mustache, always tastily dressed and would easily bear the palm among the gentler sex as the handsomest man in town. He took an active interest in city affairs and any matter of public concern was incomplete without the colonel as a prominent figure. His paper, with Charles W. Butler as editor, was easily the leading journal in town.

Irish died in the 1860s and ownership of the *Chronicle* passed to Samuel Fox, a more conservative and less aggressive man. The newspaper was quickly eclipsed by the *Star*. For awhile, the competition between the two papers was fierce and was grist for local debates in grocery stores and over checkers matches. The subjects on everyone's minds were slavery in the South and impending civil war, issues that as sharply divided the city as they did the nation.

The *Star* bitterly struck out at Republican leaders and the *Chronicle*. One of the *Star's* favorite targets was Augustus Brandegee, a lawyer, politician, and ardent abolitionist. In 1858, Brandegee, as a municipal judge, freed a fugitive black slave who had stowed away aboard one of the ships that entered the port and who had been captured in the city. The *Star* alluded contemptuously to

Brandegee and the other "black Republicans" who had granted the man, who became known as "Stowaway Joe," his freedom.

Ruddock found himself increasingly under fire as the war approached and antagonisms toward the South and against slavery intensified in the city. Angry mobs protested outside the newspaper's offices, and once threatened to burn the building down, according to a shaken Ruddock. Dray, in his 1896 historical sketch, speculated that Ruddock had made up the story, but there is no question that the editor was under attack. The situation became so precarious for the owner of the *Star* that he hired a police officer to guard him en route to and from his office.

In 1860, when the Democratic Party split over slavery, the *Star* supported the ticket of the Southern wing headed by John C. Breckinridge for president. The paper made light of Abraham Lincoln's candidacy and was incredulous when Lincoln won. The newspaper continued to pound away at the anti-slavery movement in an increasingly shrill voice. The city sponsored a lecture series called the Citizens Course, and when the Reverend Henry Ward Beecher, the famous abolitionist, delivered one of the talks in December 1860 at Lawrence Hall, the *Star* stated in an editorial:

> *He spit out some of his dark-colored wormwood on the present federal administration (James Buchanan) and the South—a deliberate insult to an assemblage of all kinds of persons and all sorts of opinions. His incendiary abolition harangue in times like these is beneath the contempt of every patriot and well-bred person.*

As late as 1862, the newspaper went on record in favor of a resolution, passed by the local Democratic Town Committee, that opposed arming slaves to fight against the South. The pressure eventually got to Ruddock, though, and he underwent a startling metamorphosis. Having entered the period as a rabid pro-slavery Democrat, he emerged during the conflict as a Radical Republican. The rival *Chronicle* described the change in an editorial:

> *Less than a year ago there was a newspaper in this city that did the best it knew how to defend and support the southern rebels and oppose and denounce anything like coercion of the rebels by the government. That sort of thing was kept up until the rising indignation of the community could not longer tolerate it, and then the mayor of the city administered to the nominal proprietor of the sheet a reprimand and a warning. The frightened traitor hired a police officer to go with him through the streets between his printing office and his home, to protect him from possible physical demonstrations such as he felt his conduct might provoke. And*

that, finally, he couldn't stand the pressure but caved in and suddenly came out a flaming unionist—for which piece of treachery to his former friends he was read out of the Democratic party.

Ruddock later reprinted this and responded:

We were out of the city Friday and Saturday. Otherwise we would have given the above lying and malicious paragraph such a reply as its mendacity seemed to warrant.

The war fervor swept aside the differences. The newspapers reported the details as, one by one, the local army units assembled at Fort Trumbull and marched to the docks to be ferried away in steamboats on the first leg of their journey to the Army of the Potomac. Bands played and politicians delivered patriotic speeches. Ruddock, witnessing this excitement, saw the great business potential the war offered to sell newspapers.

The *Star* boosted its circulation by publishing extras at noon every day with up-to-date dispatches on the war. The instant success of this tactic prompted Ruddock to try a morning newspaper, but the experiment was short lived because the advertisers rebelled at the idea of paying double rates.

WITH THE END OF the war, the newspapers were left to their own resources to maintain reader interest. In a few years, the *Chronicle* went out of business and the *Star* faced an uncertain future. These early newspapers had a careless, thrown-together quality about them. They devoted most of their news space to national and international news that came over the telegraph wires, and devoted few of their resources to finding out what was going on in the city. The "local reporter" often was the bookkeeper in the office, who gathered news by taking a stroll across the Parade to find out what the topics of the day were. The local news, such as it was, more often than not was merely gossip, and there was no attempt to verify the information. In fact, it was often labeled as "gossip."

The early newspaper proprietors were most closely in touch with politics, for they were invariably engaged in political activities and used their newspapers to support their political views. The newspapers published the entire speeches of the president and United States senators and the governor's opening addresses to the legislature. Despite their limitations, the newspapers stayed in touch with what was going on in the city in significant ways. Their owners and minuscule staffs were active in many facets of community life. While the editors did not go to great lengths to gather and analyze facts, the news routinely arrived at their offices in the hands of people of all walks of life—judges, doctors, and businessmen. Alfred H. Chappell, a member of a wealthy merchant family and music store proprietor, and his brother Frank H. Chappell, owner of a local coal company, paid daily visits to newspaper offices with tidbits of information and opinions on the issues of the time.

For all their shortcomings, the city's early newspapers presented a picture of what was going on in the city: the shipping news in the active port, the conduct of justice, the city's setbacks and triumphs, the humor and the tragedy. They also provided, with increasing clarity, a running commentary on significant public affairs in their editorials. These principally addressed political issues, but the editors also attempted to instruct the city on the course it should follow to get out of its economic slump. They fought for a railroad through the region and later wondered whether this might have been a mistake insofar as it reduced the importance of the port.

They were the first to notice the decline in the whaling businesses and to focus attention on the deteriorating condition of the docks. They also continually reminded the city of the importance of its past. Each year, the local newspapers retold the story of the Battle of Groton Heights. A weekly, called *The Repository* put out by William S. Starr (no relation to George Starr), published sketches of the city's early history by the woman who remains the city's most distinguished historian, Frances Manwaring Caulkins. After the Civil War, *The Repository* also published articles by a young, charismatic lawyer in town who had recently returned from military service, Major John A. Tibbits.

This local tradition was tangible to Bodenwein's early mentor, George Starr, who still remembered Colonel Samuel Green, the editor and publisher of *The New London Gazette*. Green had lived through Benedict Arnold's attack on the city in the Revolution and did not die until 1859. The stories Bodenwein heard about these men left a lasting impression on him.

The past collided with the present on the *Star* after the Civil War. Without war news, the paper's sales slumped. To remedy this, Ruddock, on the recommendation of Alfred H. Chappell, enlisted the help of John Tibbits.

Tibbits was good-looking, wellborn, and well connected. His maternal grandfather was Ezra Chappell, a wealthy New London businessman in the early 19th century who had made his fortune as a maritime merchant in the West Indies trade. "Uncle Ezra," as he became known, later made even more money as a local banker, stocks and bonds trader, and real estate developer. He had large land holdings in the undeveloped southern end of the city. He was, in short, very rich. His youngest and favorite daughter married Tibbits' father. She died shortly after the birth of her son. Tibbits' cousins, Frank H. and Alfred H. Chappell, were also up-and-coming figures in the city. Both understood the importance of the local press to their business ambitions.

Tibbits attended Williams College. In 1862, he enlisted in the army, where he rose to the rank of major. He was wounded in engagements at Antietam and Gettysburg, neither time seriously. When he returned to New London after the war, he studied law under Augustus Brandegee and practiced law briefly with Thomas M. Waller, a leading Democrat in the city who later would serve as mayor and governor. But Tibbits became active in the Republican Party and developed a reputation in the state and national party for his skills as an orator and tactician. When he had a falling out with Waller, he left the practice to go into the newspaper business.

This was a logical course. From the time he had been in college, Tibbits loved writing and displayed a literary flare. One of his first outlets for this talent had been the weekly *Repository*, next to Miss Caulkins' tales of old New London. He was just what Ruddock needed to prop up the flagging *Star*. Tibbits joined the newspaper as editor and part owner in November 1866.

This was bad news for the local Democrats. It was bad enough that Ruddock's earlier conversion left the party without its own newspaper. Now it had to contend with a beefed up Republican newspaper with a strong and skillful editor. Under Waller's leadership, the Democratic Party had regrouped after the war. It was deriving new strength from the city's growing population of European immigrants, including Anton Bodenwein, who became an American citizen and New London voter October 22, 1878. Without the benefit of a newspaper to advance its views, the party relied on the oratorical skills of Waller, who regularly denounced the *Star* at Democratic rallies and wherever he traveled.

Tibbits added spirit to the political contest with his former law associate by enlarging the *Star* to six pages and enlivening the local coverage. He also wrote all the editorials, which were focused and eloquent.

As the Republican Party came under the influence of business interests and the Democrats in the North became the party of the new American arrivals and the working class, New London became a political seesaw for its two major parties. The *Star*, in its reincarnation as punchy local newspaper, seemed to delight in its coverage of both the serious public issues and lighter stories emanating from this healthy political environment.

In 1869, the Democrats were in control of City Hall, while the Republicans were in power in Washington. That June, a committee from Washington paid a visit to the city to inspect a new railroad bridge across Winthrop Cove. Since there was a Republican administration, it fell to the New London Republicans to make all the arrangements, and these did not include the newly elected Democrats, including the mayor (Tibbits' former law partner) Thomas Waller.

The *Star* reporter reported in detail how the delegation from Washington and the local Republicans enjoyed a sumptuous dinner at the posh Pequot House and then traveled by steamboat to the site of the bridge while the Democrats "looked on glumly from the shore."

But Tibbits was also mindful of the city's failure to progress economically while other cities in Connecticut were taking off as a result of the post-war expansion of manufacturing and trade. Tibbits, in between editorials advancing Republican Party interests, recognized in his newspaper the need for the city to build an industrial infrastructure. He called for the development of a water system and for other public works improvements. He pushed to have the streets paved. And, on another front, he lobbied to persuade Yale and Harvard and their wealthy and influential alumni to bring their boat race to New London.

Ruddock, who had amply feathered his own nest in politics, became a railroad director. His health deteriorated and he sold his interest in the newspaper to Courtland I. Shepard, whose family owned a dry goods business in the city and had other large investments. On May 10, 1873, the *Star*, under its new management, changed its name to The New London *Evening Telegram*. Before the year was out, the newspaper moved into a new building around the corner from the site of the city's first press on Green Street.

Tibbits stayed with the *Telegram* for eight more years, but as time passed, he grew restive. He was not happy with the new partners, whose interests turned out to have more to do with the business of the newspaper rather than its higher purpose. By the time the Bodenweins arrived in New London, he was already giving some thought to operating his own newspaper.

FOUR

THE DAY IS BORN

When The Day *was born July 2, 1881, in a makeshift printing office on*

the second floor of an old stone building on Bank Street,

upon opening its weak eyes to take a peek at its surroundings,

it found New London a small and insignificant place.

—Theodore Bodenwein, 1931

IN 1877, THE YEAR the Bodenweins moved to New London, John Tibbits was appointed customs collector for the port, a coveted federal patronage position. He was 33, dashing in appearance and charming. The appointment illustrated Tibbits' growing stature in the inner circles of the Republican Party after the war. The advancement, coincidentally, occurred during a national scandal over the federal spoils system that originated during the Grant administration. Tibbits' good fortune in politics had emanated from that same provident fountain of political benefits.

President Rutherford B. Hayes tore into the corrupt system, which rewarded party workers with government jobs regardless of ability. Congress refused to pass legislation reforming the civil service system, but Hayes succeeded in arousing the public's interest, and civil service reform clubs cropped up across the United States. The most notorious corruption occurred in New York City, where Hayes angered New York Republicans by dismissing Chester A. Arthur as the collector of the port of New York. Untouched by the scandal, Tibbits carried out his duties at the Custom House on Bank Street and remained editor of the newspaper. It was not uncommon then for editors to have second jobs, usually of a political variety. Politics and journalism were philosophically intertwined. John C. Turner, Tibbits' city editor, was city clerk in New London.

During that time, Tibbits focused the attention of the *Telegram* on the agenda of the Republican Party and the business prospects of New London. His most cherished cause was to bring the Yale-Harvard rowing race, an enormously popular sporting and social event among the fashionable set on the East Coast, to the city. Leaders hoped the race, with its infusion of wealth, would bring prestige and business to New London and further help awaken it from its doldrums.

The newspaper conscientiously documented the goings and comings of the rich, stopovers by the flotilla of the New York Yacht Club on its passage to Newport every summer, the annual count of fashionable guests to visit Pequot House and the city's other summer hotels, and the Long Island Sound excursions aboard steamboats. But the local news scattered in bite-size pieces on the inside pages also provided a picture of the seamier side of the old port, much of it connected with alcohol. Alcohol flowed freely in the city—too freely, many argued. The local temperance movement, centered in the city's churches, staged rallies and lectures regularly. The champions of the cause blamed the rise of alcohol-related problems, including disorderly behavior, family violence, and suicides, on the city's growing population of European immigrants, notably the Irish and the Germans.

On March 22, 1870, a Scottish stonecutter and father of eight by the name of John Muir supported this stereotypical theory and added to the unhappy statistics of alcohol abuse by literally drinking himself into the grave. Muir was 52 when this occurred. The city medical examiner could not resist editorializing in his scrawled notes on the death certificate. He described the official cause of death as "three pints of gin and two quarts of ale."

Muir's widow, Mary, and six daughters and two sons settled in an apartment at 88 Bank Street. Thomas, the oldest son, was 15. John was 13. The daughters were Annie, 18, Maria, 17, Frances, 10, Christina, 8, Sarah Jane, or Jennie, 6, and the baby, Elizabeth, 11 months. The mother took in washing. Maria and Thomas helped support the family by working in the New London Horse Nail Factory. Thomas later worked as a baker. As they grew into womanhood, the girls were pretty and popular with boys. Jennie would grow up to marry Theodore Bodenwein. Thomas died in the 1930s in Norwich State Hospital, an institution for the mentally ill.

The city responded to the outcry from the temperance movement by attempting to license saloons. The law was regarded as a joke for the most part. But it had enough weight to give rise to a lively local debate over whether beer ought to be regulated under its provisions. The *Telegram* argued that it should not be, and tended to make light of the temperance efforts. In one editorial, Tibbits wrote that beer was good because it made people sing. The temperance society responded that it also made them fight.

With all its problems, the old whaling port managed to attract favorable outside attention as the city entered the final quarter of the 19th century. The New York *Sun* ran a feature story in the summer of 1877 on the Pequot Colony, the shoreline resort area developing in the city's south end that was becoming popular with the wealthy set in New York. The story noted the decline in whaling, but speculated that New London might reemerge as an eastern resort destination rivaling Newport, Rhode Island. The New York *Evening Mail* that spring noted in an editorial: "New London now claims to be, and not without good grounds, an important auxiliary port to New York City." The newspaper pointed, in particular, to a new wharf built for the railroads and the city's convenient rail connections.

New London in 1877 still possessed many of the cultural furnishings of the wealthy whaling era. Its lecture and concert halls, built in the flush times before the Civil War, were faded but still attracted famous lecturers and performers who traveled the circuit from Boston to New York. The most popular of its halls was Lawrence Hall, built in 1856 by Joseph Lawrence, the wealthy whaling merchant who had emigrated to America from Italy and changed his name from Guiseppi Lorenzo. The spacious hall was a favorite location for political rallies. Famous lecturers like Harriet Beecher Stowe and Frederick Douglas appeared there, as well as leading entertainers and popular stage shows. But by the 1870s, the building, much like the rest of New London, was run down and in need of repairs.

One of the performers to appear at the hall during this period was Bertie LeFranc, who billed herself as a "pedestrienne." She entertained local audiences that summer by walking 50 miles in less than twelve hours along a course within the hall that had been marked out by a surveyor. The performance received enthusiastic reviews in the local press.

New London claimed a cultural kinship with New York City and constantly had its eyes on the big city. The railroad and the steamboat lines formed a link between the swelling metropolis and the lazy New England port at the eastern end of Long Island Sound. The New York newspapers were dropped off at the train depot every morning for local distribution, and the New London papers paid close attention to New York gossip.

The *Telegram* brought the first word to New London about a scandal involving one of the country's up-and-coming dramatic stars, James O'Neill.

O'Neill, who had just married Ella Quinlan, was sued by a woman in Cleveland who claimed also to be married to him. Nettie Walsh alleged she started an affair with O'Neill when she was 15 and that she bore him a son in 1875. Playwright Eugene O'Neill was born thirteen years later in New York City, the legitimate son of James and Ella. His father bought a summer home in New London in 1884 in part to get Ella's mind off myriad troubles, including memories of this embarrassing interlude in the actor's past.

The efforts by Tibbits and others to snag the Yale-Harvard regatta for New London paid off in 1878. The promoters and the city reached an agreement that April. Both the railroad and the steamboat companies, which stood to profit from the huge crowds and were the major financial interests backing the event, were parties to the deal that Tibbits helped broker.

The first race on the Thames River took place on June 28, 1878, and attracted more than ten thousand spectators, roughly equal to the city's population. Many of these observed the event from twenty-five platform cars lined up along the shore, each carrying eighty passengers. Steamboats carried spectators from New York, and there was a special train from New Haven. Hundreds of others watched from the shoreline and from yachts that filled the harbor. Harvard won the race, which continues as an annual event to this day. The regatta became the occasion for huge gatherings of yachts and boosted business in the local restaurants and hotels.

The same year, 1878, Buffalo Bill's traveling road show appeared in the city and was a huge success, the *Telegram* reported. The city was paving its main streets with Belgian stones at the rate of twenty-five feet a day and building a new road into the Pequot section. Early in 1879, a long legal dispute finally entered the court over whether lager beer was intoxicating, and therefore subject to city licensing. After abundant and contradictory expert testimony, the jury declared a deadlock and the case was thrown out.

IN 1878, TROUBLE BEGAN to brew at the *Telegram*. Readers got their first inkling of unrest that November. A letter was published at the head of the news columns signed by Tibbits and Courtland I. Shepard, president and business manager of the New London Printing Company, noting the unexplained disappearance of John C. Turner, the city editor and city clerk. The letter noted that Turner departed for New York without explanation. It assured the readers that the accounts of the newspaper were in order and that Turner did not appear to be in any financial difficulty.

Turner, 33 at the time, was the son of a New London postmaster and merchant. He had been a reporter for the *Star*, then the *Telegram*, after the Civil War, where he became a close friend of Tibbits. The two had similar tastes in journalism and politics. Turner, like Tibbits, did not get along with the Shepards and in 1878, he had abruptly left for Yonkers, New York, to work on a newspaper there. Tibbits stayed three more years, but his relations with Shepard and the *Telegram* went downhill, not that they were ever particularly good. In the spring of 1881, he quit without warning. He announced his departure in a message to readers on May 21:

> *As my connection with* The Telegram *ceases with this present edition, I desire to say good-bye to the readers of the paper. I thank them for their courtesies and much forbearance. It ordinarily falls to the lot of an editor to incur the censure of more or less the people in the community where he does his work, and I cannot expect to be an exception to the general rule. I should like to shake the hands across the chasm with those who feel that I have done them injustice. I can at least assure them that I retire with kind feelings toward everybody.*

His resignation occurred on Saturday. The following Monday, the *Telegram* stated in an editorial:

> *The editor who succeeds him (Tibbits) assumes his duties with little experience and with a profound sense of his inability to supply the place unfortunately left vacant.*

However, the newspaper pledged to serve the best interests of the Republican Party, even if this meant disagreeing with the party's national leaders. The newspaper would be staunchly opposed to bossism and corruption, it stated, and would make it clear when it favored and opposed local patronage appointments. On the issue of religion, it would take a stand against bigotry. On local issues, it stated:

> *The* Telegram *will identify with all that makes for the city's prosperity and the development of its businesses and commercial advantages. This is the chalk line it has stretched for itself …*

The comments suggest Tibbits and the management of the *Telegram* had political as well as personal differences. Tibbits had been a party regular since the Grant administration and owed his patronage job to his connections with the party bosses. Another factor may have been the different dispositions of the Shepards, who were dry goods merchants, while Tibbits was a polished politician, newspaperman, and somewhat of a romantic.

Whatever the case, Tibbits had the idea of starting his own newspaper in his mind when he left the *Telegram*. He immediately started making preparations, and worked all that spring and summer readying the second story in a stone building on Bank Street for the city's newest newspaper, *The Day*.

Theodore Bodenwein, 17 that year, was busy across town working on his own newspaper venture, a single-page Sunday paper. One edition marked the 100th anniversary of the burning of the city by Benedict Arnold. The publication was printed on George Starr's press at night and distributed in Anton's shop for a penny a copy.

That same summer of 1881, as Tibbits began preparing to launch *The Day*, yet another career in journalism was being launched. At The Young Ladies High School in New London, 17-year-old Charlotte Holloway, the school's valedictorian, and a petite, outspoken Irish beauty, attracted the attention of the *Telegram's* editors with her talent for expression, evidenced in her senior composition, "The Quest of the Grail." The newspaper described her work as "especially mature." Walter Fitzmaurice, an Irishman who replaced Turner as city editor of the *Telegram*, took note of her talents with a pen and prevailed upon the newspaper to hire her as a reporter.

The Holloways were members of the city's growing population of Irish immigrants. Her parents, Thomas and Honora Moran Holloway, had, by their daughter's account, taken part in the struggle for Irish independence and Charlotte retained a lifelong passion for the cause along with her gift for words. Honora, widowed by that time, lived on Cole Street with her three children, Charlotte, Edwin, and Mary. Edwin supported the family as a shoemaker until Charlotte was old enough to go to work as a journalist.

That summer, Henry P. Haven, one of the city's leading whaling merchants, announced his plans to endow a new public library for the city. This signified the start of a remarkable period of cultural expansion in the city, in which new schools, parks, monuments, and cultural and social institutions would sprout from the wealth the maritime merchants had accumulated in the whaling industry.

The 1880s were the start of what many felt was the beginning of a renaissance in the city. But the hope of such change conflicted with the quiet qualities that made the city charming and appealing to outsiders. The dairy farms, old warehouses "still faintly redolent of whale oil," the long, comfortable bar at the Crocker House, a State Street hotel, the fire companies, clambakes, the foghorn, picnics, and patriotic celebrations on the Fourth of July were all ingredients of a New London that attracted the likes of actor James O'Neill to the city from New York. Wrote Eugene O'Neill's biographer, Louis Sheaffer:

By the 1880s, New London presented a drowsy face alongside the Thames River, its life quickened only in summer by a host of vessels on the broad, well-trafficked river, by an influx of tourists and part-time residents. The life of the town otherwise drifted along peaceably in street after street lined with overarching elms; elms flanked even State Street, the chief business artery, as it climbed away from the river and the railroad station.

That was the city into which *The Day* was born, a place of wistful hopes and sleepy contentment. For his newspaper's first home, Tibbits selected quarters in the bawdiest and most colorful section of Bank Street. The street was the main route past the wharves of the whaling firms, as well as part of the post road from New York to Boston. Theodore Bodenwein later remembered it as a "long, unkempt thoroughfare with mostly wooden residences on each side." Many of the residences had been remodeled and contained stores. More than half the city's saloons of the time were located on the street. But the street also possessed an elegance. Wealthy whaling merchants made their homes in comfortable mansions along the street. South of *The Day's* first home was the Revolutionary War era homestead of Nathaniel Shaw, Jr. The Shaw Mansion was the headquarters of the Connecticut Naval War Office at New London and is the home of the New London County Historical Society today.

The street was unpaved, and parts of it did not drain well, leaving it muddy much of the time. In addition to whaling firms and all the related maritime businesses, its commerce included carriage making and repairs, grocery shops, and furniture stores.

Charles L. Klinck, a German immigrant, operated one of the city's most frequented butcher shops there. The amiable Klinck and his family lived over the shop. His daughter, Daisy, later married a young engineer, the son of a traveling salesman from Rhode Island. The young engineer, Waldo Emerson Clarke, would play a major role in New London development.

Tibbits set up his newspaper on the other side of the street from Klinck's market, on the second story of a granite building north of the customhouse where he was the government's top official. The building, which is still standing, had a saloon next door. There were so many watering holes on the riverside of Bank Street proper women made a point of walking on the other side. People entered the newspaper by a flight of stairs on the south side of the building.

John Turner returned to New London to join Tibbits as city editor. However, he only stayed at *The Day* for a year. He left the newspaper and worked on the Paterson, New Jersey, *Guardian* for 15 years and then he returned again to New London to be the managing editor of a weekly, *The Pinnacle*. He also served as town clerk in New London. He was good-natured and widely liked. He died a bachelor, October 28, 1921, at age 76, after he was struck by a trolley car as he crossed State Street. A witness said he started to cross the street near the New London County Courthouse, then suddenly turned back into the path of the train. His death occurred two days before *The Day*, as part of a special 40th anniversary edition, published his reminiscences of working as a newspaperman in New London. In the article, Turner explained some of what was going through the minds of the founders of *The Day*:

> *In the 70s, it was tardily realized that the city needed more than anything else a real newspaper. It had something worth telling of but no medium through which to tell it. Up to that time, New London was not blessed with anything in the journalistic line that was looked upon as a marvel. But that was not wholly due to a lack of effort on the part of the publishers or lack of talent on the part of editors. The public had not been educated to a high standard of journalism and business people had not yet learned the great value of advertisements.*

The men Tibbits brought together to run *The Day* also included William J. Adams, a local wheeler-dealer who had been the circulation manager of the *Telegram* and who leased and managed Lawrence Hall. Adams appears to have put up most of the modest initial capital to start the newspaper, about $2,000.

Tibbits recruited John McGinley, then 37, to be the newspaper's first reporter. McGinley was the son of a New London whaling captain, John "Strong Arm Jack" McGinley. He had been a buyer in the linen business in New York, a job that frequently took him to Europe. But the firm he worked for went out of business and he was unemployed when Tibbits persuaded him to work for him. Bodenwein, who became an adoring friend of McGinley, explained Tibbits' unlikely recruitment:

> *He had no previous experience, but he did have a large fund of information, a ready command of language, a genial personality and a happy faculty of making friends and keeping them. He also had a sense of humor and he took to reporting easily and wrote many clever things.*

William J. Adams prevailed upon Tibbits to hire Adams' brother, Samuel T. Adams, to be the newspaper's chief printer. Samuel Adams had been the composing room foreman at the *Telegram*. William H. Rolfe, a handsome, hardworking telegraph operator, also went to work for *The Day*. Bodenwein later claimed Rolfe went several days without sleep taking down the details of the shooting of President James A. Garfield over the telegraph. But on another occasion, Bodenwein said *The Day* had no telegraph capacity when it started, and got its telegraph news on the train every day in metal sheets.

Bodenwein and Rolfe became good friends, and married sisters, daughters of John Muir, the stonecutter who had drunk himself to death in 1870. Rolfe's wife was Christina Muir. Bodenwein married Jennie Muir. Rolfe would become one of the first stockholders and directors of The Day Publishing Company when Bodenwein incorporated his newspaper in 1909. He died at work of nervous exhaustion related to his demanding and stressful job at *The Day* November 8, 1921, less than a month after Turner was killed by the trolley car.

Tibbits named the morning newspaper *The Day* because he wanted a name that was different. And he was successful. The name of the newspaper has never since rolled easily off the lips of those who pronounced it. Bodenwein was fond of telling a story of the attempts to keep the name secret before publication. The story, as were many of his stories, may be apocryphal:

> *To keep the title a deep, dark secret, not even the compositors setting advance copy were let in, and wherever the name should have appeared, three letters were substituted, whatever letters the imagination or fancy of the writer dictated. The idea on the night of publication was to take these out and insert "Day" This was done, but so well were the dummy titles distributed and so numerous that not all of them were eliminated when the paper went to press very late, with the results that as the combined office force seized the first copies off the press and eagerly scanned the freshly printed pages, there were exclamations like this: 'Hey, stop the press; it says here The Cat, or 'Here's another title that hasn't been changed, The Bat or "Oh Lord, here's one more—The Dog.' At last, however, all the corrections were made, and* The Day *began its career.*

The *Day*'s first press had a capacity for six pages. But *The Day* started out as a four-page newspaper, similar in appearance and content to the *Telegram*, which Tibbits also designed. It was printed on a flat-bed press, in which sheets of paper were fed into the press by hand and printed on one side at a time, two pages to a side. It was powered by a steam engine, which did not work at the inaugural press run, making it necessary to operate the machinery by hand and causing the paper to come out late. *The Day* started out with forty advertisers. The advertising filled ten of the paper's twenty-four columns. The newspaper printed about one thousand copies a day initially.

The Day was launched on the morning of Saturday, July 2, 1881. The lead story had to do with the Yale-Harvard regatta, in which Yale beat Harvard. But during the holiday weekend, *The Day*, with only a skeleton crew, could not muster enough printers to turn out a more significant story that day: The attack by a gunman against President James Garfield. The city's newest newspaper could not get the story in the paper until Monday. Garfield would die from his wounds in September.

That was not the only time that Tibbits and *The Day* failed to report a major story in a timely or complete way. Once one of the newspaper's reporters, John Lynch, got drunk and failed to return with the story about an important Democratic political rally. At another time, Tibbits, who had been reporting on a celebrated murder trial (brilliantly according to Bodenwein), disappeared to embark on political business and missed a critical development in the trial.

The longest running local story at the time had to do with a proposal to build a railroad bridge across the Thames River between New London and Groton. Many feared such a bridge would handicap the campaign to establish a Navy yard upriver from where the bridge was planned. Both the Hartford and Norwich newspapers, as well as the *Telegram*, published fervent editorials against the bridge. *The Day* remained on the fence. The *Telegram* accused Tibbits of being in the pockets of the railroad interests. The Norwich *Bulletin*, a morning newspaper in the city 15 miles upriver from New London, chimed in with brutal personal attacks on the customs collector and publisher.

The *Telegram* charged in an editorial February 1, 1882, that Tibbits compromised his integrity as a journalist for the sake of his business partners: his cousin, Frank H. Chappell, coal dealer and the new president of *The Day*, and Robert Coit, president of the New London Northern Railroad. Late in 1881, realizing that he needed more capital to wage a war against the rival newspaper, Tibbits had gone to Chappell for financial backing. Chappell and several other local businessmen, including Coit, put up $10,000 to form a stock company, The Day Company. John McGinley also owned several shares. The *Telegram's* implication was that Tibbits had been bought out by coal interests and the railroad, which the newspaper said were in cahoots.

With these fresh financial resources, Tibbits inaugurated a new afternoon paper called the *Penny Press* to compete with the *Telegram* and tried new ploys in the circulation war. *The Day* dropped its price to a penny and, taking advantage of the city's new railroad connections to the rest of Connecticut, began selling *The Day* in other parts of the state. The newspaper abandoned the experiment eighteen months later.

The debate over the bridge continued until a compromise was reached in March 1882 that quieted local fears. The community agreed to the construction of a bridge if the railroad would include representatives of the Navy and War departments on a committee planning the project. Tibbits helped broker that arrangement and construction on the bridge began the following year. The bridge, described by *Scientific American* as the largest drawbridge in the world when it was completed, cost $1.4 million. An estimated four thousand people watched as the first trains crossed the river in October 1889.

The Day was more straightforward in its coverage of manufacturing. Tibbits was appalled at what he viewed as the city's failure to attract factories as successfully as other cities in the state. The paper covered existing manufacturing intensely and carried editorials calling for greater efforts to encourage new firms to locate in New London.

Not everything at *The Day* was deadly serious. McGinley made certain of that. To add some color to the news columns, he invented the Jibboom Club. Early in the *Day*'s history, he began writing about the activities of an organization of retired seafaring characters who met regularly, elected officers, exchanged colorful stories, and had spirited debates on various subjects related to the sea. The Jibboom Club formed chapters in surrounding communities and had special events. The Groton chapter went roller skating once, and the *Day* account pictured a rink full of aging mariners rolling ungracefully about the place on wheels. They staged a big parade through the middle of New London once, concluding with a huge catered banquet with a band and clever speeches. Invariably at Jibboom events, there was considerable drinking and conviviality. One account read: "The Jibboom club held its annual meeting on Saturday and elected officers. …. After the election the club adjourned to splice the main brace and get one or two sheets in the wind."

The stories were the product of McGinley's fertile imagination, though the accounts were based on real characters who gathered in a junk shop in the basement of Lawrence Hall, told many of the stories that were retold in *The Day* and drank to each other's health. The feature excited so much interest that in January 1891, a real Jibboom Club was formed and met well into the 1930s. *The Day* devoted a regular column to its activities and reflections on the city's maritime past.

Theodore Bodenwein, who was still living with his parents, abandoned his little newspaper and went to work for *The Day* in November 1881 as an apprentice printer. That's when he met John McGinley, who would become his closest and most influential lifelong friend.

Only seven years older than Bodenwein's father, the good-natured and kindly city editor and business manager of the newspaper became a father figure for Theodore. The relationship flowered when Bodenwein bought the newspaper in 1891. McGinley became the father Bodenwein would have preferred to have, someone who would open doors to New London society for him. The romance of the newspaper world in New London awakened Bodenwein's ambitions, and began to draw him away from his parents and the past they represented. As a 17-year-old printer's devil, he began to peer into a world that valued wealth, position, and power. McGinley, not Anton, had the ability to introduce him into that world. Bodenwein wrote at the time of McGinley's death in 1915:

> *...he was not only my chief reliance and always loyal friend, but almost a father to me. He was years older than I and more experienced in the ways of the world. I was young and impetuous; he was mature in judgment and imperturbable in temperament. I learned to love and respect him. His advice and his good counsel I found well worth heeding.*

Theodore Bodenwein's early employment with *The Day* coincided with the beginning of a spirited competition with the rival afternoon paper, the *Telegram*. The *Day*'s circulation rapidly spread across Connecticut and the newspaper established a firm foothold in New London and the surrounding communities. Its growing influence and its rabid anti-Democratic posture provoked a strong reaction from the *Telegram* and the local Democrats, including Tibbits' former law partner and the local party's last hope, Thomas Waller.

THOMAS WALLER WAS BORN in New York State in 1839. Orphaned at the age of nine by an accident that took the life of his parents, he had been raised by an uncle, Robert T. Waller of New London. He studied law, and entered the New London County Bar in 1861. He served in the Civil War, but was discharged as the result of serious vision problems and returned to New London. He became an icon of the local Democratic Party. The party was looking for someone of his stature, for it had suffered serious setbacks in the Civil War.

Waller's fortunes in politics had risen rapidly as a result of his clear conception of the growing liabilities of the Republican Party, led in New London by Augustus Brandegee and John Tibbits. During and after the war, the Republican organization increasingly fell under the influence of the ascending industrial interests, and Waller could clearly articulate that fact and exploit it to gain support among the city's growing immigrant population. The Civil War had empowered a class of ambitious industrialists who made use of the Republican control of the government to expand their railroads and manufacturing empires. The idealism of politicians like Augustus Brandegee was, in the view of Democrats like Waller, being corrupted by their influence.

The last Democratic newspaper in the city had been the *Star* up until the time of David Ruddock's conversion during the Civil War. Without a Democratic newspaper to back him, Waller was nevertheless able by his own devices and rhetorical powers to rise on the ladder of state politics. He was secretary of the state in 1870-71. He was elected for three terms to the state legislature and served as speaker of the House of Representatives in 1876. And in 1878, he was elected governor.

That crowning achievement invigorated and galvanized the city's Democrats, and led to the successful buyout of the *Evening Telegram* by Democratic investors. On February 12, 1883, when *The Day* was still in its infancy, the *Telegram* announced that it had been taken over by new management, including several prominent Democrats, and would thereafter be an organ of the Democratic Party. The investors included Henry P. Dudley, president of a fertilizer company; William A. Holt, of Holt & Avery, a local grocery and liquor dealer; William Belcher, the judge of probate; Mathias Moran, a railroad executive; and William M. Stark, a lawyer.

Julius Shepard, son of Courtland I. Shepard, who had been president of the New London Printing Company that published the *Telegram*, became the president; Stark the secretary and Moran the treasurer. For a new manager, the backers imported a heavy-hitter from New York, F. Dana Reed, the editor of the Brooklyn *Eagle.*

The Democratic takeover of the *Telegram* intensified the newspaper's battle with *The Day*. But the national political struggle that grew more combative in the 1880s increasingly distracted Tibbits from focusing on his newspaper. Late in 1884, he answered the call of his party to help in the presidential race between James G. Blaine, the Republican presidential candidate, and Grover Cleveland. The year before, he had hired Charlotte Holloway away from the *Telegram* to be a reporter. He was impressed enough by her abilities to leave *The Day* in her hands so that he could go forth to assist his party. He named her assistant editor, and placed her in charge in the fall of 1884.

This was not a mean accomplishment for a woman, particularly one who was at the time only 20 years old. Women editors were surfacing on American newspapers in that period and the women's suffrage movement was in its ascendancy. But New London was still a conservative sanctuary. The *Telegram* complained at one point of women participating in a political rally. But Tibbits believed in women's suffrage, and he admired Holloway, as did Augustus Brandegee, the Republican leader and close associate of Tibbits.

In the political turmoil of 1884, the *Telegram* reprinted an attack that had been made against Brandegee, ridiculing a political speech he had made at the National Republican Convention. Brandegee got his revenge the following year by securing delinquent notes on the newspaper and shutting it down. Bodenwein recalled the day this happened:

> *The time for retaliation had arrived. Forthwith he (Brandegee) secured a writ of attachment and walking down the street, he waved the papers in his hand and after explaining to an acquaintance what the purpose was, exclaimed: 'And vengeance is mine, saith the Lord.'*

Tibbits and Frank Chappell, the president of The Day Company, seized the opportunity and dove into the more desirable afternoon-newspaper market. Bodenwein left *The Day* to help start a new morning newspaper, the *Morning Telegraph*, with three others: Walter Fitzmaurice, the *Telegram's* city editor; John Lynch, who had recently been fired by *The Day;* and George A. Sturdy, who had been the composing room foreman of the *Telegram*. In the next years, Bodenwein assisted in building the *Telegraph* into a formidable competitor to *The Day*. The more lively *Telegraph*, with its collection of strong, young talent, nearly drove *The Day* into the ground, helping set it up for Bodenwein to return and take over ownership seven years later.

FIVE

In Charge at 27

I had always nourished an ambition to own a daily newspaper.

—Theodore Bodenwein, July 2, 1931

THEODORE BODENWEIN LEARNED THE printing trade in George Starr's shop and at *The Day*, but he got his real start in newspaper publishing on the *Morning Telegraph*, which gathered steam with a flamboyant collection of talent from the moment it appeared on the scene in 1885.

Walter Fitzmaurice had already earned a reputation as an aggressive editor on the *Telegram* in its politically driven battle with *The Day*. He also was a local customs collector, as well as a reformed alcoholic and leader in the local temperance movement.

Bodenwein later recalled Fitzmaurice's epiphany as an alcoholic as well as the newspaper culture of the time. Fitzmaurice had enjoyed the company of the small cadre of reporters in town who frequented the local saloons. He was short and frequently found himself on the losing side of barroom brawls. One Sunday morning, he found himself coming to in an alley near a downtown livery stable, hung over and disheveled from a night of revelry and brawling. Bodenwein remembered him saying:

> *I sat in the alleyway watching people come down State Street from St. Mary Church. They were all bright and cheerful and the young men of my age were clean and well dressed and respected. I compared their looks and condition with mine. I was dirty and disheveled in appearance and had a bad headache and but little change in my pocket. I thought to myself, "I earn better wages than most of these fellows and there is not any reason why I cannot be as well dressed and as much respected as they are." The thought stuck. I made a sudden resolve to stop the use of*

> *intoxicating liquor entirely—a resolve which was hard to keep but which I never broke from that day.*

John Lynch worked in the same building with Fitzmaurice at the Custom House as the United States signal officer, the official who issued weather reports with flags on top of the building. When *The Day* had reorganized as a stock company late in 1881, Tibbits had made John McGinley the business manager and hired Lynch as a reporter. Lynch could have learned a lesson from Fitzmaurice. He was talented but drank too much and was unreliable wherever he worked. His long-suffering wife ran a rooming house on Bank Street.

His downfall had occurred during the fall presidential campaign in 1884 when he had been sent to cover a large Democratic rally on State Street. He met a drinking buddy on the way, they adjourned to a saloon and Lynch never returned with the story. The next day, Tibbits had a letter published in the rival *Telegram* apologizing for not covering the event. Tibbits personally fired Lynch.

George Sturdy, a native of Dublin, Ireland, had worked as a printer in New York before migrating to New London in 1881 and going to work for the *Telegram*. A kindly and personable man, he was well liked in the city. After helping start the *Telegraph,* he would leave that paper to help start still another newspaper in New London in 1890, the *Globe*.

Bodenwein claimed the *Telegraph* was his idea and he rounded up the partners. There is more evidence supporting the view that Sturdy, Fitzmaurice, and Lynch started it, and Bodenwein joined them shortly afterwards. Bodenwein and Sturdy took charge of production of the new newspaper, which they originally thought of calling the *Telegram* but decided against it because of possible copyright infringements. Lynch was the city editor and reporter. Fitzmaurice was the business manager and backup reporter during the day. They operated the paper in Sturdy's house on Green Street and for three months printed it at Starr's plant on Main Street. That fall, the partners bought the *Telegram* plant on Green Street for $1,500.

Lynch remained only a short time before falling off the wagon. He went to work on one of the Norwich newspapers before leaving the area for good to live in New York. Fitzmaurice took over as editor and hired Charlotte Holloway to be a reporter and editorial writer. Sturdy managed the production of the newspaper and Bodenwein became the business manager. That became the team that led the *Telegraph* in a spirited rivalry with *The Day* for five years.

This early staff of the *Morning Telegraph* formed a creative chemistry that would characterize the paper, on and off, for its thirty-five-year history. It had a style and flare that was spunky and irreverent toward the local Republican establishment. Except for the period between 1901 and 1906, when Bodenwein, owner of *The Day*, took charge of it in an attempt to control competition, it was both Democratic and populist. But it also ministered to the city's culturally discerning readers in literary and theatrical reviews and news and commentary on the arts. It would be the only newspaper where James O'Neill could get a job for his son, Eugene, when the future Nobel Prize winning playwright was just getting started as a writer. Louis Sheaffer, O'Neill's biographer who studied the two papers intensely for his book, observed the difference in the newspaper's heyday in 1912, when Eugene O'Neill was a cub reporter, "Unlike *The Day*, a more conventional daily, the *Telegraph* encouraged its reporters to get color, humor and some individuality into their writings."

His years on the *Telegraph* from 1885 to 1890 were a professionally and personally fulfilling period for young Theodore Bodenwein. He developed both skill and confidence as a newspaperman, consolidating his knowledge of all the facets of the business. During that period, he met Jennie Muir. Jennie lived with her mother, brother, and sisters on Bank Street, in a two-family house south of the *Day's* original quarters, near what today is Columbus Square. One of Jennie's sisters, Frances, was a clerk in a department store in the city. Her brother, Tom, was a baker. Jennie was in her early twenties. She had dark hair and was fair complexioned. She was pretty and popular, as were all the Muir sisters. She was one of two of the young Muir women to be courted by a New London newspaperman. Her sister, Christina, married William Rolfe, the good-looking telegraph editor of *The Day*. Jennie and Bodenwein, who had grown a stylish mustache and was handsome and somewhat cocky, were married on February 3, 1887, in St. Mary Star of the Sea Church. They moved into a rented house on Tilley Street, in the center of the city.

The *Telegraph* was at full throttle that year. The newspaper reveled in a culture of competition with *The Day*, relishing the opportunities to outshine and outmaneuver it. In the summer of 1887, the *Telegraph* outperformed *The Day* in covering the biggest news event of the *Day*'s history right in its own building. The same newspaper that managed to miss an assassination attempt on the president of the United States let itself be trounced by the rival newspaper in covering the murder in broad daylight of the *Day*'s business manager in the newspaper's business office.

FREDERICK A. S. PERRY was the sort of visitor who spooks newsrooms, a crackpot with a chip on his shoulder looking for the editor. He was a loaded gun, cocked, and set to go off, the type of character reporters and editors try to pass off on to others or otherwise escape. In 1887, Perry lived with his mother on Franklin Street, a pleasant neighborhood lined with Greek Revival houses. The Perry home was on the corner of High Street, at the bottom of a hill from the city jail. Perry was intelligent, well spoken, and well educated. He had traveled widely.

But everyone in the neighborhood knew Fred Perry was odd, not to mention angry. He had been institutionalized several times. Some sympathized and protected him. But others were afraid of him, and most of the neighbors were irritated over the racket of his barking dogs. He behaved strangely in public and this summer of 1887 had been arguing frequently and loudly with his mother. She fled home after one of their fights, sending Perry into a fury. Soon afterwards, a sign appeared in front of the house that caused concern: "Dogs starving in backyard. One from Blossom Kennel, N.Y. This house of 'hell' vacated. Defiance. Tyranny is endured by fools alone."

Word reached *The Day* of Perry's bizarre behavior and Oscar Hewitt, a city judge and part-time correspondent for the newspaper, went to the Perry home to report on the strange events on Wednesday, August 3. Hewitt said he rang the front doorbell repeatedly and went around the house knocking on windows, but there was no sign of Perry, only dogs barking violently inside, probably as a result of the ruckus the reporter was creating outside. Hewitt speculated that Perry either had had a fit or had killed himself. With these frightful but unsubstantiated theories in the back of his mind, Judge Hewitt returned to *The Day* and filed a story for next edition of *The Week*, the weekly newspaper published by *The Day* on Wednesdays.

He described Perry's good qualities, including his intelligence and youthful interest in boating in the harbor. But he added that Perry's behavior had become erratic. Then the judge carefully, or not so carefully, selected words that probably led to the worst tragedy ever to befall *The Day*. He said Perry "exhibited signs of dementia."

It turned out that Perry neither had had a fit nor killed himself. He returned late Friday, August 5, from a trip to New York and read about himself in *The Week* the following day. All weekend, he raged against the newspaper. He climbed onto the roof and shouted his outrage to imaginary multitudes, and as late as Monday morning, August 8, he was observed chopping limbs violently from the trees around the house for no apparent reason. He told a concerned deputy sheriff who visited the house that he wanted revenge on whoever wrote the story. "Fred, don't do anything rash," the deputy counseled him.

Later in the morning, Perry walked into the *Day* office at 16-18 Main Street. There was nobody in the business office in the front of the building. So he stormed into the pressroom in the rear and confronted William Corcoran, one of the pressmen, demanding to know where the editor of *The Week* was. Corcoran told him to get lost. Perry retreated, by now trembling with anger, to the business office, and started toward the stairs to the newsroom when he encountered John McGinley, the city editor of *The Day*. Perry persisted with McGinley in his demands for the identity of the editor of *The Week* and a retraction of the article. McGinley, not wishing to waste his time with a crank and his boring story, told him to wait for someone to arrive in the business office and tell him about his problem, and left.

That someone turned out to be Ezra Chappell Whittlesey, cousin of Frank Chappell and John Tibbits and the business manager of *The Day*. Whittlesey, 54, entered the room with a newsboy, and Perry immediately accosted the manager with his tirades about the story. Whittlesey pointed out he was the business manager and did not have anything to do with the news. Perry kicked the wastebasket near the desk and pulled a gun from a jacket pocket. A pressman who was standing in the door shouted a warning. Perry fired the gun twice at the manager. One bullet entered Whittlesey's chest; the other passed through his arm and lodged in the wall. The wounded man rushed into the pressroom, where he collapsed. Perry walked calmly out of the building and then ran through the downtown, where he was captured by police.

Whittlesey did not lose consciousness, and *The Day*, in its edition that afternoon, held out hope for his recovery in an editorial that also defended the *Day*'s actions in printing the story. In its account of the shooting, *The Day* reprinted Judge Hewitt's story. Doctors were unable to locate the bullet that lodged in his chest, and Whittlesey died of his wounds the following day.

The incident was devastating for the *Day*'s small staff and the community, where Whittlesey was widely known and well liked. The son of a Congregational clergyman, he was, as were Tibbits and Frank Chappell, a grandson of Ezra Chappell, the early 19th century maritime merchant and business leader. He had served on the New London City Council and the local school board, and was chairman of the Republican Party in the city at the time of his death.

The Day published several editorials praising the fallen manager, condemning Perry, and attacking authorities for letting him run loose. Perry was found guilty of second degree murder and sentenced to life in prison but spent most of his sentence in a mental institution. *The Day* wrote:

> *He (Whittlesey) was shot by a maniac, who, if the authorities had done their duty, would not have been allowed to roam about where he could do harm to any body. The shooting carries with it a lesson to them. They should not in the future allow such characters as Perry to be at large carrying weapons to attack any one against whom they may have a fancied grievance.*

But the *Telegraph* wrote circles around *The Day* from its first story the morning after the incident to the funeral and trial. The original account of the murder in the *Telegraph* contained far more detail and color than *The Day* provided and was closer to the picture of the incident that was revealed in Perry's murder trial. The *Day*'s story portrayed Perry's original encounter with McGinley as calm and civil, whereas later accounts at the trial and the story in the *Telegraph* described Perry as highly agitated.

After ferreting out the facts in the murder, the *Telegraph* reporter went to the police station and interviewed Perry in his jail cell and ran a transcript of the interview. Judge Hewitt also visited Perry that afternoon, but only to harangue him for his deed, not to interview him. The *Telegraph* described Perry in rich and detailed prose:

> *He was a tall and gaunt man, about 45, with high, smooth, jeweled, delicate, blue veined temples. His eyes were deep-set under overhanging brows and are on occasion steady or shifty, sparkling or lusterless as the different sensations or sentiments are translated through them for the diseased brain; and that Perry's brain is demented no sane man who converses with him for five minutes can doubt.*

The Day also neglected to mention Whittlesey's connections with the prominent Chappell family in its obituary, as well as his age and his survivors, all details that were contained in the *Telegraph* story. The *Telegraph* also went into more detail about the funeral, and ran a better reasoned editorial that cited the similarities between Whittlesey's murder and one that had just occurred in Washington, D.C., and faulted the laws that allow the mentally ill too much freedom.

Whittlesey's death helped further drain life from *The Day*, which already had grown languid from Tibbits' increasing absences. In addition to practicing law, he was becoming more and more preoccupied with politics and less interested in journalism. He was elected to the General Assembly, where he became speaker of the House of Representatives and surrendered much of the editorial control of the newspaper to Samuel T. Adams, the former *Telegram* compositor. Adams was distinctly unqualified for his new responsibilities.

Above, Agnes and Theodore Bodenwein entered the U.S. through the processing station at Castle Garden, at the Battery in New York, shown here in a Currier & Ives lithograph in 1872. *Eno Collection, Miriam and Ira D. Wallach Division of Art, Prints and Photographs, the New York Public Library Astor, Lenox and Tilden Foundations*

Left, New London's waterfront was still busy when Theodore Bodenwein and his mother arrived in New London. This photograph, taken shortly afterwards in the early 1870s, shows the steamboat *City of Worcester* departing for an excursion to Newport, R.I. The building at the far right is the railroad station. Local ferries sit at the dock.
New London Public Library

Right, Whaling brought great wealth to New London, but the industry's decline after the Civil War led to a long effort to find a substitute. This painting by Thomas Petersen shows the Lawrence Wharf, one of city's busiest berths for whaling ships, in the 1850s.
New London Public Library

Left, The Pequot House, at left, was a popular stop-off for the wealthy visiting New London in the 19th century. The hotel burned to the ground, and Theodore and Edna Bodenwein built a house on the spot. *Lyman Allyn Museum of Art at Connecticut College*

Right, George Starr, New London mayor and printer, introduced Theodore Bodenwein to the newspaper business in his print shop on Main Street. *Picturesque New London*

Above, John Bolles led a drive to locate a Navy coaling station in New London. The station became the site of a major naval submarine base. *New London Public Library*

Right, John McGinley was *The Day's* first reporter, later became the city editor and was a mentor and father figure to Theodore Bodenwein. *The Day*

The Parade, near the New London waterfront, was an important gathering place in the city in the 19th century, as shown in this 1868 photograph of a political rally for presidential candidate Ulysses S. Grant. The view is looking up State Street. The offices of the *Daily Star*, one of New London's daily newspapers at the time, is to the left of the American flag.
New London Public Library

The Bodenweins lived at Douglas and Bradley streets, not far from the present location of *The Day*. The buildings survived until the 1960s, when this picture was taken just before the structures were razed for the Winthrop urban renewal project. The tenement where the family had lived is to the right.
The Day

Upper left, Thomas Waller was a law partner of John Tibbits, but they parted company over politics. Waller later became the only Connecticut governor from New London. He was also a land developer, Ocean Beach having been one of his ventures.
Picturesque New London

Lower left, Augustus Brandegee was an abolitionist and after the Civil War, an early Republican leader in New London. John Tibbits studied law under him, and Brandegee's son, U.S. Senator Frank Brandegee, became a close friend of Theodore Bodenwein's.
The Day

Above, Frank H. Chappell, who operated a New London coal firm, was a cousin of *The Day's* founder, John Tibbits, and an early owner of *The Day.* He arranged the deal in which Theodore Bodenwein took over the failing newspaper in 1891.
Frank H. Chappell III

Left, Charlotte Holloway briefly served as the editor of *The Day* in the early 1880s and later became both a colleague and rival of Theodore Bodenwein on the *Morning Telegraph*. She is shown here as a young staff member of the *Morning Telegraph* and popular lecturer. *Morning Telegraph*

Above, Theodore Bodenwein appears here as the young manager of *The Day*, shortly after he acquired control of the newspaper from the Chappells. *The Day.*

Left, Major John A. Tibbits, a Civil War veteran, started *The Day* in 1881 with financial help from his cousin, Frank H. Chappell.
The Day

Right, Jennie Muir and Theodore Bodenwein were married in St. Mary Star of the Sea Church on Huntington Street in New London in 1887. The church had been built in 1872 to accommodate New London's growing population of European immigrants.
New London Public Library

***bove,** The Day* was born on the second story of this Bank Street, New London, building, shown here in 1873, ght years before the newspaper got started. The building is still standing.
ew London Public Library

THE DAY.

VOL. I. NEW LONDON, CONN., MONDAY, JULY 4, 1881. NO. 2.

THE WORLD BY WIRE.

THE ASSASSINATION.

Latest Reports From the White House.

THE PRESIDENT'S CONDITION

More Precarious This Morning.

A CHANGE FOR THE WORSE.

The Final Dispatches Less Hopeful.

SYMPATHY FROM ALL QUARTERS.

Patriotic Utterances of the Southern Press.

An assassination attempt on President James Garfield occurred after *The Day* went to press with its inaugural edition on July 2, 1881, but because the printers had dispersed for the holiday weekend, Ne London's latest newspaper couldn't get the story to its readers until July 4. The front page of that edit is shown here. *The Day*

With Bodenwein's business skills starting to become apparent and a stable of creative writers and editors on hand, the *Telegraph* charged ahead of *The Day* in circulation and advertising revenue. By 1890, the *Telegraph*, while not listing its actual paid circulation, was claiming to advertisers to reach fifteen thousand individuals. *The Day* did not allude to its circulation, but Bodenwein years later said it had sunk to below two thousand by the mid-1880s, and fewer than one thousand in 1891. That represented a plunge from a statewide circulation of sixteen thousand as a one-cent paper, an experiment that had been abandoned in 1884 because of the high costs of transportation, mechanical limitations, and generally bad management.

Ironically, good fortune for the Republican Party contributed further to the decline of *The Day*. In 1885, Grover Cleveland had become the nation's first Democratic president in a quarter of a century, but the party's hold was short-lived. Partly on the basis of the contentious free trade issue of the time—Cleveland advocated lowering tariffs—Republican Benjamin Harrison of Indiana narrowly defeated Cleveland in the election of 1888. Republicans also gained control of both houses of Congress.

New London Republicans were jubilant at the results, conducting torchlight parades and putting on fireworks displays for several days. The political turn of events charged the battery of *The Day*, which described the Republican festivities as the biggest event, bar none, in the history of the city. The newspaper listed everyone who had specially illuminated his house for the glorious victory. John Tibbits, the editor, would have a special reason to be grateful for the Harrison victory. The following year, he was rewarded for all his hard work for the party with a presidential appointment as United States consul in Bradford, England.

Tibbits' departure probably saved *The Day* from the same fate that befell some of the city's earlier failed newspapers. Had he not left, his growing indifference would have destroyed the paper, for no one would have seen fit to replace him. Nonetheless, Major Tibbits' departure reminded the city of his real accomplishments as an editor and induced a genuine feeling of loss at *The Day* and in the community.

In eight years as editor, Tibbits had struck a chord in the community with *The Day*. He had employed the newspaper to promote his brand of politics, but also to further the cause of progress in New London. The civic spirit to which the newspaper contributed was just beginning to produce results, in the swelling and expanding factories in the city, new office buildings, an explosion of home building, and a surge of philanthropy. The city now boasted about the new railroad bridge Tibbits had been accused of promoting for the railroad interests. And his newspaper's support of building a new train station in front of the Parade, blocking the river view from State Street, was no longer considered an act of diabolical collusion with the railroads. Union Station was designed by the well-known American architect Henry H. Richardson and today is a designated historic landmark. The Yale-Harvard regatta he had fought hard to bring to the city was firmly established in New London, where it remains to this day. He did all this with a sense of decency that won him and his newspaper many friends.

The afternoon he and his wife were to leave on their way to London, just before noon on July 23, 1889, the Major was summoned into the composing room, where he was greeted by a sea of smiling faces of the entire *Day* crew. Samuel Adams, managing editor, delivered a warm and impassioned going-away speech, pointing out the long and kindly relationship between the editor and the employees. The *Day* staff presented the Major a traveling bag and umbrella. Tibbits responded emotionally. The community also felt the same strong feelings. There was a large crowd at the Union Station platform to see the Tibbitses off.

Tibbits was to spend four years as the United States consul in Bradford before returning to New London in 1893 in declining health. Tibbits was only 49, but he had contracted Bright's disease, a progressive and usually fatal kidney affliction. He and his wife arrived back in the city on the first day of summer. He displayed signs of fatigue, but managed to visit with a few friends, including John McGinley. *The Day* noted that on leaving England, Tibbits had been given a warm send-off. "Indeed, no predecessor in the Bradford consular office was ever the recipient of so many evidences of regard or assurances of esteem as Major Tibbits."

The Tibbitses moved back into their old cottage on the northern end of Pequot Avenue, near the river. Tibbits had hoped the familiar surroundings and curative sea air of New London would bring him back to health but his condition worsened. Even before becoming ill, he had confided he bitterly missed New London and had even considered turning down an earlier reappointment.

In the middle of July, he fell into a coma. He died in his sleep at 8:30 in the morning of July 22, 1893. *The Day* wrote that same day:

> *To the wide circle of his political acquaintance, he was the brave soldier, the ardent partisan, the ready and effective orator, the gifted and versatile journalist, the resourceful leader or the dreaded though admired*

> *opponent, but to his intimates, he was the warm-hearted companion, the hopeful and hope-inspiring adviser, and generous friend. To those who knew him best he needs no other encomium.*

St. Mary Star of the Sea Church was crowded for the funeral. His casket was borne into the church by his three half brothers and his three cousins, Alfred H., Frank H., and William S. Chappell. Veterans of the 14th Connecticut Infantry Division, his outfit in the Civil War, attended. A wake took place at his Pequot Avenue cottage. "The service was sad and simple and at its close, the friends departed, leaving the family with their dead for the few hours that remained."

TIBBITS' DEPARTURE FOR ENGLAND in 1889 had been bad news for his cousin Frank Chappell and the other businessmen who owned *The Day*. Chappell, the president of The Day Company and principal investor, could not have been pleased with the paper's declining revenue. Tibbits had responded to his cousin's entreaties as best he could by trimming the expenses of the newspaper. One way he had lowered the overhead was by moving into several smaller and less expensive, but unsuitable, buildings. In truth, the newspaper was going under, and all that kept it afloat was Tibbits' reputation and skills as an editor, as scantily as they were applied to *The Day*. Adams, the managing editor Tibbits named, had little talent for running a newspaper, and *The Day* continued in its downward spiral over the next two years.

While *The Day* was failing, the Bodenweins were beginning to reap the benefits of their citizenship in a rich land. And Theodore was not the only one in the family to benefit. Anton was also prospering, both financially and socially. He expanded his business on Main Street to include a larger line of shoe supplies. No doubt taking a cue from his newspaper son, he began advertising his business more aggressively in both local newspapers.

Meantime, Theodore joined in the local real estate stampede that was engulfing New London as an explosion of new business development and hopes drove up land values. The opportunities for personal profit this created were said to have been one of the reasons actor James O'Neill, father of playwright Eugene G. O'Neill, moved to town. Rich new investors like J. N. Harris, Morton Plant, and New York publisher Frank Munsey would join in. In 1888, Harris developed the Harris Block, a huge building on State Street, which is still standing, that contained large stores, offices, apartments, suites, and quarters for the local YMCA.

Bodenwein, with limited means, at first merely dabbled in the market by buying several lots on Clover Court, a new subdivision on the outskirts of the downtown. In 1890, he gave one to Anton and Agnes, who had lived in rented quarters all their lives. Thus his parents had their own home at 1 Clover Court even before Theodore and Jennie owned their own home. Anton, at 50, was in his glory. America had delivered on his dreams. His business was doing well. His son was becoming important and prosperous. And he, too, had become important as a leader in New London's German-American community. On June 12, 1888, Anton and several of his friends founded a German social club called Harweigh Lodge No. 12. It met twice a month in the Knights of Columbus Lodge. Anton became its first president and was a lifetime trustee.

Theodore was gaining a reputation as a "smart young fellow." He mastered the mechanical side of newspapers, but also showed a natural flair for marketing. Personable, good looking, and earnest, he was a natural promoter. That would be one of his great strengths. He had keen, practical instincts and would become an artist at sales gimmicks to boost circulation and attract advertisers. Color the newspaper blue on Memorial Day. Promote newspaper sales with boat excursions and gifts. Exploit special occasions, milestones, important historical anniversaries. Give people reasons to buy the newspaper and advertisers cause to advertise. This was a knack he began to display as early as his teens, when he had published a special edition of *The Thames Budget* marking the anniversary of Benedict Arnold's burning of the city.

In the local newspaper business, he was a prodigy, and with his talent he had a sizable ego. He was not alone in that regard on the *Telegraph*. Charlotte Holloway, the other prodigy on the newspaper—and a cheeky, outspoken one—could well have helped account for "temperamental differences" Bodenwein later referred to at the *Telegraph*. A conflict between the two might explain why Bodenwein, in his repeated recitations of the history of the city's newspapers, never mentions her despite the fact that she was the first female editor of not one but two newspapers in the city with which he was associated.

Charlotte Mollyneux Holloway was among the most gifted writers ever to work on New London newspapers. Tibbits recognized her flair with words and encouraged her to leave the city and pursue a higher destiny. While she was still working for *The Day* in 1885, he wrote a recommendation that read:

> *Miss C. M. Holloway has been connected with the editorial department of* The Day *for the past two years. She is a ready writer and has, in my opinion, a decided aptitude for newspaper work. During the last presidential campaign, in my absence, she had full control of the editorial*

columns and acquitted herself with much credit. She has done nearly all the editorial work on the paper for many months past and has also written the book notices which have always been well done. I cheerfully recommend her to any editor who wishes a bright and competent assistant.

At age 25, while she was an editor of the *Telegraph*, she wrote a biography of the Revolutionary War hero Nathan Hale, which was published in New York. The opening words illustrate her descriptive powers and enjoyment of words:

Seldom has there been a more gloriously beautiful day even in the month of the poet's song, of flowers and sunshine, than was the 6th of June, 1755. The sun shone with a steady warmth agreeably tempered by the west wind which sent scurrying whiffs of perfume from the roses on its every breath and the birds sang in the leafy bowers with the joyous fullness and triumph of the spring, whose promise was beginning to mature into fulfillment. From the hour that the first pale tinge of pink streaked the gray sky, the thrifty New England farmers had been busy in the fields, and though they silently drank in the elixir of the sparkling day, there was small converse about its beauty.

She could just as easily skewer a target of her anger, as she had the British, one of her favorite targets, in an editorial in *The Day* in 1884 in connection with the conflict over Ireland:

One thing (Queen) Victoria has ever done, she has regarded her colonies, and Ireland, as so many producers, and the governments as supply agents who should help fill the coffers which must sustain profligate sons and dissipated sons-in-law.

She could also be coolly analytical, as she exhibited in an editorial defending organized labor in the January 22, 1888, *Telegraph*:

Education of the masses is the only means to surmount the obstacles in the way of a proper assertion of the rights of labor and the recounting of this principle is the best feature in the constitution and methods of the Knights of Labor.

Holloway never left New London, instead she stayed and supported her aging mother and sister, Mary. She remained as an editor and editorial writer on the *Telegraph* until it folded in 1920. She was active in Republican politics, got a state job as a labor investigator in the 1920s and 1930s, and wrote frequent letters to the editor on various subjects. She died in a nursing home on February 3, 1939, nearly a month after Bodenwein's death.

While Holloway was comfortable there, the *Telegraph* was growing too small and limiting for Bodenwein in 1890. And if that was not enough to shake him loose from his first management position, a personal tragedy may have provided the extra push he needed to move on. Jennie bore their first child in September 1889. It was a boy, and they named him Theodore R. Bodenwein. The couple moved from the center of the city into a rented house on Williams Street, a quieter section of town, to begin raising Theodore's first male heir. Early the following fall, the child became violently ill. For a week the parents watched helplessly as the baby suffered from high fever, diarrhea, and spasms before dying of infant cholera less than two months after his first birthday.

Shortly afterward, Bodenwein sold his interest in the *Telegraph* to Walter Fitzmaurice for $3,000 and for a year "cast about New England" for a newspaper of his own. New London was a small city, and Frank Chappell and the directors of The Day Publishing Company were no doubt aware of his movements and quick to spot an opportunity to rescue their investment in *The Day* with help from the young man whose competitive spirit had helped to nearly sink their newspaper. Bodenwein had already demonstrated the ability to get a newspaper off the ground. Maybe he could rescue a dying one. Bodenwein, at the same time, had heard that the owners of *The Day* were looking for a buyer. They were predisposed to welcome an offer from this young man. Indeed, they were eager for such a break.

The drawback was that Bodenwein, for all his skills, did not have enough money or collateral to buy a newspaper. The Chappells were sharp Yankee businessmen. They were not in business for charity. They had sunk thousands of dollars into the paper when their cousin John Tibbits had run it and they hoped to recover their investment. But Frank Chappell was smart enough to recognize there were few within view other than Bodenwein who could save the newspaper, with its dwindling circulation and advertising revenue.

Bodenwein met with Frank Chappell at the Chappell Coal Company's New York offices in the summer of 1891 with an offer to buy the newspaper: "I hardly expected that it would be considered seriously. But to my gratification, it was taken up and accepted in a few months." They signed an agreement on September 5, 1891. Bodenwein bought *The Day* for $25,000 with $3,000 down and a mortgage for the rest with The Day Company, which retained control until the loan was paid off at $1,000 a year. Bodenwein was not permitted by the agreement to change the politics of the newspaper without the consent of the directors. In other words, he would have to switch parties and become a Republican, something he did without hesitation.

SIX

BOOM TIMES

I had neither great experience, influential friends nor financial backing. Most of my education had been acquired outside the schoolroom. But I had plenty of faith in New London's future. As I look back upon the episode, I must also have had plenty of assurance as to my own judgment.

—Bodenwein, September 13, 1916, on his purchase of *The Day*

THE FIRST THING THE 27-year-old Bodenwein did after he took control of *The Day* was to fire managing editor Samuel T. Adams. Adams, who was 38, went to work for the Meriden *Journal* in Meriden, Connecticut, for several months but returned to the city and purchased a part interest in the *Daily Globe*, a new newspaper established in 1890 by two businessmen, Samuel Prince and Oliver Gardner. George Sturdy joined him as a partner at the *Globe*, which became one of Bodenwein's biggest worries as well as the *Day*'s last local competition. The paper did not go out of business until 1930, ten years after the demise of the *Morning Telegraph*. Samuel T. Adams died in 1935 at the age of 82. The two founders of the *Globe* also died in the decade that saw the death of their newspaper. Prince died in 1930 and Gardner in 1936.

The *Globe* described itself as an independent newspaper, reflecting the growing drift of newspapers away from partisanship in their news coverage. Both *The Day* and the *Telegraph* maintained their party loyalties, but also placed a greater emphasis upon objective journalism and the concept of fairness. The *Telegraph*, though considered Democratic, asserted its independence in the following droll way:

The ownership of this newspaper is in the hands of a Democrat and two Republicans, each with different personal bias and political tendencies as between conservatism and progression. Among these three are the editor and the business manager.

Our genial chief newsgatherer, Joseph Smith, 2nd, is a wildly enthusiastic Democrat. For a long time he said his prayers as often as not to Camp Clark, and his democracy is just as much a part of his religion as his ideas of marriage .... There is a faint suspicion that Mr. Smith attended the Democratic rally the other night.

Another important staff official may be a mixed socialist and anarchist. As far as possible we keep him off political assignments. But he writes satirical verse which is so really clever we feel obliged to print it, albeit with the blue pencil in pretty constant use.

There are others.

Out in the composing room we have every shade of political opinion known since Brutus slew Caesar.

The resurgence of newspaper competition reflected a growing prosperity and exuberant confidence in New London. The mood was accompanied by a growth in population and potential readers. Bodenwein took on the unassuming title of manager. For under the terms of his agreement, he still did not own the newspaper. His agreement with The Day Publishing Company was, as he later pointed out, more of a lease until he paid off his debt.

The Day occupied half of a two-story stone building at 92 Bank Street owned by the Chappells that had been a family house. It was not big enough and was poorly arranged to accommodate a newspaper. Nor was the printing press adequate to serve the growth Bodenwein envisioned. Frank Chappell and the directors had invested nearly $15,000 in a new press for John Tibbits' gambit at statewide circulation. The press had the speed to print twelve thousand copies an hour, but only four pages at a time. Printing an eight-page edition required two press runs, and the papers had to be folded by hand.

Newspapers were becoming more sophisticated in their content and adding pages filled with news, splashy display advertising, and features. This was particularly true of the expanding number of evening newspapers, which were becoming the equivalent of what today would be called family entertainment centers, with comics, puzzles, romantic stories, and homespun advice as well as news and editorials.

Bodenwein realized he needed additional pages to build readership and enlarge advertising revenue. So the second significant step he took was to purchase a new press from a local firm, the Babcock Printing Press Company. The new press, mounted next to Tibbits' white elephant, could turn out two thousand additional copies an hour, and Bodenwein thought that set-up would be more than sufficient to carry him into the future. He was happily wrong. Within two years, he put the press up for sale and went shopping for an even bigger and faster machine.

Bodenwein made another, more subtle change in *The Day* that reflected his deeper purpose. He redesigned the newspaper's familiar nameplate, making the old English lettering of *The Day* on the front page bolder and changing the pictorial logo completely. The old symbol of *The Day* showed the sun rising over a bucolic Thames River with mythological figures on either side and beneath it the words, "It Shines for All." It was oriented to the 18th century. The new logo, which first appeared October 17, 1891, gazed into the 20th century, picturing the icons of the city's recent progress: its new railroad bridge, "the biggest of its kind in the world," and Union Station. No additional words were necessary. Bodenwein had assumed the risk of buying *The Day* with a strong faith in the future of the city and its material progress, which was most tangible to the city at the time in these things of brick, steel, and mortar. He was determined from the beginning not only to be part of that progress, but also to contribute to it as its foremost booster.

He set out with a clear plan to develop a loyal readership from the shambles in which he had found the *Day*'s circulation. At the time, the local newspapers published full-page advertisements in the City Directory that made extravagant, unsupported claims about circulation superiority. Bodenwein challenged the veracity of these assertions. He published what he claimed were hard figures and opened the *Day*'s circulation books to anyone's scrutiny. He also announced a new creed for the newspaper, the *Day*'s first clear statement of purpose in its history:

> *Good Evening! Have you Read* The Day*? This is a question very often heard. Why? Because there is always something bright and interesting in* The Day. *It excites comment. It is handsomely printed, ably edited and prints more news and better stories than any local newspaper. It is the Paper of the People, because it is published in the evening, a time when a majority of the people do their reading. It is a newspaper that prints the news. It is Republican in politics, but it fights fair. It is full of vim, vigor and vitality. It is winning new friends and new patrons every day. It is for the interests of New London, first, last and all the time and it confidently believes that in its efforts to give this city the best paper ever printed here, it will be firmly and loyally supported by the public.*

Bodenwein said he found peddling advertising in person distasteful. But he pitched in anyway. He had no choice because there were few others to do the job. And under his direction, the newspaper aggressively marketed its advertising columns and services as a commercial printer. The head of the *Day*'s printing shop was John Dray, who was considered one of the best printers in the city. The quality and quantity of Dray's work had helped Tibbits keep the newspaper afloat. *The Day* continued to promote itself as a commercial printer that offered the best machinery, type, and printers in town. The newspaper also packaged and marketed the new genre of classified advertising under the heading "Wants of the People" and underbid the other local newspapers on rates.

John McGinley stayed on with Bodenwein as a reporter and city editor. Bodenwein brought aboard John G. Crump, a municipal judge and former editor on the *Evening Telegram*, to head the editorial operation. The rest of the staff consisted of ten typesetters, eight of whom were young Irish women, two pressmen, and an office boy, who was sort of circulation manager. Bodenwein's brother-in-law, William Rolfe, one of the few people in his wife's family he seemed to like, later became Bodenwein's telegraph operator.

At first *The Day* purchased its telegraphic news in precast, six-column metal plates shipped every morning from New York and sawed up into pieces of whatever *The Day* chose to use. Bodenwein had put most of his initial efforts into local news gathering. But he quickly saw the advantages the unfolding wire services offered, purchased various part-time telegraphic services, and eventually became the second newspaper in Connecticut to subscribe to the full service of The Associated Press. He did so in time to provide the *Day*'s readers with timely dispatches from the Spanish American War.

McGinley played a crucial role in Bodenwein's plans. Though he was not a particularly good editor, he "wielded an exceedingly clever and facile pen" and had excellent reporting skills, Bodenwein later said of him. Bodenwein came to believe that the best reporters were "local boys" who knew the city because they had grown up there and had many contacts.

> *A good reporter is hard to find, at least one who will fit into the life of a small city like New London, where it is necessary for him to know everyone in order to go after news.* The Day *is fortunate in that respect. The best material for reporters is found among New London boys. Once taught the fundamentals of reporting, they are better able to pick up news than those secured from other cities.*

John McGinley also was Bodenwein's closest confidante and friend and remained so for twenty-five years. At 47, he was only a few years younger than Anton Bodenwein was, and Theodore Bodenwein remembered years later looking upon McGinley almost as a father.

Bodenwein's warm sentiments toward McGinley later were mirrored in a young Eugene O'Neill, who became a close friend of two of McGinley's sons, Arthur and Thomas. Art was a young reporter for Bodenwein at the same time O'Neill was a cub reporter for the rival *Morning Telegraph*. The amiable and unflappable editor and family head in O'Neill's play *Ah! Wilderness* was modeled partly on John McGinley, who had become city postmaster by the time O'Neill came to know him.

Bodenwein's family life, as was the case with O'Neill's, was in marked contrast to McGinley's. Agnes, his mother, already was elderly by the time Bodenwein was a teenager. Bodenwein's family life had been further stunted by his having gone to work when he was 13. This was more often than not the case for the children of working-class families because free schooling only existed for the primary level. He had no brothers or sisters. The McGinleys, in contrast, were a large, and from all appearances, conventional and happy family under John's tutelage.

It was generally true of Bodenwein's adult life that he found more fulfilling companionship in his work than he did at home. The men and women he associated with professionally at all levels became more of a family to him than his real family. It became a working credo for him that his employees, including the newspaper's many news carriers in later years, were part of the *Day* "family," which meant his family. This sentiment was particularly pronounced toward McGinley.

McGinley, son of whaling Captain Strong Arm Jack, filled an emotional void for Bodenwein, but the genial man-about-town also served an important practical purpose as well. He helped Bodenwein move into the upper chamber of New London society and power. McGinley, who was well liked and wired into all the right places in town, became Bodenwein's ticket to the social clubs, political inner circles, and boardrooms of New London, where the German shoemaker's son still had yet to be admitted in 1891. Bodenwein's circles of friends and colleagues up to that point in his life were many of them untouchables in the city's Yankee caste system. The Chappells recognized him only as a business partner, not yet as their equal. His forgetful and dowdy mother-in-law, the aging widow Mary Muir, and Jennie's troubled brother Tom were not people he would bring to dinner with any of the Chappells. Anton and Agnes were similarly disadvantaged socially despite their more comfortable circumstances. Bodenwein did not necessarily look down upon these people, but he surely realized he needed to get out of their shadow to achieve real success in New London.

John McGinley was ubiquitous and beloved in New London society. He helped organize The New London Board of Trade, a precursor of the Chamber of Commerce, to drum up business and industry for the city. He became a warden in St. James Episcopal Church, the house of worship for many of the city's blue bloods. Bodenwein abandoned his Roman Catholic upbringing to join the prestigious and socially prominent church. In the years that followed, many of Bodenwein's underlings at the newspaper, Baptists, Methodists, Roman Catholics, and agnostics, would experience a similar spiritual conversion.

McGinley also belonged to the prestigious Thames Club, to which all the local barons of business and industry belonged. He was named to all the important ceremonial committees, including the citizens' group that was formed in 1896 to arrange the city's 250th birthday party. And he was a leader in the local Republican organization. He was elected city treasurer in 1892. Bodenwein may have been McGinley's manager on *The Day*, but McGinley was Bodenwein's social and political manager and guide to New London's elite, providing the boost, advice, and connections the young German immigrant needed to get into Victorian New London's fanciest parlors.

But before that could occur, Bodenwein needed to prove himself to the city with *The Day*. This took him only a few years. He increased the size of the newspaper to sixteen pages and added many new features. He ran baseball box scores on the front page, the forerunner of a full sports page that would appear later, concentrating on the local baseball league and other New London sports. He compartmentalized the news into state, local, and county sections, giving each a clever sounding title. The roundup of brief state news items was referred to as "Assorted Nutmegs." He began gathering news from far-flung correspondents in the little hamlets outside New London, places with quaint names like Mystic, Niantic, Noank, Poquonnock Bridge, and Salem. He introduced coupons, which readers could cut out to obtain free or reduced price items like books and sewing patterns. He ran roundups of news from fraternal organizations in town, of which there were many. He started publishing all the births and marriages each year on New Year's Eve. The object was clear: to amuse, entertain, and inform families as they gathered in the evening and to make *The Day* a part of the family routine. He was relentless in going after new readers and advertising. *The Day* promoted its advertising next to the editorial column every day. The promotions were mostly of a gentle variety, designed to explain the utility of advertising and how to best exploit it.

Bodenwein's cardinal approach to building advertising was to establish a faithful readership, and there was practically nothing he did not try to achieve this. *The Day* more than made up for its generally pedestrian content with sales gimmicks. The newspaper regularly published special editions on occasions that were important to the community. One of the most striking of these was a special edition honoring the Grand Army of the Potomac on the occasion of a 30th reunion in New London. For two days in June 1895, thousands of Civil War veterans gathered in the city for that occasion, and Bodenwein provided them with an airy, attractive six-page souvenir edition, with dozens of crisp and beautiful photographs of local scenes and scenes from the war along with a schedule of events. It cost five cents. As he did at every opportunity, he used the publication to tout the advantages of life in New London:

> *New London is halfway between New York and Boston and within 50 to 100 miles of the large cities of Connecticut, Massachusetts and Rhode Island. The air is pure and bracing, moderate in temperature, epidemics are unknown and the most frequent cause of death is old age.*

Bodenwein also sponsored expense-paid family steamboat excursions and picnics for readers late in the summer, just before the start of school. All one had to do to participate was clip a coupon from *The Day*, which entitled a family to one round trip to Bushy Point, a resort and picnic area where there were swings, a merry-go-round, picnic tables, swimming, fishing, and clamming. One of his most idiosyncratic promotions was a "Beautiful Baby Calendar," which contained pictures mailed in of New London babies and was distributed to readers on New Year's Day. An editorial in January 1897 called attention to the feature:

> *New London has been from way back to the present time famed for fair women and brave men and there has been no change to make the representatives of the city any less enviable in that particular. We not only have pretty babies, but lots of them.*

New London responded enthusiastically. The *Day's* circulation tripled in the first three years under his control. With evidence of growing readership, Bodenwein persuaded the Chappells to invest in a new headquarters for the newspaper. In this endeavor, he found it more advantageous to deal with Alfred H. Chappell, who had joined his brother Frank in the coal and towboat businesses. Bodenwein found Frank Chappell crusty and difficult to deal with.

Alfred, who was a church organist and musician, on the other hand, seemed to Bodenwein the kindlier of the two and appeared to have been a softer touch and more attuned to Bodenwein's theories about building the newspaper. The theories boiled down to the idea that to make money *The Day* needed to spend money. Bodenwein described this approach a couple of years later as "a combination of practical economy and lavish expenditures." Behind it was the notion that *The Day* would grow with New London by promoting New London's growth. Bodenwein felt a personal loss when Alfred died in 1912:

> *In the early days of my ownership of* The Day, *now 20 years ago, when I had assumed a heavy burden of indebtedness, I came to close business relationship with him. A few words of encouragement were worth much to me in these days and I will always cherish his kindly attitude toward me. As a newspaper publisher, necessarily linked in my work with every movement seeking to improve social and industrial conditions in New London, I cannot forbear giving testimony to the leading part Mr. Chappell has always taken.*

Everybody who had the money was building new and more ostentatious buildings in New London in the 1890s, so it was not a wild stretch for the Chappells to embrace Bodenwein's speculative proposal. Any real estate venture was considered a good investment in the building frenzy taking place. Everybody was a real estate genius and financial wizard.

In 1893-4, the Chappells built a four-story building *The Day* would share with the Boston Furniture Company. It was located on the east, or water, side of Bank Street. Years later, on May 10, 1921, after *The Day* had left it, the building was badly damaged in a fire suspected to have been arson. It was finally completely destroyed by the fire caused by the 1938 hurricane. The Chappell Building had been *The Day*'s first real home, and for Bodenwein it was a forceful symbol of the newspaper's progress. *The Day* had sold the Babcock press and installed in the new building a brand new Cox Duplex Press, custom-made for the newspaper, that was capable of printing five thousand, five hundred copies an hour. Bodenwein bought a second new press for the job-printing department. "Money," the newspaper declared in its breathless announcement of its move up in 1894, "was no issue."

Instead of steam engines, which were dangerous and unreliable, *The Day* used electric motors to power its presses. For the first time in his life, Bodenwein had his own office, with a desk suitable for a newspaper executive and a boardroom table with matching chairs to meet with his staff and important visitors. The newsroom had desks, telephones, typewriters, and a library with enough room for twenty more years of bound editions of *The Day*. There were pictures of famous journalists from Europe and America hanging on the wall.

Bodenwein announced the move in the May 12, 1894, edition of *The Day*. He was like a child with a new toy. Characteristically, he exploited the occasion to promote himself and *The Day*:

> *For more than two years, in fact ever since* The Day *threw off the shackles of conservatism and started to occupy its proper place in the front row of journalism, the old quarters in the stone building hampered the efforts of the management of every department and change became an absolute necessity .... The success of* The Day *in the past two years has been nothing short of marvelous. From a moribund journal, it has been transformed into the most influential in its field and territory, first in news, first in circulation, first in advertising patronage, first in enterprise, first in everything that goes to make up a successful modern newspaper.*

He declared that his success was consistent with his original plan to give New London the best newspaper it ever had. He compared the occasion to the time the original Hoe Press was introduced at the New York *Sun* and important figures in the newspaper world were invited in to witness its first run. He recounted the history of the New London newspapers, from the *Connecticut Gazette* on, and placed himself and *The Day* at the cutting edge of that tradition. And he invited everyone in town to visit the new building and see the presses in nightly open houses that lasted for weeks.

The Day could not completely escape its curse of personal misfortune. In July 1894, two months after the newspaper debuted in its new building, Bodenwein's editor, Judge John Crump, locked himself in an upstairs bathroom in his house on nearby Tilley Street and took his life with a shotgun. Crump had been showing signs of depression for months. He returned home from the Thames Club that Tuesday in a fit of despair and, in a frenzy, tried to slit his jugular vein with a razor in the kitchen before his horrified wife and father-in-law. When his father-in-law stopped him, Crump went upstairs and shot himself. Crump's death was the second untimely death of a popular and respected *Day* executive in seven years. Like Ezra Whittlesey, who had been murdered in the *Day* offices, Crump was well liked in the city. He had replaced Tibbits as editor of the *Evening Telegram* when Tibbits left to start *The Day*, and had remained in that position until the newspaper was taken over by the Democrats. When he was appointed to the Court of Common Pleas in 1889, he was the youngest judge serving in Connecticut. Bodenwein greatly admired his writing skills, although he often complained the judge was distracted from his newspaper work by his responsibilities on the bench. *The Day* nevertheless commented on his death:

> *In the shadow of the sudden tragedy that has robbed the city of one of its best intellects and kindliest natures, the associates of John G. Crump on* The Day *feel the impotence of mere words to express what he was to the journal on which they labored together with a common purpose, nor the measure of his abilities as a writer. From early manhood he had warmed to the profession of journalism and felt the fascination of the pursuit, but to him its power was never underestimated nor did he take up the pen without feeling the responsibility that inspires the born journalist.*

Bodenwein struggled in these years to build a staff equal to the mission he had set for *The Day*. His misfortunes had an almost tragicomic quality to them. An editor he hired from a Massachusetts newspaper to replace Crump turned out to be suffering from tuberculosis and tried unsuccessfully to commit suicide before dying of the disease. That editor's successor found *The Day* too provincial and boring for his tastes, and left to work for Joseph Pulitzer in St. Louis. Bodenwein was more successful in trusting to his instincts to hire local men. In 1894, he enlisted Walter Slocum, a clerk in a State Street dry goods store, as a reporter. Slocum turned into a more reliable hire, and in 1896, Bodenwein made him the *Day*'s managing editor, a post he held until 1925 when he was appointed postmaster.

Bodenwein meantime took a hands-on role in the editorial operations of the newspaper, and began writing the newspaper's first local column, which he called "The Tattler." The column was a rambling product filled with gossip about local politics and city life. It had sparse literary merit, but that did not stand in the way of its popularity. It was successful because of its directness and personal approach. Bodenwein inaugurated the column in 1892, but turned it over occasionally to Walter Slocum from 1902 to 1921, when Slocum left the newspaper. Bodenwein resumed writing all "The Tattler" columns until shortly before his death in 1939.

"The Tattler" was always written in the first person, and dealt with a subject or many subjects in a breezy, conversational, often wry style.

"Why don't the park commissioners get busy with the parklet at the Parade?" demanded "The Tattler" in one column. "It was turned over to their tender care some time ago, and they have apparently forgotten it entirely." In another, he told the rambling story of a case of mistaken identity a hotel clerk had related, observed the extent to which horse carriages were being replaced by electric cars, and described the grace and kindness of an Irish immigrant he sat next to on a trolley car. Local politics and city development were frequent topics throughout the history of the column. The writer entered the living rooms, parlors, and kitchens of the city at suppertime and carried on a personal conversation with its readers. "The Tattler" was another way Bodenwein found of connecting *The Day* with the family life of the city and cementing loyalty.

A later *Day* manager, Orvin Andrews, copied Bodenwein beginning in the 1920s with a personal column called "Sentences by the Judge," borrowing the nickname the staff had given the bespectacled business manager for his stern, judicial demeanor.

New London was upbeat in the 1890s, although a national financial panic in 1893 would dampen that spirit. The national depression of the 1890s gave rise to local relief and charitable activities, which *The Day* supported in its editorial columns. But life went well for the Bodenweins in those years. Late in 1892, Jennie became pregnant with their second child. Gordon Bodenwein was born May 10, 1893. The couple moved into a larger rented house on Montauk Avenue, a wide boulevard that extended into the south end of the city, where the growing number of prosperous families were settling. The couple began looking at property to buy in that prestigious end of town.

In 1896, Bodenwein threw the weight of his newspaper behind an event of significant local importance. For more than a year, the city had been preparing to celebrate the 250th anniversary of its incorporation. The observance was to be more than merely a historical commemoration. The city anticipated it as a coming-of-age party, in which to celebrate its new promise of prosperity and progress. Bodenwein saw it as an opportunity to make his own debut into the circles of power and prestige in his adopted city. He was 32.

SEVEN

POWER BROKER

Charles B. Whittlesey of New London presented the name of Theodore Bodenwein for secretary of state, his speech being interrupted by the arrival of Mr. Roberts. The latter was immediately presented to the convention. He thanked the convention, briefly reviewed state and national issues and bespoke a solid vote for the entire ticket .... Mr. Bodenwein's nomination for secretary of the state was at once made by acclamation.

—*The Day,* September 14, 1904

NEW LONDON HAD BEEN settled in 1645 and 1646 by English Puritans led by John Winthrop, Jr., the son of the Massachusetts Bay Colony governor. The new arrivals referred to the area as Pequot, after the powerful Indian tribe that dominated the area until 1637. That year English troops and warriors from the Mohegan and Narragansett tribes led by Captain John Mason attacked and came close to annihilating the Pequots in a brutal, genocidal campaign called the Pequot War.

This was the first and one of the most barbaric of the wars waged by European Americans and rival Indian tribes against native Americans. The Pequots were resourceful, aggressive Algonkian-speaking Indians who had migrated to the Thames River valley from what is now upper New York and had taken the area by force. The tribe and the Mohegans were ruled by the Pequot chief Sassacus until a rebellion by the leader Uncas led to the independence of the Mohegans.

The murder of two English traders that was attributed, some argue falsely, to the Pequots led to the outbreak of the war in 1637. In reaction to the murders, the Puritan leaders in Massachusetts ordered a punitive expedition to destroy the native villages and crops on Block Island, Rhode Island, and in the New London, Connecticut, area. In response to that expedition, the Pequots attacked several settlements in Connecticut. The General Court of Connecticut then ordered an offensive war against the Pequots. Christian clergymen, who regarded the Pequots as savage infidels, supported the conflict.

Mason and his Mohegan and Narragansett allies staged a surprise attack June 2, 1637, on a Pequot fort on a hill in what is today the village of Mystic. More than five hundred Pequots, many of them women and children, were burned or otherwise slaughtered. Many Pequots, who had been at another fort, including Sassacus, were eventually killed or captured by other Indians or the English. Many were sold into slavery.

But the tribe was not wiped out. One survivor, Robin Cassacinamon, became an indentured servant in the Winthrop Jr. household in the Massachusetts Bay colony. He later took advantage of his connection with Winthrop to obtain land concessions for the Pequots when Winthrop moved to Connecticut. For a time, the Pequots were prevented by law from dwelling in their old homes and visiting the graves of their fathers. They could no longer call themselves Pequots. Nobody expected that the decimated tribe would ever return to southeastern Connecticut, let alone regain its powerful influence in the area, which it did in the closing years of the 20th century.

The conquest of the Pequots removed the last obstacle to the settlement of Connecticut. After that, European settlements began proliferating throughout the region. New London was among the first of the new English communities to benefit from the more secure conditions that followed the elimination of the perceived Pequot threat.

New London's early settlers eschewed sites on the immediate waterfront and established their homes on a hillside overlooking what was first called Pequot Harbour or Faire Harbour. On the hill, they buried their first dead and built their first meetinghouse. Winthrop settled in a house near the Thames River, at the head of Winthrop Cove, just north of the later site of the train terminal. Cassacinamon helped him select the location. Winthrop built a grist mill for the town next to his house. Although the first settlers had arrived in 1645, they did not receive their charter to govern themselves until May 6, 1646.

THAT WAS THE BACKGROUND of New London's birth, whose 250th anniversary was celebrated with much fervor and hope for the future on May 6,

1896. New London spent months preparing to celebrate this anniversary. It was a period of gushing business optimism and an overpowering sense of destiny. Theodore Bodenwein looked forward to the event with the anticipation of an up-and-comer in the city and the emotions of a new father. The Bodenweins' third child, Elizabeth, was born in January 1896. Gordon was 2 and already a precocious and attractive child adored by both his 33-year-old mother and his grandparents. The Bodenweins this year purchased a building lot from the Brandegees and built their first house, a three-story Victorian mansion overlooking the Thames River. The property was listed in Jennie's name.

Agnes' health by that time was failing. She suffered from a stroke and died two years later on March 12, 1898, at age 76, and was buried beside Theodore R. Bodenwein, her son's only namesake. It had been twenty-nine years since she had stepped off a German steamship in New York with her five-year-old son and entered America.

Citizens named to prepare the arrangements for the 250th celebration included Bodenwein and John McGinley, his city editor. My grandfather, Eben Stone, a recent arrival in town, was on one of the committees. Stone was one of the owners of the city's newest and most posh jewelry store. He and his father-in-law, Isaac Perry, had established a branch of their western Massachusetts business in the city three years earlier, participating in the mounting migration of commerce to New London in the 1890s. Investors were finally being drawn by word of the city's commercial boom. Eben Stone, then 28, had a heart problem and his doctor told him to move closer to the ocean for his health. Word had reached Great Barrington, Massachusetts, where he lived, of a shorefront city called New London where the air was pure and healthy. Perry & Stone, Jewelers and Silversmiths, opened its first store on State Street in the Bacon Building. *The Day* published several stories about the new store, noting that its arrival signified the city's growing importance and prosperity.

Bodenwein was eager to please the local movers and shakers and signaled his uncritical willingness to be a cheerleader and his readiness to become a player. The newspaper jumped onto the bandwagon of each business campaign that came along. When the Bath Iron Works, a Maine shipyard, nearly burned to the ground and was rumored to be looking for a new home, *The Day* suggested that New London would be the best location for the business. The newspaper backed the extension of trolley lines into the towns around New London. There was considerable controversy over this, as there was over many developments of the time. The New London Board of Trade and many of the local business leaders, including Bodenwein, believed the trolleys would bring new commerce. The rest of the nation was beginning to feel uneasy about the railroads and other big business interests. National politics were dividing along lines of pro- and anti-big business sentiments, and the New London Democratic Party was fueling its tanks with anti-big business feelings, which were particularly strong among the city's immigrant population.

Bodenwein had his first big chance to show off his newspaper in the city's elaborate celebration of the 250th anniversary of Winthrop's settlement. The *Day*'s staff worked for weeks preparing copy, taking pictures, and selling ads for an ambitious souvenir edition that would blend stories and pictures from the city's past and present. Practically the entire regular edition of the newspaper was dedicated to the event. *The Day* published the detailed line of march for the parade through town that day. It listed the names of all the school children participating in the program, and singled out all the local businesses that were decorated with patriotic bunting. It displayed on the front page the full, six-thousand-word text of poet and banker Walter Learned's address on the founding of the city, next to a three-column picture of Winthrop.

The city was favored with a radiant spring day to celebrate its birthday. The temperature was in the fifties but the sun shone brilliantly. Packed trains had been unloading passengers at Union Station for days. Steamboats from New York poured out throngs of visitors. Businesses and homes all over the city were decorated in red, white, and blue bunting. First thing in the morning of May 6, the entire sixty-five-member band of the Mission of the Immaculate Virgin disembarked from the steamship *The City of St. Lawrence* along with a huge crowd from New York. The group marched behind a unit of Hibernians up State Street and along Huntington Street to St. Mary Star of the Sea Church where they performed before a large crowd. Children from all the city's schools filed into the center of town led by their schoolmasters. Farmers from across the area came with their families in wagons that had been scrubbed for the occasion. Crowds packed in around the waterfront railroad station, where visitors arrived by the hundreds. More than three thousand tickets were sold before noon on the train from Norwich to the city, *The Day* reported. "Everybody beamed good nature," a reporter for the *Morning Telegraph* noted.

A big parade through town was led by the Masons. Charlotte Mollyneux Holloway wrote the text for the day's official program. The most unusual sight was the arrival of a small band of Mohegan Indians who had been invited to take part by Ernest E. Rogers, one of the youngest members of the organizing committee. Attitudes toward Indians then were ambivalent at best. The United States was engaged in military conflicts with Indians in the settlement of the

West. Indians still captured the imagination of Americans. As a matter of curiosity, Native Americans were featured in rodeo side shows and traveling carnivals. But the Indian culture also was an object of serious interest. Social clubs were formed devoted to the study of Indian culture.

The local Native Americans, in fact, were living in the dark age of their history. A handful of descendants of the once powerful Pequots subsisted in poverty on two thousand acres of land in Ledyard, a rural town along the eastern shore of the Thames River. The General Court gave this land to Cassacinamon's people when it forced them to leave land in Noank that Winthrop, Jr., had given them. The Indians called the swampy, wooded land in Ledyard "Mashantucket," which means "well-wooded land." It was located near Lantern Hill, one of the highest elevations in the region.

The Mohegan tribe lived under more favorable circumstances. It had not been banished and did not have to go underground, as the Pequots did. The tribe ingratiated itself with the early English settlers by adopting their religious faith. The Mohegan Samson Occum became a well-known Congregational preacher in early New England. The Mohegans organized a Puritan church in Montville, north of New London, and retained their ancestral identity. The Montville Mohegans represented this indigenous people in the ceremonies that day in May of 1896. The chief wore war paint and a feathered headdress. Two others wore Indian costumes and one was on horseback.

The newspaper reporters who recorded the event described the mixed reaction to the scene. *The Day* reported:

> *They made an eloquent picture, representing the passing of the aboriginal tribes of red men who once inhabited this country, and the all-conquering advance of the pale faces.*

The *Morning Telegraph* was more inclined to feel sorry for the "last of the Mohegans":

> *That was indeed a sad and striking comment on the pride and pomp and power and rank which was presented by this spectacle of the last of the Mohegans. They were a mere handful, whose pacific faces refused to assume their old fierceness, even with war paint and feathers.*

That morning, the city marked the placing of the cornerstone for a statue of John Winthrop at the site of the city's first meeting house, next to the first burial ground. *The Day* had surveyed leaders of the community about the best location for the statue. Mayor George F. Tinker picked the site near the Bulkeley School pointing out that it offered a clear view of the Thames River and easy access from a main street. The large crowd gathering for the cornerstone dedication included Theodore Bodenwein, Jennie, Gordon, and the baby, Elizabeth. Alfred H. Chappell, the president of the board of trade, delivered the main address, which began:

> *Two-and-a-half centuries ago, upon this hill, our forefathers laid the foundation of the town destined to become the mother of thousands of fair, true hearted women and brave young men.*

A four-hundred-voice schoolboys choir sang *America* after the cornerstone had been dedicated in a Masonic ceremony. The rolling community shindig next proceeded to the dedication of the Soldiers and Sailors Monument, for which Sebastian Lawrence, whaling merchant and descendant of Italian immigrants, donated $20,000. The monument was built from granite quarried in nearby Westerly, Rhode Island. It stood on a thirteen-foot-square pedestal. A soldier at parade rest and a sailor stood at either side. On top was a nine-foot-tall statue of the goddess Peace.

The monument had several layers of meaning. It represented the end of a long quest, led by a succession of local newspapers including *The Day*, to beautify the Parade area. It was located in the middle of the unsightly gravel lot, which was the first sight to greet visitors when they got off the trains and boats. Everyone agreed the new monument was a decided improvement over the old flagpole that had stood there for years. This act typified the City Beautiful movement, in which cities in America strove to clear away blight and mimic the great cities of Europe.

The monument also was an indication of the unfolding philanthropy of the wealthy survivors of the whaling era. Lawrence, whose family owned one of the city's leading whaling firms, would later endow the city's only public hospital. These were steps toward immortality for the successful heir of Italian immigrants who had ascended to wealth and power during the whaling era.

Finally, the Soldiers and Sailors Monument was yet another public improvement to promote the city's downtown commercial growth, a symbol that New London was recovering from the disabling illness that afflicted it with the decline of whaling.

New London genuinely appreciated Bodenwein's thorough and enthusiastic coverage of the anniversary activities. His newspaper rose perceptibly in popularity in the city, and his stature ascended with it. The *Telegraph's* early burst of energy, on the other hand, turned out to be short-lived. The newspaper had the spirit but not the resources or the business acumen to keep up with *The Day*. Bodenwein's greater worry was the *Globe*, run by George Sturdy and

Samuel T. Adams, whom Bodenwein had fired upon taking control of *The Day*. The *Globe* came onto the market at one cent. But, to Bodenwein's surprise, even that could not stand in the way of the *Day*'s growth in circulation. Bodenwein expanded his reach still further by spreading into the surrounding towns, making use of the new trolley lines and of local correspondents who were paid by the inch to submit news from the region's hamlets.

NEW LONDON AND *THE DAY* received another jolt of adrenaline four years after the anniversary, when James J. Hill, an eccentric financier and railroad builder, arrived with a fabulous get-rich plan that instantly captured the imagination of the community. Hill had crisscrossed the northwest with his railroad tracks and was president of the Great Northern Railroad when he showed up in New London. He had a plan to sell wheat to Asia, shipping it from the Midwest on railroad cars and carrying it to the Orient in gigantic steamships. His search for a place to build the ships brought him to the shores of the Thames River in Groton, where he learned there already was a shipyard near the opening of a deep harbor. It would be perfect for ships of the size he contemplated. This was the old railroad ferry landing.

Moses himself could not have caused more excitement than Hill did in New London. The city was already in a mode of thinking that naturally accompanies the transition from one century to the next. It was in the midst of a minor burst of prosperity, and many felt Hill had arrived to lead New London into the Promised Land.

Hill set up a subsidiary, Eastern Shipbuilding Company, at the Groton shipyard, and began preparations to build the first two ships, the *Minnesota* and the *Dakota*. The efforts were extensive. The little village where Bodenwein had grown up had to reorganize itself by an act of the legislature to sell gas and electricity to the shipyard. Housing was built to quarter thousands of shipyard workers. Everyone thought the Great Millennium had arrived, including Bodenwein, whose newspaper covered the progress closely each step of the way.

The day the *Minnesota* was launched, the banner headline across the front page of *The Day* read, "Biggest Ship in World, the *Minnesota*, launched at 2:15 p.m." According to *The Day*, forty thousand people witnessed the ship slide into the river. Hill watched from his yacht, one of hundreds of luxurious vessels that crowded into the harbor. The newspaper used the occasion to tout the advantages of New London, its harbor and its favorable climate for other investors in visions of grandeur:

The fleets of the world could find anchorage within the boundaries of the harbor of New London and therein ride safely no matter how severe the storm, for Fishers Island forms a natural breakwater and inside is at all times comparatively smooth water and always good holding ground.

The Day noted the convenient links to the railroads and the healthfulness of the climate and natural beauty:

New London is situated in the very center of that section of the United States between the Connecticut River and the Pawcatuck River, which Baron Von Humboldt pronounced the healthiest section of the world.

"Summer visitors from New York would," *The Day* said, "attest to the beauty. Visitors come year after year by excursion boat and train. There are parks, winding streets in the old part and long, new avenues, with beautiful examples of all styles of architecture."

Local businesses filled the newspaper's pages with congratulatory advertisements. T. A. Scott & Company, the city's leading marine engineering and towboat company, bought a large display ad noting the importance of the event and the skills it offered in the city's future development. The Brainerd & Armstrong silk mill, the city's largest industrial employer with nine hundred workers, and the F. H. & A. H. Chappell Company also purchased big ads. The Chappells emphasized in bold lettering the company's major product, coal. Some argued it was coal that accounted for the *Day*'s early support of the railroads, and it was coal that may have made the launching of the *Minnesota* so endearing to Frank Chappell that day.

Coal, it turned out, also became one of Hill's biggest problems. There were not yet sufficient coaling stations in the Pacific to fuel ships as large as the *Minnesota*. Nor had trade with the Orient progressed to the point at which it could fill the gigantic holds of the ship with cargoes to return to America. As a result, the dreams of the Great Millennium in New London were quickly dashed by the rapid collapse of Hill's enterprise, leading to the shuttering and bankruptcy of the Eastern Shipbuilding Company.

While the setback shocked Bodenwein and the rest of the city, the collapse of this early shipbuilding scheme did not alter the course Bodenwein had set for his newspaper, nor slow him down, although he encountered a minor business setback of his own. Caught up in the boom mentality in 1901, he bought the ailing *Telegraph* from Walter Fitzmaurice for $12,000 in an attempt to monopolize the morning and afternoon newspaper markets and keep the newspaper out of the hands of a strong competitor. Fitzmaurice went to work in Norwich for the Norwich *Bulletin*. He died in 1921 at the age of 70.

The purchase of the *Telegraph* was, by Bodenwein's own later admission, a stupid business decision. What the purchase succeeded in doing was to emasculate the *Telegraph*, which grew dull and neutered politically. The Democratic Party once again lost its voice with the press. And Bodenwein lost $4,000, by his own estimate.

DURING THAT EVENTFUL PERIOD, Bodenwein plunged into local politics. McGinley, who had been appointed the city's postmaster in 1900 and ruled the Republican Party, helped him get appointed to several local boards and, in 1903, nominated and elected as a city alderman. Bodenwein's prestige grew with the *Day*'s circulation, which had climbed to nearly four thousand in 1900. The newspaper finally became audible to the city's ruling class. In 1904, Bodenwein burst upon the stage in state politics.

He could not go wrong then. The dawn of the 20th century was a blessed period for the Republicans. Theodore Roosevelt had captured the nation's imagination with his assertive foreign policy and aggressive populist stance against big business. His positions on issues disarmed the Democrats, who already were divided over the populism of William Jennings Bryan. A strong economic recovery after the Panic of 1893 had made a Republican landslide in 1904 virtually inevitable. The Democrats in New London sensed the problem they faced and had difficulty finding candidates for any office. Thomas Waller, the former governor and the party's elder statesman, actually was mentioned as a candidate for the legislature to run against his own son, Charles B. Waller, so desperate was the situation.

The generations were changing guard in that period. The younger Waller, like his father a lawyer, was growing in popularity, but he had joined the Republican Party, the dominant political organization in the city at the time. Augustus Brandegee's son, Frank Brandegee, also a lawyer, was another up-and-coming Republican. The Democrats in the city were led by Mayor Bryan F. Mahan, an audacious and popular Irishman and born politician who managed to earn affection in both camps by latching onto the one thing both parties had in common: the craving to get rich and put New London on the map again. Mahan succeeded Thomas Waller as the voice and the hope of the Democrats. Mahan was the first Democrat to come along in the city to make a political career out of economic development. Mahan capitalized on the movement to make New London New York's surrogate port, and campaigned to build a huge pier on the Thames River for East Coast ocean traffic. He also was an aggressive land developer and was a partner with Bodenwein in several investment schemes.

But 1904 was not his year, nor a year for his party, although its ranks were swelling with new European arrivals to New London. The Democratic Party was handicapped by such obstacles as an antiquated system in the state legislature that awarded every community the same representation regardless of its size. That unrepresentative apportionment ensured small town Republicans dominated the legislature.

The Democrats were not so disarmed that they were unable to raise compelling social issues. Theodore Roosevelt was neutralizing the opposition by raising Democratic concerns like the evils of business monopolies and business corruption. His "Square Deal" clearly conflicted with mainline Republican ideals by calling for greater regulation of business and broader controls of the railroads. But his aggressive foreign policy increasingly raised cries of imperialism, and the Democrats seized upon this issue in the 1904 elections. They offered as evidence the example of imperial Russia, which was being pulverized in its campaign against the Japanese in the bloody Russo-Japanese war, the dominant international story in *The Day* at the time. The Russian czarist government, the Democrats argued, showed how imperialistic powers exploited the common people and squandered resources to carry out their international aggression.

But the party had lost its voice in the media. The *Telegraph*, under Bodenwein's ownership, bit its tongue and silently sat out the election. This situation must have evoked memories for Tom Waller, who had had to outshout the *Star* in the 1870s, when there was no Democratic newspaper in town. He had not lost his gift for political rhetoric. The aging war-horse appeared at a party rally in the Quaker Hill section of Waterford, the rural town neighboring New London, one night before the election and delivered a booming oration on how he had helped Grover Cleveland sweep the state. He acknowledged that he had not voted for William Jennings Bryan, but would if he ran again. He attacked the Republicans who boasted about prosperity, fuming that the wealth was concentrated in the hands of a few. McGinley best represented his party on the local stump, defending the record of the Roosevelt administration in rallies throughout the region.

The southeastern Connecticut Democrats' greatest, if not only, hope was attorney Christopher L. Avery, the son of Bodenwein's childhood neighbor in Groton, who ran for the state senate in the state's 18th District. It really did not matter much, though, who was running in the state races. The controlling influence was the contest between Roosevelt and Judge Alton B. Parker of New York, his ineffectual Democratic opponent from the Tammany machine. The Republicans in the state were confident of a victory, and the local party organizations headed for the convention in New Haven ready to carve up the spoils of a Roosevelt landslide.

Bodenwein had already gotten his feet wet in politics as an alderman from the city's south end. He enjoyed certain advantages on his home turf. He employed one of the major political players. The chairman of the city nominating convention was John McGinley. On the motion of Attorney Charles B. Whittlesey, a former business manager of *The Day* and son of the late Ezra Chappell Whittlesey, the convention appointed a nominating committee that included Frank Brandegee, a close friend of Bodenwein's and associate in real estate ventures, and Frank V. Chappell, a son of Alfred H. Chappell. The committee backed, and the convention unanimously supported, a delegation to the state convention prepared to back Bodenwein as the party's nominee for secretary of the state. Whittlesey delivered the nominating speech for Bodenwein at the state convention, taking note of Bodenwein's achievements as a newspaper executive and citizen active in the city's interests. *The Day* published an editorial the next day praising the choice, stating of Bodenwein:

> *His courage and enterprise are known and admired here and he has made an exceedingly good impression on the representatives from all parts of the state, who by hundreds, congratulated him on his nomination and promised him their good will and support.*

In the final days before the election, *The Day* pounded away at the Democratic ticket, excoriating Parker, extolling Roosevelt, and supporting the Republican ticket daily on its editorial page.

Every public event seemed to be an opportunity for Bodenwein to enlarge the following of *The Day*, and this included elections. The newspaper displayed the election results to crowds outside its Bank Street headquarters. As fast as the results poured in from The Associated Press over the newspaper's telegraph wires, they were placed on slides and projected on a screen across the street.

That's how New London first learned of Bodenwein's victory on November 8, 1904. During that evening, a crowd of several thousand outside the *Day* building witnessed news of Roosevelt's landslide victory, which swept the entire state Republican ticket into office. In between returns, *The Day* entertained the audience by showing motion pictures of the Spanish American War and comedies. Bodenwein trailed Roosevelt by twenty-four votes, but led the rest of the Republican ticket in New London. Frank Brandegee was elected to

Congress. Christopher Avery lost his bid for the state Senate, while Tom Waller's turncoat son, Charles, won a seat in the legislature.

Bodenwein was elected for two two-year terms as secretary of the state. During that period, 1905-1909, local politics turned nasty and drew the *Day*'s publisher and the newspaper into the struggle. The Republicans in the city split into two camps, with the supporters of Mayor Benjamin Armstrong on the one side and the old Brandegee wing of the party, which included Bodenwein and the Chappells, on the other. The Chappells' presence signified that wing's close and long connection with coal and railroad interests. Armstrong, owner of the Brainerd & Armstrong silk mill, one of the city's largest employers, had succeeded Democrat Bryan Mahan in the city's top office. He accused Mahan of leaving the city's finances in shambles, and charged his Republican opponents and the Democrats with being in league in cozy and corrupt deals involving city business and real estate speculation. Favored individuals were securing lucrative franchises, he claimed. City money was going to support private real estate deals. Materials purchased by the city were being diverted for private use. Favors were being handed to the local trolley companies. Those were among the charges Armstrong made.

He sacked a number of the city commissioners, including former Governor Thomas Waller as parks commissioner. He also attacked Waldo E. Clarke, the young streets commissioner who had just been hired by the city, charging that funds were being spent on construction work that was not getting done. The Democrats looked on merrily as the Republicans began to self-destruct in an internecine battle that eventually engaged the three local newspapers. In a letter to the editor of the *Globe* October 2, 1907, Armstrong attacked Bodenwein and *The Day*, charging the newspaper was siding against him not only in its editorials, but also on its news pages:

> *The only way for the mayor to reply to his critics in* The Day *is to buy an advertisement for $1 an inch or $18 a column ....* The Day, *persistently from the time I was elected, followed a definite policy of misrepresenting the mayor and his official acts and policies with the view of leading the public, if possible, to the point where they would have a feeling of distrust of the administration. The owner of* The Day *has been even more unjust than any of his greatest enemies ever could have anticipated.*

Armstrong suggested Bodenwein's conduct might have had something to do with the fact that the city no longer was awarding coal contracts to the Chappells. This was the second time a head of *The Day* was accused of compromising his news judgment in the interests of the Chappells. The first was when the *Telegram* accused John Tibbits of catering to railroad and coal interests over the issue of building a railroad bridge across the Thames River in the 1880s. Bodenwein shot back at Armstrong in an ad of his own:

> The Day *is not the issue. Its moderation has been extraordinary. Armstrong is saying all this because he can't control the paper. He has not been able to command its praise nor to purchase its silence. That he is charged $1 an inch for space in* The Day *in which to reply to his critics is a tender spot, no doubt. That, however, is* The Day's *regular rate.*

The *Morning Telegraph*, which Bodenwein had just relinquished control of, supported Armstrong. The battle was waged in caucuses that October in the city's five wards. The most spirited of these occurred in the Second Ward, where Ernest E. Rogers, a young clerk for Brainerd & Armstrong, challenged Alfred H. Chappell. The caucus at the Konomoc Hose Company firehouse on Union Street got so raucous the police had to be called. Rogers won by twenty-five votes, sending him on his way on a political career that would see him becoming mayor, state senator, and lieutenant governor. But Armstrong men won in only one other ward. Anti-Armstrong candidates prevailed in the three remaining wards prompting *The Day* to declare a victory against the Armstrong "dictatorship." Mahan returned two years later to take back the mayor's office for the Democrats and lead the city into another period of expansion.

Bodenwein's elections as secretary of the state helped change the course of his life for better and worse. The pace of his life quickened. He traveled to Hartford to perform his new duties, and he gained influence among the editors and publishers of New England newspapers. As Gordon and Elizabeth grew up, the Bodenwein family life became increasingly strained. *The Day* and politics consumed Bodenwein's life and increasingly took him away from home. Jennie's mother's mental and physical health deteriorated. Bodenwein traveled to New York, where he had become active in the expanding business of The Associated Press. The wire service reorganized and settled in New York at the turn of the century. Bodenwein became a charter member and director.

The Day continued to grow during that period. Bodenwein added to his reporting staff Alfred Ligourie and John McGinley's son, Arthur, who became one of the closest friends of Eugene O'Neill. Arthur did not stay with *The Day*, but went on to become the sports editor of the Hartford *Times*. Ligourie stayed and was part of the staff that took over *The Day* after Bodenwein died.

The Day was, by that time, becoming a close-knit organization, somewhat of a family. The newspaper formed its own minstrel team, which performed at picnics and outings throughout the newspaper's circulation area. Both young

McGinley and Ligourie performed in those shows. Theodore, by then in his 40s, had come into his own as a member of the upper crust of New London and the state. His biography appeared in books about the state's business leaders, which invariably noted his rise from humble beginnings to a position of importance in newspaper publishing. By 1910, he had dispensed with his financial obligations to the Chappells and other original directors of the newspaper and formed a stock company of his own. He became a member of the city's leading social clubs, including the Thames Club and the Harbour Club.

Jennie benefited from her husband's increasing importance. She saw that her children received the best educations; she took part in the social life of wives of successful businessmen in the city. She was an organizer of the Faire Harbour Club, a women's auxiliary to the exclusive Harbour Club, where Theodore developed a taste for poker and hobnobbing with the city's most powerful citizens. Elizabeth was on her school tennis team and active in dramatic productions. Gordon attended the Bulkeley School, a classical high school formed from an endowment during the expansion of philanthropy in the late decades of the 19th century.

The Bodenwein children, offspring of working class families, were brought up in an entirely different world from their parents' early lives. They had no contact with the struggling immigrant backgrounds of Theodore and Jennie other than through Jennie's mother and sisters and their grandfather Anton. Anton, now retired, moved out of his house on Clover Court and spent most of his time with his German-American cronies, living in a boarding house operated by Anna Hanson on Main Street.

A year or two after Theodore was first elected secretary of the state, Jennie began to suspect her husband was seeing other women and their marriage began to fall apart. The 23-year-old relationship collapsed in 1910. In October, Jennie and the children moved out of their home on Montauk Avenue into the Mohican Hotel, the city's new luxury hotel built by Frank Munsey, a New York publisher. Theodore moved into an apartment in the Crocker House, another local hotel, the same day. Jennie filed for divorce on the grounds of multiple instances of adultery. Through her lawyers, the firm of Hull, McGuire & Hull, she claimed damages of $150,000 and filed attachments against her husband's stock in The Day Publishing Company and The Day Printery Company, the newspaper's commercial printing operation, as well as five tracts of her husband's real estate holdings. Theodore had already made plans to marry a woman he had met on a business trip to New York, a young divorcee twenty years younger than he was, by the name of Edna Simpson Winfield.

EIGHT

Scandal & Progress

The defendant on divers days between the first of January 1906 and the first of October 1910 has committed adultery at divers places to the plaintiff unknown with persons to the plaintiff unknown.

—Divorce decree in the case of

Jennie Muir Bodenwein vs. Theodore Bodenwein, February 1911

THE DELICATE NEGOTIATIONS OVER the divorce were carried out by two of the city's most ambitious young lawyers, Frank L. McGuire, who represented Mrs. Bodenwein, and Charles Whittlesey, by then a New London prosecutor, who represented both *The Day* and Bodenwein. This is not to suggest that the divorce had partisan overtones, but McGuire was a leading Democrat. He was a partner with attorney Hadley Hull in the firm of Hull, McGuire & Hull. Whittlesey, who became the business manager of *The Day* after his father was murdered at the paper, was a leader in the Republican Party.

The handling of the divorce concerned Bodenwein because the scandal threatened his hard-won respectability and, perhaps more important, the good name of *The Day*.

Gossip was inevitable in the small city. Bodenwein could do nothing about that. Jennie, a pleasant and attractive woman, was well liked and many would regard her as the victim, take her side, and hold that position for years. She had a reputation for being a devoted mother. She focused on preparing her children for privileged lives in keeping with their new status in New London society. Elizabeth went to Williams Memorial Institute (WMI) and Gordon to Bulkeley School, which were two exceptional classical public high schools. New London highly valued education and in the 1890s went on a tear of building new schools. Elizabeth gravitated toward art and drama, while the more withdrawn and somber Gordon developed interests in history, philosophy, and religion. Both were above average students, though not at the top of their classes. Elizabeth appeared in plays at WMI and in dramatic productions put on by the Faire Harbour Club. Gordon won the German prize in his graduating class.

Bodenwein minimized the damage by not contesting the divorce and thus avoiding a potentially embarrassing trial that would be covered in rival newspapers in New London and in Norwich, where the court was located. The lawyers hammered out a settlement in private. Jennie won custody of Gordon, who was 17, and had graduated the year before from Bulkeley, and Elizabeth, 15, who was a freshman at WMI. Jennie received $20,000 in alimony, and the house on Montauk Avenue, which was already in her name. Bodenwein agreed to secure a loan for $15,000 of the alimony with *Day* stock. Under the agreement with his ex-wife, he would have been required to surrender the stock, representing a fifth of the newspaper's holdings, if he failed to meet any of the $3,000 annual payments. Bodenwein and his lawyer later negotiated a new agreement in which the publisher put up land that he owned near the newspaper as collateral, alleviating the danger that Jennie could become a significant stockholder. The divorce was granted in the Superior Court in Norwich on April 3, 1911.

Practically before the ink had dried on the decree, on May 25, Theodore married Edna Simpson Winfield, 27, in the living room of her widowed sister Mrs. Cora Mitchell's house in a working class neighborhood in Trenton, New Jersey. Edna's niece, Edna Mitchell, a stenographer, was the maid of honor. There was no best man. The ceremony was performed by the Reverend C. H. Elder, pastor of the Trinity Methodist Episcopal Church. A German restaurant catered a dinner for the party. The newlyweds left the same night for New York, where they sailed off for Europe on a honeymoon that would take them back to Bodenwein's homeland in Germany. There were brief announcements of the wedding in the Trenton newspapers and in both *The Day* and the *Morning Telegraph* in New London. The Trenton papers emphasized both Bodenwein's past role as secretary of the state and the fact that he published a newspaper. For Edna's family, there had been no more auspicious an occasion. Edna, without any doubt, had elevated the family's outlook with her new husband.

Edna probably met Bodenwein in New York. He often traveled to the city on business. How, where, and when they met remains a mystery. Jennie alleged that Bodenwein's adulterous behavior began in 1906, the year he completed his first term as secretary of the state. Whether Bodenwein fully understood what he was getting in for is anyone's guess.

Edna was spunky, willful, adventurous, fun-loving, warm hearted, generous, thoughtful, genuine, a romantic, volatile, common, stylish, a bitch. All these descriptions would attach to her during her lifetime. Her marriage to Bodenwein was clearly a critical break for her. She had been born poor and had devoted considerable effort to trying to escape the hold of the area where she was brought up around the Trenton waterfront.

That effort included moving to New York after a divorce from her first husband, Lewis Winfield, a Trenton laborer, whom she married when she was only 14. Edna declared she was 18 on the marriage license.

Edna Simpson had been born at home in a dreary industrial area of downtown Trenton, near the Delaware River, on September 19, 1883, the thirteenth child of John S. and Augusta Simpson. Only seven of the children survived. Her father worked in various jobs as a laborer before becoming a Trenton fireman in 1896. His closest son, Philip, also was a laborer and later a carpenter. Augusta died in 1903, John ten years later.

The Simpsons were a hard-working family, and a few from among them attained better lives, and would have done so even without Edna's advantageous second marriage. Her brother Will went to work for a paint store in Trenton, stuck with it, and built a respectable middle class life with his family. Will's daughter, Edna, married Albert C. Lambert, a prominent Trenton businessman.

Edna Simpson was a leader in the family, both respected and adulated by her brothers and sisters even before she came into money. Both her brother Will and sister Cora named daughters after her. Edna doted on these young women and they adored her, referring to her affectionately as "Auntie." She was what some might call a soft touch. Both relatives and friends, sometimes shamefully, took advantage of her generosity. Later in her life, her vacation home in Florida would fill with freeloaders every season she was there, some of whom even had the nerve to ask her for the plane fare to get to Florida.

Years later, after Bodenwein died and she had just sold their house in New London, Edna demonstrated her most admirable trait, her instinctive thoughtfulness, by inviting the young daughter of the couple who were buying the house to have tea with her and tour the big house to give the child a chance to pick out her own bedroom. For all her faults, Edna was magnanimous.

She was not beautiful, but she presented a nice appearance. Those who knew both Jennie and Edna felt the former was more attractive, not to mention nicer. Edna's nose was slightly too large for her slender face. She had angular features. But a warm smile and plucky personality obscured these imperfections.

She could be tough. Her conversation was often spiced with expletives, both in her anger, which was mercurial, and in her exuberance, which was displayed frequently. She bet on the horses and played cards. She enjoyed drinking and was a chain smoker. She sometimes employed a long cigarette holder for dramatic effect. Switchboard operators at *The Day* grew used to her demanding, occasionally abusive phone calls, sometimes late at night when she had had a few drinks. Alma Wies, the daughter of Waldo E. Clarke, a prominent resident, remembers her as being pushy. That impression came from the time Edna attended Wies's wedding in 1934 with an uninvited guest, one of Edna's nieces.

Finally, she was a social climber, one of the best. And that suited Bodenwein's needs. He had achieved professional and political success, and the time had arrived in his life when he needed to consolidate his position in New London society. A man of his importance required a wife who would help him advance socially. Edna's background was as socially inferior as was Jennie's, perhaps worse, plus she had had a teenage marriage to a laborer. Presumably no one in New London was aware of her background and she was skillful at climbing the social ladder. Jennie, whose background was known in New London, had not been very good at that. She was more interested in raising her children. Some would say she was too nice for such a job, with all the affectation and pretensions it involved.

The Bodenweins traveled in Europe for three months. When they returned to New London, they moved into an $8,000 Victorian house on Nathan Hale Street in a fashionable neighborhood with tree-lined streets on a hill overlooking the city. Edna quickly pushed her way into the local social scene. She staged opulent dinner parties at their home and gathered around her a circle of wives of the local business barons, preferring those who shared her tastes in cards and having a good time. Jennie sent Gordon to a private school in New York State to prepare for Yale and she and Elizabeth left the Mohican Hotel and moved back into the house on Montauk Avenue while Elizabeth completed high school.

WHEN BODENWEIN, 47, RETURNED from his honeymoon in the summer of 1911 rejuvenated in the company of a young wife, he enthusiastically reassumed command of *The Day*. He had disposed of the *Telegraph* after experiencing persistent financial losses. He claimed to have given it away in 1906, after which it went through a succession of management and ownership changes before it met its destiny in 1910. That was the year Frederick P. Latimer became the editor. The 33-year-old Latimer briefly restored the *Telegraph's* old spirit and brought out the best in its gifted staff, which still included Charlotte Holloway and had as its city editor Malcolm Mollan, a tough, skillful newspaperman.

Latimer, a Yale graduate who studied English literature and law and was something of a renaissance man, would best be remembered as the editor who hired young Eugene O'Neill as a reporter against everyone else's better judgment in the summer of 1911. Biographer Louis Sheaffer related this story:

> *Eager to gain some writing experience under editorial guidance, Eugene had his father speak for him about a job at the* Telegraph, *New London's morning paper. When James broached the matter to Judge Frederick P. Latimer, the editor in chief, and business manager Charlie Thompson, they pointed out, as everyone knew, that the paper was chronically hard up. What, they wanted to know, could they use for money in paying the boy? After James agreed to reimburse them for his son's salary, Eugene went to work in mid-August for the* Telegraph *for ten dollars a week, unaware that his father was subsidizing his formal start as a writer.*

Whereas *The Day* was provincial in its style and approach, the *Telegraph* was cosmopolitan and literary. It went after news aggressively and brought out the color and human drama in a city that was bustling with both in its Irish taverns, along its streets, and on its waterfront. The newspaper provided the most detailed coverage of the activities of the Socialists, who had recently moved their state headquarters to Mystic. And it turned its editorial page into a strong and articulate forum for ideas, prompting Bodenwein to attempt the same thing on *The Day*. For a while it rivaled *The Day* in its advocacy of progress, with more literary flare, as demonstrated in a front-page editorial in April 1911 on the state's need for more "business patriotism:"

> *The matter transcends politics or the picayunes of the ballot box. Those of our municipalities which most prosper are those fortunate because more than their pedestrian contemporaries they have understood the meaning and potentiality of cooperative business effort. They have a community spirit that vitalizes their every undertaking. We need a manifestation of the same rugged energy and conscientiousness that leveled the forests of our colonial days, that in later days by ship, by rail and in our manufactured products, made known our name from the*

Baltic to Peru. We lack these things because as a state we have failed to realize the need and the value of business patriotism.

The Day, not always with as much literary skill, but with the advantage of a considerably larger circulation and Bodenwein's substantial business and political connections, plunged into the same quest for New London's elusive economic progress. That search was intensified by Bryan F. Mahan. Mahan was mayor of the city from 1903 to 1906, and again from 1909 to 1915. This uncommon Democratic leader pushed the city to build for the future. Even the dyed-in-the-wool Republican Bodenwein could not resist liking him. When Mahan was considering running for Congress, *The Day* urged that he stay in New London, where he could do more good for the city. Bodenwein and Mahan became not only good friends but also partners in several land development schemes.

Mahan's pluck had no limits. When city politicians were dead set against spending the money to build a new City Hall, which was badly needed, he persuaded them to "renovate" the old one. The city built virtually a new municipal building around the old one. The city under his leadership built miles of new sidewalks. But his greatest feats had to do with persuading the state to invest $1 million in a state-operated pier for ocean commerce and to win for New London a new college for women. Bodenwein placed the weight of his newspaper behind both these efforts.

The notion of the grand pier stemmed from the idea, which the city had been discussing for decades, of rivaling New York City for ocean commerce. Mahan turned the project from a pipe dream into a reality when, as a state senator in 1911, he got through the legislature a bill making $1 million available for the "ocean pier." Bodenwein assisted both with the backing of his newspaper and his substantial clout with the state Republican Party. It helped, in this regard, that Frank B. Brandegee by then occupied a seat in the United States Senate. Rarely in its history was New London as well armed to demand political favors.

Critics were quick to attack the investment, which was lambasted by envious politicians in other parts of the state as political pork for New London. But others outside the city appreciated the possibility that the project might prove to be valuable for the rest of Connecticut. The New Haven *Union* wrote:

Senator Bryan F. Mahan of New London did a splendid day's work for Connecticut in the Senate last week. We use the word "Connecticut" advisedly because it is a nearsighted person who can see only a mere New London benefit in the proposal to build state docks to accommodate ocean-going vessels in that harbor. It is true New London is to get a million dollar harbor improvement at state expense because nature favored New London with one of the finest harbors on the Atlantic seaboard; because New London has admittedly the best harbor in Connecticut. Connecticut, however, the whole state, is to be an equal gainer with New London by this contemplated improvement. Everywhere there are evidences of an expansion of the foreign trade of the United States. Reciprocity and tariff concessions and an effort to upbuild our merchant marine are going to open up to American commerce vast foreign markets.... Why should not Connecticut benefit from this splendid boom by anticipating the almost certain demands of commerce by utilizing New London's splendid harbor.

In 1912, the state hired Waldo Emerson Clarke, a 29-year-old civil engineer, to be the chief engineer for the massive project. Clarke was married to Daisy Klinck, the daughter of a well-liked New London butcher and civic leader. The two had eloped to the Panama Canal Zone, where Clarke worked for two years for the United Fruit Company. Before that, he worked briefly as a city engineer in New London, but left in disgust over the corruption he encountered in the city government. That was when he first met Bodenwein.

The state's steamship pier was a massive project. *International Marine Engineering*, a trade publication, referred to it as the first attempt in America at comprehensive, scientific harbor marine engineering. The approach, which was developed in European ports such as Liverpool and Antwerp, united advanced marine engineering and the most up-to-date methods of operating a port. The key to New London's success, the publication said, was in its ability to connect rail and water transportation effectively.

The port of New London has the opportunity to place itself far ahead of New York, Boston and every other American port as the proper place for steamships from all parts of the world to discharge their cargoes expeditiously and economically and reload correspondingly.

Bodenwein and Clarke became close friends, two men united in their vision of New London's progress as well as a shared concern over the ineptitude and corruption they saw in the local government. Bodenwein was not satisfied with having helped to get the project off the ground. He behaved like a clerk of the works, following the plans in minute detail, both in the news coverage and on the editorial pages. *The Day* interested itself in the layout of the buildings and the pier and in the plans for the rail and road connections. The newspaper, and the city, had visions of the port becoming as important as some of Europe's leading outlets to the Atlantic like Liverpool and Antwerp. Bodenwein advocated careful and scientific planning of the construction and operation of the pier to achieve the maximum advantage.

During this period, he joined a competition among Connecticut communities to be the site for a new women's college. The effort had started when Wesleyan University in Middletown, Connecticut, closed its doors to women. Cities and towns across the state were raising funds to try to attract the new institution. New London appropriated $50,000 to buy land for this purpose. Bodenwein had prodded the city to make the funds available and then praised the people when they followed his advice. *The Day* wrote on October 19, 1911, when the Court of Common Council approved the appropriation:

> *New London may fail in getting what she is after, but it is to the credit of the place that there is such a willingness to do what can be done influencing a favorable decision on the part of the committee. The city shows that it has the progressive spirit, when it is willing to work for its own interests and such a spirit cannot fail to bring good results.*

Offers came from communities across the state. New London, in fact, was the last to join in the competition, which was judged by a committee of thirteen based in Hartford. Mahan, in his usual brash style, pushed the funds through the City Council. Harriet Allyn, the daughter of a local sea captain, Lyman Allyn, and prominent philanthropist, donated the land on a hill overlooking the Thames River. And to sweeten the pot, the city pledged to raise an additional $100,000 for the first construction. Bodenwein was one of the leaders of the campaign. He had a giant wooden clock attached to the front of the *Day* building to mark the progress of the drive.

The committee agreed to establish the college in New London. Connecticut College opened its doors to its first classes in three stone buildings in 1916.

The impact his newspaper had must have astounded even Bodenwein. It emboldened him to use *The Day* to shape the development of New London in ways small and large. The newspaper broke open its narrow, gray editorial columns to wage an editorial campaign to raise funds for a new YMCA in 1914. An editorial in the final days of the fund drive pleaded:

> *Don't wait an hour for the call of a hustler. Sign your check or write a pledge and send it in—right now. And let every citizen become for this last day a volunteer hustler. Ask all your friends if they have subscribed. If any of them hasn't, take personal charge of him and see that he does.*

He lobbied for the federal government to transfer the training schools for cadets in the revenue service, later known as the Coast Guard, from Baltimore to Fort

Trumbull. This former Army installation where John Tibbits and many other young men had assembled to go off to the Civil War and that once had been the core of the city's military activity was now lifeless. *The Day* editorialized:

> *What is needed most emphatically is a spirit of cooperation of all classes in the community in every effort that promises to build up the city and a spirit of that sort cannot fail to have a good effect and bring results.*

Bodenwein felt sufficiently secure to scold his peers in the business community on the pages of his influential newspaper with full confidence that they would take what was said to heart. In an age in which great philosophical debates raged over the moral purpose of America, in which materialism and social justice were pitted against one another in a spirited conflict, Bodenwein believed without qualification in the good of capitalism. His views were grounded not in abstract ideas but in the practical day-to-day activities of New London and the region around it. He believed that New London's earlier decline arose from the sloth and contentment of the men who had grown rich on whaling and had failed to invest in the city's future.

That course, he understood, was reversed with the aggressive activities of the Board of Trade and strong leadership from the business community in the 1890s. But Bodenwein feared the business leaders were retreating dangerously from the city's political life and leaving matters too much to avaricious politicians who had their own venal interests at heart. He was not the only person with these sentiments. The theme had been sounded as early as 1908 by Alexander J. Campbell, manager of the New London Gas and Electric Company, in a passionate speech before the New London Businessmen's Association. Campbell charged the city was again in the hands of old men "who have made their money and are content with having the city remain as it is—dead." On the other hand, he said, the young leaders in the city were stifled and held back.

Colin S. Buell, the principal of Williams Memorial Institute, repeated the theme two years later in a plea for support for the Municipal Arts Society, an organization devoted to promoting public art and architecture in the city. Buell argued that the city's wealthy leaders had devoted too much attention to turning New London into a resort home for the rich, and not enough attention to developing new forms of commerce.

> *In spite of state pier and other commercial developments, the people who could do so retired from business to live upon their incomes and New London became a city of homes instead of a thriving business town. The 19th century wharves became tumble down skeletons, except when*

patched here and there in a spasmodic effort to shut in the ghost of former times and to keep up appearances. They symbolized stagnation in business and decadence in trade. No one seems to have appreciated that a city of homes cannot remain a city at all for more than one or possibly two generations.

Bodenwein took up the cause from the pulpit of his newspaper. His tools were the news pages, the editorial page, and "The Tattler," the column he started, but turned over to Walter Slocum during his busy engagement in politics. But Slocum's skills never equaled the clever writing skill Bodenwein developed. Bodenwein, who read voraciously and learned to write from the classics, composed in clear, crisp prose that used muted humor, irony, and penetrating arguments that got directly to the point. He never learned to use a typewriter, and wrote in longhand his many stories, columns, and editorials, only later employing a dictating machine. His style was clearly recognizable in an editorial in 1911 urging the city's businessmen to run for offices on the City Council:

The council is composed of 18 members. Just four of them are State Street businessmen. Main Street businessmen furnish one member, and Bank Street merchants contribute two. Here are seven business men in a body of 18 members. About one third—hardly enough to leaven the lump.

Bodenwein argued that it was in the business interest of the merchants to involve themselves in politics. There was a time, he argued, when each alderman represented some important business or industry. And that was a time when the city was smaller, and there were fewer men upon which to draw for political service. New London was entering a critical point in its history, and the city had great opportunities to do great things.

We should consequently put our best men forward. The selection of the ablest men for city officials should not be a mere matter of politics. The government of a city like New London should be a business proposition, not a political one. The Day, *usually partisan, does not care whether an alderman is Republican or Democratic so long as he is an able man who represents something tangible in the community and who has shown a capacity to successfully conduct his own affairs before attempting to transact the business of the city … .In the old days, no representative businessman was permitted to shirk his obligations to this community as to refuse to serve the city in the capacity of alderman.*

Approaching his 50th birthday in 1914, Bodenwein began to contemplate his legacy. The newspaper he had taken over in 1891 provided him with a comfortable income, much of which he invested in New London real estate. He purchased land in the growing expanse of subdivisions in undeveloped parts of the south end of the city, where New London's population was expanding. He now enjoyed the company of the city's elite in its most upscale business clubs, the Harbour Club, which was headquartered on the riverfront, and the Thames Club. The *Day*'s circulation had climbed beyond five thousand, and the paper reached out to the four corners of the region surrounding New London. The growth of the newspaper was enhanced by new trolley lines, such as the one that opened with great fanfare in the village of Old Mystic in 1911. In the new granite buildings of Connecticut College and the long state pier that extended far out into the Thames River, he could see the fruits of his efforts. But his progress did not fill him with contentment. Instead, it caused him to worry about how long it would last.

NINE

MUNSEYVILLE

As a newspaper owner and publisher, Mr. Munsey was an iconoclast.

He destroyed one cherished tradition after another.

He seemed to delight in smashing precedent.

—Theodore Bodenwein, upon Frank Munsey's death in 1925

IN 1895, MONTHS BEFORE the city's 250th anniversary and while Bodenwein was still married to his first wife, a new character had appeared in New London who was to have a major influence on Bodenwein: Frank A. Munsey, who became one of Theodore Bodenwein's biggest worries. Munsey, a New York publisher, arrived in New London to set up a magazine publishing house free of labor troubles and other such annoyances he faced in the big city. Just as he later would cause an upheaval in the newspaper industry, he turned New London on end, and left an indelible impression on Bodenwein that was a mixture of fear and wonderment. More than anyone, Frank Munsey aroused Bodenwein to think seriously about his legacy and the future of *The Day* after his death.

Munsey, like Bodenwein, was a poor boy who made good. Within several years he had amassed a large fortune by adapting the techniques of the popular dime novel to pulp magazines. He imagined compounding his fortune by moving his printing operations from New York to some small New England town near the water, where he envisioned transportation and labor costs would be much lower.

Bodenwein first learned of Munsey's intentions early in the summer of 1895. Alfred Chappell visited Bodenwein at the *Day*'s office in the Chappell

Building on Bank Street, informed him he had a chance to locate a big industry in New London, and asked Bodenwein how he would feel about moving his newspaper somewhere else if it were necessary. Bodenwein did not know what to say. After all, he had just moved in the year before. He had equipped the building with the latest machinery. He had made a major production of moving into the new headquarters. He could not have been happier than in the *Day*'s shiny new headquarters, in his impressive new office.

"What industry?" he asked Chappell. When Chappell told him *Munsey's Magazine*, Bodenwein was flabbergasted. Bodenwein was in the vanguard of economic progress in New London and the last thing he wanted was to stand in the way of such a boost to the city's development. But he was not eager to move. His immediate response was to suggest to Chappell that the building was not suitable for Munsey's purpose.

He told his august landlord, "This is no place for a fine printing plant. It's too near the salt water and too close to the railroad. Every day clouds of heavy smoke and cinders settle over everything no matter how tightly the doors are closed. Alfred, this would spell ruin for a magazine printing plant." That was not what Chappell wanted to hear, but he knew better than to push the issue with the visibly agitated Bodenwein, who could be a bulldog. The conversation planted slowly germinating seeds of insecurity in Bodenwein. He later remembered: "It gave me a jar. Nothing came of it, but it gave me some restless nights and I began to lay plans for a home for *The Day* which it could call its own."

He lost trust in the Chappells for so cavalierly considering taking back what they had only recently provided. And he developed a healthy fear of Munsey for putting him in such a potential predicament. That summer, Bodenwein began to plan to get out from under the Chappells' grip and find a new home for *The Day*, someplace where its future would not be at the mercy of someone else's whim.

Alfred Chappell, who was president of The Board of Trade, had a network of business contacts in New York and was the one who had led Munsey to New London. After Bodenwein's reaction, he proceeded to show Munsey and his architects and minions numerous sites in the city, including two the city could offer him for nothing. Chappell volunteered to have constructed whatever kind of building the publisher wanted, and, in their discussions, consented on behalf of The Board of Trade to pay the taxes on the property for ten years. Munsey accepted Chappell's deal and agreed after some tough negotiations to buy the old Bacon homestead on upper State Street from Morris W. Bacon for $30,000.

That summer, Munsey visited Bodenwein at *The Day*. The two instantly developed a respect for one another. You would not exactly call it a liking, though. They were both relatively young men, seriously ambitious, with similar backgrounds and extensive knowledge of the publishing industry. Bodenwein was 32, Munsey ten years older. They discussed the labor situation in the city and some of the issues Bodenwein had raised with Chappell regarding problems of printing a magazine in New London. Munsey had brought along an engineer to inspect the *Day*'s press to determine whether salt air and the soot from the trains caused any damage. The salt air was good for the health, but would not harm the machinery, rollers, ink, or the finish of the paper, they agreed. Munsey left satisfied that the corrosion issue was a red herring, as indeed it was. Munsey, by now, had taken a liking to the little city that tried so hard and naively to please him. The week before Christmas, he sent a telegram to Chappell announcing his decision to build in New London. Bodenwein, who had agreed to sit on the story until the deal was concluded, ran the first account of Munsey's plans on December 18, 1895.

The Day ran an ecstatic story on the announcement, though not on the front page. It explained to its readers it had known about the story for weeks, but had been pledged to secrecy. Munsey, it reported, was embarking on a bold innovation in magazine publishing that would elevate both his and New London's fortunes. The magazine would provide employment for hundreds of skilled workers. Munsey would erect a tall and elegant eight-story building unlike anything the city had ever seen. The magazine in New York used twenty-six Cottrell presses built in Westerly, Rhode Island. That number would significantly increase in New London. The railroad would be kept busy with huge shipments of paper, hundreds of tons every month. And the business would be a boon to the post office, which might have to expand and would assume a greater importance in the postal system to handle the huge shipments of magazines to all parts of the country. The smell of money was again in the air.

The project proceeded with a speed that astounded the local populace, who were used to things taking a more leisurely pace. The Munsey Building went up New York style. Within days, the site was cleared, a huge hole was dug for the foundation, and as the city prepared to celebrate its 250th anniversary, the steel superstructure began to rise above the city's humble skyline. Crowds gathered around the construction site every day, marveling at and critiquing the progress. A debate arose among the sidewalk superintendents over whether the great superstructure would collapse upon itself from such unconventional construction techniques. The downtown merchants exploited the excitement, welcoming Munsey to the city and calling attention to their merchandise in the same breath in advertisements in *The Day*. The Metropolitan News Depot, a retailer on Bank Street, proclaimed: "Frank Munsey has made a hit and so have we. Our stock is up to date, the finest line of Christmas cards in this city."

When it was finished in 1896, the new eight-story building towered over the city and was visible for miles. Immediately the presses began to arrive at the city docks. They were loaded on wagons and hauled up State Street to their new home. Printers, engravers, and binders from New York arrived to live in New London, and the magazine hired many more skilled workers locally, creating a momentary boom in the economy. Munsey envisioned creating a little industrial paradise of happy workers uncorrupted by the influences of labor unions. As Bodenwein later described the plan: "It was Mr. Munsey's idea to create a sort of home community for his people; the Munsey plant was to form a nucleus around which would spring up in time a sort of Munseyville, where peace and harmony would dwell and labor troubles be reduced to a minimum."

The assumption that he could pull off something like that was Munsey's biggest miscalculation. Along with the New York printers came organizers for the International Typographical Union. Practically as soon as they got off the train, they went to work to set up a local in New London. They called upon the printers at the three local newspapers, *The Day*, the *Globe*, and the *Morning Telegraph*, and at local commercial printing shops to join them. They arrived at an auspicious time, for Bodenwein had just introduced one of the latest innovations in newspaper production: typesetting machines.

These new machines caused the first technologically related layoffs on the newspaper. Rapid strides in technology threatened the security of the printers, particularly women hired to set type by hand. One out of every four of the first members to join the union were women, who constituted the largest number of the printers laid off when the new machinery was installed at *The Day* in 1895. The local printers did not have to have their arms twisted to join the ITU. Local 159 was organized September 17, 1896, at *The Day*.

Because of this and other problems, Munsey's utopian scheme quickly unraveled. Munsey had thought that he could have the magazine postmarked with the prestigious New York address although mailed from New London, but postal regulations did not permit this. How could he succeed with his magazine if everyone viewed it as originating in a one-horse town and not the great metropolis? He had to ship the magazine to New York for mailing, seriously compromising one of his purposes for moving to New London: to save money.

At about the same time, he got into a quarrel with the union regarding overtime. In the rush before the monthly publishing deadlines, a great deal of evening overtime was required. Munsey was outraged to learn that the workers were charging him overtime for the time they took for their evening meals. When he posted an announcement that he was putting an end to the larcenous practice, the union went on strike. Munsey immediately shut down the magazine, six months after it started operations. George Britt, his biographer, described Munsey's characteristic speed at making up his mind:

> *By six o'clock the same evening (of the strike) the first of the big new presses was lifted off its foundation and set onto a boat; before midnight, the greater part of the equipment was afloat on Long Island Sound. Before the next monthly publication time, everything was back in New York, set up and ready to go. … The Munsey publishing plant arrived in New London and departed, all in a few months, leaving behind only a vast pile of brown pressed brick on a prominent corner, forlorn as a temple in a desert, echoing the gathering dust.*

Thus ended New London's chances for becoming the hub of a giant publishing empire. But the failure of that scheme did not diminish the contribution Munsey made to New London's development. Bodenwein remarked when Munsey died:

> *Probably no man with the exception of Bryan F. Mahan had so much to do with establishing New London in the favor of the world at large. That it was not done in the way he originally contemplated matters not.*

Whereas publishing had become more than a business for Bodenwein, it was merely another business for Munsey. Magazines, newspapers, grocery stores, hotels, what was the difference? Exhibiting his remarkable business versatility and resourcefulness, Munsey transformed the building he had constructed for his magazine into a fancy hotel, and named it the Mohican after the local Mohegan Indians. Every room had its own bath, something then still a novelty for a small place like New London. He brought in chefs from New York and built a ballroom and roof garden with a view of New London Harbor. He opened a department store on the street level, which he described as "a little piece of 23rd Street." It sold everything from furniture to pins. For awhile, he sold a line of umbrellas from a shop in the building. And he installed a giant refrigerator and opened the city's first supermarket, the Mohican Market, which could offer a large selection of fresh meats and vegetables. This became the parent store for the Mohican Market chain that spread across New England. Hardly a day went by when there was not some dramatic change at the Mohican. Munsey became a metaphor in New London for mutability.

The hotel became Munsey's hobby, and New London became his fondest retreat from the big business world, somewhat as it had become for the actor James O'Neill. He was not sociable like O'Neill, but he enjoyed the pleasant pace, the city's simplicity, and the deference it paid to him. He visited the Mohican frequently, and every time he showed up, he ordered some change or other. Whenever Frank Munsey got off the train at Union Station and marched briskly up State Street, his shoulders back, his posture ramrod straight, everyone knew something big was going to happen. An elevator shaft here, an addition there, major renovations, a new business. Munsey's fertile mind never stopped producing ideas. In the course of several years, he spent several million dollars on the Mohican. He became a familiar, though not universally beloved, figure in New London. Popularity never seemed to be a serious concern of his. He was too busy with his business deals. He found New London a good place to make money and prodded Bodenwein to do more to boost the city in his newspaper. He turned to real estate and made large profits buying and selling downtown properties for development. New Londoners remembered him as one who never engaged in small talk and did more talking than listening.

Some in the city did not like him, just as there were people across the country who were not enamored of his methods. After the initial rush of enthusiasm, downtown merchants, in particular, complained that he was competing unfairly with them with his various business enterprises. Bodenwein more than once crossed swords with him, usually over stories in *The Day* that Munsey did not care for. Munsey once got so angry over the *Day*'s coverage that he threatened through an agent to start his own newspaper or buy one to get fairer and more accurate treatment. Bodenwein took everything Munsey said seriously. He learned from experience to fear Munsey's hair-trigger impulses. He bought the *Morning Telegraph* from Walter Fitzmaurice in 1901, at least partly out of the fear Munsey might buy it.

Soon after he moved his magazine out of New London, Munsey resumed publishing it in New York and made vast profits. With these gains as a capital war chest, he turned his attention to acquiring metropolitan newspapers. He bought the Washington *Times* and the New York *Daily News* in 1901. These were followed the next year by the Boston *Journal*. Six years later, he bought the Baltimore *Evening News* and founded the Philadelphia *Evening Times*. He brought to his acquisitions the same furious and unpredictable creativity that he brought to the Mohican. He completely overhauled and, some said, improved the dowdy Boston *Journal*, but to the point that its readers did not recognize or like it. He had no problem with investing huge sums of money on new machinery and other big improvements, but would vehemently resist buying such things as new office furniture. He drove the employees of the newspapers crazy with new rules. He banned smoking at the *Journal* because he felt it wasted too much time. He had a reputation for discharging employees for whimsical reasons. He was known to dislike fat employees, and preferred his newspapers staffed by slim and fit people like himself. He showed a genius for innovation, but his changes invariably took place faster than the public could absorb them. Munsey's biographer George Britt observed:

> *The rapid succession of his changes made it impossible for any single popular idea to take hold. Newspaper choice is a habit. Munsey tore up established habits by the roots, and before new ones could form, he was tearing up again. His impatience kept him from reaping any fruit from his planting.*

He eventually sold the Boston *Journal* at a loss after nearly driving it into the ground. In 1917, it was merged with the Boston *Herald*. He caused similar havoc with the New York *Daily News*. He killed the Philadelphia *Evening Times* in 1914 after it failed to make a profit. The rare newspaper property he owned that did well in that phase of his life was the Baltimore *Evening News*, and that was one with which he meddled the least.

These attempts at building a powerful newspaper chain preceded a period of newspaper mergers that would earn Munsey the reputation as the "grand high executioner of newspapers." This later development occurred during the massive consolidation and adjustment of the World War I period. He provided a clue about his thinking when, in the midst of his troubles with the Boston *Journal*, he ventured the opinion that Boston would be better off if it trimmed the number of newspapers in town from eleven to four. He had written in *Munsey's Magazine* as early as 1903: "In my judgment, it will not be many years—five or ten perhaps—before the publishing business of this country will be done by a few concerns—three or four at the most." He felt before the outbreak of World War I that large newspaper chains were the most efficient method of organization. During the war, when wartime conditions were driving up newspaper costs, he turned to consolidation as a guiding principle. He put it this way:

> *The same law of economics applies in the newspaper business that operates in all-important business today. Small units in any line are no longer competitive factors in industry, in transportation, in commerce, in merchandising and in banking.*

Using the profits from his grocery and magazine enterprises, he set out on a frenzy of mergers. Many of the papers that were traded in this furious activity had distinguished pasts, though many had fallen upon hard times. Some of the products of his deals actually were improvements, such as the New York *Herald Tribune*. After unsuccessfully trying to buy the New York *Herald* from the family of Ogden Reid, Munsey sold them the New York *Tribune*, a highly successful newspaper for many years. His merger of the New York *Globe* and the *Sun* was his most successful venture, and his last. Munsey died unexpectedly on December 22, 1925, of complications from appendicitis.

During his lifetime, Munsey gained widespread disfavor in the newspaper industry he had invaded with such force and impact. The prevailing sentiment was summarized in William Allen White's gleeful epitaph as he danced on the grave of the deceased. He became known among newspapermen who were not fond of him or what he stood for as "The Grocer." But Bodenwein, who was strongly influenced by Munsey, was more sympathetic and understanding although maybe not approving of all his methods or his politics.

Bodenwein was incensed at Munsey's views in the *Sun*, and *The Day* lambasted the paper regularly. But the two men had a great deal in common. Both set out in the publishing field with nothing: Munsey the son of Maine Yankees, Bodenwein the son of German immigrants. Both struggled for about ten years before making a breakthrough, and they did this during roughly the same period. Both were innovators with a brilliance for business and were not afraid to take risks. And contrary to what many felt about Munsey, he, as much as Bodenwein, felt there was a greater purpose to newspapers than making profits.

Munsey, for all his predatory instincts, had strong political and moral principles. He was convinced that the two major political parties had outlived their usefulness and that America required a political realignment to carry it forward in the 20th century. He went against the grain of the conservative newspaper owners of his time, including Bodenwein, in backing Theodore Roosevelt and the Bull Moose Party over the Taft Republicans and he used his newspapers to advance these values, often writing the editorials himself.

Bodenwein saw in Munsey's drive a motive that was purer than most of his contemporaries would have acknowledged: to build a secure base for newspapers, where they could exercise their responsibilities in the democracy, on the foundation of capitalism. Munsey thought the best way to make a free press secure was through consolidation, building huge business trusts like the railroads and banks and liquidating unprofitable ventures. Bodenwein said of this:

> *Mr. Munsey in his newspaper ventures played with millions where others before had only played with thousands. That he shook up the metropolitan newspaper business with a tremendous upheaval is true. His purpose was to stabilize it by reducing the number of papers. He accomplished that no doubt, but in the end others profited by it the most.*

Munsey described his higher vision to the journalist and columnist David Lawrence, who later wrote:

> *He (Munsey) was criticized for extinguishing newspapers, but he believed it good business and stuck to his theory to the very end. On the other hand, he told the writer on one occasion that it would be a mistake for captains of wealth to buy and sell newspapers in the belief that they could be made profitable without considering the human equation. He said that there would develop some day a sort of trusteeship whereby men of genius in editorial writing, in news management and business administration would be given a free hand by owners. He thought that unless an owner possessed all three elements in his own personality, he would be better off with a system of three administrators whose power to manage a newspaper properly was not limited by owners.*

Munsey, who never married, thought of the future of his publishing empire, including the *Sun*, which he was fond of. After his death, his closest associate, William J. Dewart, revealed that Munsey had been planning to place the newspaper into a trust that would enable the employees to take it over. *The Day* published a story about these plans, and Bodenwein recorded them in the back of his mind as a possible pattern he could follow. Munsey remained in good health up to the time of his death and never got around to changing the will he had written in 1921. The plan ended with his death. Without heirs, his empire was liquidated. Most of his fortune, estimated from $20 million to $40 million, went to the New York Metropolitan Museum of Art.

Munsey's funeral illustrated the tremendous impression he had made. Thousands passed by his bronze coffin, which lay in state in the Cathedral of St. John the Divine. Bishop William J. Manning, a close friend, presided at the funeral. The honorary pallbearers included Governor Alfred E. Smith, John D. Rockefeller, Jr., and Adolph S. Ochs, publisher of the New York *Times*. Munsey's death was a front-page story in *The Day* for two days. *The Day* published a full-column editorial on his death, and on Christmas Eve, Bodenwein wrote a long first-person account of Munsey's life and the influence he had on New London. Walter Garde, president of the New London Chamber of Commerce, sent a telegram conveying the city's sorrow at his death:

The late Mr. Munsey was probably the largest individual property owner in the city and our citizens are at once abruptly stunned to learn we are no longer to have the valued advantage of his personal direction and wise counsel in promotion of matters in which his interest and that of our city are so closely and amicably associated.

Frederick P. Latimer, the editor of *The Morning Telegraph* from 1911 to 1913 and now an editorial writer for *The Day*, wrote a column showing a gentler, more public spirited side of Munsey than the one that accompanied his public persona. Latimer recalled visiting Munsey when the *Telegraph* was in the midst of one of its many financial crises. He dropped in on Munsey without an appointment at his office in the Flatiron Building in New York City. He found Munsey pleasant and helpful. Munsey told Latimer that if Latimer was in the newspaper business just to make money, he was in the wrong business. During a second visit several years later, Latimer said he learned that several veteran editors and other staff members were being kept on the staff of Munsey's newspapers even while the papers were going through financial difficulties due to a recession because Munsey feared they could not get jobs elsewhere. Latimer wrote:

Mr. Munsey's other enterprises in the financial way were businesses. He had magazines and stores and buildings and stocks and banks for profit. But the newspapers he had primarily to render a service. He owned them in the course of being a good citizen according to his light. He had a firm conviction that the best epitaph placeable on anybody's tombstone is this: "A Good Citizen." That ideal was an obsession with him as with some people the passion is to get rich or with others to be famous or powerful.

Bodenwein wrote of his death:

The passing away of Frank A. Munsey removes a strong and virile character from national life. He was a positive man. He had courage, will and vision. He hated sham and pretense and he loved to break precedent. He never was shackled by prejudice or tradition. He was a pioneer. He blazed the way for others to follow. He played a lone hand. He made successes out of failures.

But Munsey's life sent a complex and mixed message to Bodenwein. The fierce trading in newspaper properties that took place during that era in which Munsey was so heavily involved, demonstrated how mortal and vulnerable local newspapers were to the whims of big money. How could newspapers that stood for something, as *The Day* did, survive for very long in that environment? But

Bodenwein also appreciated that Munsey understood that risk as well and was toying with the idea of creating financially secure trusts to sustain free and socially responsible newspapers. He was aware that Munsey, with no blood heirs to inherit his newspapers, had contemplated leaving them in trust to his employees and the only thing that prevented him from so doing was an unexpected attack of appendicitis. He also never forgot that Munsey, at the drop of a hat, could have forced *The Day* from its home.

IN ITS YOUNG LIFE before 1907, *The Day* had meandered about downtown New London from one rental home to the next. Born on the second story of a granite building on Bank Street, it moved from there to Main Street, not its present site and a location best remembered as the site where a crazed reader murdered the business manager, Ezra Whittlesey. It also was there that the sorrowful employees had bade John Tibbits farewell when he left to become the United States consul in Bradford, England. As the newspaper sank into debt, the Chappells moved it into cheaper quarters they owned on Bank Street, an old stone house known as the Brown mansion. That is where it was when Bodenwein and the Chappells concluded the deal under which Bodenwein took control of *The Day*. Shortly afterward, the Chappells erected a new building at 240 Bank Street, overlooking the water, which *The Day* shared with a furniture company. Only a short time after Bodenwein moved in, Alfred Chappell suggested that *The Day* might have to move out to make way for Munsey.

Bodenwein began hunting in earnest for a new home for *The Day* in 1905. He found it was not an easy task. There were few suitable sites available. He tried to buy an old building on Bank Street owned by Sebastian Lawrence, but Lawrence was not interested in selling it. After months of searching, he found a site on Main Street. The property was occupied by an ancient one-and-a-half-story wood building containing a confectionery shop and a Chinese laundry. A black family lived upstairs. It was two buildings down from where the Savings Bank of New London had just constructed a building. He paid $8,500 for the property, which had 36 feet of frontage and extended back from the street 90 feet. He bought a second lot to the rear to provide access to a back street called Bradley Street. He hired New London architect Dudley St. C. Donnelly to design a four-story brick and stone building whose front slightly curved to conform to the contour of the street.

The construction began in the winter of 1906, and drew to a close in August of the following year. *The Day* began moving on August 12. Crews hauled the Linotype machines out of the Bank Street building over the weekend, after the Saturday press run. The machines were disassembled and hoisted to the fourth floor composing room in pieces by a huge block and tackle attached to a plank and eye bolt fastened to the roof of the new building. A large crowd of employees and others watched as the machines inched up the rear face of the building. A team from the Hoe Company supervised the work of taking apart and reassembling the double-deck press.

It took all weekend to move the machinery the quarter mile between buildings into the new pressroom. Two of the crew fell into the old press pit and suffered minor injuries. But by late Sunday night, the entire mechanical department of *The Day*, as well as the newsroom, had made the move. *The Day* was printed at the *Morning Telegraph* for the week it took to get its own press reassembled and operational again.

The Day moved into its new home in 1907. "We all thought we were fixed for life," Bodenwein later recalled.

TEN

VIEW FROM THE TOP

It has always been my ambition to make The Day *something more than a mere business proposition.*

—Theodore Bodenwein, September 13, 1916

ON SATURDAY, JANUARY 24, 1914, Theodore Bodenwein celebrated his 50th birthday with his wife Edna, 31, and their closest friends and colleagues at an exclusive dinner party in one of the private banquet rooms at Munsey's Mohican Hotel. Bodenwein had many reasons to feel content and happy that night. He had a young and attractive wife at his side. New London was prospering. He was now well situated in the local social order. And *The Day* was solidly planted in the community and spreading its influence into the countryside. Bodenwein, a son of humble German immigrants, seemed to be at the top of the world. The printed program for his 50th birthday party carried this verse:

He found New London in the woods
Developed it and got the goods
No single move of civic pride
But found him standing by its side.

John McGinley, the city postmaster and *Day* editor, who had been at Bodenwein's side for nearly twenty-five years, acted as the master of ceremonies. McGinley was 70, but still fit and capable of bringing a smile to Bodenwein's face with jokes delivered at the publisher's expense. Some of the city's most important citizens turned out to help Bodenwein celebrate that milestone in his life. The guests included Ernest E. Rogers, the former clerk for the Brainerd & Armstrong Company, the silk manufacturer, who had been propelled into city politics during a fierce power struggle between Republican factions in 1907. He later was to be elected mayor of the city with Bodenwein's backing. Bryan Mahan, at this point a congressman from New London, was there, as was Walter Slocum. Slocum, the managing editor of *The Day*, was also gaining ground in the local Republican Party and in ten years would be postmaster. He presented Bodenwein gifts of a silver water pitcher and an engraved cigarette case on behalf of friends and employees of *The Day*.

A remarkable half-century had passed since Agnes Bommes Bodenwein and her husband, the shoemaker Anton, had brought Theodore Bodenwein into the world. The world had changed dramatically. When Theodore was born in Dusseldorf, Germany was still a loose and weak confederation struggling to unite and become a European power. After the Bodenweins left their homeland and migrated to New England, Otto von Bismarck had succeeded in molding the German states into a formidable world power. In a few years Germany would be at war with the United States in the world's first global conflict.

For Agnes and Anton, their gamble in leaving Germany for America had paid unimagined rewards. They had found a better life in America where Agnes had lived for nearly thirty years in increasingly comfortable circumstances before she died in 1898. She raised a good son, a serious, polite boy who was always eager to learn and had a passionate ambition to succeed. She lived long enough to see him become the manager of his own newspaper and an important figure in the small city where they had settled. She suffered the death of one grandson, but saw the birth of two other grandchildren, Gordon and Elizabeth. Both of these children would live wealthy, cultured, upper middle-class lives, beyond anything she probably imagined when she and her five-year-old son had stepped off a boat at Castle Garden, New York, in 1869. When his grandmother died, Gordon was roughly the same age as his father had been when he reached America. Elizabeth was three.

Anton had closed his shop on Main Street and retired in 1902, devoting all his time to his German social club and his cronies. He was in generally fit health, but suffered from asthma. Anton was not listed among the guests at Theodore's 50th birthday party. This was not unusual. Bodenwein was solicitous of his parents' needs, but did not go to great lengths to advertise his background to the snobbish local elite. When Agnes had died in 1898, there was no obituary for her in *The Day*, only a brief death notice. Anton fared better in his son's newspaper. His death, at age 80, January 30, 1917, was announced in a one-column obituary beneath a studio photograph. The picture, taken several years earlier, shows a handsome, kindly elderly man wearing a suit with a pin, probably of the Harweigh Lodge, in his lapel. He had a full handlebar mustache, like the one Bodenwein sported in his 20s and 30s, and he was wearing spectacles. He had a full head of hair, parted and combed back in the same style as the son.

Jennie, Bodenwein's first wife, who was also 50 in 1914, was still living with Elizabeth in the house at 302 Montauk Avenue. Her mother, Mary Muir, had died February 20, 1908. Mary Muir had passed her last years in fairly comfortable circumstances, compared to her past struggles, in a house on Montauk Avenue that Jennie and Theodore had helped finance. She had three grandchildren: Gordon and Elizabeth and Robert A. Graham, the son of her daughter Annie. Robert became a New London fireman. The causes of her death were listed as paralysis and senility. She was buried in a grave beside her husband's in Cedar Grove Cemetery, thirty-eight years after John Muir died of alcohol poisoning. Theodore personally attended to the details of the funeral.

Gordon, Jennie and Theodore's son, had graduated in the class of 1910 at Bulkeley School. Each senior was required to prepare an oration, and Gordon's was entitled "The Valley of The Shadow of Death," suggesting both an interest in theology that would develop into a vocation in the Roman Catholic priesthood and an introspective, if not sometimes morbid, disposition. Gordon prepared at a private school in Dobbs Ferry, New York, and went to Yale, where he was a member of the Class of 1916. Gordon revered his mother, resented his father, and totally disliked Edna, who felt the same way toward him. He had a warmer relationship with his aunt, Christina Rolfe and her husband, Bodenwein's Associated Press telegrapher William Rolfe.

The year her father celebrated his 50th birthday, Elizabeth was in her senior year at Williams Memorial Institute. She picked up the nickname "Tuts." She was short and athletic, with a mischievous glint in her eye and a warm grin. Her best friend was Roberta Morgan, who later married Tommy Troland, a Bulkeley boy. Years later, Troland and Elizabeth would sit on the board of directors of *The Day* together.

ON HIS 50TH BIRTHDAY, Bodenwein could look back at a city that had grown considerably and still was growing, though never fast enough to suit him. For a long time, it had troubled the publisher that inland cities like Meriden and New Britain, without the bountiful benefits of a deep-water port and other natural advantages of New London, nevertheless were so much more successful as industrial cities. This did not make sense to Bodenwein. The only answer, he thought, was that the city needed stronger leadership, and he continued to thrust *The Day* into that role.

In 1907 *The Day* had joined forces with local developers and financial interests in a controversial attempt to lure a large manufacturing plant to the area. The effort had been led by Leroy Harwood, treasurer of the Mariner's Savings Bank, and James R. May, a local real estate agent with strong political inclinations. There was strong local opposition, which *The Day* branded as backward antigrowth sentiment. In an editorial on August 17, the newspaper said:

> *One of the things that has interfered very seriously with the growth of New London in the past and is at present holding back the era of prosperity, that those who have the interest of the place at heart are longing for, is the desire of a surprisingly large number of its citizens to keep the city a very quiet place. There are quite a few for whom the busy hum of industry is a disturbing element. Factory whistles jar their nerves. They would like to have New London simply a large village, with city conveniences in the way of public service, and look upon the industrial growth of the place as something to be dreaded.*

The editorial charged that the attitude had a long history.

> *Since the dying out of the shipbuilding across the river there has been a season of dullness that has been anything but enjoyable. Now there is a chance to stir up a renewed activity, and it is combated by that spirit of exclusiveness that has never yet done anything to help the community.*

Some of the pro-development harangues of *The Day* and the business community had paid off in 1910 when the New London Ship and Engine Company moved into the empty shipyard of the Eastern Shipbuilding Company, bankrupt after James Hill's scheme to build steamships to carry wheat to the Orient had collapsed. The new company built diesel engines, which led eventually to the construction of submarines at the shipyard by the Electric Boat Company. The submarine shipyard would be the dominant industry in the region through two world wars and the Cold War.

Bodenwein appreciated these little advances, understanding better than many that progress was incremental. The Navy coaling station the region had fought so hard to obtain became an important submarine base. The transfer of a small school to Fort Trumbull placed the city closer to becoming the site of the United States Coast Guard Academy.

Connecticut College was scheduled to open with three main buildings a year after Bodenwein's 50th birthday. Frank V. Chappell, who was one of the first trustees, took the opportunity to sell the college all its coal. His father was Alfred H. Chappell, who had been a leader in the drive to bring the college to the city. New London's elite felt a sense of ownership in the college and was taking advantage of its proprietary rights by installing favorites in jobs and positions of importance at the new college. A city hospital endowed by the Lawrence family had opened in 1912, carrying on a history of philanthropy in the city in which wealthy families attached their names to significant and lasting public institutions—a practice that could not but raise in Bodenwein's mind the question of what he would leave behind. New London was talking about building a highway bridge across the Thames River to replace the ferry, the same ferry that had brought the Bodenweins to their home in Groton and had carried them to their second home in New London.

For Bodenwein and others, the single greatest hope for New London rested with the $1 million ocean pier being constructed on the Thames River under the watchful eyes of Waldo E. Clarke. New London felt its time had come as a major port. The New London Businessmen's Association had maneuvered to make the city the site for the national convention in 1912 of the Atlantic Deeper Waterways Association. This group had been formed to promote development of an inland waterway from Maine to Florida along which goods could be shipped by water protected from the perils of the open Atlantic Ocean. New London, with its pier, inland rail connections, and protected waters, was expected to be a key piece of that plan. President William Howard Taft visited the convention and inspected the work on the pier when the delegates met in April 1912. Congressman Mahan spoke before the large group of business leaders from around the country and made a pitch for New London.

The time had long passed since Bodenwein had to curry favor in New London. Now, leaders sought his advice and favor. His stature was reflected in his selection as president of the New London Businessmen's Association in 1914. In that position, Bodenwein campaigned to merge the association and the Board of Trade into a stronger organization to promote the city. This effort eventually paid off in the formation of the New London Chamber of Commerce. Bodenwein would become its first president in 1920. His name had been published as early as 1898 in *Men of Progress*, which contained sketches of Connecticut business leaders, and in *Men of Mark in Connecticut* in 1910. The latter described him as "a striking example of American citizenship."

AT 50, HE STILL had time left. Bodenwein was determined to use it to complete his work with *The Day*. He had not always been attentive to that task. His family had competed for his attention soon after he bought *The Day*. Later family troubles distracted him. And when he entered politics and ran for office, he left the newspaper in the hands of others, an action he later regretted. The newspaper showed the effects of his absences in its bland and predictable pages from 1904 to 1908. He later acknowledged this problem and resumed a more hands-on approach to managing *The Day*. The period from 1911-1916 was a period of great activity at *The Day*, much of it emanating from Bodenwein's presence at the helm.

Bodenwein had laid the foundation for his work by incorporating The Day Publishing Company as a stock company. On August 13, 1909, the state authorized the company to issue one thousand shares of capital stock with a par value of $50 a share. The Day Publishing Company was formally incorporated September 15. The original incorporators, in addition to Bodenwein, were his brother-in-law, William H. Rolfe, Walter Slocum, Joseph T. Chapman, and Alfred W. Newman.

With new capital, he set out to modernize the newspaper in all its aspects. One of his first concerns was to build up the newspaper's advertising to correspond to the rapid business growth in the city. Until 1905, *The Day* had not systematically pursued this task. New London's growth at the turn of the century brought with it a proliferation of small retail businesses, many of them run by immigrants. While the established businesses often were parsimonious with their advertising dollars, Bodenwein saw great raw potential for new advertising revenue from these newcomers whose shops were crowded along Bank and Main Streets. He also sought to make the jump from patent medicine advertising to the growing lucrative market in national brand advertising. He organized a full-service advertising department to help businesses prepare ads. The *Day* advertising staff studied store conditions and provided business advice as well as sold advertising.

The new department drifted along without demonstrable results until 1914, when Charles C. Hemenway, one of Bodenwein's earlier reporters who left *The Day* to work for the Hartford *Times*, tipped Bodenwein off to the existence of an eager young clothing salesman with a background in retail advertising: Orvin G. Andrews. Andrews previously had worked in advertising for department stores in Newport, Rhode Island, and in Peoria, Illinois. Bodenwein wrote Andrews to ask if he would be interested in joining *The Day* as an advertising solicitor. Several letters were exchanged and in the winter of 1914, Andrews agreed to go to work for *The Day*. He was 26. It took him eight months to make that decision, he recalled more than 40 years later. He was aware that leaving Rhode Island to work in Peoria had been a big mistake. Job security was poor there and the managers required that he be a floorwalker as well as an advertising solicitor. He didn't want to move his wife and children again without some assurance that he was taking a job where he'd be comfortable in staying. Bodenwein interviewed him on a Sunday afternoon:

> *I'll never forget that drizzly Sunday I came for the personal interview. The wind was whipping around the Taylor Drug Store corner. In those days, I wore glasses that pinched into the nose; no temples over the ears. Rounding that corner, the wind caught me on the tack and away went the glasses when I grabbed onto my hat. One lens lay in smithereens on the brick pavement. Atop this misfortune, I had to wait for the boss to show up for the appointment. I was kind of a sorry mess.*

Bodenwein nevertheless hired him from among scores of applicants, four hundred according to his own account. In Andrews, Bodenwein quickly discovered that at last he had found a business mind that worked like his own.

BODENWEIN ALSO TURNED HIS attention to selling more newspapers. That task was a challenge from two standpoints. Trolley lines had enabled *The Day* to expand its circulation to outlying towns and villages, where the newspaper enjoyed the greatest advantage compared to its rivals. But the trolleys did not go everywhere, were often unreliable, and, worst of all, the companies began to charge the newspaper to carry its bundles whereas the service had once been free. To solve these problems, *The Day* purchased its first black delivery trucks, on which the newspaper's familiar logo was painted in white. To provide the outlying territories with news coverage, Bodenwein relied upon a corps of town correspondents who were paid by the inch to provide copy. They performed their jobs with a wide range of literary and reporting talents. *The Day* had suburban reporters in twenty places around the southeastern corner of Connecticut and on Fisher's Island, New York, a small residential island off New London's shore.

By 1916, the *Day's* circulation had climbed to more than nine thousand, compared to the one thousand level it had when Bodenwein bought *The Day* in 1891. Nearly half his base was outside New London. The only area Bodenwein could not seem to crack were the towns to the west along the Connecticut River, where Middletown and Hartford newspapers controlled the territory.

Bodenwein had a full-time staff of forty, with a weekly payroll of $850 in 1916. He had six reporters, including Alfred Ligourie, who had been hired out of high school in 1908, and Lillian Lamb, who reported on society news and looked the part with the colorful big hats she liked to wear to work. He also took Malcolm Mollan, a much-respected newspaperman in Connecticut, away from the *Morning Telegraph* to be the *Day*'s editor in charge of writing editorials. Mollan was an intimate of the millionaire Morton Plant, who put some of his own money into the *Telegraph* in a futile attempt to keep the paper afloat. Mollan left *The Day* in 1920 to become editor of the Manchester (Connecticut) *Herald*.

Bodenwein did most of the hiring, and he paid close attention to the quality of the reporters *The Day* enlisted. Because of his preference for hiring young, local men, the Bulkeley School was for years the most provident spawning ground for *Day* reporters. Such employment became a coveted prize for new graduates, and Bodenwein had the luxury of being able to pick from among many applicants. Of this task, he would remark in 1916: "I have found a strong desire among men of all kinds to take the position of reporter, but few of whom had the slightest qualification for the work."

Bodenwein tried to hold onto the best, but he was not always successful. He was often proud of the ones that got away and went on to greater work in bigger cities. One of his favorites among these was the aforementioned Charles C. Hemenway, editor of the Hartford *Times*. Arthur McGinley, one of John McGinley's sons, became the sports editor of the same newspaper. Bodenwein called *The Day* a graduating school for reporting talent. But in 1916, a more permanent staff, one he felt comfortable to trust his newspaper to, was forming. The core included Ligourie, who would become the city editor for many years; George Grout, the news editor; and Andrews, whom Bodenwein later named general manager. These were not necessarily the best minds to pass through *The Day*. Mollan was far better an editor than, say, Grout would be. But these men were trusted. They developed a loyalty to *The Day* that was almost familial, and that was important to Bodenwein. Loyalty was a quality he sought among advertisers, readers, and staff, for he felt it ensured a long life for his newspaper. Grout had been with the newspaper almost from the time Bodenwein took control of *The Day*.

Bodenwein was strict and demanding, but he respected his workers, and believed throughout his life that if he treated his employees well, they would return the favor. He had a Republican antipathy toward unions, but maintained excellent labor relations with the International Typographical Union that had formed in New London in 1896 when Frank Munsey arrived in town. He did not always agree with the International representatives from out of town, but the local officers found him, if not always agreeable to their terms, at least reasonable and, more important, respectful. Their first dispute had occurred during contract negotiations in 1902. While Bodenwein, who owned both *The Day* and the *Morning Telegraph* then, agreed to the union's wage proposals, he objected to its demands to make Labor Day a holiday. He complained that it would be an "injustice" to force the newspapers to close that day, though he offered to let the workers have time off to attend the Labor Day parade. He won that battle. And the union still felt kindly enough toward him to endorse his candidacy for secretary of the state in 1904, noting in a resolution:

> *Theodore Bodenwein ... has always acceded to every just demand or request by the New London Typographical Union No. 159, and has treated his employees with the greatest consideration at all times. It was principally through and by him that the present satisfactory scale of our union is in operation. He has been unreservedly genial and friendly to all members of our craft, and it is but justice to ourselves and Mr. Bodenwein that we reciprocate his manifestations of good will toward printers in particular and organized labor in general.*

Bodenwein was not always as pleased with the outcome of negotiations. He only reluctantly assented to wage increases, which placed the local printers in a higher scale than several other cities of the same size in the state. He also complained that the local printers were slow learners of the new technology he was introducing. He regarded this as a national problem.

> *It seems to me that the inventors of labor-saving and improved machinery have outdistanced the ability of the average workman. Newspaper publishers invest great sums in modern machinery and are not able to obtain the full degree of efficiency out of it.*

Bodenwein looked forward to the day when the newspaper unions would establish training schools for apprentices.

Bodenwein remade *The Day* into a modern product, but he was careful not to make some of the same mistakes Frank Munsey made that offended readers. The changes were introduced gradually. *The Day* again changed its logo from the busy montage of local engineering marvels Bodenwein started with to the official New London seal, which had on it a clipper ship. The change made the front page of the newspaper cleaner and more appealing to the eye. Bodenwein also divided the paper into clearly defined sections and set them off from one another with attractive headlines. The newspaper offered a full sports section, under the editorial direction of George Eshenfelder. Half the section was devoted to local news. New London was an avid sports town, with a preference for baseball and boxing, and *The Day* covered both closely and thoroughly.

He also overhauled the *Day*'s dull editorial page. He enhanced its substance with stronger editorials that were in larger type and more attractively presented at the top of the page. He further dressed up the page with political cartoons, which were run large. The section also carried feature stories and columns.

It was a departure from the earlier days when the editorials were written by anyone on the staff who had extra time to write them and the page was a sea of gray type. The way was shown by the *Morning Telegraph*, which under Frederick Latimer's direction, had taken to running lively editorials in a more flamboyant page layout. In 1912, before Bodenwein completely overhauled the section, *The Day* started copying the *Telegraph's* practice of featuring more important editorials in larger type at the top of the page. Bodenwein not only borrowed the *Telegraph's* style, but recruited Latimer to be the editor of the *Day's* editorial page.

> *I came to the conclusion that a strong editorial department could be made a special feature of the paper. I think that we have succeeded in lifting* The Day's *editorial pages out of the commonplace rut. I believe one or two editorials with inspiration and force—with some punch behind them—hold the attention of newspaper readers better than a page of matter merely written to fill space.*

Bodenwein boasted that he had mastered every facet of running a newspaper—mechanical, business, and editorial. He had started as a printer. He was a student of press technology from a very young age inspecting the machinery in George Starr's print shop. He understood the dynamics of newsgathering and he was capable of writing well. He was a meticulous and demanding editor. He attributed his success largely to his well-rounded grasp of the business. He never had to rely on others to make decisions. His skills enabled him to buy the best new equipment. In 1914, he bought his fifth press, a Hoe Company product that could print twenty-four thousand sixteen-page editions or twelve thousand thirty-two-page editions an hour. *The Day* had to tear down an old building and build an annex to the rear to accommodate it. Gradually, the growing newspaper spread out in all directions in adding to its Main Street plant.

Two years after his 50th birthday, Theodore Bodenwein passed another

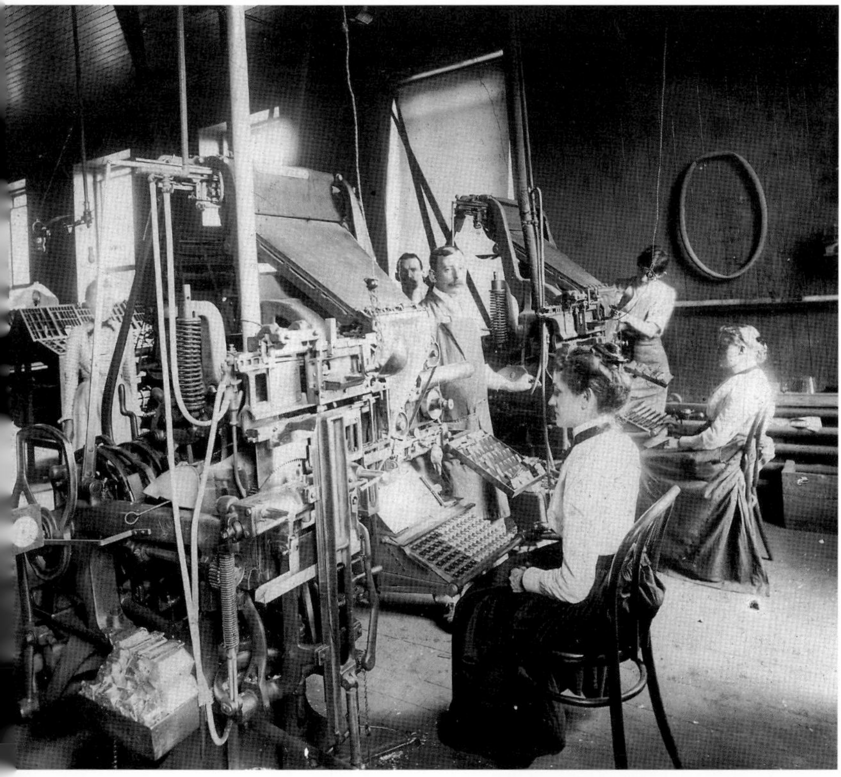

Left, Many of the early printers at *The Day* were women, and some of them stayed on when Linotype machines replaced hand setting type. One of the women Linotype operators was Mary Sheridan, foreground, in this 1896 picture. *Ralph Daniels*

Above, To save money, *The Day* moved into this building, known as the Brown House, on Bank Street before relocating to new quarters in the Chappell building also on Bank Street in 1894. *New London Public Library*

Left, Main Street was lined with small businesses when Theodore Bodenwein built a new plant for *The Day* there in the early 20th century. The site, where *The Day* still is located, is on the right, near the middle of the photograph. The street has been renamed for Eugene O'Neill, the playwright, who spent his childhood in New London. *Lyman Allyn Museum of Art at Connecticut College*

Left, Frank H. Chappell and Alfred H. Chappell built this home for *The Day* in 1894. The building, at 240 Bank Street nearly burned down early in the 20th century and was finally destroyed in a blaze caused by the 1938 hurricane. *Picturesque New London*

Left, *The Day* printers posed for this picture in 1900. James P. Neilan, the composing room foreman, is seated. Julian Moran who later owned the *Morning Telegraph*, is third from the left. *Ralph Daniels*

ight, Theodore Bodenwein had recently been
lected Connecticut's secretary of the state
hen this photograph was taken in 1905.
he Day

elow, Theodore Bodenwein still in his 20s, is
eated at the far left in this picture taken in
he Day newsroom in its quarters at 240 Bank
treet. George Grout is leaning against the
esk. Reporter Charles H. Thompson is
tanding to the right. The man seated in front
f him is Malcolm Mollan. Both Thompson
nd Mollan went on to distinguished careers
utside the city. *The Day*

Left, After Alfred H. Chappell suggested he might want Bodenwein to vacate the *Day's* headquarters on Bank Street to make way for Frank Munsey's magazine, Theodore Bodenwein built this new headquarters for the newspaper on Main Street in 1907. The original building was doubled in size in 1928. *The Day*

Right, Pressmen and printers posed for this photo in front of the *Day's* building on Bank Street, the Brown House, in the late 1880s, before *The Day* moved into a new building down the street. *The Day*

Left, Spectators watched the Yale-Harvard crew race, which John Tibbits campaigned to bring to New London, from the railroad bridge across the Thames River in the summer of 1893. *New London Public Library*

bove, American magazine and newspaper ıblisher Frank Munsey, a familiar figure in ew London for his business ventures there, ·uck both fear and respect in Theodore ɔdenwein. *AP / Wide World Photos*

Below, Bodenwein felt more comfortable going to Alfred H. Chappell rather than Chappell's brother, Frank, in broaching the subject of a new building in the 1890s. The Chappells turned *The Day* over to Bodenwein in 1891. *The Day*

Above, By 1916, the *Day's* news staff had grown considerably, as this photo of the newsroom shows. William Rolfe, the telegraph editor, is at the far left. Others, from left are, George Grout, the news editor, Alfred Ligourie and Mark Staples, reporters, Malcolm Mollan, the editor, John H. Smith, a reporter and George Eshenfelder, the sports writer. *The Day*

Above, Anton Bodenwein, Theodore's father, had become a popular figure in New London's German-American community when this photo was taken before his death in 1917. *The Day*

Above, John G. Crump was a judge and managing editor of *The Day* until he committed suicide in 1895. *Picturesque New London*

Right, The year after he worked for the *Morning Telegraph*, Eugene O'Neill posed for this picture with a nurse and a friend at a sanitarium, where he was treated for tuberculosis. *New London Public Library*

The Day

Left, One of Theodore Bodenwein's promotions for *The Day* was a "beautiful baby" contest. This 1894 page displayed some of the winners that year. *The Day*

Above, Edna Bodenwein kept three photographs in a small red cloth case, those of her second husband, Theodore Bodenwein, her third husband, Victor Heimbucher, and this one believed to be of her first husband, Lewis Winfield, a laborer she married in Trenton, New Jersey, when she was a teenager. *Donald Mitchell*

Above, Jennie and Theodore Bodenwein had this house on Montauk Avenue, (shown as it appears today,) built in 1896, before their marriage broke up. *Skip Weisenburger, The Day*

Right, Work on an eight-story building for *Munsey's Magazine,* shown here in its early stages, attracted considerable attention. When Frank Munsey ran into labor difficulties, he turned the building into the Mohican Hotel. *New London Public Library*

Above, John McGinley, seated far right, was the patriarch of this large family and a source of inspiration for playwright Eugene O'Neill and Theodore Bodenwein. The McGinley's are shown here shortly before John McGinley died in 1915. The others are, seated from left, John's wife, Evelyn Essex; and sons Morgan, whose so Morgan years later became editorial page editor of *The Day*; John and Winthrop. In the back row, from left, are sons Lawrence, Arthur, Thomas and Stephen and daughter Evelyn. Arthur and Thomas were sidekicks of O'Neill. *Morgan McGinley*

important milestone as the United States drew closer to war. In 1916 he observed the 25th anniversary of his September 1891 agreement with Frank Chappell and others to take over the operation of *The Day*. Bodenwein had a consuming preoccupation with history and his role in it, and each anniversary was, for him, an occasion to look back at the progress he had made and to peer toward the future. In September 1916, *The Day* published an expansive anniversary edition marking the twenty-five years Bodenwein had owned it. In this edition, he laid out the newspaper's history, and ruminated upon its future and upon his legacy.

Mortality is an issue that suggests itself to one in his fifties, and the subject may have had a greater immediacy to Bodenwein at the time. The previous fall, he had lost his best friend, the man who had been a second father to him, who had worked at his side for a decade, who had smoothed his way into New London society and had helped him gain political importance, the man who the year before had entertained the guests at his 50th birthday party. John McGinley's health began to fail early in 1915, when he experienced a minor stroke. He suffered a more serious stroke the following October and never regained consciousness. His obituary in *The Day* began: "John McGinley, than whom no man in New London was better known or better loved, died at his home, 46 Jay Street, at 4:15 this morning. *The Day*'s lead editorial on October 2 was a tribute to McGinley:

> *To merely assert that John McGinley was one man in 10,000, that his creator endowed him with a singular sweetness of character and with a broad and tolerant charity as rare in quality as in comprehensiveness, is to but touch the borderland of justice. The kindliness of the man, the magnanimity of him, the native culture and sunniness of his disposition, combined with a rare and widely comprehending intellect to make his personality as distinctive as a prismatic color.*

In addition, Bodenwein wrote his own, deeply personal tribute:

> *He radiated geniality and sunshine. He was always optimistic and seeing only the bright side of everything. His keen wit was never punctured with acidity. He never knowingly injured the feelings of even the most humble. Enemies he had none.*

The pallbearers at his funeral included United States Senator Frank H. Brandegee, Postmaster Bryan Mahan, and Bodenwein. With a clear sense of his own mortality, Bodenwein wrote in September 1916:

> *I wanted to make* The Day *a recognized public institution in New*

London—something everyone would be proud of and turn to as one of the big things of the city—something which the community would be noted for. I do not know whether I have succeeded. I know people say The Day *is a remarkably fine paper, as good as many issued in much larger cities. But in my mind, the paper is yet capable of improvement. I hope to make many changes for its betterment before I am compelled to retire from the scene of newspaper activity. I have my ideals and aspirations well in mind, but carrying them out concretely is another matter.*

Bodenwein briefly recounted his own experiences with the newspaper, mentioning both his successes and failures. He mentioned that more than ten years earlier he had hoped to turn over the operation of the newspaper to others. But he found there was much more work that demanded his attention. He said he worried about the future:

I begin to wonder now what will be the fortunes of The Day *ten or 20 years from now. Man's span of life is limited. But no matter who may be at the helm or what politics may be guiding it, my earnest hope is that* The Day, *unlike us poor mortals, will be able to go on forever.*

ELEVEN

THE WAR YEARS

I was born in New London and for years we went down to the banks of the river and saw nothing but a vacant sea. By the coming of the Deutschland, *we see a commercial undersea line between the U.S. and Germany.*

—Bryan F. Mahan, November 8, 1916

THE CLOUDS OF THE war that was raging in Europe drifted across the United States late in 1916. Theodore Bodenwein and his associates in New London hoped that the United States would remain out of the conflict. For Bodenwein, the sentiment arose partly from his German heritage. But for this circle of practical men, national loyalties and lofty values had less influence than sound business sense.

The war in Europe presented New London with a surprising opportunity to prove the value of the big ocean pier that Senator Bryan Mahan had won for the city five years earlier. Its construction was nearing completion in 1916, but unfortunately without any promising commercial prospects. The project had been attacked from other parts of the state from the beginning. Early on, legislators had tried to take back the funds. Newspapers, led by the *Hartford Courant*, attacked the project as folly and waste.

The war posed a vexing problem for Bodenwein, Waldo E. Clarke, Mahan, and the other leaders who envisioned New London as a major Atlantic port. A British naval blockade hampered shipping, which seriously threatened New London's grand plans—at least until the arrival of an unusual German submarine. German U-boats had been wreaking havoc on Atlantic shipping. On May 15, 1915, one of those undersea warships had sunk the British liner *Lusitania* killing 128 Americans. The attack inflamed American public opinion in favor of entering the war, though not *The Day*, which steadfastly supported the American policy of neutrality.

Existing combat submarines were new, small, and even thought by some to be of dubious military value despite the damage they were causing at the time. The significant exception was the larger German *Deutschland* class of U-boat. The Germans built two of these, the *Deutschland* and *Bremen*. Each was 315 feet long, with two large cargo compartments. They carried eight officers, twenty-one enlisted men, and had a capacity for seven hundred tons of cargo. They were capable of speeds of fourteen knots on the surface and seven knots undersea. The lead ship was commanded by Captain Paul Koenig, 45, an urbane and respected naval officer. Germany maintained that these large submarines were noncombatant, undersea mercantile vessels designed to elude the naval blockade. The British charged, without proof, that they were engaged in espionage.

The *Bremen* was lost at sea. But the *Deutschland* made two visits to the United States before America entered the war; the first to Baltimore, the second on October 31, 1916, to New London. German officials said New London was chosen because of its harbor's deep waters and accessibility from the Atlantic. It also undoubtedly helped that the city's leading newspaper, *The Day*, was friendly toward Germany and was owned by a German American. There was also a vocal German American community in the city, which included Charles Klinck, father-in-law of Waldo Clarke, the resident engineer at the State Pier. Germans had established velvet mills in the region, including the Rossie Velvet Mill in Mystic. Part of the *Deutschland's* cargo was dye for these mills.

The visit was enveloped in secrecy. Local officials were briefed only days before the ship was to arrive. *The Day* did not report on the plans until Tuesday, October 31, eight hours before the boat's arrival. Arrangements for berthing at the State Pier were made by the Eastern Forwarding Company, also known as the Ocean Navigation Company, a German firm acting as agent for the *Deutschland*. A representative met secretly with the mayor, Ernest E. Rogers, and Clarke, who were stunned by the news but deeply appreciative. Instructions from Washington were to accommodate the ship, and there was no reluctance to do so. In fact, there was a great deal of joyful excitement. A long section of the pier on the north side was sealed off and large floating barriers with barbed wire across the tops were towed in to create a secure berth for the vessel.

Everyone had a slightly different reason to derive satisfaction from the submarine's arrival. Mahan and Clarke were the prime movers behind the State Pier and were briefed with other city leaders about the Germans' intentions of making New London a principal port of call for the "undersea merchant ships." They were ecstatic, for here was the big chance they foresaw for making New London into another Liverpool.

For Mayor Rogers, it was the first big event of his administration. With the strong backing of Bodenwein, whom he had met as a young clerk for the *Telegraph*, Rogers had been elected mayor only the year before, when Mahan left office to become postmaster. A methodical, intelligent man, an accountant by training, Rogers, just turned 50, had driving personal ambitions and a sense of self-importance. He never reached his goal of becoming governor, but the *Deutschland* thrust him, in the infancy of his political career, upon the world stage. Suddenly, he, Ernest Rogers, was dealing with Washington, Hartford, and the German government, in the person of Captain Frederick Hinsch, manager of the Eastern Forwarding Company, a subsidiary of the North German Lloyd Line. Hinsch moved into the Mohican Hotel and motored around in a German-made limousine with American and German flags flying from the front fenders.

It was clear from his writings that Bodenwein was awash with emotions. As a German American, he shared the feelings of other Germans in the country who opposed American involvement in the war. He had submerged his immigrant past, but the thought that Germany might become the key to New London's prosperity unleashed his sense of pride in his roots. Anton, now 78, fanned the flame of his son's fervor with his own exuberance, which resonated through the local German community. As a leader in the effort to develop the State Pier, Bodenwein also saw this visit as a validation of the oft-ridiculed project.

The *Deutschland* had left Bremen October 1 but rammed a tugboat on its way out of the harbor and had to return to port for repairs. It set out again on October 10, running submerged and dodging steel nets and British warships to break through the blockade. It surfaced in Fishers Island Sound late in the evening of October 31, to the astonishment of the crew of a trawler who first spotted the submarine in the glare of their searchlight.

The *Telegraph* scooped *The Day* on the story of the *Deutschland's* arrival. As he was leaving O'Leary's saloon late at night, a reporter for the morning newspaper literally stumbled into two government health officers who had just visited the submarine to conduct routine physical examinations before the ship berthed. The reporter had the presence of mind to ask why they were out so late and they told him scarcely in time for him to file a story for the morning edition. By Wednesday morning, November 1, the story was in the streets and on The Associated Press wires, causing excitement and controversy.

The New London Chamber of Commerce prepared elaborate plans for the *Deutschland*, whose arrival, leaders decided, would mark the grand opening of the State Pier. Bodenwein arranged a lavish dinner for the officers and crew at the Crocker House. He was assisted by George Sturdy, publisher of the *Globe*, Waldo Clarke, and Charles Klinck, Clarke's father-in-law. Germany's increasingly bold submarine attacks on Atlantic shipping were turning public opinion against Germany. Rolling out the red carpet for a potential belligerent did not please everyone. One who took offense was George S. Palmer, whose family owned Palmer Brothers, a local manufacturer of comforters. Palmer was also among the New London businessmen who invested in the *Morning Telegraph* in its long struggle to stay afloat. A righteous man and a leader in the temperance movement, Palmer questioned the patriotism of his fellow New Londoners who were going to such great lengths to entertain the Germans. In a letter November 7 to the *Telegraph*, he obliquely chided German Americans like Bodenwein:

> *During the past several days, many New London people have noted with surprise and regret not unmixed with indignation what seems to them the extraordinary social activities of certain citizens toward the personnel of the German submarine now barricaded and guarded by intricate systems of electricity and barbed wire at the Connecticut wharf in our city. It is commendable that they put it to use for foreign commerce. I have no criticism of people of German descent who … are especially drawn toward the daring countrymen who have risen from the depths of the sea at their very doors. Let them rejoice together. Such are the natural outlets of racial feeling. But when our Chamber of Commerce and our municipal authorities, supposedly standing for the whole body of our citizenship, join in such festivities … they are heard to convey to the German visitors assurance of cordial approval and sympathy … We cannot be giving loving cups to the officers of German submarines who at some future time may possibly make their presence known torpedoing without warning American merchant ships in sight of our shore.*

Bodenwein was sensitive to the perception that his newspaper's objectivity was compromised by his German past. He made a point of reporting the events surrounding the *Deutschland* thoroughly and impartially. The day after the ship arrived, he attended an afternoon press conference conducted by Koenig at the Mohican, and *The Day* published a detailed story under his byline. Ordinarily, John Mallon, the newspaper's leading reporter, would have covered the story. But the publisher wanted to make sure to get it right.

He recounted details of the *Deutschland's* voyage to the city. The story referred to several sensitive issues raised by the press, including the value and nature of the ship's cargo, an incident in Baltimore Harbor in which two fishing vessels allegedly violated American neutrality by spreading their nets in the submarine's path, and the fate of the *Bremen*. Bodenwein noted Koenig spoke English well and was "a diplomat of the first order."

The same day, the *Day's* lead editorial lashed back at nonbelievers for holding New London and its State Pier up to ridicule, noting that one no less authoritative than Captain Paul Koenig had declared that New London had "one of the finest harbors in the world." For some time, the newspaper said,

> *There had been a pronounced disposition on the part of an element in Connecticut newspaperdom to deprecate the idea, to belittle the potentialities of a Connecticut seaport, to employ sarcasm whenever the subject of the New London ocean port came up in any form for discussion. To these newspapers and the gentlemen who control their policies,* The Day *points out the fact that New London was selected by the Ocean Navigation Company as its terminal for the reason that its approach from the sea is more direct and through a greater depth of water than that of any other port on the Atlantic seaboard; and because, arrived at, it is, in fact, as Captain Koenig says, "one of the finest harbors in the world."*

All that week, crowds flocked to the waterfront to get a peek at the submarine. Koenig and the crew became celebrities overnight. There was a parade in their honor in Mystic. The New York *World* invited Koenig and several of his officers to spend the night at the newspaper on election night that week (they politely turned down the offer). Theatrical promoters poured into the city with offers to the officers and crew to make guest stage appearances in New York. One New York theatrical producer offered to take the whole crew on an all-expense-paid trip to the city. All the invitations were declined, for the crew had to be on hand for the submarine's secret departure, whenever that was to be.

Under Bodenwein's supervision, the Crocker House was transformed into what a *Day* writer referred to as "a veritable Garden of Eden" for the welcoming dinner Wednesday, November 8. The event was sold out. Freshly cut flowers filled the big room of the old hotel. German and American flags were draped over the walls. Each crewmember received a sterling silver match box and solid gold fountain pen engraved with his name and the date. Koenig received a gold watch with the seal of the city engraved on the back. Ernest Rogers noted in presenting it to him that the motto on the seal was "Mare Liberum," Latin for a free sea. The gifts came from Perry & Stone.

The Day proclaimed the reception was "unquestionably the biggest and friendliest gathering given guests by the citizens of the whaling city." The speakers looked forward to a long and flourishing trade relationship with the

Germans, one that would transform New London, at last, into the great seaport it was destined to be. Frank V. Chappell, Alfred H. Chappell's son and chairman of the Rivers, Harbors and Bridges Commission, spoke of how the *Deutschland's* arrival validated the need for the State Pier:

> *We see in Captain Koenig and his crew the first recognition of the facility of the state pier. He and his men crossed the Atlantic in a submarine and came to this port. Governor Winthrop, the founder of New London, walked from Boston to the site of the Old Pequot Indian village. Since then New London has developed and we believe in having facilities for enterprise.*

Germany and southeastern Connecticut had much in common, Chappell said. Both depended on great rivers for commerce. The arrival of "the most wonderful ship that has sailed the seas" marked the beginning of the commercial development of the State Pier, he said. With the opening of the Panama Canal, New London would become homeport for vessels trading with Hawaii and the Pacific coast. Cargoes of lumber from the West Coast and wheat from Canada would arrive on the Great Northern and Central Vermont railroads for shipment from New London. A huge grain elevator would rise on the city's waterfront. "The day has already come when we have a return on our State Pier."

Koenig responded with gracious words for his hosts, sending spirits soaring by describing New London as one of the greatest ports in the world. He said that if it weren't for the British naval blockade, he would like to bring the kaiser to the city to see this wonder for himself. In that day's issue, Bodenwein described Koenig in "The Tattler" as a hero, regardless of his nationality.

> *Every day the state pier has witnessed throngs of people from far and near, watching for a chance to get a glimpse of him. Admiration for a man of courage is inherent among the American people. In Captain Koenig this quality is recognized and appreciated.*

The week saw more serious business, as the ship prepared for its return voyage. Rumors circulated that British and French warships lay in wait for the *Deutschland* in the waters of the Atlantic off eastern Long Island. That week, the German ambassador to the United States and his wife visited the ship, staying overnight in the Mohican. The last of the returning cargo, consisting of $2 million worth of nickel, rubber, and silver bars, was loaded onboard and the city speculated when the submarine would leave.

On November 16, Koenig visited throughout the downtown. He visited the Crown Theater and dropped in at the Crocker House bar. This turned out to be his way of saying goodbye without letting anyone know he was about to leave. At one-thirty the next morning, the *Deutschland* left its berth at the State Pier, accompanied by the tugs *T.A. Scott Jr.* and *Cassie* of the T.A. Scott Wrecking Company, which was employed by the Germans as towboat operator for the submarine. The ship headed south pursued by launches *The Day* and *Telegraph* had rented to keep tabs on the submarine and had manned around the clock. They followed the submarine into open waters and then turned back, thus missing the opportunity to be eyewitness to a huge story.

A full moon illuminated the smooth waters. The *Deutschland* headed into The Race, a turbulent channel between Fishers Island and Long Island that provided an entry to the Atlantic. The tide was running strongly. The submarine was preceded by the *T.A. Scott Jr.*, serving as the pilot boat since there was no pilot on the sub. Captain Hinsch, manager of the Eastern Forwarding Company, was on board the *T.A. Scott Jr.* to see the submarine to safety. The tugboat *Cassie* had fallen a half-mile behind as the two vessels picked up speed. Koenig and the crew of the sub were anxious to get into the Atlantic and submerge before any enemy ships spotted it. The *Deutschland* turned toward Montauk Point, the easternmost tip of Long Island, intending to make a dash for open sea. Just as it picked up speed, the strong current turned the *T.A. Scott Jr.* broadside into the path of the submarine. The *Deutschland* struck the tug in the rear, upending and sending the boat and its crew to the bottom of The Race in a matter of minutes. All five of the crew lost their lives trapped inside the boat. But Hinsch, who was standing on the deck, was thrown into the water and pulled to safety by the crew of the *Cassie*.

That afternoon, *The Day* published an editorial honoring the memory of the men who died. It was, indeed, a hard fortune, the newspaper observed, that such an auspicious occasion, the very first opportunity for the employment of its new ocean terminal, should be marred by tragedy. Only those who understood what it meant to a community to see its highest aspirations within reach after many years of striving could understand what this meant to the people of New London, the editorial writer continued. But in the end, he wrote,

> *the men aboard the* T.A. Scott Jr. *didn't die for nothing. They gave up their lives for a great ideal. They were part of a vast enterprise … an enterprise that will have its effect and will build its monuments long after all of us have gone to join them in the great beyond. For they were helping to make a new center of commerce of the world, a new mart where the work of the hands of man will meet the work of the hands of man in barter from the four corners of the earth.*

The *Deutschland* returned to port, but departed several days later, leaving behind bittersweet memories but little of consequence to help the city become a new center of international commerce. The port call was the last significant commercial activity the facility would see for years. Hinsch remained in New London to supervise the nonactivities of the Eastern Forwarding Company until America entered the war. The hubbub over the *Deutschland* must have been a proud time for Anton Bodenwein, as it was for his son. Theodore had escaped his background as a poor immigrant and become successful in America, but then found it possible to feel genuine pride in his past in the economic miracle offered by a trade relationship between New London and Germany and the celebrity of Captain Paul Koenig.

Bodenwein and other New Londoners awaited anxiously the return of the *Deutschland* as the months passed and the United States was drawn more deeply into the conflict. Stories appeared regularly speculating about the ship's return. Such a story appeared in *The Day* on January 30, 1917. The newspaper reported a rumor that the *Deutschland* was headed for New London. Hinsch, as he always did, denied knowing anything about it. Next to the story was a photograph of Anton Bodenwein, accompanied by his obituary.

Anton died of complications from an asthma attack. He had been in good health until several days before his death, but then his health deteriorated rapidly. Following breakfast, he fell asleep in his chair and died at the age of 79, forty-eight years after he had brought his wife Agnes and son Theodore to eastern Connecticut from Germany. He had been living in retirement in a rooming house on Main Street, down the street from his son's newspaper and from the block where he had run his shoemaking supply business.

The *Deutschland* never returned. George Palmer was right. The Germans fitted it with torpedo tubes and turned it into a warship. But the city never forgot the ship, and especially Koenig, the charming skipper. After the war, Koenig began corresponding with Waldo Clarke, and the Clarkes visited him in Germany in the 1920s, where he renewed efforts to establish commercial relations through Koenig's contacts with the North German Lloyd line.

The *Deutschland* was among thirty-seven submarines that ended up in the hands of Great Britain after the war. It was overhauled and taken on a tour of British coastal towns in the fall of 1919. The French later used it for target practice. An accidental engine-room explosion in Liverpool in September 1921 destroyed the ship.

The *Deutschland* haunted New London long after its departure. By a strange coincidence, late in 1918, a unit of American soldiers drove out a squad of Germans from a trench in France. As the victorious Americans ransacked the place for souvenirs, Fred Swanson, a doughboy from New London, discovered a book written by Captain Paul Koenig in which Koenig described the voyage of the *Deutschland* from Bremen to New London in the fall of 1916. The American military authorities would not let him send the book, but he mailed home a flyleaf showing a picture of Koenig. Swanson's name had been the first one drawn in his hometown when the draft was instituted in June 1917.

As the war developed, it looked more and more as though the state ocean pier would become a white elephant. The United States entered the war in March 1917, ending any prospects of significant trade. The Navy leased the facility from the state. New London was a strategic location in the Atlantic, and the pier was used for allied submarines and other vessels, government shipbuilding, and as a base for naval reservists. None of this returned the fabulous profits its developers had envisioned.

NEW LONDON AND THE area around it increasingly took on a military character and an industry took root that nobody had foreseen, nor fully appreciated as it developed. It was the business of war. The shipyard where James Hill had planned to build giant merchant ships that would turn New London into a world port became the site for the construction of the first diesel submarine engines, as the United States began to develop its capability in that field.

In March 1917, Congress approved a $1.2 million appropriation to build a submarine base at Groton, across the river from New London. The site for this was the tiny foothold of a naval base New Londoners had lobbied for after the Civil War. The installation had started as a coaling station. In the late 19th century, the region had strongly resisted plans to build a bridge over the Thames River out of fear this would be an obstacle to its future as an important naval installation, turning on John Tibbits, then editor of *The Day*, for supporting the railroad's interests in building the bridge. In September 1917, the Navy Department began buying additional property around the base.

Ernest Rogers reveled in his new role as a wartime mayor. Much of the task of mobilizing for the war fell to local governments, and Rogers attacked the job with zeal and efficiency. An officer in the National Guard, he formed and headed the New London Committee for Preparedness and Defense, which was principally responsible for recruiting members for the local Home Guard. More than five hundred attended the first drill at the state armory on Washington Street. New London organized the state's first battalion of the Home Guard.

The United States had only about 208,000 servicemen in uniform when it entered the war. To make up for this inadequacy, it instituted a draft. The first registration took place in June. Draft committees were set up in communities across the region and arrangements were made to prepare for the registration day, June 5, 1917. Rogers feared the worst, and police and National Guardsmen were stationed across the city as a precaution against violence. One fear was that the Socialist Party, which had a headquarters in Mystic, would foment disturbances. But the fears were unfounded. The Socialists could not agree on a position. New London and the area around it responded to the call with an outpouring of patriotism.

Registration Day was heralded with the ringing of church bells and sounding of fire whistles throughout the city shortly after dawn. Thousands of young men poured into the registration stations in the five voting wards in the city. The officials included *Day* reporter Alfred Ligourie, who as assistant city clerk was on duty at City Hall to register nonresidents. Mayor Rogers traveled from station to station to inspect the progress. That day, Judge Frederick Latimer commented with an eloquence and beauty that shines brilliantly in the history of the newspaper in an editorial entitled, "It Makes Us Glad." Latimer had left the flagging *Telegraph* in 1913 and returned to the fulltime practice of law, writing for *The Day* on the side. He wrote:

> *This morning's early blare of whistles and bells seemed to be the ushering in of a joyful holiday rather than a time of trouble and pain. Abundant sunshine, the sweet odors and bright appearance of June offered no temptation to gloomy thoughts. At the registration booths, even with the presence of military guards and their sharp bayonets, it was difficult to realize the grimness of the hours. We do not comprehend them. Perhaps that is a mercy. Troops with heavy hearts have a hard handicap on the march to victory. The nation would be in a bad case to tire itself out with emotions of sadness at its very entrance into the strain of war. We do right to begin our duty cheerfully. The best in life is the doing of duty. Life is a school for manhood and womanhood. Its triumph is the production of character. Except for their testimony of good lives lived, of hardships overcome, of evil things vanquished, not even flowers and flags could bring honor to the cemeteries; the monuments of antiquity would be no more of account than crumbling stones of the field, or the debris of broken forests.*

Bodenwein rallied behind the war effort. *The Day* documented its human drama and supported America's cause on the editorial page. It pushed the citizens to buy war bonds. The newspaper chronicled the hundreds of requests for exemptions that went before the draft board. It kept track of the many recruits and draftees who went to Camp Devens in Ayer, Massachusetts, to be shipped overseas to the war. Mayor Rogers, Colonel Christopher L. Avery of the National Guard, and Henry C. Chappell of the Defense Council presented each of the draftees with gold pieces before they left. Recruits from throughout New England passed through New London enroute to training centers. And as the war ground on, the newspaper began recording the mounting casualties, as well as the happy reunions and acts of heroism.

New London and its harbor were teeming with military activity. At the height of the conflict, more than ten thousand men in uniform were at installations in the area or aboard ships here. There were ships from around the world berthed at the State Pier next to the yachts of millionaires like Cornelius Vanderbilt that were pressed into service chasing submarines off the coast. The harbor filled with submarines, submarine chasers, and torpedo boats. At night, searchlights swept across the harbor looking for unwelcome vessels. During the day, the city filled with sailors of all stations and walks of life, including the very rich who entered the service of their country. No local industry benefited more than the local saloons, which swelled in number to eighty-four to accommodate the thirsts of the new arrivals, prompting a reconstitution of the temperance movement.

Among the first New London draftees to leave the city for military service was Andrew Satti, a second-generation son of one of New London's earliest Italian immigrants, grocer Charles Satti. A younger brother, C. John Satti, would later become a physician and powerful Democratic leader in the city. On November 19, 1918, *The Day* reported that Andrew Satti was the victim of a German gassing. He recovered and returned home, later to operate the confectionery shop his father started on Bank Street.

Dr. Joseph Ganey, a sidekick of Eugene O'Neill's, was ordered off to Fort Oglethorpe, Georgia, to serve in the medical corps. A year after their father's death, four of John McGinley's seven sons entered the war, a fact noted in *The Day* on October 3, 1917.

> *Seldom is a mother called upon to furnish four sons for her country's defense in the early days of the war, yet Mrs. John McGinley of Ocean Avenue has four sons who either are or will be shortly in the military service of the United States. This is a record of which any mother may be proud, and one which is yet unequaled in New London.*

Winthrop McGinley entered the medical corps as a surgeon. Thomas

McGinley, who was head of McGinley Brothers, a real estate firm, became an Army officer. Lawrence McGinley served in France in the medical corps. Arthur failed the eyesight test for the naval reserve, but was accepted into the Army. Playwright Eugene O'Neill, who was staying with his father on the day of the draft, successfully appealed for a medical deferment. He had suffered from tuberculosis. Earlier, he had mistakenly been arrested as a socialist agitator in Provincetown, Massachusetts, where he resided. John Mallon, who was among Bodenwein's favorite reporters and who mixed journalism with politics, and George A. Eshenfelder, sports writer, both left for military service. Both returned safely after the war to resume their jobs, although Mallon would work briefly in the office of Second District Congressman Richard P. Freeman.

In 1916, Jennie Bodenwein had moved to Brooklyn, New York, with Elizabeth, who entered Pratt Institute as an art student. Elizabeth met and later married Eugene Miles, a well-to-do artist from the Shaker Heights section of Cleveland. Gordon, who graduated that year from Yale, signed up with the naval reserve in 1917 and was stationed in Philadelphia performing administrative duties until his discharge when the war ended the following year. Gordon had turned into a strapping, handsome young man.

The war was both a problem and an opportunity for *The Day*. It created a scarcity in two critical commodities the newspaper needed, newsprint and gasoline. Bodenwein had to reduce the size of the newspaper and trim back distribution. But the paper still sold more copies because of the demand for war news. Eventually, higher costs of production forced Bodenwein to raise the price of *The Day* from two to three cents. But that did not occur until December 1918.

Bodenwein supported the war in most of its aspects, but he chafed at the government's obsession with secrecy and censorship. The practice reached deep into American life and was particularly intrusive in military areas like the region around New London. Army censors went so far as to monitor all telephone calls in the little waterfront village of Niantic, west of New London, where there was a small National Guard encampment. The government was concerned callers would disclose troop movements. "It's enough to make angels weep, this censorship stuff," Bodenwein huffed.

WHILE THE WORLD AROUND it shook with international turbulence, New London found time to devote to its ritual parochial concerns. Connecticut College, which had opened its doors in the fall of 1915, quickly became embroiled in a war of its own between Frederick H. Sykes, its first president, and the board of trustees, headed by Frank Valentine Chappell. The dispute was precipitated when Chappell raised the price he was charging the college for coal. This evoked the question of what the chairman of the board was doing selling coal to the college. Before long, charges were being hurled back and forth. Sykes accused Chappell and others on the board of feathering their own nests at the new college's expense. The college, one letter writer to *The Day* commented, had become "a mighty good thing for the Chappells." Chappell and the board counter-attacked, threatening Sykes, who originated most of the accusations, with removal from office. The students rallied to Sykes' defense, but he resigned in 1918 and was replaced by Benjamin J. Marshall. *The Day* supported the trustees and appealed for reason during the controversy. The *Hartford Courant* more pointedly questioned the propriety of the Chappells doing business with the college while Frank V. Chappell was serving as a trustee, notwithstanding the fact that his father, Alfred H. Chappell, had headed the drive to establish the institution.

The Chappells also found themselves in the middle of another controversy, this one about whether the city should take over the operation of the ferry to Groton. This was a perennial issue, going back to when Theodore Bodenwein had arrived in Groton, in fact even earlier than that. It seems everyone complained at one time or another. It made no difference who operated it. One as innovative as Maro Comstock, who installed the first steam engine aboard the boat to Groton, could not dispel the general perception of rotten service.

The advent of the automobile brought the issue to a climax. New London was on the main road between Boston and New York, and all the traffic had to cross the river on the ferry. The growing number of cars was creating huge traffic snarls in downtown New London and along the Groton waterfront. Vacation traffic in the summer compounded the problem. The problem was intensified because the ferry company, operated by the Chappells, had only one boat, which had a capacity for only seventeen vehicles. The ferry was cramped and it smelled, people complained. But the family still had plenty of political influence and almost blocked an attempt to take over the service. That battle came down once again to a fight between the Armstrong and the Chappell wings of the Republican Party.

In September 1917, the City Council voted to continue leasing the service; then, a week later, turned around and by a vote of 9-6 decided to take over the ferry. The verdict should not have come as a surprise. *The Day* commented in an editorial September 7, 1917:

The city was always stupid about the ferry, from a time that reaches back to antiquity. A right motive would have been to give the public the best obtainable accommodation. Instead the motive about the ferry has been either to make as much money as possible out of it, or to avoid as much as possible the expenditure of any money on account of it.

The war and the military presence in New London re-ignited another old debate in the city. In 1917, a fight broke out over whether or not the government should shut down the scores of saloons essentially by de-licensing them. The no-license campaign, as it was called, was fought in the fall of 1917. Nationally, the temperance movement that would lead to Prohibition in 1920 was gaining momentum during the war and in 1918, the federal government would outlaw the sale of liquor. This action preceded the enactment of the 18th Amendment, which created Prohibition in 1920. But in 1917 the "no-license" champions in New London argued that the city should not wait for the possibility of prohibition. They warned that New London had so many saloons that the Navy might decide to leave the area and not maintain a major base there, reflecting a national trend that tied prohibition to the war effort. The arguments were reminiscent of the ones that echoed through the city's history, going back to the debate in the 1870s over whether the sale of beer should be licensed. An advertisement in *The Day* September 29, 1917, supporting the continued licensing of saloons, noted that the consumption of beer hadn't done any harm to the fighting ability of the Germans. *The Day* opposed the no-license initiative, which was put to a vote on Election Day, September 30, 1917, and went down in defeat. The newspaper argued that the saloons would not be such a large problem if New London had more wholesome attractions for the soldiers and sailors. The enlisted men in the city were generally well behaved, the newspaper asserted.

An armistice ended the war November 11, 1918. The church bells rang, and the fire whistles blared. There was a huge and spontaneous parade through the downtown. That night, a fireworks display launched from Williams Memorial Park lit up the sky. Hundreds of sailors poured into the area and danced wildly. In front of City Hall, a group of American sailors hoisted a French sailor into the air to the cheers of the crowd. The French sailors in town started their own parade down State Street.

In one of the last editorials he would write for *The Day*, Judge Latimer filled the column with pyrotechnics of his own in capital letters:

.... The war is ended! The war is ended! The war is ended! Swing your partners one and all. ... The German people are LICKED! And yet they are FREED. ... The hell of war is DESTROYED ... Ah, what a day, what a day!

TWELVE

The Iconoclast

It is not using extravagant or unkind language to say that our city meetings are fast degenerating into a joke. A million dollar budget is too big a business to be subject to the caprices or passions of a mob.

—Theodore Bodenwein, September 20, 1919

THE WAR'S END WAS a great relief to everyone, but it also left Bodenwein and New London's other business leaders somewhat uneasy. The war economy had propped up the city's fortunes. Military business had kept the ocean pier busy, even if it was not making money, and it had even resurrected the Groton Iron Works, left over from James Hill's grand scheme to build a fleet of super-steamships. The shipyard, though it was in receivership, got contracts for six new merchant ships that raised the hope of averting bankruptcy. Charles E. Morse, the shipbuilder who had helped pick out the Groton site for Hill, led the government back to the banks of the Thames River to construct the new ships for the nation's wartime merchant marine. Peace ended the orders.

Morale had been kept up by the patriotic effort, embodied in such endeavors as the United War Work campaign, to raise funds to carry on the war. But worrisome cracks were forming in the city's foundation again. The civic spirit that had soared at the turn of the century was being supplanted, in the view of the New London burghers, by selfish and contentious politics. This had been foreshadowed as early as 1907, in the internecine Republican battle during the administration of Mayor Benjamin Armstrong.

Typical of old cities of the time, machine politicians milked the government for jobs and business. This conduct was encouraged by the way the government was set up. A dozen different committees of the City Council ran the city, each responsible for a different function. One committee was in charge of maintaining and building streets, another of fire protection, another of the police force. Significantly, each committee had its own politically appointed purchasing agent and auditor. The fox was in charge of the hen house. The Court of Common Council and the people of the city, in town meetings, appropriated money, but the committees spent it more or less as they wanted, and where the funds went nobody knew. Often, the money was not spent on the purposes for which it was intended. This tendency was particularly evident in the Street Department, as Waldo E. Clarke had found out as the new superintendent of the department beginning in 1907. Mayor Armstrong had called Clarke onto the carpet because specifically approved street repairs had not been made. Clarke's defense was that he had not been able to find any money left in the budget to perform the work. It had been spent on something else.

The fight during Armstrong's administration, which preceded the 1907 city elections, underscored the weaknesses of the existing system. Armstrong occupied a strong position as elected mayor. Mayors, the only elected office holders who enjoyed the backing of the entire electorate (the councilors had been elected from wards since 1889), had considerable power. Mayors like Bryan Mahan had used this power to accomplish great good for the city. But, on the other hand, Armstrong was virtually helpless to prevent the corrupt and inefficient practices that he charged were occurring because of the city council's control over the departments of the city government.

Both political parties took part in this game, and contributed equally to the problem. The parties competed for support by providing jobs and other political favors. The Irish-dominated volunteer fire companies became strong political machines capable of delivering votes to ward politicians in return for favors.

The war accelerated changes in New London that already were under way. The city's immigrant population grew quickly, prompting the community to make extraordinary efforts to assimilate the new arrivals. The fast growth of the immigrant population alarmed Americans across the country, leading to an "Americanization" civic movement. The city organized volunteers to help foreigners learn English and find jobs. Local industries, however, could not provide jobs for them. And not all the people already there were totally reconciled to the arrival of these new citizens. They were becoming worried about their own security and many saw the new arrivals as threats.

The worries were compounded by the danger, real and imagined, of anarchists and Bolsheviks. The Bolshevik Revolution in Russia in 1918 spread alarm across America, and small cities like New London did not escape the "Red Scare." There were numerous stories in the local newspapers about alleged Bolsheviks who were tracked down and deported. In New London, such instances were particularly numerous in the area known as East New London, the part of the city where John Winthrop had originally settled. It was not far from the present site of *The Day*. Many eastern Europeans were settling there because the housing was old and inexpensive. On December 22, 1919, three men with Slavic names were arrested in that section of the city and charged with being Bolsheviks and inciting workers to oppose the U.S. military expedition in Russia after the revolution. The word "Bolshevik" was a pejorative. A New London policeman was disciplined for referring to a worker as a Bolshevik.

Former Mayor Benjamin Armstrong, in a letter to the New York *Evening Sun* in November 1918, appealed to employers to show their patriotism after the war by making room for the returning soldiers. Unfortunately, Armstrong's firm, the Brainerd & Armstrong silk mill, was hard-pressed to hold onto the workers it had. In 1919 and 1920, it cut back drastically on its hours and let workers go. Bodenwein worried on the pages of his newspaper about what would become of the new submarine base and other military installations and industries in the area. The conclusion of hostilities cut off the work for the Groton Iron Works, and the shipyard began laying off workers.

But nothing devastated the spirit of the city more than the fizzled *Deutschland* scheme to create an underwater trade route between New London and Europe. As outrageous as it sounds, the city actually believed that would happen. And when it did not, the confidence of optimists like Theodore Bodenwein, Waldo Clarke, Bryan Mahan, and Ernest Rogers imploded. The ocean pier was to have been the solution to the city's quest to restore life to the New London waterfront after the collapse of the whaling industry. But at the end of the war, other than as a Navy dock, the pier lay idle—all one thousand feet and $1 million of it.

Clarke tried hustling business for the pier, but it was almost impossible. Late in 1919, he reached an agreement with the U.S. Grain Corporation in New York to ship flour through New London on a trial basis. Clarke appealed to dock workers in the city to turn out in large numbers to unload the ships to show the company New London's capabilities. The workers showed up in substantial numbers, but refused to work overtime, foiling the chief resident engineer's plans to land bigger contracts.

A deeply worried Bodenwein sent a letter to his friend, United States Senator Frank Brandegee asking for help in drumming up business. He petitioned him to have the city designated as a port for the United States Shipping Board, the government agency in charge of the nation's merchant marine. The board responded to Brandegee that while New London had satisfactory harbor facilities, there was no cargo to send there at the time and no shipping concern in the city to receive cargo if there were.

These setbacks shook the confidence of the same leaders who not long ago had felt so sure of themselves and the city's future. The business community increasingly felt the problem resided with political leadership and the government. In this regard, Bodenwein was in an ambivalent position. He had his feet in both the political realm, as the Republican town chairman, and in the business community, as a businessman and leader in the Chamber of Commerce. But he could see the problem growing. It was all he could do to maintain order in his own party. And while he reflexively supported the status quo, he was growing disillusioned, if not fearful, that the old local ruling class he had struggled most of his life to enter was losing control.

Before the war, he had believed the city's deteriorating situation resulted from a shortage of good candidates, by which he meant fellow businessmen. So in 1911 and 1912, The Day had tried encouraging more businessmen to enter political service. But the facts did not really support his theory. The mayors who occupied office during the first decades of the 20th century were, by and large, respected leaders with good minds. Rogers generally was acknowledged to be an excellent mayor, so good that Bodenwein boasted about having brought him into politics. The Court of Common Council was not totally inhabited by nincompoops, either. In fact, Bodenwein played an important role in picking many of these men.

It seemed to matter little which party was in charge, or what mayor was in office; the city kept going downhill. The infrastructure, the roads, schools, and public accommodations deteriorated. The neglect was starkly evident after the war, when the city turned to rebuilding a peacetime economy and took a closer look at what it had to build on. Most of its downtown streets were congested and badly in need of repairs. The old water and sewer mains that were built in the 1880s needed to be repaired and extended into newly developing parts of the city. Bank Street, which became a major thoroughfare through the city, could not handle the growing traffic. The old railroad bridge, once acclaimed as an engineering marvel, had become inadequate for the trains and had been replaced by a new one. The state turned the old span into the first highway bridge across the Thames River. It opened in 1919. But traffic to this bridge still had to cross a narrow and ramshackle bridge over Winthrop Cove, and the city was hard-pressed to find funds to replace it.

After the war, the Chamber of Commerce undertook a campaign to widen Bank and Bradley streets. Bradley Street was a busy commercial back street that passed the rear of the *Day* building on Main Street. But at the same time, the school district was clamoring for funds to build new schools and repair the existing buildings. There were pressing needs wherever the bewildered aldermen looked. They balked at the street improvements. Taxes were already rising just to cover existing expenses and the waste. They faced a tax rebellion.

In 1920, the Chamber, distressed by the government's unresponsiveness to what it viewed as a crisis, would form a committee to explore changes in the city charter to make the government work more in the interest of the city's development. The Chamber named Bodenwein chairman. There was a certain amount of irony, if not humor, in this choice, for Bodenwein was known to be a protector of the establishment, one who used the power of his newspaper to support the good work that was taking place in the city, not tear down its leaders. What the business leaders were suggesting was a direct assault on the status quo, of which Bodenwein was an important player as leader of the Republican Party. *The Day* by and large stood for things as they were. It was the struggling *Telegraph* that more often challenged the existing order and raised embarrassing questions about the local ruling class. Bodenwein did not like such displays of disrespect, as he had written on September 20, 1918:

> *I haven't much use for the people who are constantly harping on the deficiencies of this city—the place they live in. If they happen to be natives, they ought to go away from home for awhile and see how they will fare in other places. I notice that most of them who do are mightily glad to get back when they can.*

Bodenwein was merciless in his treatment of the underdog *Telegraph*, which even in its darkest hours could be a scrappier paper than *The Day*. He lorded over the rival newspaper, referring to it contemptuously as "a nearby paper." He delighted in ridiculing it, as he did in on September 25, 1918:

> *The editorial oracle of a nearby paper has just discovered that Liberty Loan bonds are a tangible asset and can be converted into money by the holder at any time. He is so impressed by his profound discovery that he calls upon the government to change the character of its official Liberty*

Bond advertisements and ask four-minute speakers in their talks to lay great stress upon the point he has found, so that the public will be raised out of its dense ignorance … No wonder people are ceasing to look upon newspaper editorials for guidance.

While political reform had been a topic of discussion for a number of years as a means of improving the city, as late as the fall of 1918 Bodenwein was opposed to wholesale changes to the city charter.

I have about come to the conclusion that our poor, old, much despised charter is a pretty efficient instrument after all, through which to govern this city … The authority to regulate our affairs is all there—it is simply up to us to take advantage of it.

But by 1920, Bodenwein found himself in the position of the iconoclast as the head of a committee that would turn the city government on end. *The Day* would lead in scaling the barricades. The discouraging situation that faced New London at the end of the war finally convinced Bodenwein and the circle of businessmen around him that nothing short of a sweeping government overhaul, action that would shatter the existing order, was going to get the city moving ahead again. The men and women (women had just gained the vote) who participated in the movement were intent on seizing power from the political machines that controlled New London's government.

The weapon they chose to use in their assault was wheeled into New London by one A.R. Hatton, head of the department of political science at Northwestern University and former city councilor in Cleveland. Hatton enthusiastically espoused an idea that was gaining popularity at the time in small and medium sized cities across the country called the council-manager form of government. In such a system, instead of a popularly elected mayor, a professional manager was the chief executive. The city manager was hired by the City Council and answered to it. The council did not have to wait for the next election to get rid of a manager with whom it was not satisfied. The council could fire the manager. On the other hand, managers who were doing a good job could stay on in the government beyond elections, and plan far ahead for the needs of the city rather than from one election to the next. And cities did not have to settle for local talent. They could compete with private business for the best executive talent there was, anywhere in the country.

Over the summer and fall of 1920, Hatton helped the Chamber draft such a plan for New London. Under it, there would be seven city councilors elected from at large in the city. This was a radical change in the way councilors were elected. Up until then, the aldermen were elected from the city's five voting wards. It was not difficult for politicians to develop effective ward organizations, often headquartered in the volunteer fire companies, that could turn out votes efficiently at elections. Now candidates would have appeal to all the voters in the city. The change, its sponsors hoped, would break up the concentrated and entrenched power of the existing ward machines and benefit the city's commercial interests, who would sponsor strong, brilliant, citywide candidates more attuned to the public good.

The system Hatton put together for the Chamber ended the authority the old eighteen-member City Council had for administering the government, in which services were provided by council committees. Instead, administrative authority would be centralized in the city manager and exercised through professionally run departments. This not only would bring more professional management to the city; the smaller council and hired administrator also would make it easier for the business interests to influence the government.

Authority to determine tax assessments would be taken out of the political realm of elected assessors and placed in the hands of an appointed assessor. This, the sponsors hoped, would end the favoritism and corruption that pervaded the existing tax system.

The changes also would eliminate the local town meetings, at which the municipal budgets were approved. This ancient artifact from John Winthrop's time was a particularly sore point with Bodenwein, who saw the town meetings increasingly dominated by "riffraff" who did not understand the complex and important financial issues they were deciding. The new form of government would take the budget approval out of the hands of the mob and place it under the control of a more enlightened council and board of finance. There also would be a planning board, which would guide development in the city rather than allow growth to proceed helter-skelter.

The proposals threatened hundreds who had a stake in the status quo. Opposition was voiced from top to bottom, from E. Frank Morgan, the mayor, right on down to the humble tax assessors. Real estate speculators did not like the idea of anyone messing with the pliable tax system that had served their individual needs up to that time. The fire companies were not eager to see their control over the government compromised. The police, firemen, and City Hall workers and all their relatives feared losing their bountiful advantages. Every piece of the existing government that was to be chopped up had a constituency that had reason to object to the change, both seekers and givers of favors.

Bodenwein and the Chamber knew the formidable job they would have getting the proposal over these political hurdles. It had to be authorized by the state legislature, and by a vote of the people in a referendum. The sponsors developed a strategy that was sweeping in its scope and amazing in its intricacy and effectiveness. In a few short months, the champions of change formed the machinery by which to outmaneuver the city's most canny political pros. Bodenwein and newspaper publishers across the country had seen, during the war, the power of the media blitz in the government's propaganda campaign. Bodenwein and the leaders around him also appreciated the potential for leading public opinion from the pulpit of *The Day*. Choosing the *Day's* owner as chairman of the Charter Committee did make a lot of sense. In the fall of 1920, *The Day* began an editorial campaign that went nonstop until the referendum in June 1921, and that grew bolder as time passed.

The Rotary Club and the Chamber brought Hatton in from Chicago to speak before civic organizations. The charter movement copied from the opposition and formed political organizations in each of the five wards. The largest of these was in the south end of the city, where Bodenwein and many of the city's most prosperous and powerful men lived. The committee met at the Harbour Club, one of the city's most elegant social clubs.

Bodenwein also courted support among the city's recently enfranchised women, for whom the referendum was their first opportunity to exercise their new political clout. On women's issues, Bodenwein could hardly have been called a progressive. But he was a practical man and one who had a clear vision. He had an opportunity to display his support for the suffragists in 1920, when the legislature passed a bill giving women the vote and Governor Marcus H. Holcombe refused to sign it. *The Day* lambasted Holcombe in an editorial on September 23. Later, Bodenwein appealed to the women to support the political reforms. Just before the June 1921 referendum, he wrote:

> *You women voters of New London can approach this subject of adoption of a new charter with an open mind. You are not fettered by tradition. You are not steeped in prejudice through previous attachment to political parties. You are not bound by preconceived notions of forms of city government. You have not been voters long enough to become infected by office seekers' virus. You are therefore free to exercise your own clear judgment. You have a great chance to signalize your entrance into the right of suffrage.*

In this campaign, Bodenwein pulled out all the stops. The newspaper ran a fourteen-part series by H.S. Gilbertson of the National Municipal League making the case for the council-manager form of government. Daily for weeks before the vote, the newspaper ran a column of commentary, entitled "Short Talks Upon the New Charter," answering criticisms as they arose and supporting the reforms.

Unfortunately for him, Bodenwein was handicapped on the editorial page at that critical point by the departure of Frederick Latimer. Latimer had left *The Day* and his law practice in 1919 to work as a full-time feature writer for the New York *Evening Mail.* He worked there on and off as a feature and editorial writer until 1928, when he returned to Connecticut to be an editorial writer for the Hartford *Times.* While he was at the *Times*, he wrote a daily column for *The Day*. He died in 1940 at the age of 64.

Latimer's departure took the wind out of the sails of the *Day's* editorial page. The lead editorials shrunk in size and were drained of their vitality. The page turned gray again. Only Bodenwein's fervor to get the reforms through and direct involvement restored some life to the pages. When the charter campaign began in the spring of 1921, Bodenwein pitched in by writing many of the commentary articles on the charter. His stiletto style is clear in this passage on May 18, in which he warns voters to beware of lies from the opposition:

> *Scurrility, coarse abuse, foul language and malicious slander are not argument—and the intelligent men and women of New London will not be affected by it. There is no class of people in this city so dull or stupid as not to see through the false arguments of the little clique of office seekers who are going around trying to poison the minds of the voters.*

On May 21, he went into more detail about these untruths. Fraternal organizations that refused to support the new charter would be raided and have their liquor confiscated. The proprietors of gambling establishments were promised protection for their support. The volunteer fire companies would lose their engine houses and be replaced by a paid department. City employees were being forced to contribute to a slush fund to pay for the charter campaign. All lies, Bodenwein declared. Bodenwein used the pages of his newspaper, often shamelessly, as a propaganda instrument. But this was war, he felt.

When Mayor E. Frank Morgan wrote a letter to *The Day* questioning the accuracy of some its claims, Bodenwein printed the letter, but ran a response taking up nearly half a page. On May 28, the newspaper published a front page story alleging that funds earmarked for repairs on one of the city's streets were diverted into equipment purchased from a politically favored garage in the city. As was commonplace then, *The Day* did not seek opposing views or corroborate the charge. Still, it furnished readers with a lot of information, and at the end could claim that it had educated the voters thoroughly, if not impartially, on the issues. In the final stretch, *The Day* ran banner ads on the front page urging voters to support the changes. *The Day* published lists of all the supporters, who were asked to sign up for the cause by filling out cards.

The well-oiled campaign brought down the old government. On June 6, 1921, voters approved the new order of things five to three, with two-thirds of the eligible voters casting ballots. The measure lost, and by the slimmest of margins, in only two of the city's five wards—the third and fourth, the Irish wards. Bodenwein was ecstatic:

> *Of course I feel satisfied with the result. It shows that the people of New London are ready at all times to support with their hearts and their votes a genuine movement for the betterment of the community.*

That's not all the successful charter fight showed to the 57-year-old publisher. The victory demonstrated to him and to the city the power *The Day* had amassed during his thirty years at the helm. Bodenwein had joined in civic campaigns before—in the struggle to bring Connecticut College to the city and to get state funds for the ocean pier, and other efforts to develop the city. But never before had he been so clearly at the head of a movement, a movement that succeeded against considerable odds

---

THE DAY WAS CLOSE to being a monopoly in the area of eastern Connecticut it covered. Its circulation in the region had reached eleven thousand five hundred at the end of 1920. This was audited circulation, Bodenwein emphasized. *The Day* had joined the Audit Bureau of Circulation, an organization to which newspapers subscribed that provided an honest picture of newspaper sales. The count did not include unsold, damaged, or leftover newspapers. The newspaper reached six thousand seven hundred households in the city. That was a quarter of all the people in New London. It reached a tenth of all the population in the area around New London. It would be a "sheer waste of money" for advertisers to employ any other medium but *The Day*, Bodenwein declared.

In 1920, the *Globe* was limping along. Early in 1921, the *Telegraph*, which Bodenwein had helped start and which had provided him with his formative experience in newspaper publishing, went out of business. It was 35 years old. The *Telegraph* had been a valiant adversary. Its editors valued good writing and attracted writers who excelled in literary talent. Charlotte Holloway, who left the newspaper before it closed to write books and magazine articles, blazed the way for women journalists in the city. Eugene O'Neill, America's foremost playwright, developed his writing skill and gathered some of his material from his tenure on the newspaper. Judge Frederick Latimer, the part owner and editor of the newspaper who had hired O'Neill, was one of the finest writers ever to serve on a New London newspaper.

Except for the time between 1901 and 1907 when Bodenwein owned the *Telegraph*, it was a Democratic newspaper, and in that role it provided a perspective that *The Day* eschewed, that of the city's growing population of European immigrants and African Americans and its blue collar class. *The Day* tended to see the world through the eyes of the Chamber of Commerce and Rotary Club. The *Telegraph*, on the other hand, reported on the life of the city around the docks, in the saloons, and on the street. Its reporting was often more thorough and accurate than the *Day's* and invariably more colorful. It paid more attention to the arts and to the fringes of politics of the time.

As Bodenwein built *The Day* into the dominant newspaper in the city, the *Telegraph* and the *Globe* had became sanctuaries for opposing views. Bodenwein boasted about his newspaper's independence and objectivity, but everyone knew *The Day* stood for the Republican machine and the city's business interests. So when Mayor Benjamin Armstrong felt it necessary to strike out against his Republican opponents, he had turned to the *Day's* rival newspapers. Bodenwein later related he gave away the newspaper to Frank J. Brunner, the *Day's* managing editor, in 1907.

Brunner sold his interest three years later and moved to New York, where he went to work for the New York *Herald Tribune*, and later became editor for the *Army & Navy Journal*. He died in 1934. In 1908, the year after his battle with the Republican organization led by Bodenwein and the Chappells, he had bought a part interest in the *Telegraph*. Two years later, George S. Palmer, exasperated by the *Day's* dominance, invested in the newspaper in an attempt to keep it afloat as an independent voice in the city. That's when Frederick Latimer joined the paper and later hired Eugene O'Neill in 1912.

Telegraph editor Malcolm Mollan and Latimer turned to millionaire Morton F. Plant to help keep the newspaper on its feet. Plant, who had built an office building on State Street across from the Mohican, invested in the newspaper and provided it a new home in his building. In 1915, Plant sold the newspaper to Julian D. Moran, a former linotype operator for *The Day* and the Norwich *Bulletin*. Plant, who continued to own the *Telegraph* building, died in November 1918 and Frank Munsey purchased the building from his estate.

The estate foreclosed on the *Telegraph* for an unpaid note early in 1921, closing down the newspaper for good. Moran, who ran the newspaper from 1915 to 1921, became the city clerk in New London when the city, under Bodenwein's leadership, changed from a strong mayor to a council-manager form of government. Bodenwein composed the obituary of the *Telegraph* in a story under his own byline in *The Day* on February 8, 1921.

> *The New London* Morning Telegraph *is dead. After 35 years of constant struggle for existence, it departed this life one day last week. The end came suddenly and reporters, not having been paid wages for some time, and seeing no prospects of any forthcoming, decided to quit work and the paper had to suspend. Hence it was cut off without any chance to print its own obituary or sing its own swan song. Sad, indeed, that a paper which has so long tenaciously clung to a precarious life should finally pass away, unwept, unhonored and unsung.*

Bodenwein said the death of the *Telegraph* supported his view that there was not room in New London for another newspaper, especially a morning newspaper. It was a good newspaper, he acknowledged. He paid tribute to the talented writers and editors, mentioning specifically Frederick Latimer, Malcolm Mollan, and C.C. Hemenway (but not Charlotte Holloway). He noted in particular Latimer's conscientious effort to revive the paper. But the people of New London were not interested, he said. He said tastes and the size of the city favored an afternoon paper. The newspaper situation in New London, he felt, would remain unprofitable for any morning publication until the city reached one hundred thousand population. "Perhaps after New London has grown to that extent there will be sufficient demand for a morning newspaper here to warrant the issuance of one." He said that would take at least thirty more years. He concluded with a note of smugness:

> *Over $1 million of good money has been expended in New London during the past 30 years in operating unsuccessful newspapers. Over 90 percent of this huge sum was contributed by local merchants and for their outlay they could not possibly have received anything like adequate return. If there is any moral to be applied I am content to let others undertake it.*

Without the *Telegraph* nipping at his feet, and with the satisfaction of having just led a sweeping government reform movement to victory, Bodenwein sensed his power and importance in the city as never before. He was possibly the most powerful figure in the city. He had toppled the old order and played a strong role in picking the men and women who would make up the new government. *The Day*, as an institution, had become a force for change. With a brand new form of government in place, Bodenwein began to see ways in which the newspaper could set the agenda for the city's future. And with the business boom that lay ahead, he and *The Day* would make some money, in fact quite a lot of it.

THIRTEEN

THE BOOM

Some persons may have the idea that if and when the four-day ocean line comes to New London we are going to be millionaires overnight. This is folly. In the first place, as soon as the news spreads that the line decides to make New London its base, there will be an influx of every kind of business man.... They will migrate to the boomtown. The result will be an overcrowding and a survival of the fittest.

—Orvin G. Andrews, April 14, 1928

THE REFORMS OF 1921 brought about their sought-after results, creating a political situation more favorable to the Chamber of Commerce. The new City Council elected in the fall of 1921 contained a majority of business-friendly councilors, including Waldo E. Clarke, the resident engineer at the ocean pier, and Lucius Whiton, a manufacturer. For Clarke, this was a moment of sweet justice after being forced by the old government to resign as street commissioner fourteen years earlier.

Whiton, owner of the Whiton Machine Company, received the most votes and thus was selected to be the first mayor under the new system. The council also included New London's first woman ever elected to public office, Annie Fenner, a widow and one of the owners of the Babcock Printing Press Company. Councilors William C. Fox and Malcolm Scott, both Democrats, were the only members who had been opponents of the reforms. "The friends of good government can rest content with the consciousness of their duty to the community faithfully and successfully performed," *The Day* said in an editorial that appeared on September 27, 1921.

The new government got off to a raucous start. There had been nearly forty contenders for the council seats and fifty applicants sent in resumes to be city manager. When the new council appointed an assessor, the three elected assessors refused to vacate their offices. They argued that they could not legally do so until the city manager named the new assessor, and there was not yet a city manager.

The council solved this problem by appointing the law director city manager temporarily and he dismissed the recalcitrant officials, the last vestiges of the old order. Thus for awhile, the city's lawyer was furnishing himself legal opinions. In November, the council had narrowed the list of manager applicants to three and from them hired James A. Barlow, a municipal executive in Dayton, Ohio, to be the city's first manager. A die-hard Democrat attempted to force another vote on the manager form of government in 1926, but didn't obtain enough valid signatures. The system survived its early tests and made it into the 21st century, supported all that time by *The Day*.

Having a government that was more responsive to their wishes calmed the fears of Bodenwein and the business leaders. And a roaring post-war economy that burst forth in the 1920s did wonders for their outlook, as well. Business boomed, and *The Day* flourished in the new environment. The growth in consumer spending and in particular the development of more aggressive national advertising for cars, appliances, and other popular consumer goods opened lucrative opportunities for advertising revenue. At the end of the 20th century, looking back, television newscaster Peter Jennings and Todd Brewster describe this expansive new medium in their book, *The Century*:

> *Up until the 1920s, most advertisement had appeared in newspapers and read more like announcements, providing the simplest information about a product ("P & G Naphtha Soap: The White Naphtha Soap in the Blue Wrapper"). But as people entered the new age, a new form of advertising lured them on. Whether it appeared on air, in one of the many flashy new national magazines crowding the news stand, or on billboards being propped up on country roads, the commercial message of the day operated as a kind of gospel proclaiming the news rules of modernity. With dramatic flair, it told people what new things they needed and what new habits they must undertake.*

Newspapers across the country benefited from this development, and *The Day* was ideally situated to cash in on the opportunities. Bodenwein was close to wiping out his only local competition (the *Globe* survived another nine years before it, too, perished), and commanded the loyalty of readers throughout the city and across the region. *The Day* ventured into the national advertising marketplace with the services of Gilman, Nicoll & Ruthman, an advertising firm with offices in New York, Boston, Chicago, and San Francisco. To stay abreast of the rapidly developing industry, Bodenwein joined newspaper associations, including the American Newspaper Publishers Association and Bureau of Advertising. He became president of the New England Daily Newspaper Association.

The *Day's* publisher had organized a team of loyal and seasoned managers in both the business and news departments, men in whose hands he felt confident leaving his newspaper while he was away for increasing periods of time. In 1923, when the 59-year-old publisher bought a winter home in Florida he placed Orvin Andrews, who was 34, in charge as general manager and secretary of The Day Publishing Company. Andrews had hired Charles "Charlie" or "C.J." O'Connor, the former sports editor at the *Telegraph* and well-known New London sports figure, as an advertising salesman in 1922. Legendary for his mercurial temper, O'Connor would take charge of the advertising department in 1935 and retain that position until his retirement in 1967.

Walter Slocum was editor until 1924, when he was appointed postmaster. George Grout, Bodenwein's most senior and trusted executive, took over the newsroom. Late in 1928, Bodenwein sent Grout, then 50, to a seminar at Columbia University to learn how to set up a library, or newspaper "morgue." When he returned, he set up the *Day's* first library filing system on index cards. This was Grout's most durable contribution to the newspaper. His system was maintained without any changes until 1977, when his card system was replaced by a clip-filing system. Grout, whose greatest passions were bridge and American history, was the first of only four librarians who worked at *The Day* in the 20th century. He also served in the 1930s as state and county editor, responsible among other things for riding herd over the rag-tag army of part-time town correspondents.

Alfred Ligourie, a bespectacled, methodical man by whose movements others at *The Day* set their watches, became city editor in 1927. He held that position until his death in 1947. The newspaper had a half dozen full-time reporters at any one time in the 1920s, but the one who left the biggest footprint was John Mallon. Johnny Mallon's name became part of New London legend, which favored colorful characters over geniuses. Mallon, handsome and cocky, always seen with a cigar, covered police, fire, and politics. Mallon was active in Republican politics in the state and was regarded by Democrats as Bodenwein's mouthpiece-in-residence for the Republican Party. But everyone liked him anyway. The *Day's* truck drivers came to know him as the one on the paper who would get their speeding tickets fixed. He was a generous man who did numerous political favors for his friends. He also could rise to the occasion as a reporter, bringing to his job insight into and detailed knowledge of the characters and the plots of the political world he loved.

Mallon, a star athlete at Bulkeley School, had started working for *The Day* as a school correspondent. He served in the Army during World War I and had gone to college in Washington, D.C., afterwards, where he got a job as an aide to Congressman Richard P. Freeman, the representative from the district that included New London. He went to work for *The Day* as a full-time reporter in 1923. He served for several years as a clerk in the police court. He was elected once as a state representative, held the post of Republican town chairman and ran for Congress, all while working as a reporter at *The Day*. He would remain in that position until his death in a car crash in New London September 7, 1947. The car he was driving smashed into the rear of an oil truck in New London, pushing the truck forward twenty-one feet. When Mallon lay dying at Lawrence & Memorial Hospital and a call went out for blood donors, two hundred persons responded, including most of the police force. After his death, *The Day* wrote in an editorial:

> *A great number of his friends reflected upon the many impulsively generous things "Johnny" had done for them, of his genial attitude toward life and his love of congenial companions.*

In 1920, Gordon Bodenwein, discharged the year before from the Navy quartermaster corps, returned to New London to join his father's staff. The staff believed the handsome 28-year-old Yale graduate would step into his father's shoes someday and the father did nothing to discourage that perception. He made Gordon assistant editor and put him to work writing editorials. But the son, erudite, moody, and more refined than the editors and reporters who surrounded him, was unhappy there, and the staff did not warm up to him either. Gordon and Edna had no use for each other. He was tormented by self-doubts and lingering resentment toward his father for his role in the breakup of his parents' marriage. He felt a strong bond with his mother, Jennie, who returned to the city in the 1920s and settled in an apartment in the Mohican Hotel. He eventually explored with great interest his Scottish roots of her side of the family. He was troubled by his growing sense of his homosexuality. Not long after he arrived, Gordon left the newspaper in 1923 to study to be a Roman Catholic priest. He was ordained in Rome in 1926.

The Day continued to grow stronger in the fertile environment of the 1920s. Late in 1922, The Day Publishing Company issued 4,000 new shares of stock, raising its capital value from $50,000 to $250,000. The shareholders included Bodenwein, Slocum, Andrews, Grout, and Helen F. Foss, a young and attractive cashier in the business office. Foss later resettled in California, where she died in 1976. As the decade unfolded, Bodenwein bought a new press, a Hoe straight-line, four-unit model, which cost $75,000. In 1928, he doubled the size of the *Day* building. The addition was built to the north of the existing building, along Main Street so as to look like part of the original building. Facing the front of the building today, one who didn't know the history would think the structure was built all at once, but it's really two buildings joined at the middle and made uniform by a new façade.

The Day used the additional space on the street level to create a modern lobby and business office. It was lined from floor to ceiling with marble. The office featured a sea of desks facing the front of the building occupied by a beehive of clerks with typewriters and other modern business machines. This was the area many in New London, from the newsboys and their parents to the advertising customers and job applicants, became most familiar with as "*The Day* Office." Andrews had an office on one side of the room where he met with every job applicant. For the people of the city, *The Day* was still associated with Bodenwein, but he had grown bigger than life and was more or less out of sight of the common horde. Orvin Andrews, or "Mr. Andrews" as he was better known, became the human face and voice of the newspaper. He was a stern but kindly man. His colleagues called him "Judge" because of his serious demeanor and the name stuck with the public in his column, "Sentences by the Judge."

Bodenwein moved into the second story of the new half of the building, occupying a dark wood-paneled office overlooking Main Street. The sanctuary insulated him from the public and from other parts of the newspaper. In addition, it provided him a refuge from Edna, with whom he quarreled at home with increasing frequency. It is not clear whether their quarrels, overheard by servants, were the result of Bodenewein's spending too much time at *The Day* or whether Bodenwein spent increasing hours at *The Day* because of the tongue-lashings that awaited him at home. Visitors reached his office by the stairway on the north end of the building, and that was the passage through which he made his way about the building. It was generally understood that people were not to use the door at the north end of the building unless they had business with the publisher.

For many employees in the 1920s and 1930s, the only time they could remember seeing Bodenwein was bumping into him on that stairway between the second floor and the composing room. The only communication many had with the publisher occurred on the stairs in awkward conversations that the publisher initiated with the question, "What do you do here?"

IN THE 1920s, NEW LONDON once again was swept up in feverish business speculation, a condition to which it almost seemed to have a genetic disposition. There was a housing boom, particularly in the increasingly fashionable south end of the city, where those who could afford it eagerly bought lots and built new houses or bought and sold property to make money. In New London, real estate rivaled the stock market as the road to riches. Home building was proceeding with such fury that it became a staple of the news. *The Day* listed all the houses that were under construction in the city going into detail about some of the plans. The newspaper also ran a regular feature on popular home-building plans of the time. The building page became one of the best read parts of the newspaper. Andrews, in a column on April 14, 1928, took note of the home-building frenzy:

> *Have you noticed in the recent building applications how many local people are building cottage style houses and how few are building two-family houses? It's but a few years ago that only the so-called well-to-do thought they could afford single-family houses.*

The most coveted residential real estate in the city in the 1920s was in the vicinity of the Pequot Colony, the local playground for the wealthy in the 19th century. Many of the big estates that made up the colony were being broken up into expensive building lots. One of New London's most beautiful spots was on a bend in the road along the river, where in the 1850s the Pequot House hotel had been built. The hotel had reached the peak of its popularity in the 1880s and 1890s when the Yale-Harvard Regatta first became an annual spectacle on the Thames River. The Pequot House offered fine cuisine and one of the most striking views of the harbor. Fire had destroyed it in 1908. U.S. Senator Frank Brandegee, who had joined the city's other real estate speculators, carved building lots out of the site. In the 1920s, several prominent New Londoners purchased these lots. Among them were Ernest Rogers and Edna and Theodore Bodenwein, who built neighboring homes suitable for their stations in life. Rogers built his palace out of brick. The building had an elegant classical portico with a balcony over it. Rogers, who went from mayor to state senator to lieutenant governor, had still higher ambitions: to become governor. A popular, but unsubstantiated, story says that Rogers designed the balcony from which to greet the public after his election as governor.

Next door, the Bodenweins had something different in mind for their new home, which they would call Pequot House after the old hotel that had stood on that site. It was Edna, actually, who came up with the idea, and saw it through to completion. Of all the things she did in her life, this singular undertaking was perhaps her most extraordinary achievement. Edna chose to build their house in the French *manoir* style that was in vogue among the rich at the time, a style that reproduced the look of ancient country mansions in Normandy. To carry out her plan, she hired Frank J. Forster, an architect noted for his work in this genre. Edna was in control every step of the way as the house was designed and took shape in 1928 and early 1929. Even in the unlikely event that she wasn't consciously trying to capture the attention of New London with her new house, the unusual and extravagant undertaking was the talk of the town. The project was the 1920s home-building equivalent of the construction of Munsey's building, the Mohican, on State Street in the 1890s.

Edna was not content to rely upon Forster. She traveled to France several times to study early precedents for the style of house, returning with strong views on how it should be built. For example, it was commonly known that the roof of such a house should sag gracefully to imitate the aging that had taken place in the originals. Everyone who had read, even casually, about such houses knew that. Builders and architects knew how to achieve this effect. But Edna, having seen the real thing, knew precisely how much the line of the roof ought to bend and would not be content until just the right curvature was achieved. As neighbors watched in amazement, the builders erected and demolished two roof frames before the right effect was achieved on the third try.

She demanded slate shingles that were curled upward and cracked as if by centuries of exposure to the sun. There was only one company in the world, a firm in California, that produced such a product, and that's where the shingles for Pequot House were obtained. She also was exacting about achieving the proper appearance of aging interior plaster, having workers mix and remix the whitewash with ashes until the color and texture made it appear it had been darkened by the burning of lamps over many years.

Edna was similarly focused on furnishing her house. She traveled to Europe three times, combing England and France for antiques. She acquired an authentic Louis XIV roll-top desk, a Louis XV daybed, Louis XIII armchairs and side chairs, antique French andirons, Yorkshire chairs and tables, Elizabethan-style oak sideboards dating to 1850, an antique oak wig stand, and eighty-eight pieces of French pottery, among other rare and expensive objects. Edna designed separate bedrooms for herself and her husband, and hers was by far the bigger and more elegant of the two. Her suite had a Louis XIV commode, a gilded, ceiling-length mirror and a huge, carved antique bed. Bodenwein's bedroom was small and stark by comparison, furnished with a more functional maple bedroom set. When the house was completed in the spring of 1929, the Bodenweins had a lavish house-warming party to which all the city's important citizens were invited. The gifts the Bodenweins received that night included a medieval bishop's robe that had hung in the Cloisters in New York. That summer, John Wallace Gillespie, a photographer for *House Beautiful*, spent a day taking pictures for a photographic layout on the new house. The article mentioned, among other things, the slight sag in the ridge, which it noted "is pleasing when it is done, as here, without exaggeration."

WHILE EDNA WAS ENGAGED in overseeing the development of her home, Theodore Bodenwein occupied himself with real estate investments in Florida and New London. In addition to their winter home in Coral Gables, they also invested liberally in Florida land. As with their bedrooms, they kept their finances separate. Bodenwein purchased shares in various real estate endeavors and provided Edna with handwritten receipts. But Bodenwein's most daring and significant venture was in New London, where he took part in a commercial development that changed the face of the city's downtown business district.

Until the 1920s, the business district of State Street stopped where the Mohican Hotel was built on the border of property owned by the Williams family, a dynasty of wealthy merchants. Whaling merchant Thomas W. Williams had built a mansion on the hillside overlooking New London. He was one of the original promoters who brought the railroad to New London. His son, Charles Augustus Williams, was the benefactor responsible for the development of an elegant city park near their estate and Cedar Grove Cemetery. The family's wealth also went into Williams Memorial Institute, the high school for young women that Elizabeth Bodenwein had attended. But after Charles Augustus Williams died in 1899, the mansion was abandoned and fell into disrepair. The future of the property on the western end of State Street became a matter of grave concern. Bodenwein and several other businessmen conceived and executed the idea of developing a commercial super-block, with offices, retail businesses and a modern theater there.

They bought the Williams property and inaugurated the ambitious project. Bodenwein's partners were Frederic Mercer, a New London manufacturer, and J. P. T. Armstrong, the president of the Chamber of Commerce. The land was carved into commercial building lots. Along with buildings and retail stores, a modern vaudeville and movie theater was built. The theater was named the Garde after one of the businessmen involved. Walter S. Garde was a partner of Arthur S. Friend, a New York developer in the 325 State Street Corporation, which built the theater at the top of State Street. Construction for the $700,000, eighteen-hundred-seat theater started in the fall of 1925 and was completed a year later.

The Garde was one of the city's most laborious construction projects. To build the foundation, crews had to blast into the solid shelf of granite that extended downhill toward the Thames River. The rock that was removed was trucked to another part of the city to fill in a swamp. One of the contractors went bankrupt in the middle of the project. The construction was beset with disputes between the builder and the city, which had to be smoothed over through political channels. The end result was at the time the most modern theater in Connecticut. The interior was decorated in a Moroccan motif then popular in Hollywood, with desert murals on the walls of a dull orange. The art was the product of Vera Leeper, a Colorado artist and decorator. The Garde had a giant pipe organ and the biggest stage of any theater in the state.

These were heady times for Bodenwein and the other businessmen as they saw their influence start to produce concrete results. Bodenwein had emerged from the 1921 city-charter campaign with the conviction that the city could shape its future through deliberate, scientific, businesslike planning. More important, he strongly believed that he and *The Day*, which helped bring a new form of government into existence, could guide and promote that process. In the early 1920s, *The Day* began running "An Agenda for New London," a list of planning goals at the top of the editorial column. One goal was to develop and implement a comprehensive city plan. The charter set the city's sights on such an approach by creating a planning board, only the second in the state. Hartford had formed the first planning board in 1906.

The City Council, following the lead of many other cities, in 1923 introduced zoning, legal standards governing the use of land. Development no longer could proceed at the whims of property owners, but had to follow rules. In 1926, the city spent $11,000 to hire a prominent New York urban planner, Herbert S. Swan, to prepare a blueprint for future development. Swan completed his work in 1928. The New London Plan, or Swan Plan as it became better known, was one hundred and ten pages and Bodenwein published the whole thing in serial form during October 1929, even as the stock market and national economy were collapsing.

The Swan Plan focused on the concerns of old cities across America, particularly those among their business interests. One of their biggest problems was traffic. The streets had evolved haphazardly before the invention of the automobile. Swan found the city an exasperating tangle of narrow, badly maintained streets that did not meet contemporary needs. Main streets in the downtown area were built to serve the ferry and other waterfront activities, not the new crossings for rail and cars upriver. As a result, motorists using the Thames River Bridge had to negotiate narrow, congested old streets and compete with trolley cars. The plan proposed a network of wide boulevards and streets including a sweeping parkway from the northernmost end of the city to the southern tip at Ocean Beach. Swan recommended more than doubling the width of Bank Street. Most of the buildings that would stand in the way were out of date and of little architectural distinction and eventually would be torn down with few to mourn their loss, he felt. Similarly, major streets throughout the city needed to be widened and extended, creating a pattern of thoroughfares. The trolley system was inefficient in a modern city, he felt, and he proposed replacing it with buses—not only within the city, but also between the city and its suburbs.

Swan was struck by New London's generally dowdy architecture, which he felt contrasted surprisingly with the elegance and grace of other New England communities. But what it lacked in grace, he felt, the city made up for in quaintness. And the one thing that set the city above many other communities was its outstanding waterfront. He proposed both to exploit the advantages of the harbor and to preserve the view of the waterfront. Pequot Avenue, where the Bodenweins' house was located, was still built up only on the upland side of the street, and he recommended the city buy all the property on the river side and preserve it as parkland before people got the idea of building there. As for the harbor, he believed the city needed to attract more manufacturing, particularly in the area around the State Pier, before it could expect to capitalize on the ocean pier. However, he did think it was worthwhile to pursue the tantalizing idea for realizing the unmet potential of the port, the "four-day ship line."

As America drifted blissfully toward the Crash of 1929, Congress kept busy inventing ways to protect American business from the worsening vicissitudes of the global economy. One such measure was the Smoot-Hawley Tariff. Another was the Jones-White Act to rebuild the U.S. merchant marine through generous outpourings of cash for shipbuilders and mercantile interests. Attracted by the glitter of huge government loans, Lawrence R. Wilder, a New York shipbuilding executive, devised a plan to put into service faster steamships that could traverse the Atlantic in four days, bringing passengers to shore on ship-to-shore aircraft. The two key elements to his plan were a $100 million federal loan from the funds that were made available under the new legislation to build the ships and a port in the northeast easier to reach from the North Atlantic than New York.

That news sent the regular crowd at the Thames Club into ecstasy. Waldo Clarke and the other business barons wasted no time in getting the word out that an ideal port for this purpose existed east of New York known as New London, where the air was pure, the harbor deep, and a fine, one-thousand-foot-long pier was awaiting. The port was closer to Liverpool than New York and not handicapped by the overcrowding and high costs of New York.

It wasn't long before Wilder's name became a household word in New London. He joined publisher Frank Munsey, James Hill of the Eastern Shipbuilding Company, Captain Paul Koenig of the *Deutschland*, and Captain Frederic Hinsch of the German Eastern Forwarding Company in the procession of messiahs whose plans ignited the imaginations and elevated the hopes of New London's business leaders.

New London's courtship with Lawrence Wilder was framed by a combination of circumstances that began with a local tragedy, became entangled with a national scandal, and ended, in the usual fashion, with Wilder's disappearance. On October 12, 1924, United States Senator Frank Brandegee, one of Bodenwein's best friends, the first United States senator ever to serve from New London and the one in whose power and influence the city was basking when the state legislature agreed to spend $1 million on an ocean pier here, wrote a note to his chauffeur:

> *Dear George:*
> *I enclose $100 for you and $100 for Emma and Rufus.*
> *I am up in the bathroom on the top floor, near 17th Street.*
> *The top floor. The floor above the one I sleep in.*
> *If you or Lundy come up there beware of the gas.*
> *Goodbye.*

Brandegee put the note on a hall table with two $100 bills then walked upstairs to the bathroom over his living quarters in his house in Washington, D.C. He reclined on the floor, resting his head on a crumpled bathroom rug, placed the end of a gas tube in his mouth and killed himself.

Brandegee was the son of Augustus Brandegee, the abolitionist and jurist under whom Major John Tibbits, founder of *The Day*, had studied law. The father was the most powerful man in the Republican Party in New London when Theodore Bodenwein was just getting his feet wet in politics. John McGinley had inherited his power from Brandegee and his wing of the party, which also included the Chappells and eventually Bodenwein. The earliest Republican leaders in New London were, in chronological order, Augustus Brandegee, who did much to establish the party, McGinley, and Bodenwein. It was Augustus Brandegee who, by calling in a note against the afternoon *Telegram*, had killed the newspaper, prompting Tibbits to turn *The Day* into an afternoon paper and opening the way for Bodenwein and some other aspiring young journalists to start the *Morning Telegraph*. Augustus Brandegee, in effect, created the opening by which Bodenwein got his start as a newspaper publisher. Bodenwein and Frank Brandegee were about the same age, enjoyed each other's company and paralleled each other in their ascents in New London. Brandegee had been a partner of Charles Whittlesey, the *Day's* lawyer and former business manager. Bodenwein was shattered by the news of his friend's death. It came, he said, "like a thunderclap from a clear sky." While there were many theories concerning Brandegee's death, including a conspiratorial one that he was murdered, the prevailing view was that he had gotten in over his head financially and suffered setbacks from real estate deals that had gone sour.

Hiram Bingham III replaced Brandegee on December 17, 1924, less than a month after Bingham had been elected governor. Bingham was the grandson of the 19th century Protestant missionary, Hiram Bingham, who had colonized Hawaii. The grandson earned fame himself as the explorer who rediscovered Machu Picchu, the famed Inca citadel in Peru. Only weeks into his first term as governor, he resigned to run for Brandegee's Senate seat.

In Washington, Bingham set out to protect the business interests of his home state. Part of that effort involved ensuring that Connecticut industries were advantageously treated in the tariff legislation that was taking shape. He also pounced on the idea of the "four-day line" and put his weight behind efforts to back Wilder's Transoceanic Corporation with a hefty loan from the Jones Act. Originally, Wilder's plan had called for $75 million in loan funds, but the figure rose to nearly $100 million by mid-1928 and Bingham was responsible for increasing the total available for loans so that Wilder's needs could be accommodated. The events brought to New London the usual amount of excitement, all documented on the pages of *The Day*. The newspaper wrote editorials, gasped at every new development, and followed the progress in Washington in great detail. Waldo Clarke made frequent trips to Washington, and Wilder paid a spectacular visit to New London aboard his yacht to "take scientific readings."

The venture fell through. The United States Shipping Board, to Bingham's chagrin, reported to Congress that most travelers probably were not eager to cross the Atlantic in four days. Wilder, meantime, found himself in a growing scandal over influence peddling similar to the one that nearly destroyed Bingham. On November 4, 1929, Bingham became only the third United States senator to be censured by his colleagues. He had placed Charles Evanson, a paid lobbyist for Connecticut Manufacturers Association, on the Senate payroll and brought him to closed tariff committee meetings. The Senate resolution said that Bingham's conduct, while not corrupt in intent, "is contrary to good morals and senatorial ethics and tends to bring the Senate into dishonor and disrepute." *The Day* defended Bingham, arguing that he was only properly looking after Connecticut's interests. Wilder was accused of unethical lobbying to secure advantages under the Jones Act. Nothing came of the charges.

A breakthrough at the ocean pier remained an elusive dream. The facility continued to be used mostly for military purposes. It was, among other things, the berth for the growing fleet of United States Revenue Service vessels used to go after liquor smuggling ships, the so-called "Dry Fleet."

The 18th Amendment, which brought about Prohibition, was never popular in New London. But it did create an unforeseen benefit for the city. Enforcing the ban on liquor turned out to be a big job for the Coast Guard, and Congress responded by increasing its manpower and resources dramatically. This called for more and better trained officers. The training academy that had been established at Fort Trumbull in 1910 was unequal to the task of creating a full-scale, four-year officer academy for the service. To a large degree, through lobbying led by Waldo Clarke and supported by Bingham, Congress decided to spend $2.5 million to build a new Coast Guard Academy on New London's shores, across the street from Connecticut College. The government's plans were predicated upon the city's promise to put up $200,000 to buy the land.

As 1929 drew to a close, New London was optimistic. The wild swings that began to occur on Wall Street that October went largely unnoticed. Beautiful photographs of the house Edna built appeared in the November edition of *House Beautiful*. The Coast Guard cadets had their annual fall formal dance at the Mohican roof garden. Montgomery Ward opened a new department store on Bank Street, and Bodenwein rejoiced that Prohibition at least had substantially cleaned up that street of its past unsavory character. At Connecticut College, ground was broken for a new building. Judge Christopher L. Avery was the speaker. Plans were moving ahead for the Coast Guard Academy. Could things get any better?

FOURTEEN

The Depression

Boy Oh Boy, I guess the bottom didn't fall out of the old market this week after all.

—Orvin Andrews, November 2, 1929

NOBODY WOULD HAVE GUESSED from reading *The Day* in the fall of 1929 that a calamity was about to happen. Bodenwein's overwhelming confidence, reinforced by his own successes in America, was hard to shake, and he refused, despite mounting evidence to the contrary, to acknowledge that the nation's industrial system was collapsing.

The facts may have been hard for him to see from the high perch he occupied. He was living in the lap of luxury, in a big house in the fashionable end of town. He had started with nothing more than a grammar-school education, and he now worked in a splendid, paneled office overlooking downtown New London. His community admired him. His newspaper had brought political change and economic good to the city and surrounding area.

Bodenwein entertained still bigger plans for New London on the eve of the Great Depression. He foresaw a "greater New London" that would incorporate surrounding territory and whose population someday would rise to one hundred thousand (it was approaching thirty thousand in 1930). New London, he believed, would become an international center of commerce centered on the State Pier, if only the state would invest more money to build warehouses. And he looked forward to the day when Ocean Beach, the city's bustling but aging and congested summer resort on Long Island Sound, would be enlarged and improved and draw visitors from all over New England. He was determined that a passing storm in the financial markets was not going to get in the way.

The country was in the secure hands of Republicans, and New London was moving forward under the benevolent guidance of *The Day* and the Chamber of Commerce.

The news about the disaster's approach appeared inside on the newspaper's stock page. Reports on the free-fall of stock prices flickered amidst the soft light of stories about the routine and rituals of the communities of southeastern Connecticut. The features there seldom changed: the club reports, the sports pages, Dorothy Dix's advice to the lovelorn, real estate transactions, and comics.

Throughout October 1929, stock prices fluctuated wildly until the bottom fell out on Thursday, October 24, "Black Thursday," as it would be remembered in history. Nearly $30 billion in losses were recorded in several days. *The Day* dismissed the developments as a reality-check on overvalued stocks. On October 30, the newspaper assured its readers that the economy overall was too healthy to succumb to the whims of Wall Street, unlike the situation in an earlier financial panic in 1907.

> *The most important thing about this near panic is that it seems not to have an effect on the welfare of the majority of people. It is a financial flurry, pure and simple, and not an industrial overturn.... Credit is due somewhere for the immense stability which has been shown by Uncle Sam during a period when his financial nervous system was under great strain.*

Orvin Andrews, as many others, attributed the problems on Wall Street to greed and manipulation by big investors:

> *The trouble with playing the market is that we small fry don't know what's going on behind the lines and just how soon our victory is going to be turned into defeat.*

Judge Frederick Latimer offered the most insightful observations in *The Day* about the actual depth of what was taking place. In his column the day after the stock market crash, Latimer noticed that people of all stations in life, including stenographers at the Hartford *Times* where he worked, were in a panic. Just what do stenographers have to worry about? he asked, then answered his own question.

> *A great deal. There are bootblacks involved in it, barbers, truck drivers, country farmers, an immense army of people of humbler resources all over the country. The stock market never in its history had drawn patronage from such a colossal number of individuals. Multitudes seemed to be making great profits in this way. Multitudes more were attracted into the game. The gossip of communities dealt with the "rights" and*

> *"tips" and this stock and that and almost anything with a seal and engraving on it could find customers somewhere.*

The happenings on Wall Street, however, were not what held the *Day's* attention in the closing months of 1929. The newspaper was more intently following the scandal enveloping Republican United States Senator Hiram Bingham who was censured for having hired lobbyist Charles Evanson to be on his staff in the midst of tariff deliberations.

That fall another important event took place in New London: a new president took charge of Connecticut College. She was Katharine Blunt, a 43-year-old professor of chemistry from the University of Chicago, a Vassar graduate, and daughter of an Army colonel. She had a commanding presence, a toughness, and confidence that earned the respect of Bodenwein and other business leaders. Bodenwein saw in her a kindred spirit. She was a doer, equal to the task of building the campus and the reputation of the women's college. In the next few years, they became close friends as well as civic allies. Blunt defied the Great Depression and embarked on one of the most ambitious building programs in the college's history. Katharine Blunt was among the few women leaders Bodenwein openly admired. She turned to him for help, and he remained at her side, encouraging her, and helping her, as she set out to build that institution while the financial underpinnings of the country were being severely shaken by an economic cataclysm.

That fall also found Bodenwein trying to figure out what to make of the newspaper's latest competition: the brash, increasingly popular, new medium of radio. That concern and puzzlement would occupy the conservative managers of *The Day* for another thirty years. In a column in November 1929, Bodenwein predicted radio would greatly expand the audience for good music but probably not accomplish much more. He noted that another benefit of the medium would be to free *The Day* and other newspapers of the chore of announcing instant election results, at least in national elections. Radio could do that a lot better. "It will save newspapers a lot of trouble and expense," he said.

New London's business leaders entered the 1930s full of confidence. The Rotary Club's annual lunch program at the Mohican Hotel on the economic outlook was entitled "The Silver Lining Beyond the Clouds." Bodenwein exuded optimism in his speech. He said America was too vast and rich a country to suffer a setback from the stock market crash. If necessary, the country could support itself. "After all, several foreign nations could fit inside a single large state in this country," he said. The crash was the product of too much speculation among people who had too much money. It wasn't worth getting upset over. So be happy, he said. "Laugh and the world will laugh with you. Weep and you weep alone." He repeated that message at the same affair in 1931. It would not be until 1932 that his outlook became at all somber.

As the spring of 1930 rolled around, *The Day* began ambitious preparations for a special edition that would mark its 50th anniversary the following year. Bodenwein, an impresario of self-promotion, relished these milestones. He had published an impressive souvenir magazine marking the newspaper's 13th anniversary in 1894, only three years after he took over. To add to the number of opportunities for special editions, he observed two distinct *Day* anniversaries: one marking the newspaper's founding by John Tibbits in 1881, and another marking his acquisition of *The Day* in 1891.

For the *Day's* half-century mark on July 2, 1931, Bodenwein set out to surpass anything he had ever done and to produce the most lavish special edition of his lifetime. As the nation entered the worst financial crisis in its history, Bodenwein produced a two-hundred-four-page, 50th anniversary edition for the newspaper's nearly fifteen thousand subscribers. He charged only three cents a copy, the newsstand price of the regular edition. The mere task of delivering this hefty, encyclopedic production was daunting. Hundreds of extra drivers and newsboys had to be recruited. At a time when the newspaper faced the need to cut its overhead, it paid its mechanical crews overtime to print the massive edition.

The publication traced the history of the city from its founding in the 17th century. It chronicled the careers of the city's most distinguished leaders. It told the story of each town that made up the *Day's* circulation area and the villages and enclaves within these towns, as well as each business and industry of importance. In each of these places, *The Day* noted "extraordinary progress" was occurring. The headlines announced "vast improvements," "great natural beauty," and "courage and determination."

Writers went up and down the main streets in New London noting every change that had occurred in the past fifty years, building by building, lot by lot. There was a photographic layout of the finest houses in the city, including the Bodenweins' mansion on Pequot Avenue, but also many ordinary looking homes. And it contained Bodenwein's often-told version of the early history of *The Day*, with all the familiar, quirky embellishments such as the story about the efforts to keep the *Day's* name secret until the newspaper was published. Bodenwein not only wrote much of the copy for the edition himself, he supervised the production. It was no doubt clear to him at 67, that this was his grand finale, the testimonial to his life's achievements, and he wanted it to be flawless.

The special edition was called "A Half Century of Progress," and its purpose was to show in the physical evidence—the buildings, factories, and public works that were pictured in rich abundance—that New London had become an important and progressive city. The edition compared the modern surroundings to the dusty, backward "unkempt place" he remembered from his youth. Bodenwein calculated that the edition would showcase the city for investors across the country, and he made sure it was widely distributed outside New London.

The edition highlighted the leadership of the past. It noted, for example, how earlier leaders had had the sense to buy reservoirs in the neighboring town of Waterford to accommodate the city's development. It told of how hospitals, libraries, and schools sprang up from the philanthropy of the region's leaders, including its wealthy whaling merchants. It devoted two full pages to describing how New London became the first city in the state to adopt the city manager form of government. It described how men of vision had seized upon the advantages of the harbor to attract commerce and make New London an important maritime port and naval headquarters. *The Day* ran photographs of all the mayors and important community leaders during the periods of expansion following the Civil War. It charted New London's colorful sports history and the spread of prosperity to the towns and villages that surround New London. In a preface to his history of *The Day*, Bodenwein repeated what had become a catechism for him:

> The Day *has had a long and eventful life. It has earned an enduring place in the hearts of the people of eastern Connecticut. It has had its vicissitudes, its tragedies, its triumphs. On the whole, it has been fortunate in surviving the critical period of evolution in the past 50 years, which blasted the hopes of so many of its contemporaries. It has grown and prospered beyond the most fanciful dreams of its founders. It has been more than a business venture. It has become an outstanding New London institution.*

It required four press runs to publish the anniversary edition, all of the work occurring during off-hours. President Herbert Hoover sent a letter of congratulations to Bodenwein, who was one of the president's staunchest supporters, and it was printed on the front page. The edition was subsidized by hundreds of advertisements. In the midst of a financial meltdown, merchants and factory owners enthusiastically purchased congratulatory advertisements to be a part of this extraordinary promotional undertaking.

But the fifty years of progress ran into a stonewall in the 1930s. The Stock Market Crash of 1929 was an early symptom of the deep hardship that followed, and New London did not escape the effects as Bodenwein had predicted and hoped it would. If there had been a delay of the Depression's onslaught on the city, Orvin Andrews theorized in 1932, it may have resulted from the large military presence. The Navy and the Coast Guard and the Electric Boat shipyard in Groton maintained significant payrolls. Electric Boat benefited both from submarine production for the United States and a market for its products in Latin America. Neither Prohibition nor the Depression diminished the taste for alcohol, and the Coast Guard expanded to carry out its mission to chase down rumrunners.

The construction work at the Coast Guard Academy and Connecticut College was also a hedge against the Depression. Relying upon support from rich philanthropists like Mary Stillman Harkness, the wife of a wealthy Standard Oil Company heir who had a summer estate near New London, President Katharine Blunt moved forward with her ambitious construction program at Connecticut College. And work proceeded on building the Coast Guard Academy across the street. In addition to this, Bodenwein finally saw one of his goals realized when the federal government decided to construct a new regional Post Office building in New London.

The growing military, government, and institutional presence in New London proved to be a two-edged sword though. Although this produced jobs when employment in private industry was shrinking, it weakened the city by removing real estate from the property tax lists. The civic leadership, dating back to the men who had persuaded the Navy to build a coaling station in the area after the Civil War, had been brilliantly successful at attracting largely nontaxable activities to the area. Colleges, military bases, parks, schools, and institutions proliferated, as Bodenwein graphically documented in his 50th anniversary edition. But the leaders had not been as successful at finding big businesses and manufacturing companies that would support the schools and local government with property taxes.

The one great commercial hope for the city, the state's Ocean Pier, remained only marginally successful and largely given over to military uses. Owned by the state, it paid no taxes. And, just as the country was entering the Depression, the city revalued its real estate using 1920s data. Thus, as taxable property was being taken off the tax lists by government and tax-exempt institutions and businesses were failing, homeowners saw sharp increases in their tax assessments. This led to growing middle class discontent and a taxpayer revolt.

The year 1932 was a turning point in New London. Bodenwein's outlook changed as he witnessed the growing unemployment. The mounting poverty placed great strains upon the local government. The Red Cross mobilized a drive to distribute free flour to distressed families. The electric company gave its needy customers more time to pay their bills before turning off the power. Observing the crippling impact on local budgets that helping the jobless was having, Bodenwein suggested setting aside some of the city's parkland for the unemployed to have gardens to support their families. The city and towns were forced to cut spending significantly to make up for deficits that arose from business failures, bankruptcies, and the general shrinkage of commerce. Business owners asked workers to accept substantial cuts in pay and this placed pressure upon schools and local governments to do the same for teachers and municipal workers.

In June 1932, Bodenwein presented a proposal to the typographical union at *The Day* asking it to accept a seventeen percent cut in wages. The union, which had not negotiated a pay increase with the publisher since 1922, rejected the proposal. Rather than risk a strike, Bodenwein agreed to extend the existing contract for six months. One of the stipulations was that the workers would accept scrip, a form of locally issued paper money that could be exchanged for food and other goods, as pay. When the six months were up, Bodenwein told the union he wanted an open shop and would no longer recognize the Local. On February 1, 1933, the *Day's* management posted notices that the newspaper was an open shop and wages would be reduced ten percent. A representative from the International Typographical Union arrived and averted a strike with an agreement that left the union intact, and that settled for an unspecified wage cut of less than ten percent. It was the worse labor trouble Bodenwein had encountered since 1907, but somehow the union and the publisher emerged from it on cordial terms again. This rather strange relationship infuriated other unions in the city who were trying to organize the labor movement.

By the 1930s, *The Day* had a reputation as a trusted institution in the community and the Depression enhanced that quality. In a desperate land where jobs were fast disappearing, *The Day* became a place where men and women—even children, who served in the newspaper's corps of newsboys and did odd jobs around the newspaper—could find steady work and sometimes rewarding careers. Bodenwein boasted about the longevity of employees on his newspaper. Arthur Russ, a machinist in the composing room, had joined the newspaper in 1898. George Grout, the city and county editor and librarian, had joined as a reporter in 1900. Alfred Ligourie, the city editor, had been on board since 1908. Francis Ham, a linotype operator; Orvin Andrews; George Kent, the press foreman; and Walter Crighton, the composing room foreman all had been there since before

World War I. And Johnny Mallon and Charlie O'Connor were on the cusp of becoming *Day* veterans.

The *Day's* popularity as a place to work made Orvin Andrews, the business manager, one of the best-known men in the city. He screened and interviewed many of the job applicants. He was the man to see "down at the *Day* Paper." Morton Kenyon, who began working at odd jobs when he finished grammar school in 1932 and later worked as a driver in the circulation department in the late 1930s, recalled why people were so eager to get work at the paper:

> *The work was steady. And if you did your job, they'd keep you. In a normal union job during the Depression, when your time was up, they threw you out and hired someone else. But here, the people were different. Mr. Andrews would keep people and give them the advantage of staying.*

John W.R. "Jack" Cruise arrived in 1931 to work on the sports page immediately after he graduated from the Chapman Technical High School in New London. He stayed at the paper for sixty years. His boss was John L. DeGange, the sports editor, who had started in 1924 and stayed on for fifty years. James A. Watterson started as a sports writer the same year Cruise did. He became news editor and did not leave until 1970. In November 1931, Bodenwein hired George A. Clapp, the telegraph editor of the New Britain (Connecticut) *Herald*, to replace Howard E. Lee as managing editor. Clapp stayed until he retired in 1970. Barnard L. Colby, who one day would become publisher, and Thomas Elliott, who retired in the 1980s as head of the mechanical departments, both arrived in the early 1930s.

The board of directors that would guide the newspaper after Bodenwein's death took shape in the 1930s. It already included George Grout and Orvin Andrews. In 1931, the publisher asked Earle Stamm to be a director. Stamm was the 34-year-old vice president of the National Bank of Commerce, Bodenwein's personal banker, and the husband of one of Edna's closest friends. He remained on governing boards of *The Day* until his death in 1950. Charles Smiddy became a director when he took over the legal affairs of the newspaper upon the death of his law partner, Charles Whittlesey. Smiddy, a leading corporate lawyer in Connecticut, played a central role in shaping the course of the newspaper after Bodenwein's death.

Whittlesey, 61, had died November 1932 in a Boston hospital after abdominal surgery. He was a son of Ezra Whittlesey, the business manager who had been murdered in the *Day's* offices by the mentally disturbed Frederick A. S. Perry in 1883. Charlie Whittlesey was a close friend of Bodenwein, as well as a political ally in the Republican Party. The son of

Frank and Alfred Chappell's cousin, he was the last member of the Chappell family to be associated with the newspaper.

The Day had the vitality and stored-up fat to survive the hard times, but the Depression killed the struggling *Globe*, which found itself unable to meet payrolls in 1933 and 1934. The Central Labor Council, an alliance of labor unions in the region, was concerned that the newspaper's failure would be a blow to labor's strength among typographers and urged the workers to stay on the job even though they were not being paid. The council, on the other hand, refused membership to Local 159 at *The Day* because of its coziness with management.

Todd Barton, a businessman from New York, bought the *Globe* from Samuel T. Adams and his son, Harry, and made an unsuccessful attempt to revive it as a flashier, morning paper. He solicited small investors in New London but the attempt failed and the newspaper died in the hands of a receiver, Waldo E. Clarke, in 1934. Barton's venture lasted only six months. Bodenwein welcomed the end of the *Globe*, his last real competition. In a "Tattler" column December 15, 1934, he tore into what he called Barton's "great adventure." Barton, he charged, was little more than a fly-by-night promoter who had no money of his own and had misrepresented the financial condition of the newspaper to attract local investors. Bodenwein said Barton even approached him about buying control of the failing newspaper. Why would he, Bodenwein, be interested in such a ridiculous proposal? The *Globe* had no advertising revenue and its printers "refused longer to be goats and work for nothing." Bodenwein wrote:

> *This is a free country. Others will come along no doubt to start another daily newspaper in New London. The field is wide open. There is no monopoly about it. But as an investment for people to put in their small savings it should not be considered. And before any well-dressed stranger from New York proposing to bring a newspaper into the world here is accepted in the community as something more than an irresponsible promoter, let him be looked up in Dunn & Bradstreet and let tradesmen and artisans demand cash for their goods and services. There will be less sorrow and bitter reflections.*

There was a great deal more disappointment in town over the disappearance of the *Globe* than Bodenwein would like to have believed. The *Globe's* death once again left the Democrats and anyone else who disagreed with the Republican, Chamber of Commerce line touted by *The Day* without a friendly newspaper. The *Day's* publisher was virtually the titular leader of the Republican Party. In fact, soon, he would be considered as a Republican candidate for governor.

Two of the *Day's* leading writers, John Mallon and George E. MacDougall, were leaders in the local Republican Party. And Mallon, of all things, was the newspaper's political writer. How could Democrats expect fair treatment from such a newspaper?

This issue came to a head during the New Deal administration of Franklin D. Roosevelt, when the Democratic tide dealt New London's Republican organization startling setbacks. *The Day* became strident in its criticism of the New Deal and of the emerging Democratic juggernaut led by Dr. C. John Satti. The perception that *The Day* was not as politically independent as it professed to be created tensions that lasted for decades.

Satti was a physician with passionate political interests, who for several years had been building a political base in the city's Italian neighborhoods. The son of one of New London's earliest Italian settlers, he studied medicine at Yale in the 1920s, and returned to New London to set up a practice. Satti and his wife, Dorothy Heffernan Satti, the daughter of a New York journalist, ran a school for immigrants in his medical office to teach English, arithmetic, and other basic skills. They became enormously popular in the Italian community, not to mention powerful.

After several years of preparations, Satti staged his march into city and state politics in the summer of 1932, when the parties in New London were picking candidates for the fall elections. At the time, the Democratic Party was in the hands of Irish bosses. The Italians were not yet a political factor, and many voted Republican. But in August, Satti filled the ward caucuses with Italian supporters and promised to deliver the entire Italian vote in the city to the Democrats if he were granted a significant berth on the state ticket. Satti theorized that with his name on the ballot, and with the Democrats enjoying the advantage of the top line on the new-fangled mechanical voting machines, he could turn the tide for the party in New London.

The Democrats were still a loose-knit, undisciplined party split into factions and accustomed to losing elections. Democrats had won only two significant election victories in New London in the last twenty-six years—in 1910 when Bryan Mahan won an upset victory in a state senate race, and in 1912, when Theodore Roosevelt's Bull Moose Party split the Republican vote. But Satti understood history better than the other city Democrats. He was the family doctor, teacher, counselor, and helper to hundreds of newly arrived immigrants who worked in bottom-rung jobs were they lucky enough to have jobs at all in those hard times. He understood the great fear and pain that was gripping the country, and where it was leading. Satti was confident that Roosevelt would lead Democrats across the country to victory, and that is why he chose 1932 to make his first big move.

The New London Democrats did not support Satti for a state office, as he had hoped, but he settled for a place on the ballot as a presidential elector. Bodenwein followed this political melodrama from his second-floor office on Main Street with mild disdain. He was certain that the Democrats would go down in defeat because, first of all, they always had, and second, Roosevelt did not have a clear program as far as he could see. The Republicans, on the other hand, had charted a straight course out of the Depression, based on tariff protection, restrictions on immigration, and tax cuts. He was perceptive enough to observe that Satti would have an impact in the election, but not keen enough to appreciate that history was about to change course in New London. Just before the election, Bodenwein advised in "The Tattler" how Italian voters could vote for Hoover and still support Satti by splitting their vote. "Some of them surely have mechanical ability," he said. Appreciating the significance of the Satti challenge, *The Day* also carried a diagram and a story illustrating how to vote a split ticket.

The Saturday before the election, the doctor and the local Italian Democratic social clubs staged a huge demonstration. Satti, riding in a convertible, led a boisterous torchlight parade through the city's Italian neighborhoods, separated according to the regions of Italy where the residents had been born. It started at Garibaldi Square and ended up near the statue of Christopher Columbus, which had been erected in 1928 and had become a symbol of the Italians' yearning for respect in the city. A marching band played and hundreds of children joined in. All the leading Democratic candidates, including U.S. Representative Augustine Lonergan of Hartford, who was challenging Hiram Bingham for the Senate, appeared on the speakers' platform. Satti, a short, stocky, expressive man, delivered a passionate speech condemning the Republican record of the past twelve years. Francis J. Conti, a Hartford lawyer, addressed the crowd in Italian, stating, "We are now paying the penalty for the campaign of 1928, when the public was tricked into believing the Republicans had the key to continued prosperity." The speakers condemned Prohibition. Timothy J. Sullivan, the Democratic town chairman, swallowed hard and praised Satti, although the two now were at war with each other for control of the party.

On election night, November 8, 1932, one thousand people crowded outside the *Day* building to see the results projected on a screen across the street. Franklin D. Roosevelt swept into office in a landslide that buried the

Republicans in New London. President Hoover, who had won New London by three hundred sixty-eight votes in 1928, lost the city to Roosevelt by more than five hundred votes. Hoover won in only two of the city's wards, including the fifth ward, the silk stocking district where Bodenwein lived. Satti's handiwork was evident in the Italian wards, the third and fourth, where the support for Roosevelt was more than two to one.

The Republican casualties were stunning. Wilbur Cross beat Governor John H. Trumbull, who had succeeded Hiram Bingham in the office when Bingham ran for the Senate. Cross had been an upstart in the state Democratic Party, challenging the Democratic machine led by boss James Spellacy of Hartford. Hiram Bingham's political career, already soiled by scandal, ended on the scrap heap in the Roosevelt landslide as Congressman Lonergan replaced him. New London lost the foothold it had in Washington since Bodenwein's best friend, Frank Brandegee, had begun serving there in 1912. *The Day* noted as much in its editorial the next day. Bingham's loss, the newspaper said, "is a personal loss to the city." New London would no longer benefit from his affinity to the area, and the state would lose the benefit of his seniority on key committees in the Senate. He was being replaced, the newspaper said, by a "routine member of the lower house, seldom heard of and seldom displaying any qualities of leadership."

Democrats, with red torches left over from Satti's parade Saturday night, marched through the city in a spectacular demonstration of their euphoria at suddenly being on top in New London. The numbers grew as the procession moved down State Street and up Main Street past *The Day* where the crowd there joined in. The parade made its way to Satti's house on Huntington Street. The crowd serenaded the leader who had had a large role in making the victory possible. Satti had run ahead of Roosevelt in New London.

There was little joy at *The Day*. Bodenwein now had to reconcile himself to a new, alien political order in Washington, as well as the emasculation of the Republican Party at home. Roosevelt left him little time to gather his thoughts. The dizzying pace of the president's new programs was quickly felt in New London. An early New Deal measure created the National Recovery Administration (NRA), which attempted to get management and labor to cooperate on prices and wages. Bodenwein was skeptical of the federal government thus reaching into the province of private enterprise, but *The Day* became one of the first businesses in the city to display the NRA blue eagle, signifying it agreed to adhere to the federal guidelines.

New London leaders were intrigued by the potential benefits to the city of New Deal loans for public works projects to provide jobs. But, beset by political rifts, the leaders had difficulty agreeing on how best to take advantage of the help. The city's needs were mounting. Most of its schools had been built in the 19th century and needed repair or replacement. It had a long list of desired capital improvements, including the proposals in the 1928 Swan Plan. Bodenwein was one of those Mayor Alton T. Miner named to a committee to suggest projects to finance. Bodenwein was skeptical about what strings would be attached and the costs to the city. The committee haggled for months over projects and even over whether New London should get involved at all.

Nevertheless, to some degree, the New Deal created a sense of excitement and confidence in the city, a belief that the country was doing something about the Depression. Soon all the advertisements in *The Day* carried the blue eagle emblem. The New Deal supported a military construction program that awarded two submarine contracts to the Electric Boat shipyard. Work started on the *Shark* and the *Tarpon* in the fall of 1933, producing several hundred jobs. Work projects to put the jobless back on their feet sprouted up across the city. Streets were paved, basketball courts constructed, parks developed. On October 24, there was a big parade, six thousand strong, to celebrate the work of the NRA.

Bodenwein's concerns about the New Deal grew nevertheless, and by 1934, his patience with the Administration in Washington had run out. He had come to passionately dislike Roosevelt and General Hugh Johnson, head of the NRA, comparing the two to Adolf Hitler. He shared the worries of his fellow newspaper publishers across the country that the government would misuse its "dictatorial" authority to muzzle the press under the authority of the NRA. He feared that child labor laws under consideration in Washington would extend to newspaper carriers. The carriers, of course, were a source of cheap labor, but he felt they also were part of the culture of *The Day*, members of the vast extended family of the newspaper. Some of the city's most distinguished citizens had started out delivering *The Day*.

Bodenwein appealed in *The Day* to former and present newsboys and their parents to send letters to Congress urging that it reject a proposed law banning child labor unless it excluded newspaper carriers. *The Day* started running pictures of prominent men in New London who had started out as young men delivering the newspaper. Bodenwein included himself among these, suggesting either that he delivered the paper for Tibbits before or during the time he became an apprentice printer in 1881, or that he was making up the story, another embellishment to a growing legend he had painstakingly fashioned over many years.

He was 70, now, and still had some finishing touches to add.

FIFTEEN

THE ELDER STATESMAN

It means a hard fight to beat this machine. But I have faith that the American people do not want to be regimented from birth to death.

—Theodore Bodenwein, December 10, 1935

EDNA ARRANGED A SURPRISE party for her husband's 70th birthday. More than one hundred well-wishers attended the affair at the roof garden of the Mohican Hotel on January 25, 1934. Edna, 51, had, by this time, made a comfortable niche for herself in New London society, though many in the provincial Yankee aristocracy still regarded her as a pushy and coarse woman, one who, though she had married into money, still lacked the social graces.

But Edna had admirers as well as detractors. People enjoyed her humor, grand showmanship, and generosity. In the midst of the Depression, she dressed and acted like a movie star, favoring mink and expensive jewelry. She did not care what people thought about her, for she did not have to; she was Theodore Bodenwein's wife. She found security in a wide circle of friends from the upper rungs of New London society. Many of their closest friends were at the Mohican that night at her beckoning.

Among Bodenwein's closest associates at the newspaper and their wives attending were George Grout, the county editor; Orvin Andrews, the general manager, Charles Smiddy, the newspaper's lawyer, and Earle Stamm, Bodenwein's banker. Each of these men, who would set the unusual course of the newspaper after Bodenwein's death, cultivated Edna's friendship, and she reciprocated with her loyalty, and more significantly for the future of the newspaper, her trust, although that trust would eventually erode. Andrews and Smiddy, in particular, nurtured a close relationship with Edna and they included her in discussions on the future of the newspaper after her husband died.

Dr. Joseph Ganey also attended. He had been a friend of Eugene O'Neill's before the war and later was active in local politics. Proper and conservative New Londoners once regarded Ganey's office in New London as a center of "Bohemianism." The source of this reputation amounted to little more than late-night whiskey drinking and card playing. But Doc Ganey's reputation as a libertine was further enhanced by his having a mistress. Later in life he married and built a house on the Niantic River near the Oswegatchie colony in the neighboring town of Waterford, a wealthy enclave where social life centered on a waterfront casino.

Another guest was Martin Branner, an artist whose syndicated comic strip, "Winnie Winkle," began appearing in *The Day* in the 1930s. The heroine was a stunning but malleable young woman who was forced by the Depression to go to work to support her elderly parents and found her way through opportune jobs into high society. Branner lived on Long Island, but had a summer home near Oswegatchie. Moss Baratz, a prominent local businessman in the city, and his wife, Lydia, were close friends, and rarely missed a special occasion of the Bodenweins. This event was no exception.

Thomas E. Troland was the new director of law in New London. His wife, Roberta, was a long-time friend of Bodenwein's daughter, Elizabeth.

No *Day* gathering would have seemed complete without reporter-politician Johnny Mallon. His hairline was receding and he had put on weight, but he was still entertaining. Charlie O'Connor, the advertising director, whose influence at the newspaper was growing substantially, and Tom McGinley, one of John McGinley's nine sons, were there too. McGinley handled much of Bodenwein's real estate and insurance dealings through his agency, the McGinley Brothers.

Former Lieutenant Governor Ernest Rogers, the Bodenweins' neighbor, and former Congressman Richard Freeman were among the state Republican celebrities who added prestige to the event. Bodenwein was one of the state's most prominent Republicans, but Edna also had made her mark in political circles. She represented New London County on the executive board of the McKinley Association, a select group of Connecticut Republicans.

Bodenwein was starting to feel his age and his compulsively ambitious life. He had become lame from hardening of the arteries and required a cane to get about. He had lost weight and paid regular visits to his physician, Dr. Albert Labensky, for mounting physical ailments. It had become a part of the routine of drivers at *The Day* and maids in the Bodenwein household to take him to the doctor's office. In 1936, Bodenwein asked Smiddy to prepare a will for him.

He had stopped playing golf, his only athletic pastime, but still made winter visits to Florida. His life still revolved around *The Day*, New London, and the Republican Party. Although Andrews and other managers of *The Day* assumed increasing control over the operation of the newspaper, Bodenwein continued to go to work every day. He was usually chauffeured by a maid, and often stayed after most of the employees had gone home. He cherished, in particular, writing "The Tattler" column, in which he kept a critical eye on local, state, and national politics. He also had a keen interest in a new feature he had introduced in the newspaper, "The Junior Day," which included essays by young readers. Bodenwein was always on the lookout for ways to boost circulation, and this page was his method to entice future *Day* readers. "The Junior Day" was published on Saturdays, and, until he died, Bodenwein supervised its production in the composing room every Saturday morning. It would be the last feature he added to *The Day*. In addition to young writing, it offered puzzles, games, tricks, and magic. Bodenwein invented it and he delighted in it like a child.

Edna loved and respected her husband. But she fretted over his long hours at *The Day*. She kept busy with activities in various organizations, including the Little Slam Club, a bridge club. Her club's triumphs in competition were regularly chronicled on the Social Page.

But she still exhibited symptoms of loneliness and isolation, including daytime drinking. Household employees often found her disagreeable when she was drinking. She also had a habit of turning up at *The Day* late at night, banging on the door, demanding to know where her husband was. She also harangued the newspaper's telephone operator with her insistent demands to talk to Bodenwein. She was disliked among the employees of *The Day*, whereas her husband, though he became distant from much of the routine, was held in the affection accorded a man of great stature and advanced years. In contrast to the brash manner of his youth, he was soft-spoken and kindly in his twilight years, reserved even in anger.

The elegant dinner party at the Mohican, on the illuminated rooftop high over New London, belied the grimness of the time. Bodenwein was celebrating his 70th birthday during the darkest days of the Depression. That year, violence from a national strike in the textile industry spilled into New England. Later in the year, troops were called out in Rhode Island to quell riots in the industrial city of Pawtucket. The threat of violence at the Brainerd & Armstrong mill and the Rossi Velvet Company mill in Mystic, a village to the east, necessitated calling out state troopers in September, 1934.

The adversity affected Bodenwein and brought out his generosity. He experienced both stock and real estate losses and, according to Orvin Andrews, he made a point of reimbursing his investment associates for their losses. In 1933, Christina Rolfe, Jennie Bodenwein's sister and the widow of William Rolfe, Bodenwein's Associated Press telegraph operator, was in danger of losing her house because of delinquent mortgage payments. Bodenwein always liked Rolfe, who had been a sidekick in his younger days. Rolfe, who had married Christina in 1883, introduced Bodenwein and Jennie. He was a director of The Day Publishing Company from 1910 until his sudden death in 1921. The Rolfes, in fact, were Bodenwein's only cordial connection with the Muir family after the divorce. The publisher asked Charles Smiddy to arrange a deal in which *The Day* bought the Rolfes' house and allowed Christina to live there rent-free for the rest of her life. The arrangement also provided her a monthly income of $43.

Jennie Bodenwein, who never remarried, spent her last years in a rooming house on Broad Street, near downtown New London. Her health deteriorated sharply in 1933 and she underwent surgery at Lawrence & Memorial Hospital two years later. A month after the operation, on March 30, 1935, she died. She was 70. Her death was marked in a matter-of-fact, three-paragraph obituary in *The Day* under a one-column headline known in the newspaper industry wryly as a tombstone head. Gordon, now a Roman Catholic priest in Bridgeport, Connecticut, had moved back to southeastern Connecticut to Old Lyme, a town west of New London, to be near his mother. He supervised the funeral and burial arrangements. Jennie, the personable, beautiful young woman Bodenwein had married in St. Mary Star of the Sea Church at the dawn of his career, was buried in Cedar Grove cemetery separate from most of the rest of her family. Her grave was next to that of her brother-in-law, William Rolfe. Christina Rolfe died in 1940 and was buried beside her husband and Jennie. Gordon's aunt, Elizabeth, died in 1942, and was buried beside her sister. Eventually Gordon was buried next to his mother's grave when he died in 1967. The separate burial plots, signifying the different phases of the lives of the Muirs and the Bodenweins and the differences that divided them, form a curious triangle in the city's foremost burial ground.

The spare and indifferent report in *The Day* of Jennie's death did not do justice to the substantial legacy she left and the important role she played in the life of the Bodenweins and *The Day*. At the time of their divorce, she held sway over a substantial interest in the newspaper in a legal arrangement to guarantee her alimony. She would have obtained part control of the newspaper if Bodenwein had defaulted on his obligation. She brought Bodenwein's children into the world and raised them: two bright, perhaps brilliant, children who matured to live fascinating, cultivated lives that enlarged their horizons far beyond the small-town confines of New London. The mother retained custody of the children when she and Bodenwein divorced in 1911, and she saw to their education and upbringing. The children looked more like her than their father. Both parents were handsome, but Gordon and Elizabeth were imbued with the dark, soft, and wistful facial characteristics of their mother. They also inherited her gentle and generous disposition. But the very qualities that she instilled in them carried the children away from New London and estranged them from both their father and the city that meant so much to him. Neither Gordon nor Elizabeth shared Theodore Bodenwein's affection for New London and the loyal, though narrow and materialistic, vision of its leaders and *The Day*.

Elizabeth kept aloof from both her parents whereas Gordon gravitated toward his mother. After she died, he researched the family line that led John Muir, the stonecutter, to America from Scotland and to New London, where he had died in 1870. He became a member of the Gordon Society, an organization devoted to Scottish ancestry. Eventually, Gordon had a large monument placed at his mother's gravesite. The stone bore, in letters that were vertically arranged in a striking, modernistic format, his name and Jennie's. This occurred after Edna, Andrews, and the other directors of *The Day* had one of the most striking and unusual monuments placed at the gravesite of Theodore Bodenwein. It had a rolled-up edition of *The Day* chiseled on the face. It is not difficult to imagine that Gordon was making a statement that his mother, too, despite her humble origins and difficult youth, had made an important contribution in her lifetime.

IN 1934, THE YEAR of Bodenwein's 70th birthday, the city separated into opposing political camps. Dr. C. John Satti, son of an Italian immigrant, had turned around the fortunes of the New London Democratic organization in the 1932 elections and put the Republicans into an unaccustomed position as underdogs. He set out in 1934 to consolidate his power. That summer, Democrats engaged in one of the fiercest internecine struggles in New London's history. The ranks of the Democrats, which had been dominated by the Irish, had filled with new arrivals from eastern and southern Europe and the resulting factional differences had made the party unwieldy for its poorly equipped leaders. That summer, Satti mounted an assault to take over the party based on a simple principle that carried him into power and kept him there for thirty years: unity. He united the fractious party and through his skills as a back-room negotiator, he kept it that way for the rest of his life. He made his mark by balancing national, ethnic, and family factions against one another in a political technique he virtually patented in New London—the "balanced ticket." Run candidates who reflected the national and ethnic makeup of the city, he taught.

He held the balance of power through the Italian families who had been pivotal in the 1932 Democratic upset, and brought that leverage to the party caucuses that summer. Among other things, he used his influence to change the party rules to depose T. J. Sullivan, the party chairman. The Satti forces rammed through a new rule that prevented federal officials from serving as town chairmen. Sullivan, by a strange coincidence, was the district manager of the federal Home Owners Loan Corporation.

That rule left the party without a leader to summon members to its city convention in August. Mayor Alton T. Miner appointed Satti the acting chairman. This placed the physician in an advantageous position against the Irish bosses who opposed him for control of the party. The opposition was led by former state Senator William C. Fox. The climate was so emotionally charged that City Manager William A. Holt detailed police to the meeting halls where the nominating caucuses for the fall elections were taking place. The school board was worried because of the risk of damage to the buildings.

The rival leaders struggled all week before the caucuses to resolve the leadership dispute, and in the final hours, they reached an agreement that made Satti the permanent chairman. At the city convention, Fox, having already capitulated in private, nominated Satti to head the party convention, stating, "It is only fitting that one who was an enthusiastic Democrat and one who could conduct the city convention with dignity, honor, and impartiality ought to be its chairman." The Democrats unanimously approved, marking the official beginning of a political dynasty that would influence New London politics and its government for the rest of the century. The settlement averted a violent showdown, disappointing many in the city, including Bodenwein, who had looked forward to fireworks.

With more good news to come, one of the worst years in the Depression turned out to be a banner year for the newly united New London Democrats. Connecticut's Democrats held their convention to nominate a governor and other state officials that summer at the Griswold Hotel in Groton. Bodenwein did not allow his political prejudices to stand in the way of his instincts as a journalist. The honor the convention afforded the region was to him not only a good news story, but a boost to the prestige of New London. *The Day* heralded the gathering with bold headlines on its front page, one of which noted that

Satti had been nominated to be his party's candidate for secretary of the state, the post the doctor unsuccessfully had sought two years earlier. Governor Wilbur Cross was nominated to run for re-election. The only setback Satti experienced was the nomination of Mayor Alton T. Miner for the state Senate. Satti favored City Councilor Alfred Lamden, the business manager at Connecticut College and a strong Satti voice on the City Council.

In their dire moment, the New London Republicans turned to Bodenwein, a former secretary of the state and their most esteemed elder statesman, to restore them to their rightful place and lead them out of their adversity. Overshadowed by the notoriety of the Democratic State Convention in Groton, Republicans in the area launched a campaign to nominate the 70-year-old publisher and civic leader as a favorite son to be governor. "No man in New London has occupied a more enviable position, and no man has done more to promote every worthwhile civic or municipal project," P. Leroy Harwood, the Republican chairman in the city, declared. The honor, as well as the insidious threat to the American republic that Bodenwein saw in Roosevelt's New Deal, aroused the war-horse in the venerable publisher. He gratefully accepted the party's support and traveled to the convention in Hartford with Edna that summer half-expecting to capture the honor.

That hope did not come to pass. New London, the hometown of the late United States Senator Frank Brandegee and base of support for the tarnished former United States Senator Hiram Bingham, had lost its luster and authority in the beleaguered party. The leaders offered Bodenwein a place on the state ticket as the nominee for lieutenant governor as a consolation prize, an honor Bodenwein respectfully declined.

It was probably just as well. The same forces of social and political change that propelled Franklin Roosevelt into office in 1932 swept across a still more radicalized Connecticut again in 1934. Connecticut re-elected Wilbur Cross governor, and in the landslide, Dr. C. John Satti became secretary of the state. Satti began his tenure by appointing Mary Romano, the daughter of one of New London's Italian first families, to be the secretary in the secretary of the state's office, a position she went on to hold for more than three decades. This marked the start of a new, Democratic political machine in New London powered and held together by the enticement of political jobs. Happy days were there again. Upon his election, Satti declared:

> *I feel that the voters of New London acted independently of party affiliations and that they felt that the New Deal under President Roosevelt was worthy of support.*

Leroy Harwood, the Republican leader in the city, commented:

> *I don't think the weather had anything to do with the results. It would seem that the Republican program of conservatism, with reduced public expenditures, does not appeal to the majority of our voters and that the certainty of heavy taxation and delayed recovery has no fears for them.*

That year, two years after the *Globe* had closed, Bodenwein came under fire for partisanship as a newspaper publisher, particularly in the *Day's* critical treatment of the New Deal. Bodenwein reacted in August 1934:

> The Day *tries to give all parties fair and impartial treatment in its news columns. … We are presently living under peculiar political conditions. Elected as Democratic, the administration has adopted policies and ideas for national government totally different from any ever subscribed by the Democratic party platform … The president's advisors are not Democrats, but socialist dreamers. …* The Day *for one does not believe that the people of this country need to be regimented. It does not want the individualism of the people destroyed.*

Ideology had only partly to do with the importance of that year's elections and the divided sentiments in the city. A new style of politics was taking shape, one that conflicted with the plans of Bodenwein and other business leaders who had crafted the city-manager form of government. That system was designed to remove political influences from the governance of the city, but the political interests never accepted the passage of the new charter in 1921 as the end of their way of doing things. The new charter reduced the City Council's role, which once included hiring, awarding contracts, and spending the city's tax revenue, to hiring and supervising the city manager. Under the new charter, the manager did the hiring and the administration awarded contracts. However, for much of the 1920s and 1930s, the politicians worked to circumvent the charter.

One of their methods was to harass and undermine the city manager. James E. Harlow, the administrator from Ohio, had lasted only two years under the constant political fire. In his place, the city hired William A. Holt, who remained throughout the 1920s and into the Depression. But the council, under Democratic control, did its best to make Holt's tenure an interminable nightmare. Holt, backed by *The Day* and the local Chamber of Commerce, set out to make significant changes in New London. The first targets of this effort were the most sensitive: Ocean Beach and the fire department.

Ocean Beach, including a two-thousand-foot stretch of beach the city had bought from former Governor Thomas Waller earlier in the century, had become a raucous and disorderly clutter of cottages and business concessions that bred crime and increasing blight on the city's southernmost waterfront. The Swan Plan, the city's blueprint for the future, called upon New London to clean up and enlarge the beach and turn it into a presentable and attractive local amenity. That was a threat to the real estate and business interests that profited from the honky-tonk attraction as it overflowed with humanity every summer.

Holt, Bodenwein, and other city leaders also set their sights on reorganizing the city's fire-fighting system. The system had as its foundation a proliferation of volunteer fire companies scattered across the city, each with its own political machine to guard it. This was the greater challenge for the reformers, for the fire companies possessed enormous political clout. The reformers had attempted to undercut the volunteer firemen's influence by having city councilors elected at large. In response, the firemen concentrated upon increasing their influence over the City Council. Their first and most successful ploy was to unite with the Taxpayer's League, which formed as a result of the discontent over the mounting tax burden homeowners experienced during the Depression.

In 1934, Holt triggered his own execution by proposing a plan to close four of the fire stations and to replace many of the volunteers with professional firemen. Bodenwein and the other advocates of the new charter in 1921 had soft-pedaled this threatening idea and lied that they had no intention of undermining the volunteer system. Holt, in making his recommendations, cited support from the National Board of Fire Underwriters. *The Day*, at the same time, vigorously advocated centralizing and professionalizing the fire department. The result of this threat to the volunteer firefighters appeared in the outcome of the local elections, two months before the state elections in November 1934. Emily O. Spiers, a Republican activist in the taxpayers' group, had made several unsuccessful attempts to be elected to the City Council. That year, she won a seat after forming a pact with the volunteer firefighters. The results were gratifying to the firemen, who saw all four candidates they endorsed for the council elected.

The local election was the beginning of the end for Holt, who endured some months more of torture from the council before resigning. Holt had been as talented a city manager as the city ever would have. A city native and Harvard graduate, he had become city manager in 1923, and led the city through both the roaring '20s and the worst days of the Depression. By most accounts, he did well, but late in the spring of 1936, the councilors met with him secretly, and emerged to announce, without any explanation, that he was leaving.

The council later issued a statement saying that Holt had not been guilty of any wrongdoing. The statement contained a list of complaints it had with his administration, none of which were new. Holt and the city engineer had proposed an expensive solution to a water main problem when a less costly alternative was available. He had appointed supernumeraries in the police department the council felt were not necessary. Certain department heads were not performing well. The harshest charge they lodged was that the manager was awarding too much overtime. Bodenwein was enraged at what he saw as a flagrant assault on the city manager form of government. He wrote on June 13, 1936:

> *It has been no secret that a majority of the present council has been working for some time to get City Manager Holt out of office. And it is no secret that the city manager has become so sick of being badgered by members of the council in his conduct of the city affairs, particularly in the matters he deems to be of petty concern, that he has been on the point of throwing up his job more than once.*

The council appointed Thomas E. Troland, the law director, to succeed him temporarily, and the job eventually devolved to John Sheedy, the city purchasing agent. But Holt had served thirteen years, displaying the extent to which the city manager could stand up to the political storms.

The struggle that led to Holt's resignation was not the last of its kind. The history of the city from then on became largely a competition for advantage between the professional appointees and the political parties, with *The Day* steadfastly defending the former. The political conflict, among other things, retarded the orderly implementation of Bodenwein's agenda to build a greater New London, expand its commerce, and reconstruct Ocean Beach. It would take another forty years to close the volunteer firehouses.

But the city manager position, which was guarded in the charter by a provision that required an enormous effort to fire a manager, still had great potential. At that very moment, in the middle of the Depression, a young lawyer in the city was attracting attention who later would develop the potential power of the city manager's office into an art form. He was then gaining the public's attention in sports, not in politics. In 1934, Edward R. Henkle won his fifth consecutive city tennis championship in singles, as well as winning the title in doubles. My father, Perry Stone, presented him the doubles trophy, which was sponsored by the family store, Perry & Stone Jewelers. My father, then 36, was a popular businessman in New London. The store had quarters in the former Plant Building, across from the Mohican, where the *Morning Telegraph* had been located. The shop was patronized by people who still had wealth, such

Top, Bryan Mahan was one of New London's most influential mayors, having forged a political career by promoting the city's development. As a state senator, he helped bring about the legislation that financed the construction of an ocean terminal in New London. *The Day*

F. V. CHAPPELL

Above, Frank V. Chappell, Alfred H. Chappell's son, helped Bryan Mahan get a pier for Atlantic commerce built in New London and later became embroiled at Connecticut College over selling coal to the college while he was chairman of the board. *The Day*

Center, William Rolfe was Theodore Bodenwein's brother-in-law, the *Day's* telegraph operator, and a director of the newspaper's board until he died in 1910. Bodenwein later went to the assistance of Rolfe's widow, Christina, during the Great Depression. *The Day*

Above, Captain Paul Koenig mailed this photograph to Waldo and Daisy Clarke after the Clarkes visited him in Germany after World War I. *Alma Wies*

Bottom, Theodore Bodenwein had disposed of his handlebar mustache and was a powerful figure in New London when this picture was taken in the 1920s. *The Day*

Above, The German submarine *Deutschland* and its skipper, Captain Paul Koenig, had become such celebrities in New London just before the outbreak of World War I that this postcard was printed marking the occasion of the vessel's arrival in New London in 1916. *Alma Wies*

Above, *The Day* bought a fleet of black trucks to distribute the newspaper after the local trolley company began charging to deliver the newspaper. *The Day*

Right, U.S. Senator Frank Brandegee was one of Theodore Bodenwein's closest friends before Brandegee killed himself in 1929. *The Day*

Left, Elizabeth Bodenwein Miles in her early 20s, after her marriage to Cleveland artist Eugene Miles. *The Day*

Below, Gordon Bodenwein, right, was a young sailor recently out of Yale and serving in the Navy in Philadelphia when this photograph was taken with a friend. *The Day*

Above, Governor Thomas Waller made a profit developing this settlement known as Ocean Beach in New London, selling the beach in the forefront to the city and developing the land behind it. Most of the buildings were destroyed in the 1938 Hurricane and New London made it all into a city park. *William Brutzman*

Below, The force of the 1938 Hurricane hurled large boats onto the shoreline in downtown New London. *William Brutzman*

Left, *The Day* resumed publishing after the hurricane with the assistance of this portable generator. A line was extended to the neighboring bank so the vault could be opened. *William Brutzman*

ight, Fire whipped by hurricane winds :stroyed many of the buildings along ank Street in New London, including e former headquarters of *The Day*, the ghest structure third from left. *'illiam Brutzman*

elow, *Day* photographer William rutzman took this picture of New ondon ablaze from the roof of the lohican Hotel during the 1938 urricane. *William Brutzman*

Right, Theodore Bodenwein had become an elder statesman but an enfeebled and aloof figure at *The Day* when this picture was taken in the late 1930s. *The Day*

Above, Ernest Rogers got to know Theodore Bodenwein when they both worked on the *Morning Telegraph*. With Bodenwein's help, Rogers rose in politics to become lieutenant governor, but he never got the job he coveted — governor. *The Day*

Right, Politician and reporter John M. Mallon, Jr., was a favorite of Theodore Bodenwein and was a pall bearer at his boss's funeral in 1939. He's shown here with his trademark cigar in his mouth, preparing to catch a fly ball at a picnic in the 1930s. He later died in an automobile accident. *Terry Mallon*

The House in Good Taste

RECALLING THE MANOIRS OF NORMANDY
THE RESIDENCE OF THEODORE BODENWEIN, NEW LONDON, CONNECTICUT
FRANK J. FORSTER, ARCHITECT

Photographs by John Wallace Gillies

THE KITCHEN AND GARAGE EXTENSION *as seen from the garden court. The walls of this house are of whitewashed brick and half timber. The casement windows have varying forms of lights with both lead and wooden muntins. The roof is of handmade tile in colors of red, Burgundy, and moss-green. At the gable end of the kitchen is plain pine boarding*

[719]

Above, This is the way the Bodenwein house on Pequot Avenue in New London looks today. *Skip Weisenberger, The Day*

Left, Edna and Theodore Bodenwein's new house on Pequot Avenue was featured in the Christmas 1929 edition of *House Beautiful. Andrew Freedman*

Above, Waldo Clarke went after the Pacific coast lumber trade after World War I to boost business at State Pier in New London. *New London Public Library*

Katharine Blunt, the president of Connecticut College, was a close ally of Theodore Bodenwein and later spearheaded a drive to build Ocean Beach Park. *Connecticut College*

Judge Frederick Latimer's long and diverse career included work as an editor at both the *Morning Telegraph* and *The Day*. He hired Eugene O'Neill as a reporter. *Louis Sheaffer Collection, Connecticut College Special Collections*

Dr. C. John Satti stormed the Democratic Party in New London during the New Deal and ruled politics in the city until 1968. He frequently clashe with the Republican-oriented *Day*. *Eleanor Satti Butler*

as Mary Harkness and Edna Bodenwein. In 1937, my father appraised about $4,000 of Edna's jewelry for McGinley Brothers to prepare an insurance policy.

Bodenwein, in his 70s, had one last political battle to wage. As the titular head of the Republican Party in southeastern Connecticut, he would spend his remaining life's energy tilting at Roosevelt's New Deal. In November 1935, delegates to the convention of the 18th senatorial district elected him to the party's state central committee, placing in his hands the responsibility to run the election campaigns in 1936. Election to such a post, ordinarily, was not an earthshaking development. But the event was surrounded with mysticism that elevated its importance. Ernest E. Rogers, one of the delegates, said that if anyone, it was Bodenwein who could lift the party out of its adversity. The delegates, meeting in the Mohican Hotel, sent a group to Bodenwein's room to inform him of the momentous decision. He graciously accepted and treated the group to a pre-arranged lunch in the Dutch Room. The following month, Bodenwein spoke before a group of Young Republicans in Groton, urging them to carry on the fight to save the nation from Roosevelt and the welfare state. If the national government were allowed to continue in its state then, he told the youths, the national constitution would be destroyed.

> *The president, who swore to uphold the constitution when he was inaugurated, is not a Democrat. He is more of a Socialist. He has ignored the planks of the Democratic Party, but has introduced and passed measures regulating the lives of the people and the industries of the country.*

He said the 1936 election was a perfect opportunity to drive out the "crackpots and theorists." His political leadership, unlike his earlier drives for change, had no impact. But this was less a time in his life to make things happen than to cash in on what he had made happen already. Those who were appreciative of his remarkable accomplishments had honored him in his final years with an offer, empty though it was, to be governor and with the hollow but flattering title of titular leader of the party. In 1935, New London presented him with his final honor. On the 20th anniversary of the Chamber of Commerce, the business community recalled his role in the founding of the organization. The old man was summoned to the front of the room at the Mohican Hotel to accept a gift, a walking stick. He rose, and moved slowly forward, displaying his advanced years. He spoke slowly, and some had to crane to hear:

> *I have always felt I owed an obligation to the people of the community and the surrounding towns. They have always been kind to me and generous in my newspaper enterprise. No service I could render, I felt, could repay for all the favors I received from them.*

SIXTEEN

THE STORMS

You looked out the window and could see roofs flying by.

—Thomas Elliott remembering the 1938 hurricane

THE DEPRESSION STILL HELD the country in its grip in the late 1930s, but New London adjusted to the hardship and federal intervention to the point at which those unusual circumstances came to seem normal. *The Day* did what it could to cheer up its readers and restore confidence in a city that had become drab and despondent once again.

On its editorial page, the newspaper preached the Republican credo that the big-government programs of the New Deal were delaying recovery and that private enterprise would rise from the ruins and lead the country out of the darkness. There may have been some truth to this partisan viewpoint. The economy was just as stagnant in the late 1930s as it had been when Roosevelt first was elected in 1932. The editorial page, under the control of Managing Editor George Clapp, seldom dealt with local matters anymore. Clapp wrote prolifically about issues and affairs that were usually far removed from New London's pressing parochial concerns.

The Day initiated a feature that spotlighted successful small retail businesses and manufacturing companies. A story on August 16, 1938, focused on a clothing merchant, Isodore Tarnapol, who declared:

> *I can honestly say business is better than last year. My number of daily customers has increased. I'm employing one more in help than a year ago and of course my total payroll is higher. I have enough confidence in New London's future to open what I think is the finest men's shop in this part of the state.*

During this time, *The Day* kept up the spirits of its young readers with the avuncular presence of "Uncle Andy" on the "Junior Day" pages every Saturday. Uncle Andy was Orvin Andrews, and every week the general manager, under his popular pen name, answered letters from young readers that arrived at "Uncle Andy's Post Office." The column was an uninhibited conversation between the *Day's* Uncle Andy and kids in the community that continued for more than a decade. Andrews later turned the job over to others and it eventually lost its appeal in the face of Saturday television and disappeared.

The summer of 1938 was a busy one. A new economic opportunity appeared on New London's doorstep in August. Ezekiel Spitz, chairman of the Chamber of Commerce's industrial committee, announced that an unnamed manufacturing firm was interested in building a million-dollar plant here. The chamber offered free land to the company and sought tax concessions for it.

The same summer, reporter John Mallon, 38, announced plans to run for Congress on an anti-New Deal platform. And *The Day* published an architect's drawing of a new firehouse for the Thomas Hose Company, one of the volunteer fire companies. This underscored the influence the volunteers still had despite attempts to consolidate the fire department into a few modern stations. The new post office had been completed and inside, funded by the Work Progress Administration (WPA), artist Thomas LaFarge had painted murals of life on a whaling ship.

During the summer, Bodenwein's health deteriorated, and it became painful for him to get around. He appeared at *The Day* during the week, but was seldom seen by the employees, except for the few who drove him to the doctor's office. For all practical purposes, Andrews ran the newspaper. Gordon, 41, resettled in southeastern Connecticut in 1938. In the spring, he delivered a mass at St. Joseph's church, according to John DeGange, then the newspaper's sports editor. Employees at *The Day* thought he planned to settle in the city as a priest, DeGange said. But in July, *The Day* published a brief announcement that Gordon had left the priesthood, and shortly after, he appeared in the newsroom of *The Day* to work with George Clapp as an editorial writer. Edna busied herself with social activities. Her bridge club conducted a tournament at a cottage near Connecticut College owned by Florence Fitch, one of Edna's friends and founder of the Little Slam Club. The weekly matches, in which Edna and her partners apparently did little to distinguish themselves in the competition, continued from July until mid-September.

In August 1938, the publisher's mortality and the future of *The Day* after his death occupied the attention of the directors of *The Day* and Bodenwein's family. Issues arose then that were subsequently debated in conflicting court testimony for several years. Charles Smiddy, who had prepared a will for Bodenwein in 1936, began a new one that summer. Within the inner circle at *The Day*, the idea arose of transferring control to a trust after Bodenwein's death rather than having the family inherit control.

The directors of *The Day* brought Edna into their confidence and persuaded her that summer to give up control of six hundred shares in the newspaper that Bodenwein had set aside in a trust fund for her. She did so in August. Bodenwein held most of the balance of the nearly two thousand outstanding shares. This was not a minor concession on Edna's part, for the stock had been producing about $12,000 in annual income. She consented to the changes in the will in return for assurances that she would be protected financially after her husband's death. Gordon was not privy to these discussions and the full extent to which Bodenwein, in his failing health, governed them became a matter of legal controversy after his death. Gordon's relations with Edna, which had never been friendly, became more contentious as he began to suspect a conspiracy against him over control of *The Day*.

August brought with it a heat wave, with temperatures rising into the upper 90s. In the sweltering weather, readers of *The Day* learned of the stirrings of another global war. "War talk persists in Europe. One spark may start a world struggle. Keep in touch with the situation in *The Day*," a boxed promotion on the front page read. In early September, Associated Press photographs of protest demonstrations by the German population in the Sudetan area of Czechoslovakia appeared in the newspaper. This was an area that Germany had had to give up after World War I. On September 15, a front-page story reported that Sudetan leaders demanded Germany annex the Sudetanland. British Prime Minister Neville Chamberlain made plans to travel to Munich for a second round of discussions with German Chancellor Adolf Hitler over the future of the Sudetanland. On September 19, the governments of Great Britain and France consented to a plan that would transfer the Sudetan territory to Hitler in return for assurances of peace in Central Europe.

Torrential rains in Connecticut brought relief from the heat. But the rain, which started in a massive trough of low pressure over the eastern half of the country on Saturday, September 17, lasted for five days. The downpours sent rivers and streams throughout southeastern Connecticut over their banks. Dams everywhere broke, pouring floodwaters across towns and cities. Major roads, including the highway to Hartford, were washed out. Areas of Hartford along the Connecticut River had to be evacuated.

The rain let up on Wednesday, September 21. As the *Day's* staff arrived at work that morning, the major story was the floods of the days before. The newspaper, which was to go to press early that afternoon, contained a full page of photographs of the damage. Mail that ordinarily would have been shipped by the Central Vermont Railroad had to be transferred to trucks because some tracks north of New London had been washed out. Little else was going on. The newspaper contained a routine story about the Republican nominating convention for probate judge. The gathering at the Mohican Hotel, presided over by Charles Smiddy, nominated S. Victor Prince, son of one of the founders of the old *Globe* newspaper, for reelection. By a coincidence, in less than five months, Prince, reelected that November, would preside over the future of *The Day*, represented by Charles Smiddy, at the New London-Waterford Probate Court.

The Day was printed early in the afternoon. The last page sent to press was the front page, in order to accommodate late-breaking stories. That morning, The Associated Press editor kept his eye on the delicate situation in Central Europe. He also monitored a tropical hurricane that was advancing up the Atlantic coast. The storm, off North Carolina, threatened Atlantic shipping, but appeared to pose no threat to the mainland. Storm warnings were issued as far north as Eastport, Maine, but the *Day's* editor was indifferent enough toward the storm to be satisfied with a United States Weather Bureau report issued at 9 am, three hours before the *Day's* deadline. The brief, one-column story, set in the middle of the front page, noted that the hurricane had passed about two hundred miles east of Wilmington, Delaware, at 8:30 am. "High tides and heavy seas were the only effects noted in the vicinity," the story said.

After the afternoon deadline, the newsroom emptied except for a few staff members, who stayed to check the first copies off the press for errors and to be on hand for late-breaking stories. Most of the reporters and editors gravitated to the nearby saloons along Main Street and behind *The Day* to unwind.

William Brutzman, 22, an apprentice photographer, had been sent to Colchester, a town twenty-five miles north of New London, to take pictures at a factory for the *Day's* series on successful businesses. Brutzman was among three apprentices who were learning the trade under Leo Lonergan, head of the *Day's* photoengraving department. As he was returning from Colchester, it started to get very windy.

> *I decided I'd better get back to the office. Just outside Colchester, a tree had fallen across the highway. Two gentlemen were cutting the tree. I got out to help remove the limbs. When I finally got back to the paper, everyone was scurrying around.*

The hurricane that had gone almost unnoticed at nine o'clock that morning had been drawn into a low-pressure area over the northeast. It had picked up speed, crossed Long Island, and smashed into southern Connecticut with one hundred twenty-five miles-per-hour winds. It hit at 2:30 pm and the fury lasted for four hours, leaving the city, as well as much of New England, in ruins. The hurricane took seven hundred lives and left sixty-three thousand homeless.

Arriving suddenly and unexpectedly, the storm trapped school children and teachers in their schools and held workers hostages in offices, businesses, and factories. Many who tried to get home as the storm struck were trapped in a maelstrom of wind, water, fallen power lines, and flying debris. Barnard L. Colby, a *Day* reporter and son-in-law of Orvin Andrews, had headed to his house in the southern end of the city with Alfred Ligourie, the city editor. They went up and down streets littered with fallen trees and debris looking for a clear path before abandoning their car and continuing on foot. When he finally reached home, Colby remembered:

> *I blush to record it, but I fell down after I'd been let into the house, so tired were my legs, and I sat right down on the linoleum with my back against the wall until I had downed two shots of medicinal spirits.*

The storm wrecked reporter Angus McKay's house. Trees crushed the cars of two other reporters. Pressman Richard Shea's house burned down. Nevertheless, before the afternoon ended, these and others on the staff, including Colby and Brutzman, had returned to work to help take part in covering the *Day's* story of its lifetime. Nothing in the 20th century equaled it for the newspaper. Colby had walked back to the newspaper from his home a mile away. The *Day* building on Main Street that had risen in several phases over the last three decades proved to be soundly built. All afternoon, the wind and sheets of rain pounded it. Even the thick walls of the building could not muffle the sounds of the violence outside. Through the rain- and wind-swept windows, the roofs of buildings could be seen flying by.

The skylights over the composing room shook violently and the plate glass windows on the street level vibrated under the pressure of the wind. Workers, fearing the glass would shatter, evacuated the business office for other parts of the building. At the height of the storm, the staff worried that the roof would blow off. This did not happen, but the power went out, quieting the Linotype machines and incapacitating the press. Ordinarily *The Day* would have produced an extra edition for such an event. But this was impossible.

The storm's force was stunning. It pushed before it a giant tidal wave, which hit Long Island, Connecticut, and Rhode Island shorelines at high tide.

Spray from the huge waves was felt as far away as Vermont, according to *The Day*. The gigantic waves dislodged buildings and railroad tracks and tossed large boats onto the shore like bathtub toys. Witnesses on the shore reported seeing a wall of water moving up the Thames River toward New London. The floodwaters from the hurricane collided with the deluge from streams and rivers swollen from the earlier rains, inundating areas along the shore that never in memory had been flooded before.

At the peak of the storm, a fire broke out in one of the coal pockets of the Chappell Coal Company on Bank Street. The flames quickly spread to neighboring buildings, soon engulfing Bank Street in an inferno. One of the first structures destroyed was the building constructed by Frank H. and Alfred H. Chappell for *The Day*, which had occupied it from 1894 to 1907. Those brand new quarters had been a source of pride to young Theodore Bodenwein as he began his publishing career. After the fire, all that was left of the building, which was then occupied by the Plaut Lauden Furniture Company, were the four walls.

The fire illuminated Bank Street most of the night. Firefighters considered dynamiting buildings in its path to stop it, but luckily, the wind shifted. Had the wind not changed, the flames would have consumed much of the center of the city, including where *The Day* was located. The shifting wind produced another danger, however. The gale sent sparks and burning debris in all directions. Workers went onto the roof of *The Day* building with ash cans filled with water to extinguish flying embers. Early in the evening, reporters and photographers ventured into the streets. They had to crawl over debris to reach the worst scenes of devastation. William Brutzman made his way four blocks to the Mohican Hotel and climbed the flights of stairs to the top to photograph the city in flames.

Most telephone service had been knocked out early in the storm, but *The Day* had a private line to The Associated Press in New Haven, fifty miles to the west, and this became New London's lifeline to the outside world. Officials used it to get word to Governor Wilbur Cross about the severity of conditions in the city. Cross, using the same line, ordered National Guard troops into the streets to prevent looting. The *Day* office, with its lone telephone connection, became an emergency communications center, where authorities were able to summon firefighters from outside the city and to deploy other emergency equipment.

As the storm raged and the fire spread along Bank Street, Andrews and the other managers turned their attention to printing a newspaper to explain to a fearful population the catastrophe that had taken place. The city, cut off from the outside world by fallen phone lines and engulfed in darkness, was in need of information to quell uninformed rumors that were spreading.

As soon as the winds subsided around 6:30 pm, printers, accompanied by a reporter, headed in a convoy of cars east to Westerly, Rhode Island, about twenty miles away, in the hope of printing a storm edition on the press of the Westerly *Sun*. But the devastation in Rhode Island was even more severe than that along the Connecticut shoreline. The *Sun* also had no power. The *Day* crew headed to Providence. They arrived there at 1:30 am, finding the Providence *Journal* and most of the city's downtown under water.

In its desperate search for a place to print, *The Day* made arrangements with the Hartford *Times* to fly printers to Hartford so they could run off the edition on the *Times*' presses. But that plan had to be abandoned because the nearest airport, in Groton, was under four feet of water. Still another crew from *The Day* headed west in a caravan of cars, and eventually managed to reach Bridgeport, where the newspaper was finally printed on the press of the Bridgeport *Post*. The edition used a clashing mixture of *Day* and *Post* typefaces through the combination of trays of type that had already been set in New London and freshly set stories prepared at the *Post*.

The September 22 edition, which contained only four pages and brought the first news and pictures of the storm to New London, would not be distributed until the following day. The newspaper had on the front page a photograph of the Bank Street fire and a page of storm pictures without captions. The scenes did not require words. A Coast Guard lighthouse tender thrown up across the railroad tracks in a sea of debris. Waterfront houses under water up to their second story with the flames of the Bank Street fire in the background. Stunned crowds surveying the damage or watching part of the city burn from their yards.

Scrolling through microfilmed pages of the editions published on September 21 and 22 makes one aware of the dimension of the disaster. The Wednesday edition that had barely come off the press when the storm blew out the power depicted a city at peace, going about its comfortable routine. Moving from the ordinary day chronicled in the September 21 edition, with its gentle, elegant front-page headlines, the reader abruptly encounters a front page in which bold and unfamiliar type screams, "City Ruined, Hundreds Homeless in $4 Million Fire-Storm Disaster."

The Day eventually obtained an electric generator that provided enough power to publish an eight-page edition Friday night. *The Day* let the neighboring Savings Bank of New London run a line from the generator to its building to furnish enough power to open the bank's vaults. In the days following the hurricane, large crowds in front of *The Day* became a familiar sight, as New Londoners gathered to read notices dealing with the storm posted on the front windows or to buy copies of the newspaper. It was not until five days later, on Monday, September 26, that *The Day* was able to publish a complete, thirty-page edition, with all the regular features, including the comics. Power had been restored the day before.

The newspaper ran an editorial that conveyed the city's sense of relief that life was returning to normal and praising the many acts of heroism. An editorial the next day explored a newspaper's role in a disaster. The editor took note of the fear that swept the city when electricity went out and *The Day* was unable to print a timely evening edition. As the fire raged on Bank Street, there were rumors of other fires. The worst rumor of all was that another hurricane was approaching the city. The desire for solid information was so great that the stacks of newspapers printed in Bridgeport "melted like a late spring snowstorm before a warm May sun." With power from the generator, the newspaper published another, eight-page edition, and that, too, rapidly was consumed. *The Day* stated in an editorial that week:

> *The experience during this storm again proved, in short, what most experienced newspaper workers have long known – that suspension of newspapers, even for a day in time of emergency, gives rise to all sorts of wild rumors and general public anxiety, and that the surest way to calm the fears of the people is to get newspapers in circulation as quickly as possible.*

On Wednesday, September 28, a neatly typed letter, on *Day* stationery, with what appeared to be Theodore Bodenwein's signature at the bottom, was posted complimenting the staff, as well as the contractor and electricians who supplied and hooked up the generator, for their efforts during the storm:

> *Even the newsboys outdid themselves in circulating* The Day *in New London and surrounding towns, and the* Day's *regular circulation staff did marvels in covering their routes, overcoming floods of water and felled trees everywhere.*

Whether Bodenwein was physically or mentally fit to prepare such a letter remained an open question. The letter could have been composed by someone else and signed by the old publisher, or dictated, or even could have appeared over a forged signature. It was written when all, including the *Day's* managers, acknowledged that Bodenwein's health was failing rapidly. The executives at *The Day* later emphasized in accounts of his death that Bodenwein appeared at the office daily until he was hospitalized in October. He was there during the hurricane, they claimed. They went out of their way to repeat this mundane point, as if it had a deep significance. Their strong suggestion was that Bodenwein was in charge both of his faculties and the newspaper that fall of 1938, when his last will and testament was prepared. But while he may have been cognizant, it's not likely in his frail health he played a dominant role in the extraordinary effort with which *The Day* confronted the worst disaster in the city's history and the newspaper's biggest story. Andrews and the others who had largely taken control of the newspaper had met this moment of destiny in the newspaper's history on their own and conducted themselves admirably.

There seemed to be no end to the stories and pictures accumulated by the newspaper's writers and photographers. News and photographs dealing with the storm and its aftermath appeared for days, and later that fall, *The Day* published a tabloid edition on the hurricane.

WHILE MOST ACCOUNTS OF the Hurricane of 1938, as dramatic as they were, followed the normal progression of events from disaster to recovery, one story developed that had a more profound and unpredictable impact—the destruction and renewal of Ocean Beach. Ocean Beach was one of New London's greatest paradoxes, a source of local pride and affection, yet also an object of controversy and embarrassment. The paradox stems, on the one hand, from the beach's natural advantages, with its graceful crescent of clear, white sand, and stunning view of Long Island Sound, and, on the other hand, the avarice of the humans who have exploited it.

Originally known as White Beach for its pure, white sands, the area had gone unnoticed and remained pristine until a company formed by former Governor Thomas Waller had purchased the tract for $25,000 in 1892. Waller then had subdivided the land along the shoreline into building lots that he sold to wealthy families who built cottages and businesses. At the same time, he sold the city the narrow stretch of beach just above the high tide mark for $25,000, the amount he paid for all of White Beach before subdividing and selling much of it. This was the first instance, though hardly the last, in which New Londoners with political connections prospected for gold at Ocean Beach. Waller merely set the process into motion—not to mention setting the standard. The belief lingered for years that the cagey politician had pulled a fast one. A man known for his blustery oratorical skills, he afterwards was frequently shouted down by adversaries when he was delivering a speech at City Hall with the scornful refrain, "Last car leaving for Ocean Beach!" As odd as that sounds today, everyone recognized the oblique reference to Waller's connection with Ocean Beach.

Without question this had been a sweetheart deal for the developers, providing little in comparison for the taxpayers who had paid for the beach. The city's purchase entitled the public to use the narrow strip of beach and a small park upland of it. Waller and the other investors had sold the lots quickly for substantial profits and the city was left with the problem of maintaining the beach. The new owners of the lots built cottages that had formed, in the beginning, a pleasant waterfront community. But the growing summer crowds at the beach would drive many of the new cottage owners away. They sold their properties, which then were developed into various types of businesses. Many were turned into boarding houses and illegal bathhouses. The development created a whole new proprietary class at Ocean Beach that profited from the proliferation of custard concessions, dance halls, stores, and amusements. The character of the beach declined so much that it began to concern nearby homeowners, and "nice people" began to avoid the beach.

By the 1920s, a hand-wringing debate had broken out over what to do about Ocean Beach. Nature, in the form of the Hurricane of 1938, eventually answered that question in a few hours. The hurricane vented some of its most violent mischief at the beach, pushing bathhouses, stores, and concessions off their foundations and leaving them in heaps of rubble. The narrow boardwalk that separated the overcrowded boarding houses from the beach was swept away. Few buildings were left standing. The hurricane, in effect, carried out one of New London's earliest urban renewal projects. *The Day* began its story on the destruction on Friday, September 23:

> *People of New London who deplored the "deterioration" of Ocean Beach and wished for the good old days when it was just a few cottages along a sandy white beach can come into their own now. There is no Ocean Beach in that modern conception thereof. What is left can be acquired cheap.*

New London attacked the Ocean Beach issue with a swiftness the city seldom exhibited. The City Council hired the New York engineering firm of W. Earle Andrews and A. K. Morgan to prepare a plan for the restoration and expansion of the beach, hoping to follow a path set in the earlier Swan Plan. The beach plan was completed before 1938 drew to a close. Orvin Andrews attended a briefing on it and took prolific notes.

The engineers concluded that it would be impractical and undesirable to rebuild Ocean Beach as it had been prior to the hurricane. They warned that another amusement park with rides, shows, and other carnival features, which was essentially what the beach had become, would continue to erode the residential character of that part of the city. Instead, they recommended a massive public works program to acquire all the shoreline property and develop it as a municipal park similar to Jones Beach on Long Island.

The beach would have to be widened by pumping in clean sand and lengthened by filling in adjoining marshland. In place of the narrow, old boardwalk, there would be a new one thirty feet wide. Behind it, the city would build a modern bathhouse for thirty-six hundred bathers. The park would have a swimming pool twenty-five meters by fifty meters, with a wading pool for children. Other amenities would include a cafeteria along the boardwalk, a roller skating oval, and a recreational area for shuffleboard, deck tennis, and archery, where admission would be charged. The whole operation, except for the cafeteria and a beach store, would be managed by the city. If New London followed the recommendations to the letter, while the city would not make a profit, it would break even and cover the costs of borrowing the $1 million to complete the project.

Not make a profit? City management? Neither of these quaint ideas appealed to the politically connected business interests in New London who had exploited the strip of city-owned beach for years. The struggle over the Ocean Beach Park plan turned into a battle over real estate that attracted attention from across Connecticut.

IN THE AFTERMATH OF the hurricane, the makings of still another legal fight in New London developed that would parallel the conflict over Ocean Beach Park. This one was over the future of *The Day* Paper. Unlike the battle over Ocean Beach, which was precipitated by the storm, the hurricane did not give rise to the fight over who would own *The Day* after Theodore Bodenwein died. The storm merely interrupted those deliberations and the intrigue that surrounded them. Until the storm struck, the directors of *The Day*, Edna Bodenwein and Theodore Bodenwein had their minds focused on the *Day's* succession of ownership. Gordon had moved onto the staff to protect his interests as the eldest child of Theodore and busied himself demonstrating his fitness for the job as an editorial writer. He kept watch on the enemy, particularly his stepmother. Charles Smiddy, George Grout, Orvin Andrews, Earle Stamm, and Bodenwein were, in some fashion or other, formulating a complicated and unusual will. Edna was collaborating with them. This activity had begun in earnest in August, when Bodenwein's health began to worsen.

It is unlikely that in the immediate period following the storm much attention was paid to the future of *The Day*. The effort to publish the newspaper absorbed an enormous amount of energy. In addition, the storm affected the personal lives of the managers with its hardships and demands. George Grout's cottage on Bentley Avenue near Ocean Beach had been severely damaged. His housekeeper had nearly drowned in the hurricane.

But Bodenwein's failing health restored their attention to the will. On October 19, Andrews obtained power of attorney to handle Bodenwein's personal and business financial affairs. Five days after that, Bodenwein was hospitalized in serious condition, and he signed a will that disinherited his wife and children of the newspaper and turned it over in trust to the employees and directors to run. Gordon Bodenwein later alleged that his father's mental and physical capacity had been seriously impaired earlier in Theodore Bodenwein's 74th year.

Smiddy had prepared the will, which became the blueprint for the *Day's* development, but initially pitted Gordon against the directors and Edna in a legal battle for control of the newspaper. Bodenwein signed it on his hospital bed. The shaky signature was witnessed by George Clapp; Dr. James Shay, a dentist; and Josephine Gomes, a nurse. Ernest F. Whiton notarized it.

The will was seventeen pages long. It began as a statement of Bodenwein's philosophy. He had clearly articulated the ideas expressed in it on many occasions: in speeches, in his columns, and in his writings in commemorative editions of *The Day*. It stated how he had spent nearly all his life building up a newspaper in New London that "should become a recognized institution in the community, a leading factor in the growth, development and improvement of the city and vicinity and the happiness and prosperity of the people."

It asserted his belief that a newspaper should be "more than a business enterprise. It should also be the champion and protector of the public interest and defender of the people's rights." His will also noted that the *Day's* success had benefited from the confidence and support of the people of Eastern Connecticut. He wished "the profits of the large business I have created with their help should, except for the provisions I have made for my dear wife and for my children, be returned to the community … "

The will created The Day Trust, turning over to it Bodenwein's stock and the six hundred shares Edna had controlled. All of the newspaper's dividends were to go into a foundation, the Bodenwein Public Benevolent Foundation. As long as they lived, Edna, Gordon, and Elizabeth were to get ninety percent of the proceeds. Edna would get half of this, and Elizabeth and Gordon would split the other half. The rest was to be distributed to charities in the newspaper's circulation area. While there was no such provision for Gordon and Elizabeth, Edna was to receive $1,000 a month from *The Day* while the will was being administered. Edna would also receive the balance of his personal property.

Five trustees were to preside over The Day Trust, and the directors of *The Day* at the time of Bodenwein's death would be the first trustees, as well as the executors of the estate. After that, the trustees would fill vacancies. There was to be one trustee from the National Bank of Commerce, which would administer the Bodenwein Foundation, and two employees from *The Day*. The trustees would be entitled to compensation as well as bonuses whenever they paid more than $100,000 to the Bodenwein Fund. If The Day Trust failed to turn over $25,000 to the Bodenwein Foundation for two consecutive years, the will instructed that the trust be liquidated and the proceeds turned over to the foundation. The Day Trust would govern The Day Publishing Company, but could dissolve the company and operate the newspaper directly if there were later tax advantages to such an arrangement.

The will left specific instructions to the trustees and their successors. They were to hold the stock and manage *The Day*, as well as a morning or Sunday newspaper, or both if growth in the area warranted it. They were to make sure the employees received liberal pay and benefits, including insurance, bonuses, and pensions. They were to add to the *Day's* physical plant, and do so in a way that was "a credit to the city architecturally" and to continue investing in modern equipment. For that purpose, the will specified that they maintain adequate capital reserves.

Finally, the will expressed the desire that Gordon someday become publisher, but it left that choice to the discretion of the trustees. That discretion, perhaps significantly, was the only loophole in a will that otherwise left little to chance.

SEVENTEEN

Gordon's Appeasement

My son, Gordon Bodenwein, is now employed by The Day Publishing Co. Although I give full discretion to my trustees, I trust and believe that at some future date his services may justify his being employed as publisher and being made a trustee.

—Theodore Bodenwein's last will and testament, October 24, 1938

THEODORE BODENWEIN DIED AT Lawrence & Memorial Hospitals in the middle of the night on January 12, 1939; his frail, 74-year-old body finally conquered by the assault of heart disease, kidney failure, and related complications. Gordon and Edna were with him during his last hours. Elizabeth had set out for New London from Ohio as soon as she had learned of his worsening condition. A Roman Catholic priest was called to administer the last rites. Bodenwein had been christened a Catholic in Germany, but spent most of his adult life a social Episcopalian. He and Edna had been married in a Protestant ceremony in Edna's sister's house in New Jersey in 1911. Bodenwein had never exhibited strong religious convictions. Gordon, until earlier that year a Roman Catholic priest, probably was the influence behind his father's last-minute settling of accounts with the Church. This would be consistent with the eagerness Gordon displayed to take charge and assert his authority as dutiful son and rightful heir.

Even the solemnness of the moment—the final minutes of Theodore Bodenwein's exceptional life—did not rouse any kindly feelings between

Gordon and Edna. Nothing could transcend their mutual dislike. Gordon suspected that his stepmother and the directors of *The Day* had plotted to turn his father against him and usurp his rights as the eldest child and legal heir. Edna publicly accused Gordon of going through his father's desk and pilfering an agreement between Edna and her husband dealing with the apportionment of personal expenses. Gordon refused to allow Edna and the directors to erect a monument on his father's grave, and as a result, for two years, the remains of Theodore Bodenwein lay in an unmarked grave next to those of his parents and first son.

The will was filed in the Probate Court January 24, 1939, Bodenwein's 75th birthday. Beginning in March, Gordon mounted a series of legal challenges that continued for three years. He retained George Curtis Morgan, a bombastic, attack-dog New London lawyer, to represent him before Probate Judge S. Victor Prince. Edna was represented by Thomas E. Troland. Charles Smiddy argued the case for the executors of the estate, who included Smiddy, Earle W. Stamm, George Grout, and Orvin Andrews. Morgan established the tone during a stormy hearing in June 1939, when he questioned whether Edna had been legally divorced from Lewis Winfield, her first husband, and thus, whether her marriage to Bodenwein was legal. Troland jumped to his feet and exclaimed that Morgan's comment was disgraceful. Prince ruled that according to the evidence in the court, Edna was Bodenwein's legal widow, and that was that. Morgan boomed that he would have more to say about the issue later. The comments were not reported in *The Day*, but appeared the next day in the Norwich *Bulletin*, the *Day's* rival out-of-town newspaper. Edna was, in fact, legally divorced and had copies of her divorce papers, which were stored in a safe deposit box until her death in 1952.

This flare-up occurred during a hearing on whether the estate should pay Edna a $1,000-a-month widow's allowance provided for in the will while the document was being appealed. Elizabeth Miles, who was a guest of the Trolands while she was in New London, consented to the payments. Gordon was opposed. Morgan contended that the disbursements would be improper while the will's legality was being challenged. Hardship was not an issue, he argued. Edna was not a poor widow. She owned an expensive house and was the beneficiary of $50,000 and $100,000 life insurance policies, he pointed out. Edna told the court that she had an agreement with her husband under which she had to pay for the household expenses out of the $12,000 income from six hundred shares of *Day* stock, which no longer was available to her. Morgan demanded to see the agreement. Edna charged Gordon had taken it from her husband's desk. Prince ruled in Edna's favor, but Gordon appealed, and Edna went without the allowance until the case was settled in 1942.

Gordon also sought to have the *Day's* directors removed as executors of his father's estate, charging they had been derelict in compiling a complete inventory of Bodenwein's property and had entered into contracts and spent money from the estate without legal authority. When an inventory was filed, Gordon challenged its accuracy and completeness, as well as its honesty. After hearing arguments on both sides, Prince ordered additions totaling $35,000, including a $10,000 personal checking account, a monthly salary check to Bodenwein amounting to $1,100 and some jewelry and personal effects that originally had been overlooked.

These were only minor skirmishes, artillery fire to soften the enemy's resistance. In the midst of the probate hearings, in July 1939, Gordon mounted his major offensive in Superior Court in Norwich. He set out to invalidate the will, charging that it was the product of a plot by Edna and the directors to take over the newspaper at his expense. Gordon claimed that at the time his father was supposed to have signed the will, he "was not of sound and disposing mind and memory and was incapable by reason of physical infirmity, diseased condition of mind and body, and lack of mental capacity to make any will." Edna and the *Day's* directors had turned Bodenwein against his son and manipulated the elderly publisher into consenting to a document he did not have the mental alertness to comprehend, Gordon maintained.

The truth of those charges was never subjected to the test of evidence and sworn testimony. The case was settled out of court, leaving unanswered the questions of how much influence the directors actually had in shaping the will and the degree, if any, to which they took advantage of Bodenwein's failing health to feather their own nests. The directors, particularly Orvin Andrews, certainly stood to gain substantially from the arrangements. They wrested control of *The Day* from Bodenwein's legal heirs. They had been in a position to exploit Bodenwein's feeble condition. They enjoyed the publisher's trust. Smiddy had control of his legal business, and Andrews not only held sway over *The Day*, but by October, had begun to administer the publisher's personal finances. Smiddy charged $20,000 in legal fees to the estate. The probate judge hearing the case, Victor Prince, was a political colleague and friend of Smiddy's. Edna and Elizabeth Miles sided with them.

The directors were unlikely conspirators. Smiddy was a wealthy and civic-minded public utilities lawyer. He was the lawyer for the Connecticut Power Company, was well-known and respected in Hartford and Washington, and admired in New London. He was founder and president of the local Community Chest and active in Boy Scouts and other community activities. Andrews was New London's kindly Uncle Andy. Few lived more exemplary lives than George Grout and Earle Stamm. They did not fit the profile of sinister men. And even if they had been inclined to, it is doubtful they could have made up this original will on their own, as Gordon strongly suggested. The document was imprinted too thoroughly with Bodenwein's thinking, motives, and style. And it was so intricate and imaginative that it had to have taken far longer than the summer and fall of 1938 to prepare.

Edna testified that the first time she had heard about a trust was in August 1938, when she had been asked to turn over her six hundred shares of *Day* stock to her husband. That was three months before Bodenwein entered the hospital, but when Bodenwein's mental capacity was a matter of dispute. Bodenwein's records indicate that he and Smiddy had been discussing a will at least since 1936, when the publisher unquestionably was still active and alert. That more probably was when Bodenwein began seriously planning for the future of *The Day*, and when the ideas that went into the final will began to take shape.

Bodenwein, in his own way, loved his family. He kept pictures of his children in his office, a snapshot of Gordon as a young sailor in uniform, a studio portrait of Elizabeth in her 20s. He hired Gordon twice, the first time as one of the newspaper's top editors when the son had no newspaper experience. He patiently put up with Edna's volatile personality and probably loved her as much as he loved anything other than his newspaper and his work. But when it came down to a choice, he always placed *The Day* before his family. *The Day* was his family. He felt personally responsible for the men and women who worked for him. He had to have been cognizant of the perils of leaving the stewardship of his newspaper to his family. None of his heirs was as equipped to run *The Day* as were the men already in charge. Not one of the heirs cared as much as he and his colleagues did about the newspaper, the people who worked for it, and the communities it served. He had to have worried that the friction between his headstrong wife and his son would result in a continuing conflict that would weaken the newspaper and leave it vulnerable to purchase by a newspaper chain. He feared that fate ever since he had met Frank Munsey.

The idea of putting a newspaper into a trust was not new to Bodenwein. He knew that Munsey had considered such an arrangement to protect his last and favorite newspaper, the New York *Sun*, but that the publisher died unexpectedly in 1925 before he had a chance to carry out the plan. It is not hard to suppose that Bodenwein's physical ailments, which required almost daily attention by a physician in his last years, served as a warning that he needed to prepare better than Munsey had.

Bodenwein also would have known of the 1931 court case that broke the will of Joseph Pulitzer and allowed for the sale and merger of the New York *Evening World.* Pulitzer had died in 1911 and his will, similar in many ways to Bodenwein's, tried to perpetuate his paper as an independent one operated by his heirs. In his will, Pulitzer said he had sacrificed his health and strength to building up the newspaper and stated:

> *Nothing in my will shall be taken to authorize or empower the sale or disposition by the trustees of my stock of the Press Publishing Company, publisher of the* World *newspaper. I particularly enjoin upon my sons and my descendants the duty of preserving, perfecting, and perpetuating the* World *newspaper, in the same spirit in which I have striven to create and conduct it, as a public institution, from motives higher than mere gain.*

One can thus surmise that the decisions made that summer and fall of 1938 were the final stages of months of painstaking deliberations in which Bodenwein was actively engaged. The spate of activity at the end was a desperate race to finish the work before Bodenwein died. The will addressed all of Bodenwein's clear, vital interests. It protected *The Day* and assured its independence. It placed the newspaper in the hands of people he trusted and repaid the debt he felt he owed the community for the newspaper's success. And it took care of his family. Under the terms of the will, Edna, Elizabeth, and Gordon lived in luxury the rest of their lives with their income from *The Day*. The Day Trust held the stock, but the three heirs remained the principal beneficiaries of the dividends of The Day Publishing Company's stock. The only drawbacks for them were that their dividends depended on the good will and frugality of the management and trustees and they had to share the dividends, to a small degree, with charities.

In addition to not inheriting the paper, Gordon did not gain a position of authority at the newspaper, and these facts upset him. Owning and running *The Day* was a privilege to which he felt entitled by birth. His mother, Jennie, in her solicitude toward her only son and bitterness left over from her divorce, had planted the idea in his mind that the paper ought one day to belong to him. Gordon implied in his appeal, and may actually have believed, that his father was sincere when he stated that he wanted him to be publisher. The two discussed this. But his father really would have to have been mentally impaired to feel confident that Gordon could have filled that role, at least right away.

Gordon was an unpopular interloper at *The Day* from the moment he stepped in the door. Most of the staff disliked him and many probably would have walked off the job if he had become publisher. Gordon had spent most of his adult life outside the city. He did not understand New London and the territory around it, nor was he interested. He knew nothing about running a newspaper, about presses, the price of newsprint, Linotype machines, newspaper circulation, and advertising. His interests were in world politics, philosophy, and theology, not New London's mundane affairs and material ambitions. His only friend on the staff appeared to have been John DeGange

The directors may have settled the case with Gordon just to prevent him from doing any more damage to the *Day's* reputation and theirs. Gordon's aggressive lawyers wore down Smiddy and the others. Curtis Morgan, by himself a handful for anyone, brought in reinforcements. In January 1940, Arthur M. Brown of Jewett City, Connecticut, joined him. And in the final weeks, late in 1941, Morgan brought on board Samuel Parsky of New Haven, a well-known Connecticut litigator. On the opposite side were Smiddy and Troland. Smiddy was busy with his duties as chief counsel of the Connecticut Power Company. Troland had to divide his time between the *Day* case and the legal quagmire he faced as New London law director over the development of Ocean Beach.

The skirmishing in Probate Court over Edna's allowance, the inventory, and the integrity of the executors strengthened Gordon's bargaining position, for it prolonged the *Day's* humiliating public exposure. The case nourished local gossip and cast doubt on the legitimacy of Bodenwein's successors on the newspaper. *The Day* reported only the essentials of the legal proceedings, but the Norwich *Bulletin* hung on every word and nuance of the drama as it unfolded. Morgan exploited the presence of reporters with bold rhetorical flourishes, prompting Troland to complain that Morgan was playing to the press. The *Bulletin* not only reported the testimony in minute detail; it occasionally spun the stories to Gordon's advantage. In a story in June 1939, the *Bulletin* referred to Gordon as a former city editor; a position he actually never held, and editorialized that he was a "capable newspaperman." When the agreement was reached in January 1942, *The Day* ran a one-paragraph story reporting that the case had been settled, while the *Bulletin* ran a more extensive story, which appeared under a headline that declared, "Gordon Bodenwein Wins Probate Case; To Be Director of Trust."

That is probably what Gordon and his lawyers told the reporters. But it is not accurate. The settlement was generous to Gordon, but it nevertheless left the Bodenwein will in force. The trustees really were the winners. They would have final word over whether Gordon would be publisher, and Gordon had guaranteed that that would never happen by having alienated Smiddy and Andrews. The agreement provided Gordon $26,000 in cash, a job for at least twenty-five years as editorial writer, and a seat for life on the board of trustees in place of George Grout. If there was a loser, it was George Grout, Bodenwein's most loyal and veteran soldier, who had to give up his position as a trustee.

Under the terms of the will, there were to be five trustees to supervise The Day Trust. As a practical matter, the trustees also served as directors of The Day Publishing Company. However, the newspaper's bylaws eventually permitted up to nine directors. One could be a director while not a trustee. The directors, in practice, conducted virtually all the business of the newspaper, then adjourned into a trustees' meeting primarily to receive the dividends from the newspaper. The trustees were, in effect, the stockholders.

For his part, Gordon dropped his appeal, consented to the back payment of the widow's allowance to Edna, and agreed to allow the executors access to Bodenwein's burial lot for the placement of a memorial stone, which had been ready for more than a year.

In the spring of 1939, Orvin Andrews and Edna had made arrangements with the Odgers Monumental Works of Norwich, an agent for the Rock of Ages Corporation of Barre, Vermont, to design a monument that would reflect Bodenwein's lifetime achievements. They wanted something that was tasteful, but at the same time would stand out in a cemetery that already contained the statuary of New London's most prominent leaders. The firm proposed decorating the stone with a Roman lamp, a symbol of enlightenment, courage, and divine inspiration. Such a symbol had always been used on fine memorials by people of culture and discriminating taste, designer Dan. D. Haslam explained. There also would be a laurel branch, suggesting victory in life, as well as victory of eternal life over death, he went on. There was just enough of the decorative to lend a bit of cheer and comfort, and enough of the simple and plain to give freedom of imagination or meditation—in short, a balance of all moods where hope, joy, and reverence mingle into a perfect harmony. He apologized that it would be impossible to follow the specification that the lettering of the loved one's name be in Roman script, because the name Theodore Bodenwein would not fit on the stone in such letters.

This first attempt pleased neither Andrews nor Edna. Andrews was particularly unhappy with the proposal. The design did not have a thing to do with Bodenwein's life, which was *The Day*. Andrews visited the offices of the Odgers Monumental Works to straighten out the people there. He sketched a design of his own. There was no Roman lamp burning eternally or laurel branch signifying a victory over life. It was far more to the point than that. At the top of the stone was an edition of *The Day*, rolled up as if by a newspaper carrier, with the familiar *Day* logo displayed. That was all.

Haslam found the idea absolutely brilliant. He wished he had thought of it himself. "Your fine suggestion gives this memorial an individual touch it needed, and we wish to compliment you on your very unique idea," he wrote Andrews. The stone would contain the newspaper page and directly below it Theodore Bodenwein's name in the Rock of Ages "patented screen background" process. The stone had been completed in April 1940, but could not be placed until Gordon agreed in the settlement reached January 3, 1942. The stones that marked the graves of Anton, Agnes, and the infant Theodore were removed, their names having been carved on the back of the new monument, which became one of the most distinctive monuments in the cemetery.

Gordon's challenge had been costly. With the *Day's* ownership in question, the newspaper had fallen under the leadership of a committee consisting of the four existing directors and trustees. Shortly after Bodenwein's death, Thomas E. Troland, the city's law director, was named the fifth trustee and a director of The Day Publishing Company. Smiddy acted swiftly in filling the position to make sure Gordon did not have a chance to take his father's place on the board. For the same reason, the directors did not convene an annual meeting in 1939, as their corporate charter required. Troland gratefully accepted his position, writing: "I thank you very much for the honor that you have conferred upon me in inviting me to become associated with you in the operation of this important public trust."

For at least several months before Bodenwein died, Andrews had been running *The Day* with little or no guidance from the publisher. He, his managers, and the staff knew how to publish a newspaper, as they had demonstrated admirably during the hurricane. But now they faced for the long term the task without Bodenwein's strong presence and without a clear legal mandate to run the newspaper. Decisions that Bodenwein would have made on his own were now being made collectively by the directors. Smiddy played a strong role because of the legal issues. The directors not only supervised the business, they also had to look after Edna. This situation established the trust's pattern of conservative, collegial management, in which Orvin Andrews, the chief executive, was to a large degree first among equals but with no one individual named to be in charge. This arrangement continued even after the case was settled and lasted for more than two decades. Andrews never chose to adopt the title of publisher. The paneled office on the second floor, into which Bodenwein had moved in 1928 when an addition was built, remained unoccupied after his death until 1961.

The legal battle not only left the newspaper without strong leadership, it seriously depleted the *Day's* capital reserves as World War II began. This could not have occurred at a worse time. The trustees had had to withdraw more than $300,000 from capital funds for legal expenses, taxes, and settlement costs. The newspaper's surplus had been $359,974 when Bodenwein died, and it dropped to a perilously low $55,115 in 1942. This capital shortage and the wartime hardships placed the newspaper in a twenty-year holding pattern during which few improvements or changes were made.

The *Day's* trustees referred among themselves to the interregnum between January 1939 and January 1942 as the period of "Gordon's appeasement." The newspaper continued its editorial orientation of the past. It remained Republican and its interests stayed aligned with the city's business interests and conservative power brokers. It espoused the civic agenda Bodenwein had established and was not timid about speaking out on any of these fronts.

In the months leading up to and following Bodenwein's death, the newspaper was swept up in the mounting controversy over Ocean Beach. The voters of New London approved the plans for Ocean Beach Park in a referendum, January 30, 1939, by a ratio of eight to one. With that clear mandate, the city moved quickly to raise the capital and develop the government machinery to move the project forward. But the plans soon were bogged down in politics and litigation. Property owners challenged the city's appraisals and went to court seeking better deals. Of the one hundred three properties appraised, there were sixty-six appeals. Six judges and dozens of lawyers eventually became involved in the real estate appeals.

On top of that, several large commercial property owners went to court to oppose the city's method of acquiring land by condemnation. They charged there was no great need for the park that would justify such methods. And politicians fought for advantage on the new commission, the Ocean Beach Park Board, which had been set up to govern the park. The board would have control over all the design and construction contracts to develop the park, and later over all the new city jobs the enterprise would produce. Dozens of new positions were to be created, from park superintendent to bathhouse attendants and lifeguards. There would be concession and restaurant contracts. The Bridgeport *Herald*, an irreverent statewide paper that published a New London edition, characterized the resulting political strife as "one of the most violent patronage wars in the city's history." The newspaper's sensational characterization turned out to be not far from the truth.

Thomas E. Troland, the city's lawyer and newly appointed trustee of *The Day*, was from the beginning at the center of the action surrounding the park's development, along with Edward R. Henkle, a young lawyer and former state representative Troland had hired. Troland divided his time between the beach fight and Edna Bodenwein's defense in the battle for control of *The Day,* which progressed through the courts simultaneously.

The *Day's* position on Ocean Beach had a long and familiar history. The newspaper had favored major public improvements even before the hurricane. It backed the Swan Plan, which called for enlarging the public park by buying additional beach in the neighboring town. In the early 1930s, the newspaper had supported an initiative by Mayor Frank Morgan, which went nowhere, to clean up the beach "physically and morally." Immediately after the 1938 hurricane, the City Council had created a committee of business and civic leaders to develop plans for the city's reconstruction, and Orvin Andrews served on the subcommittee for Ocean Beach. The newspaper endorsed the plan that came out of that group's work.

Politics and self-interest enveloped the project from the start. When the City Council agreed to create an independent board to manage the park, both major parties made certain a section of the proposed law that would have prevented party leaders from serving on the board was removed. Dr. C. John Satti, the city's Democratic leader and one of his ward bosses, Richard Sheflott, thereupon were appointed to the new board. Troland sparked an immediate controversy by ruling that these appointments violated the City Charter, which made it illegal for political officers to serve on city boards and commissions.

Satti's minions on the Council were incensed by the ruling. William J. Brady, Joseph A. St. Germaine, and Samuel Selleck demanded an investigation into all the city appointees for possible conflicts of interest. The resulting survey revealed that dozens of city officials had possible conflicts, including Orvin Andrews, who served on the Zoning Board of Appeals while *The Day* did advertising business with the city. George MacDougall, a *Day* reporter and park-board member, faced a similar problem. Charles Smiddy would have had to get off the Zoning Board of Appeals because the company he represented, the Connecticut Power Company, had a street-lighting contract with the city.

Meantime, Satti and Sheflott claimed that neither of them was any longer a party leader. During a party struggle the year before, in which two factions claimed to be in control, the party failed to elect any officers. The matter was settled in the summer of 1939, when the party elected Francis L. McGuire, a 34-year-old lawyer, to succeed Satti as the town chairman. Satti and Sheflott retained their foothold on the park board, which later would become a source of political patronage for the Democratic Party under Satti's rule.

Democrats occupied most of the seats on the City Council, but this was misleading because it did not reflect the actual, complex configuration of power in New London. Satti's three men comprised a minority, while the other three Democrats and one Republican member formed a majority coalition that supported the city administration and the city's business leadership on Ocean Beach. This situation led to a fight over the appointment of architects to manage the project. The Ocean Beach Park Board picked the local firm of Payne & Keefe for a fee of $60,000, although another New London firm had offered to do the work for $12,000 less. Payne & Keefe was well connected in the city's power structure, as well as with *The Day*. Morris Payne was a major general in the National Guard and commanding officer of the 43rd division. Colonel Thomas Troland was his chief of staff, Lieutenant Colonel Alfred Ligourie, the *Day's* city editor, his adjutant. Payne also was chairman of the Planning Board until he stepped down in May 1939 over a possible conflict of interest. Edward Keefe, the other partner, was a well-liked and respected architect. His role in history was as one of playwright Eugene O'Neill's best friends. The firm had designed the new post office in the city and was the choice of the New York engineers who prepared the park plan.

The three Satti Democrats on the council opposed the choice of Payne & Keefe in the first of many patronage struggles over Ocean Beach. They held up the funds to hire the architects. Meantime, referendum petitions were circulated opposing not only the $60,000 appropriation for the architects but the entire beach project.

Orvin Andrews was the likely author of a "Tattler" column on July 29, 1939, that tore into the three politicians for trying to obstruct progress on the $3 million park project. The column claimed that the three condoned alleged acts of fraud by challenging the city officials who uncovered the scandal. A city investigation had found cases in which signatures had been obtained under false pretenses. More than a dozen names on petitions had been taken from gravestones at Cedar Grove Cemetery. Five of the signatures were of long-dead, famous city leaders, one of whom was said on the petition to be living at Law

Director Troland's father's address. The "Tattler" accused St. Germain and Brady of trying to discredit the city officials who uncovered the improprieties, and *The Day* for writing the story. The writer also faulted them for undermining the park board over the selection of architects and in so doing causing additional costs by delaying the project.

> *If Councilors Brady and St. Germain would pursue their appointed duties half as diligently as they hatch lurid dreams of dire and dreadful plots behind every development at Ocean Beach, they would serve the city much more effectively.*

The "Tattler" appeared on Saturday, and the Democrats had all weekend to prepare their counterattack. Brady led the assault at the end of a City Council meeting the following Monday night. He condemned the *Day's* scurrilous attack on his character and the reputations of St. Germain and Selleck. "I consider any paper that would resort to such contemptible tactics is a lying, vicious menace to the community." Then he added: "If Mr. Bodenwein had lived I don't believe I or anyone else would be forced publicly to question the policy of the paper he worked so hard to build." There was loud applause from the large audience in the gallery. Then Selleck took the floor. He said he did not know who wrote the "Tattler," but if that person drove an automobile, he'd be charged with reckless driving. Several in the audience rose to berate *The Day*. The following Saturday, *The Day* fired back in another "Tattler" column, accusing the three councilors of diverting attention from the real issue: their attempts to discredit city officials for uncovering fraud in the referendum petitions. *The Day*, the column said, would continue to champion the best interests of the people.

The Satti Democrats expected little sympathy from a newspaper they had long been convinced opposed their interests. The two out-of-town newspapers in the city, the Norwich *Bulletin* and Bridgeport *Herald*, offered a more sympathetic ear, filling the vacuum left by the *Telegraph* and the *Globe*. The *Herald* featured the Ocean Beach story as a juicy political scandal, "the now famous Ocean Beach stinkeroo," as it referred to the matter on July 30, 1939, in a story about the trial of four charged with fraud in the beach referendum case. A later story carried the headline, "Council wolves battling for seaside spoils as patronage mess is bared." Much of the reporting, mixed liberally with commentary, did not justify the sensational headlines. But the newspaper's coverage helped put much of the controversy, downplayed by *The Day*, in a clearer perspective that illuminated what it was: political intrigue stemming from self-interest.

The *Herald* did not take sides. The *Bulletin*, on the other hand, gave vent to the point of view of Satti and the minority Democrats on the City Council. The newspaper had a reporter, George R. Morris Jr., stationed in the city. Morris believed city officials and *The Day* unfairly used the fraud issue to kill the referendum, and he suspected political favoritism in the selection of the architects. Morris wrote stories in melodramatic prose about the "minority Democrats" and the diabolical forces arrayed against them. One of his best stories, published on the morning of September 8, described in sixty column-inches how he was thrown out of a meeting of the Ocean Beach Park board despite the objections of Dr. Satti.

The board, meeting at City Hall, was getting ready to discuss the proposed contract with Payne & Keefe for architectural services. Joseph C. Keefe, (no relation to Edward Keefe, the architect) the chairman of the board, called for a vote to close the meeting to the public. Keefe was the president of a local food wholesaling firm and Charles Smiddy's brother-in-law. He was supported by members Katharine Blunt, president of Connecticut College, F. W. LaForge, and George MacDougall, who was a *Day* reporter, but also a voting member and secretary of the beach board.

Morris refused to leave and a debate broke out between Satti and Keefe over whether the reporter should be allowed to stay. Morris noted in his story that this was the first board meeting in two months and would be the occasion for the board's "steamroller vote" to award the contract for architectural and engineering services. Satti spoke in the reporter's favor:

> *Up to now there has been little business by this board that would greatly interest the public. But now the situation has changed. This board has become colorful. It has a majority and a minority; some of us are supposed to be biased and some of us are supposed to be unbiased; some of us have been accused of being political and some are supposed to be non-political. The power of our body is to let the public attend our meetings or keep them out. To do the latter, in my opinion, is in extremely bad taste.*

Satti then promised Keefe that if the reporter were ejected, he, Satti, would tell Morris what happened after the meeting. One by one, others from the public in the cramped little room including some disgruntled city architects, went to the reporter's defense. Keefe was unmoved. Morris said that as long as MacDougall, a reporter, was in the room, he would stay unless he was forcibly removed. Satti declared that he was making Morris his personal secretary. Keefe said there was nothing in the City Charter about board members having personal secretaries. Satti said there was nothing about not having secretaries, either, and if the meeting was going to be closed, he needed a secretary to make sure he was not misquoted. Keefe called for another vote on his ruling that Morris had to leave, and he was supported four-to-three. Morris said that now that he was Satti's personal secretary, the matter was out of Keefe's hands. Keefe asked John Sheedy to call Troland for a legal ruling. Troland ruled that the board could have an executive session by a 4-3 vote, and that members could not have private secretaries present during closed sessions. "I'm sorry George, now you'll have to leave," Keefe said.

The obstacles in the path of the Ocean Beach project eventually gave way, and by the end of 1939, the city owned most of the real estate and work began to demolish what was left of 150 buildings and to clear away the debris. This work, which was completed in 1940, added to a building boom that already was well under way. With the United States entry into World War II only a year away, new buildings were nearing completion at Connecticut College and more were being planned. Hundreds of building permits had been granted to repair the hurricane damage. Roads were widened and repaved. And the approaching war brought with it, along with apprehension, hope for the end of the Depression and a return to prosperity.

The Day entered a new era at the same time. On January 10, 1942, the month after the Japanese bombed Pearl Harbor, *The Day* announced a settlement had been reached with Gordon. That same day, Gordon's name appeared on the newspaper's masthead, which lists its executives, as editorial writer. The listing was just below the name of his father, publisher of *The Day* from 1891 until 1939.

E I G H T E E N

Peace & War

There doesn't seem to be much point in writing sports these days, because like everything else, our indoor and outdoor pastimes have been pushed so far in the background by the conflict raging in the Pacific that they can hardly be located.

—James A. Watterson, sports column in *The Day,* December 8, 1941

DURING HIS THREE YEARS of strife with his stepmother, Edna, and the men his father left in charge of *The Day*, Gordon Bodenwein assumed an awkward presence at the newspaper he had thought was his birthright. Although the settlement of the will bestowed upon him authority and wealth far beyond the means of the other reporters and editors, he continued to occupy a humble post in the middle of the newsroom. When John W. R. "Jack" Cruise, a sportswriter, left to serve in the Army in April 1942, Gordon, 49, attended his going-away party at the Gondola Restaurant, in the city's Italian district. Gordon was assigned Cruise's desk next to the switchboard. Here he wrote learned but sometimes stilted and abstract editorials on national and international issues.

His sister, Elizabeth Miles, managed to stay out of the fray over the will, responding to legal issues through depositions and notarized documents. She returned to her home in the Shaker Heights suburb of Cleveland after her father's funeral and continued her life as a wealthy socialite with her husband, Eugene Miles. Miles was a lampshade manufacturer as well as an artist and prominent patron of the arts. His paintings had been exhibited at the Cleveland Museum of Art on five occasions between 1928 and 1935. Elizabeth was pretty, multitalented, and outgoing, though on occasion haughty. She had stumbled upon photography when she borrowed a friend's movie camera to photograph gardens during a visit to Europe in 1935. This led to an interest in black and white still photography and an avocation in which she gained local recognition for her work. She became known for innovative darkroom techniques. She was a well-known lecturer on horticulture and European and American gardens. She also had a reputation as a popular party giver in the wealthy enclave. Beginning in 1942, her wealth was compounded by large quarterly checks from *The Day* under the terms of her father's will.

Edna moved out of the house on Pequot Avenue after her husband's death and lived in a suite of rooms in the Mohican Hotel for three years, during which time she rented the house and it fell into disrepair. In the spring of 1941, she drove with a friend cross-country to California, stopping in Death Valley; Albuquerque, New Mexico; and Palm Springs, California. They returned aboard the ocean liner *S.S. America* by way of the Panama Canal. When she got back in April, the Little Slam bridge club had a welcome-home party for her at the Mohican. Her friends presented her with a bouquet of roses, and she recited a poem she had composed as a tribute to their friendship.

World War II transformed New London and its surroundings from a stagnant victim of the Great Depression into a busy hub of military activity. The driving force behind this was the advance of submarine warfare as an important part of U.S. naval strategy. The earlier civic campaigns to attract industry and military installations had resulted in making southeastern Connecticut a major participant in this strategy. In 1940, Congress approved $2 million for additional construction at the Submarine Base in Groton. The activity at the Electric Boat shipyard picked up dramatically as the government set out to launch a submarine a month, a pace that was increased to one at least every two weeks.

In 1942, the federal government took over the old Groton Iron Works south of Electric Boat to accommodate the crush of new submarine orders. The development of the new facility, known as the Victory Yard, squelched another private shipbuilding plan spawned in the early days of the war. Alfred Holter, a well-known Norwegian industrialist and naval architect who had escaped after the Nazi occupation of Scandinavia in 1940, had planned to acquire the shipyard to build merchant ships out of concrete. When the Navy got wind of the project, it sent a telegram to the Norwegian Shipbuilding and Trade Mission in New York expressing its disapproval. The Navy claimed the shipyard was "not in the national interest" because a foreign-owned shipyard would jeopardize the Submarine Base. That was just before the government took over the failed shipyard. When the Navy condemned the property, Holter and Shell Oil Company, which owned part of the property, clashed with the Navy in federal court over the $220,000 price.

The war reduced shipping at the State Pier in New London to a trickle once again. The number of cargo ships calling at the pier fell from fifty-eight in 1939 to thirty-three the following year, and the figure dropped to only a handful after that. The Navy once again took over a large part of the pier. But few other than Waldo Clarke, the resident engineer, worried about this, as other bountiful sources of wartime employment flourished. The Victory Yard created five thousand new shipbuilding jobs. The Electric Boat Company had to empty out its truck garage across the street from the shipyard to interview job applicants, who lined up by the hundreds on Thames Street every day for several weeks. The federal government also awarded Connecticut a $685,000 grant to develop the area's little state airport in Groton into an Army airfield. New London's Fort Trumbull, the 19th century Army post, was filled with naval activity. The government invested nearly $1.5 million to double the size of a school it had established there to train merchant marine officers. The Navy, with scientists employed by Columbia University, began performing secret research dealing with antisubmarine warfare at the installation. The Groton estate of Morton Plant, which had been purchased by the state after the millionaire's death, was turned into a training center for Coast Guard petty officers. New military housing bloomed across the landscape for thousands of new arrivals taking part in the war effort.

The city approached the war in an optimistic frame of mind. Its business district along State, Bank, and Main streets recovered from the Depression and was thriving. The family-owned businesses attracted large numbers of patrons from the surrounding region. New London, with its department stores, shops, drug store soda fountains, bars, restaurants, and movie theaters, was nearing its height as the area's hub of activity. Students from surrounding communities still attended the three privately endowed high schools in the city, Chapman Technical School, Bulkeley School, and Williams Memorial Institute.

New London was the region's transportation center. Union Station, though it was growing old, swarmed with travelers. The state had started the construction of a new steel highway bridge across the Thames River in 1940 and its highway approaches passed through the city. The state just barely finished the project in 1943 before the war cut off the supply of steel.

THE CITY EXPLODED WITH pride in July 1940, when the new Ocean Beach Park opened. In an astonishingly short time, contractors had cleared away the rubble from the hurricane and built an elegant park modeled after Jones Beach on Long Island, which had been engineered by Robert Moses, New York's public works czar. The Ocean Beach project had gotten started when Katharine Blunt, Connecticut College President, led a delegation from the city to visit that park on Long Island. Preparations for the opening took place that spring and into the summer, as the cashiers, attendants, lifeguards, and other workers were recruited, trained, and outfitted in crisp, stylish uniforms with a nautical theme. The cashiers wore identical tailor-made suits. Bathhouse attendants were issued starched sailor suits. The new park superintendent wore a white commodore's uniform with brass buttons and epaulets. Concessionaires had been painstakingly screened to assure the best quality. Orvin G. Andrews noted in *The Day*, July 6, 1940, "The miracle has happened. Ocean Beach Park has been dedicated and has turned out to be a splendid recreation center that was promised when it was but the paper plans of expert park engineers."

The plans for Ocean Beach eliminated the worst qualities of the old beach and borrowed the best. Boarding houses were banned by new zoning regulations in an attempt to restore the residential quality of the surrounding neighborhoods. The boardwalk, unlike the narrow, ramshackle walkway that preceded it, was a broad and handsomely designed pedestrian boulevard. In the middle was a large expanse for dances and other community activities. A lofty clock tower that overlooked the park became a landmark. As at the old beach, a restaurant, The Gam, served "shore dinners," and there was a cafeteria and ice cream and frozen custard stands. The beach was bigger and, it seemed, the sands whiter. This was the happy dawn of Ocean Beach, before the city's politicians discovered ingenious ways to exploit it and drag it down again.

More than twelve thousand people attended the opening ceremonies, including Thomas E. Troland, the law director and *Day* trustee, who had carried out the mammoth task of loosening the land from the clutches of the reluctant property owners and business interests. The experience convinced Troland, Orvin Andrews, and others of the importance of retaining the park under public ownership and management and keeping the property out of the hands of profiteers. The people's representatives had gone to a great effort and obligated future generations to pay the $3 million cost, and the citizens were entitled to hold on to the fruits of that effort, they reasoned. Leo B. Reagan, the mayor, told the audience the city at last had, by building the park, reclaimed its birthright. Dr. C. John Satti, leader of the city's Democratic Party, described the park as a lasting monument to the courage and spirit of the people of New London after the devastating hurricane. Katharine Blunt, a member of the governing board for the park, said the development of the park demonstrated the strength of democracy, which was being questioned in other parts of the world:

> *We have built it ourselves, we of this by no means large city of 30,000 people. It seems to me a really remarkable performance. We hear much talk these days about the ineffectiveness of democracy. Yet right here on this beach we have an excellent demonstration of real accomplishment by democracy.*

Ocean Beach, immaculate and gleaming new, filled with visitors in the summers of 1940 and 1941. The opening days were its brief moment of innocence, before politicians in the city resumed fighting among themselves over jobs and concessions and before wartime gas rationing limited automobile traffic to the park. The country's entry into the war, though it was not unexpected, quickly banished that mood.

The day after the Japanese attacked Pearl Harbor, December 7, 1941, the military plants and installations were surrounded with security forces. Guards were posted at the entrances to the State Pier, and state police lined up shoulder-to-shoulder along Thames Street to guard the entrances to the Electric Boat shipyard. The day after that, air raid sirens sounded as reports came over the newspaper's AP wire that enemy bombers were within striking distance of New York. The alarm sent the city into a panic. Children were sent home from school, and off-duty firemen and police were ordered back to work. The Coast Guard manned shore guns. For two hours, the alarms blasted periodically in varying bursts that nobody could figure out. The city had developed no plans for an attack, and nobody, including the police and firemen, knew what to do. The episode turned out to be a test, but it brought home to New London for the first time the gravity of its new situation as a military stronghold for a world war.

New London was preoccupied with the conflict for the next several years. The city, which was the postal address of the submarine base although the installation was located across the river in Groton, soon acquired a national name for itself as an important military port. Wartime Hollywood movies about the submarine service referred to it. Bars along Bank and Main Streets proliferated to oblige the thirsty throngs and the city filled with men and women in uniform from all parts of the country. Most were sailors, but many in the other services returned to the city on leave. A whole generation of New Londoners, the children of the Depression, headed off to war. One of the city's movie houses changed its named to Victory Theater. A big USO recreation center was opened on Coit Street.

The Day struggled to cover this epic story under a rigidly conservative management, wartime shortages, and a staff depleted by the draft and enlistments. Newsprint shortages forced it to cut back from twenty to twelve pages. The sports section was reduced from three pages to less than one. This had to do as much with the reduction of male sports activity as it did with the availability of paper. Metal shortages made it necessary for the newspaper to reduce the number of photographs, whose images were transferred to press through the use of zinc plates. On top of these disadvantages, the newspaper was guided by a former advertising solicitor and a board of directors with less of the grasp and enthusiasm for the mission of a community newspaper than Theodore Bodenwein had possessed. *The Day* chronicled the dramatic events with diminishing depth. The editorial page expressed no emotion, in contrast with the passionate editorials of Judge Frederick Latimer during World War I. George Clapp, the managing editor, relieved by Gordon of some of the editorial writing, took up the task of writing "The Tattler" most of the time, and this, too, lost the bite it had in the hands of its originator.

Gordon loathed Andrews and had a chilly relationship with the reporters and editors. He confided to friends that he dreaded going to work in the morning. Often he did not show up, writing his editorials at home. He could get away with this because he was a trustee and was guaranteed his job for twenty-five years. The terms of his settlement with the *Day's* trustees required that he write at least one editorial a year. He lived for eight years in Old Lyme, a fashionable rural town west of New London and an artist colony where famous American Impressionists like Childe Hassam had gathered since the beginning of the century. In 1943, enriched by his settlement with *The Day*, he moved into a large and elegant stone house in Jordan Village in Waterford, the town next door to New London. Although the move was facilitated by his augmented means, it also may have been motivated by the need to reduce his commuting distance because of wartime gas rationing, the same reason that made it necessary for *The Day* to pull back the boundaries of its circulation territory.

Gordon, the owner's son who might have been publisher of *The Day*, cut a sad figure at the newspaper. Elizabeth Latham, the *Day's* switchboard operator for many years, recalled of him:

He had a desk in the newsroom near the switchboard. The others didn't pay any attention to him. The reporters wouldn't have anything to do with him. He was quiet and minded his own business. If I helped him with something, he'd leave candy for me on the switchboard.

He tried his hardest to be friendly with the others at *The Day*, as indicated by his presence at Jack Cruise's going-away party in 1942 and later appearances at newspaper gatherings. He attended most of the newspaper social events. He also invited the staff to several parties at his house in Waterford. But he had few real friends in New London in or outside the newspaper. He escaped whenever he could to New York City. One of his few close friends in New London was Elsie Bishop, the widowed owner of a music and photographic studio next to *The Day*. The store sold photographic equipment and sheet music. Raymond Izbicki, a 20-year-old announcer for the city's first radio station, WNLC, met Gordon there and they became friends for several years. Izbicki remembers Gordon as a gifted intellectual but a troubled man. "He was not a friendly person, not outgoing. He was sometimes morose. He didn't laugh readily. He could be cheerful, but it was always short-lived."

Gordon shared his father's proclivity for self-promotion without the advantage of controlling a newspaper. Until he died in 1967, he sent *The Day* press releases about articles he wrote for learned publications and of honors bestowed upon him. The June 1941 edition of *Connecticut Circle*, a stuffy magazine published by Harry Morse of New London, carried a story characterizing Gordon as an up-and-coming editorial writer. Morse was a friend of Gordon's. The writer asserted that Gordon was an accomplished, but modest journalist, whose arm had to be twisted to consent to an interview. It claimed that Gordon had contacts among diplomats in Washington, some of whom had recently arranged a dinner in the nation's capital to consult with him. It concluded with three samples of his work published in *The Day*. The best, entitled "Orations," described how skilled orators, Winston Churchill, Benito Mussolini, Adolf Hitler, and Franklin Roosevelt were manipulating public opinion.

National and international events today are being run on oratorical lines. Contemporary great leaders are all great talkers and their conduct of the war includes periodic outbursts telling the world what they are doing and why. Every home in the land has thus become the setting for domestic and foreign contention and recrimination … It is only the sad comment upon the vociferous scene that seductive speech seems oftentimes to pile confusion upon confusion and to increase, rather than diminish, the distraction and the distress of the human mind.

Gordon, like his father, mixed fact and fiction in describing himself. His intellectual credentials were real, but his ability as a journalist and his influence in Washington were questionable. He had gone to Yale, studied in Italy, and spoke several foreign languages, including Italian. He was an engaging conversationalist on intellectual issues, though he could not carry on a casual conversation. He was moody and exhibited signs of bitterness. He confided to his closest friends his distaste for Andrews and told them he had been cheated out of the newspaper by the men who ran it. He was bitter toward his father, reverential toward his mother. He implied that he was disenchanted with the Roman Catholic Church and experimented with other religions, including Buddhism. He set up a Tibetan Buddhist shrine at his house in Waterford. Even to those he confided in, he was secretive about his personal life, but most who knew him realized that he conducted a covert homosexual lifestyle in the conservative community where he worked and lived. He never fit into the practical and provincial setting of *The Day* and the community it served.

THE NEWSPAPER CARRIED ON with few changes in management or style during the war. Some of the editors still wore old-fashioned green eyeshades. George Clapp, a shy, conservative newspaperman who eschewed controversy, remained the managing editor for nearly twenty years after Bodenwein's death. Alfred Ligourie, an officer in the National Guard who insisted upon being referred to as Colonel, continued as the city editor except for a brief period of active military service. He felt privileged as one of the staff Bodenwein had hired. John DeGange, who along with Clapp, had been a favorite of Bodenwein's, stayed on as the sports editor. George Grout, whose wife, Frieda, was a proofreader, doubled as the county editor and librarian, keeping up to date the card filing system he had established on the eve of the Great Depression in 1929. James Watterson remained as a sports writer. Under their influence and under the constraints imposed by the war and Gordon's appeasement, *The Day* operated largely from habit.

Some thought Clapp, the foremost news executive under Bodenwein for many years, would someday become the editor and publisher. But it became obvious that Andrews had something different in mind. He and the directors postponed a major change by leaving the newspaper without a publisher for more than twenty years. Meantime, Barnard L. Colby, Andrews' only son-in-law and the favorite of the newspaper's management, stood by and was nurtured to begin an ascent up the ladder that would move him past Clapp,

Watterson, DeGange, and others Bodenwein had hired and favored. Colby would become publisher in 1961.

As *The Day* moved cautiously forward, clutching the rail of the status quo and living fearfully within its limited means, a liberated Edna struck out on a new life, choosing, if not reveling, in change and spending her wealth lavishly. She was not one to remain alone for long. After living as a widow for a respectful four years, she remarried. Her third husband was Victor Heimbucher, 51, comptroller for the Babcock Printing Press Company. Edna seemed to cherish her collection of husbands. She retained until she died a little, red pocket photo container with pictures of her three spouses. These were Bodenwein, Heimbucher, and Lewis Winfield, her first husband who in the photograph is a handsome young man attired in a Sunday suit with a derby hat looking out at a beach on the New Jersey shore.

Heimbucher, eight years younger than Edna, was a widower from Chicago, whose wife had died in 1940. The two lived in the Mohican Hotel, where Heimbucher proposed in the winter of 1943. On January 29, Edna said, Heimbucher and several other couples burst into her suite at the hotel. One of the men in the party placed a pillow on the floor, and Heimbucher knelt on it, declared his affections, and asked her to marry him. Heimbucher asserted during later divorce proceedings that Edna had induced him to marry her and promised to support him. Edna provided a different account. Edna said Heimbucher had led her to believe he was independently wealthy.

The two were married at a friend's suite at the Waldorf-Astoria Hotel in New York in a Lutheran ceremony at 5 pm, April 24, 1943. The suite was decorated with a profusion of spring flowers. About 50 friends from New York, Philadelphia, Boston, Long Island, and New London were present. Edna wore a gray suit with a matching hat, a watermelon colored veil, and a corsage of white orchids. Josephine J. Mitchell of New London, one of Edna's closest friends, was the bridesmaid. Her husband, Irvin Mitchell, Jr., was a New London businessman and had been a political and personal associate of Theodore Bodenwein. Harry Faeber, the vice president of the Babcock Printing Company, was the best man. The couple spent their honeymoon in Annapolis, Maryland, before returning to New London.

Edna and Victor moved into Pequot House, the house she had built with Bodenwein, but they lived there only briefly. Edna rented the house again, and put it on the market. In 1945, she sold it to David Elfenbein, a wealthy Jewish businessman in New London, for $30,000. Most of the furniture Edna had purchased in Europe was sold to the Elfenbeins for $6,300. The sale, which followed months of tortuous negotiations, had a deep personal significance to Elfenbein according to his grandson, Andrew Freedman. Freedman said his grandfather told of rowing a boat in the Thames River near the original Pequot House hotel when he was a child in the 1890s. He lost an oar, and paddled up to the dock to get another but was ordered away by an attendant. He believed this was because he was Jewish. Buying the house built on the site of the Pequot House had, for that reason, great symbolic importance to David Elfenbein, his grandson said. If this was true, David Elfenbein shared a spiritual kinship with Theodore Bodenwein, the German immigrant, who along with Edna, the daughter of a Trenton stone cutter, chose the site of the old Pequot House partly as a way to validate their position in New London society.

Edna engaged the services of a young lawyer, Edmund J. Eshenfelder, an assistant law director in the city, to help her with the sale. But she personally took charge of the negotiations with Elfenbein, wrangling over myriad issues ranging from the furnishings to the garden hoses. Edna and David Elfenbein haggled for months, but during the discussions, Edna and Elfenbein's wife, Miriam, took a liking to one another. While the house had been rented the gardens and grounds had become overgrown, and Edna proposed a plan to replant them, even prescribing methods to restore the proper soil chemistry. The Elfenbeins found her to be a bawdy but admirably strong-willed woman, one who could be obnoxious, but could be fun as well. When the house finally was sold, Edna invited the Elfenbein's 12-year-old daughter, Joyce, to the house for tea, to give her an opportunity to pick out her own bedroom.

In 1946, Edna bought a winter house in Fort Lauderdale, Florida, and a summer home in the Oswegatchie section of Waterford, and she and Victor carried on an active social life in public and a troubled relationship in private at both locations. The house in Florida was filled during the winter months with Edna's friends and family, to the extent that it was later nicknamed "Friendship House." In private, Edna and Victor battled with each other from the time of their brief honeymoon in Maryland. Each claimed the other drank too much, and Edna charged during her divorce that Victor was abusive.

Her tempestuous third marriage, for the time being, kept her mind off the affairs of the newspaper. During the war as the newspaper labored under unusual conditions, she had not questioned that her checks did not increase appreciably. After the settlement in 1942, she had received the accumulated amount of her widow's settlement, $23,000, which along with her life insurance and later Victor's income, helped her maintain the lifestyle to which she had become accustomed as Theodore Bodenwein's wife.

The Day struggled under increasingly difficult conditions to keep its readers informed. Its mechanical equipment badly needed to be replaced and required constant attention. The ancient furnace in the basement blew up once. With advertising sharply curtailed, the directors voted on April 20, 1942, to increase the retail price of the newspaper from 18 to 24 cents a week.

Within the limitations of a smaller newspaper, features thinned out, and the news columns grew leaner. The human drama of the war came across nevertheless in the fragments of information that were reported. Little elaboration was necessary. The newspaper employed its scarce supply of zinc to publish group pictures of each new group of young men who were inducted into the military. It was filled with stories about individual servicemen. One such story, on May 4, 1943, appeared under the picture of a young man in uniform, Naval Aviation Cadet Deane C. Avery of Mystic, who had been transferred to the Naval Air Station in Pensacola, Florida, after completing flight training in Massachusetts. Avery, who served as a combat pilot during the war, later became one of the publishers of *The Day*.

The launching of submarines at Electric Boat was another news staple. At first, the launching ceremonies had elaborate programs, but as the pace picked up and submarines were sent into action almost every week, the finer points were dispensed with. Soon, the newspaper was reporting the casualties and acts of heroism aboard these submarines. On June 24, 1943, *The Day* reported that six submarine officers, including a native of Groton, were decorated for exploits in "sending Japanese submarines to the bottom." Among them, Lieutenant Commander William H. Brockman, 38, the husband of the former Carolyn Hanover of Groton, was decorated for having sunk a Japanese destroyer, a 9,000-ton enemy transport ship, and a 5,000-ton cargo ship, as well as damaging a heavy cruiser and a 10,000-ton tanker. Lieutenant Commander Thomas B. Klakring, 38, whose wife lived in Mystic, near New London, received a medal for valor after he "daringly attacked and sank two Japanese destroyers and a large cargo vessel." The newspaper was soon compiling long lists of war casualties.

The routine of war, with its shortages of food, gasoline, and other necessities, penetrated every aspect of life. A debate broke out on the City Council over whether the authorities ought to enforce the rules that forbade the use of automobiles for recreation, since the restriction was cutting into the parking lot receipts at Ocean Beach. The Twentieth Annual Eastern Connecticut Interscholastic Conference track and field championships took place in the city rather than at the University of Connecticut, thirty miles to the north, to save gasoline. New London Junior College, a two-year institution that had opened in 1939, was forced by the scarcity of students to close in February 1943. "More than half of our students are young men and most of them seemed destined to enter the armed services during the next several weeks," Waldo E. Clarke, chairman of the board of trustees, said. Sports events, which played an important role in the life of the city and even politics, were unsettled by the departure of able-bodied men. Colonel Thomas E. Troland declined an offer by supporters to sponsor his nomination for the United States Senate at the Republican convention in 1942, explaining that his military unit, the 43rd Infantry Division, would be mobilized for the war that November.

Troland's decision probably did not make much difference in the outcome of the senatorial race, for he had little name recognition outside New London. But his absence while he served in the military may have had a profound significance for New London politics in the decade after the war. Troland was replaced as director of law by his assistant, Edward R. Henkle. Then, in April 1944, John W. Sheedy, the city manager, became ill and went on a leave of absence, and Henkle moved up to acting city manager. These flukes placed Henkle in a favorable position to be permanent city manager when Sheedy died in November. Other names were mentioned for the post: George E. MacDougall, the former *Day* reporter and then special assistant to the Connecticut Reemployment Commission; Major General Morris B. Payne, the architect of Ocean Beach; and even Waldo E. Clarke, whose name was thrown in without his knowledge while he was out of town. But Henkle had the advantage of having been in the position for eight months already, and the City Council appointed him city manager in December 1944. This ushered in what would be known in the city's history as the "Henkle Era" for the deep imprint he made after the war as the strongest city manager since this form of government had been created in 1921. Henkle, who had been a Democrat, and Dr. C. John Satti became the two most powerful figures in the city. The City Council fell into Republican hands during the war, but real authority became concentrated in the hands of these two men.

These developments would have been thoroughly analyzed in *The Day* had Theodore Bodenwein still been alive. But while they were mentioned, they escaped detailed analysis under the existing management. The interest Bodenwein showed for politics disappeared. George Clapp, the managing editor, seldom ventured into the community and never engaged in politics as Bodenwein had and underlings such as John Mallon and George MacDougall did. Orvin Andrews was a Republican, but possessed little of the political insight Bodenwein had. Barnard L. Colby wrote about politics, but kept a professional distance from it. He was, in that sense, the newspaper's first modern political reporter, one who observed political events with total impartiality. This detachment may have been refreshing to political leaders like Dr. Satti, but it did not occur without a price. The newspaper lost its feel for the significance of politics and the other forces that were bringing change to the city. Without the strong and involved presence of an editor of Bodenwein's stature, the *Day's* perspective on politics became more distant and less forceful.

The Day demonstrated in the fall of 1944 that it still could perform the basics of its mission in the community. In an eerily familiar pattern of developments, heavy rains fell in mid-September, ending a long drought. The rain was followed by a powerful tropical hurricane that struck the region on the night of September 13. This time, everyone was prepared, including the weather service, the municipal governments, and *The Day*. The newspaper carried weather-service warnings, and detailed extensive preparations to avoid the catastrophe caused by the 1938 hurricane. The 1944 storm had many similarities to the earlier one. It halted rail, bus, and automobile traffic, uprooted trees and poles, leveled beach pavilions, and caused heavy damage and some loss of lives. But it was not nearly as violent as its formidable predecessor. The day after the hurricane, *The Day* departed from its practice of ruminating on national and world affairs and published a rare local editorial entitled, "The Big Blow." *The Day* expressed the community's relief at having escaped a second calamity in six years.

> *The big hurricane seemed to expend itself in three hours; this little hurricane blew and blew and blew, over a period of more than five hours, and ended on the incongruous note of a whistling wind long after midnight, roaring through the tortured trees while the stars shone innocently above and seemed to wink at the cowering people, who wondered if it was all coming back again.*

Other serious matters occupied the minds of New London's leaders as war slowly drew to a close. As early as 1943, Waldo Clarke and other business leaders worried about the future of New London when the industrial demands of the war dropped off. Orders for submarines were already falling off so sharply that Electric Boat began making plans to close its South Yard. That year, Clarke proposed a concerted effort to promote the development of the New London port after the war, possibly through the formation of a port authority. He also began following leads for new industry for the area. He heard that a small pharmaceutical company, Charles Pfizer & Company, was looking for room outside its Brooklyn, New York, headquarters to expand its business.

Clarke also was aware of the concerns across the country over the movement of business and industry out of the cities and the dangers this posed to New London. At the end of the war in 1945 the community was confronted with many promises and many questions.

Unfortunately, *The Day*, which Theodore Bodenwein had hoped in his will would take the lead in the community's advancement, had few suggestions other than the stale list of goals in its agenda for New London left over from before the publisher died.

NINETEEN

Still a Family Newspaper

Gentlemen, brace yourselves, as no one has a corner on gripes. For the third year in a row, you have reduced my dividend while you continue to do a greater volume of business.

—Edna Bodenwein, January 13, 1951, letter to the *Day's* directors

SHORTLY BEFORE THE END of the war, a reporter for *The Day* asked Captain Frederick H. Warder, the new commander of the Submarine School in Groton, whether he believed that World War II would be the last conflict in which submarines would play an important role. This was a question that was on everyone's mind in New London. He answered, "They said that after the last war and the German U-Boat came close to winning this one by itself."

The officer's response was predictably no, that the nation always would need submarines. However, at that time, nobody knew what would become of the military industry that had infused so much energy into the wartime economy. The little universe in the southeastern corner of Connecticut that *The Day* covered emerged with apprehension from a conflict that had brought it prosperity as well as personal hardship.

In the months following the war, the Navy proceeded to mothball many of the nation's subs at the Groton base, taking the boats out of commission and storing them for future use. Goss Cove, the inlet near the submarine base, filled with submarines back from the war. The Navy shrouded them from the elements in mysterious looking spherical bubbles over their conning towers.

Sightseers traveled out of their way to view this odd sight from Quaker Hill, the village across the river from the base.

The decline in submarine orders starting before the end of the war, meant that the government no longer needed the Victory Yard, the old Groton Iron Works property on the south end of Electric Boat that it had purchased in 1942. By a fortunate coincidence, just as this was occurring, in November 1944, John L. Smith, president of Charles Pfizer & Company, asked the company's board of directors to build a new plant someplace beyond its cramped quarters in Brooklyn to accommodate its post-war expansion. The company began a search for a site for a new plant across the eastern half of the United States. It surveyed 80 spots. But Waldo E. Clarke led the company to the Victory Yard, which turned out to be just what it was looking for. Pfizer purchased the yard and surrounding property in 1946, establishing a foothold that would make it one of the area's leading industries.

Clarke had not lost his masterful touch as a dealmaker, though he no longer had Theodore Bodenwein at his side to blast away the obstacles for him. The two had been a crack team as civic leaders. In the past, Clarke would have gone to Bodenwein whenever he was working on a deal to make sure that: (A) *The Day* would support him; (B) the Republican Party would back the idea; and (C) *The Day* would keep a lid on the news until Clarke said it was OK to tell the public. When that time came, Bodenwein would boost the proposition on the editorial page, in the news coverage, and in the "Tattler."

Without Bodenwein's leadership as an editor and owner, *The Day* was drifting into the postwar era doing little more than keeping up with the news and providing scarce guidance. Ocean Beach turned out to be the *Day's* last big battle for many years. George Clapp had no taste for local controversy, and Orvin Andrews deferred to Clapp's conservative judgment on editorial policy, which coincided with the directors' cautious business approach.

Without Bodenwein at his side, Clarke lost some of his political clout. He had been the target of the corrupt political system as a young superintendent of streets in the early part of the century and he shared Bodenwein's zeal for political reform. The two had joined forces in the struggle after the First World War that led to the 1921 City Charter. Clarke had served on the first City Council under the new arrangement and was mayor once. Just as Bodenwein drew political strength from John McGinley, Clarke derived his influence in politics from Bodenwein.

Clarke, in his 60s as the Second World War ended, still enjoyed enough respect as an elder statesman to persuade the New London City Council to create a development commission to bring new industries to New London and to try yet again to establish the port as a shipping center. The council named him one of that commission's first members as well as a member of the Board of Finance. Clarke also became a member of a state commission formed to recruit industry.

Clarke was worried about what would happen to New London after the war. Returning GIs and expanding businesses and industries were expected to gravitate toward the suburbs, where land was cheaper, taxes were lower, and living conditions were not as congested as they were in the cities. New London needed a post-war plan for its survival as certainly as the world did, he felt.

Clarke feared a flight of business and industry from the cities that would leave urban centers wastelands. In notes he kept in 1944, he quoted the National Association of Real Estate Boards: "The decentralization movement in American cities threatens to become the most wanton waste of wealth this country has ever known through the destruction of land and building values of business properties."

He believed the only solution to this problem was good planning and regional cooperation. He knew the New England communities around New London would never buy the idea of political consolidation. But he felt it would be practical to create a metropolitan council encompassing New London, Groton, and Waterford that would plan for their mutual needs, mainly to develop the Port of New London with shipping and manufacturing. The regional council he envisioned mirrored a plan *The Day* had been touting in its Agenda for New London since before Bodenwein's death, only *The Day* proposal had not included Groton. Eventually, he felt, the city could extend municipal water and sewerage to the other communities to service new industry. He was one of the first to advance the idea of regional cooperation in this New England bastion of small-town parochialism.

Clarke believed it would be necessary to provide subsidies for industry, such as tax reductions and free land. The state would have to help. It could do so by compensating the city for its tax losses from its vast tax-exempt government property. New London, with its tiny, six-square-mile land area, would have to be particularly resourceful in its development, he felt. It could make use of Riverside Park, near the Coast Guard Academy, as an industrial site, and reclaim additional land for industry that was not being used to its full potential. New industry was critical to the development of the pier. He believed the lack of manufacturing was why the port facility had failed in the past. He proposed forming a development organization with the capital to take over blighted sections of the city and redevelop them for a combination of housing, business, and industry. This was Waldo E. Clarke's assessment of New London's needs in 1944, one that turned out to be remarkably close to the mark.

But for one who had such a grasp of what was needed for the future and who had had such an enormous impact on New London already, Clarke was singularly unappreciated. He spent his last years fighting off critics and immersed in humiliating controversy. Clarke could honestly claim credit for delivering to New London's doorstep the Coast Guard Academy, the New London Junior College, and now a growing pharmaceutical company, Charles Pfizer & Company. But these contributions did not spare him from attack by perennial adversaries like state Senator Perry Shafner, a spunky Democrat from New London. Shafner single-handedly mounted an attack on Clarke as head of the state pier in the late 1940s.

Shafner accused Clarke of being a total failure in promoting shipping at the pier and intimated that Clarke had personally profited at the state's expense. The charge that the state pier was a white elephant was an old tune, but the claim gained fresh currency after the war when New London went to the legislature to recover its tax losses from the pier. City Manager Edward R. Henkle demanded some of the money he thought the pier was taking in. What money? Clarke retorted. The state pier had never been a moneymaker, he said. He recited his thirty-year struggle to turn the venture around, beginning after World War I when he had tried to secure a long-term contract to ship lumber from the northwest into New England and failed again when the longshoremen refused to work overtime to unload flour. The pier Bryan Mahan had won for the city had been handicapped by one setback after another, he said, including two world wars in which the Navy took over much of the facility. Shafner seized upon Clarke's remarks as an admission that the pier actually was a failure, and he demanded that Clarke either produce some results this time or be replaced by someone "who would take steps to put New London back on the map."

Had Bodenwein still been alive, he would have expressed his rage in "The Tattler" at the suggestion that Clarke lacked the astuteness to promote the city. Bodenwein had been loyal and never afraid to rush to a friend's assistance. He had defended Senator Frank Brandegee when Brandegee was under attack for dragging his feet on the issue of women's suffrage. And he berated the American public for supporting the censure of Senator Hiram Bingham. He had stood by Clarke during one of his darkest hours, when he was under attack by New London politicians as a young city engineer. Bodenwein would have wasted no time in pointing out that it would be hard to find anyone in the city's history with a greater record at developing the city than Clarke. Clarke's only problem, as Clarke admitted, was that he dealt in a world that had to be secretive and therefore often was suspect by the public. Bodenwein always had the advantage of knowing the truth as one of Clarke's closest confidantes and could address public criticism with the benefit of inside information.

Bodenwein also would have shown more passion and involvement than the editors of *The Day* did in the postwar efforts to court industry, including an unsuccessful drive Clarke led to bring a steel mill to the region. And the editors did not so much as crack a smile when the city put in a bid to become the site for the United Nations headquarters late in 1945.

"This Section Boomed as Site for Capital of World Peace Group," a headline in the December 28, 1945, edition, announced. That movement got underway when the Chamber of Commerce asked City Manager Edward R. Henkle to promote New London as the site for the United Nations. The City Council eagerly embraced the idea, as rumors about it mushroomed. One story had it that Mary Harkness, the area's most wealthy and prominent philanthropist, had offered her summer estate in Waterford to the world organization. But *The Day* was unable to confirm this in a telephone call to the mansion. "They would not even say whether Mrs. Harkness was at her Waterford residence or out of town or where a message could be directed to her," the newspaper said. Still, the reporter continued, it was a logical possibility, considering Mrs. Harkness's many philanthropies.

Four days later, Mayor James May sent a telegram to President Truman appealing for his support, describing New London's often repeated advantages: the city was halfway between New York and Boston, with rail lines east and west, north and south, and one of the best ports on the Atlantic. Selectmen Charles T. Crandall of Groton and Monroe L. Beckwith of Waterford also placed their names on the telegram. Rather than get into the middle of this, Gordon Bodenwein wrote several editorials in the following months that dispassionately examined the actual course of the search, which led to New York City. He never mentioned New London or Westerly, Rhode Island, which also sought to become the peace capital of the world.

An event of more immediate concern at the *Day* office occurred on November 3, 1947. That morning, Alfred Ligourie, the city editor for twenty years and a member of the news staff since 1908, collapsed from a heart attack at his mother-in-law's house in the south end of the city and died. He was 64. Ligourie's death followed by only two months the death in an automobile accident of John Mallon, the *Day's* most veteran reporter. *The Day* gradually emptied of the men who had been at Bodenwein's side in the early days. In a few years, George Grout, one of Bodenwein's earliest hires would pass from the scene, leaving only one major player from that bygone era: Orvin G. Andrews.

While Mallon was remembered as happy-go-lucky, Ligourie was recalled for his stiff demeanor and mechanical predictability. During the years he served on *The Day*, he divided his interests between the military and the newspaper, and as reporters remembered, seemed sometimes to confuse the two in his role as a newsroom executive. He had a reputation for order and discipline, a quality that contrasted with the freewheeling lifestyles of most of the reporters. Reporters out on morning assignments usually stopped off at Hammy's, a nearby saloon, on their way back to write their stories. As the morning wore on, Ligourie would begin pacing the floor waiting for them, occasionally glancing out the window. The telephone operator's duty was to place a call to the bar to summon the wayward staff. Shortly, as the city editor watched from the window, the reporters raced back to *The Day* along Main Street like soldiers rushing back from liberty. This was almost a daily occurrence. George Clapp wrote in a rare local editorial that appeared the day after Ligourie died:

> *Colonel Ligourie was a meticulous man for detail in the handling of news stories, and often drew upon his wide acquaintance for information not otherwise available. A man of fine appearance he took considerable care with dress and prided himself upon being punctual in reporting for his hour of work.*

Ligourie's death created the first significant opening in the news organization since Bodenwein's death eight years earlier. Until then, the editorial staff had been immutable. Not much had changed since George Clapp wrote a job aspirant on May 6, 1940, "I would be guilty of misleading you if I indicated that there is the slightest chance of a summer job, or a permanent one for that matter ... There has been no change in reporters in five years, and none seems likely at this moment."

To no one's surprise, Barnard L. Colby, Orvin Andrews' 35-year-old son-in-law, rose to the position of city editor. Everyone called him Bar. The son of a New London ophthalmologist, he was courtly and charming and better educated than the rest of the newsroom staff. Shortly after he had been hired as a reporter in the 1930s, he began courting Ruth Andrews, Orvin's daughter, and a graduate of the Katherine Gibbs School. The popular young woman worked in the *Day's* business office. They were married October 23, 1937. They had three children, Robert, the oldest, and twins David and Dorothy.

Colby was a favorite in the office even before he married Ruth. In the 1930s, he wrote a series of articles on the city's famous whaling captains based on the articles written for *The Day* by W. B. Wall, a local historian. He also wrote profiles of interesting characters in the area, of whom several had close ties to *The Day*. One of these, Martin Branner, was the Waterford artist who created Winnie Winkle, the comic strip. Colby also profiled Don Fraser, the *Day's* correspondent from Salem, a farm community north of New London. Colby was not the most talented journalist to have worked for *The Day* up to that time. He was not in the same league as Judge Frederick Latimer, Malcolm Mollan, Arthur McGinley, Charles Thompson, and Charlotte Holloway. He did not have the appreciation for politics that distinguished Johnny Mallon, George MacDougall, and Bodenwein himself or the empathy for New London's people and knowledge of the city that characterized James Watterson. But he was skillful and precise with words, possessed a sharp wit, and was likable. He had a college education, unlike the others on *The Day*. And as much as he attempted to minimize the fact, he was the boss's son-in-law.

The only one who took umbrage at Colby's promotion, a week after Ligourie's death, was Watterson, who harbored a grudge the rest of his life. In the normal course of events, he, and not Colby, would have been the next in line for the important newsroom command post. He had four years' seniority over Colby and had filled in as sports editor during the year and a half Ligourie was on active duty with the National Guard and John DeGange was acting city editor. Watterson did not attend the office party to celebrate Colby's promotion. John DeGange was the toastmaster at the event. Other guests included George Grout, Gordon Bodenwein, and George Clapp.

THE MID-1940s MARKED a turning point in Edna Bodenwein's life. It was the end of the romantic phase of her marriage to Victor Heimbucher and the beginning of a five-year period in which the marriage fell apart and she became a gadfly to the trustees. If one is to believe Edna's later assertions in her divorce battle with Heimbucher, the honeymoon between the two actually ended with their honeymoon in 1943. Heimbucher left his job with Babcock Printing Press Company as the distressed company, which had furnished Bodenwein with one of the *Day's* early presses, prepared to close its New London operations. He went to work for the company's parent organization in Chicago, but left the job under circumstances that became an issue in their divorce. Edna later asserted that her third husband took to a life of idleness. Heimbucher countered that Edna had gone back on a promise to support him when he gave up a well-paying job to devote his full time to their marriage.

While they were married, both, in truth, lived lives of idleness, spending winters at a home in Fort Lauderdale and summers in the Oswegatchie colony of Waterford. Edna bought the Waterford house in 1946 with assistance from one of her closest friends, Forrest Budd, a New London banker. Budd handled all the arrangements, including the furnishings and interior decorating. He also took care of her personal finances, and in turn the Budds were among the credentialed guests at "Friendship House" in Florida. Edna's generous instincts overflowed. Friends and relatives descended regularly upon the house in Florida, as though it were their own. She lavished gifts upon her brother, William Simpson, and her nieces, including shares of stock.

Her generosity was made possible by her income from the Bodenwein Public Benevolent Foundation, which dispersed ten percent of the dividends from the newspaper to charitable causes in the *Day's* circulation area and ninety percent to her, Gordon, and Elizabeth. Edna, who would receive upwards of $20,000 a year and more under the arrangement after the settlement, carefully kept track of the *Day's* business, poring over financial reports that Andrews sent her. Her marital difficulties seemed to awaken her interest in the newspaper. By 1946, she was asking questions and making suggestions that one would expect of an owner or major stockholder.

The directors were attentive, understanding that if Edna was unhappy, she could appeal to the Probate Court with her grievances. It might have occurred to them also that she was privy to a great deal more knowledge about the newspaper's transition from a proprietorship to a public trust than ever came out during the court case. In a letter March 9, 1946, Charles Smiddy responded patiently to a wide array of issues she had raised. He explained that while *The Day* had done as well in 1945 as it had the previous year, her dividends dropped because the newspaper had had to liquidate two mortgages it held, one that had been secured by a house owned by one of the newspaper's executives for a personal loan on which he had defaulted.

Smiddy also noted that the directors feared a drop in circulation in 1946, but said he was confident the newspaper's earnings nevertheless would be strong enough for her to receive $22,000 to $25,000 that year. That was more than double what Andrews was receiving. *Day* employees had not received pay increases for some time, and the newspaper would have to grant raises or face labor trouble, he said. The directors hoped that increased advertising after the war would make up for shrinking circulation. Smiddy assured Edna the directors intended to increase the quality of the newspaper and, in particular, would increase the amount of local news. He told her the directors had followed her advice to insert the programming for the local radio station. The letter had all the reassuring elements of a stockholder's report, although *The Day* no longer had stockholders in the usual sense.

Edna always worried about money. She kept a detailed ledger of expenses and bickered persistently with vendors. She bought new Buicks regularly and hounded the New London dealer by mail with complaints that sometimes questioned his integrity. Her focus on *The Day* and on her income from the newspaper was interrupted briefly in 1949, when she and Heimbucher were separated, and she sued for divorce. The divorce battle, which was adjudicated in a Florida court, lasted from that October until June 1950, when she was awarded a divorce on her own terms. During those months, charges flew back and forth between the two. Edna hired a professional writer to launch her opening salvo against Victor, in a five-page letter that laid out in fine detail her grievances over money, Victor's alleged idleness and dependency, and other matters. At one point, she held up the example of Theodore Bodenwein to her third husband:

> *The money you have enjoyed spending is not earned by me. It would serve me right if it was out of my hide. But it was earned by a fine, good man who slaved for years, 14, 16 and 18 hours a day through blood, sweat and tears. Certainly his hard-earned money could do more good in some medical research or for crippled children, rather than supporting you in idleness and allowing you to indulge yourself until death.*

Victor painted an unflattering portrait of his second wife. It was she, not he, who lived a dissolute life, requiring him to take care of all the household chores and serve as nursemaid to her while she stayed in bed all day. Victor claimed that Edna had demanded that he give up his job in Chicago to live at home with her, and in turn, she had agreed to support him financially the rest of his life, even if they were separated or divorced. Victor said that his doctor had prescribed daily doses of liquor for a heart condition, whereas Edna was constantly engaged in partying in which there was heavy drinking that had nothing to do with medicinal purposes. On June 19, 1950, the 15th Circuit Court for Brevard County, Florida, dismissed Victor's claim and granted Edna a divorce and the right to recover her former name.

Thus liberated at the age of 67, Edna resumed her life of entertaining friends and keeping an eye on the directors of *The Day*. In the latter pursuit, she returned with a vengeance despite failing health brought on by her lifestyle of easy living. While her major concern always seemed to be her dividend checks, she also scrutinized the quality of *The Day* and its editorial operations.

CHANGE BEGAN TO STIR at the newspaper, which had emerged from the war stodgy, dull, and predictable. In November 1949, Colby, who was being groomed to replace his father-in-law, was promoted for the second time in two years, this time to the new position of assistant general manager. James Watterson was promoted from reporter to city editor. Although the change moved Colby out of the newsroom into the business office, he retained his influence over the news operation through influencing hiring decisions as job opportunities began to open slowly after years of remaining closed.

Colby hired Deane C. Avery as a reporter. Avery was a World War II combat aviator and younger brother of Colby's best friend, Latham Avery. When Colby moved out of the newsroom in 1949 and another reporter vacancy opened, Duncan H. Fraser, son of Donald A. Fraser, the town correspondent and feature writer from Salem for forty years, was hired to fill it. Duncan Fraser, who was in his 20s and trying to start his own printing business, represented a new breed of college-educated reporters Colby was bringing to *The Day*. Fraser was a graduate of Wesleyan University, a prestigious Connecticut institution. Next, Joseph G. Ryan, then the 22-year-old news editor of the *Trentonian*, a daily newspaper in Trenton, New Jersey, was hired to replace Gordon Bodenwein as editorial writer. By 1950, Gordon had tired of the routine of working in a place where he was not wanted, sold his house in Waterford, and took up permanent residence in Mexico, using his reliable stream of wealth from *The Day* to begin a new life. Ryan had risen to that position while still a student at Ryder College. George Clapp officially hired both men, but Colby really made the decisions.

In his new position, Colby had yet another duty: humoring Edna, who was firing off letters regularly about what was wrong with *The Day*. Colby was particularly effective at this. Edna was growing suspicious of Andrews and the others, but she was charmed by the general manager's son-in-law. She harped about her dividends to Andrews, but she wrote motherly notes to Colby, tendering compliments and suggestions with mild criticisms. She had been reading the columnist Walter Winchell in the Fort Lauderdale newspaper and sent Colby clips as a suggestion for enlivening the wooden editorial page. She complimented *The Day* for a feature called "What is a Newspaper?" and told Colby she liked the review of the last year's news that appeared on New Year's Day.

"It was most pleasant to receive that touch of sun, light and sweetness from the Southland," Colby responded on January 10, 1951, to one of her letters. He acknowledged that he had a small role in "What is a Newspaper," but credited his new hire, Joe Ryan, for the work. He told her that *The Day* had briefly run Winchell, but discontinued him in the belief that his type of reporting clashed with the more conservative style of news handling and other features in *The Day* columns. "Hope you're having a pleasant winter. You deserve all the best because you are a very kind lady." Kindness wasn't exactly a quality that shone through to Andrews and the other directors, who were susceptible to the reverse side of Edna's generous temperament.

The years following the war were astonishingly good for *The Day*, with both circulation and advertising revenues rising with post-war economic prosperity and suburban population growth. All the while, Edna carefully charted this growth using the steady stream of financial reports Andrews sent her. The data, which she examined in great detail making notes in the margins and underlining passages, raised in her inquisitive mind the logical question of why her income was not rising proportionally. Wasn't there something they could do, perhaps raise the price of the newspaper from four to five cents or some equivalent measure, she was asking in 1949.

In 1950, just after her divorce went through, she made a more forceful and threatening demand. This occurred shortly after another significant death in the *Day* family. Charles Smiddy died of a heart attack on July 5, 1950, at the age of 59. His obituary noted his roles as an important public utility lawyer and civic leader. But his most important legacy was the will he helped engineer for Theodore Bodenwein. The document had turned *The Day* over to a group of community leaders, including himself, and *Day* employees to run on behalf of a community trust. An editorial in *The Day* after his death did not mention this, his most significant, professional and civic accomplishment, although it alluded to the seventeen years he spent as a director of *The Day*.

Smiddy's death not only left a void in the leadership of *The Day*, it created a vacancy on the boards of directors and trustees. Edna wanted to fill one of these. She brought the subject up in public at a dinner gathering in New London. Andrews was infuriated. He told her she should not be discussing such private matters in public. He told her that the next time she needed to discuss a matter this sensitive, he would talk with her at her house. Andrews assured her he was not trying to keep her from trying to influence the way *The Day* was run. But there were some problems associated with her interest in becoming a trustee. For one, while Gordon had resigned as an employee, he wanted to stay on the board of trustees. There was some question whether he could get away with that, since he filled a trustee slot reserved for a *Day* employee, and it was unclear whether he could transfer to the slot Smiddy had held. Possibly the other trustees might want to elect Gordon to the Smiddy vacancy. But that would leave an employee vacancy, and George Grout, who was squeezed out of the board in the settlement with Gordon, had said he wanted to retrieve his seat if the opportunity arose. However, Andrews went on, Grout was a gracious man and knew he was not going to be around forever, and he felt that maybe Bar Colby ought to be considered for that position. And Andrews said he was "in accord with Mr. Grout's thinking in the matter that Colby would be the logical man to elect as an employee trustee, since he is in a position where undoubtedly he will head up the company. He should be the man." Actually, the last thing the trustees wanted was to have Edna on the board. It was bad enough having her input from her residences in Waterford and Florida. Eventually, the trustees elected Waldo E. Clarke to fill Smiddy's vacancy.

On September 12, 1950, George Grout, one of the first reporters Theodore Bodenwein hired, and the man who invented the *Day's* library filing system, died after fifty years with the newspaper. He was one of Bodenwein's most trusted employees and had been a director since 1910. He started out as the Groton reporter, taking his bicycle across the Thames River on the ferry every day to gather the news and returning the same way to write it. Grout not only developed the newspaper's library system, but also inaugurated a feature that listed everyday news events of twenty-five and fifty years earlier. *The Day* wrote:

> *George was an old timer's newspaperman—the despair of the younger generation when it came to sturdy health and energy, inclined to give no thought to hours of work; a digger for details and a stickler for accuracy.... His familiar green eyeshade gave him the appearance of a newspaper worker of some years back ... He even wore it at times at bridge tournaments.... He had a tolerant view toward the somewhat informal, happy-go-lucky attitude usually noted in a newspaper city room, unlike some older workers who at times, in such circumstances, begin to show some annoyance at a little good natured horseplay in their advancing years.*

Bar Colby replaced Grout as a director and was elected the secretary of the board of directors in October 1950. The changes added to Edna's apprehensions that she was being cut out of the loop. Her temper rose over the 1950 Christmas and New Year's holidays. In January 1951, her rage burst forth in a letter to all the directors. Edna wrote several drafts on the backs of old letters and envelopes, each successive one more furious than the earlier one. For the third year in a row they had reduced her dividend, she bristled. "All the while you continue to do a greater volume of business." Andrews had apologized that there would be a "slight reduction" in her dividend. Did they consider $7,000 a "slight" reduction? "As I have written you before, you cannot continue to cut my dividend and expect me to like it."

What was going on up there, she demanded to know? Some of the directors now were paying themselves fees as "officers." The directors had increased the price of the newspaper in 1949, but why wasn't the new revenue reflected in her dividends? There were vacancies on the board, so why wasn't she sharing in the savings? "Gentlemen, I don't mind sharing, but to take from me, that smacks of socialism." Andrews kept talking about "the lean years ahead," she went on. "Please remember it's not lean years for the heirs and fat years for others. Wasn't it Charles Smiddy who was always talking about the rights of the heirs? I hope you gentlemen continue thinking in that vein."

Even before he replied formally to her letter, Andrews dashed off a personal letter, typed on the cheap copy paper used in the newsroom, on January 17, 1951. He said that in the years following her husband's death, the newspaper should have been putting aside money to replace machinery. But it had not because it had to appease Gordon. Now it was necessary to take the savings out of earnings. Gordon's case had drained the treasury of the newspaper, placing the newspaper in a precarious position, he said.

Andrews told Edna she was receiving a far better yield in her dividends than she would in the stock market. The stock market yield was about six percent; the yield on dividends on *Day* stock was forty-six percent in 1950. She was wrong to think *The Day* was extravagantly operated. He cited a 1949 newspaper survey indicating that the average expense of six newspapers of comparable size to *The Day* was $685,224, compared to *The Day* expenses of $522,928. The *Day's* earnings were higher than those newspapers, its total salaries and wages lower. As to her question about the officers, *The Day* needed corporate officers to fulfill its legal duties, but had held off electing them because of Smiddy's fear Gordon would take the occasion to gain power:

> *The point I want to make clear is that for* The Day *to continue to properly function, replacements of machinery are a must. While depreciation set up on the books allows for about one half the replacement cost, it is only a book entry and doesn't represent cash. In order to have cash to pay out for these capital improvements, it can only come by setting up some reserves from part of current earnings. Because it was not done, and because of the drain on surplus, we have reached the point where it is a necessity.*

Two days later on January 19, Earle Stamm wrote:

I do not for a minute believe that you think that either the board of directors of The Day Publishing Co. or the trustees have been reckless or miserly in the manner in which the activities of the paper have been conducted, and I am certain that after the annual report has been prepared by the independent auditors, you will feel as proud of the earning ability of the paper as do those men who meet regularly to consider the matters that come before them at their meetings.

The last to write was Thomas E. Troland, now a Superior Court Judge. On January 24, he explained that the dividends had been as high as the directors felt was prudent and still enable them to build up capital reserves. Failing to do that would not be in the interest of Edna or any of the heirs, he said. As for the fact that there were suddenly officers receiving salaries, he explained that the directors had not had an annual meeting as Connecticut law required since her husband died. That was the way Smiddy had wanted it, he said. "I don't know the real reason Charlie Smiddy did not want to call a meeting to elect officers, but Orvin thinks it was because he did not want to elect Gordon president." The directors elected their first full slate of officers in 1950. Earle Stamm, the president, and Orvin Andrews, executive vice president, each received $1,000. Bar Colby, as secretary, was paid $250. Orvin Andrews, in his January 17, 1951, letter, attempted to answer Edna's concerns about the officers' compensation:

The trustees are doing good work. Their meetings are long and spirited. They contribute a great deal to management. They are trying hard to keep the earnings high and the dividends continuous and high. They are mindful of the heirs' rights .... I think that all the trustees feel that it is an honor to be connected with the paper, and that although they all enjoy being compensated for the work, that is really secondary.

Edna and the directors continued to correspond, alternating flattery and light-hearted banter with serious concerns over the newspaper and Edna's benefits from it. But her health deteriorated during the early months of 1951. She died in October. Her death was reported in a sketchy obituary on an inside page. As she requested, her body was cremated. An urn containing her ashes was buried next to Theodore Bodenwein, his parents, and the son he and Jennie had brought briefly into the world. By her own request, there was no funeral. For reasons that are unclear, her name was never added to the monument Orvin Andrews designed and the Rock of Ages Corporation of Barre, Vermont, prepared. In keeping with her generous spirit, she left much of her estate to charity, including a substantial bequest to the Lawrence & Memorial Hospitals in New London.

T W E N T Y

REAWAKENING

My chief complaint was that the newspaper needed more starch.

—Joseph G. Ryan, *Day* editorial writer 1950-57

EXCEPT FOR THE PART about Gordon becoming publisher someday, the trustees conscientiously followed the instructions "the boss" had left them. But they had been hampered by the world war, by the long struggle over the will, and by their own limitations. They were, basically, businessmen without the vision and will of a strong editor to guide the newspaper. They followed Theodore Bodenwein's directions as explicitly as possible. They were solicitous of the employees' welfare. Considerable labor unrest existed elsewhere in the newspaper industry, a concern that Andrews repeatedly voiced at board meetings. The trustees, who also were directors of the newspaper, maintained cordial relations with the *Day's* employees. In the 1940s, they had set up a noncontributory pension plan, developed a group health insurance program, and increased paid vacations for the newsroom from one to two weeks.

They had granted a $3-a-week war bonus because of the high cost of living and granted Christmas bonuses of one or two weeks' pay. They usually acceded to wage and benefit demands, although they delayed doing so as long as possible. A family-like benevolence characterized much of what they did. They repeatedly agreed to extend paid sick leave to employees whose normal sick time had run out. When the board granted a pension to one of the compositors, it also voted to increase the pension of an earlier retiree to match it. The newspaper lent money to its employees, a practice that Bodenwein started. This generosity left the newspaper with a portfolio of mortgaged real estate and bad debts.

In 1944, despite efforts by Edna and Gordon to extract more generous incomes for themselves, the trustees had begun putting aside money for badly needed plant and equipment improvements and for the newspaper's growing pension liability. The *Day's* building had not been significantly improved since 1928. Its Hoe press had been installed in the 1920s. Some of its staff had been there even longer.

The trustees did not need the will in front of them to remember to attend to Bodenwein's widow and his son and daughter. Edna and Gordon would not let them forget for a minute. Edna's death on October 1, 1951, raised the directors' hopes that the pressure from the heirs would diminish, and that they would have more flexibility to spend money. Her death provided a windfall for Elizabeth and Gordon, who split her fifty percent share. But it was not long before Gordon began needling the board about its extravagant spending habits, and even Elizabeth began expressing a deeper interest in the newspaper's finances. On October 10, 1952, Gordon wrote to complain about the "meager dividend." Gordon even hired a New London accountant to review the newspaper's financial records.

After several years of sitting on the money while the estate was being decided, The Day Trust had begun distributing the charitable funds. The National Bank of Commerce trust department mailed out checks for such purposes as painting churches and furnishing television sets for rest homes. Lawrence & Memorial Hospitals received a grant in 1949 to help with a new oil burner. The fund paid to drill a well at the Camp Wakenah Boy Scout camp. The fund paid to send the choir at Williams Memorial Institute to the All-State Choir Festival in Hartford. The bounty was small but spread widely across the community.

If *The Day* trustees fell short of fulfilling their public trust, it was in carrying out the charge to be "champion and protector of the public interest and defender of the people's rights." Without Bodenwein's forceful and authoritative presence, *The Day* had become a champion of very little on the home front during the war. As an example of how tepid the *Day's* editorial policy had become, the directors, before the United States entered World War II, once admonished George Clapp for not being evenhanded enough in his treatment of Germany in his editorials.

Clapp, who had been managing editor since 1931 and who had written most of the newspaper's opinion for those decades, was prolific in his output of editorials. He also continued writing the Saturday "Tattler" column. But despite its volume, his writing seldom had a distinguishable point of view or local perspective. One of the few contemporary issues that excited him enough to come down on one side or another was automotive engineering, a subject that fascinated the editor. Gordon, who had supplemented Clapp's work from 1938 until 1950, did not add noticeably to the level of excitement on the page. It was not that Gordon did not try. He worked hard, wrote extensively, and occasionally interestingly, on many subjects and brought a sophisticated view to *The Day*. The trouble was that *The Day* management, including Clapp, neither cared for him nor took him seriously.

The newspaper, nevertheless, had slowly come to life after the war. *The Day* went to battle stations early in 1946, when City Manager Edward R. Henkle proposed selling the government's downtown real estate holdings, including City Hall, and building a civic center elsewhere to house the government and police. The city chose Williams Park just north of the downtown on the road that leads out of town to Hartford. The site had once been the city's burial ground and had been turned into a park through the philanthropy of Charles Augustus Williams. The city was to use a $24,000 federal grant for post-war development to prepare the plans.

The directors viewed the proposal as an extravagance as well as wanton destruction of a historic park that was an object of great local pride. They took extraordinary steps to block it. At their meeting November 18, 1946, they voted to recruit retired City Manager James Barlow, who was living in Portland, Maine, to do a study of New London's government building needs, a study that subsequently reached the same conclusion the directors had. Before the study was commissioned, the directors ordered a front-page editorial, to be reviewed by the board prior to publication, opposing the move. The newspaper invited readers to comment, and ran dozens of the responses, most of them attacking the plans and Henkle. The controversy, which created the bitterest relations between *The Day* and a city manager since 1921, went on for months. The proposal was abandoned.

Despite the unfriendliness he experienced, Gordon had clung tenaciously to his perch on *The Day* until 1950 when he departed for Mexico. He had enough interest as editorial writer to join the National Conference of Editorial Writers the year it was formed in Washington, D.C. He was one of the charter members and attended the first conventions of the organization in Washington in 1947 and in Louisville, Kentucky, in 1948. At the 1948 convention, he had participated in an editorial-page critique group that included, among others, editors from the *Hartford Courant*, *Christian Science Monitor*, Boston *Post*, and Worcester *Evening Gazette*. Gordon had taken with him for review editorial pages Clapp had prepared. Later, he seemed to enjoy reporting on the pummeling that the *Day's* managing editor's work took. He summarized the results in an article that appeared on the editorial page November 23, 1948:

> *When it was the turn of* The Day *to come up for notice, the chairman remarked that its editorial page was a "nice, clean open looking thing." Then he called attention to the fact that the page carried no editorial cartoon. Its absence, as well as the presence of the crossword puzzle and a whole column of news on that page, had to be explained as due to the newsprint shortage. It is to be feared that the others rather looked down their nose at this, since only one other paper in the group offered this reason for a very lamentable invasion of the editorial page. The chairman criticized one editorial in* The Day *on foreign automobiles for an obvious statement about their high prices being due to import duties, and he said that the author, in this case, should have been shorter* (sic).

Gordon was, by legal agreement, a trustee for life, and he came and went more or less as he pleased. He traveled to three national political conventions in 1948, including the one held by the Progressive Party in Philadelphia, and wrote commentaries on them for *The Day*. He also wrote a twelve-part series on Mexico during his extended visit there in 1949. Clapp opened the series with an editor's note informing readers that Gordon had written twelve articles on Mexico and that they would run daily until they ran out. His work, regardless of its merits, was viewed with indifference at *The Day*. Most of his contributions were crammed into the bottom of the editorial page, undistinguished from their cluttered and nondescript surroundings despite their local origin and fresh and interesting insights. Gordon's writing went to waste. It was both literary and perceptive. A half-century later, *The Day* sent me on a trip to Mexico sponsored by the National Conference of Editorial Writers. I read his series after I returned, and it was still fresh and relevant.

Whereas Gordon genuinely viewed the editorial page as an important medium of free expression to stimulate readers to think about what was going on in the world around them, Clapp often seemed more disposed to view it as a space to fill every day. The reporters called Clapp "Guv" for governor, a nickname Colby had given him years earlier. He was humorless as a rule and kept to himself. He seldom socialized outside the newspaper. His greatest passion in life was the fishing trips he took every summer to Maine. The page, along with the rest of the newspaper, reflected his conservatism. Day after day, there were four editorials and each was the same length. There were few photographs anywhere in the newspaper. The headline type was antique. There was no design to the inside news pages; printers basically stuffed lead type onto the pages as it fit. The newsroom on the second floor was dowdy and old fashioned, a reflection of the late 1920s, when the last addition had been built.

As much as he may have tried, Gordon had little impact on his father's newspaper. Neither his well-developed intellect and his extensive writing, nor his professional contacts outside the parochial world of the newspaper made any difference. He discovered in Mexico a friendlier environment and spent increasing periods of time there. He became the benefactor of a Benedictine monastic order in Morelia, in the state of Michoacan, and presided over the construction of several new buildings for its monastery in 1947, according to a necrology he prepared for the Connecticut Historical Society. He wrote to his friend in Stonington, Raymond Izbicki, that the monastery had to be fortified for some unexplained reason, Izbicki recalls. His resignation from *The Day* in 1950 brought much relief to the newspaper's management and directors; although they were still doing battle with another Bodenwein. Edna was still alive at this time and seeking to fill one of the board vacancies.

After Gordon resigned his staff position, the board debated whether he could continue to serve as a trustee and director. At their December 16, 1950, meeting at Stamm's house, the directors corrected the record of the previous meeting by crossing out the statement that Gordon was absent. He was not absent, the amended minutes said, because he was not eligible to be on the board in the first place. Gordon's permanent exile ended any chance that his father's wish that he someday become publisher would be fulfilled.

COLBY VIEWED GORDON'S DEPARTURE as an opportunity to charge the newspaper's batteries by hiring a replacement. The trustees looked upon the development as a blessed deliverance. The assistant general manager carefully broached the subject of hiring someone from outside the newspaper to take Gordon's place. There was never any question in Clapp's mind that Colby was in charge, but Colby always had to be circumspect in bringing new ideas like this to the newspaper's veteran editor, a former colleague of Theodore Bodenwein, and a member of the staff who had witnessed the signing of the will. Clapp protested that he did not need any help. He worked better alone. Gordon had been, frankly, a nuisance, he felt. Clapp could turn out four editorials a day effortlessly and had a backlog in the bottom drawer for the days the Muse did not show up for work. But Colby gently persuaded him of the advantages of an extra hand. *The Day* advertised the position in Editor &

Publisher, a newspaper trade publication, and it was in this way that Joseph G. Ryan was recruited from his job in New Jersey in 1950. Clapp and Colby interviewed Ryan and offered him more pay than he was receiving as news editor at the *Trentonian*. Also, Ryan was eager to return to Connecticut where his ailing father lived.

Although he became fond of Clapp, Ryan, then in his early 20s, quickly realized that the newspaper lacked a sense of mission under the editor's direction. "I felt the newspaper wasn't fulfilling its role as the conscience of the community," he recalled nearly fifty years later. "There was little advocacy. Even the 'Tattler' was passive commentary." He described Clapp's editorials as being often "Afghanistanian," that is to say, having to do with remote subjects that had little relevance to the rapidly changing region of southeastern Connecticut.

Ryan maintained the requisite respect for Clapp's position, but Colby encouraged him to introduce changes whenever possible. Such authority from the top had been the one thing Gordon had lacked in his efforts to improve the newspaper. Clapp's annual fishing trips to Maine gave Ryan chances to innovate. He introduced shorter and more straightforward editorials and occasionally snuck in pieces on timely state and local issues. Something as simple as varying the length of the editorials constituted a revolutionary change.

The newspaper's dreary, cluttered appearance had reflected a deeper disorder. Without an editor who was active in the community, *The Day* had lost touch with what was going on. Even in politics, the medium in which *The Day* was born and in which Theodore Bodenwein vigorously participated, the newspaper had become indifferent. The Republican directors had distanced the newspaper from political activity in 1947 by voting to bar editors and reporters from holding political positions while they presented readers with purportedly unbiased accounts of politics. This ended the tradition of the newspaper staff being politically active that had begun with John Tibbits, the founder, and continued with John Turner, John McGinley, Theodore Bodenwein, John Mallon, and George MacDougall.

The prohibition was designed to do away with the *Day's* unfavorable reputation for political partisanship. The newspaper had come under persistent attack from Dr. C. John Satti and other Democratic leaders for its political biases. John Mallon pushed the practice to absurd limits by covering politics while he was a leader in the Republican Party, a city official, and, at one point, a candidate for Congress. But an unfortunate side effect of the change was to further distance *The Day* from the civic life of New London. Although the newspaper's top news executive and editorial page editor eschewed controversy, the newspaper continued to reflect a Republican leaning. But it no longer attempted to influence political outcomes in the robust fashion of Theodore Bodenwein. It no longer had a strong point of view on politics or much of anything else.

Colby set out to refocus the *Day's* attention on the mission of community service that had been laid out in the will. The first significant evidence of this effort was a full-page manifesto of the *Day's* purpose in the community on December 29, 1950, entitled, "What is a Newspaper?" The statement, which Ryan composed, was presented in a handsome, airy layout with graceful, modern headline type and crisp, clear prose that explained the *Day's* policies and its role as Bodenwein had specified before he died.

> The Day *throughout its history has sparked the progress of New London and its surrounding communities, the fortunes of which, in the last analysis, are closely tied together. Believing that, in this age of industry, stimulation of technical activity in this area is of genuine benefit economically, socially and politically,* The Day *has repeatedly advocated the location here of more industrial activity. The steel mill proposed for nearby location is an example of the type of industrial stimulus which we believe to be of advantage to the community …* The Day *has long stood for the advance of everyday, practical measures which will further enhance the enjoyment of living for every individual. To effect good government, of the greatest benefit to the most people; to bring about harmony and cooperation on civic affairs; to further those causes which arise in furtherance of the growth of a healthy community: these things reflect the practical applications of the* Day's *policy.*

The statement said that while *The Day* still considered itself "independent Republican," the newspaper would endeavor to rise above ordinary politics. It would advocate good government without regard to party. It described how the newspaper was set up, both as a newsgathering organization and as a business. It explained the Bodenwein will that had established The Day Trust, and listed the charitable projects the newspaper already supported through the Bodenwein Public Benevolent Foundation. It described how the newspaper's continued growth would serve the community, both by sustaining an independent newspaper and enlarging the charitable benefits from the Bodenwein foundation. It was the most explicit explanation of how The Day Trust worked to appear since Bodenwein's death in 1939.

The Day sought ideas for improvements both from the staff and from its readers. The directors conducted a contest among the employees in January

1953 for ideas on how to improve the newspaper. Winners received government bonds. Reporter Duncan Fraser won one of these prizes by recommending a more efficient plan to organize the newsroom. The layout of the old second-floor newsroom had evolved haphazardly over the past twenty-five years. Fraser suggested, among other things, organizing the reporters' desks around the city and county editors and creating a separate section for the Sports Department. The directors even agreed to pay for new desks. The layout formed the basis for the *Day's* modern newsroom, as the staff continued to grow.

In October 1953, *The Day* conducted its first readership survey, asking what people liked and disliked about *The Day* and its various features. The survey was not scientific, but merely sought opinions. Readers could use forms the newspaper printed and return them anonymously. Newspaper carriers were paid five cents for each form they returned. *The Day* printed the criticisms and questions it received and responded to them, more often than not defending present practices. Colby, who had begun writing "Sentences by the Judge," wrote a column devoted to criticisms of the column. He did so with self-effacing humor that had become his trademark:

> *Just so you'll be aware of my low standing with some subscribers to* The Day, *let me tell you what they think of my efforts. Here are the whole eight of 'em. "Used to be interesting, now it smells." "No good." "Fatuous in general." "Quite corny." "Dull." "Amateurish." "Bores me sometimes." And one woman wrote, "Obnoxiously folksy."*

The managers drew the conclusion that while the readers as a rule liked *The Day*, there was room for modest changes. Based on the survey, comic strips were added, others dropped. The appearance of the newspaper was changed, but only gradually and slightly.

Life poured back into *The Day* in the early 1950s. The editorial page recovered its punch as well as a writing elegance under the influence of Ryan. He restored a style and strong point of view to the page that largely had been missing since Judge Frederick Latimer had written for *The Day* at the beginning of World War I. *The Day* began getting under people's skin once again, as indicated in an angry letter to the editor published August 26, 1952. Alfred M. Bingham of Salem, a son of Senator Hiram Bingham and publisher of the radical journal *Common Sense* during the New Deal, wrote to denounce *The Day* for its bias against Democrats.

> *In your issue of August 22 … four out of five editorials are devoted to proving that our government is rotten to the core. The first describes the administration as "a gang of political bloodsuckers." The second attacks*

Left, Barnard L.Colby, shown here shortly after he was hired as a reporter in 1933, was groomed by Orvin Andrews and the *Day* directors to take over *The Day* when Andrews retired. *The Day*

Above, Orvin G. Andrews directed the unusual design of the monument for Theodore Bodenwein's burial site in Cedar Grove Cemetery. *Skip Weisenburger, The Day*

bove, After the 1938 Hurricane, the old Ocean Beach was reborn in the 1940s as a modern municipal ark, shown here, patterned after Jones Beach on Long Island. *The Day*

Above, In a court settlement, Gordon Bodenwein won a place among the directors and trustees, who posed with *Day* employees in this picture at a dinner gathering in the 1940s. The six men on the boards are all seated in the front row. They are, from left, George Grout, Charles Smiddy, Earle Stamm, Gordon, Thomas Troland and Orvin Andrews. The woman seated center is Eleanor Leather, a bookkeeper.
The Day

Above, Orvin Andrews was firmly in charge o *The Day* in 1944, when this picture was taken with his first grandson, Robert Colby, in his lap. *Robert Colby*

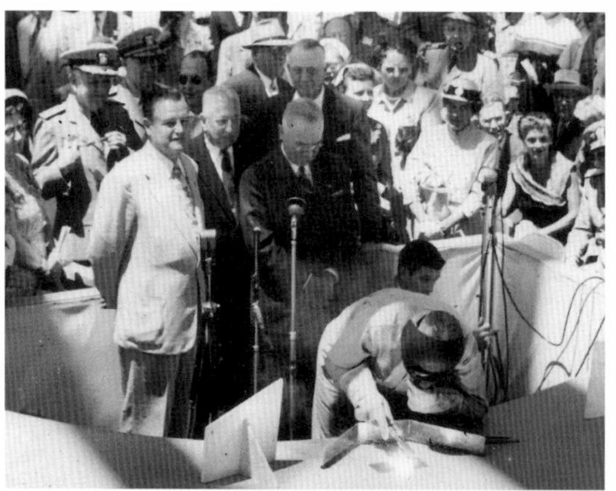

Above, *The Day* mobilized its whole news staff when President Harry S Truman visited Groton for the keel-laying of the nation's first nuclear submarine, the *Nautilus,* in June 1952. A shipyard welder engraved the president's initials into the keel after Truman wrote them in chalk.
New London Public Library

Left, Bar Colby was still a young reporter in this photo with his wife, Ruth, Orvin Andrews' daughter, and their son, Robert. Four years later, Bar Colby became city editor. *Robert Colby*

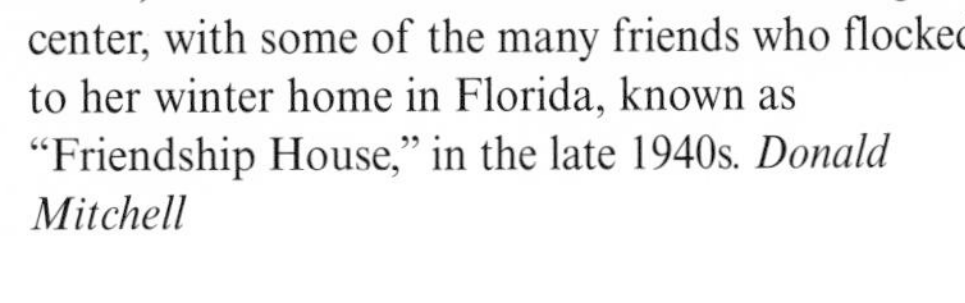

Above, Edna Bodenwein Heimbucher, standing center, with some of the many friends who flocked to her winter home in Florida, known as "Friendship House," in the late 1940s. *Donald Mitchell*

Above, Edna and Victor Heimbucher smile at one another in a rare moment of affection in their generally turbulent marriage. *Donald Mitchell*

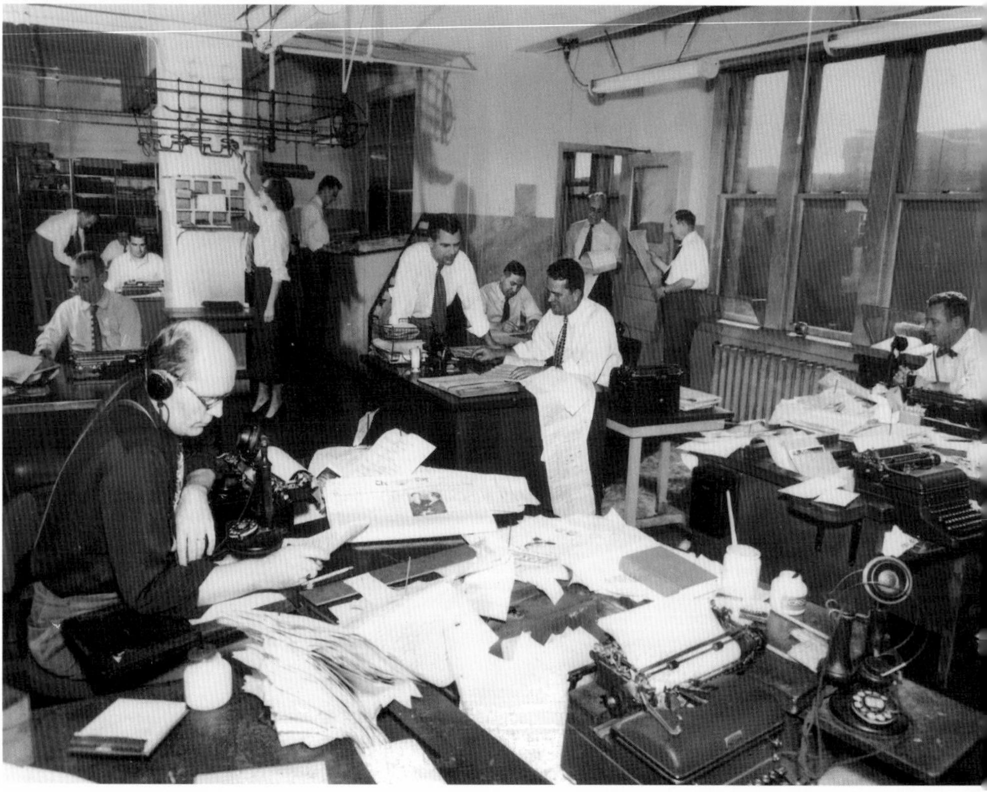

Above, The newsroom was located on the second floor of the building from 1928 until the early 1960s. This is how it appeared several years before it was moved into new quarters on the fourth floor. Reporte Jim Cunningham is in the foreground left. Deane Avery is to the far right. To the left of him is Jim Watterson. Reporter Helen Floyd reaches toward the conveyor belt to the composing room. *The Day*

Right, *Day* trustee Waldo Clarke, a close associate of Theodore Bodenwein, predicted a catastrophe for New London from the movement to the suburbs after World War II. He turned out to be right.
Alma Wies

Above, Gordon Bodenwein, far left, and Waldo Clarke, next to him, were guests on a visiting naval vessel in the late 1940s, shortly before Gordon left *The Day* and settled permanently in Mexico.
Alma Wies

Left, To protect its territory in the rapidly growing town of Groton, *The Day* opened a satellite office there. The early staff consisted of, from left standing, reporters Raymond Rancourt, Gerry Chapman and Ivan Robinson, and seated, office manager Judith Sinton, Deane Avery's sister. *The Day*

bove, *Day* press foreman George Kent posed with the touring "Rheingold Girls" in the newspaper's essroom shortly before his retirement. Kent selected the *Day's* new press in 1960 and supervised all the anges associated with the new building. *Ann Cupello*

Right, Generations of young carriers like these shown in the 1940s delivered *The Day* in New London and surrounding communities. Interest in paper routes diminished in the 1980s, and the carriers on bicycles gradually were replaced by adults in cars. *The Day*

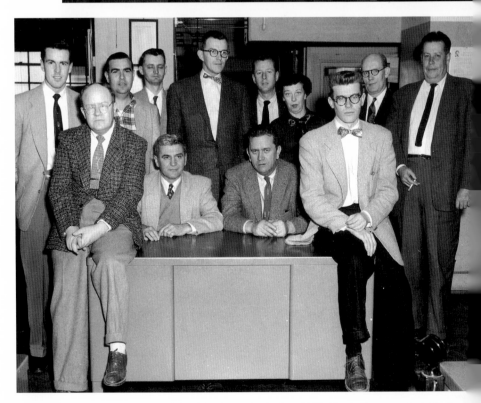

Above, *The Day* news staff posed for this picture in the late 1950s. In the front are Jack Cruise, John DeGange, Jim Watterson, and Curt Pierson. Behind them are John Foley, Bob Nauta, Bo Craigue, Joe Ryan, Deane Avery, Evelyn Archer, Jim Cunningham, and Paul Walcott. *The Day*

bove, Waldo Clarke played an important role in attracting the pharmaceutical company Charles Pfizer Co. to Groton. This is what the Groton plant looked like in 1946. The company became one of the rgest pharmaceutical firms in the world and reawakened New London's hopes in the 1990s when it panded in the city. *Pfizer Inc.*

bove, Orvin Andrews received a movie camera at his retirement in 959. The others are John DeGange and Max Fox. *John DeGange*

Above, George Clapp, who was managing editor of *The Day* from 1931 to 1958, towed the editorial line from the Bodenwein era and kept the newsroom on an even keel through the difficult years after Bodenwein's death. *The Day*

Right, *The Day* pioneered urban renewal, as it tore down buildings behind it on North Bank Street for its addition in 1960. *The Day*

Left, Elizabeth Bodenwein Mil turns the first shovelful of soil for the *Day's* first building addition in more than 30 years in 1960. Earle Stamm is at far left. *The Day*

> *"the corruption-breeding curtain of secrecy behind which so many tax frauds were spawned." The third takes a sweeping crack at congress and "the nonsense that goes to make up a congressman's oratorical stock in trade." The fourth indicates the main campaign issue is "Trumanism," which you seem to define as "corruption, fixing and favoritism." Maybe your editorial writers are suffering from ulcers.*

In the early 1950s, the directors had decided it was time to begin augmenting its staff. It reached again beyond its territory to recruit experienced reporters. Paul Walcott, 52, was hired as a reporter and editor November 11, 1951. He had been an overseas correspondent for The Associated Press and was the editor and owned a part interest in the Greenfield, Massachusetts, *Recorder-Gazette*.

Ryan redesigned the editorial page in 1953. He removed the masthead, the listing of information about the staff and newspaper operation that had always appeared at the top of the editorial column. The newspaper introduced a new column by Jane Eads, an Associated Press writer, to provide a woman's viewpoint on national affairs. It added more letters to the editor and began running guest editorials from other newspapers.

Colby, who was a stickler for precision in language, established rules of style in 1955. Colby explained the changes in the "Tattler" on March 12:

> *In essence, the aim of any publication is to be read and to any degree that it can make this easier, it believes it and its readers benefit. That's the basic philosophy of any set of rules pertaining to what to write and how to write it. And it is the* Day's *belief that the alterations effective today along this line will produce an improved newspaper for its readers.*

The trustees looked upon these changes approvingly. They continued to oversee the running of the newspaper, but gave Colby increasing room to manage *The Day*. His authority expanded even more after his father-in-law, Orvin Andrews, had a serious heart attack in June 1951 and Colby gained a dominant hand in setting policy, although Earle Stamm presided over the board of directors. A new vacancy opened May 16, 1953, when Waldo E. Clarke, a trustee since Charles Smiddy's death in 1950, died of a heart attack. The directors reached again into the business community to replace him, electing Charles R. Sortor, 51, a New London automobile dealer.

Clarke, 71, had been found dead in a bedroom chair at the home of his son-in-law and daughter, Dr. Carl H. Wies and Alma Wies. He had been working in the garden earlier in the afternoon. Clarke had been engaged in his latest industrial crusade at the time of his death, the effort to bring a steel mill to the region. The State Pier, which he had helped build and had managed for more than forty years, was closed for a day in his honor. *The Day* wrote in its lead editorial, "Few men indeed have been as inspiring of their own time, abilities and efforts on behalf of their fellow citizens as Waldo E. Clarke." John E. Kelly, an industrial consultant based in Washington, wrote:

> *Certainly few among the living have done more than Waldo Clarke to build New London and the Thames Valley, and the roster of those plants and educational institutions whose selection of eastern Connecticut was due in large part to Waldo Clarke's efforts is an impressive one.*

Clarke had shaped New London as few others had, bringing to the city important industries and institutions. A less known fact is that he also helped shape the purpose and character of *The Day* as an associate of Theodore Bodenwein in political and civic undertakings over a period of nearly 40 years. Bodenwein had shared the view of Clarke and the local Chamber of Commerce that the key to the region's future would be the ocean pier. New London, they had believed, would someday become a leading world shipping port, connected by sea to Europe and Asia and by rail to Canada and the Middle West.

Clarke and Bodenwein had shared a belief in three issues—developing New London as a major shipping port, preserving the city-manager form of government, and regionalism that would establish a "Greater New London." These, along with the preservation of Ocean Beach Park as it was conceived and developed in 1938 and 1939, were sacred to *The Day*.

The *Day's* adherence to these beliefs was made evident in 1955 when Dr. C. John Satti, the *Day's* political nemesis, mounted a new campaign to change the government structure he despised. Satti's target this time was Section 146 of the City Charter, which prohibited political officers from holding appointive positions in the government. This was the rule that Thomas E. Troland, as law director, had invoked in an attempt in 1939 to drive Satti off the Ocean Beach Park Board. Satti and his party had a long and ardent interest in holding positions of influence on such boards, where there were opportunities for distributing political favors and gaining an equitable position for the party's working-class constituency. This interest was heightened in the 1950s as the city began to examine forming a new government agency to redevelop older parts of the city. Satti and other Democratic leaders wanted to be sure to be in on the ground floor of such a powerful government commission.

Satti had state Senator Duane Lockhard, a Democrat and Connecticut College professor, introduce a bill in the legislature to remove the Section 146 restriction. The legislature had passed a similar measure two years earlier, but the Republican governor in office at the time, John Lodge, vetoed the measure.

But now Abraham A. Ribicoff, a Democrat, was governor, and Satti took advantage of the improved circumstances to try again.

For the board of *The Day*, this amounted to a declaration of war. The move by the Satti Democrats drove Colonel Troland into a heightened level of military readiness. For Troland, more so than any of the others on the board, the charter was sacrosanct, second in importance perhaps only to the Ten Commandments. He could not let the Democrats undermine the government in this fashion. Nor would *The Day*. The newspaper opened fire just days before a public hearing on the bill at City Hall in editorials at the top of the front page. The first of these got immediately to the point. "*The Day* is unalterably opposed to the proposition that more politics in New London's council-manager form of government will result in better government." It went on:

> ...The Day *is strongly opposed to tinkering with Section 146. The tinkering would give the politicians a foot in the door. After the manner of politicians, they'd soon be inside. Changing this section would mean they would have "influence"—to say the least—on appointments to city boards, etc., non-paying positions but posts that nevertheless have much influence over government.*

Before long, the editorial continued, all the boards would be stacked with political hangers-on. Imagine what it would be like, it asked the readers, to have to do business before such boards. The citizens would have to see the ward bosses first, get their approvals, pay them their respects if not more. The ward boss would pass each request up the ladder to "Mr. Big," presumably Dr. Satti. In the second barrage entitled, "Do you want this?" that appeared on the evening of the hearing, *The Day* warned that the change would undermine non-partisan government in the city forever. "Non-partisan government is the coming thing, yet New London is asked to take a backward step by amending its charter to permit more rather than less political maneuvering." *The Day* urged people to turn out for the hearing and denounce the change. If they didn't feel like making speeches, they could just register their disapproval and sit down.

A. A. Washton, a lawyer and one of Satti's favorites, led off at the hearing with an animated attack on *The Day*. Just what does the newspaper mean about keeping politics out of government, he demanded to know. The charter itself was a political document, wasn't it? Wasn't Theodore Bodenwein politically motivated? There has to be control somewhere, he said. At least with party control, there was responsibility, he argued. The parties have to answer to the people. Satti rose and argued that the very opposition to the change was politically contrived. He contended that Governor John Lodge had vetoed the bill two years before after several political leaders from the other party "got to him." However, on balance, only eleven speakers favored the change. Thirty-three, including downtown business leaders Ezekiel Spitz and A. A. Camassar, spoke against the bill. Satti, knowing defeat when he saw it, instructed Lockhard to withdraw the measure. The senator did so, but first took a final shot at *The Day* for poisoning the public's view of politicians.

The Day had recovered its old spunkiness. The newspaper also went on the offensive against a move by business interests to rezone property surrounding Ocean Beach Park for hotels and other commercial uses. Troland led that charge as well from his seat on the board. And when the city began discussing a serious downtown-parking problem, reporter Paul Walcott was assigned to investigate the issue. The newspaper published his report on October 1, 1954, along with a front-page editorial calling for the use of eminent domain to acquire property for parking. It declared, "The time to lick the parking problem is NOW—before New London withers on the vine." *The Day* noted that New London's future was closely tied to the success of its downtown retail district. The city had little room for manufacturing and needed to preserve its preeminence as a commercial center for southeastern Connecticut, a trading area with more than one hundred thousand consumers. "If New London's business area goes to seed now, the merchants will no longer be able to carry the tax load they do now. They'll move out or close down. And what about their workers who will lose their jobs? And who will take over the city's tax burden? Those property owners who remain, including small homeowners, including YOU."

NEW BLOOD AND A policy of change had animated the newspaper. But the *Day's* renewed vitality and adventurous spirit had financial causes, too. An explosion of consumer spending after the Korean War created a bountiful advertising market. Advertisements for consumer goods such as cars and appliances helped push the *Day's* revenues to a record level by 1955. Colman Street, until recently a quiet country road, became a busy strip of car dealerships as America renewed its love affair with the automobile. The *Day's* advertising revenues increased from $296,489 in 1945, to $762,787 in 1950 to $1.1 million in 1955. The three-fold increase occurred in local, national, and classified advertising.

The *Day's* advertising was not the only thing in southeastern Connecticut that was affected by the automobile. Just as Waldo Clarke had feared, the period after the war saw a movement of business and population into the suburbs, a movement made possible by the automobile and the development of new roads. The little farm towns and fishing villages became suburbs for the region's increasing population. And nowhere was this trend greater than in the town across the Thames River from New London. Groton, which Theodore Bodenwein's family had left in the 1870s to live in the city, was beginning to rival New London as a center of development, with its growing military, industry, and naval presence.

Suburban development created a dilemma for the *Day's* directors. While they were concerned over the damage it could cause to New London, they did not want to lose out on the commercial advantages it offered. Those advantages came into focus in 1952, when a developer for the First National supermarket chain, who was moving up the coast developing suburban shopping centers, reached Groton in 1952. Martin Olson developed the Groton Shopping Plaza, a complex of stores centered on the supermarket, and then built another one in New London, known as the New London Shopping Center. The *Day's* directors may have been hazy in their knowledge of the newspaper industry, but they understood money and what this development meant to a business like *The Day*. As a result, at the same time they were worrying over New London's future in retailing, they began courting readers and businesses in Groton. *The Day* spread a streamer headline labeled "Groton News" across the front of the second section of the newspaper, creating a daily Groton section. It opened a satellite operation in Groton in May 1954, with a news staff, advertising representative, and business office. The outpost was located on North Street, halfway between the Thames River and Long Hill Road, the country route where Olson's shopping center overnight rose on land he had purchased from a local farmer. The move drew the newspaper physically closer to the region's biggest story, which was unfolding on the riverbank where Anton Bodenwein had settled with his family more than eighty years earlier.

TWENTY-ONE

NUCLEAR POWER

If the launching of the atomic submarine Nautilus *is met with the same enthusiasm that accompanied the launchings in 1903 and 1904 of what were then the largest ships in the world, this area is due for excitement Thursday.*

—Arthur Jenkins, *The Day*, January 16, 1954

EARLY IN 1950, WHEN the directors of *The Day* still were preoccupied with Edna Bodenwein's complaints about her dividends and worried about New London's downtown parking problems, the Navy made a decision that would have a tremendous impact on the region. It went ahead with plans to develop a nuclear-powered submarine and decided to build it at the Electric Boat shipyard in Groton, which had been downsizing after having built so many submarines during World War II.

The Cold War dictated that the United States strengthen its naval defenses, particularly in the area of the polar ice cap separating the Soviet Union and North America. Interestingly, New London's connection to the Arctic goes back to the 19th century when its whaling ships were among the first to head toward the North Pole. Conventional submarines, which operated on the surface with diesel engines but were powered underwater by storage batteries, were not able to operate under the ice cap because of their short traveling ranges underwater. Nuclear power offered a way to surmount that obstacle.

The atomic submarine was conceived and promoted by Hyman G. Rickover, a brilliant, eccentric young naval captain. Rickover had intended that the new submarine be built at the Navy's shipyard in Portsmouth, New Hampshire. But when an officer there rejected the proposition, Rickover on the spot turned to the Navy's most prolific submarine builder in Groton for help. A company history related:

> *When the admiral in charge declined, Rickover in his impudent fashion, picked up the admiral's phone and called O. Pomeroy Robinson Jr. (general manager of the EB yard)… "Can you build a hull for an atomic submarine?" he asked him. "Why, sure, sure," Robby replied, "but what the hell do we have to do?" "I don't know myself," said Rickover, "but we'll work it out."*

This was a decision over which neither *The Day* nor the region's leaders had any influence. But it nevertheless capped the efforts of civic leaders, which had begun after the Civil War when they worked to establish shipbuilding and a naval foothold in the form of a modest coaling station on the Thames River. The Groton shipyard subsequently played the leading role in the development of the modern submarine. The diesel engine had been adapted for submarine use in the waters off Groton and New London before World War I. The shipyard had developed improved techniques for welding and had gathered thousands of shipbuilders uniquely skilled in constructing submarine hulls. It had built nearly two hundred submarines. The coaling station had become a major Atlantic submarine base. Together, these installations set the stage for the development of atomic power in southeastern Connecticut.

The Navy's selection of Groton to develop the nuclear submarine transformed the *Day's* territory. Within months, EB hired more than four hundred new engineers and draftsmen. This was more than double the number of ship designers the company employed when its business was at its peak during World War II. Some of the nation's most accomplished engineers moved into southeastern Connecticut to work on the project. The new arrivals included Carleton Shugg, a former deputy commissioner of the Atomic Energy Commission, who became the assistant general manager at Electric Boat and later was promoted to general manager.

Their work was surrounded with secrecy, and several years passed before the magnitude of what was taking place at the shipyard became at all clear to *The Day* and its readers. The only visible evidence of what was going on at the outset was the increasing traffic around the shipyard. But Electric Boat already had begun to recover from its post-war slump with new contracts to build submarines for the Peruvian navy and several experimental diesel submarines for the United States Navy and the new activity was not considered unusual.

As the project progressed, the Navy and Electric Boat alternated a policy of secrecy with a patronizing form of public relations. They invited the press on visits to the local installations and on short trips aboard submarines. The progress at Electric Boat was kept before the public's eyes through harmless press releases and the ceremonies that marked the stages of shipbuilding: keel-laying, launching, sea trials, and commissionings when the ships were formally turned over to the Navy. *The Day* did not attempt to explore the remarkable story systematically. Jim Cunningham, the waterfront reporter, usually handled the routine news. Paul Walcott, the newspaper's most experienced writer, wrote the big stories. Joseph Ryan recalled:

> *EB was the tail wagging the dog as far as the news was concerned. When the company was building the old diesel boats, the military aspect was very pronounced and didn't get much treatment in the press. Not much changed.* The Day *got news releases, and used them based on their news value and space available. There was no effort to develop any sympatico with the company, or solicit information. EB wanted to be left alone.*

One did not have to know what was happening inside the shipyard to appreciate the impact it was having outside the gates. The shipyard's expanding work force settled across the region. A new, well-to-do, and privileged class formed around the Electric Boat payroll. Electric Boat, with a blank check from the Navy to develop the nuclear submarine, offered premium salaries and benefits to attract engineering talent to the project and keep the employees happy under demanding working conditions.

The new arrivals were well educated and generally good neighbors, but they did not talk to their neighbors very much about the work they did. They bought new cars and built houses. Even if they were disposed to talk about their compelling roles, they did not have time to. Tradesmen worked forty-eight-hour weeks and designers worked more than fifty hours a week as pressure grew to meet construction deadlines. Engineers often were required to travel across the country on short notice for indefinite periods of time. The reactor for the first of the submarines was developed on an Idaho desert in a simulated submarine hull and many of the engineers divided their time between the Idaho site and Groton.

The trade union formed at the shipyard after the war, the Metal Trades Council, demanded increased wages and benefits for the skilled tradesmen at the shipyard. They felt they were entitled to the rewards because they worked under difficult conditions and had to master sophisticated new construction techniques to fashion the new submarine hull.

The Cold War brought other changes. The cocoons came off the submarines at the Submarine Base, and the boats resumed their patrols and training maneuvers in the North Atlantic. A 531-foot submarine tender, or mother ship, the *Fulton*, moved into a permanent berth on the north side of the State Pier in New London in 1951. Its crew of twelve hundred submarine mechanics and maintenance workers became a prominent part of the rowdy bar scene along New London's Bank Street. News coverage of the undisciplined conduct of sailors created strains between *The Day* and the Navy. To improve relations, *The Day* and the Chamber of Commerce cooperated in honoring a "Sailor of the Month." Fatal automobile accidents involving sailors at the Submarine Base became both a continuing story and a public issue.

Congress invested fresh resources in the naval laboratory at Fort Trumbull for research into new technology to mask the noise of the submarines and to detect the presence of enemy vessels. The laboratory, which had been run by Columbia University during the war, attracted leading acoustics engineers and scientists. Their number grew to nearly one thousand by the 1950s, as the race with the Soviet Union over submarine warfare technology accelerated. The Naval Underwater Sound Laboratory eventually occupied all of the government property at Fort Trumbull, including the coastal fortification built in 1839. The Electric Boat shipyard, the submarine base, and the naval laboratory formed a triangle of military activity and technology that would drive the region's growth for more than thirty years and permanently change the character and outlook of the area.

The first important news event connected with the development of the new submarine occurred on June 14, 1952. President Harry S Truman traveled to Groton for the keel-laying ceremony for the *Nautilus*, the first of the atomic submarines. A special nine-car train carried Truman and the presidential party to Groton. The train made a brief stop in New London to allow members of the press to disembark onto a boat that took them to the shipyard across the river. *Day* reporter Deane Avery wrote a story about the New London stop where three hundred spectators greeted Truman. The secretaries of the Army and Navy, chairman of the Atomic Energy Commission and Connecticut Governor John Lodge were on board the train for the event, he noted. The train traveled across the river to an old rail yard at Poquonnock Bridge, then to the shipyard along a siding.

The Day reported that an audience of ten thousand gathered in the south yard at Electric Boat for the ceremony. Truman said, "The day that the propellers of this new submarine first bite into the water and drive her forward will be the most momentous day in the field of atomic science since that first flash of light down in the desert seven years ago. Then we knew we had a bomb for war. Now we know we have a working plant for peace." Truman initialed the hull in chalk and Theodore Risch of New London, a veteran welding foreman, burned them into the metal with a welding torch.

Paul Walcott wrote the leading front-page story that day. He not only described the ceremony, but also explained as best he could the principles of atomic propulsion. Walcott's story also alluded to the massive local effort that would go into the submarine:

> *Massed around the president by the hundreds were the mechanics, engineers and draftsmen whose combined skills are to produce this unprecedented craft. Also there were some of the scientists who developed this new and terrible power in which most people stand in as much awe as did primitive man of the sun and fire. There were also top executives of two giant electrical manufacturing firms whose resources are concentrated on making the power plant for this A-Submarine and another to follow.*

It took two more years to build the *Nautilus*. Simultaneously, work proceeded on a second submarine, the *Seawolf*, which was designed to try out a different type of nuclear reactor. The two reactor designs were in competition with one another. *Nautilus* employed a hot water reactor, while the *Seawolf* reactor was to use liquid sodium for cooling. There were plans for two additional submarines, *Skate* and *Triton*, the latter to have two reactors. Announcements of new submarine contracts became a staple of the *Day's* news.

But because of the secrecy, details of the epic drama involved in building these vessels largely escaped the attention of the local populace and *The Day*. Introducing a nuclear reactor into the cramped confines of a submarine was an engineering feat that was entirely unprecedented. The problem of cooling the reactor was daunting. The hull design, ventilation, piping, and electrical systems and instrumentation required for an atomic submarine were vastly different from those in conventional submarines. The designers and tradesmen who worked on the *Nautilus* were, in many respects, heroic inventors.

In addition, operating the new submarines required highly trained and disciplined officers and sailors. Rickover handpicked the officers, who had to meet demanding standards in leadership, technical knowledge, and character. Rickover's idiosyncratic system of interviewing candidates for the nuclear service became legendary. One method he employed to test the responses of an officer was to seat him in a chair in which one leg was shorter than the others.

He selected as the first skipper of the *Nautilus* Commander Eugene Wilkinson, a veteran of submarine service during World War II. Wilkinson and his family rented my grandparents' summer home in the Quaker Hill section of Waterford, across the river from the Submarine Base. Wilkinson made history when the *Nautilus* telegraphed that it was under way on nuclear power for the first time on January 17, 1955.

What was occurring in Groton mirrored a phenomenon that was taking place across the nation as the United States mobilized for the Cold War. Secret military and industrial enclaves formed across the country to build and operate new defenses, just as secret towns formed in the Soviet Union. The inhabitants were privileged. The recruitment for this task benefited southeastern Connecticut with an elite, well-paid new class of citizens as well as a skilled and highly specialized work force. It also helped the region to avoid the effects of a recession that struck the country later in the 1950s.

From the *Day's* standpoint, the new arrivals created a significant group of potential new readers and, consequently, new advertising business—that is, if the newspaper could entice these discriminating, more cosmopolitan arrivals to read it. But the prosperity had a downside, as well. As the effort to develop submarine technology consumed more energy, the region became increasingly reliant upon military industrial spending. Smaller businesses and industries often found it difficult to compete for labor with the defense plant, with its high wages and interesting work.

The pay and benefits of the military industrial complex drove up costs for other businesses, which accelerated the flight of manufacturing that was taking place in the state. But for some time these negative consequences were largely unforeseen and invisible. Nobody felt the slightest apprehension. *The Day* agreed with the general sentiment when the *Nautilus* was christened by First Lady Mamie Eisenhower on January 21, 1954, that only good would come from this marvel of technology.

It snowed heavily the week before the launching, and workers were kept busy clearing the snow from the south yard. But on the day of the ceremony, the temperature rose into the fifties, melting the remaining snow but shrouding the shipyard in fog all morning. *The Day* mobilized practically its entire news staff for the event. That day's edition compared the event to the launchings of the *Minnesota* and the *Dakota*, which had been witnessed by crowds of fifty thousand in 1903 and 1904. The day before the launching, *The Day* published an editorial on its front page urging its readers to mark the occasion by flying American flags. *The Day* declared:

> *The launching of the world's first atom-powered submarine at Groton tomorrow will take place in history alongside such notable achievements as application of steam to railroad travel, the invention of the internal combustion engine, the first airplane flight at Kitty Hawk–perhaps even the invention of the wheel.*

While it stated the event "belonged to Groton," the newspaper pointed out that people in neighboring towns had reason to celebrate. "The men and women who had a hand in building this historic submersible come from all parts of southeastern Connecticut." Westinghouse Electric Corporation, which developed the reactor, passed out press releases to reporters stating that the power plant for the *Nautilus* could provide electricity "indefinitely" for Groton and New London. The company added that the successful adaptation of nuclear power to the submarine "indicates the feasibility of a civilian atomic power plant to produce electricity for home and factory." *The Day* ran a story based on the release under the headline, "Wow! *Nautilus* Engine could Illuminate City." *The Day* said in an editorial the day the *Nautilus* was launched:

> *Groton and Electric Boat Division, as well as other industrial firms involved, the Navy and the scientific wizards who have tamed the atom all rightfully share the acclaim on this occasion. It's no brief flash of fame, either, for their joint efforts have wrought a change in the world that ranks among the weightiest to be contributed during the age in which we live.*

IT WASN'T LONG BEFORE the military and industrial network that took shape in southeastern Connecticut in the early 1950s brought a weighty change to the local landscape in the form of fresh development. Martin Olson purchased the Drosdyk family's pig farm in Groton along U.S. Route 1, the old highway to Boston, to build another of his shopping centers. This created interest in developing commerce along the rest of the road through the rural center of the town. The development gave rise to zoning controversies and the town's rapid growth prompted the town to change its government from the selectmen form of its rural past to a town manager system. All of this was fodder for the new Groton section of *The Day*, alongside expanded news of Cub Scouts and women's clubs in the town.

The Day eagerly embraced the new businesses that sprouted up to serve this bustling defense community. The First National chain supermarket became one of the newspaper's heavy advertisers, joining the growing number of car dealers along Colman Street in New London. These high-volume businesses blossomed upon the landscape and filled the *Day's* coffers. But the development also posed troublesome problems for the managers and directors of the newspaper. The directors worried about competition from the Norwich *Bulletin* for control of this wide-open new territory. The *Bulletin*, with its home turf battered by mill closings, was deeply interested in entering the *Day's* prosperous circulation area in Groton. Constant rumors that the rival newspaper planned to open a Groton office generated lively discussions at *Day* board meetings.

The Day was not yet equipped to go to battle with another newspaper. While it suddenly had more money than it knew how to spend, it had not invested in any significant improvements in nearly thirty years and the results were apparent. Its old, four-unit Hoe press was not equal to the task of increased circulation and larger editions. To launch a significant offensive in Groton, it badly needed room to enlarge and modernize its composing room, where the newspaper was set into type. It needed more space to store newsprint. It required a bigger mailroom. It needed a new press. It settled, for the time being, for adding a fifth unit to the old press in 1956.

The venerable board of directors were by now, prodded by Colby, ready at last to make significant investments in plant and equipment. Colby routinely brought out Theodore Bodenwein's will to persuade them that its provisions made it imperative that they invest in the newspaper. He said:

> *The old conservative board of directors didn't take too kindly to any of this. They had not spent any money on capital investment since Bodenwein in 1928 doubled the size of the building. This was all new to them and they were a little nervous. I said, "This is what Bodenwein wanted us to do." I'd get out the will, which I kept in the files. In those days, I wasn't sure they remembered it. Every time we discussed improvements, I'd say, "It wasn't my idea. It's Bodenwein's idea."*

They had been putting aside $2,000 a month and had built a capital reserve of nearly $300,000. They could pay for substantial improvements in cash, and that's the only way they would consent to make new investments. But the issue had become not whether to invest funds, but how and where to do so. In particular, did it make sense to add to the old building, which had been expanded in every direction and seemed to have little space available to go any further? Should the company look for another site, possibly outside New

London? They seriously discussed that possibility in the 1950s, even though the terms of the will would seem to have prohibited such a move.

But on July 16, 1955, Orvin Andrews and Bar Colby made their position clear when they proposed staying put on Main Street and building an addition, rather than locating a new plant somewhere else. That was the hard way. The plan they proposed was byzantine and problematic. Their plan called for an addition over the existing pressroom, mail room, and garages on a split-level between the second and third floors of the main building. This would become the new composing room. Two existing buildings on North Bank Street, the street behind *The Day*, would be razed, and another addition would be constructed there for paper storage. In a later stage, *The Day* would acquire a building to its south, along North Bank Street, raze it, and build an addition to the pressroom. It bought a lot across the street, the site of the city's old police station, for parking.

The bewildering development plan underscored the strong sentiment on *The Day* to remain in New London despite the manifold difficulties the newspaper and many other businesses faced in the cramped, congested quarters of New London's ancient downtown. The newspaper was hemmed in by decrepit buildings and handicapped by the narrow, congested street serving its loading docks, where newsprint was shipped in and newspapers were dispatched to the various corners of its circulation area. *The Day* struggled for nearly five years to improvise a practical way to expand, employing architects to study and restudy what it could do with the limited space. Meantime, it negotiated—at a distinct disadvantage unfortunately—with the neighboring property owner, Arthur Wilinski, to buy his property for the newspaper's expansion. The *Day's* predicament was duplicated many times over among the property owners and businesses in the city's aging central business district, which helps explain the newspaper's later readiness to support sweeping urban renewal projects as uncritically as it did.

While *The Day* struggled with these problems, its Groton office and two pages of Groton news made up the totality of its Groton strategy. The Groton office added to the *Day's* visibility in the town, but it did not fundamentally change the pedestrian and old-fashioned way the newspaper went about covering the news. The motive for the move was not to revolutionize the *Day's* approach to news but to harvest new advertising revenue and readers before the Norwich *Bulletin* got to them. The *Day's* management pursued its business aims in Groton aggressively. Reporters and newspaper executives went on the speaking circuit before local business and service clubs in the town. *The Day* frequently conducted advertising workshops for businesses. The directors weighed the success of the Groton office in terms of revenue. In the first year, the office took in more than $20,000.

While Andrews and Colby endeavored to enhance the *Day's* appeal in Groton, the news managers worked at cross-purposes. They still regarded the town across the Thames River as the boondocks. New London news was not always necessarily more interesting or important than the news in the towns, but it enjoyed superiority in the eyes of the editors and senior reporters. Their universe was New London. Their attitudes and tastes toward the news were shaped in New London, in their professional contacts and daily visits to watering holes like the Crocker House and Mohican Hotel bars. The leading newsmakers, those who were most frequently mentioned and quoted, were part of New London: City Manager Edward R. Henkle; Marshal Ginther, the executive head of the Chamber of Commerce; and Dr. C. John Satti, the city's leading political power broker. Others as powerful, men like Representative Nelson Brown of Groton, speaker of the State House of Representatives, still were treated as supporting actors.

Henkle was so important a figure at the newspaper that a reporter who did not get along with him was yanked from his beat and replaced. It became standard practice to seek Ginther's spin on practically any city news story. The *Day's* relationship with the hometown Chamber was so cordial that the organization was bold enough to request that the newspaper pay to publish the Chamber newsletter. The directors politely refused, but *The Day* still wrote stories about the contents of the newsletter, "News and Views," every week. Political control in the city went back and forth between the two parties, but Satti was in the middle of it all, controlling the deals, and he was considered by the *Day's* editors and reporters the kingpin of politics for the entire southeastern corner of the state. The Satti family was big news whether it was winning or losing, as in 1956 when Satti's wife, Dorothy, experienced a humiliating defeat at the hands of state Representative Ella T. Grasso in a fight to be the state party's representative on the Democratic National Committee.

While the activity around the city desk was full of drama, the routine in Groton was reminiscent of earlier times, when the town actually was a backwoods. The basic pattern probably was established when George Grout covered the community at the turn of the century, crossing the river every day on the ferry and traveling to the various stops along his beat on a bicycle. Instructions for covering the beat were passed along from one reporter to the next. Groton always was the least of the assignments on the newspaper, and the appearance of a new reporter in town usually meant there had been a series of big changes at *The Day* higher up, as, for example, in 1949, when Bar Colby had been appointed assistant general manager and Jim Watterson had left his beat as City Hall and court reporter to replace him as city editor. Deane Avery then ascended from the Groton beat to a choicer assignment reporting on police, fire, and politics in New London.

Duncan Fraser, who was hired as a replacement in Groton, remembered Avery taking him on the rounds for a week before starting his new assignment in New London. The daily routine, as Fraser remembered it, started at Poppe's General Store on Thames Street, the drop-off spot for news about clubs and fraternal organizations and the place to pick up local gossip. From Poppe's store, the reporter walked to the borough police station to pick up the arrest and accident reports. He drove to the town hall in Poquonnock Bridge, paying visits to Irving J. Poppe, the town clerk, and the irascible first selectman, Charles T. Crandall. He met with the school superintendent, Sylvester B. Butler, who was preoccupied with securing federal grants to build new classrooms for the town's exploding population. He picked up the court dispositions by phone. Several nights a week, he attended town and borough meetings. During the summer, he filled in for vacationing reporters on other beats.

The Groton office carried on in this time-honored routine, although the club news now was hand-delivered to the *Day* office and the messengers often hung around to talk. "The name they gave the [Groton] office is some indication of the attitude toward it," Raymond Rancourt, who had been the first reporter assigned to the new Groton office remembered. "We all called it 'Siberia.'" The addition of reporters did not necessarily improve the depth of the stories, but added to the breadth of the coverage. The biggest stories were the sale of World War II government houses in Poquonnock Bridge, the growth around the new shopping center, and the disappearance of the selectman form of government, which ended the thirty-year regime of Charles Crandall.

The outpost lumbered along without change until February 1958, when the *Day's* worst fears were realized and the Norwich *Bulletin* finally opened its long-rumored Groton office. This put the managers at *The Day* into a state of high alert. At the directors' meeting that month, Colby presented the board with a plan to counter the threat and "identify more fully *The Day* in and with Groton." Part of the strategy, to enlarge the Groton section and conduct circulation and advertising promotions, awaited the completion of the elusive addition to the New London building. The managers also proposed a public relations campaign, including a series of dinner meetings with local leaders.

They also considered investing *Day* funds in a local bank as a good-will gesture. And they even considered changing the name of the newspaper to *The New London Evening Day and Groton News* but did not.

The Day had already celebrated its anniversary on July 1, 1956, by publishing a forty-page tabloid edition. The company had entertained all the employees and their spouses at a dinner dance at the Mohican Hotel roof garden that night. It produced a half-hour color slide presentation entitled "Dayland," which boosted southeastern Connecticut as an ideal place to live and work. Just as the 50th anniversary edition was Theodore Bodenwein's swan song, the 75th anniversary was Orvin Andrews' last hurrah. He remembered Bodenwein's reflections in 1916:

> *Forty years have passed since the day when Mr. Bodenwein wondered about the future of* The Day *and hoped for its continuance. It is a better newspaper—carrying more news and advertising, having doubled the circulation of those days, employing a far larger number of persons and proving a profitable venture in spite of ever increasing costs and higher taxes.*

Andrews was 66, a year older than Bodenwein had been when *The Day* marked its 50th anniversary. Just as Bodenwein by that time in his life had turned over much of the authority to Andrews, Andrews had relegated most of the control to his son-in-law, Bar Colby. Andrews wrote in his "Sentences by the Judge" column on the Saturday before the *Day's* anniversary:

> *Those who are employed by* The Day *over the next 25 years are going to witness undreamed of changes in the methods of operation—due to greater knowledge in photography, electronics and atomic power.*

But, characteristically, he added that despite all the changes, *The Day* had made no radical changes in the way it gathered and presented the news. "The same steps are still necessary to produce your good evening newspaper."

Bar Colby actually disagreed. In 1957, he began making significant changes in the operation of the newspaper. With the board's consent, he orchestrated a shakeup of the newspaper's management. He pushed George Clapp, the last of Bodenwein's news managers, upstairs, appointing him editor of the newspaper. This reduced Clapp's responsibilities to writing editorials and removed the operation of the newsroom from his control.

Joe Ryan, then the assistant managing editor, saw the handwriting on the wall and left *The Day* that year. Ryan sensed the growing hold the "family" had on the newspaper. "I got the impression that the newspaper was pretty wired and there wasn't any place for me to go," he remembered. *The Day*, then, was under the control of a close-knit group of relatives and friends concentrated around Orvin Andrews and his son-in-law, Bar Colby. In the changes, Colby made Deane Avery, brother of his best friend, Latham Avery, managing editor. Kenneth Grube was appointed an assistant editor, assuming copy-editing duties and taking charge of the newspaper on Saturdays. The changes were delayed for several months because of difficulties encountered in hiring a reporter to replace Grube. To hasten the changes, the directors agreed to a recommendation by Colby to increase the wages for the position.

Colby, as secretary of the board and assistant general manager, pushed on with his campaign to improve the newspaper. In the 1950s, newspapers in the United States combined their resources to form a press-training center at Columbia University, the American Press Institute. Colby persuaded the directors to support the organization and send *Day* employees there. *The Day* was a charter member and sent newspaper executives to the institute from its outset. *The Day* was among the smallest newspapers in the nation to take part in the creation of API. The first employees from the newspaper to attend the institute were Jim Watterson, the city editor, and Raymond Bracci, the circulation manager. This was the first formal professional training at *The Day*, as well as one of the newspaper's first out-of-town junkets for its employees.

On September 19, 1959, Orvin Andrews announced to the board his intention to retire as general manager the following month. At the same time, he announced that title to the Wilinski property next to *The Day* finally had changed hands after four years of haggling and the plan for the addition was going forward. Andrews stayed on the board, both as a director and president of The Day Publishing Company. At an earlier meeting, the board had agreed upon a salary increase, to $17,500 for Andrews. He received a pension of $7,500 a year.

Orvin Andrews had worked forty-five years for *The Day*. Theodore Bodenwein hired him near the outbreak of World War I as an advertising solicitor. In that role, he developed a modern advertising department for *The Day*, hiring a staff and training both employees and advertisers in the art of using the newspaper to promote business. In the beginning, Andrews' pay was so low he had to work in a second job as a shoe salesman to support himself and his family. But Theodore Bodenwein quickly formed a respect for him, and placed him in charge of the newspaper business as general manager. Andrews had hired his daughter, Ruth, to work in the business office, and there she had met Bar Colby, a greenhorn reporter. The two had been married in the 1930s.

Andrews, with help from the newspaper's lawyer and trustee, Charles

Smiddy, led the battle to carry out Theodore Bodewein's will. Gordon Bodenwein charged that Andrews took part in a conspiracy to disinherit the Bodenwein children of the newspaper, but that issue was left unresolved when the directors reached an out-of-court settlement with Gordon. Orvin Andrews carried out the terms of the will, but also made sure his son-in-law and not Gordon Bodenwein would take over the newspaper after he stepped down.

Andrews, in many respects, imitated Theodore Bodenwein. He remained aloof, and some felt he was unfriendly. But he continued the paternalism Bodenwein had begun toward "*The Day* family." At his insistence, the directors continued to lend money to employees, care for their needs when they were sick, and maintain competitive wage scales. When compositor Thomas Elliott was wooed by a rival newspaper in 1957, the directors, at Andrews' suggestion, promoted him to composing room foreman and created a new position for the existing foreman, Walter Crighton. Andrews also persuaded the directors to overhaul the entire wage structure of the newsroom to make it more competitive. His severe countenance, which earned him the name "Judge," belied both a wry sense of humor and deep compassion. Andrews was remembered as one who tried to find other jobs for job-seekers during the Great Depression if nothing was available at *The Day*. If anyone, it was Orvin Andrews to whom Bodenwein entrusted *The Day*. Andrews was loyal, loved *The Day*, appreciated Bodenwein's goals for the newspaper, and was practical and professional in his management of the newspaper. Andrews ran the newspaper from 1939 to 1959, trying to conciliate the heirs and build *The Day* into the kind of newspaper Bodenwein called for in his will. The *Day's* editorial on the occasion of his retirement stated:

> *Sizing up his service—evaluating it—can be a very difficult task. It means, for instance, that employees who have known him for years suddenly review their association with him and realize that he has been an exceptional boss in many respects. It's but part of it to say he's been a fair man to deal with, that he always seemed to have an inexhaustible source of patience and that he has shown a feet-on-the-ground characteristic when sudden difficulties have surfaced.*

TWENTY-TWO

Change Knocks

It was the end of a wonderful period, before the city was turned upside down. It was the last we'd see of the old New London, the place where I grew up.

—John Foley on his early years at *The Day* in the 1960s

WHEN ORVIN ANDREWS RETIRED as general manager in the fall of 1959, *The Day* plant still looked much the way it had for decades despite the directors' fitful efforts to modernize in the 1950s. Were he to return at that time, Theodore Bodenwein would have had no difficulty recognizing the old building inside and out and the neighborhood around it. He would have noticed the newspaper was struggling to get by with the press he had purchased in the 1920s, and he would have been troubled by the newspaper's failure to keep up with the times. He would have noticed the rundown condition along the streets around the newspaper, but also would have appreciated the vitality that still existed there and the strong sense of tradition that survived at his newspaper. He might have recognized some of the people who had worked for him, though they had aged by more than twenty years.

The newsroom hadn't been remodeled significantly since it had opened in 1928 and still had the look and feel of the 1930s when Bodenwein had died. Tobacco smoke created a thin haze in the room. There was still no passenger elevator. The office was crowded and cluttered. It was noisy from the racket of manual typewriters, phones ringing, and general human commotion, which resonated off the plaster and wood walls and ceilings at peak hours before the

2 pm deadline. Dusty, old-fashioned light fixtures hung from the ceiling. Water pipes and iron radiators were exposed. An unsightly overhead conveyor belt that looked like an elaborate clothesline noisily carried edited and rolled up stories to the composing room on the fourth floor. Ashtrays, glue pots, and heaps of paper littered the desks. Each reporter had a Royal typewriter bolted to a steel tray on one side of the desk that could be folded back on spring hinges and slid into a compartment, a modern innovation introduced when the directors adopted Duncan Fraser's plan for reorganizing the newsroom and took the radical step of buying new desks. However, most of the reporters used this space to keep old newspapers and personal belongings. Fastened to the other end of the desk was a rotary-dial telephone with headsets.

Nobody realized it then, but *The Day* was in the twilight of an age of printing technology that had begun with Johann Gutenberg's invention of movable type in the 15th century. Within the next three decades, computers would displace the skilled printers who set type with machines. Electronic imaging would make paper largely unnecessary in writing and editing stories and foretell the day when editors would dispatch whole made-up pages from their computers to the pressroom. The new technology would have no noise, no odor.

But the future had not yet entered the *Day's* consciousness. Paper was piled everywhere. On top of the desks were sharp metal spikes, where reporters impaled their notes and the copy desk stored stories ready to be edited. These fixtures, symbols of their time, were usually stuffed high with unruly-looking piles of copy paper, old news releases, and newspaper clippings. Copies of recent editions were spread across a counter in one corner, held together by cumbersome steel binders with sharp spikes. Stationed nearby in the newsroom was Phyllis Bankel, who was hired to replace George Grout as librarian in 1951 after Grout's death. Bankel pored over every page of the daily editions, as Grout had begun to do in 1929, circling every name and topic, and then typing the entries on three-by-five index cards to be filed in alphabetical order. Each entry included the topic, the gist of the story, and the date of publication, page and column. There was no more painstaking a job at *The Day*, nor one more unappreciated or important. In all its history, *The Day* has had only four librarians to map the daily editions for future explorers of history.

Reporters kept notes and typed their stories on 8.5-by-11-inch sheets of newsprint. The writers cut and pasted their stories together from pieces of this cheap material, of which *The Day* seemed to have an endless supply. The reporters carried the finished products, untidy and sometimes long enough when fully extended to touch the floor, to the editors' desks and deposited them on spikes. In most newspapers, the process of typing an insert or cutting off a story at the end was performed with scissors. But in 1949, John DeGange, the sports editor, invented a "shear bar," which enabled the writers to cut off copy paper neatly and efficiently with one swift motion of the hand as it was yanked from the typewriter. The invention was merely a strip of steel strap from paper bales. It was fastened with machine screws to the moving carriage of the typewriter just over the roller. Editors used it when they wrote headlines and sent them to the composing room to be set. It even facilitated interoffice communication. Bar Colby and his successors dashed off notes to editors and reporters on sheets of copy paper that were neatly ripped from their executive typewriters with the assistance of John DeGange's shear bar. Dyspeptic notes, complimentary messages regarding stories, insistent questions, all on familiar-looking little strips of copy paper folded neatly and placed in used envelopes. The staff knew when these appeared on their desks that they either were about to be humiliated or exalted with praise from above. DeGange patented his device and offered it for sale to various other firms, including the Burroughs Adding Machine Company.

The desks were rearranged to improve efficiency and college graduates from other parts of the country began to appear in the newsroom in greater numbers. But the "old New London" order still had a commanding influence. Bulkeley School and Chapman Technical High School, though they had closed in the early 1950s when New London had opened its own public high school, remained a defining experience in New London's culture. Their influence survived at *The Day* as it did throughout the city, where generations were shaped by their classical instructors and athletics. Judge Thomas E. Troland, who was a *Day* trustee and director, reminisced at board meetings about the days when the Bulkeley teams "strove mightily" against scholastic adversaries.

While Deane Avery was the managing editor, Jim Watterson, Bulkeley '29, ran the city desk, the nerve center of the newspaper, with dictatorial authority. The staff lived in trepidation of the irascible editor, still a handsome and athletic man who had played both baseball and football in high school. No questions were asked when he sent reporters out in the morning to bring him several cans of beer from Gordon's Package Store on Main Street, nor did his taste for saloon life diminish the respect that was held for him. Bringing back booze to the newsroom and visiting saloons were part of a long tradition at the newspaper. So was getting names right. Watterson obsessively challenged the spelling of every name in a story that did not look right, ordering the writer to look it up in the city directory. He had been at *The Day* nearly thirty years by

1959 and seemed to know practically everyone in the city, as well as the proper spelling of each name. This extensive personal knowledge of the community was shared and valued by most of the senior reporters and editors.

It surprised no one when Colby, Chapman Tech '29, was appointed to replace his father-in-law as general manager on October 2, 1959, the day Andrews retired. Colby's salary was advanced to $14,000 a year. Colby had been a director since April 18, 1959, and secretary of The Day Publishing Company since 1950. He had essentially managed the newspaper. Announcements and edicts about the newspaper had for some time contained both Colby's and Andrews' initials, "OGA per blc," indicating the degree to which Colby was running things. But the elders, consisting of Andrews, Troland, Earle Stamm, and Charles Sortor were not ready quite yet to name a publisher. There still was nobody on the board, including Bar Colby, bold enough to make such a radical move.

The Day had grown after the war, but was still small. There were only about a dozen reporters, counting the ones in Groton. Some stood out over others. One who already was on the way up was Bob Craigue, 34. Craigue was serious and methodical. He was a 1949 graduate of the University of Missouri School of Journalism and had been an Army officer during the Korean War. These credentials and his solicitude toward his superiors helped him to rise quickly in the newsroom hierarchy until 1967, when he abandoned his wife and children and ran away with the *Day's* 24-year-old society page writer, Gina Muzzi.

John Foley, 27 in 1960, and David Carlson, 25, would stay longer and rise higher in the organization. They were among the most capable reporters and advanced quickly. The two developed a close friendship and became the newsroom cut-ups. They thrived in New London's barroom culture. They were both natives. Carlson had grown up in Groton, Foley in New London. They met at Mitchell College, the successor to the junior college Waldo Clarke had helped establish in the city. Both had served in the military, Carlson in the Navy, Foley in the Coast Guard. Foley was a graduate of New London's new public high school, but he could still claim a Bulkeley lineage, having enrolled there before the school went out of existence.

Males still dominated the newsroom, but women were starting to gain a foothold. Evelyn Archer had been secretary at the naval sonar laboratory at Fort Trumbull when she was hired as the writer for the social page. A tough-talking and dogged journalist who could out-drink some of her male peers, she later became the military writer, a tough job involving dealing with unions and closed-mouthed defense industry executives. In the late 1950s, *The Day* hired another woman, Suzanne "Suzie" Cole, to write feature stories. Colby had liked feature writing himself and emphasized it at the newspaper. The newspaper discouraged turning routine news stories into something they weren't, but frequently ran short "brights" based on the news, which offered reporters a chance to be clever. These were signaled typographically by headlines with borders around them. For example, when the Navy announced that it was going to name its new class of missile submarines after famous Americans in history, the newspaper ran a story in this format that began, "It won't be long before George Washington and Patrick Henry join the local submarine fleet."

The Day also enlarged its offerings of columns written by staff members beyond Andrews' turgid and increasingly irrelevant "Sentences of the Judge," which he continued to write from his retirement home in Fort Lauderdale, Florida, until his death in 1973. Curt Pierson started a political column called "The Political Pitch." Reporter Arthur Jenkins wrote a fishing column called "Biting Comments." Margaret Stacy, a proofreader, wrote elegant historical articles, noting, among other things, the effects of road building and other changes that were taking place on the region's historic landscape.

Ken Grube, who worked at the Greenwich *Time* when Clapp hired him in 1957 and had ten years' experience on New York and Connecticut newspapers, emerged as the *Day's* star reporter. He had the additional title of assistant city editor and was in charge of the city desk on Saturdays. Grube was naturally curious and got along with everyone, regardless of social station. He liked people and luxuriated in the populist atmosphere of the saloons around *The Day*. He was not a native of the city, but he absorbed its history and culture, and learned the intricacies of the *Day's* history better than some of the older staff.

John DeGange, Chapman Tech '24, was responsible for sports coverage, but doubled as the Groton editor in New London even after the Groton office opened. In this role, he trained new reporters. He was demanding, but patient, and liked by the reporters. Duncan Fraser, whom DeGange trained, wrote:

> *John was a crackerjack newspaperman, and, if he thought his successive pupils were capable of learning the craft, he took pains to be a good teacher. He ran a hard school and wasn't easily satisfied. If the meaning wasn't crystal clear in a story I put on the spindle on his desk, or if I had buried a lead or committed any other journalistic sin, John made me write the story over. And over again, until it satisfied him and until I had learned thoroughly the right way to do it.*

DeGange prepared a training exercise for copy editors that underscored the *Day's* conservative policies on writing:

> *This is your first day as a copy editor for a conservative newspaper that strives for pure, but simple English, concise, crisp, exact, logical. It prefers short words to long ones, proper usage to common usage, Anglo Saxon words to foreign imports. But only if they will do a better, more precise job.*

He also established himself as an authority on the Yale-Harvard crew regatta, which he had reported on for *The Day* almost since he arrived in the 1920s.

The daily news staples of *The Day* were politics, traffic accidents, and crime. While the political writers ventured to the state Capitol occasionally and started to report more on the unfamiliar politics in the region outside New London, they understood New London best and concentrated their attention there. This was before the press assumed a more critical posture toward politics in the 1970s. It was also before freedom of information laws. Political reporters like Pierson, and later Foley and Carlson, depended solely on their resourcefulness as reporters and cordial relations with politicians to ferret out the news. This meant, among other things, drinking until late at night with politicians at the Kozy Korner, a bar and restaurant on Truman Street, where the City Council gathered after its meetings.

The *Day's* political coverage dwelt on the machinations of the Satti Democratic organization, which in 1960 still had formidable power although Republicans controlled the City Council by one vote. The Republicans had gained power during the Eisenhower administration, but still had to do business with Dr. C. John Satti and his lieutenants, attorney A. A. Washton and Anthony Facas, to secure advantages from the government and divide political spoils.

This accommodation between the two parties grew with a change in Republican leadership. In 1956, Angelo G. Santaniello, the law partner of one of Satti's sons, seized control of the Republican Party from the old guard in the city's first primary. Santaniello, who practiced law with C. Robert Satti in an office at 40 Washington Street, was part of a crop of postwar politicians in New London who rose to prominence in the 1950s and 1960s and consorted with one another over the city's business. Charming and clever, Santaniello made friends throughout the city. He was known to everyone simply as Angie, even after he became a State Supreme Court Associate Justice in the 1980s.

Another in this group was Harvey N. Mallove, a Democrat and the son of Morris Mallove, a New London businessman and leader in the city's Jewish community. These younger politicians, many of whom had been servicemen during the war and in many cases were Bulkeley boys, formed a new power structure that looked after the city's business interests, which were often intertwined with their own. Their dealings diminished the significance of party lines and often took place out of public view. They came to rival both the old Democratic families with immigrant backgrounds who gained power with Satti's ascent in the 1930s and the old Yankees whose influence in the Republican Party dated back to Bodenwein's time. The *Day's* political reporters found these men friendly and accessible and formed close bonds with them.

The newspaper cultivated a friendly and, by later standards, respectful rapport with the police as well. *The Day* ran a story about each fresh recruit and kept an up-to-date file of photographs, or "head shots," of all the local police and state troopers. These were stored on zinc plates on which the pictures were photoengraved. Whenever the opportunity presented itself, *The Day* ran pictures of police who played parts in solving crimes or had just been promoted. The newspaper also maintained cordial relations with the police by printing flattering feature stories.

The newspaper also kept a file of photos of naval officers, whose pictures appeared frequently in the newspaper. These portraits of unsmiling men in uniform looking straight at the camera became a familiar part of the daily appearance of *The Day*, adding to its generally dreary and cluttered appearance.

The Day presented a view of the world largely through the prism of the police and the political leadership with whom reporters hobnobbed after hours. It was an interesting world filled with everyday drama. The police reporter sat through daily sessions of the police court and related stories about the colorful parade of humanity that passed through that chamber, stories that would barely interest today's newspaper editors. John Blotsky, 44, was a regular character in this drama. Blotsky both drank a great deal of cheap booze and had a chronic disrespect for authority. On September 28, 1960, he was the subject of a three-column story in *The Day* for having raised havoc in the police court the previous afternoon. This was nothing new for him, but always a matter of great interest and concern to the police and *The Day*. Blotsky started out by shouting obscenities to a reporter in the lobby outside the courtroom. He then burst into the court and created a commotion. The judge ordered the sheriffs to bring Blotsky before him and cited him for contempt. Later Blotsky invaded the office of attorney Griswold Morgan, nephew of Curtis Morgan, Gordon Bodenwein's lawyer in *The Day* case, and threatened him. *The Day* reported that Blotsky was sentenced to one hundred twenty days in jail for these offenses. Through his exposure in *The Day*, Blotsky, who otherwise would have died anonymously, became a well-known and colorful figure.

One of the most sensational crime stories in the 1950s was about Annie M. Sadd, 50, who dragged the dead body of her two-hundred-fifty-pound boyfriend downstairs and outside after he succumbed to a heart attack at her summer retreat in February 1955. She fastened the body to the bumper of her car with a piece of clothesline and dragged it seven miles to a secluded spot near a lake, leaving a trail of blood and torn flesh. Mrs. Sadd, whose husband was 90, said she panicked after she couldn't revive her companion. Reporter Seymour Katz wrote of how the one-hundred-twenty-pound woman used "terror strength" to move the body outside. *The Day* ran a picture of Resident State Trooper Leland Cable, who got the credit for solving the mystery.

Time had stood still throughout *The Day*, as it had to some degree in New London. The composing room, where the pages of the newspaper were organized and prepared for the press, was using technology that had not advanced significantly since Linotype machines displaced the Irish women who had set type by hand in the 1890s. Basically the same machinery was at work in the same place on the fourth floor of the newspaper where the paper's original typesetting machines had been hoisted by block and tackle when *The Day* moved from Bank Street to Main Street in 1907. One of the printers, Dan Donovan, was the son of one of the early women printers at *The Day*.

The Linotype machine had been a wonder of printing engineering in its time, a marvel of intricacy. It tripled the speed of setting type from the manual method. Linotype operators worked at keyboards similar to typewriters, but unlike typewriters, these formidable machines towered over the operators. The machines filled the composing room with the racket of the clattering metal machinery and the odor of molten lead.

As the printers typed at the keyboard, the Linotype machines released movable brass type into a mold for each line of type that would appear in the newspaper. The machines squirted molten lead into the molds. The molten lead lines of type were cooled and pushed into a tray one after another. Another printer carried the loose lines of type, or galley, to a "dump bank," or galley, where burs of metal were trimmed off, patented ink was rolled over the lead type and a copy of the story was created for the proofreaders. The corrected proof was returned to another Linotype operator, who typed corrected lines. Another printer replaced the lines containing errors with the corrected lines, reading the mirror-image lead-cast copy upside down. Some of the *Day's* printers were legendary for their speed and accuracy. Bill Campbell, who was hired in the 1920s, was so fast the machine slowed him down. The machines could set seven lines a minute, Campbell could have set more than that, but he had to wait for the machine to catch up with him. In the 1960s, *The Day* introduced several machines on which printers typed stories onto punch tape, which was fed into new, automated Linotype machines, and set type at a higher rate of speed. Only then were the machines able to equal Campbell's speed.

The stories that had been set in type went to makeup men, who laid them out on metallic trays, or chases. These rested on movable carts, which were called turtles. The printers filled the pages with the molded lead type. An editor stood by as the printer placed the lead-cast stories and headlines into place. Headlines were set by hand until the 1950s, when *The Day* introduced machines to do this. Photographs were transferred onto metal "cuts" by a process of photoengraving. This work was performed by printers under the supervision of Leo Lonergan, a commercial engraver, who rented space from *The Day* on the third floor. Until after World War II, Lonergan had been in charge of the photographers and did all the *Day's* photographic developing.

An editor usually determined where to cut stories to make them fit into the available space. But the printer was in charge of laying out the inside pages of the newspaper. The printers were craftsmen who fashioned each page with the advantage of skills that took years to master, and they had enormous pride in their workmanship. Apprentices spent six years learning the trade before they became journeymen printers. Their training engaged them in each facet of the complex process of printing the newspaper. Although there was occasional friction, their authority was unquestioned. They frequently alerted the editors to errors, not to mention perceived stupidity in the content of stories.

The work was difficult and hazardous. There was so much machinery in motion that printers were frequently injured. The workers inhaled lead vapor, a presence they treated so casually that many rested lunch sandwiches on the pots where the lead was melted. The composing room was stifling in the summer because there was no air conditioning and the machines and lead pots gave off tremendous heat. The pace and deadline pressure were intense and stressful. Yet young men in New London coveted these jobs, which provided both unusual job security and pride in workmanship. Paul Libera, who started work as a printer apprentice in 1967, remembered what attracted him to the work, "It was a craft. Not everyone could sit down and do that stuff." Robert J. Donovan, the composing room foreman from 1979 to 1988, recalled a great influx of young printers in the 1960s:

> *Being a printer at* The Day *was a very promising career.* The Day *had a reputation for growing and not laying off people. Turnover was minimal, especially in the mechanical departments.*

Stereotypers pressed fiberboard impressions from the metal pages. These were used as molds for lead castings that went onto the press. The castings transferred the relief images of the pages onto rolls of paper that flowed at a high speed in continuous webs through the cylinders of the press.

Producing the newspaper depended not only on the efficiency of the machinery, but also on the cooperation of editors, printers, and press operators. The human collaboration was particularly critical in the late 1950s and early 1960s when the old machinery Bodenwein had bought had reached its limits and required enormous resourcefulness to meet the expanding needs of the newspaper. The *Day* managers needed additional press capacity to produce larger newspapers and meet greater circulation demands. The more than 30-year-old Hoe Company letterpress, which Bodenwein had bought for $75,000, was pushed to its limits by doubling up and attaching plates of the same pages next to each other. In the early 1960s, the old-time printers reached the height of their importance at *The Day*. There were more than fifty printers in the composing room to meet the augmented demands to print more advertisements, more pages, and more copies.

The daily work created a close camaraderie among the crafts in the newspaper, including the writers and editors. Workers from the editorial and production departments came into contact with each other regularly. As deadlines approached, editors assisted the printers in the composing room. The printers in the composing room delivered the mats to the pressroom, and also helped cast the metal plates that were fastened to the press.

After the newspaper went to press in the afternoon, the relationship spilled over into the little bars and restaurants that surrounded *The Day*—Danny Doyle's, Dudeens, Hammy's, and Skrigan's. The surroundings mirrored the newspaper in their reassuring familiarity. *The Day* had been at the same spot for more than fifty years and most of the buildings near it had been standing at least that long. A few actually had survived the burning of the city by the British during the Revolutionary War. Gorra's Fruit Market, the city's last open-air fruit and vegetable store, and Beit Brothers supermarket, which Theodore Bodenwein had helped finance and which served the needs of the busy neighborhood, were across the street from *The Day*. The Learned House mission, which cared for generations of the city's disadvantaged children, occupied an old Victorian mansion several blocks north of the newspaper.

From a distance, these buildings formed a quaint and beautiful picture of an old New England city. But up close, many were decaying from old age and neglect. A survey done for the city by real estate agents in 1955 found that sixty percent of the housing in the area along the waterfront was unfit for habitation. Many of the buildings were vacant. Many of the old houses had dirt cellars and were unheated in the winter, musty and decaying. These included the tenement where Theodore Bodenwein had grown up in the 1870s and 1880s. Nonetheless, this section of the city still had a strong pulse. The waterfront continued to be busy. The State Pier produced work for longshoremen, many of whom lived nearby. The district had filled up with immigrant families from Eastern Europe in the early 20th century. They built churches and enriched the city with their customs and their labor. These families were joined by blacks who had migrated north looking for work after World War II and had moved into the worst housing available. Several of the streets had rows of attractive 19th century mansions that had been well maintained, including a line of whaling-era homes called Whale Oil Row.

The neighborhood continued to have a comfortable feeling for the people who worked at *The Day*. The perception was clouded by nostalgia and sometimes the pleasant influence of alcohol that blurred the actual rotting and rat-infested condition of many of the ancient wood-frame buildings. Many successful New Londoners had grown up in the neighborhoods near *The Day* during the Depression and retained favorable memories from that era while forgetting the bad. One of the worst slums in the city in 1960 was located on Stony Hill, which ascended a steep hill away from the water. Roger Dennis, a well-known American impressionist painter, later romanticized the street in a well-known 1968 painting based on a *Day* photograph taken just before the neighborhood was cleared for an urban renewal project.

Main Street, which passed in front of *The Day* building, was lined with rows of shops, bars, and little restaurants as well as a growing number of vacant storefronts. The *Day* workers' favorite retreat after the afternoon deadline was Hammy's, a bar run by Steve Downey and Andrew Hamilton, or Hammy. As in many local watering holes, yellowing pictures of sports figures lined the walls. These pictures of New Londoners who had achieved fame or outsiders like Yogi Berra who had played baseball in the city during World War II reflected the city's strong attachment to sports. Hammy's was dominated by the personality of Downey, who was known for his brutal, irreverent humor. "Downey would always be yelling at someone, usually some insult dealing with someone's nationality and skin color," John Foley, then a 23-year-old reporter, remembered. Nobody took him seriously, for they knew the five-foot-seven, rotund bartender meant no harm. Humor, which would be considered tasteless, insensitive, or politically incorrect in later decades, formed a bond between the races and nationalities that were cramped into the tiny city. Downey's favorite target was Palmerlee Tilton, a venerable bellman at the Mohican Hotel. Tilton, whose skin was deep black and who had a rich bass voice, always sat in the same place, at one end of the bar. A typical exchange between Downey and him:

Downey: You know you're nothing but a no-good, worthless nigger.
Tilton: I'se no nigger. I'se Portuguese.

The *Day* workers spent so much time at Hammy's, the bar became known as The *Day* Annex. Foley remembers being taken there on his first day at work. "They said, 'Come on, we're going to The *Day* Annex.' *Day* Annex? Where the hell was that?" The *Day's* news staff began drinking in the afternoon. That was the norm at *The Day* then. The bulk of the daily work was finished at the 2 pm deadline. The news staff gave little thought to the next day, but instead unwound and socialized over beer and whiskey until the bars in the city closed. The routine, which strained family life and shortened life expectancies, was part of the job. That's how reporters and editors met news sources, picked up political gossip, and stayed in touch with life in the city. Edward R. Henkle, the city manager, could be found at Hammy's playing cards virtually every afternoon, before his secretary, Ella Howard, summoned him back to City Hall for an appointment or merely to exert her storied authority.

Skrigan's was another popular spot among the news staff. The bar was in a decrepit wood frame building behind *The Day* on North Bank Street, the street that previously had been called Bradley Street and had been the site both of the city police station and a red light district. Sam Skrigan, the proprietor, was among the many Russians and Ukrainians who had settled there. Skrigan was a burly Russian who developed enormous strength as a young man delivering ice to homes in East New London and later in life made a lot of money in the stock market. He operated the bar with his wife, Olga, a tall, gentle woman who looked after the *Day* reporters as though they were her own children. Their son, Paul, was a high school teacher. The clientele consisted largely of Eastern Europeans, *Day* workers, and Coast Guard cadets, who had discovered and adopted the bar. When an urban renewal program began tearing down buildings in the neighborhood, Skrigan's was the last building to go.

These were some of the favorite spots, but hardly the only bars the *Day* crew visited. New London had places to drink so numerous one could have spent a career without having visited them all. For more genteel surroundings, the city offered the Crocker House and Mohican Hotel bars on State Street, where the city's business leaders and political elite unwound. Marshal Ginther, the executive vice president of the Chamber of Commerce, could be found at the Mohican bar late in the afternoon imbibing his favorite cocktail, the Manhattan, and holding forth. Both aging hotels were in the terminal stages of their illustrious histories, but the pleasant and reassuring atmosphere of their bars and restaurants lived on for another 15 years.

The city also was filled with social clubs with liquor licenses. Everyone belonged to a club or knew someone who did, entitling him to drink the cheap whiskey and beer there. The Polish Club, Knights of Columbus, Elks, Veterans of Foreign Wars, American Legion, Retired Armed Forces Association, Order of Eagles, and various Italian clubs all offered friendly sanctuaries to meet people, which, more than drinking, was what the barroom culture in the city was all about.

The drinking often did not stop in one establishment. Practitioners of this style of life migrated from one bar to the next to such a degree that a person could meet dozens of people in a night, and hundreds in a week. An evening might start at the Crocker House, continue at the Elks Club, and end up in the last throes of a going-away party for a retiring New London cop. The next afternoon, a story would appear in *The Day* about the cop's heroic career. The city gathered at testimonials at the Knights of Columbus Hall or nationality nights at the Elks Club on Washington Street. There were no class distinctions in these gatherings. The rich and powerful drank with working men. They all knew one another by their first names, or more often, their nicknames, like Lefty, from a distant past in the city's Morgan baseball league, or Duke or Bones, names that probably harked back to Bulkeley or Chapman Tech days. Everyone's life was an interesting story, and these often wound up on the pages of *The Day*, in a retirement story, a feature, or obituary. The city was, to a large degree, like a large family. And the same environment still existed at *The Day*, where the managers, editors, printers, pressmen, office workers, and business staff worked and played together and the company shared the concerns of the staff both on and off the job.

But change was at hand. Early in 1960, work began on the North Bank Street addition to *The Day*. The directors invited Elizabeth Miles, Bodenwein's daughter, to attend the groundbreaking ceremony and gave her the honor of turning over the first shovelfull of dirt. The second, third, fourth, fifth, and sixth shovels were manned by newsboys. The new building would provide larger quarters for the composing room on the second floor, and give the editorial department a modern, more spacious newsroom where the composing room had been.

The two-story building was also built to hold a new press. In anticipation of this, George Kent, the press room foreman, was promoted to a newly created position of mechanical superintendent and building supervisor and was placed in charge of shopping for a new press as well as supervising plans for the space that it would occupy. Colby and the directors had been struggling for several years with the press problem. They had installed a fifth unit to the old press in 1956 to augment its capacity, and when they did that, they added a color unit to meet demands of advertisers.

Still other, bigger developments were in store for North Bank Street, where Bodenwein and other business leaders had once clamored for public improvements. And they were coming, faster and more dramatically than anyone anticipated.

TWENTY-THREE

REDEVELOPMENT

The taxpayers have but to walk many of the streets concerned to realize how outworn their ancient structures are—beyond renovation, scarcely put to one tenth their efficient use.

—*The Day,* September 27, 1961

WHILE *THE DAY* WRESTLED with its needs to expand in the 1950s and prospected for customers in the suburbs, New London placed the familiar old neighborhoods around the newspaper under a microscope and concluded that radical surgery was required. Discussions begun in 1951 led to the idea of a sweeping slum clearance program to make room in the cramped downtown for new buildings, wider streets, and off-street parking. *The Day* needed each of these. The newspaper had to expand its plant to make room for new production machinery and a growing work force. It had purchased an abandoned police station and neighboring lot on North Bank Street behind the *Day* building for parking for its employees, but that was inadequate for its long-range needs. And North Bank Street for years had been too narrow and congested to efficiently service the loading docks, where newsprint arrived in trailer rigs and bundles of newspaper were loaded onto trucks for delivery into the newspaper's circulation area. As early as 1921, the Swan Plan had raised the question of how businesses could survive on that street under such adverse conditions. The conditions grew worse in the next forty years.

Urban renewal, by holding out the promise of the space it needed in the future, kept *The Day* in downtown New London and earned the strong and unqualified backing of the newspaper from the outset. From its beginning, the *Day's* history was intertwined with the city's development but never as clearly as it was with redevelopment. The conflicting notions of suburban development and urban renewal received their impetus from Washington. Congress authorized the development of a national highway network to carry the country's increasing automobile traffic. The added mobility this afforded Americans helped drain the cities of business and people. At the same time, Congress passed housing legislation in 1949 that led to the creation of urban redevelopment authorities to grapple with the resulting problem of blight in older cities.

City Manager Edward R. Henkle and the Chamber of Commerce were interested almost immediately in redevelopment, primarily for business reasons. Henkle knew the city had to make room for new business, but worried about the social disruption this would cause in the crowded downtown neighborhoods and in the rest of the city, where many of the working class families of various races and nationalities would have to move. New London created its first redevelopment commission in 1951. It was headed by Bertram F. Rossiter, a politically inclined telephone company employee, who along with his wife Eleanor, was a protégé of Dr. C. John Satti, the Democratic leader. Its focus was limited to creating new off-street parking for the business district. This led to the first slum clearance program in the city, along Golden Street and Green Street. But New London's plans ran into a snag. The federal government would not pay for a plan that created only parking lots and the city had to finance the project. That first agency was disbanded in a maelstrom of controversy.

This did not end the city's interest in urban renewal. A committee of real estate agents appointed by the City Council in the mid-1950s had been studying various ways to rebuild the city's deteriorating tax base. F. Jerome Silverstein, a 37-year-old real estate appraiser, was the chairman. The group reexamined an idea in the 1921 Swan Plan to build a new road along the city's western boundary from the downtown to the south end of the city to stimulate development and accommodate a new sewer line. But they concluded the swampy conditions along the proposed route made this prohibitive. The committee also looked at filling in part of Winthrop Cove, where Governor John Winthrop had landed in the 17th century, to create new industrial land. Charles P. DeBiasi, the city's public works director, squelched that idea as well, arguing it would cost more than it was worth. The committee's third recommendation met with a more appreciative response. The committee proposed an urban renewal plan to clear decaying neighborhoods up and down the ancient waterfront district as a way of creating new land for new businesses and housing in the tiny city.

The real estate community was enthralled with the possibilities urban renewal presented to revive the city's downtown real estate market after decades of stagnation. The City Council endorsed the idea, and in 1958 created a new redevelopment commission, this one headed by Silverstein. He held that influential and gradually more controversial position for twenty years. *The Day* applauded the action and the choices to serve on the group. "Despite the caliber of the committee, redevelopment will never get off the ground without the wholehearted support of the council and other officials and the public at large. The results, which can accrue from such a program, make it worth the effort," the newspaper said.

Silverstein was a son of Jacob Silverstein, a local real estate agent and appraiser. He had grown up in a house overlooking the old Ocean Beach, where his family was a large property holder. He had been a teenager and star football player at Bulkeley School when the 1938 hurricane struck the city. His father had been one of the appraisers who established the values of property when the city bought the land for Ocean Beach. Silverstein had followed his father into the real estate business after graduating from the University of Connecticut. The son was interested in the impact postwar changes were having on real estate values and became an authority on the subject. He had carried out a survey of the impact turnpike construction was having on land values. He understood thoroughly the economics of the changes that were overtaking the city and the potential of urban renewal to generate new wealth. He had the additional advantage in city politics of old-school ties with a circle consisting largely of Bulkeley alumni who were rising in politics at the time. The leader of the group was Harvey Mallove. Others were attorneys Francis T. Londregan, Joseph F. Regan, C. Robert Satti, and Angelo G. Santaniello. Santaniello and Satti, son of the Democratic leader Dr. C. John Satti, would become the lawyers for the Redevelopment Agency.

Bertram Rossiter, who had been chairman of the earlier commission, was installed on the new agency primarily to keep an eye on things for Dr. Satti. Gordon Tuthill, another real estate agent and head of a civic group that was promoting an effort to bring new development to the city, The Citizens Action Committee, also became a member of the new agency. The citizens group was made up of New Londoners from the comfortable south end of the city, where the city's power was centered. They were worried about New London's waning importance as a result of the changes taking place outside the city.

New highways through the region and suburban development were driving up real estate values in the suburbs and depressing the value of the city's downtown business district, which had been the region's center of commerce. In 1958, work was finished on the Connecticut Turnpike, which ran from the New York state line on the west to Rhode Island. Eastern Connecticut politicians successfully lobbied the state legislature to continue the four-lane expressway from East Lyme through the northeastern part of the state in hope of stimulating growth there after the area lost most of its textile industries. That fight had been led by John N. Dempsey, executive aide to Governor Abraham Ribicoff and mayor of Putnam, an economically distressed mill town in that region. The legislature authorized that section of the turnpike over strong objections from lawmakers from other parts of the state, who felt it would be a waste of money because the region was so rural and sparsely settled.

Another new highway was planned that would run along the southeastern coast of the state, from the Connecticut Turnpike through New London to Rhode Island. This was to be a section of the new Interstate 95, an expressway that eventually would carry traffic from Florida to Maine. The road followed the route through southeastern Connecticut of an older road known as the Blue Star Highway, which crossed the bridge between New London and Groton.

The Day followed the story of the new highways with interest, though not much insight. Its coverage was sometimes superficial. When the Connecticut Turnpike still was under construction, *Day* editor Joseph Ryan flew over the one-hundred-twenty-six-mile course of the road to prepare a feature story. Leo Lonergan, operator of the commercial engraving company at the newspaper and once chief of the photographers, was the pilot. When the road opened, the newspaper said in an editorial,

> *The new road seems certain to give Connecticut an economic lift. Industries may follow the highway which will place them within easy reach of New York and Boston markets. The turnpike can be expected to bring more tourists into the state.*

Nobody anticipated the real impact the roads would have in driving suburban growth and helping in the decline of the old city. A 1960 study by the state did not shed any light on the impact the new roads would have. *The Day* did not attempt to analyze the ramifications. An editorial on April 2, 1960, stated that the turnpike had not been open long enough to make any meaningful predictions.

New London had its hands full figuring out how to make room for its own business growth and renewal, a concern that was mirrored on the board of *The Day*. The city is unusually small. It has only six square miles of land area. New

London business leaders surveyed the city for new commercial land. They turned once again to the area around Ocean Beach as a site for new businesses. In the early 1960s, Mallove led an unsuccessful drive to rezone the area around the beach for hotels and other businesses, but *Day* director Thomas Troland made it clear that he would die rather than let that happen. *The Day* opposed the change.

In its quest for room to grow, the city also became embroiled in a controversy over plans to make use of newly available property on the outskirts of the downtown. Attorney Lazarus S. Heyman, a Danbury developer, proposed building a shopping center at the site of Williams Memorial Institute when the school moved to the Connecticut College campus in the 1950s. The property, north of downtown New London on the road to Hartford, was near Williams Park where City Manager Henkle and some other leaders had wanted to establish a civic center. *The Day* vigorously had opposed that earlier plan. But this time, the newspaper supported the new plan, although the downtown New London merchants vociferously opposed it. The *Day's* position may have reflected the powerful influence of the newspaper's lawyer, Francis McGuire, who was a member of the WMI board of trustees. The newspaper reasoned in a front-page editorial that the shopping center would add to the city's tax revenues at a time when the money was badly needed and bring about more good than harm for the downtown businesses. The additional revenue would offset some of the costs of the new parking lots in the downtown. *The Day* added:

> *It's only a question of time before this area on the west bank of the river has a shopping center. If it's not in New London, it will be outside the city. Is it not logical to suppose that a center within the city, only a few blocks from the city, would bring shoppers into the city?*

The *Day's* exhortation had no impact. The opposition was so strong that the proposal was abandoned. Dr. Ruby Turner Morris, an outspoken economics professor and political activist at Connecticut College, suggested the city buy the property for government use. But it was purchased, instead, by the Roman Catholic diocese, which opened St. Bernard High School on the former Williams Memorial Institute campus in 1957. The diocese was yet another of Francis McGuire's affiliations. He had been a member of the Diocesan Bureau of Social Service, so well thought of for his service to the church that he was later awarded the Knight of St. Gregory Papal Order by Pope Paul VI in 1965.

It was only a matter of time before a new shopping center developed by Martin Olson went up outside the business district on the south side of the Interstate 95 highway. Construction began in September 1955 and the retail complex opened in the spring of 1957. The old retail district struggled on, buffeted by the winds of change and imprisoned by its own limitations. Although it remained busy at the outset of the 1960s, it felt choked in a tangle of outmoded buildings and congested streets. Parking remained a problem despite the new off-street lots on Green and Golden Streets. The new shopping centers like Olson's offered vast fields of free parking.

Other problems remained. The city had never followed the advice in the 1921 Swan Plan to build wide boulevards to accommodate the age of the automobile. Although it was easy to drive to the shopping centers, it was a headache to get in and out of the city on its narrow main arteries. Business leaders were calling for an expressway to connect the highway and the business district. The department stores desperately needed additional room to compete with mass merchandisers in the shopping centers. There was little room for delivery trucks to unload and no space for stores to expand. New London had six major department stores: Sears Roebuck & Co., G.M. Williams, Montgomery Ward, Kresge's, F.W. Woolworth & Co., and Genung's. Only Genung's and G.M. Williams were locally owned. The rest belonged to national chains, which had no sentimental attachment to downtown New London and were becoming frustrated with conditions there. The city, although it was entering a program that would make large parcels of land available to developers, did little to persuade these businesses to stay. Sears wasted no time in relocating to the new shopping center. Woolworth's stood fast for the time being. Kresge's kept open its State Street store while it built a second one in the shopping center. First National, the chain supermarket, abandoned its downtown store to be in Olson's shopping center.

The downtown merchants increasingly were hard pressed to compete with the new stores in the shopping centers. Robert Hall, a discount men's apparel store that opened in the Groton Shopping Plaza in 1960, advertised quality men's suits at a fraction of what they would cost in New London's apparel stores. And parking was free. The new stores, with vast advertising budgets, fattened the *Day's* advertising revenues, while the downtown stores, never extravagant spenders to begin with, accounted for a diminishing share of the newspaper's revenues.

On top of external obstacles beyond their control, many of the owners of the family businesses in downtown New London brought on some of their own problems. They had become complacent after years of monopolizing the region's marketplace. They shrugged their shoulders at the more aggressive retailing that was taking place in the shopping centers, which was reflected in full-page advertisements in *The Day*. They were reluctant to keep their doors open longer hours and on holidays as a convenience to shoppers. They defiantly stuck to their old ways, without trying to improve their quality of service, keep up with consumer tastes in an age of exploding consumerism, or advertise in the newspaper aggressively. The businesses in the shopping centers, under the conditions of their leases, had to cooperate, whereas New London's downtown businesses went their own ways, rarely agreeing on anything. But some of the city's leaders viewed urban renewal as a way to reverse this business decline. Harvey N. Mallove, who had taken over the management of his family's State Street jewelry store and held a position on the City Council, led in espousing the need for action. F. Jerome Silverstein summarized their hopes in a *Day* interview in 1961:

> *This city has a wonderful future ahead of it. Redevelopment is the key to the future. It can renew the city's importance as a trading center, an important asset, by creating a better, new center through better buildings and stores, better traffic conditions and more parking. These in turn will enable the city to draw customers from a wider area.*

Both New London's city manager, Edward R. Henkle, and Mayor Wilfred A. Park at the time expressed the same view. New London could not grow until it made room in the cluttered, rundown center of the old city. This limitation dictated that if government did not act quickly, New London homeowners would have to shoulder the increasing financial burden of operating the government and running the schools. The worst-case scenario of which Waldo Clarke had warned during the closing days of World War II was descending upon the city, some felt.

In his spring budget message in March 1960, the city manager repeated Clarke's call of fifteen years earlier for a concerted government effort to exploit the scarce vacant land the city still possessed and create additional space for development to hold down property taxes. Mayor Park, who was a banker and one of the new wave of Republicans who followed Angelo Santaniello into power, felt New London's future would be as a service center for the region, with its schools, hospital, and banks. Urban renewal, the banker believed, would help the city expand into that new role by stimulating new investment.

The Day looked on the changes that were taking place around it with growing puzzlement. Its goals, once clear, no longer seemed consistent. For example, the newspaper always placed New London's downtown business interests ahead of other priorities. But historically it also had favored a regional approach to economic growth. Theodore Bodenwein had always felt that what was good for the communities around New London was good for New London. Confident in that notion, he espoused a metropolitan form of collaboration among New London and its neighbors. His own business instincts had told him that growth in the suburbs would boost the newspaper's advertising and circulation. But the interests of the suburbs increasingly competed with the interests of New London. There was no place in which this conflict came into greater focus than it did in the institution Bodenwein helped bring into the world: the city's Chamber of Commerce.

In the spirit of regional cooperation espoused for years by *The Day*, the chamber had set out to expand its influence to adjoining towns. This new orientation caused it to change its name, first to the Greater New London Chamber of Commerce and eventually, in the 1960s, to the Southeastern Connecticut Chamber of Commerce. But this was viewed as a threat by suburbs that already had their own chambers and had little interest in New London and its problems. With their own stores and budding supermarkets and the convenience of shopping centers in the region, a growing number of suburbanites could spend their lives without ever visiting downtown New London.

It was not evident at first, but the chamber's expansion also became a practical threat to New London's downtown business community. The trend watered down the business group's interest in downtown New London. As the group reached out to embrace the business growth that surrounded New London, the chamber became less concerned with New London. The organization, which up until then had played a strong role in bringing about economic and political changes in New London, started boosting competing business interests elsewhere. As early as the 1950s, it supported expansion of the city's water system into Waterford to advance economic growth there, a cause *The Day* strenuously supported over angry objections by many in the New London political community. New London leaders such as City Councilor Thomas F. Griffin feared water lines would lead to growth outside the city that would rival the city's business interests.

"It is important to New London that there is water in Waterford. Nothing can happen in Waterford that cannot help but benefit New London," banker Henry L. Bailey, the new president of the Chamber, said in his inaugural address February 5, 1957. Of course Bailey, like a growing number of leaders in the business community, lived outside New London, and his bank, the New London Federal Savings & Loan Association, was benefiting greatly from the suburban growth in home mortgages. Mayor Park was an officer in the same bank. *The Day* adhered to the same logic, which had been a matter of faith to

Bodenwein and Waldo Clarke. Development outside the city, they believed, would benefit the city. When New London politicians refused to appropriate a few thousand dollars for a study into the water issue, the newspaper stated in an editorial arguing for the study,

> *...many factors combine to link closely the fortunes of New London and its neighboring towns, especially since New London is so limited geographically. If anyone wants to come here to live, or to establish a business, the chances are excellent he'll find no room to do so except in one of the adjoining communities. New London can't help but benefit from progress anywhere in the area.*

The Day, like the New London banks, nevertheless faced a moral dilemma that pitted its sentimental attachment to the downtown against its interests in the suburbs. The directors were confronted with the need to make real choices not only about the newspaper's location, but also about its very identity. While its investment, its home, its history, its very heart were concentrated in downtown New London, its potential for growth in circulation and advertising lay outside the city limits. This was not very different from the situation Theodore Bodenwein had faced, but in Bodenwein's time, the two realities were not inconsistent because New London still was the unchallenged business and service center of the region. Automobiles, highways, and suburban shopping centers after World War II changed this. The changes turned this interdependence between the city and its suburbs into competition. As the 1950s had drawn to a close, *The Day* still believed that the interests of New London and its neighbors were compatible but it became more difficult to reconcile the two. *The Day* bought into the popular idea of "regional cities," in which groups of communities worked together and shared their wealth for the common good. It stated in an editorial March 5, 1957:

> *Just what form America's spreading suburbanization will take is largely a matter of guessing thus far. But there are plenty of signs that regardless of its form, the trend will continue and with it will grow the interdependence of towns within these regional metropolitan regions. It foreshadows what may be the most sweeping change in municipal thinking since the town meeting began to fall short of supplying the growing needs of government.*

The editorial page was not the only place at *The Day* this subject was debated. On the *Day's* board it was more than a topical concern, another casual current-events issue on which the editors felt compelled to take a learned position.

Regionalism touched the vital interests of the newspaper, and the directors agonized throughout the 1950s over the *Day's* identity as either a New London or a regional newspaper. The regional view won out in December 1959, when the board voted to change the newspaper's registered trade name from the *New London Evening Day* to *The Day*. But the directors were so reluctant to make this drastic move that they waited until January 21, 1963, to change the newspaper's front-page nameplate.

ALTHOUGH THE NEWSPAPER BOTH championed and relied upon growth in the suburbs, practical considerations as well as sentimentality kept the newspaper where it was in one of the oldest and most congested sections of New London. *The Day*, in truth, was stuck where it was, and was pleased when urban renewal came along at the time it did to make room. *The Day* was not anxious to move, and the last thing the redevelopment agency wanted was to relocate *The Day*. Acquiring the newspaper's buildings and moving the heavy and intricate printing machinery somewhere else would have exhausted the agency's relocation budget several times over and cost far more than it was worth for the small amount of land it would make available. *The Day* estimated it would have cost more than $2 million to move. As the new renewal project approached, the redevelopment agency assured *The Day* that it did not intend to acquire the newspaper property, and it made similar assurances to the Savings Bank of New London, next to *The Day*, and to St. James Episcopal Church. The renewal plans, in turn promised to make available new land for their needs.

A grateful *Day* clutched urban renewal to its bosom, while the newspaper engaged in continuing discussions with the Redevelopment Agency to get the best land deal it could. After several years of negotiations, Francis McGuire reached an agreement with the Redevelopment Agency in 1964 under which the newspaper sold the old police station property to the agency. In turn, *The Day* was promised land to its south, the site of Bishop Studio and the Salvation Army, when the property was later cleared. The agreement guaranteed the newspaper there would be a wider street behind the *Day* building, along North Bank Street, to serve its loading docks. *The Day* agreed to share in the responsibility for maintaining the service road.

The Day already had taken a lead in boosting the program in a referendum campaign in 1961-62. The newspaper allowed C. Francis Driscoll, the executive director of the Redevelopment Agency, wide space on the news pages to expound the advantage of the program in a seven-part series. *The Day* followed this with a series of front-page editorials supporting the program. The newspaper candidly acknowledged the newspaper's self-interest in the project, not that it was any secret in the small, gossipy city. In an editorial on April 21, 1962, *The Day* pointed out that it had become aware of the importance of urban renewal while it was attempting to secure land for expansion. "The city must always perfect itself to mean something to everyone who has anything to do with it," the newspaper said. Piecemeal, private renewal such as *The Day* had attempted, required too much effort. The city needed the redevelopment project to make room for new business development. If the city failed to accomplish this, homeowners in the city would confront escalating taxes. On April 24, it said:

> *Redevelopment will rescue forlorn business property, long since unrentable, set up new, modern homes, widen streets, untangle traffic, establish parking, clear waste land for commercial use—in short, revive a region largely run to decay.*

The job of selling redevelopment to the city had turned out to be easier than anyone anticipated. Even those who started with reservations about details of the plan wound up supporting it. The author of the city's renewal plan was city planner Maurice Rotival. Rotival had helped draw up renewal plans both for New Haven, Connecticut, and Paris, France. He adhered to the school of urban planning of the time that called for remaking cities so that they would gain the advantages of suburbs—garden apartments, wide streets that could carry many cars and an abundance of places to park cars. His proposal for New London called for clearing most of the nearly five hundred buildings in the waterfront neighborhoods and business district around *The Day*. Rotival's plan would create a network of boulevards to carry cars efficiently in and out of the city from the highway. Some streets would be widened while others with familiar names, like Hallam, Shapley, Richards, and Douglas Streets, would disappear. On the western boundary, along Huntington Street, high rise luxury apartments with views of the Thames River and New London Harbor would replace the clutter of 19th century wood-frame structures along Huntington Street. Below these buildings there would be townhouse apartments for middle income families. Off to one side, near the bridge, new apartments for the poor would rise from land around John Winthrop's colonial mill, then largely a Polish neighborhood served by two churches. In that way, a utopia of mixed housing would bring all classes of people into the city.

The plan pictured new industries and warehouses near the State Pier to bring new business to that still languishing facility. Parking garages and new parking lots were interspersed among the development. Near *The Day*, office buildings and a resplendent new department store would take the place of the 19th and early 20th century brick buildings that were clustered there.

Harvey Mallove, who became mayor of the city in 1961 (New London's mayors are selected by their colleagues on the city council for terms of one year), had headed the R-Day Committee formed to win approval of the project in the April 1962 referendum. Angelo Santaniello helped with organizing the Republicans. The Chamber of Commerce backed the plan, though its support was tepid compared to the energy it had shown in earlier civic campaigns in New London. Support came from service clubs and civic organizations, including the League of Women Voters.

The NAACP, which was in the midst of a struggle with the city government over housing discrimination, was at first skeptical. But after debating the issue, it concluded that on balance renewal would be a plus to black families by providing better housing. However, some leaders, particularly the local organization's president, Linwood Bland, were worried that blacks dislocated by the program would have trouble finding housing in other parts of the city because of racial discrimination. Before they would support the program, they pressed Mallove for assurances, which he gave, that the City Council would pass a fair-housing law.

Even the New London County Historical Society eventually embraced the program, which proposed to level the city's oldest and most historic neighborhoods. Some of the structures had been built before the Revolutionary War and survived the burning of New London by Benedict Arnold. These included the pre-Revolutionary Fox & Grapes Tavern north of *The Day* on Main Street. The building was then the home of a grocery store where reporters from *The Day* bought grinder sandwiches at lunchtime. Shapley Street and Stony Hill, which ascended a hill from the river, evoked the city's past in their shingled and decaying structures. Captain Adam Shapley, a hero at the Battle of Groton Heights, had lived on Shapley Street. Stony Hill, located on the route from the waterfront to the center of government on Bulkeley Hill in colonial times, once had been a fashionable street. The very names of these streets and others that preserved the memories of New London's past would disappear from the city's map. The significance of this possibility prompted the Historical Society to suggest that some of the new buildings and projects be named for the disappearing streets.

The story of succeeding eras was told in the architecture of other neighborhoods slated for demolition. Federal Street was lined with elegant, though sometimes rundown, houses built before the Civil War, nearly all of which are gone today. Sebastian Lawrence, the philanthropist son of the whaling captain Joseph Lawrence, lived in the mansion at the corner of Main and Federal Streets. This was home of the B. P. Learned Mission in the early 1960s. Later the Redevelopment Agency took it over for its battlefield headquarters before tearing it down in 1970. Acors Barns, a whaling master who became president of the National Bank of Commerce in the 1850s, had lived in a mansion on Federal Street, near St. James Church, in the 1830s. Francis McGuire and his wife, Helen, bought the house in the late 1950s, and had turned it into offices for the law firm. That building, too, was headed toward demolition under the renewal plan.

Buildings on the urban-renewal hit list also included a brick mansion built in the 19th century that had been the childhood home of City Manager Edward R. Henkle and his brother, Dr. Robert Henkle. One of the city's early synagogues, Congregation Ahaveth Chesed, was on Federal Street. Before it was a synagogue, it had been one of the city's early Methodist churches.

Huntington Street, located along the western boundary of the urban renewal area, had been another fashionable district in the 19th century. Alfred H. Chappell lived in a mansion on the west side of the street when he was helping to finance the expansion of *The Day* in the 1890s, and later when he led the drive to found Connecticut College in New London. Bodenwein had visited that house several times. The house, still stunning in its elegance, had survived as the then local headquarters of the American Red Cross. A row of Greek Revival houses that had been built in the 19th century, known as Whale Oil Row, formed a line of white columns along the east side of the street near the downtown. These houses were developed by Ezra Chappell, grandfather of Frank and Alfred H. Chappell and John A. Tibbits, the founder of *The Day*. They, too, were to be torn down. One of them was the medical office of Dr. Carl Wies, the adored physician for the city fire department and son-in-law of the late Waldo Clarke.

The area to be cleared also included some of the most striking buildings in the downtown. The most conspicuous of these was the Victorian-era Neptune Building, which had towered majestically over the parade since 1905. The building was so distinctive that three decades after it was torn down, the city considered reconstructing it. Others included the brick and granite façade of the Union Bank & Trust Company, and Union Station. Silverstein was particularly fond of the idea of razing the train station to open up a view of the Thames River. The agency began discussing those plans with the New York,

New Haven & Hartford Railroad, the owner, in 1960, even before the Winthrop Urban Renewal Project had been approved.

Buildings were not the only heritage endangered by renewal plans. Neighborhoods there still tangibly reflected the waves of European immigrants who had arrived earlier in the century. Although these neighborhoods were constantly changing, the lingering imprint of the Eastern Europeans was still evident in the names of the residents along North Bank Street: Bitok, Lawski, Miastowski, Dembrowski, Kawalcczyk, Malenowsky, Makarewicz. The working class neighborhoods there had low crime rates, and neighbors knew one another. Residents still bedecked their houses in flowers on the holiday of the Pentecost. The neighbors supported shops, small grocers, restaurants, and bars that were also patronized by the office workers in the city. The streets, although lined with a growing number of vacant buildings, had life flowing through them and were, on the whole, interesting and attractive. These neighborhoods were, in a way, landmarks by themselves. Many New Londoners could look down these streets and recite the names of the people who lived there, or used to reside there.

The New London County Historical Society, which had become a shadow of the organization Ernest E. Rogers had headed when the organization celebrated the city's past as the naval headquarters of the American Revolution, was deathly silent on the plans until Dr. Carl Wies and attorney Francis McGuire challenged the agency's plans to demolish their buildings. Embarrassed into action, the society formed a committee to study the buildings in the area to see if any were worth being preserved after all. Dwight Lyman, the president of the society and chairman of the group's redevelopment committee, was skeptical. He stated in September 1961 that he doubted there were a dozen, and probably there were fewer, buildings in the project area worth saving. His committee conducted a cursory review. "It became quickly evident that there are pitifully few buildings in the area in a condition which would allow economic preservation," he said.

McGuire, held in awe and reverence by New Londoners, demanded the agency leave his building where it was. The McGuires invited the Redevelopment Agency to tour the Barns house, where Helen McGuire served them tea and cookies and her husband attempted with increasing impatience to force their retreat. McGuire spoke almost in a whisper, but with authority that usually caused people to shrink before him. But the agency did not shrink.

Wies, whose friends included Dr. C. John Satti and virtually the entire fire department, suggested the city form a historic district to preserve at least some of the city's past contained in the renewal area. It encompassed all four houses on Whale Oil Row, including his offices, as well as McGuire's building and all the other buildings in an area bounded by Huntington, Federal, Meridian, and Church Streets. The agency was unmoved by this display of resistance by two of its most influential citizens. It responded that if it made exceptions for these buildings, other owners of old buildings might demand similar concessions. The local garden club, as well as a colleague of Wies's, Dr. Elsie Tytla, joined in supporting Wies and McGuire. The garden club issued a statement in August 1961:

> *Other cities carried away by enthusiasm and the glowing picture presented by redevelopment plans, have made the mistakes of destroying irreplaceable old landmarks. We hope that the city, whose welfare we all have at heart, will not do the same.*

The Historical Society, caught between these forces, vacillated. It could not win no matter where it turned. When it endorsed a more modest version of Wies' plan, the group was attacked for having come under undue influence from Driscoll, the redevelopment director. When it endorsed the whole historic district plan, the Redevelopment Agency accused it of going back on its word. In the end, on the eve of the referendum, the Redevelopment Agency approved a compromise that was even more modest. The agency agreed to leave Whale Oil Row standing, along with McGuire's building and several other structures. All the rest were to go.

This compromise silenced the last opposition to the renewal plan. *The Day* hailed the compromise and looked forward to a brilliant future for the city. Both political parties lent their organizations to the R-Day Committee to make phone calls and transport voters to the polls. Automobile dealers made cars available to help get out the vote. And the Star Democratic Club, a black organization headed by a Jewish ward boss of Dr. Satti's, Seymour Manheimer, sprang into action to get out the vote.

On April 30, 1962, the city embraced urban renewal by a vote of four to one, scarcely realizing what it would mean to the city. The decision cleared the way for great and unforeseen changes for the city and for *The Day*.

TWENTY-FOUR

Change Enters

You don't enlarge a newspaper plant without throbbing drama.

—*The Day,* November 8, 1960

THE 1960s UNLEASHED A cascade of changes at *The Day* after twenty years in which there had been few alterations in its appearance and habits. Construction on the North Bank Street addition had moved ahead rapidly during the spring and summer of 1960 and resulted in one of the first high-profile face-lifts in the old waterfront quarter since Bodenwein had doubled the size of the *Day* building in 1928.

Another four years would pass before the city's urban renewal program would begin a more alarming transformation there. But *The Day*, and not F. Jerome Silverstein's Redevelopment Agency, introduced the derrick and wrecking ball to the neighborhood. In 1959, a *Day* contractor leveled Arthur Wilinski's dry goods store, H. Marcus & Company, and an old restaurant next door for the expansion. The *Day's* expansion in partnership with redevelopment transformed North Bank Street from a cluttered neighborhood of shops, vacant frame buildings, bars, and brothels into a neater, but desolate service road for the newspaper.

In October 1960, riggers moved the heavy printing machinery from the fourth floor to the new composing room. This task was performed with the same fanfare that had accompanied the *Day's* earlier move from Bank Street in 1907. Through a hole that had been cut in the roof, a rigging firm from Berlin, Connecticut, hoisted the fifteen Linotype machines from the old composing room on pallets and deposited them in the new composing room. Each bulky machine weighed nearly two tons and consisted of thousands of movable parts. They were handled "as though they were so many pieces of Dresden china,"

The Day wrote on November 8, 1960. The stereotype press and nearly one hundred other pieces of printing equipment were removed by a derrick from the old composing room to their new quarters in twenty-four hours, so that the newspaper could resume publication on schedule.

The old composing room was remodeled into a modern newsroom, but the knotty pine décor popular then gave the room more the feel of a rustic suburban rec room or a hunting lodge than a city room. *The Day* installed a passenger elevator and replaced the mechanical conveyor that carried copy to the composing room with quieter and more efficient pneumatic tubes. The building finally was air conditioned, except for the pressroom and mailroom.

Betty Latham, the switchboard operator since September 1936, was relocated from the newsroom to the downstairs lobby. From that station, her trademark voice would greet callers for another ten years.

For more than sixty years, *The Day* would have only two full-time telephone operators, Betty Latham and her successor, Anita Louise Taylor. Upon Latham's retirement in 1978, Taylor, who had just been laid off from her job at the Millstone nuclear power station in Waterford, would take over the switchboard. Taylor had applied at *The Day* to produce proof for the state unemployment service, just down the street from the newspaper office, that she was looking for work. Latham's dispassionate greeting each time someone called the newspaper and Taylor's cheerful North Carolina drawl were engraved over the years in the city's memory as the voices of *The Day*. Men who called the newspaper fell in love with Taylor merely from listening to her say, "Good day, *The Day*" and "Thank yeeoo."

The Day opened offices in Mystic in 1961 and Norwich in 1963. Until then, James McKenna had run his one-man Mystic news and advertising operation out of his house. *The Day* moved its Groton office into more spacious quarters on Long Hill Road, closer to the new shopping centers. E. Curtiss Pierson, hired as a reporter in 1952, took charge of news operation there.

Bar Colby, now in his early 50s, was gaining confidence and respect not only in New London but also in the American newspaper industry for his initiatives as a newspaper executive, particularly in the area of training reporters and editors. In April 1960, he was elected a director of the American Newspaper Publishers Association. The ANPA, founded in 1887, was one of the most powerful newspaper organizations in the country. *The Day* was one of the smallest newspapers represented on the board.

The directors of *The Day* still were cautiously following Colby's lead. There had been no significant changes in the group in a decade. Earle Stamm still was president, a position he had held since 1950. Charles Sortor, the auto dealer, had become vice president and assistant treasurer; Colby was now treasurer and secretary. One of the significant aspects of these titles, as Edna Bodenwein had complained bitterly when alive, was that the officers received extra compensation for performing the additional duties; $1,200 annually on top of their $100 a month salaries for attending board meetings. While Orvin Andrews was president, on April 27, 1965, the board doubled the compensation for the president. In addition, under the will Charles Smiddy had written and Bodenwein signed, board members awarded themselves bonuses of "additional reasonable compensation," as high as $3,000, for delivering $100,000 or more in a year into the Bodenwein Public Benevolent Foundation. Officers and directors could make more than $6,000 a year for the honor of serving.

In the early 1960s, Stamm's health began to fail and the board conducted meetings at his house because he was too frail to go out. On April 15, 1961, he retired as president and the directors appointed Andrews to replace him. Stamm died on June 4, 1963. He was 68. Stamm and Andrews had been the last active holdovers on the board from the era of Theodore Bodenwein. The others who had served on the newspaper when Bodenwein was alive were George Grout and Charles Smiddy. Gordon Bodenwein, who replaced Grout in the settlement of the estate, retained his position as employee trustee in absentia while he lived in Mexico, but played no role other than as a distant gadfly.

An executive for the National Bank of Commerce, Stamm had been both the publisher's personal financial advisor and executive vice president of the institution that handled all the newspaper's accounts. Stamm had believed that local banks had an important responsibility in advancing the interests of the community, and he had helped formulate the provisions in Bodenwein's will that would create the Bodenwein Public Benevolent Foundation. His bank and the successors that absorbed it in a procession of mergers administered the fund and remained the depository of the *Day's* continuously mounting wealth from its monopoly in the region around New London.

BODENWEIN'S WILL SPECIFIED THAT the National Bank of Commerce continue to have one representative on the board of trustees. But by the time of Stamm's death, the bank had merged with an out-of-town bank, becoming Hartford National Bank & Trust Company. More than a year would pass before Hartford National named a replacement for Stamm, a fiscal conservative and the director who most often had tangled with Colby on spending issues.

The brief period after Stamm left the board provided a breather for Bar Colby. Colby enjoyed unchallenged authority. His father-in-law was retired from the business and only nominally in charge. Besides that, Andrews often was absent from the newspaper's deliberations during the winters he spent in Florida. Charles Sortor, an old friend of Colby's, and Thomas Troland went along with the general manager on most matters. This enviable situation ended for Colby on September 12, 1962, when Hartford National bank finally assigned Francis McGuire to be its representative on the *Day* board of trustees and directors. McGuire, who had been the *Day's* lawyer for twelve years, had asked for the appointment, and he generally got what he requested.

McGuire's arrival at *The Day* turned out to be a mixed blessing for Colby. McGuire, like Colby, was a progressive thinker and open to change if it met his exacting practical standards. McGuire liked *The Day*. He was fascinated with the newspaper and its potential both to bring about change and wield power. He would in the years that followed, support Colby and his successors in modernizing the newspaper and improving the product. But this benefit came at a price. McGuire was a very powerful figure in the city and not a shrinking violet. While Colby was Andrews' heir to the control of *The Day*, McGuire soon single-handedly outweighed Colby in the balance of power on the board. A staunch Democrat, he also brought an alien political point of view to the newspaper.

Francis McGuire came from a lineage of strong, Democratic politicians in the city. His paternal grandfather had emigrated from Ireland and settled in the city in the 1880s when *The Day* was getting started and Theodore Bodenwein was beginning his career in newspapers. His father was Frank L. McGuire, who had been city clerk. The elder McGuire's prestigious law firm represented Jennie Bodenwein in her divorce from Theodore Bodenwein in 1911, arranging the deal in which Bodenwein put up equity in *The Day* as security for his alimony payments to his former wife. Francis McGuire built his influence in the city both as a good lawyer and adroit behind-the-scenes power broker. McGuire and Stamm were alike in commanding respect and having footholds in the city's most important institutions. New London enjoyed two levels of power: the mundane political level and above that and out of sight of the public, the institutional level. The institutions reflected the sum of the city's greatest wealth and personal power in the memberships of their boards. McGuire was a trustee of Connecticut College, Hartford National Bank & Trust Company, Lawrence & Memorial Hospitals, and Williams Memorial Institute, among others. He led the first fund drive for Mitchell College and was close to the Roman Catholic bishops assigned to the eastern Connecticut diocese headquartered in Norwich.

He also maintained his family's influence in politics. While the McGuires were part of the local Irish aristocracy and socialized with the city's most affluent and established elite, they felt it important to maintain a foothold in the party of the people. Dr. Satti and other Democratic leaders valued this connection with the mysterious center of power in New London's South End, or Fifth District as it was called from its voting district number. McGuire found his association with the party similarly advantageous. When the party was split asunder in a factional battle in the late 1930s, the Democrats chose Francis McGuire to be the compromise town chairman. He filled that post from 1939-41, enjoying the support of all the factions.

McGuire was not one to collect prestigious affiliations as mere trophies. In whatever capacity he served, he insisted upon being in charge and took his work seriously. He had a droll sense of humor and was dignified and good looking, highly intelligent, and charming. He loved good company and having fun. But he was always in control, both of himself and the people in his presence. One tested his patience and challenged his authority at great risk of a withering put-down or worse. He was capable of expressing rage without raising his voice or changing his expression. Francis Driscoll still remembers the day in the 1960s when McGuire and his wife entertained Driscoll, then the executive director of the Redevelopment Agency, and other agency members at the Acors Barns house in an effort to save the house. "You felt fear in his presence," Driscoll remembered.

McGuire brought the same commanding presence to the *Day* board, where he provided a critical but constructive and progressive voice. He served as a check on the influence of the Avery-Colby family circle that had secured control of the public-trust newspaper. Orvin Andrews had passed his mantle of authority to his son-in-law, Bar Colby. Colby's closest friend was Latham "Late" Avery, a dairy farmer. This benevolent connection yielded a bounty of jobs at *The Day* for the Avery family. Latham's brother Deane eventually would become co-publisher; Late's son-in-law, E. Curtis Pierson, would become managing editor; another son-in-law, Arthur Weber, would become city editor. Latham's wife, Edna, was a proofreader and his sister, Judy Sinton, served as the *Day's* office manager in Groton. On the Colby side, Bar's son, Robert would become news desk chief in the 1970s.

These were not necessarily unsuitable additions to *The Day*, but it was healthy for *The Day* to have someone unrelated to the Avery-Colby family group and who had a critical bent to counterbalance their influence. McGuire, for his part, became an advocate of another rising star on the newspaper who was related neither to the Colbys nor the Averys: E. Wesley Hammond, who started in the business office in the 1950s as a payroll clerk and rose to become a co-publisher with Deane Avery in the 1970s and 1980s.

McGuire was not immune from the charge of serving his own interests on The Day Trust. He continued to be the *Day's* lawyer while he was a trustee and director. He held similar dual positions at the hospital, Connecticut College, and Williams Memorial Institute. Such self-serving situations, more likely to be criticized today than at that time, were commonplace. But in McGuire's case, the advantages he obtained in legal business were vastly outweighed by the benefits his keen mind and connections brought to the institutions he represented. The same could be said of Charles Smiddy. Smiddy had made more than $20,000, a large amount of money in the early 1940s, in legal fees executing Bodenwein's will, but he also had helped engineer The Day Trust.

McGuire combined his legal knowledge and his influence in ways that helped Williams Memorial Institute move to Connecticut College and become a fully private school, and that enabled Lawrence & Memorial Hospitals to get around legal restrictions and dispose of decaying and useless surplus property it inherited from the Lawrence family in downtown New London. But the most important battle he led was on the *Day's* behalf. This would begin in the next decade, and continue after his death in 1982. In the end, it would save The Day Trust and preserve Theodore Bodenwein's legacy. It is safe to say that most of the important decisions made at *The Day* until McGuire's death, bore the imprimatur of his practical and analytical mind. These included changes that were, for a newspaper that had hardly budged from dead center since Bodenwein died, rather breathtaking:

In 1964, the board elected Colby publisher, restoring both a title and position that hadn't existed at *The Day* since Bodenwein had died in 1939. Colby occupied Bodenwein's office and *The Day* remodeled a room next to it in the same dark-paneled décor as a place for the board to meet. It was called the Bodenwein Room.

The directors had strengthened the business side of the newspaper by creating a new position. Wes Hammond, then the office manager, became the *Day's* first controller on December 29, 1962. This restored the balance between the business and news operations that had been lost when Bodenwein died and Andrews took charge of both ends of the newspaper business. Andrews had little understanding of news and his son-in-law and successor, Colby, had tenuous business skills. Colby would now devote all his attention to the editorial department and Hammond would fill the vacuum in the business office. A young accountant and Korean War veteran at the newspaper and favorite of Deane Avery's, Alcino Almeida, replaced Hammond as office manager.

The Day faced the dilemma of whether to continue with letterpress printing or convert to offset printing, which many newspapers were then doing. Following the recommendations of veteran pressman George Kent, *The Day* opted for letterpress printing and on June 20, 1963, bought a new, five-unit rotary press capable of printing more pages and color advertisements. Kent was traditional in his thinking and had close connections with the Hoe Company through its long association with *The Day*. Bodenwein swore by the company, which had developed the modern rotary letterpress. Convinced he had found a bargain in a piece of equipment left over from a deal that had gone sour, Kent opted for another Hoe press.

Unfortunately, the press was obsolete before it arrived and the decision turned out to be an expensive mistake on the company's part. As more publishers switched to offset printing, the Hoe company went bankrupt in July 1969, sending the *Day's* mechanical supervisors scurrying to buy spare parts. In fairness, many newspapers, caught in the middle of the technological revolution taking place then, made the same mistake. Nevertheless, the problems that beset the press led to the inside joke: Question: What kind of press does *The Day* have? Answer: She's a Hoe (more or less rhyming with whore).

The press made its first run May 22, 1964, three days before Colby became publisher. Soon it was printing color ads and fat editions in a single run. This was George Kent's last big assignment in his forty-seven-year career at the newspaper. Theodore Bodenwein's top pressman retired at the end of 1964. George "Red" Kent had begun work at *The Day* in 1914 as a janitor. He had been so devoted to his work that he spent many of his vacations looking at presses in other parts of the country, to the extent that his wife became knowledgeable about the technology. He was referred to often as "Mr. *Day*" for his importance and loyalty. Now both the printer and the pressman who had been pallbearers at Bodenwein's funeral were gone. Walter Crighton, the foreman of the composing room, had retired in 1963, after having been bumped upstairs to make way for Thomas Elliott. Elliott replaced Kent as mechanical superintendent. Wilfred C. Rogers, a printer at *The Day* since 1940, became the composing room foreman, and John Mirtle was named his assistant.

In February 1963, *The Day* asked the Redevelopment Agency for additional land south of its building for future expansion and requested that North Bank Street be widened some more. McGuire negotiated the deal that gave *The Day* the space it needed, including room for a parking lot. The agency modified its plans for North Bank Street to accommodate the newspaper, although it was a tight squeeze and the agency and *The Day* haggled for years about the newspaper's access. Before the agency would sell *The Day* the land south of the building along Main Street, it demanded *The Day* furnish a master plan detailing how the newspaper planned to develop the new land. *The Day* hired William Ginsburg & Associates, a New York engineering firm, to do the work.

By then, the new press already was approaching its limits, and *The Day* planned to buy two new units, which would require still more space. The *Day's* advertising bloomed in 1966, when a new shopping mall on the north side of the highway through the city opened containing two new department stores: Two Guys, a discount store, and higher-end Outlet Company, a Providence, Rhode Island, company. The Outlet Company became the newspaper's biggest advertiser, often running multiple full-page display ads in a single edition.

The directors began to improve the *Day's* employee fringe benefits program, following Bodenwein's wish that the workers be well taken care of and that pay and benefits be attractive enough to draw talented employees. *The Day*, up to that time, provided its employees pensions, but these were small and paid directly out of the newspaper's revenues. The newspaper's benevolence to its employees was informal and fiscally unsound, relying on the discretion of the management. Colby carried on a practice dating back to Bodenwein of caring for employees as though they were family members. The newspaper continued to grant no-interest loans to employees, subject to the approval of the board. When workers had used up their sick time, their pay usually was extended by votes of the directors. Colby, whose kindness and solicitude toward the employees were generally agreed to have been abundant, rarely turned down a request for help, and the directors never denied his recommendations. Significantly, the board occupied itself discussing these matters, sometimes at great length.

McGuire insisted that the newspaper systematize its benefits and brought in representatives from the Hartford National Bank & Trust Company, where he remained a director, to develop a funded pension plan to replace the newspaper's primitive pay-as-you go system. *The Day* also started providing major medical insurance and paid life insurance.

One of McGuire's most distinctive contributions was in the realm of politics and in the political orientation of the newspaper, which had been conservative and Republican. At his urging, in 1966, the newspaper began endorsing candidates for state and national offices after years in which the newspaper had stayed clear of politics. *The Day* had, until then, presented itself as a newspaper that was "independent Republican." While its editorials reflected a knee-jerk Republican point of view, *The Day* never took positions in elections. Kenneth E. Grube, then the editorial page editor, accurately summarized that posture in 1972:

> *For many years,* The Day *deliberately refrained from direct endorsement of political candidates. Our paper generally reflected Republican viewpoints on its editorial page, for this was an era when even small cities supported more than one newspaper, the newspapers openly labeled themselves as Republican or Democratic and partisan editorial pages were the rule rather than the exception. The* Day's *own late owner was a Republican and for decades* The Day *was listed as a Republican paper. Even without formal endorsements, there was no doubt about whom the paper supported.*

Grube went on to explain the change that McGuire brought about:

> *… The* Day's *editorial policy has become independent of partisan ideology. We attempt to provide a variety of opinions on the Editorial Page and are wedded to neither party in analyzing and commenting upon public issues. Thus in recent years,* The Day *has endorsed candidates for public offices ranging from state senator to the president of the United States. These endorsements are not made according to political affiliation. Rather, they attempt to weigh the way we feel they would respond to the particular office they seek.*

Although he was able to persuade the directors to endorse candidates in elections, McGuire wasn't always happy with the results. He found himself outnumbered on the board by die-hard Republicans, which led to several spirited debates over elections.

The Day favored local candidates, provided they could walk and talk. The directors usually were influenced by the recommendations of the editors, Ken Grube and Curt Pierson. In its endorsements in the fall of 1966, the newspaper supported a Democrat, Governor John N. Dempsey, for reelection. It also backed Democrats Ella T. Grasso for secretary of the state and William B. Stanley and John P. Janovic, both local candidates, for state senator. But it endorsed Republicans Joseph H. Goldberg, of Norwich, for Congress over William L. St. Onge, and Morgan K. McGuire, Francis McGuire's brother, for the state Senate.

Francis McGuire's first major political setback on the board occurred in 1968, when he found himself the only director to vote against supporting Richard M. Nixon for president. The choice followed a raging debate, during which the directors almost decided not to endorse anyone. In 1972, when Nixon ran for re-election against George McGovern, the directors were deadlocked, and the newspaper this time did not make any endorsement. *The Day* explained on October 26:

> *The position in which we find ourselves in regard to a Presidential endorsement is akin to that of many families in which the members are divided as to the choice between President Nixon and Senator McGovern. While the family itself may not be voting as a unit, its members can and will vote their choices as individuals.*

THE DIRECTORS MADE A series of management changes in this period that had an even more dramatic effect on the *Day's* editorial policy and on its approach to newsgathering. On November 1, 1965, the directors created a community relations department, placing Deane Avery, who had been the managing editor, in charge. *The Day* had begun an effort to reach out to the community through service organizations and leaders in May 1964. Avery's change of duties began a year later, when he was placed on a leave of absence from the newsroom and given the new title of executive editor purportedly to add to the stature of his office as community relations director. Avery later was given the additional assignment of personnel director.

The move served three purposes. It provided the opportunity to advance Avery in the organization. It placed him in contact with the public, a role the affable executive performed best. And it brought about a change in style in the way *The Day* covered the news. Kenneth E. Grube, more liberal in his social views and aggressive as a newsman, became the new managing editor.

Under Avery's management, *The Day* newsroom had continued in the gentler, old school of reporting characterized by cozy relations with the cops and politicians. Grube advocated asking more hard questions, even if it meant stepping on the toes of those in authority. He had a willing student of his point of view in Curt Pierson, who left his position in the Groton bureau to become Grube's assistant. Of all the family members who rose to positions of authority at *The Day* under Orvin Andrews and Bar Colby's watch, Pierson was clearly the most talented as a journalist. When he left his job in Groton, the Town Council passed a resolution praising his work.

Grube would manage the newsroom for only two years. But during that time, he began to fortify the news staff with a fresh supply of young, well-trained, and more aggressive reporters.

One of the first of these was Morgan McGinley, who arrived in 1965 at the age of 23. McGinley was the grandson of Bodenwein's early mentor and father figure, John McGinley, and nephew of Arthur McGinley, the former *Day* reporter, sidekick of Eugene O'Neill, and sports editor of the Hartford *Times*. Morgan McGinley, a graduate of Colby College in Maine, had started at the Providence *Journal-Bulletin*. Grube hired Stanley DeCoster, a Boston *Globe* intern, who would become one of the newspaper's most accomplished investigative reporters. He also hired Janet Roach, a Barnard College graduate. During her short stay, Roach crafted the routine business before the police court into daily poignant and colorful stories about life in the area. She later became a documentary film producer. Grube hired me as a summer intern while I was a graduate student at Boston University School of Public Communication in the summer of 1966.

I remember the day I arrived. Gina Muzzi, the pleasant women's page editor whose desk faced the elevator, was the first to greet me. Grube's desk was next to hers, along the side of the room that faced Main Street. Curt Pierson sat next to him. Grube got up and warmly shook my hand. He escorted me to a corner in the back of the newsroom next to a picture window that looked out on the Thames River. There were cushioned benches along the wall and a table for staff meetings. Grube summoned Bob Craigue, who had become city editor, and Jim Watterson, the news editor, and we all sat there as Grube recited my academic credentials in an admiring and effusive way that had become his style. Craigue, puffing on a pipe, nodded as Grube continued. I noticed Grube's eyes darted about behind his thick glasses as he talked. Watterson scowled as he looked directly at me through bloodshot eyes with his arms folded during the presentation. When Grube concluded, Watterson growled, "But can he type?" That was the start of my career at *The Day*.

The Day was in the last stages of awakening from a sleep then. Nobody could have planned the events that aroused the newspaper from its long lethargy after Bodenwein's death. This rather bizarre chain of events began in 1967, the year I returned from Boston University as a full-time reporter. Colby had initiated a new training program, a series of monthly seminars that were conducted at dinner meetings at the Crocker House. At one of these gatherings, early in the spring of 1967, Watterson unleashed his pent-up dislike for Colby in an angry tirade before an audience of shocked colleagues. Colby and the other managers later attempted to pacify Watterson, but insisted that he apologize. Watterson refused and in April, the veteran editor hired in 1930 agreed to retire on a disability. He was 56.

Watterson's retirement signified a watershed in the history of *The Day*. He still had commanded respect in the newsroom, and had trained or influenced most of those who survived him in the newsroom. Morgan McGinley, who worked under him, wrote reverentially when Watterson died nine years later:

> *James S. Watterson was a newspaperman for 37 years. Jimmy wasn't simply in the business that long. He was distinguished not chiefly by length of service, but by the fact he was, truly, a newspaperman.*

Watterson's retirement was followed by a series of promotions that were altered by other untoward events. Bob Craigue was to replace Watterson as news editor. John Foley, Craigue's assistant, was to become city editor. Carlson, who had been covering politics, and Raymond Bordner, the newspaper's court reporter, were to become copy editors. The changes were to have taken place on Monday, June 9, 1967.

I was assigned to the police beat then. Part of the police reporter's routine was to have breakfast at the State Police barracks in Groton after sorting through the arrest and accident reports. The ritual was carried out in the timeworn interest of cultivating camaraderie with the police and picking up bits of news that were not contained in the reports. Before breakfast, I would routinely call the city desk to fill in the editors on the stories I'd be writing. Craigue usually answered the phone. But that June morning, Carlson's voice was at the other end. "Have a good breakfast. There've been some very interesting developments here," he told me. Carlson rolled the r in "very."

The interesting developments were that Bob Craigue and Gina Muzzi, the women's page editor, hadn't shown up for work. Craigue had abandoned his wife and children and he and Muzzi had run away together over the weekend. This was a shock at *The Day*, where Craigue was known for his reliability and ambition. His Sunday routine had consisted of going to St. James Episcopal Church, where Colby also worshipped, and later driving around the region looking for story ideas with his wife. Craigue and Muzzi resurfaced in Florida. They requested that *The Day* send them their income statements for the Internal Revenue Service. Craigue later changed his name to Robert Drake and married Muzzi. He worked at the *Times-Picayune* in New Orleans for ten years before his death on October 15, 1980.

At its next meeting, the board discussed this personnel crisis and family tragedy in the context of the need to liberalize the newspaper's pay and benefits to attract talented news executives from other newspapers. The board gave Colby the authority both to raise editorial department salaries and grant news executives fringe benefits comparable to the ones they had where they had worked before joining *The Day*. An experienced editor would not have to start over accumulating seniority for paid vacation and other benefits.

The Day set out on a nationwide search to fill the news editor's spot. The management hoped in particular to find an editor who could help modernize the design of *The Day* to improve its appearance. By August, Grube felt he had found just the person the newspaper was looking for, an experienced editor with stunning academic and professional credentials from a large newspaper in the Middle West. The selection was posted on the newsroom bulletin board, with Grube's breathless recital of his vitae. His arrival was anxiously awaited, until Grube received an apologetic letter from the alcohol rehabilitation ward of a New York Hospital. The *Day's* news editor-elect had been admitted there after falling off the wagon. He explained that he was so thrilled over his new job that he stopped to celebrate over a drink at an airport bar in New York and the next thing he knew he found himself in the hospital.

The Day quickly recovered from this setback and hired another applicant, David Anderson, a deskman at the Miami *Herald*, as news editor. Elizabeth Lengyel, a writer for the New Haven *Register*, joined *The Day* as Gina Muzzi's replacement on the women's page. The others who had been promoted took their places, and *The Day* set out on a new era of innovations.

T W E N T Y - F I V E

DEVASTATION

This community, thank the Almighty, has been spared the passions

which led to wanton destruction and bloodshed in so many cities,

uprisings which debased and destroyed the innocent who are by and far

the majority in all of the races and creeds,

which make up American humanity.

—*The Day,* October 19, 1968

ALTHOUGH NEW LONDON ESCAPED the riots that shocked so many cities, the late 1960s crashed into it with the fury of the 1938 Hurricane, shaking the city to its ancient foundations. Only this time the tempest was manmade in the form of urban renewal. It ripped apart old ethnic neighborhoods, uprooted small businesses and familiar landmarks, and rattled the political and social structures.

Internal changes also jolted *The Day* as suddenly and as dramatically as Theodore Bodenwein's death had in the hurricane's wake early in 1939. These changes, concentrated in the fall of 1967, at last freed the newspaper from its entanglement with the past and began to unleash the potential within the Bodenwein will. But the urban renewal storm that struck New London left the newspaper surrounded with devastation and a sense of bewilderment that it was unable either to explain or alleviate.

Urban renewal reduced whole blocks of the city to rubble. Some of the debris was used as fill to create new and unfamiliar streets while old streets vanished. The advance of the wrecking ball was so relentless that the disorienting transformation of the old city became part of the local routine. At first, when the story still was a novelty, *The Day* chronicled it in pictures. But with the quickening pace the editors gave up trying to keep up with the demolition crews as they moved up and down the streets with their heavy equipment and commotion. The newspaper contented itself with publishing matter-of-fact wrap-ups of the Redevelopment Agency's march to condemn property and tear down the buildings that stood there. By the time it was finished in the early 1970s, the agency had razed more than five hundred buildings within eyesight of *The Day*. They ranged in size from two-story houses to the four-story Victorian Neptune Building, a stunning and elegant brick structure the same age as the original *Day* building. The whole neighborhood where Theodore Bodenwein had lived as a teenager was leveled.

In the place of crowded and picturesque old neighborhoods and familiar street scenes, the destruction left a desert of empty lots giving downtown New London the look of a bombed-out city. After making their deadlines, *Day* reporters took shortcuts across gravel lots to get to the bars that were still standing. Skrigan's was the only old building slated to be demolished that was still left along North Bank Street behind *The Day* that summer of 1967. I spent many afternoons there in the company of friends from *The Day* and the regular crowd of old-timers from the former neighborhood. A few diehard patrons arrived in taxis from the places beyond walking distance to which they had been relocated.

To add to the excitement, the Vietnam War was closing in on us. Those of draft age (I was 24) were anxious about our futures. Stan DeCoster and Morgan McGinley each got into the National Guard. I was drafted into the Army in January 1968. Ken Grube gave me an anthology of I. F. Stone's essays as a going-away gift.

Skrigan's friendly little oasis helped make the waiting more tolerable. Living totally in the present under such absurd circumstances made the changes that were occurring outside actually appear normal to me. But others less existential in their outlooks were wounded by a sense of loss. Daylight, now unimpeded by surrounding buildings, beat in through a picture window of the bar. I remember the window framing the muscular body of Sam Skrigan in his bar apron as he looked into the vacant tracts. The man was built like a refrigerator. He had a high-pitched voice and his laugh was penetrating. He'd shake his head and curse the Redevelopment Agency for what it was doing to this small corner of the world. They used to call the area New London's Little Ukraine but now it looked like the surface of the moon. Skrigan's closed October 19, 1967. John Foley wrote the obituary. The hour it closed, the editor played an Irish drinking song on the juke box in the Russian bar so he could write in his lead the next day, "They played 'The Wearing of the Green' at 1 am today at Sam Skrigan's venerable thirst-quenching establishment at 38 North Bank Street." Coast Guard cadets who frequented the bar later had a plaque in memory of the bar placed at the entrance of a parking garage that was built at the site. The memorial still greets *Day* employees who park there, but most of these are too young to remember Skrigan's.

Small businesses were ripped out from what still had been a busy commercial area despite the blighted conditions. Theodore Bodenwein years earlier had helped several of the businessmen get started in the belief these enterprises would add to the vitality of the city and the newspaper's advertising revenue. Bodenwein had doubts about the survival instincts of the complacent Yankee mercantile class in the city, but held out great hope for the more eager, foreign-born entrepreneurs like himself who set up shop in the city in the early part of the century. Many of them were Jews who were driven from Russia and Eastern Europe by the pogroms there. Bodenwein generously rallied to their assistance. These were, in his mind, sound investments, more reliable than some of the stock and real estate he invested in.

Redevelopment forced Soltz's kosher meat market, which Bodenwein had supported with a loan from *The Day*, to move into a less convenient location in the city. The family had to give up its slaughterhouse, where cattle and chickens were killed and dressed in the kosher tradition. The market once had received its livestock from farms across the region, including Jewish farms in Colchester and Montville, but that activity ended with urban renewal.

Beit Brothers market, which also had benefited from Bodenwein's help, had to move to a less traveled part of the city. Gorra's market across from the newspaper never reappeared after its building was razed. The program ended the long life of Bishop's Studios next to *The Day,* where Gordon Bodenwein sometimes visited his friend Elsie Bishop, and countless other small businesses that had made up the mosaic of downtown New London. By late that year, the effects of urban renewal had become starkly evident. New London awoke to the reality like a homeowner returning from a pleasant vacation to find his house had burned down. Nobody had foreseen the results from the conceptual drawings of Maurice Rotival, who had designed the plan to revitalize the city. New Londoners became more anxious as the expanses of bulldozed land increased in size and little headway was made at filling them with the department store, new housing, and office buildings that had been promised. Among the few, halting signs of progress were a new automobile body shop

bove, Riggers once again had to move the *Day's* printing equipment in 960, this time from the fourth floor to the second floor of the new ddition. *The Day*

Above, Francis McGuire dominated *The Day* for twenty years, from his election to the board in 1962 until his death in 1982. He mobilized the legal effort to protect The Day Trust from a challenge by the Internal Revenue Service. *Helen McGuire*

bove, Printers set type on bulky and intricate Linotype machines before computers and advanced rinting techniques changed all that in the 1970s. This picture was taken in the *Day's* old composing oom before new quarters were constructed in 1960. Printer Bill Campbell, to the right wearing the ndershirt, was legendary for his speed. *New London Typographical Union No. 159*

Right, This distinctive monument stands over the graves of Gordon Bodenwein, his mother Jane, or "Jennie," and several of his aunts and uncles on the Muir side of the family. *Skip Weisenburger, The Day*

Above, Orvin Andrews, seated in the center, presided ove the board until his death in 1973. However the real control even before his retirement as general manager in 1959 was in the hands of Bar Colby, second from the right, and Francis McGuire, far right. They groomed W Hammond and Deane Avery, standing left and right, to take over the newspaper when Colby retired. The others in the picture are trustees Thomas Troland and Charles Sortor. *The Day*

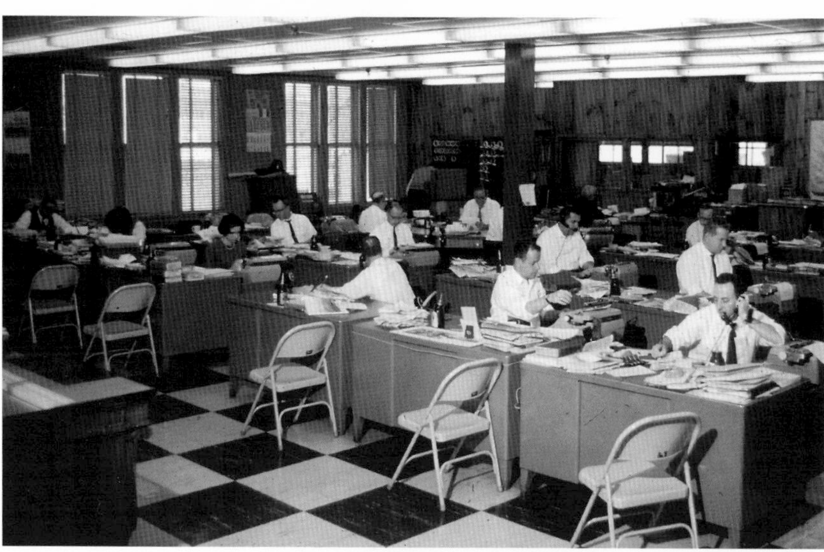

Left, Jim Watterson, just behind the post in th rear of the photo, was still a dominant figure in the newsroom when this picture was taken in 196 Ken Grube, the managin editor, is at the far left. Gina Muzzi, the society editor who fell in love and ran away with Robert Craigue just after he had been named to replace Watterson as news editor, i the third fron the left. *The Day*

Right, *The Day* opened a larger office in Groton as the town grew in the 1960s as a result of defense spending. Curt Pierson, left rear, ran the office until he was promoted to assistant managing editor. His brother-in-law, Art Weber, at the desk in front of him, was a reporter. Both were married to nieces of Deane Avery and rose to high positions. *The Day*

Left, This was the view from *The Day* looking north along Main Street, over the roof of the Savings Bank of New London, in the 1960s, before urban renewal leveled the area. Most of the buildings were razed for the project, including a Revolutionary War era tavern on the right side of the street. Hammy's, a popular watering hole for *The Day*, was on the left, beyond the supermarket in the foreground. *The Day*

bove, Deane Avery, leaning against desk, confers with rt Jenkins, the Page One editor, in this photo taken in 966. *The Day*

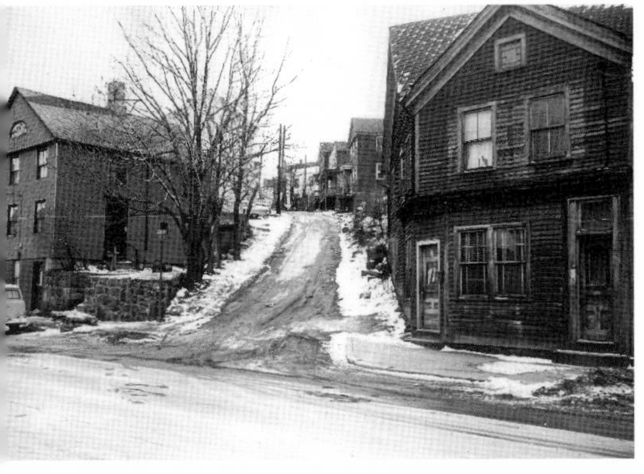

bove, Streets like Stony Hill disappeared from the ap during New London's urban renewal juggernaut the late 1960s. *The Day*

Below, Jim McKenna, right, sold advertising and reported the news in Mystic in the 1950s and 1960s. *The Day*

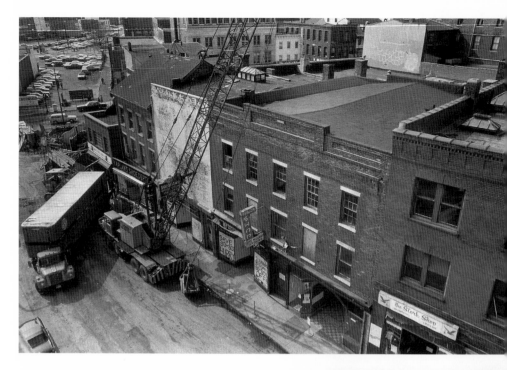

Above, A wrecking crew proceeds down one side of Main Street, opposite *The Day*. All the buildings in the foreground of the picture were razed. They included earlier quarters of *The Day*, where Ezra Whittlesey, the business manager, was shot by an irate reader, and George Starr's print shop, where Bodenwein published his first newspaper. *The Day*

Above, Jack Urwiller's polished work won *The Day* widespread recognition for the artistic quality of its photography. Examples include this picture illustrating the brooding solitude of a tree and a bird against the moonlit sky. *Jack Urwiller*

Above, Jack Urwiller assembled a team of prize-winning photographers after he was hire in 1968 as the *Day's* first chief photographer. *The Day*

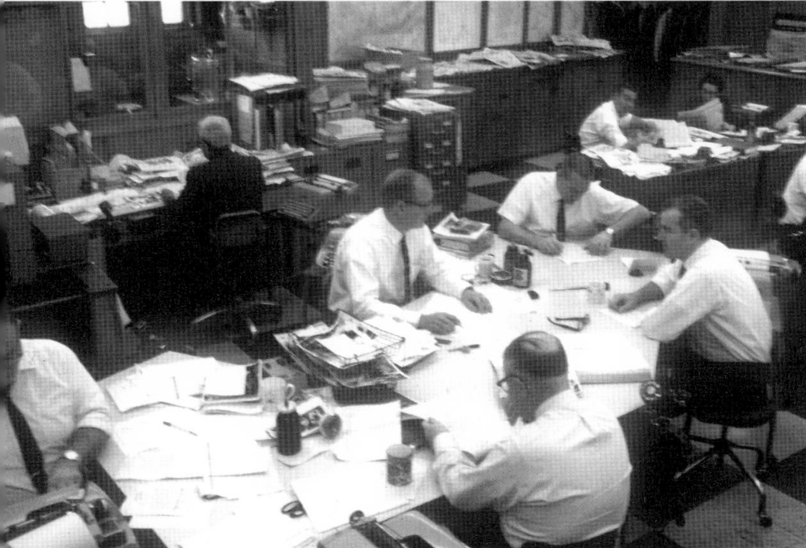

Left, Dave Anderson, center, was hired in 1967 to modernize the look of *The Day*. In a short time, he overhauled the appearance and spirit of the newspaper. *The Day*

bove, Kenneth E. Grube restored a local touch to the *ay's* editorial page in the 1960s. *Mary Ann Grube*

Above, Nuclear submarines produced at the Electric Boat Shipyard, like this one photographed by Jack Urwiller in the late 1960s, played an increasingly important role in the life of the territory covered by *The Day*. *Jack Urwiller*

Above, New London civil rights leader Linwood Bland, far right, led this march through New London in the early 1960s. *New London County Historical Society*

Right, Bill Mitchell reads the afternoon paper from an observation post on a roof while he was covering an accident for *The Day* in 1967. The intern later was fired in a showdown with management during a period of growing turmoil in the newsroom. *William Mitchell*

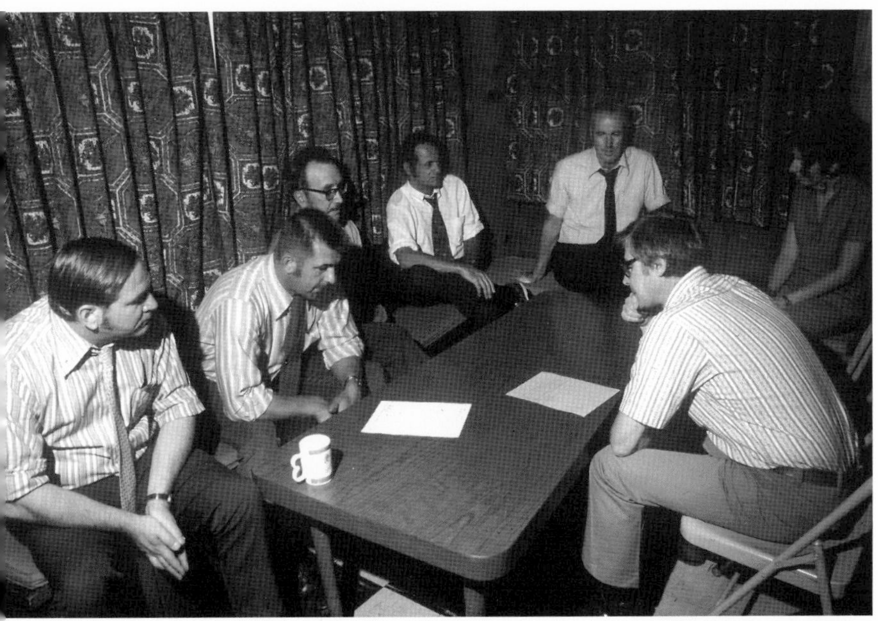

bove, Curt Pierson, right, presides over a morning editors' eeting. The others, from left, are Dave Carlson, Art Weber, Ray ancourt, Bob Colby, John Foley, and Liz Lengyel. *The Day*

bove, The news staff in the early 1970s worked hard and played ard. Pictured here from left at an office Christmas party are, ichael Bagwell, Morgan McGinley, Jack Urwiller, Norm derberg, John Foley, and John Peterson. The box being esented to Foley contained a parakeet. *The Day*

Above, Morgan McGinley, hired in 1965, belonged to the latest of three generations of McGinleys represented on the *Day* staff. His grandfather, John, became the first reporter in 1881. His uncle Arthur was a young reporter for the newspaper before World War I. *The Day*

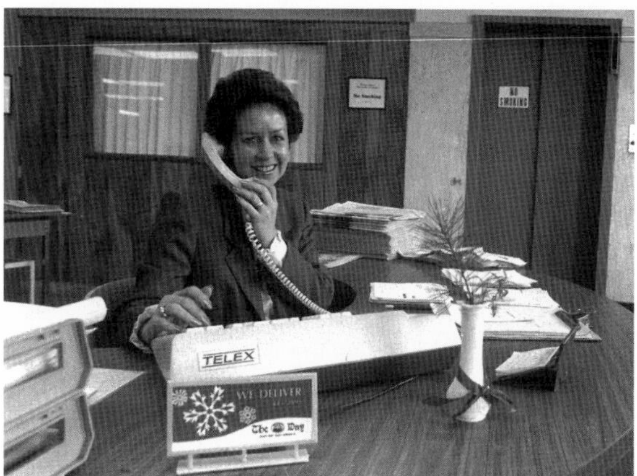

Left, Anita Louise Taylor was one of only two telephone operators at *The Day* since the 1930s. Men fell in love with her voice over the phone. *The Day*

Above, John Peterson was a promising reporter and leader in the newsroom, but left after having been passed over for a promotion. *The Day*

Above, The *Day* newsroom in the early 1970s was split into a night and day staff. That and the swift promotion of Bar Colby's son, Robert, back to camera, raised the hackles of the staff. *The Day*

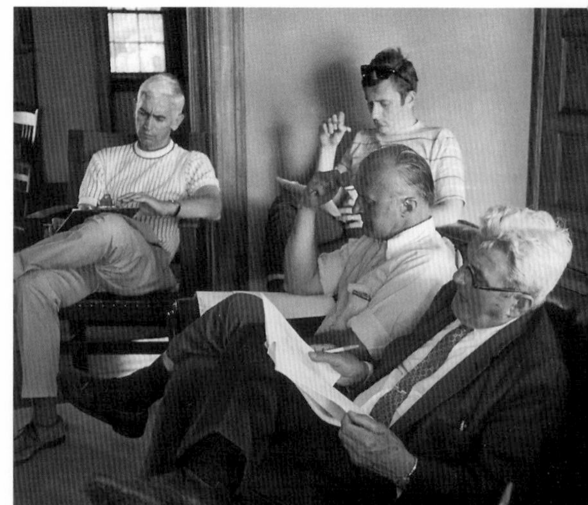

Right, John DeGange, far right, attends a press conference for the Yale-Harvard regatta, an event he covered for *The Day* for decades. *Jack DeGange*

developed by Emma Lincoln, the leader of the city's Republican Party, and a complex of high-rise apartment buildings for low-income families. The apartment buildings rose as far off to one side and out of the way as the agency could squeeze them, next to the highway bridge across the river. *The Day* enthusiastically hailed the opening of the Winthrop Apartments in the fall of 1967. Work began on an office building south of *The Day*. But little else appeared on the barren landscape.

Urban renewal wasn't the only force that was undermining the city's confidence. The Coast Guard Academy was moving ahead with a ten-year, $16 million expansion plan that reached into the quiet, pleasant residential areas near Connecticut College for fresh land. The area was near the spot where Edna Bodenwein and her Little Slam bridge club sometimes had met at Florence Fitch's secluded cottage on the Thames River. It encompassed a neighborhood where many college faculty members resided. The real estate in the path of the Coast Guard's expansion included a 19th century shipyard, owned by the Chappell family, where yachts were repaired. The city grew concerned not only over the impact this was having on its social structure, but over the losses it was causing to its tax base.

The Cold War stretched the military installations in the region to their limits. The Electric Boat shipyard swelled with new workers, who poured into the region to build a new class of nuclear attack submarines, vessels designed to hunt down and attack Soviet submarines. By then, Polaris-class submarines also were being built to carry missiles armed with nuclear warheads. The suddenness of that growth in the shipyard gave rise to new labor tensions and produced housing shortages and a competition for jobs that aggravated racial tensions with the waves of blacks who were moving north in search of shipyard jobs. Shipyard workers went on strike in the summer of 1968.

The Navy looked to the congested Italian neighborhood known as "The Fort" for land to expand its sonar laboratory at Fort Trumbull. The Navy's laboratory had become an important part of the nation's submarine defenses against the Soviet Union and required additional space for its secret work and growing force of scientists and engineers. Some of the same enterprises that Theodore Bodenwein and New London's other leaders had fought for years earlier were starting to be viewed as threats to the city's well-being. People were in the path of this new spurt of progress. Homes, stores, and meeting halls in the Italian neighborhoods where Dr. C. John Satti had campaigned for Franklin Roosevelt and the Democrats in the 1930s stood in the way of this expansion. The neighborhoods spread out along Shaw's Cove, where the Redevelopment

Agency was considering a second renewal project tied in with a federal flood protection plan for the waterfront area. The flood plain, pounded by the 1938 hurricane, bordered Bank Street, near the *Day's* earlier quarters at the turn of the century. All this would seem to be enough of a blow for a small city. But there was more in store. The state planned a new highway project through East New London that rivaled redevelopment for the impact it would have on the predominantly Slavic neighborhood. The two-lane highway bridge across the Thames River had become a bottleneck on the new interstate expressway between New York and Boston. The problem was aggravated by massive traffic jams during the rush hours at the Electric Boat shipyard. The state police were so exasperated by the daily traffic headaches they had to untangle that they considered a plan to remove disabled cars from the bridge with helicopters.

State highway engineers designed a twin span next to the existing bridge to ease the flow of traffic. An expressway from the highway to downtown New London was added to satisfy the city's demands for its share of the benefits from the new roads. The elaborate plans, with their cloverleaf interchanges and a wide artery into the city, required taking massive amounts of additional property in this congested part of the city. These plans made it necessary for the Redevelopment Agency to demand still more land in downtown New London to compensate for what it lost to highway construction.

The area was experiencing change in another arena. Social unrest from the civil rights struggle could not help but influence the area dominated by *The Day*, where about three thousand blacks now lived. The response was tame in comparison to other parts of the country, but nevertheless significant. Leaders in the black community, led by Linwood Bland, a mechanic and leader of the NAACP from 1962 to 1968, were emboldened by the national civil rights movement and became more vocal on fair housing and employment issues.

But it was a constant struggle for Bland and other young black leaders to get the conservative Negro community in the city fired up over the upheaval that was taking place in the rest of the country. The Reverend Albert A. Garvin, pastor of the city's largest black church, Shiloh Baptist Church, and elder statesman in the black community, set the tone. He favored a more conciliatory approach in securing civil rights, one that did not offend the white businesses and rich New Londoners who employed blacks in the city as domestics. Garvin quietly had been battling for greater dignity for the city's blacks since he had arrived in the city and had taken charge of Shiloh Baptist Church in 1937. But he had favored diplomacy for such causes as getting *The Day* to stop the obnoxious practice of gratuitously referring to blacks by their race in headlines and stories. Typical of this policy, when Bessie Franklyn, 38, of 45 North Bank Street, had been fatally knifed in her apartment in November 1938, the *Day's* story appeared under a headline, "Negro woman dies of slashing."

Garvin had the support of members of the Jewish business community, who had been offended that Jews were identified in this same demeaning manner in the newspaper and had threatened an advertising boycott. But their argument with the newspaper's management got nowhere until the Reverend Oliver Bell, an influential white Methodist minister, joined the cause. *The Day* had agreed to stop the practice of racial labeling on the eve of World War II. Bell had been a Rotarian with Theodore Bodenwein and Orvin Andrews.

Garvin always was cautious not to jeopardize the jobs of blacks in the city by pushing the case too hard. He was grateful for small triumphs, and appreciative of the *Day's* solicitude. He was welcome at the newspaper and enjoyed an open pulpit in his letters to the editor on racial issues. The newspaper had led a campaign in 1947 to raise funds for medical expenses for Gadwell Knowles, an eight-year-old black child suffering from tubercular meningitis. *The Day* also went to the assistance of other black families in need, including a family that was burned out of its home. On October 28, 1947, Garvin expressed his gratitude in a letter to *The Day*:

> *It is the human touch of* The Day, *and the fine people of its staff, that help number it among the outstanding newspapers in the nation. It is a newspaper at its best, emphasizing the human side of the community life, restoring faith and confidence, demonstrating democracy and instilling hope in the minds of the people. It is easily sensed that these humanitarian acts of* The Day *have no commercial intent; they are simply a spontaneous Christian gesture.*

New London was a compact city in which the races had by and large managed to get along as a matter of necessity. The older generation, which included Linwood Bland's father, Linwood Bland, Sr., eschewed militancy. Bland's father had moved to New London from the South as a baseball player in the 1920s, and as the friendly and distinguished bartender at the Mohican Hotel, he was held in high regard and affection by some of the city's most important figures.

But the son was impatient with the deference the black elders displayed toward the white community. He had found support for a more militant approach among younger blacks who attended Negro colleges in the South after the war and returned with more radical ideas. These included Garvin's son, Albert Garvin, Jr. Bland also found backing at Connecticut College in Jane Torrey, a professor there. Torrey was the voter registration chairman for the NAACP. During Bland's leadership of the NAACP, blacks and their supporters picketed the Woolworth's store in downtown New London in sympathy with the lunch-counter sit-ins that were taking place in the South. *The Day* supported the civil rights struggle in the South but spoke out against the local demonstrations on the editorial page, arguing that the New London branch of Woolworth's both employed and accommodated blacks.

Drawn into the national political maelstrom, a liberal wing began to gain strength in the city's Democratic organization. It included Connecticut College faculty, Jews from the south end of the city, and business leaders like Harvey Mallove. They began to form a wedge in Satti's more conservative and traditional Democratic organization. Satti died in 1968, leaving the problem to Abraham A. Washton, a lawyer, who had been a lieutenant in his organization since the 1940s. Washton's task over the next two decades would be to make room for blacks, Jews, Hispanics, and intellectuals in the party without alienating the old guard. Satti's large family and their confederates had by then assumed a powerful proprietary interest in the party.

The political equilibrium was disrupted further by court-ordered redistricting. "One man, one vote" rulings that demanded better representation in the legislature ended Connecticut's system of sending to the legislature two representatives from each community, regardless of its population. This move weakened the influence of the Republican Party and small towns in rural Connecticut.

THE CATACLYSM IN NEW LONDON was accompanied by changes at *The Day*. Gordon Bodenwein, whose position on the board of trustees had been left vacant since he left *The Day* in 1950, died on August 10, 1967. Deane Avery was elected to replace him as one of the two employee trustees. Gordon had left the Benedictine monks where he had helped build a new monastery and had resettled in the resort city of Acapulco with Leonardo Cèsar Padilla. A mutual friend of the two, Raymond Coté, owned a hotel in Mexico and had visited Bodenwein in New London in the late 1940s, according to Raymond Izbicki. In Acapulco, Gordon changed his will, disinheriting his sister, Elizabeth Miles, and the Benedictines. He made Cèsar Padilla, also of Morelia, his only heir. Gordon had invested money in a hotel in the Copacabana section of Acapulco in Cèsar Padilla's name, according to New London probate records. The proceeds of The Day Trust in this fashion reached at least as far as Mexico.

When Gordon died, Elizabeth had his body returned to New London. *The Day* paid the expenses. There was a requiem high mass at St. Paul's Church in

Waterford, which a small delegation of *Day* directors and managers attended. He was buried next to his mother, Jennie, in Cedar Grove Cemetery, beneath the modernistic monument he had designed. Elizabeth, now Theodore Bodenwein's last surviving heir, and Wesley Hammond took places on the board of directors. On November 1, George Clapp retired and Ken Grube replaced him on the editorial page. Curt Pierson became the managing editor. All of these changes came rapidly in the closing months of 1967 and jolted *The Day* onto a more progressive track.

Miles and Hammond joined ranks with Francis McGuire on the board as the management set out to make fresh investments and bring about innovations in the newspaper. The balance of power on the board meant the managers would have to do so on McGuire's exacting and meticulous terms. Francis McGuire, and not Bar Colby, became the most influential person on the newspaper until McGuire's death in 1982, a situation that was to the mutual advantage of Colby and McGuire and the ultimate benefit of *The Day*.

Curt Pierson, as the new chief executive in the newsroom, led *The Day* into a period of more aggressive and probing journalism. Grube, with McGuire's encouragement and support on the board, brought a fresh perspective and sense of mission in the community to the newspaper, along with an uncharacteristically liberal and Democratic orientation. As city editor, John Foley brought his raw, keen instincts as a newsman to bear on gathering the news. These changes, by a miracle of circumstances, combined to place all the right people in the right places. David Anderson's arrival marked the end of the Jim Watterson area. Anderson worked for *The Day* less than a year before he tired of the stifling small-town mentality of the top management of the newspaper and returned to Miami. But in the short time he was in New London in 1967 and 1968, he infused the newspaper with a fresh spirit.

Colby and the directors had acknowledged the *Day's* weaknesses when they had used additional resources to recruit an experienced news editor from outside New London. Hiring David Anderson to fill Jim Watterson's spot was an important step, but Anderson had good material to work with. Even before his arrival, the newspaper had become good enough to attract favorable attention. In 1963, it received the advertising industry's N. W. Ayer Award for excellence in printing, makeup, and typography. The contest judged nine hundred fifty-five newspapers in fifty states. *The Day* was among eleven winners. Others included the New York *Times*, Baltimore *Sun*, and *Wall Street Journal*. *The Day* won the recognition even with its crowded, nine-column front page and the fact that printers, not editors, made up the pages inside the newspaper.

Anderson was a flamboyant and irreverent editor accustomed to the dynamic atmosphere of a big metropolitan newspaper. In addition to his impressive professional credentials, he was friendly and helpful, mischievous, enthusiastic about the news, prompt to praise good work, and sometimes outrageous. He joyfully bellowed orders, questions, and encouragement across the newsroom. He was, to be concise, a breath of fresh air compared to his dour and stubborn predecessor. From the moment he arrived and moved into his position in the "slot" at the center of the city desk, he stirred the imagination of the newsroom. "He was a great guy. He fired up the staff. He brought out the best in everyone," Morgan McGinley remembers.

Anderson set out to dress up the front page by reducing the number of columns from nine to eight. The newspaper started using photographs more boldly. The editors left more room, or white space, around stories and headlines, giving the page a brighter and airier appearance. The push for change liberated the pent-up talents of the Page One editor, Arthur Jenkins, who went on to produce front pages that were graceful, elegant, and occasionally powerful.

The editors began planning the layout and positioning of stories on the inside pages. The pages, which in the past had been thrown together by printers in the composing room, now were laid out ahead of time on paper dummies on the copy desk with an eye toward their appearance and importance. *The Day* turned to a "modular" format in which stories were organized in neat blocks rather than wrapped around other stories in doglegs. This was the newspaper's first attempt at "packaging" stories and photographs to be more eye-catching. The improvement gave the newspaper a cleaner and more organized look and added to the impact of good stories. *The Day* started using more local stories on the front page, and began to feature the best of them across the top of the page. Anderson's knowledge extended to newspaper production, and he used it to drive the composing room and pressroom to improve the quality of reproduction in *The Day*.

The newspaper placed a greater emphasis on photography, investing additional resources unusual for a newspaper its size to hire accomplished photographers. *The Day* had not up to that time fully escaped from the years during World War II when pictures were minimized to conserve metal, or from the years the photographers worked under the photoengraver rather than the editors. Throughout the 1950s and much of the 1960s, *The Day* depended upon Clayton "Bud" Farrar, another Bulkeley graduate, one-time track star, and old-fashioned photographer who always had a big cigar in his mouth. Farrar, a technically proficient photographer, perfected the genre of the "line-up" shot, in which subjects were herded into lines, asked to smile and captured on film in that unnatural pose. The *Day's* pages were filled with these photographic cliches that gave the newspaper a gray appearance despite its good typography.

This changed on February 12, 1968, when *The Day* recruited Jack Urwiller, an Associated Press photographer who had worked in Denver and Philadelphia, to be its first chief photographer. Urwiller hired two talented young photographers to join him: John Ligos and Gordon Alexander. Together, they revamped the way *The Day* used pictures. The innovative environment even motivated Hubert Warren, a part-time *Day* photographer from the old school who traveled on assignments with a French poodle he called Pierre, to do some fine work. Urwiller and the other photographers combed the region looking for pictures that captured human drama, the area's abundant beauty, and the offbeat. *The Day* had not used photographs to portray the captivating seaside and rural scenery and life of the region since Theodore Bodenwein published pictorial special editions in the early part of the century. Such drama in pictures had not been seen in the newspaper since William Brutzman and the *Day's* other photographers in the late 1930s had documented the Bank Street fire and other ravages of the 1938 hurricane.

Urwiller moved into a house on the Mystic River, across from the Mystic Seaport museum, and often spotted his subjects as he set out for work in the morning: scenes such as the old whaling ship *Charles W. Morgan* through mists rising from the river and waterfowl in motion near the river's surface. On January 9, 1968, *The Day* showcased Urwiller's work in a layout. His pictures showed the brooding solitude of a tree and a bird against the moonlit sky; the weather-beaten face of an old woman; a seagull swooping toward the water; a Veterans Day observance in which the surroundings are reflected in a soldier's ceremonial chrome helmet.

While Anderson's charismatic presence helped set the tone for innovation, Curt Pierson furnished the drive and leadership that moved the newspaper forward. Pierson, 33, was the husband of Latham Avery's older daughter and Deane Avery's niece, Katharine. He had developed an interest in journalism in high school. He had been editor of the school newspaper and won a $1,000 scholarship, a large sum of money in 1952, for his newspaper talents. He was youthful, good looking, and got along well with the *Day's* staff. He was a natural leader.

Pierson encouraged reporting that dug below the surface without fear of authority. He freed reporters from the drudgery of their beats to delve into stories. Under his leadership, Norman Soderberg, hired from the New Haven

Register in 1964, became the *Day's* first investigative reporter, with the new title of special affairs reporter. *The Day* sent Soderberg to the American Press Institute in New York for a seminar on investigative reporting and turned him loose on two of the city's most pressing and important stories in the 1960s: race relations and redevelopment. Fast-moving events gave urgency to both these matters.

The assassination of Martin Luther King, Jr., on April 4, 1968, unleashed a new wave of violence in American cities. Even before that, *The Day* had been watching the developments in other cities with apprehension. On March 19, Grube warned in an editorial of the danger from mere rumors of violence. "Dignifying a rumor by even discussing it publicly is a dangerous thing to do," he wrote. *The Day* helped arrange a meeting at the New London YWCA to discuss the mounting racial tensions, but only twelve people attended. Grube wrote another editorial on March 23 expressing disappointment at the low attendance and warning of the consequences of indifference:

> *Before any kind of commitment can be made by the vast majority of citizens, this exchange of views must take place before audiences which number far, far in excess of 12 persons. Vast displays of disinterest will surely discourage people who are trying to do something constructive.*

The news of King's murder reverberated in New London, where racial tensions at New London High School already had been inflamed by a controversy over interracial dating. The NAACP's youth council had charged that teachers were notifying white parents that their children were dating blacks. The principal, William Foye, denied the accusations. In the days following King's murder, black students at the high school staged a walkout over the principal's objection and Foye clumsily threatened to penalize them. After a memorial service, blacks marched spontaneously through the city. The first stop was *The Day*. Just as the march that followed Dr. C. John Satti's first victory in the 1930s had found its way to the front of the newspaper, the civil rights marchers almost instinctively wound up at the front entrance of *The Day*. There they pleaded for the newspaper's involvement and prayed. The march then proceeded along the same path the earlier Satti demonstrators had followed to the courthouse, near Satti's early New London homestead, where they registered their objections to the fact that all the city's deputy sheriffs were white.

Clarence Faulk Jr., one of New London's young black civil rights leaders, telephoned Grube, who was a member of the NAACP and a friend, for advice about how to defuse the growing tensions. The two discussed the idea of creating a college scholarship for high school students in King's memory. Faulk arranged a meeting of some of the city's leaders to explore the idea. The group, which met at the Hartford National Bank, the *Day's* bank, included Grube, Ralph E. Wadleigh, Jr., the bank's treasurer, Eunice Waller, a black teacher, the Reverend Norman MacLeod, Jr., pastor of the Second Congregational Church and Richard R. Martin, the mayor of the city. The meeting resulted in the Martin Luther King Scholarship Fund, which since then has helped send scores of black high school students to colleges, some to Ivy League colleges. Grube summarized the sentiment behind the cause in an editorial that week:

> *No amount of tokenism on the one hand or violence on the other is going to make Dr. King's dream a reality. He sought a higher quality of American life for all, white and black. The effort, if it is to succeed in Dr. King's memory and to the everlasting benefit of mankind, must start locally.*

In response to the events and pressure from civil rights leaders, *The Day* assigned Soderberg to explore the city's racial problems. The result was a series published in October 1968 entitled "The Negro and The City." The journalistic effort went against the grain of local sentiment, which opposed even acknowledging racial problems in fear this would aggravate tensions. *The Day* explained:

> *Some very sincere people said this was a "bad time" to publish something like this. They feel this is a critical period, when one inexact move, one misinterpretation, could undo what already has been done. Others sense a growing reluctance on the part of the white majority to actively think, and do something about the situation which has been before our very eyes for so many years ...* The Day *submits that the only antidote to social unrest is reason and a willingness to face reality and do something positive about it.*

Soderberg's stories documented racial biases in hiring and housing in the city and generally in the way blacks were mistreated. They pointed out the dilemma blacks faced in standing up for their rights at the risk of being ostracized in the small city and possibly losing their jobs. They reported that blacks occupied no positions of importance in city government. The Redevelopment Agency, in particular, had no black employees in significant paid positions or on its policy board although its actions affected a large number of minority families who were being uprooted by the project. While the new laws supposedly guaranteed fair housing and employment, Soderberg wrote, there had been little progress in enforcing them. Even *The Day* was not spared criticism in the article. McKinley Winston, a black neighborhood leader, observed there were disproportionately few blacks in any of the city's businesses and industries, including the newspaper. *The Day* at the time had only one black employee, a custodian, although the directors had begun discussing recruiting black reporters. The last story detailed advances that were being made primarily in volunteer efforts by social service agencies in improving conditions.

The series gave Grube the hope that New London and its surroundings, whose racial problems were still small in scale, could set an example in improving race relations and ending discrimination:

> *This is a region which can, if it will, lead the nation in a demonstration of racial harmony. It is not a question of spending huge sums of money or passing a lot of new laws. Rather, it is a question of understanding the humanity of all and the basic dignity of all. Vast gaps remain between promise and performance. Closing those gaps is a human responsibility of the greatest importance. The future depends on what we recognize of today's realities so that we can correct tomorrow's course.*

The Day distinguished itself in its racial coverage by assuming a leadership role before problems got out of hand. Even before the turbulent events of the late 1960s, the newspaper had won the trust of black leaders like the Reverend Albert Garvin by opening its doors and its pages to them and supporting black causes in a concrete way, as it did with the fund-raising drive in 1947 for young Gadwell Knowles. The *Day's* directors also donated annually to the NAACP. But Grube carried this outreach a step further by developing friendships in the black community and taking the lead in the Martin Luther King Scholarship Fund.

It's true that although *The Day* made a deliberate attempt to report on black issues, it remained a white institution with a white perspective. The newspaper did little if anything to cater to the tastes of black readers. For another two decades, few black faces appeared on the obituary pages and among the wedding announcements. The *Day's* greatest utility for black leaders was the vehicle it furnished for communicating with the white community. The newspaper's commitment to help the black community brought the newspaper stature and respect, to the degree that even when the newspaper offended blacks, usually through some inadvertent slight or oversight, the black leaders went easy on the editors. This cordial relationship enabled the newspaper to remain a constructive leader on civil rights in the city.

The same wasn't true with urban renewal. Although the newspaper led in race relations, from the start it dismally trailed events dealing with redevelopment. The newspaper endorsed the program without asking any of the logical questions. It accepted the Redevelopment Agency's word that developers were waiting in the wings with plans for new buildings and enterprises—apartments for all classes, office buildings, and a big-city department store, among other things. Along with the rest of the city, it failed to divine the crushing impact the program would have on its historic character and the culture of the neighborhoods in the renewal areas. It ignored the abundant possibilities for self-serving that such a sweeping real estate undertaking afforded. By August 1968, when the city was growing disillusioned by the devastation and lack of progress in redeveloping the area and Soderberg was assigned to investigate the program, all the newspaper could do was catalogue the mess that already had developed.

The Day published a seven-part series prepared by Soderberg entitled, "The Good Ship New London Redevelopment." The series expanded the metaphor, at painful length, that the Redevelopment Agency was a ship that was taking on water and in danger of sinking. It pointed to a history of agency bungling, including its failure to follow up on a Providence, Rhode Island, department store's interest in opening a store in the renewal area. The Outlet Company chose instead to build its New London store in a shopping mall along the highway in the outskirts of New London. Soderberg suggested that one of the reasons the project was failing was that the city lacked strong leadership, a situation he theorized grew out of the city manager form of government. The city didn't have a strong mayor to promote the project and hold the agencies accountable. His stories questioned the wisdom of relying too much on a department store to revitalize the city. But the series still concluded that the project was fundamentally a sound idea and still was New London's best hope to revive its business district.

The reporter exposed the problem, but added little that people didn't already know. Significantly, it failed to address growing suspicions and anger over the central role of Silverstein and the Redevelopment Agency. Silverstein was the lightning rod for the city's disillusionment and he continued to preside over the program under a cloud of suspicion that he was personally profiting from the project in his appraisal business, an allegation he denied and *The Day* failed to prove or disprove. The city and *The Day* entered the 1970s unenlightened over the questions the series raised:

> *Is the worst over? Is it going to be downhill from now on? Will redevelopment, after all, prove to be the tonic New London has needed to assume its intended role as Southeastern Connecticut's commercial hub?*

By 1968, the city was concerned that while the Redevelopment Agency had leveled much of the city, it had lined up little new development to occupy the vacant lots. A major developer the agency had selected defaulted on its contract. The agency had been unable to bring a department store to the city, although it always claimed to have one on the hook. The prospects paled for middle-income housing to replace the neighborhoods that had been demolished between Huntington and Main Streets, along the hillside overlooking the river. *The Day* summarized the sentiment in the city on August 22, 1968:

> *Those who were vocal in support of redevelopment, including this newspaper, are all the more disheartened because implicit in their support was the promise that time itself would prove urban renewal to be the true remedy to New London's problems.*

TWENTY-SIX

REBELLION

Management personnel at The Day *are kidding themselves and their public if they claim such distortions as the Aug. 8 concoction are worthy of the trust placed in them by the late Theodore Bodenwein.*

—William J. Mitchell, 20, to *The Day,* August 12, 1969

THE UPHEAVAL AT *THE DAY* in the late 1960s, not to mention across the nation in the form of antiwar protests and student demonstrations, exhilarated and emboldened the newsroom. The writers displayed a new pluck not only toward the police and government agencies and the local institutions, but eventually even toward the established order at the newspaper. Managing Editor Curt Pierson's staff was fired up and eager to take on any story, no matter how outrageous or controversial. And it wasn't just the new arrivals who exhibited this high-spiritedness. Evelyn Archer, the military writer, cultivated sources in the shipyard unions at Electric Boat by being one of the boys and drinking at bars with them. Archer had joined the newspaper in 1954 as a social reporter. With her sources in the shipyard, she became a thorn in the side of the shipyard's management during a summer-long strike in 1968. On many mornings, she could be heard on the phone with Joseph Wornom, the public relations director at EB, shouting, "Joe Wornom, you're a goddamn liar." She was equally fearless with Joseph Pierce, the shipyard's general manager. Jim Quinn, the political writer, exulted in skewering politicians, as he did John N. Dempsey, the popular Democratic governor of Connecticut, in a column on September 13, 1969. The state had gone heavily into debt pouring assistance into the cities in an attempt to avert urban violence, and Dempsey and Democrats in the legislature were pointing fingers at each other for the state's deteriorating financial condition. Quinn's column removed the cover of amiability the governor wore in public and revealed a bitter, mean person bent upon revenge against his political enemies.

> *Dempsey's old image of the genial governor, running the state with a mixture of affability, schmaltz and good intentions is long-gone, probably never to be recovered.*

In 1968, *The Day* employed a second David Anderson, a portly Yale graduate and Army veteran who had been a Chinese interpreter for the military, to cover the region's anti-poverty program. New London had just applied for federal funds under the Johnson administration's Model City program, which poured money into cities for social programs. New London hoped the assistance could quiet some of the growing discontent in the black neighborhoods that were being torn up by urban renewal. Anderson, in the spirit of the times, cast himself as an advocate of the poor in his reporting and he vigorously carried out that role with passionately partisan articles.

The exuberant atmosphere brought the staff into conflict with the traditional minded top *Day* executives. Before he left in July 1968, news editor David Anderson tangled with Deane Avery and Bar Colby over innovations in makeup as well as news coverage. Anderson had little respect for the two, and the normally good-natured executives bristled under his irreverent treatment, which Anderson did not hesitate to display in front of others. Avery recalls the day he questioned the placement of a picture on the front page and ordered Anderson to move it. Anderson consented, but angrily told Avery in front of all the printers that the change had ruined the layout. Soon after, Anderson left *The Day* and his place was taken by a more loyal replacement, David Carlson. But the Miami editor's outspokenness left its mark. The *Day's* young reporters became openly critical of the publisher and executive editor for their alleged timidness in going after the news.

The reporters regarded anything as fair game, even the institutions that had close historic alliances with *The Day*. Notably these were Connecticut College, the Coast Guard Academy, and Lawrence & Memorial Hospitals. Whenever stories in *The Day* angered people in high places, Bar Colby heard about it in the elite circles in which a publisher normally traveled. Deane Avery received the same bombardment in his contacts with the community. Both Colby and Avery were too good-natured and, some of the staff felt, too faint-hearted not to be affected by the normal flak newspaper executives encounter. The two often put the newsroom on the defensive over complaints from high places.

People calling with remonstrances often would preface their remarks with the threat, "Bar Colby is a personal friend of mine." The truth of that assertion was often suspect, especially when Bar Colby became "Bernie Colby" in the caller's words.

Lawrence & Memorial Hospitals, where both Colby and Francis McGuire were directors, was a particularly ticklish subject in the newsroom. The institution, a not-for-profit community hospital built from the fortune of a whaling family, benefited from a steady stream of funds from the Bodenwein Fund. Through its influence at *The Day*, the hospital managed the terms of its own coverage to the consternation of reporters. Reporters felt uneasy when they wrote stories about the hospital and grumbled about it as one of the newspaper's "sacred cows." City officials, who were more exposed to the fury of the *Day's* gung-ho newsgathering force, complained about the favored treatment *The Day* afforded the hospital and the college. One of the city managers used the phrase "interlocking directorate" to refer to the *Day* directors who held seats on the boards of other institutions. The expression found a receptive audience in the newsroom, where the staff was growing restive over the newspaper's perceived special treatment of certain organizations.

There were fewer such constraints from top management over coverage of politics and the city. The newspaper held the Redevelopment Agency's feet to the fire with articles like one that appeared on January 9, 1969. Morgan McGinley had learned from a source that a street being built in the renewal area had to be built over because the agency improperly had used demolition materials for fill. The agency had not done test borings beforehand because its budget for that purpose had run out, his reporting revealed. This wasn't an earthshaking story by itself, but typical of how the newspaper was monitoring the government for wrongdoing and mistakes.

Day reporters hounded the agency with questions about fruitless, behind-the-scenes negotiations to bring a department-store developer to town, to the point that the agency accused *The Day* of scaring developers away. *The Day* reported on the delays and failures in the renewal project, including the collapse of the agreement with a firm that was supposed to develop the major part of the renewal project—the housing and department store. The *Day's* reporting halted the City Council when it tried to appoint a local bail-bondsman without any qualifications as city manager in a secret deal. The newspaper, in a series by McGinley and accompanying editorials, went after the state government and the electric company over the issue of water pollution caused by the waste deposits from a power plant. And from the start, the newspaper shadowed C.

Francis Driscoll, the former head of the Redevelopment Agency who became city manager in 1969, looking for the slightest misstep. Reporters no longer felt obliged to fraternize with the city manager and city councilors to get news. There were enough gabby and disgruntled sources in City Hall and the political parties to make such deference unnecessary.

IN THE SUMMER OF 1969, the newspaper published another investigative series by Norman Soderberg. This one dealt with the Coast Guard Academy's expansion. Concern over the plans had been building in the city since April 1968, when the federal government's General Services Administration began acquiring thirty-four properties for the project. This was on top of eleven other houses the government had purchased for the Academy the year before. The plans affected seventy-two families, and neighbors and the city suspected the Coast Guard had even more real estate in its sights. Mrs. Edwin F. Sibley, whose home at 121 Mohegan Avenue, was among the first to be taken, told Soderberg she learned about the plans on the radio. She had lived in the same house for sixty-three years. Soderberg reported that Dr. Paul F. Laubenstein, a retired religion professor at Connecticut College whose house on Oneco Avenue also was in the path of the plans, said news of the project "burst like a bombshell." The series reported complaints that agents for the government had been heavy-handed in making offers for the property. It noted the city's concern over the losses to its tax rolls. Soderberg wrote in his final installment:

> *Residents, especially those surrounding the academy and city officials, are concerned that New London, like the legendary city of Atlantis, will eventually disappear from the face of the earth as it is devoured chunk by chunk into a vast academy complex.*

These worries were vented on the City Council, in letters to the editor, and in public discourse. Another conflict that arose between the Coast Guard and the owners of the Thames Shipyard, which was in the path of the Coast Guard's plans, added to the adverse public attention the service was receiving. The normally benign Coast Guard Academy, which was unaccustomed to controversy, suddenly found itself at the center of a huge and embarrassing one. The feedback reached the top brass in the Coast Guard, who wanted to know what the Academy was doing to stop it. Rear Admiral Arthur B. Engel, the superintendent, complained to Bar Colby about the relentless pounding the institution was taking in the press and pleaded for a break. Colby was sympathetic. Unfortunately, there wasn't a news event in sight on which to hang a more flattering picture of the academy, other than maybe the 179th anniversary of the Coast Guard. Judge Thomas E. Troland had an idea, however. He reminded the directors that 1969 was the 40th anniversary of the year New London turned over to the government the land for the Academy. Troland, who had one of the longest and most voluminous memories at *The Day*, had been law director in the city and had been instrumental in acquiring the site for the Coast Guard. He knew the whole story and was eager to share it at a board meeting that summer. What a brilliant idea, everyone agreed. Nobody else would have thought of it. Even Admiral Engel later admitted he had no idea such an important milestone in the Academy's history was about to be crossed.

An order to prepare an appropriate spread in the newspaper marking the occasion was sent upstairs from Colby to John Foley, the city editor. Foley assigned the job to the youngest member of the staff, William J. Mitchell. Mitchell was a student at the University of Notre Dame and a summer intern at *The Day*. He was smart, good looking, well liked but the *Day* editors would learn to their regret, spirited, idealistic, and unafraid to challenge authority. In his five summers at *The Day*, he had been swept up by the bold *esprit* and sense of mission in the news staff. In that spirit, Mitchell turned in a story that, rather than celebrating the growth of the Academy as he had been assigned, pointed out the service's history of land-grabs in the city. Foley told Mitchell that wasn't exactly what he had in mind. "As I probed the matter, it became clear that they were looking for a more upbeat story," Mitchell, who later became a foreign correspondent and editor for the Detroit *Free Press*, recalled thirty years later. The conflict between the young intern and Foley escalated. Mitchell typed Foley a memorandum urging that *The Day* abandon this folly and notifying the city editor that he had decided as a matter of principle not to write the story he had been assigned:

> *It is clearly a compromise of good journalism, a typical attempt at pleasing still another of the* Day's *ridiculous sacred cows. Journalistically and every other way it smells very bad.*

The controversy moved downstairs to Colby's office, where Pierson, Foley, and by now Bar Colby attempted to reason with the ordinarily likable intern. Pierson particularly was fond of Mitchell and didn't want to fire him. But the superiors suspected that others in the newsroom who were attempting to organize a union had put him up to this mischief and they didn't want to betray any signs of weakness. Mitchell refused to back down. Finally, Pierson looked across the table at the young man and said, "Beverly will make out your check." Beverly Prescott was the payroll clerk. Mitchell had just been fired.

Mitchell didn't let the matter drop. He went to the City Hall and read a copy of the Bodenwein will in the Judge of Probate's office. Armed with evidence that *The Day* had strayed from its historic purpose, in publishing "puff pieces" about the Coast Guard Academy, he sent Grube, the editor who originally had hired him, a letter to the editor condemning the management for its cowardly and unprincipled conduct. He concluded by quoting Theodore Bodenwein from the will: "I believe a newspaper should be more than a business enterprise. It should also be the champion and protector of the public interest and defender of the people's rights."

Grube refused to print the letter, arguing that it was about an internal personnel matter rather than a public issue. He wrote back, angrily scolding Mitchell, reminding him that publishers frequently "interfere" in the newsroom in such fashion, and that it was common form for those who worked for them to comply with their wishes. He pointed out the newspaper had covered the Coast Guard controversies thoroughly. It was a "gross libel" to suggest that *The Day* had strayed from the Bodenwein will. The newspaper had, he said, over the years undergone a series of changes intended to carry out the wishes of Bodenwein. "*The Day* today is a better newspaper than it was five, 10, 15 and 25 years ago. It will continue to improve."

The episode with William Mitchell ordinarily would have been a minor event, hardly worthy of a footnote in the newspaper's history, little more than an overzealous intern dismissed for insubordination. The incident would have caused the usual stir in the newsroom, but it would have been forgotten the next day. But other matters gave it a larger significance. That summer of 1969, reporters and editors in the newsroom led more or less by James Quinn, the political reporter, and William Heard, a Groton reporter, had entered into serious discussions with the American Newspaper Guild over organizing the staff at *The Day* into a collective bargaining unit.

Discontent had been building up in the newsroom for months, and Colby and the other executives at the newspaper were frankly worried. The Guild, which was making headway at other New England newspapers, was, in fact, management's greatest fear. The directors had devoted most of their monthly meeting on October 27, 1968, to discussing Guild troubles in Waterbury and Hartford, Connecticut, and Woonsocket, Rhode Island. The Woonsocket *Call* had been shut down by a Guild strike. The Waterbury *Republican* was at an impasse with the union over wages and benefits. A Guild movement was moving ahead at the *Hartford Courant*. Controller E. Wesley Hammond recommended increasing the hourly wages in the newsroom at least to the level of the mechanical departments at *The Day* to counter the union threat. The board agreed to raise the wages of experienced reporters and editors. It pained Colby in particular that the staff would be so ungrateful for the advantages the newspaper had provided. The directors had been engaged for several years in discussions over upgrading pay and improving the benefits of the employees. They were also studying a reduced workweek.

But the issues in the newsroom behind the Guild movement had less to do with money than with discontent over the management of the newspaper. The concerns were not over pay and benefits, but over nepotism in hiring and promotions, a perceived lack of nerve at the top in dealing with sensitive news issues, and favored treatment of the "sacred cows." The issue of favoritism climaxed in August 1969 when the management promoted Bar Colby's son, Robert, to assistant city editor. Robert had joined the staff from the Manchester (Connecticut) *Herald* as a copy editor less than a year earlier. That same summer, the "interlocking directorate" expanded by one with the appointment of Charles E. Shain, the president of Connecticut College, as a *Day* trustee after the death of Charles Sortor. Francis McGuire, who was the lawyer for the college, recommended Shain for the post. The young, handsome college president provided McGuire with some liberal Democratic support on the conservative board. He also added to the institutional presence on the board.

In the spring of 1969, management announced a sweeping overhaul of beats involving more than half the reporters. Pierson explained the changes were healthy for the newspaper and the staff, but the sudden upheaval increased the staff's feeling of having no say in matters. The move toward excellence that Colby and the other directors had initiated was backfiring. Grievances among reporters were mounting just as *The Day* was beginning to reap the rewards for its efforts to improve. Recognition poured in for Urwiller and his photographers, the reporters, and the editors. Hardly a month passed that *The Day* did not receive professional accolades for its photography. In June 1969, Gordon Alexander won three prizes in that month's contest of the National Press Photographers' Association. John Ligos did the same the following month. Alexander took top honors in the competition in August. In September, the *Day's* front page won first place in the New England Associated Press Managing Editors' Association annual contest for newspapers its size.

The achievements elevated the staff's confidence and with it its defiance. Bill Mitchell's run-in with management over the Coast Guard stories seemed to validate the view of the news staff that the management was weak, self-serving, and beholden to special interests. The leaders in the movement wanted a stronger role in newsroom decisions, and the Guild organizers from the international's offices in Boston led the *Day* activists to believe the union could deliver such power. The union notified the newspaper of its intent to seek union recognition August 11, 1969, and asked to meet with the managers. *The Day* refused the request. Colby wrote back that *The Day* didn't believe that the committee represented a sufficient number of employees. Both sides dug in for a bitter fight that would last more than a year and eventually involved other departments. The battle over the Guild caused still more turnover in the news staff, including the loss of one of the newspaper's best reporters, Jim Quinn, and left permanent scars in the relations between management and the news staff.

Colby summoned help from the New England Daily Newspaper Association, which was confronting the Guild's aggressive thrust in the Northeast. The newspaper eventually hired a Boston law firm, Snyder, Tepper & Berlin, to represent it in the dealings and purchased strike insurance for the first time. In December 1969, the newspaper hired Robert K. Burns of the University of Chicago to conduct a survey on employee attitudes, and the consultant met with employees for months.

Colby saw the Guild effort as a personal affront. For his entire career as a manager and executive at the newspaper, he felt he had looked after the welfare of the employees as though they were part of his own family. He had brought the newspaper prestige as one of the first executives from a small newspaper to serve on the board of the American Newspaper Publisher's Association. He had initiated training programs and sent dozens of reporters and editors to out-of-town seminars to improve their professional capabilities. The very time the Guild campaign formally started, the directors agreed to pay reporter Morgan McGinley's salary while he took part in a four-month fellowship at the Washington Journalism Center. McGinley's $2,000 fellowship, one of only ten awarded in the country, was announced in September 1969. For several years, *The Day* had been taking steps to improve benefits and raise pay above the industry norm for newspapers its size. Colby and the directors seldom refused a request from an employee for financial assistance or extended sick leave. He could not understand how the staff, considering all this, could be so ungrateful.

But Jim Quinn, who led the Guild effort in the newsroom, had a less charitable view of the publisher. The perspective from the newsroom was that the management had rewarded family and friends with sinecures at the newspaper, the most egregious example being the publisher's own son, Robert Colby. Quinn and others felt Bar Colby was too "spineless" to stand up for the staff when the newspaper was under fire for its coverage. They believed the newspaper's ties with special interests in the city in the form of its leading institutions was compromising the *Day's* news coverage.

There was enough truth to these charges to attract support for the Guild from most of the reporters, including me. I was in the Army in Korea during most of the campaign, though Jim Quinn was writing letters to me to lobby for support for the union. But the backing diminished as the drive wore on in 1970. It became increasingly evident that the organizers from the union international were not as concerned with the management issues in the newsroom as the staff originally thought they were. The union maneuvered to include other departments, including the business office, maintenance staff, and proof room. This diluted the newsroom's issues and weakened the chances of winning in the final vote. Colby and other executives, including newsroom managers like John Foley and Dave Carlson, waged an effective campaign of propaganda to discourage support. Much of the effort was directed at workers outside the newsroom, where there was little support for the union idea in the first place. Bar Colby made a passionate last-minute pitch against the union in department meetings the week before the decision.

The vote took place on December 3, 1970. Employees of the nonmechanical departments voted two to one against having the American Newspaper Guild become their bargaining agent. The total vote was ninety to forty-five against the Guild, with most of the support for the Guild coming from the newsroom. The committee challenged one vote, Robert Colby's, because he was the publisher's son. His vote was counted anyway. After the vote, Bar Colby had a victory party at his house in the south end of the city for all those who had supported management, in which Colby delivered a bitter diatribe against the effort to organize the Guild. One of the reporters who had led in the Guild campaign, William Heard, the Groton reporter, left before the issue came to a vote. Jim Quinn and Sandra Young, another reporter who had been at the forefront of the effort, left *The Day* shortly afterwards.

THE GUILD WASN'T THE only serious concern facing *The Day* as it entered the 1970s. Since the disappearance of the *Evening Globe* and the *Morning Telegraph* decades earlier, the Norwich *Bulletin* had been the *Day's* major competition. Apprehension over the *Bulletin* entering the growing Groton market in the 1950s had been the reason *The Day* had opened an office there. But *The Day* easily outmaneuvered the *Bulletin*, and established command of the advertising and circulation market in the growing town and its affluent enclave of

Mystic. By early 1969, *The Day* was confident enough to close the news bureau in Groton and move the news operation back to New London, leaving behind only a business office. For years the two newspapers had been carrying on a gentlemanly competition over the news in each other's territory. *The Day* had stationed a part-time writer in Norwich. The *Bulletin* had a bureau in New London, on the second floor of the Crocker House, just above the hotel bar. In addition, the *Hartford Courant* also kept its foot in the door in New London in the person of Joe DeBona, who also was stationed at the Crocker House. DeBona had covered New London for the Bridgeport *Herald* before it had gone out of business in the 1960s and was legendary both as a colorful writer and one able to concoct a story from very few facts.

The *Bulletin* was well read in New London. Its presence in the city was sustained primarily by sports, not news, however. New London had an insatiable appetite for sports news, and the *Bulletin*, being a morning newspaper, was able to scoop *The Day* on the outcomes of all the night games in professional sports. That was to a large extent why many New Londoners purchased both *The Day* and the *Bulletin*. The competition among the three newspapers ranged from ludicrous to astounding. In the early 1950s, Deane Avery had covered City Hall in New London for *The Day*, while Robert Flanagan, who later became the city assessor, was the *Bulletin* reporter there. Once a month Avery had to attend a *Day* dinner on Monday, the night the City Council met. Under an unwritten agreement between the two, on those nights Flanagan filled in for his competitor and filed the City Council stories for *The Day* as well as the *Bulletin*.

The other extreme had occurred after a celebrated murder in New London in June 1963. Nicholas Ukraine, a 26-year-old psychopath, for no apparent reason murdered a couple next door to his home and their 10-year-old son. The crime was reported to police at 9:45 pm and *The Day* was well on its way toward covering the story for the next day by 11 pm. *Day* reporters John Foley and Dave Carlson stopped for a nightcap at the Crocker House bar, where they met Joe DeBona, who hadn't yet heard about the crime. Carlson and Foley waited until after DeBona's deadline, then mischievously asked him, "Hey Joe, did you hear about the Ukraine murder?" The color drained from DeBona's face. He rushed from the bar. The next morning, a story on the murder appeared in the *Courant*. DeBona had managed in a split second to scoop *The Day*.

Joe DeBona similarly got the best of me when I was an intern in the summer of 1966. Raymond Bordner, the court reporter who doubled as the *Day's* arts editor, had sent me to the new Eugene O'Neill Theater Center to interview the playwright Edward Albee. The people at the center told me Albee wasn't granting any interviews, but I could attend a workshop he was leading and talk to him before he returned to New York. I sat for a half-hour in the classroom where the workshop was supposed to take place waiting for Albee to appear. Finally a door opened, and out walked Albee and Joe DeBona, who had just spent an hour interviewing Albee. DeBona filed a story in the next day's newspaper describing the playwright's Connecticut connection.

This had all been considered sportsmanlike in the past, and the competition carried out in a spirit of good humor and mutual respect. But, on May 1, 1970, the rivalry grew more intense when the Norwich Bulletin Company announced plans to publish an afternoon paper in Groton, the Groton *News*, beginning on May 29. Donald L. Oat was to be the president and treasurer of the new tabloid. Oat's designs on Groton were serious and filled with ill will. Oat had made several unsuccessful attempts to raid *The Day* for talent. He asked Morgan McGinley to be the managing editor of the Groton *News*. McGinley recalls he told him: "Don, you can't run a decent newspaper in Norwich. What makes you think you can do any better in Groton?"

The Day was in a better position than it had been in the 1950s and 1960s to confront a competitor. It had a stronger editorial staff and had improved its production capabilities. It had built onto its press and the new units began operation in 1969. All seven units were used for the first time in August to publish a fifty-page edition in a single run. *The Day* had added to its variety of wire offerings by subscribing in January 1969 to the New York Times News Service.

The Day opened an office in Norwich. The territory between the two newspapers consisted of the towns of Preston, Montville, and Ledyard and the two newspapers attacked each other in the three communities. *The Day* used billboards in Norwich and Montville, which had become a prize in the heightened competition. In June 1970, *The Day* hired the *Bulletin's* two top reporters, Steven Scott and Michael Ahearn. *The Day* reorganized its news staff to confront the new threat from the north. *The Day*, which in the past had covered night meetings by paying reporters overtime, created a night staff to expand its suburban coverage, particularly in the communities over which the *Bulletin* and *The Day* were competing.

Ray Bordner was transferred from the copy desk to manage the operation. His staff included James Irvine, Michael Bagwell, a British immigrant who was hired from the North Adams (Massachusetts) *Transcript* and me. On Monday, the heaviest night for municipal government meetings, Morgan McGinley and Michael Ahearn joined the night operation to cover meetings in New London and Norwich. The plan, which was announced at a dinner meeting, was received with little enthusiasm. I wasn't happy because my wife and I had a young child and the new schedule kept me away from home afternoons and evenings. The changes added to the irritations on the staff over management's habit of making changes without consulting with the employees. But they eventually were accepted and with the streamlined flow of copy, *The Day* was able to push back its deadline by an hour to better compete with the news and soon was running circles around the competition.

A THIRD ISSUE *THE DAY* faced in the late 1960s and early 1970s was the technological revolution that was transforming newspaper publishing. Advances in commercial printing that enabled printers to set type with computers and prepare it for the press with photocomposition equipment were being adapted for the larger scale printing of newspapers. Unfortunately, *The Day* was handicapped by its decision ten years earlier to buy a letterpress, rather than an offset press, which used new photocomposition techniques.

Many other newspapers faced the same predicament. The industry was attempting to help them adjust as inexpensively and efficiently as possible by adapting the outdated presses to use the new techniques. The American Newspaper Publisher's Association (ANPA) was exploring conversion techniques at its research institute in Easton, Pennsylvania. The ANPA developed and patented a technique known as "DiLitho," a process using lithographic plates, in which the image is rendered on the surface so that some parts retain ink while others reject it. In order to distribute the ink properly, the plates had to be dampened while the press was running, and various companies, including the Harris Company's Cottrell division in Westerly, Rhode Island, developed different methods of accomplishing this.

The Day began exploring the new technology in 1968 with the International Typographical Union looking over its shoulder. The union was enthusiastic about making improvements but concerned about job security. The union embraced the conversion to cold type, but only after management agreed no printers would lose their jobs as a result of technological changes. Management appeared to be in no hurry to make a decision on cold type until the Norwich *Bulletin* announced its plans for the Groton *News* in the spring of 1970. The *Bulletin* was well ahead of *The Day* in its technology. It already had converted to cold type and owned a new Harris Graphics offset press that produced a crisp and attractive looking newspaper. The *Bulletin* published the Groton *News* at its Norwich production plant.

The Day, which had dragged its feet over these production issues, had to scramble to catch up. Despite the *Day's* fears that it would be at a competitive disadvantage with the Groton *News* because of the *Bulletin's* superior equipment, it still took three years for the management to make a decision on where to go with the new technology. The *Day's* handicap was evident in the newspaper's failure to compete successfully against the *Bulletin* to publish *The Dolphin*, the Submarine Base newspaper. But on the bright side for *The Day*, the Groton *News*, despite the *Bulletin's* technological advantages, made slow headway in advertising and circulation and continued to lose money at a rate of thousands of dollars a week. *The Day*, in effect, proved that it could compete in Groton even with one hand tied behind its back with its superior news coverage.

The job of choosing the new technology fell to a management team consisting of Deane Avery, Wes Hammond, and Thomas Elliott, the mechanical superintendent. They ruled out buying a new press, since the old one was only six years old and the two additional units were only two years old. They examined and initially rejected the DiLitho method because of problems the New Haven *Register* had experienced with the alcohol dampener, which softened the newsprint and caused frequent "web breaks." But Cottrell soon developed a method using water instead of alcohol, and *The Day* decided to buy that system late in 1973.

The newspaper had bought its first photocomposition equipment for use in setting ads in 1971. Later, it bought computerized scanners for news copy. IBM Selectric typewriters that produced copy clean enough to be scanned by the machines replaced the old Royal typewriters in the newsroom. However, until the press was converted, the scanners were equipped to produce punch tape that could be fed into the high-speed mechanical typesetting machines. With the completion of the press conversion, the scanners were connected to photocomposition equipment that would produce stories to be pasted on pages. The pages were photographed and developed into aluminum offset plates, which were mounted on the press. Eventually, the editors' IBM typewriters were replaced by computer video display terminals. The conversion to cold type was completed in July 1974.

The changes resulted in far greater efficiency, but also swept away both a trade and a culture at the newspaper. Computers replaced the skilled Linotype operators. Cameras replaced the stereotypers. Some of the printers who stayed, and didn't accept early retirements offered by the newspaper, learned higher-order skills on the computers and sophisticated camera equipment that took the place of the old machinery, most of which was sold as scrap metal. But others were reduced to cutting and pasting stories onto cardboard pages. Many accepted early retirements, including legends in the composing room like William Campbell and Will Rogers, the composing room foreman.

Despite the Guild problems and discontent over issues like the night staff, Pierson had assembled a strong and motivated group of young reporters and commanded their loyalty and respect. He began harnessing their energy, sometimes in teams, to work on investigative stories. Stan DeCoster and Michael Bagwell joined forces on a story that revealed Ruby Cohen, the powerful state legislator from Colchester, was profiting from no-bid leases to the state of property he owned. Largely as a result of these revelations, Cohen lost his seat in the legislature to a little known young Democrat, Sam Gejdenson. Morgan McGinley, DeCoster, and I worked together on an investigative series that exposed waste and financial abuses in the Model City program. The Model City Series was made possible by the city government's eager cooperation in furnishing financial documents. The white-controlled government establishment later used the series to strip the poor and minorities in the city of control over the program. We were, to some degree, used in a power play. John Peterson, a swashbuckling and aggressive reporter Pierson hired from the North Adams (Massachusetts) *Transcript* in 1971, doggedly pursued the government on oil spill stories and became the first *Day* reporter to refuse to disclose his news sources when he was subpoenaed to testify in a federal bank robbery case. Pierson backed Peterson, as he did others on the staff when they came under attack for zealous reporting.

The *Day's* work impressed James Boylan, editor of the *Columbia Journalism Review*. He was assigned to evaluate the newspaper in an ambitious survey of New England newspapers by the New England Daily Newspaper Association, New England Society of Newspapers, and the regional chapter of Sigma Delta Chi. While Boylan noticed an "old-fashioned starchiness" in the newspaper, and felt *The Day* spent too much energy on government meetings, he was impressed enough by the product to say *The Day* had "the foundation to become one of the best small newspapers in the country." He found the editorial page, edited by Kenneth E. Grube, to be the most lively and polished part of the paper.

T W E N T Y - S E V E N

THE TRIUMVIRATE

Who do you think should be publisher? Deane doesn't know much about business and Wes doesn't know anything about news.

—Elizabeth Bodenwein Miles, May 1975

THE YEAR 1973 WAS a happy and a heady time for *The Day*. It was a time for the newspaper to savor its achievements, flex its muscles, and celebrate. Although the New England Daily Newspaper Survey found some aspects of its coverage wanting, by and large it placed *The Day* well ahead of its competitors. The newspaper was compared favorably with the best dailies in New England by the evaluators. Of the Groton *News*, the survey said, "Despite its outward differences from *The Day*, the *News* gives the impression of covering much of the same ground but possibly not doing it as well." It praised the Norwich *Bulletin's* clean, crisp appearance, but added, "Behind its fresh exterior lurks small town booster journalism of fifty years ago or more."

The Day never was stronger. Its staff seldom had been more sure of itself or exuberant. Curt Pierson, 45, was a charismatic newsroom executive, arguably the best managing editor in the newspaper's ninety-two-year history. The staff believed he would be publisher one day, although it was clear to everyone he would have to wait his turn for either Deane Avery or Wes Hammond. One or the other was assumed to be next in line for the job when Bar Colby, who was approaching retirement age, left. Colby had groomed Avery to succeed him, but Francis McGuire favored his protégé, Hammond, for the job.

John Foley had keen news instincts that equipped him well for his job in the front lines as city editor. It was true he made many snap judgments. He had the irritating habit of predetermining how stories he assigned ought to turn out. He was a formula newsman and had difficulty with complex and unpredictable stories. But he had excellent reflexes. He pounced on news, as he did after spotting a wire story buried in a morning newspaper Saturday, May 16, 1970. The brief item noted that a state police investigation was underway into the slaying of two brothers a year earlier during a police stakeout in Norwich. Gene and Roger Perkins, both unpopular characters with the state police, died in a four-minute fusillade of gunfire by state troopers at a junior high school. The petty felons had entered the building to burglarize it. Later evidence showed that the two men had been unarmed and the state troopers had brought a gun and planted it at the scene to cover up this fact. *The Day* didn't uncover the story, a wire service reporter did. But the newspaper was among the few Connecticut newspapers that contributed significantly to coverage that undercut the authorities' attempts to conceal the guilt of the police. That Saturday morning, Foley sent reporters in all directions in pursuit of the story. I was sent to the country home of the state police commissioner to interview him for his reaction. Foley told me, "Christ, this is going to be a hell of a story."

RAYMOND BORDNER, THE *DAY'S* night editor, molded the mutinous night staff into a smooth-running team with his calm leadership. Bordner, 43, was a versatile writer and intelligent editor. He wrote moving and eloquent stories in the late 1960s about the trial of Antoinette Foster, a pretty, petite, battered wife accused of murdering her Navy-officer husband. As the newspaper's first arts editor, Bordner helped develop the *Day's* close relationship with the new Eugene O'Neill Theater Center in Waterford. The center, founded by George C. White, a member of a wealthy and prominent Waterford family, developed America's first incubator for American theater, naming it after the nation's only Nobel-prize-winning playwright. *The Day* supported the center in its ongoing skirmishes with the crusty Yankee natives, who resented the arrival of the big-city actors and playwrights who flocked there. Several decades later, White became a director of *The Day*.

Bordner also supervised the newsroom in the transition to the new era of photocomposition. This required the infuriating dependence on IBM Selectric typewriters to prepare stories for the early computer typesetting scanners. The process was a nightmare. Reporters and editors had to type flawless corrections above the lines of text, each set out with slash marks. A slight mistake, such as a missing space or even a smudge mark would cause the scanner to misread the copy. The pressure of earlier deadlines and ongoing problems with the converted letterpress equipment compounded the difficulties. Bordner's unflappable demeanor and good nature helped avert a newsroom rebellion over these nuisances.

The Day now had a news staff of twenty-two reporters and fourteen copyreaders and editors. These included one full-time black reporter. *The Day* had been looking for minority reporters since its confrontation with the black community over hiring and coverage after the King assassination. The newspaper sought help from the anti-poverty agencies to find qualified minority candidates. The directors agreed to make an extra effort to recruit minorities, but turned down a request from black leaders to pay to train them.

It was a different story for women. While the number of racial minority reporters stayed low, the women's movement was transforming *The Day*. Women appeared in the newsroom in ever-larger numbers. By 1973, they made up nearly half the news staff. Some of these women became exceptional journalists. One of the most talented was Beatrice Andrews, a Berkeley graduate and Peace Corps veteran. She was hired as a general assignment writer in 1969, left in 1973, and returned seven years later as a business writer. Her stories were exhaustively researched and penetrating and won numerous awards.

Joan Poro, the wife of a naval officer, joined the staff as the Old Lyme reporter right out of college in 1972. In 1974, she took over the Electric Boat shipyard beat during a period of turbulence and controversy there. Electric Boat was racing to keep up with its orders for the Navy's latest class of attack submarines. The shipyard hired thousands of new apprentices and rushed them through training programs. The effort led to labor trouble, growing inefficiencies, and cost overruns. In recognition for her work covering Electric Boat, Poro became the first woman on *The Day* to occupy a major newsroom management position outside the social desk since Charlotte Holloway had been editor in the 19th century. Poro was appointed Groton editor in 1978.

Morgan McGinley, grandson of John McGinley, Bodenwein's long-time mentor, introduced a fresh, irreverent style to the New London City Hall beat. He reminded people of his grandfather with his close associations in New London, strong affection for the city, garrulousness, and humor. McGinley had been taught in a busy urban news bureau of the Providence *Journal-Bulletin* to ask hard questions. He attacked F. Jerome Silverstein for conflicts of interest between his real estate business and work on the Redevelopment Agency and made life uncomfortable for C. Francis Driscoll, the city manager, and A. A.

Washton, Democratic leader in the city. Disgruntled City Hall workers and politicians delighted in providing the reporter a steady stream of inside information on the foibles at City Hall and at Washton's law office on Broad Street, where the Democratic leaders met every Sunday night. Washton became so furious about the leaks to McGinley that he made his ward bosses swear on a Bible to keep their mouths shut. The entire scene that night was described in McGinley's weekly column the next Saturday, including the precise dialogue. When he wasn't seriously uncovering ineptitude and malfeasance, he poked fun at it in satirical columns that starred "C. Him Bristle," his fictitious name for C. Francis Driscoll. Driscoll became so enraged over McGinley's needling that he summoned the reporter and Ken Grube to his office to dress them down. But Driscoll wound up on the receiving end of a tongue-lashing by Grube, who told the official that the time was gone when reporters for *The Day* kowtowed to City Hall.

The Day gained a statewide reputation for its hard-nosed and independent reporting of state politics. This approach was at odds with the docile school of political journalism prevalent in the state Capitol at the time. The Capitol press and the politicians they covered were joined at the hip. Jack Zaiman, the *Hartford Courant's* veteran political reporter, courted John Bailey, the state's powerful Democratic leader, and thus had a monopoly on the important political news, which came out as Bailey wanted to see it. The other reporters had to content themselves with picking up the scraps from Zaiman. Reporters literally ate out of the hands of politicians. Legislators kept the pressroom supplied with liquor and furnished the Laurel Club, the Capitol press club, with provisions. Jim Quinn and later Stan DeCoster were among the few who would have nothing to do with these practices, a fact that made them unpopular in the pressroom. Quinn became a virtual outcast among the Capitol reporters when he wrote a column comparing them to streetwalkers. For a decade after that, *Day* reporters were not assigned desks by the bureaucracy that ran the pressroom, and had to scribble their stories in longhand and phone them in from pay telephones.

DeCoster, who followed Quinn to the Capitol in 1971, added to the *Day's* reputation for critical and independent reporting as well as the newspaper's unpopularity among insiders in Hartford by helping to expose a state leasing scandal. The revelations about political favoritism in awarding state leases led to the downfall of a man who not only had been one of the most powerful legislators but also a beloved figure in the pressroom. After his fall from power in the 1974 primary, Ruby Cohen no longer was around to deliver fresh brown bread to the pressroom as he had during each session of the legislature.

THE DAY, STILL ENGAGED in a race with the Groton *News*, was paying renewed attention to Groton. James Irvine, who became Groton editor in March 1973, delved into the Byzantine politics of the town, which was made up of numerous tiny and independent jurisdictions that made covering the place mind-boggling. Whatever political gossip didn't appear in the news columns wound up in his weekly column, the "Groton Grapevine." His writing was unpolished and pedestrian, but the column was newsy and popular and helped *The Day* retain the overwhelming loyalty of Groton readers in the eight-year competition with the Groton *News*.

Ken Grube, the *Day's* editorial page editor, restored a local emphasis to the opinion section. He started an op-ed page for contrary opinions. In contrast to the reclusive George Clapp, he enhanced the presence of *The Day* in the community by hobnobbing with people of all walks of life. His acquaintances included some of the most powerful figures in the state. Governor John N. Dempsey and Secretary of the State Ella T. Grasso, who would become the state's first elected woman governor in 1974, sought his advice, even on matters like highway design. Grube was active in state newspaper circles, including the Connecticut Circuit of the Associated Press, and was a crony of editors around the state. He helped Grasso draft the state's first freedom of information law and was one of the founders of the public television corporation in the state. He appeared regularly for years on a statewide political talk show on public television called *Fourth Estate*.

Grube built bridges to the area's black and Jewish communities and had contacts and sources across the region. He stayed in touch with the people of the area through his after-hours socializing in working-class bars like Sully's in Groton, which was conveniently located on his route home. He regularly arrived home late.

The newsroom had moved past the guild insurgency and morale had risen again. Management made an effort to cultivate better relations with the staff, and Avery reported back regularly to the directors on the progress. The formal University of Chicago sessions designed during the Guild movement to identify grievances and deal with them led to regular department meetings. Avery began a series of weekly newsroom training seminars. These were followed by "anti-seminars," in which the staff adjourned to Hughie's, an Italian restaurant run by a former Irish American prizefighter, for long afternoons of drinking. These beer-soaked sessions reflected a fresh wave of robust and unruly after-hours behavior by the news staff. This spirit was exemplified in a wild office Christmas party in 1973 in which the office Christmas tree was hurled out a window. It landed on a roof outside Deane Avery's office and one of the reporters was assigned to go to work early the next morning and retrieve it before Avery arrived. Fire engines rushed to *The Day* that night when reporters flooded one of the bathrooms using the fire hose in the newsroom and setting off the fire alarm. An editor careened through the mailroom on one of the forklifts used to move newsprint. A similarly unbridled scene occurred at a picnic Avery had at his farm in Stonington. Colby and Avery grew sufficiently concerned over the rowdiness to ban liquor at office gatherings, and Avery's picnic was the last time for a long time an executive of the newspaper dared to invite the reporters to a gathering at his home. But the carousing was merely the other side of a highly motivated and close-knit staff. The late 1960s and early 1970s were a rare period in the newspaper's history when nobody in the newsroom could think of a lot to complain about. Michael Bagwell, the military reporter then, recalls:

> *It was a happy time. It wasn't just that we were cutups. We looked forward to going to work every day and participating in the life of the newsroom. It was a lively place with the noise of the typewriters and the smoke all over. But the feeling went beyond that stereotypical scene. We were doing interesting things. Everybody had a good thing to do and we felt we were putting out a damned good paper.*

THE STAFF WAS SO new and young that few took much note of Orvin Andrews' death on March 13, 1973, in his 85th year. Andrews had been living in retirement for thirteen years. The only contact the newsroom had with him was when someone had to edit "Sentences by the Judge" which arrived every week in the mail and the newspaper continued to publish long after it was of any interest to most readers. Grube wrote an editorial, entitled "The Judge," in which *The Day* spoke of Andrews' seriousness, his underlying humor, and, mostly, of his prudence. "During his tenure, *The Day* grew at a steady pace, establishing the foundation for the more rapid expansion required in the most recent past," *The Day* said.

Later that spring, the directors gave Bar Colby his father-in-law's title as president of the board, and made Judge Troland, 80, now the lone survivor of the original trustees in 1939, the chairman of the board. These changes had little impact on the operation. More significant changes occurred in newsroom management. John Foley became assistant managing editor. Arthur Weber, the husband of Latham Avery's daughter, Judy, replaced Foley as city editor. Bob Colby replaced Weber as chief of the news desk, where he was responsible for layout and the flow of copy. And David Heckerman, who had been hired only recently as a reporter, became assistant city editor.

The staff by this time no longer resented Bob Colby's privileged place in the newsroom. The son possessed his father's sense of humor, charm, and character, and earned the staff's good will despite his hereditary advantage. Heckerman's advancement, on the other hand, didn't set well with the newsroom. The promotion shattered the sanguine mood. Senior reporters resented the fact that a relative latecomer was promoted over them and faulted Avery for the poor choice. Avery, of course, was the executive editor. And he liked Heckerman from the start. They shared an interest in horses, for one thing. But Avery also respected Heckerman's judgment. Heckerman was thoroughly, sometimes painfully, even-handed. Unlike the other reporters, he was reluctant to see wrongdoing in the world. His style clashed with the brash approach of newsroom leaders like John Peterson. Heckerman's approach appealed to Avery, who had to deal with the impact of stories at the Rotary Club and in his other dealings with the public as director of community relations. Avery was sensitive to every complaint he heard, and one could argue that was his job. Peterson was furious over having been passed over for the promotion. He left *The Day* and shortly become managing editor of the Norwich *Bulletin*. Peterson competed fiercely with *The Day*, backed by *Bulletin* Publisher Donald Oat, who was delighted to go on the offensive against his archrival.

The greater significance of the changes early in 1973 was to create hairline cracks in the mortar of the newsroom organization. Weber, though the reporters liked him, didn't have Foley's instincts for news. The reporters had to tell the new city editor as diplomatically as possible what was news and what wasn't. Heckerman, as Weber's assistant city editor, lacked the killer instinct to go after stories aggressively. Weber's great love never had been journalism, but horticulture, and he eventually left to pursue that interest at a local garden business. But his shortcomings at the newspaper did not diminish the affection that was felt for him. When he died of cancer in 1995, there was barely enough room in the church sanctuary in Ledyard, not far from his farm, for all the mourners. The changes also removed Foley from a post he had filled effectively and placed him next in line for a job for which he was not as well suited. The change that would advance him to that point was nearer than anyone imagined.

Curt Pierson's leadership had motivated the newsroom to reach a high level of achievement. But his personal life created problems. After hours, Pierson joined in the regular newsroom carousing in New London's bars. He encouraged this conduct by taking part in it and fraternizing with his staff. In particular, he had a wandering eye for attractive women in the newsroom. The editors and reporters tended to look the other way because of the strong affection and respect they had for him and the prevailing mores of the time. But his romantic dalliances contributed both to the breakup of his marriage to Deane Avery's niece and to his surprising resignation in 1973.

Pierson left in the fall. More than seventy people from *The Day* attended his going-away party. Deane Avery was the toastmaster for the event at Hughie's. Every department was represented. All were sorry that Pierson was leaving because of all that he had done to build *The Day* into a strong newspaper. He went to work for the *Morgan Horse Magazine* as director of publications. He later had jobs as a news executive for newspapers in Gardner, Massachusetts; Bremerton, Washington; Spokane, Washington; Middletown, New York; and Gainesville, Florida, before retiring. Had things turned out differently, it is very likely he would have some day become the *Day's* publisher.

Foley automatically stepped into Pierson's post. Given the choice of James Irvine and Ray Bordner, management chose Bordner to become assistant managing editor. Bordner helped Grube write editorials but concentrated on the conversion to cold type, which was completed the following year. *The Day* published its first edition with photocomposition and its converted press on August 20, 1974. Foley took charge of a newsroom that, fortunately for everyone, had so much momentum and enthusiasm it almost ran itself.

It was an auspicious time for Bar Colby, now 65, to retire. When he had arrived at *The Day* in 1933, he was the only college graduate on the news staff. Now most of the staff had college degrees. He had fought with the directors to modernize the plant, and now *The Day* was speeding ahead of him into the computer age. He had campaigned to train the reporters and editors in the disciplined use of the English language, but now reporters were arriving on the job with writing style, precision, and reporting abilities superior to his, or at least they thought so. And there was not one, but two possible successors waiting to replace him. The question before *The Day* in 1974 was which of the two should succeed Colby: Deane Avery or Wes Hammond.

It was no secret that Colby favored Avery, the executive editor, and Francis McGuire preferred Hammond, who oversaw the business of The Day Publishing Company. If it came to a vote, McGuire probably could count on the support of Elizabeth Miles and Charles Shain. Judge Troland was in the middle on most matters. The other directors were Colby, Avery, and Hammond.

In other words, the board, which endeavored to operate by consensus, was more or less evenly divided over succession, just as it recently had been split over whether to endorse Richard Nixon or George McGovern for president. It decided the latter matter by endorsing neither of the candidates, reflecting the weight of the two McGovern supporters: McGuire and Shain. The directors took the middle course once again and made Avery and Hammond co-publishers. Avery would oversee the news department, Hammond would supervise the business of The Day Publishing Company, and Francis McGuire would exert his influence over both from his powerful position on the board. *The Day*, in this fashion, came under the control of a triumvirate consisting of Avery, Hammond, and McGuire, with McGuire still having the final say on most matters. Like his father-in-law, Colby remained a director after his retirement, holding on to that position all the while Hammond and Avery managed the newspaper. The directors hired him as a consultant. Avery took his place at the front of the newspaper as president of The Day Publishing Company. He moved into Colby's office, and the boardroom next door, known as the Bodenwein Room, was remodeled for Hammond and a new boardroom was built across the hall.

ON THE NATIONAL SCENE, anti-war protests, Watergate, and other events provided a steady stream of material for the newspaper's growing crew of eager young reporters. The paper was full of interesting news. The Watergate scandal had a local angle in L. Patrick Gray, an obscure New London lawyer, former naval officer, and political supporter whom Richard Nixon chose to be acting director of the FBI after the death of J. Edgar Hoover. The newspaper sent Michael Bagwell to cover Gray's testimony in the Watergate hearings. *Day* reporters wrote pointed stories about Gray's hapless role in the Watergate cover-up, such as when Nixon's aides ordered him to "deep six" critical documents in the investigation, an order he followed by burning them in his living room fireplace in nearby Stonington.

One Saturday morning, Gray appeared in the *Day's* newsroom and three reporters interviewed him for two hours. They wrote a story that highlighted his vanity more than matters of substance. He showed the reporters his badge, remarked that it had a Number 2 on it. "Mr. Hoover's had Number 1."

On the local beat, New London was still struggling with urban renewal. In an effort to compete with the outlying shopping centers, the city ripped up State Street and put in a pedestrian mall. The original idea was to develop a "semi-mall" allowing a lane of traffic along the street. But the idea quietly underwent a metamorphosis into a full-blown pedestrian walkway, a change that initially escaped the *Day's* attention. The construction, which lasted a year, drove still more retail stores out of business. *The Day* not only endorsed the idea of the mall and contributed to the fund to build it, but also sponsored a public contest to give it a name. From the hundreds of entries, the city chose Captain's Walk. The city celebrated the opening with a champagne party and ball at the Mohican Hotel roof garden, which Governor Thomas G. Meskill attended.

The activity masked a continuous business decline in the city and the failures of the urban renewal plan. The renewal program, in fairness to it, had accomplished much that was largely unappreciated. It corrected the problem of traffic congestion getting in and out of the downtown. It made room for existing businesses like *The Day* to expand and for others to locate in the city. And it began to rebuild the city's ancient sewers and water system. But it produced these results at the price of great destruction and dislocation. And it delivered less than it had promised or hoped for. The utopian mixture of housing for different classes that had been envisioned in the original Rotival Plan never materialized. High-rise buildings for the poor were located out of the way near the bridge. The "middle income" housing, sponsored by a local church group, was shoddily built and really not middle income. The "luxury housing" turned out to be subsidized elderly apartments.

The Redevelopment Agency abandoned its search for a department store and turned to locating a new hotel in the city. New London's existing historic downtown hotels were rapidly fading into history. The Crocker House closed in 1972. The Mohican, opened by Frank Munsey after his magazine plans collapsed, continued downhill for another six years. Once the elegant lodging for wealthy visitors to the Yale-Harvard regatta and other New London events, the Mohican had become a seedy lodging place for steelworkers on the new bridge across the Thames River, which was completed in 1973. Fires, bomb scares, and the murder of an elderly resident beset the 85-year-old building in its final years. The sentimental image of the old hotel as a grand place was preserved only in the bar, which continued to serve its loyal patrons, including regulars from *The Day*. The hotel and its storied bar died before the decade ended. Joseph Polimeni, a city fireman who moonlighted in real estate, bought it in 1976. He closed the bar two years later, promising to reopen it as a discotheque. But this never happened. The building was sold and converted to federally subsidized apartments for the elderly. Harold Gatheral, the bartender, opened his own bar, Harold's, down the street, and it became the last downtown hangout for *The Day* and other regulars who migrated from the Mohican.

The nation was soon to suffer through the Arab oil embargo, runaway inflation, the near bankruptcy of New York, and the decline of other American cities. Nonetheless New London awoke to new hopes and rampant speculation by the middle of the decade. The mood took a dramatic upswing when the city decided against an urban renewal plan to tear down one of the city's most prominent edifices, Union Station. The structure had been one of the early targets of urban renewal. F. Jerome Silverstein made it a personal crusade to destroy the massive building designed by the great 19th century American architect Henry Hobson Richardson and replace it with a more modest modern terminal. *The Day*, which had endorsed all the agency's other plans for leveling large parts of the city, agreed with him. Ken Grube wrote in numerous editorials that the station, with its rundown interior, filthy bathrooms, and unkempt appearance, needed to be excised from the city's landscape, opening a view to the Thames River that had been blocked since the end of the 19th century. When the National Park Service refused to designate Union Station as a national landmark in 1970, *The Day* applauded the government for its wisdom. In an editorial on November 14, 1970, it snidely observed that the building was a poor example of Richardson's work that had been put in the wrong place. On May 5, 1971, the newspaper exclaimed, "Why an eyesore should be permitted to block this view is beyond comprehension."

Claire Dale, a classical musician and outspoken and determined civic crusader, felt otherwise, and mobilized a campaign to save the building. She lobbied at *The Day* and eventually formed an organization called Union Railroad Station Trust. While Grube persisted in his contempt for the building, her point of view found its way through other routes into the news and commentary columns of *The Day*. Late in 1972, Morgan McGinley wrote a column supporting the historic building's preservation that began, "What this city needs is a good fifty-cent imagination." There were any number of new uses to which the station could be put, but the agency, with its determination to tear down everything in its path, probably never thought of them, he argued. He invited entrepreneurs to take a look at the station. And he drove a stake in the belief that *The Day* held that razing the building would create a clear view of the river.

> *Say what? A clear view of the dilapidated City Pier? A clear view of the pride of amateur public works directors ... the city of Groton's sewage treatment plant?*

By that time, the growing number of architects, preservationists, and ordinary citizens opposed to the Redevelopment Agency's plans were starting to have an impact. That same month, after Frank Scheetz, a retired Navy chief, builder, and one of Grube's cronies, offered to buy the station for $20,000 and turn it into a submarine museum, Grube retreated from the *Day's* militant stance. An editorial on November 25, 1972, argued that the agency had offered no evidence that it would put up a worthy transportation center in place of the old station. That's why so many people were coming out in opposition. They didn't trust the agency. And why should they? The agency did everything in secret. Grube didn't concede yet that Union Station was worth saving, but challenged the agency to produce proof it would build something better in its place. *The Day* sent a reporter to a conference in Indiana on putting old train stations to new uses. In an article on November 21, 1972, McGinley pointed to a successful effort in the Rhode Island city of Woonsocket.

Grube finally and reluctantly surrendered. Public opinion had turned against the Redevelopment Agency as a result of the civic campaign and the exposure it received in the *Day's* news pages. The finishing touch occurred when the agency displayed plans by a bus company to build a depot at the site of the station. *The Day* published a rendering of the squat, functional block building on the front page. Dale's group interested George Notter, a Boston restoration architect, in restoring the building as a restaurant and train terminal. *The Day* sent a reporter to Boston with Silverstein and other city officials to view Notter's restoration work. They dined in a restaurant in an old government building that Notter had refurbished. Afterwards, the agency approved Notter's plans, ending a seesaw controversy that had started in the 1950s.

The successful Union Station campaign put a halt to the Redevelopment Agency's demolition juggernaut in downtown New London. The final stage of the agency's plans called for the widening of Bank Street, which would have required tearing down many of the whaling era buildings overlooking the river. The plans were dropped soon after *The Day* published a front-page story in which Dale Plummer, one of the founders of Union Railroad Station Trust, chronicled the history and importance of the buildings. Even City Manager C. Francis Driscoll, who started the agency's blitzkrieg through the city as executive director of the Redevelopment Agency, became a preservationist.

The opening of the new Union Station in July 1976 coincided with preparations for the nation's bicentennial. Notter threw a lavish party in the station. *The Day* produced a tabloid edition celebrating the event, in which it apologized for having been originally wrongheaded about the station. "We were wrong!" one headline admitted, over an excerpt from one of Grube's early editorials. "But we changed our mind!" it continued over an excerpt from another containing the newspaper's reconstructed point of view. But even that editorial, which ran on June 7, 1975, after Notter revealed his proposal, was half-hearted. This made it all the more ironic that Grube later collected all the praise for the newspaper's transformation and received an award from Union Railroad Station Trust, when the credit should have gone to McGinley and other reporters whose work had helped the city see reason. Grube sounded more like a prisoner of war forced by the enemy to make a statement:

> *This newspaper has never championed the station as a handsome edifice its friends say it is. But the station is sound, commodious and a structure impossible to duplicate at today's prices.*

Union Station's dramatic rescue restored the flagging spirits of many and established an upbeat and optimistic mood in the city that lasted for the rest of the decade. Easy bank credit and federal tax incentives had provided fuel for a furious real-estate boom. Speculators poured into the city with plans for the city's ailing historic buildings. A bar owner, Richard Rudolph, rebuilt the old hotel building near the train station where he had opened Rudy's. The investment purchased time for the structures and created the impression the city was on the move once again.

The city celebrated the nation's 200th anniversary in 1976 with a joyfulness that hadn't been felt in years. The atmosphere matched the optimism of the city's 250th anniversary, the hopefulness that the *Deutschland* had brought to the port and the euphoria following the two world wars. The same month the train station reopened, tall ships slipped into the harbor for the nation's bicentennial, music drifted across the water, fireworks lit up the sky, and the city overflowed with people from all over, including the usual number of opportunists.

EARLY IN 1977, *THE DAY* explored a tip that a promoter hired by the Chamber of Commerce to organize waterfront events was mixed up in a large-scale, fraudulent business deal. The newspaper sent a reporter to New York and New Jersey to look into federal records involving Anthony A. "Al" Constantine, who was seeking an extension of his $20,000 contract. In his application for the job, Constantine described his background as a yachtsman and financial consultant. What wasn't generally known was that he had been founder and president of Stonehenge Ltd., a real estate syndicating operation that had collapsed two years earlier, causing losses of more than $50 million to the investors. The Securities and Exchange Commission entered a default judgment against Constantine on charges of fraud. Constantine didn't admit his guilt, but was found technically guilty because he never answered the civil complaint.

Constantine's partners included Howard Garfinkle, a Miami financier with a criminal record.

The Day, in an editorial on March 10, 1977, faulted the Chamber and other officials for not performing a better background check on someone who was hired to represent the city. But it stopped short of recommending Constantine's contract be terminated. The story and editorial didn't do Constantine any harm. Public opinion, some of it orchestrated by local business interests that supported the marine promotion program, rallied to Constantine's support, condemning *The Day* for digging into his past. The Marine Commerce and Development Committee, a civic organization the city had authorized to run the marine promotions program, renewed Constantine's contract, although the group specified that he wouldn't handle funds. Heckerman interviewed Constantine, letting him further elaborate on his side of the Stonehenge episode, and wrote a sympathetic story.

The Day then joined the party and for the next several years published special tabloid editions about the festivals and lavished daily publicity upon the events, believing that all the activity would benefit the city. In 1978, when Constantine set out to break a trans-Atlantic record with his trimaran sailboat *The Spirit of America*, the newspaper donated $500 and published daily dispatches on his progress, which Constantine radioed from the high seas.

The epicenter of the waterfront activity was Richard Rudolph's bar and restaurant, where he and his wife, Bonnie, held court. The bar became the unofficial headquarters of Save Our Seas, a purportedly environmental organization with somewhat nebulous goals that arrived in September 1977 with the crew of the barkentine *Barba Negra*. The men and women aboard the boat adopted New London as their homeport and settled into a free berth at City Pier, where they engaged in a series of fund-raising events.

One of the annual events conceived by Constantine and the MCDC was the "Flotsam and Jetsam" raft race. Many of the banks and other businesses put their employees to work building fanciful rafts during the weeks leading up to the day of the race. Even *The Day* entered the contest, which was held on the 1979 Labor Day weekend, and later published a firsthand account by one of the reporters who served on the crew. Looking on from a yacht in the harbor was a tall, distinguished looking man with a mustache. As the raft drew near, the man cheered over the ship's microphone in a thick Greek accent, "Go New London *Day*."

It was last thing anyone expected to hear from P. Takis Veliotis, the general manager of the Electric Boat shipyard and long-time target of *The Day*.

TWENTY-EIGHT

RAISING HELL

We voice our respect and compliments to southeastern Connecticut's major daily, The Day *of New London, for it demonstrates how well the community newspapers of today work to serve first all the interests of their readers, no matter how much that service displeases powerful private or political forces.*

—The Danbury (Connecticut) *News-Times,* June 27, 1979

AT SIX-FOOT-FOUR, P. Takis Veliotis, was imposing, both in size and reputation. The Greek-born shipbuilder had been a corporate vice president and general manager of Electric Boat's Quincy, Massachusetts, division. In October 1977, he was sent by General Dynamics, Electric Boat's parent company in St. Louis, to straighten out the Groton shipyard and stop its mounting losses. In a race to catch up to the Soviet Union, the Navy had dumped more submarine orders on the shipyard than it could easily handle. Productivity and financial problems threatened its future and by extension the well-being of southeastern Connecticut, where the company was the largest employer. In the defense buildup in the 1960s and 1970s, southeastern Connecticut had begun to look more than ever like a company town of Electric Boat and the allied military and defense industry activities.

The situation at the shipyard had grave national security implications as well; the crisis there endangered the Navy's strategic plans. The Russians were believed to have had twice as many nuclear attack submarines as the United States by the end of the 1960s and submarines now figured importantly in the Cold War arms race.

The shipyard had begun to get into trouble in 1974, when the Navy awarded Electric Boat the contract to build the first Trident missile-firing submarine, the Navy's latest and most important weapon, on top of orders for eighteen 688-class attack submarines. To keep up with the work the Navy heaped upon it, the shipyard nearly had to triple its workforce in the next three years. It hired thousands of untrained apprentices and attempted to turn them into skilled workers in crash training programs. The shipyard had started out with a highly trained and mature workforce in 1970. But in its frantic effort to build its numbers, the company had to lower the bar as the labor force grew from twelve thousand in January 1971 to more than thirty thousand by mid-1977. Many of the young Vietnam era workers brought with them substance abuse problems and disrespect for authority. Discipline broke down. The inexperience caused mistakes and slowed down production.

The fact that the 688-submarine was designed by Electric Boat's rival, Newport News Shipbuilding and Drydock Company, in Newport News, Virginia, exacerbated Electric Boat's predicament. Admiral Hyman G. Rickover, head of the Navy's nuclear propulsion program, distrusted the private contractors. He wanted Newport News to design the new submarine rather than let the experienced designers at Electric Boat do the job alone and to play the two against each other. But Newport News built surface ships and had never designed a submarine. Resulting delays in producing design drawings as well as design mistakes and numerous changes ordered by the Navy added to Electric Boat's burdens. Double-digit inflation in the early years of construction further compromised Electric Boat's ability to stay within its construction budget. In 1975, General Dynamics handed the Navy a bill for $220 million in cost over-runs on the first seven submarines. The claim was settled for $97 million the following year. On December 1, 1976, the company turned in a second claim, this time for $544 million, escalating the tension between the contractor and the Navy.

In 1976, General Dynamics sent Gordon MacDonald, the corporation's chief financial officer, to Groton to put the shipyard in order. He took up residence at a Mystic Ramada Inn. But after eight months, MacDonald returned to St. Louis without having accomplished anything significant. While he was in Groton, the unions filed more than two thousand grievances over steps he had taken or proposed to take to improve efficiency.

The company, with a backlog by 1977 of seventeen attack submarines and five of the mammoth Tridents, had fallen more than two years behind schedule in its orders and was losing money at a rate that alarmed the corporate managers in St. Louis. In sending in Veliotis October 24, 1977, General

Dynamics chose to administer stronger medicine. Veliotis had solved similar production problems at Electric Boat's shipyard in Quincy by slashing the size of the work force and squeezing more work out of the shipyard.

The nation was at the height of the Cold War and there was tight security inside the shipyard. But it was impossible to conceal the confusion at the defense plant when thousands of workers, many of whom unwound in bars around the shipyard after each shift, were privy to what was taking place. Joan Poro, the *Day's* military reporter, heard daily stories, primarily from labor sources, that fit into a picture of general chaos inside the yard. Early in September, a month before Veliotis' arrival, John Foley authorized her to go to work on an investigation into the productivity problems. Dan Stets was pulled off his Groton beat to help. But events overtook them. Veliotis arrived in the midst of their project with dramatic announcements of layoffs and management changes. This forced *The Day* to rush into print with the reporters' findings two weeks ahead of schedule. For five days, Stets and Poro wrote installments against deadline on the day the stories appeared. Also, they were writing front-page stories on unfolding news. Each worked nearly ninety hours that week.

Electric Boat stonewalled the newspaper from the start. It would not answer the *Day's* questions. The defense contractor ignored formal requests for interviews with Veliotis and other top managers. Electric Boat persuaded the Navy to oppose the *Day's* efforts to secure information through the Freedom of Information Act. The reporters interviewed more than one hundred Electric Boat workers and government officials for the series, "Electric Boat, Boom or Bust?" which won the two reporters professional accolades and the shipyard management's hostility. In an editorial on October 27, *The Day* summarized the problems it had uncovered at Electric Boat:

> *Anyone reflecting on these facts must conclude that the reasons for trouble are multiple, stemming basically from an inability of top management to manage. Construction errors, late deliveries, poor delivery, poor morale, ineffective supervision, bad workmanship requiring that a job must be twice sent back for corrective work—these and a host of other manufacturing malignancies led to the inevitable crisis.*

One of the newspaper's sources said, "I would say ten years ago we built submarines. Now I don't know what we're building." The reporters found examples in which the wrong welding materials were used. Torpedo tubes on the first Trident, the *Ohio*, were installed improperly twice. An inspector told the newspaper that the submarine *Philadelphia* virtually was built twice because of mistakes. The newspaper only mildly criticized the company for the manner in which it put people out of work. And *The Day* welcomed the steps General Dynamics was taking to come to grips with the shipyard's dysfunctions. In another editorial on October 25, it had written:

> *The shipyard can best be managed by a tough shipbuilder who has faced and overcome difficulties in the past. Building submarines is no ordinary exercise in production. It is a sophisticated art and a tremendous technological challenge.*

Electric Boat's irritation at *The Day* grew as fresh disclosures about the shipyard's struggle appeared almost every day. Meantime, ill will toward the company mounted. Employees with years of experience lost their jobs. Many had worked on the original *Nautilus* project. A large proportion were in their 50s. Fear mounted as rumors spread that General Dynamics would shut down the shipyard if the Navy didn't provide the money for the cost overruns. Electric Boat's embarrassment benefited the Navy and Admiral Rickover in a contractual dispute with the company in which hundreds of millions of dollars were at stake. One night, after Poro had become Groton editor, Rickover made a surprise telephone call to her. Poro remembers only that the call was flattering. Others at *The Day* recall from her accounts of the conversation at the time that Rickover hinted he could get her a job in Washington.

Early in January 1978, Electric Boat tried to put a lid on its public relations crisis, which it blamed largely on *The Day*. In its shipyard newsletter, it lashed out at the "rumor mongers" and "bad mouthers" in the shipyard, who, it charged, were undermining efforts to improve productivity and maintain its production schedules. It also took aim at *The Day* for "biased and unbalanced reporting." "Such slanted reporting makes it extremely difficult for anyone to get the facts surrounding the issues," the company said.

The antagonism against the newspaper reached a peak in March 1978. Veliotis, who had surrounded himself with executives from Quincy, signaled a change when he brought in Alex Piranian, who had been his press spokesman there, to be Electric Boat's public affairs manager. Piranian's arrival marked the start of a new era in relations between Electric Boat and *The Day*. Later that month, Electric Boat, without any advance warning or explanation, stopped talking to *The Day* and ceased advertising in the newspaper. All its classified ads for jobs and institutional ads were placed with the *Day's* competitors. Whenever reporters called the public relations office at the shipyard, they were told the company no longer had anything to say to *The Day*.

The Electric Boat news blackout became public in February 1979, when Veliotis snubbed *The Day* and granted his first interview since arriving in 1977 to the Norwich *Bulletin* and the *Hartford Courant*. *The Day* reconstructed the interview from published reports and ran a front-page story about the problem with Electric Boat on February 2 and an editorial on February 5. The blackout attracted national attention the following month when Deane Avery, reacting to the Veliotis interview, appealed to the National News Council for help. The council was formed in 1973 to help arbitrate disputes between the press and private industry. Norman E. Isaacs, editor in residence at the Graduate School of Journalism at Columbia University, was chairman. William B. Arthur, former editor of *Look* magazine, was executive director. In his complaint on March 13, 1978, Avery accused Electric Boat of discriminating against the newspaper by cooperating with other news organizations but not *The Day*. This followed months in which Avery was ignored in his attempts to discuss the issues with Electric Boat and General Dynamics officials. A. H. Raskin, the former labor writer for the New York *Times*, was assigned to investigate the dispute.

When the company refused to cooperate with the News Council, the council sought help from Michael Pulitzer, a council member whose family owned the St. Louis *Post Dispatch*, General Dynamics' hometown paper. Pulitzer talked to Fred J. Bettinger, the corporation's director of public affairs and advertising, about *The Day*. Bettinger told Pulitzer that the company was irked at what it considered the *Day's* settled pattern of taking "cheap shots" at Electric Boat based on "irresponsible statements made by disgruntled employees and former employees, often on the basis of barroom interviews." Bettinger said the company's irritation was heightened by the fact that the *Day's* critical stories were appearing just as the management team was beginning to turn the shipyard around. The company concluded that it was pointless trying to explain its side to *The Day* because the newspaper misrepresented it or played it down and so it decided just not to talk to the newspaper anymore. Pulitzer passed on to Bettinger Avery's assurances that *The Day* didn't have an ax to grind against Electric Boat, and was only interested in objectively reporting on developments at a company that was southeastern Connecticut's economic mainstay. Bettinger promised to explore the possibility of a meeting between Avery and someone from the company but months more passed with no further word either from St. Louis or Groton.

The council released its findings on June 13, 1979, after an acrimonious debate among the members. A council subcommittee had rejected in a 6-5 vote a strong resolution calling upon the Navy to require contractors such as Electric Boat to adhere to the same standards of releasing information to the press as the Navy had to follow. Instead, the 18-member group unanimously issued a weak statement that said Electric Boat, despite its many government contracts, was under no obligation to talk to *The Day*, but added that southeastern Connecticut, whose economy depended on Electric Boat, deserved better from the company. "When public funds and public interest are involved to such an extent in a company that employs a quarter of all the workers in southeastern Connecticut, the community is ill-served by Electric Boat's arbitrary silence," the decision stated. The council also offered to mediate the dispute. Isaacs was so angry he considered resigning from the council. Arthur, the executive director, said it was the worst vote in the council's six-year history.

Avery regarded the council's stand as a victory and hoped it would persuade Electric Boat to work with the newspaper. Grube and most of the reporters and editors were disappointed, if not angered. *The Day* received encouragement in the controversy from across Connecticut. Stephen Collins, editorial page editor of the *News-Times* of Danbury, wrote, "There was a time, in an earlier and what we consider a less enlightened period in American history, when there were not only company towns but company newspapers, run the way the major employer in town wanted. But that period has long gone."

Electric Boat didn't respond to the report. But the relations between *The Day* and Electric Boat already had begun to thaw that spring. The company cooperated with *The Day* in its coverage of the launching of the *Ohio*, the Navy's first Trident submarine. The day before the launching, the newspaper devoted its front page to the event, which was to be attended by First Lady Rosalind Carter and Senator and former astronaut John Glenn of Ohio. Blackout or no blackout, the construction of the submarine was a monumental achievement and a huge news story. The *Ohio* was the nation's most sophisticated piece of war machinery. It was capable of firing twenty-four powerful missiles six thousand miles, each armed with multiple nuclear warheads, from below the ocean's surface. The Trident would be the third "platform" for launching strategic nuclear weapons, the others being land-based missile installations and strategic bombers. Putting aside feelings one way or the other about its purpose, it was a marvel of technology. The newspaper's coverage acknowledged that it was also a frightening weapon. The day of the launching, *The Day* reported on its front page about the thousands of demonstrators who protested outside the shipyard against the Trident class submarine, a scene that would be reenacted numerous times during the next decade as sentiment grew against what would turn out to be the grand finale of the nuclear arms race in the Cold War.

The news boycott of *The Day* continued, however, for nearly two more years. In April 1981, Robert H. Steele, a former Republican congressman in eastern Connecticut, arranged a meeting between Avery and Veliotis. They met for dinner on April 23, 1981, at the Old Lyme Inn. When Avery arrived, Veliotis was already in the dining room, standing next to the fireplace. Avery recalls:

> *I felt intimidated. He looked eight feet tall. He was very cordial. He said, "Hello Deane," and came forward and shook my hand. He said, "We should be friends." There was someone there from the public relations department, and before we parted after dinner, he (Veliotis) told him to make sure we got an invitation to the next launching.*

The meeting formally marked the end of the news blackout and the resumption of normal relations. The blackout had benefited no one. Throughout the controversy, *The Day* didn't let up on its coverage. Electric Boat did more damage to itself, in fact, for the stories Stets and other reporters wrote without Electric Boat's response became one-sided. This deeply concerned Avery and the newspaper's editors. In Avery's repeated pleas to the company to talk about coverage, he acknowledged *The Day* was vulnerable to errors in covering the complex issues. He made it clear he wanted to discuss the company's grievances and address them. It was a complicated issue, reconciling the need to protect defense secrets during a heightened period of the Cold War with the public's economic interest in the work that was going on at Electric Boat. It was one thing to conceal legitimate defense secrets and another to hide construction errors, morale problems, ineffective supervision, and bad workmanship, all of which had been the focus of the *Day's* coverage.

By the time he met with Avery, Veliotis was in a struggle between Electric Boat and the Navy over the unsettled claims in the 688 program. John Lehman Jr., Navy Secretary in the Reagan administration, was becoming increasingly impatient with the standoff, and sought Veliotis' removal from Electric Boat. The Reagan administration, concerned that the feud between the shipyard and the Navy was endangering national security, also was eager to move aside the combative Rickover. Rickover had been urging the Justice Department to press criminal charges against General Dynamics for allegedly illegal cost overruns. Veliotis was moved into a corporate position outside Electric Boat in November 1981 and Rickover was forced to retire the following January.

What Avery and others on the newspaper and on the News Council did not know was that Veliotis had far more to hide during this period of *The Day* news blackout than anyone imagined. Veliotis later was implicated in a kickback scheme with a contractor that had begun in Quincy and continued at Electric Boat during the three years he was there. He fled to Greece to escape prosecution and lived in seclusion until his death in January 1999.

SHORTLY AFTER THE SERIES on Electric Boat had begun, on November 6, 1977, Joan Poro became Groton editor in another newsroom management shuffle. She replaced Jim Irvine, who became news desk chief. Poro showed herself to be as tough an editor as she was an investigative reporter during her first week on the job when she decided to raise some hell with the good-old-boy network in Groton. The Groton Lodge of Elks held an annual dinner honoring the military community. Many local leaders and prominent citizens were invited, including police chiefs, mayors, and city councilors. *The Day* routinely covered the event, but its stories overlooked a feature that occurred at the conclusion of the program. After the Boy Scouts who presented the colors had been sent home, the Elks brought in strippers to entertain the brass.

Poro, who knew about this practice from having been a Groton reporter, assigned Stephen Fagin to write an uncensored version of the Elks' 1977 salute to the servicemen. That year, the club was honoring disabled servicemen. According to Fagin's November 16 story, the mayor of the city presented a plaque to a former city councilor who had lost his leg in combat in Korea. The recipient received a standing ovation. There were some speeches. Around 9 pm, the dinner tables were removed, the lights dimmed, and two dancers, one from the Boston Playboy Club, the other from Australia, pranced in, threw off their clothes and danced and frolicked around the room before the appreciative audience. Fagin's account was displayed modestly on the Groton page under a bland three-column headline that said merely, "At Elks Night: Strippers Entertain Servicemen." The story resulted in a brief suspension of the club's liquor license and fine. Fagin was warned by the club he would never be able to join the Elks, and the mayor would not talk to the newspaper for several months. In later years, *The Day* probably would have run the story on the front page.

This wasn't the first time the Groton Elks, the biggest fraternal organization in town, had squirmed under the public spotlight. In 1973, the club had been the object of the *Day's* attention for refusing admission to a black civil-rights leader, Louis Cornelius. In the region blacks still had their own Elks lodge in New London. Poro had been one of the reporters who covered the story when Cornelius was turned away. Cornelius later sued the lodge. He had strong backing from the *Day's* editorial page in this fight to break the color barrier.

In the 1970s, *The Day* made investigations a high priority. It could afford to. The battle over the Guild had led to improved pay and benefits that attracted talent. By the mid 1970s, *The Day* had an experienced staff of more than forty reporters and editors. The degree of talent was borne out by the later successes of several of the reporters who left. Richard Polman and Dan Stets both eventually became foreign correspondents for the Philadelphia *Inquirer*. Avery pointed out to the board in April 1977 that the newsroom now had two reporters working on investigations at all times. Investigative reporting had become fashionable after the Watergate scandal. Aspiring young reporters were drawn into the profession by the glamour created by Bob Woodward and Carl Bernstein, the Washington *Post* reporters who broke the Watergate story. John Foley gave his reporters copies of their book, *All The President's Men*, as a how-to handbook and reporters adopted some of the techniques, including a rule requiring two sources to confirm a fact. During an investigation into the local police department in 1975, reporters met with sources in dark parking lots late at night as Woodward had met with "Deep Throat" in a parking garage.

Reporters Suzanne Trimel and Lance Johnson examined lax controls over radiation exposure at the Millstone nuclear power station in a series entitled "Radiation Roulette." Stan DeCoster and Bruce MacDonald crossed the state line into Westerly, Rhode Island, to prepare a series "Can Westerly be managed?" examining why the community couldn't seem to hold onto a town manager. In 1978, *The Day* exposed how special interests planned to kill a bottle-deposit bill that environmentalists had been attempting to get through the legislature for six years. Just before the vote, *The Day* wrote in an editorial:

> *The bill is opposed by a wily crew of well-financed container and beverage industry operators. What they lack in logical arguments and genuine concern for the public interest they more than make up in pressure tactics and parliamentary deviousness.*

The Bottle Bill was passed that year.

THE DAY COVERED SOME genuinely important stories, notably the one at Electric Boat, but it missed or glossed over others. On Christmas Eve in 1973, a college student was changing the tire of a female companion's car on a New London Street when he was struck and killed by a car. The motorist fled the scene. In its next edition, *The Day* had a routine story on an inside page about the hit-and-run, with a picture of the victim, Kevin Showalter. The police botched the investigation to the point of losing crucial evidence, and Lucille Showalter, the mother of the victim and a prominent local teacher and civic leader, suspected this was intentional to hide the guilt of somebody who was well connected in the city. She eventually theorized that the driver was Harvey

N. Mallove, a New London businessman, former mayor, and local power broker. Mallove was a member of the inner circle of politicians who had hired City Manager C. Francis Driscoll, and who remained a close friend of Driscoll. The mother spent the next two years pleading with authorities to get to the bottom of her son's death. She finally succeeded when Governor Ella T. Grasso agreed to order an investigation by a one-man grand jury. Connecticut law provided for such grand juries to gather facts about high-profile, unsolved crimes.

The Day shied away from the controversial case, covering the breaking news but doing little to look below the surface. The editors regarded the determined mother's crusade for justice for her son as a nuisance and viewed her theory about Mallove as intriguing but implausible. The newspaper never supported the mother's campaign for a more thorough investigation on its editorial page. Lucille Showalter suspected the newspaper avoided the controversy out of deference to Mallove and Angelo Santaniello, one of Mallove's closest friends and a local judge who Showalter suspected was helping cover up for Mallove. Mallove's connection with the case first became public when state police, in a hearing in a New Jersey courtroom, told a judge that Mallove was a "principal" suspect.

The *Day's* interest in the story grew when a federal grand jury began investigating possible corruption in the New London Police Department in 1974. David Burt, the police reporter, and several other reporters took part in an investigation that uncovered details of the probe, including the identity of the police officers who were the targets. The suspicions that hung over the department added some credibility to the theory that the police might have taken part in a cover-up in the Showalter case. By 1975, *The Day* was competing with the Norwich *Bulletin* for new leads in the Showalter story. John Peterson, the *Bulletin* managing editor and former *Day* reporter, had a close interest in the case and was responsible for much of his newspaper's ardor for the story. Peterson was competitive by nature and happy to embarrass *The Day*.

On February 22, 1978, Judge Joseph Dannehy, the grand juror, released an unusual report that stated that the police investigation had been so botched that it was impossible to determine guilt, but that it was "more probable than not" that Mallove was the driver of the car that killed Kevin Showalter. *The Day* ran a story under a banner headline on the front page, as well as the text of the grand jury report. The newspaper, like many people in the community, shook its head at these findings, which pointed to Mallove's guilt without providing him a chance to defend himself in a trial. His wife, Rosalind, crusaded without success to have the state legislature abolish the one-man grand-jury system. The truth remained shrouded in mystery. *The Day* had done little to shed light on the dramatic case, especially in the early stages, when investigative reporting might have made a difference. Nevertheless, the Malloves, Santaniello, and their friends remained bitter toward the newspaper for the coverage it did give the case.

THE DAY REPORTED ON southeastern Connecticut's growing influence in the legislature in the late 1970s. The person mainly responsible for the region's improving fortunes in Hartford was state Senator Richard F. Schneller, a retired manufacturer and Democrat from the town of Essex, who became the Senate majority leader. Schneller, like the *Day's* Ken Grube, was a friend and supporter of the governor, Ella Grasso. He secured support for new state assistance for the area around New London, including a plan to develop the Thames River basin and the languishing port of New London.

But *The Day* overlooked the beginnings of a story that would have a profound effect on the development of southeastern Connecticut. The 1970s were years of mounting activism by the survivors of the state's Indian tribes. Tribal members began to appear at public hearings in the state Capitol demanding the creation of a state Indian Affairs Council. In a region where Native Americans were little more than objects of quaint curiosity, descendants of the Pequots were trying to rebuild their tribe on its rundown reservation in Ledyard. The few survivors living there adopted bylaws and a constitution in 1974. Richard A. "Skip" Hayward, a shipyard worker and grandson of Elizabeth George, a tribal matriarch, was elected tribal council chairman the following year. In 1976, the Pequots filed a suit in federal court to regain eight hundred acres of reservation that, they claimed the state illegally sold in the 19th century. Hayward tried to interest *Day* reporters in the story, but often was brushed off as a crank in the same way Lucille Showalter had been.

The newspaper paid only slightly more attention to John Hamilton, who claimed to be the head of the Mohegan tribe. Stan DeCoster followed his efforts to establish his legitimacy, and Hamilton, or Chief Rolling Cloud as he was known by his supporters, made DeCoster an honorary tribal member.

Avery, Wes Hammond, and the other directors were generally pleased with the newspaper's performance despite the difficulties with Electric Boat. In fact, the directors regarded the shipyard's blackout as a badge of honor. There was seldom a meeting when Avery didn't report accomplishments by the newsroom. Hammond brought the board good tidings as well. Boom times had dramatic effects on the *Day's* financial position. The year 1977 was a banner year for the newspaper. Its revenues, approaching $7 million, were double what they had been only ten years earlier. More than $1 million of this was in classified advertising, stemming largely from the real estate boom. In light of these successes, the co-publishers recommended adding a week's salary to the customary two-week Christmas bonus, and the directors agreed.

For stockholders in a conventionally owned stock company, such revenues would have been reason to celebrate, for the earnings almost certainly would have translated into handsome dividends. But the *Day's* situation under the trust Bodenwein created didn't work that way. *The Day* spent the money on operations as fast as it earned it. While the revenues doubled in ten years, expenses tripled, as the directors plowed more money back into the newspaper and saved for future needs, notably for a new offset press, a new computer system, and the addition on the northeast corner of the building they had promised the Redevelopment Agency they would build.

The directors had this freedom to spend because the newspaper had no stockholders to satisfy. *The Day* trustees were, in effect, the stockholders. The dividends, usually set by Francis McGuire, seldom changed much from year to year. In 1977, the directors turned over $151,000 to the Bodenwein Public Benevolent Foundation, about the same amount as the previous year. In 1978, the dividends paid actually fell to $122,000. This did not trouble the Hartford National Bank & Trust Company, which administered the Bodenwein fund. After all, McGuire represented the bank on the *Day's* board. Elizabeth Bodenwein Miles, who sat on the board and was the recipient of all but ten percent of the dividends paid to the Foundation now that her brother Gordon was dead, was content with her income. And based on the newspaper's net earnings, it compared favorably with the dividend pay out of the average business. The only incentive to augment the dividends was a provision in Bodenwein's will that directors reward themselves with a yearly bonus if the amount paid to the Bodenwein fund exceeded $100,000. In 1977, they gave one another a $4,800 bonus, $500 more than the previous year, for exceeding that target.

With the flexibility it had to spend without worrying about stockholders, *The Day* had built an organization that was better able to do investigations, risk offending advertisers, and cover its large territory better than other newspapers its size. By 1977, the *Day's* news staff numbered nearly fifty, twenty percent higher than the average staff for a New England newspaper with the *Day's* circulation. Fully a quarter of the *Day's* total number of employees worked on the news staff, compared to fifteen percent typical of the newspaper industry. The *Day's* newsroom payroll was nearly twice that of the group average.

The extra resources provided the newspaper with a seasoned and versatile staff, which was put to a test early in 1978. On February 6, an uncommonly ferocious blizzard struck Connecticut, paralyzing the state for days. Storm Larry sculpted deep drifts of heavy, wet snow down highways and roads across southeastern Connecticut. The snow began to fall in the afternoon, after the newspaper had gone to press, and continued through the night. Many from the day shift couldn't get home, and joined the night staff for the duration of the storm. *The Day* filled the next day's edition with stories and photographs from the storm and still managed to get to press an hour early and distribute eighty percent of its thirty-nine thousand papers although roads were in many places impassable. The National Guard was activated to clear the roads with its heavy equipment.

The storm strengthened the bonds and *esprit* of the newsroom. But developments that spring worked in the opposite direction. Ray Bordner left to be a freelance writer. *The Day* replaced the versatile Bordner with two editors. David Heckerman, who had helped establish an op-ed page, became assistant editorial page editor and James Irvine took over the administrative duties as assistant managing editor. Neither was as popular as Bordner. Soon, Irvine's authority virtually equaled John Foley's in the newsroom. His abrasive style shortly began to erode the good will toward management in the newsroom.

Even more dramatic changes occurred on the board of directors, which was cautiously beginning to look into the future. The directors began to consider starting a Sunday newspaper, and toyed with the idea of a morning newspaper on Saturdays. Hammond also began to present figures to the directors for buying a new press and building a major addition in the next ten years.

On March 27, 1978, Thomas Troland, a director and trustee since 1939, died. At 85, he was the last of the original trustees of The Day Trust. Troland had replaced Theodore Bodenwein as a director of The Day Publishing Company. He was the lawyer for Edna Bodenwein in the struggle over her husband's will. He also represented thoroughly the institutional interests of New London for which the newspaper stood. He had helped fashion the new city manager form of government and was the city's first law director and served briefly as city manager. He handled most of the legal work connected with the development of the modern Ocean Beach after the 1938 Hurricane. He worked out the complicated arrangement by which the city acquired the land for the Coast Guard Academy in 1931. After World War I, he was among the local leaders who lobbied for Electric Boat to build its submarines at the New London Ship and Engine Company yard, the current Electric Boat shipyard, in Groton. Grube wrote in an editorial on March 29:

Judge Troland had a special relationship to us at The Day. *He had been the warm and trusted friend of Theodore Bodenwein, who built this newspaper into a strong and effective medium of public service, rescuing it from almost certain bankruptcy in 1891. The judge's appointment as a trustee of* The Day *was a natural. He knew the region and he took pains to learn the details of publishing a paper to serve the changing needs of the area. He was a force for making the paper what it is today, though there were times when he disagreed with the editorial policy.*

The trustees replaced Troland with Elizabeth Miles, Bodenwein's daughter. Miles had returned to New London after her husband, Eugene Miles, died in March 1969. Francis and Helen McGuire had visited her in Cleveland. McGuire had discussed her returning to New England and becoming a director of *The Day*. He had been Elizabeth's lawyer and saw in her another supporter on the board. Miles was eager to rejoin her high school friend, Roberta, Judge Troland's wife. Troland rented her a cottage and Elizabeth returned to her hometown in 1970, after more than fifty years away. She built a lavish French provincial house near the Trolands on Niles Hill Road and indulged her tastes in entertaining and collecting antique English silver pieces. On the board, Mrs. Miles never made waves. Deane Avery recalled her role in a 1984 interview:

Once in awhile she'd raise an issue. She wasn't difficult to get along with. She didn't object to expenditures half as much as I would if I had been in her shoes. That is not to say she wasn't interested in the newspaper. She had a strong interest in the newspaper. Every once in awhile she'd challenge something. She'd say, "Do we need to do this this year? Can't this wait?" But that wasn't very often.

Mrs. Miles, in truth, had very little to complain about. In years past, neither had Edna, her stepmother, nor her brother, Gordon, although they had complained loudly and repeatedly about their dividends. In 1978, when she was made a trustee at the age of 82, she was receiving more than $100,000 in income from the Bodenwein Public Benevolent Foundation. She had amassed an estate worth more than $1.7 million, nearly all of which she left to the Bodenwein Public Benevolent Foundation when she died on November 11, 1978, seven months after having been made a trustee. Her death ended the Bodenwein family line in America that had begun when Agnes and Anton Bodenwein and their 5-year-old son, Theodore, emigrated from Germany to southeastern Connecticut in 1869, eventually settling in New London in 1877. There being no further survivors, this event signified a watershed for her father's legacy, although there would be one more battle to fight

TWENTY-NINE

Split Interests

It's clear that the trustees here realize that the consequences of this case may be that the perpetuation of their existence as power brokers in the city will be eliminated.

—D. Patrick Mullarkey, U.S. Department of Justice, June 27, 1983

WHEN SHE DIED OF cancer November 20, 1978, at age 82, Elizabeth Bodenwein Miles left $7,000 to her household help and several close friends, including Roberta Troland. She willed her Lincoln to her driver, Alteo Severini, and her English silver collection to the Wadsworth Atheneum art museum in Hartford. She left her house to Lawrence & Memorial Hospitals and the rest of her estate, valued at more than $1.7 million, to the *Day's* Bodenwein Public Benevolent Foundation.

The Day ran a flattering obituary on the front page with a recent photo of her displaying a piece from her English silver collection. The editors' warmth in handling the story contrasted with the newspaper's indifferent treatment of the deaths of her stepmother, Edna, and brother, Gordon. Their obituaries had been placed inside the newspaper. A significant difference between Elizabeth on the one hand and Gordon and Edna on the other was that Elizabeth never caused the directors and managers of the newspaper any trouble. *The Day,* appreciative of this, wrote in an editorial November 21, 1978:

> *She was truly a lady of great dignity and perception. And she was truly her father's daughter, ready to rise to any challenge, fully prepared to sustain and strengthen the newspaper.*

In truth, her greatest importance to the newspaper did not spring from any action she had taken, but from her longevity. Her death opened the door for the full implementation of her father's 1938 will. The death of Theodore and Jennie Bodenwein's daughter, born when there was still hope in the couple's marriage, didn't receive the attention it was given in *The Day* and in the national press because of her fame as a collector, her past as a photographer, or as a millionaire patron of the arts. Her death was noteworthy because it created an unusual and substantial windfall for southeastern Connecticut that had been planned more than forty years earlier, when her father's health was failing rapidly. In addition to her substantial bequest, the nine-tenths of the dividends from The Day Trust that had accrued to her, her brother, and stepmother while they were alive now would be available for civic betterment in the *Day's* eastern Connecticut circulation area. *The Day* paper overnight became one of the region's biggest charitable givers. All of its stock dividends, averaging more than $130,000 a year, now would go into the community, as Bodenwein had wished when he stated in his will:

> *I am not unmindful that I owe the success of* The Day *in large degree to the confidence and support of the people of Eastern Connecticut, and I believe the profits of the large business I have created with their help should, except for the provisions I have made for my dear wife and for my children, be returned to the community…*

But Elizabeth's death also created serious problems for Francis McGuire and the other trustees. It aroused the unwanted attention of the federal bureaucracy that her father had intensely distrusted. By the most unfavorable of coincidences, just as Mrs. Miles was resettling in New London and entering the last years of her life, Congress had been scrutinizing private foundations like The Day Trust for possible abuses of the federal tax code. A 1965 report by the Treasury Department had pointed to many cases in which businesses improperly sheltered their assets from the Internal Revenue Service and rewarded themselves through such arrangements. Based on the report, Congress tightened the rules governing private foundations in a 1969 tax reform law.

The law addressed a number of practices tax planners used to avoid paying taxes, but the one affecting *The Day* addressed the exploitation of private foundations to perpetuate family businesses. A business could be passed from one generation to the next without backbreaking estate taxes simply by turning the stock over to a private trust, as the Bodenweins did. In the *Day's* case, however, the family didn't consist of blood relatives but colleagues. The principals also could claim a charitable deduction, as Bodenwein, Edna, and the other *Day* stockholders presumably did when they turned over their stock to The Day Trust with the intent that some of the proceeds from the dividends would go to charity.

Congress was concerned that such tax advantages, designed to encourage worthy private charities, sometimes gave businesses unfair competitive edges, in effect a subsidy not enjoyed by their competitors. Congress did not want the same businesses that had claimed charitable deductions thwarting the charitable purposes by piling up earnings in the businesses and not distributing them to their rightful destinations.

To discourage this practice, the Tax Reform Act of 1969 had imposed a confiscatory two hundred percent tax on the value of a charitable foundation's stock over twenty percent of the outstanding shares. This would have amounted to a levy on *The Day* of more than $1.6 million in 1978. This was more than twice its net earnings that year. McGuire knew that applying the new private foundation rules to *The Day* would force the trustees to liquidate the newspaper and dissolve the trust, as Congress intended. The newspaper would no longer be able to furnish the foundation even the minimum $25,000 contribution Bodenwein had called for in his will for it to continue to exist.

But Congress, champion of loopholes, created one McGuire hoped *The Day* could squeeze through. The new law applied specifically to exclusively charitable trusts—trusts that were classified as tax-exempt foundations by the IRS and were not required to pay taxes on their earnings. But in an attempt to penalize foundations that tried to evade the new rules by not applying for tax-exempt status, the law imposed punitive restrictions on foundations that retained non-tax-exempt interests. These were called split-interest trusts. Congress excluded, or "grandfathered out," such trusts that were created before the law went into effect in May 1969. To take advantage of this exclusion, McGuire and other lawyers for *The Day* would argue over the next three years that when Mrs. Miles, the last Bodenwein heir, died, The Day Trust still had a continuing, or "unexpired interest" in the form of the profit-making newspaper that made it a split-interest trust.

The federal government would counter that with Elizabeth's death, The Day Trust became an exclusively charitable trust. The trust's only remaining legitimate interest was to devote its resources to charitable causes, meaning it would have to sell the newspaper. Soon after Mrs. Miles died, the Hartford National Bank & Trust Company, which administered The Bodenwein fund, filed an application to make the Bodenwein Public Benevolent Foundation a tax-exempt charitable foundation. It had to, because otherwise it would have had to pay taxes on the dividends it received from *The Day*. *The Day,* meantime, asked the IRS to rule on the issue of whether The Day Trust was an exclusively charitable foundation or a split-interest trust. In the interest of its survival, it argued it was the latter.

In 1979, Francis McGuire's law firm made a decision that would have a significant impact on the *Day's* legal strategy over the next five years. McGuire merged his small, family-run New London firm with the larger, well-connected New Haven law firm of Wiggin & Dana, and lawyers for that firm eventually took control of the case. In the beginning, Charles Kingsley of Wiggin & Dana worked with Frank L. McGuire, Francis' elder son. But the case eventually was turned over to a young and talented team of Wiggin & Dana lawyers led by Mark R. Kravitz, 32. Kravitz had been a clerk for William Rehnquist when Rehnquist, later to become chief justice, was an associate Supreme Court justice.

D. Patrick Mullarkey, a tax lawyer for the Justice Department, would argue the government's side. Each side approached the case with a passion and level of interest that made it clear that this was more than a routine tax dispute; it was a battle of high principle between the government and *The Day,* one of the nation's last remaining independent newspapers. Although *The Day* paid and continues to pay its full share of taxes, the IRS felt the *Day's* trustees had been depriving the public of its rightful share of the *Day's* profits by retaining its earnings while taking care of themselves. The trustees argued they were battling to preserve Theodore Bodenwein's legacy to the community of an independent daily newspaper that was a champion and defender of the people's rights.

THE IRS RULED IN 1981 that The Day Trust had become an exclusively charitable trust when Elizabeth Miles died, subjecting it to the tax rules embodied in the 1969 Tax Reform Act. *The Day* filed its 1980 tax return and paid a $2,801 excise tax. Congress had authorized the tax to help administer the new rules. *The Day* paid the tax and then applied for a refund of the excise tax to trigger a decision on whether, in effect, the newspaper would have to be sold or not. When the IRS did not respond to the refund request in six months, the trustees appealed the IRS's original finding in United States District Court in Hartford. The plaintiffs were the newspaper's five trustees, co-publishers E. Wesley Hammond and Deane Avery, Charles E. Shain, Francis McGuire, and the newest member of the board, Evan Hill, chairman of the journalism department at the University of Connecticut. The trustees had just elected Hill to replace Elizabeth Miles.

The case generated a sense of drama among the board members, whose survival as overseers of *The Day* was at stake. McGuire was fearful that *The Day* would lose and the newspaper would have to be sold. The proceeds from the sale, expected to be more than $10 million, would go to the Bodenwein Public Benevolent Foundation, where it probably would produce an annual income ten times higher than that which the trustees had been allotting it. The newspaper would come under the control of stockholders and managers possibly more interested in maximizing the newspaper's earnings and dividends than being "the champion and protector of the public interest and defender of the people's welfare" as the will decreed. The trustees would forfeit their advantages, both in the influence they enjoyed through the newspaper and the financial perquisites. The liberal wages and benefits the employees enjoyed, the no-interest loans, and extended sick leaves all would be in jeopardy.

But these things were unimportant, the *Day's* lawyers would argue. What was important, they said, was that the trustees would no longer be in a position to carry out Bodenwein's wishes: that they continue to operate a quality newspaper serving the people of southeastern Connecticut; that the newspaper grow, and that a new building be constructed to accommodate its growth, and that after these purposes were taken care of, what was left of its earnings would be turned over to the people of the region for charitable and public purposes. If the government prevailed, it would thwart Bodenwein's purpose, stated as early as 1916, that *The Day* would somehow go on forever.

McGuire alerted the other trustees to the danger right away. It is anyone's guess what would have happened if he had not been there to mobilize the newspaper in this battle for survival. Hill later faulted McGuire for benefiting from the costly legal work. But it is a question whether a law firm without McGuire's roots in the newspaper and interest in its future would have reacted as quickly, or with as much determination. It is safe to say that McGuire and his predecessor as the *Day's* lawyer, Charles Smiddy, performed comparable roles in shaping and preserving The Day Trust. At the two most critical periods in its history, *The Day* had smart, committed lawyers devoted to the newspaper on its board. McGuire furthered the newspaper's chances of winning the case by linking his law firm to one with greater resources and talent just as the IRS matter was surfacing. Charles E. Shain recalled of the crisis, "It was exciting to be on the board. We didn't know whether we were ever going to be able to continue *The Day* as it had existed."

Every step the board took was carefully calculated in McGuire's methodical way. The directors, in a sense, cleaned house, taking steps to avoid any appearance that they, God forbid, were serving themselves. The newspaper already had cleared the deck on the charges of self-serving nepotism with a new personnel policy, enacted July 1, 1977, that prohibited relatives of full-time employees from being hired for full-time jobs. Nobody related to a department head could be hired for any job. The policy, however, conveniently excluded all existing employees. Bar Colby terminated his five-year contract as a consultant three months before it was to expire. The directors also ended the practice of making positions on the board of directors lifetime sinecures, setting the mandatory retirement age at 70. *The Day* hired a Washington lobbyist to see if the tax law could be changed in the event the trustees lost their case in court. Sam Gejdenson, the young congressman who had started out in politics by taking Ruby Cohen's place in the state legislature in 1974, offered to introduce a bill exempting *The Day* from the Tax Reform Act of 1969. The trustees, in a singular move designed to demonstrate that The Day Trust had an interest in *The Day,* voted to turn over $1,000 a year for five years to the newspaper for newsroom seminars. This move was intended to show that The Day Trust was supporting the newspaper and thus still a split-interest trust. McGuire also made sure *The Day* explained the situation clearly (and with the correct company spin) to its readers, inviting a reporter to his house and spending a whole Saturday morning going over the case. I was that reporter, and like all the others who have stood in McGuire's presence, remember the awe I felt.

It wasn't an easy subject to explain. Although *The Day* had described how the trust worked on several occasions, readers still had only the vaguest idea about how *The Day* operated. Some of the employees were similarly unaware. There were printers and pressmen who believed that when Elizabeth Miles died, the newspaper would distribute its earnings to the employees in a profit-sharing plan and were disappointed when this didn't happen. Except for the recipients, few knew that the *Day's* net earnings were distributed to charity, or that a trust and not a family owned *The Day*. New Londoners at various times thought Orvin Andrews, Bar Colby, Deane Avery, even Morgan McGinley owned the newspaper. Even those who understood that *The Day* was owned by a trust had the misconception that it didn't make profits or pay taxes. In truth, the business both made money and paid taxes, although it probably plowed more of its revenues back into the business than into the charitable trust and consequently paid less in income taxes than other newspapers. But nevertheless, *The Day* paid $380,000 in federal taxes in 1978. The only taxes at issue in the IRS case were, on the one hand, the modest surtax, and on the other, the gigantic 200 percent tax *The Day* would have to pay if it lost.

The case attracted little attention in the community for a matter of such importance to it. There wasn't a groundswell of fear for the *Day's* future. Maybe that was because there was little public understanding or appreciation of how *The Day* was set up or how this arrangement benefited the community. Few knew that the public was a beneficiary of the trust. In fact, the public enjoyed some control insofar as anyone could challenge the trustee's felicity to the Bodenwein will through the probate court. The potential of the Bodenwein fund after Elizabeth Miles' death hadn't penetrated the consciousness of people in the area. Some who understood better than others were happy over the threat to the *Day's* dominance. One writer wrote a sarcastic letter to *The Day* expressing his opinion that the community would be vastly better off if the newspaper were sold and the proceeds were used to benefit civic projects. And from a purely economic standpoint, he was right. The sale of *The Day* would, indeed, have greatly augmented the disbursements of the Bodenwein fund. But the trustees of *The Day* contended that the intangible benefits of having an independent local newspaper outweighed any gains from the sale of the newspaper. Patrick Mullarkey did his best to discredit that idea.

Sadly, Francis McGuire was not present to witness the final stage of the battle. While he had been making plans to launch the challenge and bolstered the strength of his small, family law firm through a merger, his health had been steadily failing. The IRS case was the last important business of his interesting and accomplished career. He died of cancer on September 9, 1982, at the age of 71.

The Day recounted in its front-page obituary McGuire's long history as a Democratic power broker and the celebrated cases he had argued. He had represented the actress Constance Bennett over the estate of the millionaire Phillip Plant, Morton Plant's son, who had a summer home in the Oswegatchie colony of Waterford. He won that case, which brought the city into the national limelight. But his most significant contribution to his community arguably was his leadership in rebuilding *The Day* after World War II and preparing the newspaper for its fight against the government in the last challenge to Theodore Bodenwein's will. Charles Smiddy led the newspaper through the fight with Gordon Bodenwein; McGuire mobilized the newspaper for its fight against the Internal Revenue Service.

THE GOVERNMENT'S ATTORNEY, D. Patrick Mullarkey, knew *The Day* well by the time he completed his legal research. And he arrived at the most unflattering conclusions about its intentions. He attributed the basest motives to Bodenwein and the trustees. And the trustees came to feel just as uncharitably toward him. Mullarkey's name was mentioned often in solemn or derisive tones in the *Day's* boardroom. He had become the enemy of everything the newspaper stood for. And he suspected the trustees were up to no good. Charles Shain remembers:

> *He became this entity. What was most interesting to us was his view of what the intentions of the board were. He took the lowest possible view of our morality. He felt we were using the paper for our own purposes.*

Mullarkey believed that Bodenwein, far from being a visionary and philanthropist, had set up the trust solely to avoid taxes on his estate after he died, take care of his heirs, and enhance the competitive advantage of *The Day*. All the rhetoric at the beginning of his will about his hopes for *The Day* were nothing more than the late publisher's "theories" about how the newspaper ought to be operated to maximize its earnings, Mullarkey felt.

The arrangement, he believed, made it possible for the trustees and directors to enjoy roles as local "power brokers." It also placed the directors and managers of the newspaper in a favorable position to squander the newspaper's income and serve themselves without being held accountable by stockholders. He felt it was ridiculous that a company with a value of more than $6 million was paying such paltry dividends to the Bodenwein Public Benevolent Foundation, less than $160,000 a year. The trustees were paying out scarcely more than the minimum Bodenwein set in 1938 for them to qualify for annual bonuses. No corporation operating under ordinary circumstances would be able to get away with such puny payouts for long without alert stockholders reacting. The trustees were, in effect, cheating the region, the supposed beneficiary of the trust, of the full benefits of the charitable trust Bodenwein created in his selfish effort to create tax advantages for his newspaper and his heirs. Moreover, *The Day* had enjoyed an unfair competitive advantage in the years since Bodenwein died because of the substantial tax breaks the newspaper received as a result of the trust. The trustees and directors had hoarded the gains arising from that advantage by retaining earnings and spending lavishly on the newspaper. The newspaper served their interests and not the intended beneficiaries of the trust.

Mark Kravitz, attorney for *The Day,* turned to the history of American journalism and the decline in the number of independent local newspapers to support his argument that Bodenwein had a higher motive: to preserve the independence of the newspaper he had spent his life building. Regional and national publishing chains had grown fat by acquiring small local newspapers and then by establishing the profit motive as their only goal. Only by establishing a trust for the benefit of *The Day* could Bodenwein have ensured that *The Day* would remain locally owned and controlled and operated for motives higher than profit.

Bodenwein's will created a unique two-trust arrangement, the lawyer argued. One trust was to carry out the publisher's vision for *The Day* as an institution that "was more than a business enterprise" and was recognized in the community as a leading factor in the growth, development, and improvement of the city and vicinity and happiness and prosperity of the people." He created a second trust, the Bodenwein foundation, to return excess profits, not needed by the newspaper, to his family while they were alive, and totally to the people of the region thereafter.

The Day had maintained its independence for one hundred years, he went on. Local independent newspapers like *The Day* were an essential ingredient of a free press. Editors and publishers of such publications cared more about their communities than the chains, he argued. While Mullarkey viewed the will as a fancy tax dodge, Kravitz saw it as a constitution for the development of the newspaper that guided the directors and managers and commanded obedience to a higher calling.

The two adversaries appeared before Federal Judge Jose Cabranes in the federal courthouse in Hartford on June 27, 1983. The case was known as *Hammond et al. v. U.S., 584 F. Supp. 163 (D. Conn 1984).* The debate there pivoted on whether *The Day* newspaper could benefit from the income of the trust when the trust consisted of nothing more than the stock of the newspaper. If that couldn't be proven, The Day Trust would be considered a single-interest trust, and the newspaper would have to be sold. The issue of whether *The Day* was a legitimate beneficiary in turn, revolved around the intentions of Bodenwein, Smiddy, and the other directors when they had contrived the scheme in the 1930s.

Kravitz argued that the publisher set up The Day Trust to protect the newspaper from predators as well as to care for his family during their lifetimes and to return some of its profits to the region where the newspaper circulated. The newspaper benefited from that legal protection, and it also received income support from the arrangement, though indirectly. The will instructed that the trustees, before they gave any thought to the heirs or charity, were to put aside money to build and maintain *The Day,* to buy the most modern machinery available, and to construct buildings that would improve the appearance and stature of the city.

Mullarkey contended that the actual purpose of the trust was to serve the selfish interests of the trustees while the only legitimate legal purpose, the reason for which it received tax advantages, was to turn over funds to the Bodenwein foundation. That end was thwarted by the trustees, he argued. The only money from the trust that the trustees ever had returned to the newspaper was the $5,000 for newsroom seminars, which Mullarkey argued was a transparent legal trick. The newspaper was merely intended to be a moneymaker for the trust.

The government lawyer argued that The Day Trust was exactly what Congress had in mind when it passed the 1969 law. He turned on its head the argument about there being a higher purpose behind the trust. Bodenwein left instructions to provide the employees "liberal compensation and various forms of assistance and rewards, such as insurance, bonuses, and pensions." Didn't this give *The Day* an unfair advantage against its competitors? Mullarkey asked. Cabranes raised the same issue when he asked Kravitz whether the idea of protecting the newspaper from chain ownership created "some kind of special economic advantage, some sort of special economic insulation, which no other newspaper would be afforded."

Kravitz replied that the arrangement didn't protect *The Day* from competition. The newspaper had plenty of competition. What it guarded against was acquisition by a competitor. The greatest threat to competition in the newspaper industry, he argued, was chain ownership, and that was the fate that would befall *The Day* if Cabranes ruled in the IRS's favor. An IRS victory would be a setback to competition.

Cabranes asked Kravitz whether the court wouldn't be getting in over its head if it became involved in the issue of media concentration and the arguments for and against it. Wasn't that issue debatable? Couldn't it be argued that media chains were beneficial to the public because they could help local newspapers do a better job? Kravitz responded that the consolidations of the 1930s were an important backdrop of Bodenwein's will and similar concerns over the consolidation in the media existed in the 1980s. One of Congress's aims in its 1969 legislation was to attack empire building by large foundations, and, Kravitz said, media chains arguably were examples of such practices. Surely Congress had no intention of furthering such empires by forcing the sale of *The Day,* he argued.

Mullarkey presented a more jaundiced view. By plowing the newspaper's profits back into the newspaper and maintaining capital reserves, he argued, the trustees were protecting themselves against doomsday "so that the charity does not get them." The newspaper existed solely to advance their interests, to the

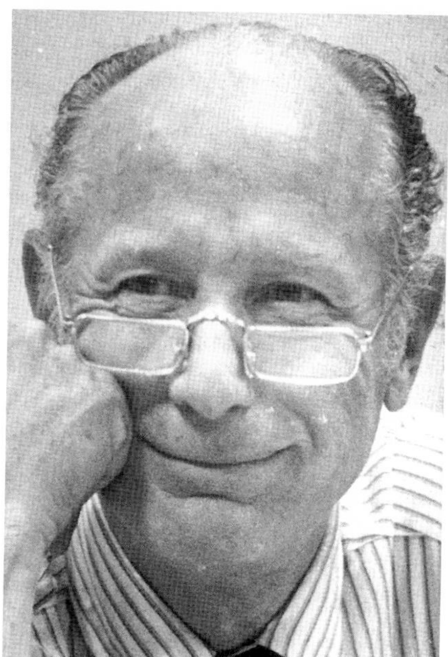

Above, When faced with the choice of a publisher between Wes Hammond, left, or Deane Avery, right, the directors chose both. *The Day*

Above, Joan Poro, left, and Dan Stets, right, conducted a *Day* investigation into waste and inefficiency at the Electric Boat shipyard in the 1970s. Their reporting precipitated a news boycott by the defense contractor against *The Day* that lasted several years. *The Day*

Above, P. Takis Veliotis, of Electric Boat, third from left, ordered the news blackout against *The Day*. He was later charged with accepting kickbacks and remained a fugitive from justice in Greece until his death in 1999. Others in this picture taken at the launching of the first Trident submarine *Ohio*, are Connecticut Gov. Ella T. Grasso, U.S. Senator John Glenn and First Lady Rosalind Carter. *The Day*

Right, Jack Sauer, the *Day's* chief photographer in the early 1980s, defied the odds when he survived this airplane crash, above, while on assignment, and later returned to work. *The Day*

Far Left, New Haven lawyer Mark R. Kravitz led The Day Trust in its successful defense against the Internal Revenue Service. *Wiggin & Dana*

Left, U.S. District Court Judge José Cabranes issued the favorable ruling that upheld The Day Trust. *U.S. Second Circuit Court of Appeals*

Above, Reid MacCluggage, right, and Deane Avery presided over the celebration when *The Day* won a favorable ruling in its case with the Internal Revenue Service in June 1985. *Inside The Day*

Vol. 1 No. 1 Published as warranted by ev

MacCluggage hires best man for job

Publisher Reid MacCluggage knew as soon as he had chosen Jim Smith as managing editor that it was a perfect matchup — the best man for the newsroom's best job.

A nationwide search for John Foley's successor ended in a solemn exchange of vows between MacCluggage and Smith to make The Day the equal of the Torrington Register-Citizen, Smith's last newspaper.

There was some grumbling following the selection of Smith, especially from those who wanted the next managing editor to come from inside The Day. But given time to thoroughly research the situation, everyone conceded that Smith was the best man.

"It's indisputable," MacCluggage said at a staff meeting. "The best man is the best man. How can anybody argue with that?"

Terms of Smith's agreement to come to The Day haven't been disclosed. Sources indicate, however, that he will be paid about $45,000 a year. MacCluggage declined to be specific but stressed that Smith will have to survive a proba-

He asked that critics give him reasonable period of time. "Let there a honeymoon period," MacCluggage clared.

Smith, upon reporting to wo propped both feet on his desk in J Foley fashion and announced that th would be only subtle changes at start. He said, for instance, that wonders why management's propag da organ is called Inside The Day.

"The new management philoso most definitely has nothing to do with side. Let's call it Outside The Day."

The arrival of Smith reunited a p tion of the old Times-Mirror fam Former members of that group Dorothy Torres and Rick Flath. "W ding bells are bringing together that gang of mine," said a smil MacCluggage.

Smith, of course, left the Hartf Courant about a year ago to beco managing editor of the Torring Register-Citizen. He immediately p mised to set a high standard of cellence with The Day. "I will make

Left, During the conflict over James Smith, *Deep Inside The Day*, an underground publication highly critical of MacCluggage and his choice to run the newsroom, appeared in staff mailboxes. It remains a mystery who published it.

Above, James Smith, a close friend of Reid MacCluggage, aroused a storm in the newsroom when he was named managing editor in 1985. *Inside The Day*

Above, James Irvine stirred up discontent among the news staff in the 1970s and 1980s for his brusque and authoritarian management style. *The Day*

bove, Lance Johnson put together the unday edition of *The Day*, but wasn't ontent to stay there. He became managing ditor in a newsroom power struggle. *acquie Glassenberg, The Day*

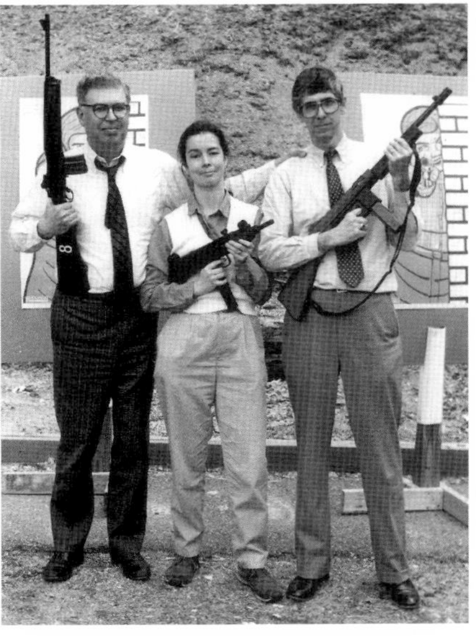

Above, The fact that there were three editorial writers rankled some in the newsroom and trustee Walter Baker, who felt it was an extravagance. The editorial staff, shown here clowning for the camera during a police demonstration on assault weapons, consisted of, from left, Morgan McGinley, Maura Casey, and the author. *The Day*

bove, Reid MacCluggage and the board clashed over changes the new editor and publisher nade after he arrived, but things later calmed down. Seated from the left are Alcino Almeida,)eane Avery, Charles Shain, Bar Colby, MacCluggage, Antoinette Dupont, Walter Baker, and :van Hill. *The Day*

Above, Bar Colby, second from left, retired as publisher in 1976, but didn't leave the board until 1991. H died in 1993. With him in this photo taken in 1991 are, from left, his son, Robert, Reid MacCluggage, and Al Almeida. T*he Day*

Left, Rick Flath, a *Hartford Courant* colleagu MacCluggage hired to be the *Day's* director of administration, became known as "Ranger Rick" fo the sweeping changes he implemented and his brash style. *The Day*

Above, Reporter Jacky Flinn distinguished herself with her reporting on scandals at the Electric Boat shipyard. She married managing editor Jim Smith following an office romance that contributed to a newsroom controversy. *The Day*

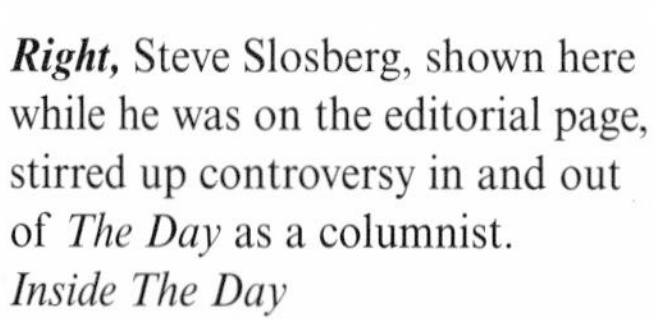

Right, Steve Slosberg, shown here while he was on the editorial page, stirred up controversy in and out of *The Day* as a columnist. *Inside The Day*

Left, Women known as "stuffers" placed pre-printed advertising inserts in *The Day* until the mid-1980s. The close-knit group of women was largely replaced by a mechanized system. Technology also drove many of the printers into early retirement. *The Day*

Left, *The Day* raced ahead with new construction in the late 1980s. The garage behind the original *Day* building and 1928 addition was razed, and a four-story addition built in its place. To the left is the 1960 addition. *The Day*

bove, Russian journalist Victor Gribachev ͻent a summer working at *The Day. The Day* ʼas one of the leading supporters of an ҳchange program between New England and oviet editors designed to bring a thaw to the ʼold War. *The Day*

Above, When Reid MacCluggage restructured the newsroom to more closely resemble a metropolitan newspaper, one of the first assistant managing editors hired was Dorothy Torres, who set up a graphics department. *The Day*

Above, Maria Hileman became the first woman city editor of *The Day* in 1985. She later took charge of special reporting projects and continued the newspaper's long-time focus on local history. *The Day*

Above, Photography continued to be one of the Day's strengths, as evidenced in this award-winning photo showing the daughter of a victim of a construction accident being comforted by a priest. *Robert Patterson, The Day*

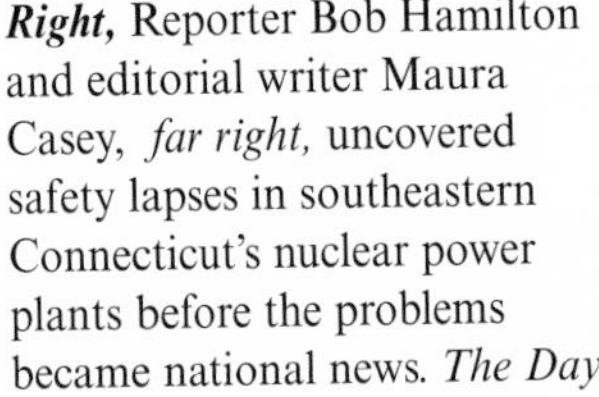

Right, Reporter Bob Hamilton and editorial writer Maura Casey, *far right,* uncovered safety lapses in southeastern Connecticut's nuclear power plants before the problems became national news. *The Day*

Above, The Pequot tribe wouldn't let *The Day* sell newspapers at its casino to protest the aggressive reporting by David Collins on organized crime's attempts to penetrate the casino. *The Day*

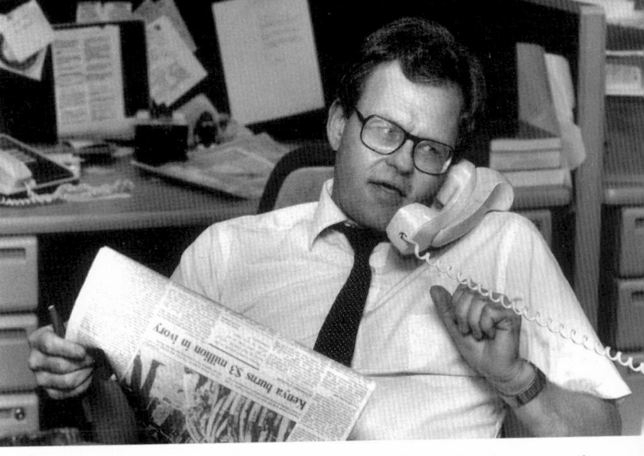

Above, Stan DeCoster set the standard for investigative reporting at *The Day* for many years. *The Day*

detriment of the charity for which *The Day* originally had received its charitable deduction. The Bodenwein foundation was hurt "because the trustees, by putting the money back into the corporation, are building up tremendous reserves so that the foundation gets $130,000 a year on capital of about $4 million, which probably has a sale value right now of $6 or $8 million."

> *The charity is getting just a pittance because the trustees are continuing to operate the business. And that's exactly the thing Congress was shooting at when it passed this legislation ... Congress did not want these businesses to perpetuate themselves at the expense of charity. That's what the law is there for.*

Kravitz pointed out that the interests of the charity were protected by the fact that the bank that administered the trust had a representative on the board. McGuire, and before him, Earle Stamm, had filled that position. McGuire was replaced after his death by Walter Baker, a bank director. However, Kravitz also made the point that Bodenwein left instructions for there to be two trustees from the newspaper. He argued this was evidence that the publisher's interest in advancing the newspaper was greater than his interest in the charity. *The Day* was not only an interest of the trust but was the prominent of the two interests. Mullarkey countered that if Cabranes conceded that *The Day* could be considered a beneficiary of the trust, the court would unleash a flood of similar appeals. But Kravitz argued that the arrangement was unique, and that other newspapers could not mimic the arrangement, because the law protected only split-interest trusts created before May 1969.

Cabranes handed down his ruling on March 23, 1984. He ruled in favor of *The Day*. The government appealed Cabranes' ruling to the Second Circuit of the United States Court of Appeals, where the appeal was argued on November 30, 1984. Cabranes' judgment was upheld on June 5, 1985. (*Hammond et al. v. U.S., 764 f.2d88 (2nd Cir. 1985*). Cabranes rejected Mullarkey's contention that the sole intent of Bodenwein's will was to maximize the income to the foundation to support his family and charity. If that had been his purpose, he could have achieved it more effectively with a single trust, with specific instructions to carry out that purpose. But Bodenwein instead created two trusts, one to take care of his family, the other to look after the newspaper indefinitely. Bodenwein left detailed instructions on how he wished the trustees to protect and perpetuate his life's work on *The Day*. It was clear to Cabranes that Bodenwein's paramount interest was to protect the newspaper so that it could carry out its higher purpose of serving the community. Cabranes also agreed with *The Day* that the Bodenwein foundation as well as The Day Trust was a split-interest trust because it could disburse funds to municipalities as well as charities. The appellate court, in affirming Cabranes' decision, was particularly impressed that Bodenwein had said in his will the trust should be terminated if *The Day* ceased to publish in New London.

> *The fact that the Trust would thus terminate if the company chose to leave the New London area or abandon newspaper publishing for a more profitable line of business gives proof that the purpose of the trust was not simply to maximize either the trust's income or the distributions available to the foundation, but was principally to further the longevity and success of* The Day *as an independent, public-spirited role that Bodenwein envisioned for it.*

One thing the IRS case pointed out was the precision with which the trustees and the directors carried out the instructions in the will. The jurists who examined the case were struck by that. The trustees followed the will to the letter. As the newspaper's lawyers pointed out, the trustees often debated the requirements of the will. Edna and her stepchildren, Gordon and Elizabeth, each lived lives of luxury on their income from *The Day*. The trustees explicitly carried out Bodenwein's directions to reward the employees with liberal wages, bonuses, pensions, and insurance benefits. The trustees actively participated in managing the affairs of *The Day*. They expanded the plant, improved its mechanical equipment, and maintained substantial reserves in the company for future needs, as they had been instructed. With Elizabeth's death, soon the region would receive its full share from the *Day's* growth. That is not to say that they had done everything perfectly, or completed all the instructions. But only a few details had not yet been addressed by the early 1980s. One of these was contained in Article 4 of the will, in which Bodenwein suggested the trustees someday consider publishing morning and Sunday papers when the newspaper's growth warranted it.

BEFORE ELIZABETH MILES' DEATH and the start of the IRS legal case, the newspaper had begun experimenting with new ideas that set the stage for a Sunday paper. In 1977, the newspaper had introduced two new pages of local features in its Saturday edition, placing Editor Lance Johnson in charge. This was followed by the creation of an op-ed page, which created a second position on the editorial page. This was filled by David Heckerman.

Even as the future of the paper was in doubt, Avery and Hammond brought up the issue of a Sunday edition in department meetings, where the reporters and editors debated it endlessly to the point few believed it would ever happen. The newspaper found support in the community for the idea in a formal survey and in focus group discussions. Advertisers favored the idea. But a host of obstacles, including a persistent newsprint shortage, delayed the decision to go ahead until September 19, 1981, when the directors voted to proceed with the plan. That followed by a short time the decision by a Massachusetts development firm to build Crystal Mall, a huge regional indoor shopping mall, in Waterford that was to have one-hundred-fifty stores, including four large department stores.

The impending opening of the Crystal Mall signaled a new wave of growth in southeastern Connecticut, along with the usual problems and possibilities. The problems, concentrated in New London and Groton, arose from a decline in their existing retail businesses, and the prospects for further difficulties caused by the new mall. Just as the new shopping centers along the highways helped drain New London's downtown of its retail business in the 1950s and 1960s, the concept of large, climate-controlled, indoor shopping malls threatened the future of the aging, outdoor shopping centers as well as the downtown business area. A severe recession in the early 1980s drove two older, large department stores and major advertisers in *The Day* out of business and a third planned to move to Crystal Mall. The loss of the two stores and the recession were severe blows to the *Day's* advertising revenue just as *The Day* was facing the need to expand and modernize to meet new competitive threats and publish a Sunday edition. For the first time in its history, the newspaper was forced to lay off workers in 1982, and reduced its Christmas bonus that year to one week. The directors took a second look at the figures in February 1983 and approved a second week's pay for a bonus.

Although *The Day* and much of the region were happily looking forward to the mall's opening, New London's downtown retail community and its political leaders were horrified over the impact they feared this would have on their efforts to rebuild the downtown. This presented *The Day* with another of the dilemmas associated with its place as a leading booster of New London and its other role as a regional newspaper.

The city's desperate experiments to restore its business vitality were not working. A downtown pedestrian mall and new access roads, the restored Union Station and the transportation center that developed there, and urban renewal didn't succeed in bringing business back. In fact, matters had gotten worse, as old businesses and even a few of the new ones were shuttered and the downtown mall began to look more like a ghost town. There were no downtown department stores any more and both its vintage hotels were gone. Two of its retail businesses soon would announce they were leaving to go to the mall.

State Representative William Cibes, a government professor at Connecticut College, led New London in a legal challenge to block the mall's construction, charging that it would produce too much traffic, create pollution, and damage New London businesses. The lawsuit led to a settlement in which the developers agreed to establish a $1.5 million trust fund for New London to use for downtown development. *The Day* criticized the city early in the controversy for threatening not to sell the water needed for the mall. But while it sympathized with the city over the impact the mall might have on its downtown, the newspaper largely sat on the sidelines during the fight.

The plans for the Crystal Mall invited renewed competition against *The Day* from outside. The Groton *News* had died in 1977, but then *Hartford Courant*, Connecticut's major statewide newspaper, had been purchased by the Los Angeles Times-Mirror newspaper chain in 1979. The new regional mall and changing management at the *Courant* set the stage for a new circulation push by that newspaper into southeastern Connecticut. It also increased the urgency at *The Day* of the Sunday newspaper, but at a time when conditions couldn't have been worse.

THIRTY

The Outsider

I was born in Norwich the week the Bodenwein will was signed.

—Reid MacCluggage, in a letter to the directors, January 13, 1984

WHILE THE MANAGERS OF *The Day* trudged ahead with plans for a Sunday edition and the newspaper still faced an uncertain future in the IRS case, two of the largest newspaper groups in America bought its two competitors, the Norwich *Bulletin* and the *Hartford Courant*. Both had histories as independent newspapers much longer than the *Day's* hundred years.

In keeping with a relentless trend of media consolidation, The (Los Angeles) Times Mirror Company purchased the *Hartford Courant* in October 1979. The Gannett group bought the *Bulletin* in August 1981. Also, another giant media conglomerate, Capital Cities Communications, purchased a string of weekly newspapers in Connecticut, including those in Old Saybrook, East Lyme, and Mystic, in the *Day's* backyard.

These transactions increased the uneasiness in the *Day's* boardroom where there already was plenty to worry about. To begin with, it wasn't a casual matter for the directors to start a Sunday newspaper. The new edition would be the boldest change in the more than forty-year history of The Day Trust and the directors were taking on this formidable risk in the midst of a recession. Furthermore, the directors were contending with the IRS case, old and malfunctioning machinery, an outbreak of staff turnover, morale problems in the newsroom, newsprint shortages, and tense relations with the minority communities.

The Day created an uproar in the New London minority community in March 1980 with an offhand assertion in a story on New London prostitution that most of the prostitutes in the city were black or Hispanic. The reporters, who based the statement on anecdotes, were unable to verify the assertion when they returned to check the records after the controversy arose. This led to the first of several showdowns with the city's minorities over coverage and staffing in *The Day* in the 1980s. Protestors, interpreting this as an example of the newspaper's racism, picketed the paper. Deane Avery endured an uncomfortable two-hour meeting with Hispanic leaders and afterwards *The Day* retracted the statement on the front page, apologized, and hired two Hispanic employees including a reporter, Michelle Lopez.

The directors and managers saw in the newspaper purchases taking place around them both the likely destiny of *The Day* if it lost its battle with the IRS and the prospect of tougher competition from the two rival dailies. The competition would now have the resources of rich national newspaper organizations behind them. Managers of *The Day* were aware that the new owners of the *Courant* on the other side of the continent in Los Angeles moved quickly on the offensive in their new territory.

The sale of the *Courant* jarred the whole state. It was the state's largest newspaper. Founded in colonial Connecticut, it had been a fixture there for more than two hundred years. It boasted that it was the oldest newspaper in continuous publication in America. It was the descendant of the *Connecticut Courant*, founded by a member of the same family of printers, the Greens, who had started publishing newspapers in New London in the 18th century. It was related through these family ties to the *Star* and the *Telegram* in New London, where *Day* founder John Tibbits got his start as a newspaper editor. As stodgy and predictable as it had a tendency to be, it was Connecticut's leading daily newspaper, a part of the routine and tradition in the "Land of Steady Habits." It was the state's newspaper of record, the only daily newspaper that thoroughly chronicled the proceedings of the state legislature. Much of Connecticut awoke ꞏ the familiar newspaper.

The impact was similarly startling at the *Courant*, where the news of the ver arrived without warning. The staff first heard about it at a hastily ɪeeting with the company treasurer. There were no representatives at the ʳrom the new owners or the old board of directors.

Murphy, the new editor from Los Angeles, where he had been metro- ꞏ of the *Times*, set out to overhaul the newspaper by expanding its ꞏng it more interesting. He named as his managing editor Reid

MacCluggage, who had been assistant managing editor under Irving Kravsow, and gave him a mandate to make major changes. Endless philosophical debates had taken place in the past over whether or not to expand the role of the *Courant*. The *Courant* had fantasies of assuming a larger role in New England, but until the takeover by Times-Mirror, it never had the impetus to do this.

The possibilities of a renaissance at the *Courant* excited many at the newspaper who had longed for such an opportunity. Under Murphy's direction, the *Courant* embarked on becoming a New England newspaper, like the Boston *Globe*. It opened a bureau in Boston. It enlarged its Washington bureau and it set its sights on covering Connecticut and New England more aggressively. MacCluggage reorganized the newsroom. The *Courant* established a new tier of middle managers and organized a Hartford desk, with eleven reporters, to improve the coverage of local neighborhoods and minority stories. James H. Smith, a longtime friend and colleague of MacCluggage's, took charge of that operation. Smith had been the best man at MacCluggage's wedding in May 1981 to Linda Howell, a reporter for the *Journal Inquirer* in Manchester and a former *Courant* reporter. That had been MacCluggage's second marriage.

The takeover in Hartford alarmed the *Day's* directors, who feared the revitalized *Courant* would step up its attack in southeastern Connecticut. The *Courant* had had a foothold there since the 1960s, when Joe DeBona covered the region. As the *Courant's* state editor in the early 1970s, MacCluggage had enlarged the southeastern bureau, which had been moved to Groton, from one to three reporters. *Courant* bureau reporters had included Michael Whalen and Jacky Flinn, who later joined *The Day.*

AFTER REPEATEDLY POSTPONING THE decision to start a Sunday edition because of newsprint shortages, the *Day* directors gave Avery the go-ahead in the summer of 1980. Several months earlier, they had reduced the size of the news hole in the daily newspaper, the space set aside for news, to conserve paper. Lance Johnson, 34, the assistant editorial page editor, became the Sunday editor. Johnson had both prepared and auditioned for that job by engineering and supervising a new Saturday feature section. That undertaking was a precursor of the Sunday newspaper, which was intended to showcase the newspaper's best writing and reporting.

Morgan McGinley moved from the night staff to replace Johnson as the assistant editorial page editor, and Avery, anticipating the increased demands of the new edition, authorized hiring a third editorial writer. The editors wanted the Sunday newspaper to feature strong, local editorials and commentary. The whole emphasis of the Sunday edition was to be on broader and more thoughtful local coverage and good writing.

Having three editorial writers on a newspaper with a circulation of less than forty thousand was unusual. Most newspapers that size had one editorial writer, two at the most. This fact became a sore subject between directors Evan Hill and Walter Baker. Baker, who replaced Francis McGuire after his death in February 1982 and was the lone businessman on the board, considered three editorial writers an extravagance. The newspaper had more pressing needs, he felt. This attitude infuriated Hill, the journalism professor, who viewed the editorial page as the heart and soul of the newspaper, and an instrument that could do much to carry out the public mission of the newspaper under the Bodenwein charter. Hill had the benefit of numbers in the debate. His supporters were Avery, Bar Colby, and Charles Shain.

I was named to fill the controversial third berth on the editorial page, leaving the state-house beat. The three of us—Ken Grube, McGinley, and me—were assigned a cramped room at the opposite end of the building from the newsroom. The reporters referred to us as Moe, Larry, and Curly after the Three Stooges, reflecting both our eccentricities and the natural rivalry between the newsroom and editorial page. The two departments engaged in an ongoing debate over which was the more over-staffed. In truth, the newspaper had staffed both departments beyond levels common for newspapers the size of *The Day.* It could afford to do so because there were no stockholders to argue differently. The same people who made the decisions, the trustees, also controlled the *Day's* more than seventeen thousand shares of stock.

Grube was 60 and, unknown to the others at the newspaper, nearing early retirement in 1982. He had made the editorial page a strong and clear voice on local issues and deepened the *Day's* community roots. Grube had powerful friends, but also kept in touch with ordinary people, including blue-collar workers and ethnic minorities. He was both liberal and Democratic in his ideals. He was suspicious of power, and clever at embarrassing those who abused it. The head of the local police union, who never rose above the rank of corporal, but had, in Grube's view, too much influence over the city police department became, in his derisive words, the "silent Captain" in editorials. The judges and sheriffs who collaborated with one another in the county courthouse over petty political matters became the "courthouse gang."

The editorial page, no longer devoted to ponderous and distant subjects as it had been for two decades after Bodenwein's death, had became highly relevant to the communities and one of the most compelling sections of the newspaper. As early as 1973, when *The Day* was critiqued in the New England Daily Newspaper Survey, the reviewer found Grube's page to be "the most lively and polished part of the paper." The page had not had such spirit since the brief period Judge Frederick Latimer had presided over it before World War I.

But for some of the same reasons it was popular, it was also a lightning rod for criticism. The region's military community, for example, would complain that it was too liberal and anti-military. Evidence of this, in the view of the Navy community and defense industry, was the newspaper's early and staunch support of Sam Gejdenson, a brash young politician first elected to Congress in 1980. Gejdenson espoused liberal causes and was thought to be, at best, indifferent toward the military and at worst a communist. But influential Jewish leaders in Grube's circle of friends adored the likable and intelligent son of Jewish dairy farmers who was born in a displaced persons camp in Germany after World War II.

New London politicians made up another group that vented a dislike for *The Day* and for Grube. In 1979, two New London city councilors who had been targets of Grube's barbed editorials, mailed out three thousand letters accusing the editor and *The Day* of being too friendly to the city administration, which they had been hounding for various reasons. Deputy Mayor Terrence Brennan and City Councilman Stephen Massad accused the newspaper of being solicitous of the city administration in turn for preferential treatment on acquiring land for expansion from the Redevelopment Agency. The two referred to Grube as a "dream writer" who was out of touch with people, and charged *The Day* was "spreading a sickness." Other critics belonged to the Satti faction of the party, which had been pummeled in *The Day* for nearly two decades for their self-serving political conduct. A school of thought formed among these disgruntled people desiring both to eliminate the city manager form of government and establish a friendlier local newspaper.

Grube, in fact, echoed many of the views of a group from the city's silk-stocking district in the south end who were alarmed at the growing rancor and circus atmosphere in city politics. The city, after a brief rush of optimism in the mid-1970s, was adrift again and engulfed in self-pity, essentially the same condition in which it found itself during the business decline after the Civil War.

There was no help in sight. The two local political parties lacked civic-minded leadership for the most part, and nobody stepped forward to take charge and attempt a rescue. The city's most important resources were in danger. Ocean Beach Park, now more than thirty years old, was showing the toll of years of neglect. For those three decades, the city government milked the public enterprise without putting any money into it or adapting the 1950s amusement park that had been built at Ocean Beach to changing popular tastes.

The schools, once the pride of the community, now were controlled by the teachers' union and the Democratic Party, and were heading downhill. Those in control were unable to deal with the needs of minority and poor children. Because of restrictive zoning and other causes, a racial divide was worsening between Connecticut's cities and its suburbs. There was growing pessimism over the downtown, once the city's pride and a primary source of its wealth, which looked more depressed with each passing day. The form of professional municipal government for which Bodenwein and *The Day* had fought in the early 1920s to advance the city's development was mired in incompetence and political buffoonery that made the city an object of ridicule.

The Day regularly called attention to these problems, making up in its editorials and news coverage for some of the leadership that was missing in the political and business communities. Its outlook amplified concerns in the south end of New London, where people were alarmed at the continuing decline in the business district and falling real estate values in the city. They faulted the political leadership, appearance of crime, and even sometimes the *Day's* reporting of crime in the city.

The newspaper shared the prevailing attitude regarding the rancid quality of politics. It bombarded the unruly politicians on the City Council on the editorial page, in columns, and in its reporting, while defending the city-manager system. The newspaper continued to put its best reporters on the City Hall beat, where they kept the issues of political chicanery and government ineptitude in the public eye. This led to a backlash from political leaders that *The Day* was responsible for the city's problems by being too "negative."

The Day supported a drive to "clean up Bank Street," which targeted the seedy bars and prostitutes along the city's busiest street in hopes this would improve the city's image and bring people back to shop. The newspaper agreed to a request by the police that it publish the arrests of "johns," men who solicited prostitutes, and assigned reporters Stan DeCoster and Bruce MacDonald to examine the two sides of Bank Street—its daytime business vitality and nighttime prostitution. This was the story that got *The Day* into trouble with the black and Hispanic communities by generalizing without the benefit of statistics that Bank Street prostitutes were predominantly black or Hispanic.

Grube's reach into the community exceeded that of most of the other managers at *The Day*. Avery and Hammond were in touch with the business and military leadership, largely through the service clubs and other organizations; Hammond was a Lion, Avery a Rotarian. John Foley and Jim Irvine were the newspaper's link to the older New London, with fond memories of the war and postwar years through fraternal organizations like the Elks lodge in New London.

Grube built bridges to the black and Jewish communities. He virtually took charge of the Martin Luther King Scholarship Fund, rescued it from insolvency, and expanded support for it among corporations in the area. These ties were invaluable whenever *The Day* got into a scrape over racial issues.

While he had a kitchen cabinet of close friends, both in the New London area and around the state, his daily contacts outside the newspaper were numerous and widespread. He scolded writers for socializing among themselves and not reaching out to meet more people. He listened to the multitudes, not just the usual sources who occupied public office and enjoyed influence. He had great empathy for people. He learned from waitresses, nurses, truck drivers, and shipyard workers, all of whom found him accessible.

On the other hand, Grube was occasionally irascible at the newspaper. He and Avery disliked each other. Grube and his two editorial writers met daily with Avery purportedly to discuss editorial policy. But Grube carefully protected the page from Avery's interference. Part of the reason was principle. He said he wanted to keep the page independent from the outside influences he felt filtered through the publisher's office. Another reason was that Grube was disorganized. He rarely planned ahead and often didn't have topics to discuss. Every morning, as the editorial writers descended the back staircase to Avery's office on the second floor to meet, Grube reviewed with his subordinates what jokes they were prepared to tell to steer the discussion away from matters of substance.

This rivalry didn't prevent Avery from influencing the newspaper's editorial policy. He tolerated most of Grube's positions and supported some of them. He also added his own views to the mix when he had the chance. Under Avery's leadership, *The Day,* which historically had supported all economic growth with a few exceptions, viewed development more warily. Avery lived in a farmhouse and raised horses. He loved the land, worried about the impact of development, and was a committed conservationist. Some of his anxiety over development was brought on by the invasive building that was taking place near his farm in Stonington. His convictions resonated for more than twenty years in the *Day's* policy favoring measures to curb growth and protect landmarks. He was among the editors who came around to support saving the landmark train station in

New London from being razed for urban renewal. He received an award for his part in this effort, and he continued to support editorial policies to preserve the area's architectural heritage. When the government decided to shutter the landmark Custom House, where *Day* founder John Tibbits once had been the customs collector, *The Day* suggested in an editorial that a maritime history group be formed to take it over, echoing the idea of local historian Lucille Showalter. There was enough interest in the idea to prompt Avery to sponsor a meeting at *The Day.* The newspaper eventually helped with the expenses of forming the New London Maritime Society, which opened a museum devoted to New London's maritime history in the Custom House.

Grube retired in August 1982. More than four hundred people attended his going-away dinner in Mystic. These included not only his newspaper colleagues from *The Day* and around the state, but also many volunteers from the charitable organizations he supported. Sam Gejdenson presented him with a congressional medal and New London and Groton proclaimed the day, August 22, a special holiday in his honor. Morgan McGinley succeeded Grube as editorial page editor, I became his assistant, and Steve Slosberg, one of the newspaper's most gifted writers in many years as well as one of the most controversial members of the newspaper's staff, became the third editorial writer.

Slosberg quickly made a name for himself for literary and perceptive work, as well as for his ability to stir up trouble both in and outside *The Day.* Slosberg despised predictable thinking, which the editorial page in many respects embodied simply by being consistent in its views. This clash of personalities created a tense atmosphere in the confining space where the editorial page operated. But the assignment also provided a regular platform for Slosberg's uncommon gift as a columnist. He reached for subjects to write about that other writers wouldn't touch, and often had points of view that were offensive to many. A local judge was brought before a state judicial board after Slosberg quoted a remark in which the judge appeared to trivialize pedophilia. Slosberg's name became a household word among the *Day's* readers, who either admired or were repulsed by his work. He sometimes seemed to write for shock value. Slosberg's columns, which often were crafted with the tightness and symmetry of poems, would bring the newspaper both controversy and distinction in the next decade.

IT TOOK A YEAR FROM the time the decision was made to publish a Sunday paper to the publication of the first edition on September 13, 1981. One of the crucial concerns during that time was how to assure that the new edition would sell. Although surveys indicated readers supported the idea of a Sunday newspaper, this was still a risky supposition with a readership that was known to be set in its ways. The managers decided to protect themselves and reassure hesitant advertisers by forcing subscribers to buy the Sunday edition with their weekday subscriptions. This decision was made with great trepidation over how the *Day's* independent-minded readers would react to this coercion.

The initial reaction to forced subscriptions confirmed the newspaper's fears. In the first month, circulation dropped by five percent as angry readers canceled their subscriptions. Average circulation for the daily newspaper fell from 38,309 in 1981 to a low of 37,471 before it began to recover in 1984. The average Sunday papers sold exceeded daily sales in 1985; Sunday circulation averaged 38,172 that year, daily, 37,837.

AN EVENT OF A more personal and poignant nature troubled *The Day* managers in the opening years of the 1980s decade. On the morning of October 15, 1981, word came over the police scanner of a serious fire on Fishers Island, New York, a wealthy colony off the coast of Connecticut just five miles from New London. Jack Sauer, the chief photographer, chartered an airplane to take him over the scene. He requested veteran pilot Richard Szalajeski, 57. Szalajeski was a favorite of the *Day* photographers because of his familiarity with aerial photography. He and Sauer made the short flight from Groton to Fishers Island and circled the burning mansion while Sauer took pictures. The fire was already under control when they arrived, and as they were about to return to Groton, the smoke began to clear with a shift of wind. Sauer asked Szalajeski to approach the house at a lower altitude. The pilot descended to nine hundred feet, just below the minimum allowable altitude, but a downdraft forced the plane down another two hundred feet. Szalajeski couldn't summon enough power from the light airplane's engine to recover altitude and the aircraft clipped the roof of a house on Sauer's side and crashed into a stand of trees.

The pilot wasn't seriously injured. But Sauer, who had released his seatbelt to lean over and take pictures, was knocked unconscious. His injuries included a broken clavicle, collapsed lung, and brain stem injury. He was flown in a Coast Guard helicopter to the Submarine Base in Groton and taken by ambulance to Lawrence and Memorial Hospital in New London.

The Day heard about the crash on the police scanner, not knowing who was involved. The first reaction was to try to get in touch with Sauer to take pictures. Even when the newsroom found out that Sauer was in the plane that crashed and that one of the two was seriously injured, it was unclear which of the two it was. Reporter Ann Baldelli was sent to the emergency room. Deane Avery also rushed there, where the scene of Sauer being wheeled in on a stretcher greeted them. Sauer's face was bloody and had turned blue. Both Baldelli and Avery were emotionally distraught, and Baldelli had trouble dictating the story to the rewrite reporter, Tom Farragher. "I was sobbing, 'It's Jack, it's Jack,' and Tom was yelling at me to tell him something more concrete and Deane, who was just as upset, had his arms around me," recalled Baldelli.

Sauer was in the hospital for three months. Doctors considered it a miracle that he even lived through the accident, and predicted that he would never be able to work again. But Sauer, an athlete who bicycled for hundreds of miles at a time, was determined to defy the prognosis and Avery, Al Almeida, and Wes Hammond told him that if he was willing to keep working, they were willing to let him. "They were like a family to me," said Sauer. Although he was replaced as chief photographer, he continued working for the newspaper part-time long enough to become inducted into the Dayvets Club of twenty-year veterans in 1998. Sauer expressed his gratitude for the *Day's* willingness to keep him on the payroll despite his disability.

THE DAY WAS BESET by mechanical problems, most of them connected with the 1961 Hoe Company press, which had been rigged for cold type printing in 1973. Delays caused by press malfunctions were a nightmare. Readers and advertisers complained of poor reproduction, including ink that rubbed off on their hands and clothing. To make matters worse, *The Day* had no upper-level managers with experience with presses. The last pressman in middle management had been George Kent. Even Tom Elliott, who retired as mechanical manager in 1982, had only a secondary understanding of presses. Management's resident expert on presses had, by the process of elimination, become Al Almeida, the controller, an accountant by training.

The poor conditions of the equipment hurt morale, and poor morale, in turn, contributed to the worsening condition of the equipment. The situation was aggravated by the fact that Francis "Moe" Grandsire, the press foreman and senior manager in charge of the press operation, also belonged to the press union and was considered "one of the boys." The pressroom became essentially unmanageable. The combination of equipment problems, poor morale, and a lack of discipline worsened tensions between the managers and the press union as well as conditions in the pressroom.

The Day was prepared to buy a new press in the early 1980s. But Almeida, who was placed in charge of looking for a new offset model, and Wes Hammond called a halt to the search in 1982. Almeida said this was because new developments in press technology cast doubt on the wisdom of purchasing an offset press. The Providence *Journal-Bulletin* had installed a new type of press, a flexographic press that was supposed to be an improvement over offset. The Atlanta *Journal-Constitution* was preparing to buy one as well. Hammond and Almeida persuaded the directors to put off a decision on a new press until the jury was in on this innovation. This delay threatened to prolong worsening problems with the Hoe press as *The Day* was starting to put out a Sunday edition. So while *The Day* delayed in buying a new press, it simultaneously sought ways to make the existing machinery work better. In April 1982, *The Day* signed a contract for more than $1 million to have the DiLitho equipment dismantled and the press converted to offset. The investment included equipment to prepare offset plates, so the money was not totally wasted. But the decision saddled the newspaper with another decade of production headaches that would be inherited by the next management generation.

The managers also wrestled in the 1980s with the challenges of covering all the towns in the *Day's* large territory. The system Bodenwein had developed of part-time correspondents who were paid by the amount of copy they produced had finally disappeared when Helen Fraser of Salem, the last of the correspondents, entered a nursing home in May 1975. With the retirement of James McKenna in June 1974, the approach of having a combined advertising representative and reporter in Mystic had faded into history as well. *The Day* had closed its Groton bureau. The newspaper now was recruiting top-of-the-line experienced reporters for starting positions. As a result, the towns along with the choicer beats were covered by experienced reporters. Steve Slosberg had begun at *The Day* as the reporter in Lyme and Old Lyme, two of the region's smallest towns, after having served as the political reporter for the Willimantic *Chronicle*. Joan Poro started out on the same beat.

The problem *The Day* faced was how to take the best advantage of this talent to cover the important news in the suburbs. As the region grew, some of the towns became almost as complex and interesting to cover as New London and Groton. The blue-collar town of Montville, for example, was outgrowing its selectman style of government as the result of its growing population. It was run by Howard R. "Russ" Beetham, a colorful former truck driver and teamster, who bought used police cars to save money and hold the tax rate down. East Lyme was among growing towns that had regulatory commissions that were controlled by land developers. Ledyard, formerly a farm community, filled with young middle class families who demanded quality schools whereas the town had little industrial tax base to support them.

The Day, which covered eighteen communities like this, struggled with how to do justice to these developing stories in its news coverage. It could no longer set aside space for each town, as it once had done, but had to make more choices in its coverage and display of news. There were too many towns and too much news. It became increasingly difficult to find room for the church and community news that had once been the bread and butter of the town correspondents and the material about the Boy Scouts and fraternal organizations that was deposited in familiar "drop boxes" every morning.

In 1982, the newspaper set out to develop a less parochial approach to the news that supposedly would make room for more and better coverage of the towns. *The Day* used a method developed in advertising known as zoning. *The Day* published separate editions that targeted news and advertising to specific territories in its circulation area. Arbitrarily, it divided the region in half, one on the east side and the other on the west side of the Thames River: Thames East and Thames West. The separate editions would feature the most important stories in these territories. In this way, there would be room for more local news on both sides of the river. There was only one flaw to this reasoning, as *The Day* would sadly discover. The region's real interests weren't separated by the Thames River. In its attempt to be more regional and provide better local coverage, *The Day* had split the region in half and nobody liked the results.

Additional problems surfaced in the newsroom, where morale suffered from past bad management choices. John Foley, who had been an exceptional city editor, was not as adept at running the newsroom. He delegated much of his authority to Jim Irvine, who was hardworking and competent but blunt and insensitive. Irvine was impatient with the shortcomings of reporters and editors who did not meet his demanding standards. His authoritarian style earned him the title "The Ayatollah," after the Iranian cleric. Morale also suffered from fusillades of withering notes from Avery over mistakes and other matters that aroused his anger.

The morale problem did not damage the general quality of the newspaper, however. Foley had put together a staff that was so good it continued to produce quality work despite unpleasant working conditions and poor management. The staff continued to win recognition for its work, including a first prize in an annual business writing competition sponsored by the University of Missouri School of Journalism. The award was for a series by

Stan DeCoster and Ann Baldelli on the awarding of lucrative cable-television franchises based on political influence.

BOTH SOUTHEASTERN CONNECTICUT AND *The Day* weathered a recession in the early 1980s, much in the same fashion as they had during other setbacks in the economy. One of the region's attractions to the developers of the Crystal Mall was that the area seemed almost recession-proof because the large volume of Cold War defense work didn't follow the normal business cycles. At the height of the recession, in 1982, Electric Boat had a backlog of more than $4.6 billion of work. P. Takis Veliotis had, to some degree, accomplished his mission to make the shipyard more efficient, although his presence didn't ingratiate the company with its customer, the Navy. In 1982, General Dynamics assigned Fritz Tovar, a German-American manufacturing engineer, to be the shipyard general manager. His management marked the beginning of a new period of stability at the shipyard, in which Electric Boat delivered nearly eleven Trident and Los Angeles class submarines on or ahead of time in the next three years.

Circumstances combined to favor the successor to Deane Avery and Wes Hammond, who announced in the spring of 1983 that they would retire in 1984. The economy recovered. The Cold War naval buildup under the Reagan administration boosted business prospects at the shipyard. The Crystal Mall promised fresh advertising revenue, and new business elsewhere in the region filled in other advertising gaps. The only uncertainty was the outcome of the IRS case, which in 1983 was still a year away from being decided. In searching for the next publisher, *The Day* applied some lessons learned from its immediate past. The management problems in the 1980s to some degree were a result of having two publishers. The board's attempt at a compromise between two candidates to lead the newspaper left *The Day* with no one solidly in command. Even Avery and Hammond realized this and they determined not to make the same mistake. Al Almeida, who later became general manager, reflected, "The system didn't work. Having two people in charge was the same as not having anyone in charge."

The directors set out on a search for one person and, for the first time in the newspaper's history, they looked beyond *The Day* office. This reflected a desire to find the best person for the job and the reality that nobody at *The Day* had been groomed for it. In the past, Bar Colby had been identified as his father-in-law's successor years before the transition actually took place. He had been the general manager's understudy before Orvin Andrews retired. Similarly, Avery had been groomed by Colby, who had taken him out of the newsroom and given him the new title of executive editor. Hammond had been brought along largely as the protégé of Francis McGuire, and already was on the board of directors before Colby retired. But neither Avery nor Hammond had a successor picked, trained, and in position.

The decision to hire a publisher confronted the newspaper with a dilemma that the *Day's* directors never had managed to resolve since Theodore Bodenwein's death: choosing between candidates who had business and news backgrounds. Bodenwein embodied all the traits of a good publisher: he had his roots in the community and had a great love of it. He was a good businessman, but also knew all facets of the newspaper, including news. He was a writer, editorialist, reporter, and columnist. He was a printer by training and kept up to date on presses. He learned about finances and management at the morning *Telegraph* before he assumed control of *The Day.* He was the embodiment of the great publishers of his time like Joseph Pulitzer and William Randolph Hearst. But his successors fell short of being such well-rounded men. Orvin Andrews knew the business end of the newspaper, but had no knowledge and little interest in the news operation. He left the newsroom in the hands of subordinates like George Clapp and eventually Bar Colby. Colby, on the other hand, had been a product of the newsroom. When Orvin Andrews made him assistant general manager, Andrews ran the business while Colby ran the newsroom. When Colby became general manager and later publisher, most of the serious business decisions, including the amount of the annual dividends, were made on the board, by Francis McGuire.

In 1983, Avery, Hammond, and the directors resolved this dilemma in a fashion that probably would have been eschewed by stockholders in some of the successful media chains of the time who favored business minds to run the newspapers. The *Day* directors set out to pick a successor from the ranks of the news profession, hoping their choice would be a quick learner regarding the business side of running a newspaper. This was a choice that strongly reflected the priority in the Bodenwein will of building an excellent newspaper over a bottom-line business approach. To ensure that the business would receive the proper attention, they restored the old arrangement that had existed in Bodenwein's time. Al Almeida was to become the general manager regardless of whom the directors hired as the next publisher.

There was little interest in the publisher job reflecting the fact that at this time, 1983, the IRS case was still unresolved and nobody knew for sure what would become of *The Day.* From within *The Day,* there was only one applicant, Lance Johnson, the Sunday editor. He did not have the experience of the outsiders who applied: Joseph M. Ungaro, the executive editor and vice president for the Westchester Rockland Newspapers, a Gannett property, and a former editor at the Providence (Rhode Island) *Journal*; John J. Monaghan, managing editor of the Providence (Rhode Island) *Evening Bulletin*; and Reid MacCluggage, the managing editor at the *Hartford Courant.*

MacCluggage was by then heading into rough seas. Mark Murphy, who had installed him as managing editor, was fired in 1983, and Michael Davies was brought in from the Kansas City *Star* to take charge of the *Courant.* This followed a fury of controversy among the newspaper's readers over the changes the newspaper had made. In its attempt to develop a more cosmopolitan newspaper, the *Courant* had changed dramatically the way it displayed town news. Even though it had enlarged its Hartford staff, it came under attack from a citizen activist, Ned Coll, and others, for abandoning its hometown by trying to become more of a New England publication. The new management had changed the familiar appearance of the newspaper, further stirring up discontent among readers. While Murphy was an exceptional editor, he did not appear to understand Connecticut.

MacCluggage, a Norwich native, had read about the job opening at *The Day,* and Maureen Croteau, a former *Courant* writer and newly selected head of the journalism department at the University of Connecticut, urged him to apply. Deane Avery had been on the selection committee that picked Croteau to replace Evan Hill, who was retiring. Avery had asked Croteau for help in the search for a publisher.

MacCluggage wrote Avery expressing his interest in the job, and he later met with Hammond and Avery in Essex. One of the subjects they discussed was the fact that the *Courant* had been named Newspaper of the Year by the New England Newspaper Association each year MacCluggage had been managing editor. That impressed Avery. He said he felt *The Day* had the resources to achieve the same distinction with its strong newsroom.

In the winter, MacCluggage was interviewed by the entire board at Poor Richards restaurant in Waterford. He remembers feeling that the meeting didn't go well. In fact, the board at the time was leaning toward Ungaro, but the sentiment wasn't unanimous. Avery in particular was impressed by Ungaro's skills with new newspaper technology, including pagination—the preparation of pages on computers. Evan Hill, however, was skeptical and vocal about it. Avery and Hammond were anxious to make a choice. But Hill was wary of hiring anyone from the Gannett chain because of its reputation for squeezing profits out of its newspapers at the expense of quality. He wanted someone who was interested in aggressive news coverage and good writing and dedicated to the community *The Day* served. On December 31, he wrote Hammond and Avery:

> *To hell with pagination if the pages' contents are trivial, carelessly thought out or sloppily ungrammatical. Ben Franklin did not have pagination, nor Jefferson, and we still read both.*

At the same time these doubts were being raised, events were driving MacCluggage away from the *Courant* and into the embrace of *The Day.* MacCluggage was becoming uneasy with Davies' leadership. Davies told MacCluggage he was appointing him managing editor for news and bringing in a new managing editor. Davies said he intended to announce the decision in the *Courant* that Saturday, which Davies knew was the day MacCluggage was to receive a prestigious award from the University of Hartford, his alma mater. Early in January, MacCluggage resigned, but stayed on for three months while looking for another job.

Not having heard anything from *The Day,* he determined to make another push for the job. On January 13, 1984, he typed a letter to the directors that, by coincidence, addressed many of the issues Hill had raised. He described his roots in southeastern Connecticut and his strong interest in the community. He enumerated his strengths as an editor and as a manager who delegates authority, plans, and listens.

> The Day *is about to enter a potentially turbulent period in its history. This does not have to be a difficult period, but the paper will need a strong, mature publisher with proven management skills. It will need a publisher with a positive attitude and a steady hand. It will need someone who really cares about* The Day. *I am that person.*

In five years, he said, he would win the newspaper recognition as one of the nation's top ten community newspapers, "unsurpassed in fairness and accuracy, thorough and thoughtful in approach and execution and written with style."

That's what the directors were waiting to hear. On February 22, 1984, the directors named MacCluggage editor and publisher, effective on July 2, when Hammond and Avery were to retire.

THIRTY-ONE

UPHEAVAL

We need more human resources. The good news is we can afford it.

—Reid MacCluggage, October 1984

The extra layer of bureaucracy has everyone who draws a paycheck from the newspaper worried about long-term financial stability.

—*Deep Inside The Day,* an underground newsletter at *The Day,* October 1985

REID MACCLUGGAGE, 46, COULD not have been more different from the two men he replaced in 1984 as the chief executive. Deane Avery and Wes Hammond were embarrassed by attention. They were so self-effacing they declined the honor of a companywide retirement party. Instead, they asked the board to donate the cost of a party to the Pequot Foundation, a recently formed charitable organization the newspaper helped establish. The gesture reflected their modesty, instinctive frugality with the *Day's* resources, and generosity.

MacCluggage, on the other hand, was a masterful self-promoter, as his eleventh hour pitch to the board in January 1984 to hire him demonstrated. His instincts to spot opportunities and market his strengths helped get him the job as publisher and largely patterned his years on the newspaper. The force of MacCluggage's personality shaped and expanded the newspaper, just as the ego and determination of an earlier self-promoter had. Like Theodore Bodenwein, MacCluggage was self-confident, forceful, devoted to his profession and unafraid to take risks, to spend money when necessary, and to make brash demands. Bodenwein had persuaded the newspaper's owners, the Chappells, that the only way *The Day* would recover its strength in 1890s was for them to stop pinching pennies and instead invest generously in the enterprise. The frugal owners acquiesced by providing *The Day* quarters in a new building and letting the new manager borrow the funds for new presses. Avery and Hammond, conditioned by the conservative temper of the past, felt it was their mission to restrain spending and make investments cautiously, whereas MacCluggage had come from a place where money appeared to grow on trees. He was prepared when he arrived, as Bodenwein had been when he took over, to recommend unprecedented new investments and changes. He had been empowered by the Times Mirror Company to force radical alterations upon a sleepy newspaper in the state capital. He brought that same impulse to his new job on *The Day*. He became the first really strong editor in the forty-five-year history of The Day Trust and it is no surprise that he became controversial.

Before he did, however, MacCluggage politely looked on throughout the spring and summer of 1984 as Avery and Hammond wound up their long careers before retiring. This was a pleasant time for *The Day* and its new publisher-elect. The self-controlled and good-natured MacCluggage was hard not to like. He asked questions and listened. He had a good sense of humor. He was an engaging conversationalist. He loved sports, particularly boxing and baseball, but he was also interested in the arts and liked interesting people, whatever they did. He understood the dynamics of newsrooms, because he had spent his career in such a setting. He was a talented writer and reporter, good storyteller, and collegial manager. What was not to like about him? The *Day* staff, which had been apprehensive about the arrival of an unfamiliar executive from outside, was relieved when several months went by and nothing unusual happened. Avery and Hammond departed quietly that summer. They wrote a farewell letter to all the employees:

> *Both of us have spent virtually all of our working life at* The Day. *One can't do that without forming strong ties to those who have worked with us. A newspaper isn't a shoe factory. It's a living thing. It has a personality. Leaving it is like saying goodbye to a family member.*

The board paid tribute to the two in a resolution on July 18, which MacCluggage composed. It referred to their contrasting styles, Avery's quick Yankee wit and sometimes flinty personality and Hammond's good-natured dependability and analytical mind.

Together, Deane Avery and Wes Hammond fought to maintain the Day's *independence; together they brought the newspaper into the computer age; and together they built a prosperous Sunday edition.*

THE FIRST TURBULENCE STRUCK in the fall of 1984, when MacCluggage, by now confidently in command, delivered to the directors his critique of the newspaper and his plans as he had promised. For the first time, the board was getting an outsider's view from a top manager, and it was not all pleasant. The new publisher didn't attempt to disguise his feelings. He had serious reservations about the management throughout the newspaper. Many of the managers were not up to the caliber of ones he had been accustomed to working with. While he was impressed by the rank and file in the newsroom, he noticed a morale problem there that he felt stemmed from poor management.

He believed that the whole organization needed overhauling. He called for the hiring of a director of administration, a position of which no one at *The Day* had ever heard. MacCluggage told the directors he and Almeida had just the right person in mind, Richard Flath, the personnel manager at the *Courant*. MacCluggage proposed a salary for Flath that was higher than that of any other manager at *The Day* at the time, other than Almeida's nearly $50,000. The publisher also recommended raising Almeida's salary to a more competitive level. *The Day* up to that time had emphasized higher salaries for reporters and editors to attract talent, but had not given much thought to the salaries of its top executives. MacCluggage started his job determined to upgrade executive pay, including his own. The time of pinching pennies was over. Travel was to become more frequent for reporters, including eventually foreign travel. MacCluggage introduced the concept of executive perquisites, including cars purchased by the company for himself and Almeida. This was the way it was done in the rest of industry, he pointed out.

The circulation and advertising departments required changes, he said. *The Day* no longer could afford to complacently count on being in charge in its business market. It faced aggressive national media chains that controlled its two daily competitors and the weeklies that surrounded it. Crystal Mall was attracting shoppers from outside the *Day's* circulation area, and the task of seizing the dominant market share of that new business required more modern management talent than *The Day* possessed. *The Day* needed a top-notch marketing manager to supervise circulation and advertising and launch a new business offensive.

MacCluggage also set out to correct problems in the production departments. Both the composing room and the pressroom needed to be brought under more skillful management, he felt. "There is a lack of discipline and some troublemakers," he told them. "The pressroom foreman, who is a union member, is a good man and a hard worker, but he is not a strong leader and the men take advantage of that. The foreman and his assistant often do much of the work and the others stand around. The room is dirty and the men lack pride in their work." *The Day* needed a production manager to oversee the two departments, he said. *The Day* also needed a new press desperately. Deane Avery had a clicker near his office that counted the number of editions rolling off the press. It stopped often, indicating the press was dead in the water.

MacCluggage also wanted to strengthen the organization in the newsroom. He was worried about the abilities of the existing managers to carry out his plans. Foley was a good newsman, but lacked planning, communicating, and motivating skills, he felt. Irvine, whom MacCluggage described as the "managing editor without portfolio," was "a powerful influence in the newsroom but not always a positive one" because of his brusque manner. MacCluggage said he wanted to modernize the beats to reflect contemporary interests, such as health, science, diet, child rearing, business, family, education, and religion. He wanted to enlarge the Living section to emphasize the arts, to get away from the "sewing and service clubs," and to explain trends and happenings in society better. "We need to be working on stories that explain what's happening in society, such as the trend toward single-parent homes, the issues facing our inner city, and how well the schools are educating our children," he told the board. He also wanted a projects editor to work with reporters and editors on investigations, series, and other more complicated stories.

Thames East and Thames West had to go, he was sure. *The Day* needed a single Region section for all the local news. He wanted to focus on good local reporting and make room for special sections on different days of the week: science and technology, arts and entertainment, business, food and living. *The Day* most of all needed to become a morning paper again. He was convinced of that. "I knew that when I walked in the door. We'd do the research, but I knew I was going to do that." The step would be necessary to compete with Gannett and Times Mirror. He could see people grabbing the *Bulletin* and the *Courant* off the newsstands in the morning. As long as *The Day* published in the afternoon, it conceded to them the advantage with night sports and all the government business that took place at night. He felt being an afternoon newspaper was sapping the newspaper of its energy and creativity. "I'd go to the morning news meetings and there was no excitement. They were mopping up. *The Day* was too good a newspaper to be a mopping up newspaper."

One of the first steps he took was to hire a consultant, Chris Urban of Urban & Associates of Sharon, Massachusetts. Urban & Associates had assisted the Torrington *Register* in changing to morning publication and MacCluggage looked to the firm to validate his belief that *The Day* could not survive as an evening newspaper.

The same month he presented his plans to the directors, he met with the reporters and editors. He told them he was setting out to "keep *The Day* on a course of excellence so that in five years, we will be recognized as one of the nation's top ten community newspapers, unsurpassed in fairness and accuracy, thorough and thoughtful in approach and execution, and written with clarity and style." He wanted a paper that was "skeptical, but not cynical." The newsroom should be open to a free flow of ideas. The managers should listen more to the reporters and editors. Managers should always be on the lookout for management talent in the ranks. In connection with that idea, he brought in a management consultant to train all the news staff in management techniques.

He wanted the newspaper to take a leadership role in the community. It was OK to scold government for mistakes and wrongdoing, but that should be done in the context of a mature and respectful relationship with the communities. He wanted more coaching of the reporters to improve their reporting and writing. *The Day* needed to place more urgency on getting news in the paper on time and to be better at communication. *The Day* had to find a new place for community news, the bread and butter of the weekly newspapers that were surrounding *The Day*. It needed to delve more into the news and explain events. And MacCluggage wanted a graphics department to present the news more attractively.

MacCluggage's plans got mixed reviews on the board of directors. Walter Baker, the bank's representative, liked what he heard. He became the new publisher's earliest and staunchest supporter. Baker, who had run several local businesses, recognized the same management deficiencies MacCluggage saw. Baker felt from the start that the newspaper needed to be run more like a modern corporation though it didn't operate under the same business constraints because of the trust. He was appalled at the sloppy conditions in the pressroom. "The place was filthy. It turned my stomach," he remembered. He agreed the production departments required stricter accountability under a manager who answered to the publisher and not a trade union. The whole newspaper required a stronger middle management to make the departments, including the newsroom, more accountable and efficiently run. To get these good managers, it needed to pay competitive management salaries. Bar Colby's salary, he recalled, was elevated only after Francis McGuire pointed out that the publisher needed enough money to dress presentably, entertain, and live a style of life commensurate with his position. Colby, Avery, and Hammond had felt uneasy about asking the board for money. Baker recalled:

> *They lived modestly and did not make big demands for salary. They weren't paid what they were worth. Once Bar recalled that if it had not been for McGuire, he never would have earned what he needed to participate in the community. This cost money.*

But MacCluggage ran into resistance from Shain and Hill. They were sensitive to the fact that some of MacCluggage's critique of the newspaper reflected on Avery and Hammond. They didn't necessarily disagree with MacCluggage on each point, but were worried about hurting feelings and violating the family culture at the newspaper. Avery still was a member of the board and he and Hammond had hired and valued the loyalty and service of some of the managers MacCluggage now wanted to replace. The disastrous decision to zone the newspaper's territory into Thames East and West had been theirs. They were the ones who delayed buying a new press and invested funds in the old, ailing one.

The board nevertheless was exhilarated by the enthusiasm MacCluggage brought and encouraged him to try his ideas. Their support and two other developments propelled the new publisher rapidly forward: an improvement in the economy and the decision of the United States Appellate Court upholding the favorable decision in the IRS case. A new executive could not ask for more favorable conditions. *The Day* was liberated from both its financial and legal restraints just as MacCluggage was learning his way around the building. The court decision was accompanied by the success of the Crystal Mall and the end of the Carter era recession.

The federal appellate court decision on June 5, 1985, came down just short of a year after MacCluggage took over. The company celebrated the event with a champagne party for all the employees in the third-floor conference room, which recently had been remodeled. MacCluggage told the gathering, "The real effect is that it allows us to survive the feeding frenzy in the industry in which increasing numbers of newspapers are being bought by large chains." He also mentioned that the decision permitted *The Day* to go ahead with plans to buy a new press. And that wouldn't be all. The 1985 verdict would be followed by a torrent of changes.

RICK FLATH HAD BEEN hired as director of administration in January 1985, and quickly became one of the most visible—and controversial—executives of the new regime. Flath had charge of personnel and before long employees began receiving a steady flow of official directives from him in keeping with MacCluggage's goal of improving communication at the newspaper. His authority eventually was expanded to include supervision of an ambitious $20 million capital improvement plan. *The Day* had not seen such lavish spending since Bodenwein had built the original building and then doubled its size twenty years later. Flath also took part in board meetings, rubbing several of the directors, particularly Evan Hill, the wrong way with his brash manner and blunt talk. It wasn't long before Flath became known among the staff as "Ranger Rick" for the rapid changes he was making and his bravado.

In April 1985, MacCluggage hired William Peterson, 32, who had worked for *Newsday* on Long Island, as the newspaper's new production manager. Peterson and Flath became the highest paid managers at the newspaper other than Almeida and MacCluggage. Peterson's salary was $47,000. Their status and salaries fed the perception that MacCluggage was building an expensive bureaucracy modeled after the *Hartford Courant's*, which was to some degree true. But nowhere did MacCluggage stir up more controversy than in the newsroom, where he inflamed ambitions and jealousies with his ideas to overhaul the operation from top to bottom using the *Courant* blueprint. He began constructing a new superstructure of newsroom managers, beginning with the appointment of Stan DeCoster as assistant managing editor for news and the hiring of Dorothy Torres as assistant managing editor for graphics and photography. Torres, hired in January 1985, had been graphics director at two Times Mirror newspapers in Fairfield County, Connecticut, the *Advocate* of Stamford and the *Greenwich Time*. MacCluggage created a new section for community news, called Neighbors, and put Bob Colby in charge of it. Colby started out with his own department of reporters who covered nothing but clubs, fraternal organizations, and neighborhoods.

MacCluggage also embarked on plans to change the way the news was packaged and presented, increasing the number of sections on Sunday and creating special sections run on different days during the week devoted to business, the arts, lifestyles, health, and other contemporary topics. The burden of printing the sections and so many more pages posed new challenges for the old press and the news staff and production crew. From the time he arrived,

MacCluggage stretched the resources of the newspaper to their limits, producing both a sense of excitement and frustration. MacCluggage didn't seem to care what it took to carry out his orders.

The new publisher also wasted no time in making good on his promise to give women a more important role in running the newspaper. In addition to giving one of the first assistant managing editor posts to Dorothy Torres, he made Maria Hileman the *Day's* first woman city editor in 1985. She replaced Bob Colby, who had held for five years the post his father once occupied. MacCluggage named Ann Baldelli, who had begun work in 1976 as the newsroom clerk, the night city editor. The most controversial change in the newsroom occurred at the top. John Foley stepped aside, moving into a newly created position as assistant to the publisher and columnist in March 1985. Two months later, MacCluggage hired James H. Smith, 38, his long-time friend at the *Hartford Courant*, to replace Foley as managing editor and to carry out the publisher's agenda in the newsroom. If there had been a single button that could activate all the hot buttons in the newsroom, MacCluggage had pushed it when he made that decision.

Jim Irvine, Foley's second in command, recognizing that Smith's appointment ended his once-promising chances of advancement, resigned and went to work for the New Haven *Register*. The Smith appointment upset those, few in number though they were, who were still loyal to Foley and Irvine. The decision thwarted other burning ambitions at the newspaper. Lance Johnson, the Sunday editor who had applied to be publisher, now had had designs on the managing editor's job. Johnson had been executive editor of the Willimantic *Chronicle* before he went to work for *The Day*. The newspaper's plans to start a Sunday paper drew him to *The Day*. He engineered both the weekend edition and the Sunday newspaper, and felt his successes in both these efforts entitled him to consideration as managing editor. "I felt I was ready for other challenges," he said. He made his interest clear to some of the directors. Smith's hiring aroused resentment even among those who weren't Johnson's fans because MacCluggage had turned again to an outsider to fill a position. The resentment was fueled by the knowledge that that choice was a close friend. What, after all, was the difference between this and the favoritism that had afflicted *The Day* in the past? The day Smith arrived, he already was in disfavor with the staff for many different reasons that had nothing to do with his qualifications for the job.

For all the ill will the decision aroused, MacCluggage was on firm ground in appointing Smith. Friend or not, Smith was a talented writer, an aggressive news professional, and an outgoing and likable manager. He was, like MacCluggage, self-confident and unafraid of taking risks. He could be abrasive and blunt. But he had a good management background to improve the newspaper and win *The Day* regional and national recognition. He had presided over a succession of changes at the *Courant* and later supervised turning the Torrington *Register* into a morning paper. He also was known to be good at coaching reporters to improve their writing and develop stories. One of MacCluggage's goals was to improve the quality of writing in the newspaper, which up to that time had not been a strong goal at *The Day*.

MacCluggage set out not only to develop good writing, but also to showcase it. The newspaper already had done this to some degree under Lance Johnson's direction in the Sunday newspaper. MacCluggage wanted to expand those gains to the daily newspaper. New section covers were intended to highlight the newspaper's best stories, which would be presented attractively with photographs and drawings. MacCluggage also authorized the newspaper's first full-time, salaried columnist. Smith gave that job to Steve Slosberg, who had already accumulated a shelf full of trophies as an editorial writer and columnist. Paul Baumann, who had left his job as a history teacher in a private school to be a reporter on *The Day*, replaced Slosberg on the editorial page. Baumann also was a stylish writer and later became an editor of *Commonweal*, the liberal Roman Catholic magazine based in New York.

Smith walked into a breaking national story in the *Day's* backyard: another scandal at the Electric Boat shipyard. Just as Electric Boat seemed to be returning to normal after P. Takis Veliotis had left as general manager and fled to Greece in June 1982, he ignited a fresh controversy by informing the FBI of alleged wrongdoing by officials of General Dynamics, the shipyard's parent company, including corporate chairman David Lewis.

United States authorities had been keeping a close and jittery watch over Veliotis, not so much because of his alleged crimes, but more because of his intimate knowledge of the submarine-building program and the fear that some of his knowledge might fall into the hands of the Russians. They stayed in touch with him through lawyers. By these contacts, Veliotis let Justice Department agents know that he had tapes of telephone conversations with Lewis, Gordon MacDonald, and other top corporate officers that, he said, would implicate them in misconduct connected to earlier cost-overrun settlements with the Navy. This aroused strong interest in Congress, which was looking closely at fraudulent charges by defense contractors. The United States Justice Department, which had dropped its investigation into possible improprieties by General Dynamics in January 1982, resumed it based on Veliotis's revelations in 1983. The investigators rented space in the abandoned YMCA in downtown New London to carry on their work.

The Day had by this time developed a degree of expertise in reporting on the complex problems at Electric Boat. Joan Poro and Dan Stets had revealed the chaotic conditions and management problems in the shipyard in the 1970s as it became overburdened with work on Cold War nuclear submarines. The newspaper's probing had continued even after Electric Boat imposed a news blackout on *The Day* and withdrew its advertising. Reporter Maria Hileman's reporting had shed light on a kickback scandal involving P. Takis Veliotis that had contributed to his flight to Greece to escape prosecution.

Jacky Flinn had taken over the story from Hileman in January 1984 when Hileman left on maternity leave. Marcel Dufresne, who had recently returned to *The Day* after completing work on a Kiplinger fellowship in public affairs reporting at Ohio State University, later joined Flinn in covering the saga. Among the subjects Dufresne had studied at Ohio State was the use of public records to develop investigative stories. This helped as the two reporters looked into the stock transactions of David Lewis on record at the Securities and Exchange Commission to see if Lewis and his colleagues were profiting from stock manipulations. Dufresne and Flinn spent several days in Washington going through SEC records and *The Day* hired a securities analyst to help them chase down this lead. Flinn recalled in an interview for this book that congressional staff members were impressed a newspaper as small as *The Day* was willing to dispatch reporters to Washington to work on the story, and as a result became extremely cooperative with her and Dufresne. Their work produced a prize-winning story January 6, 1985, that detailed the amount of money David Lewis made through his General Dynamics stock options. In a single six-month period, he had made a $1.7 million profit by buying and selling corporate stock without having to spend a penny of his own. After he was hired in May, Smith worked closely with both reporters in molding the continuing Electric Boat story, Dufresne remembered. "He was comfortable with reporters. He understood their language. He was interested in story telling, and understood when we were onto something good."

But during these months, Smith, who was married, fell in love with Flinn. While such occurrences were not unusual at *The Day*, Smith's romantic involvement with Flinn contributed to the controversy over his hiring and other changes MacCluggage was making at the newspaper. In October 1985, copies of an underground pamphlet patterned after the *Day's* house organ, *Inside The*

Day, had shown up. It was called *Deep Inside The Day* and lampooned the changes MacCluggage had made. In a possible attempt to conceal the authorship, nobody was spared criticism in the publication. But it was clear the chief target was Smith, whose picture was on the front page beneath a photograph left over from the IRS case victory celebration of the publisher holding up a bottle of champagne. The story, developed around the fact that Smith had been MacCluggage's best man at his wedding, appeared beneath a headline, "The best man for the job." The origin of the publications has remained a mystery at *The Day*. An editorial presented a laundry list of newsroom gripes about MacCluggage's management, all loosely supporting the thesis that he was creating an expensive and useless bureaucracy of upper-echelon managers while the rest of the staff was overworked and underpaid and the newspaper was jettisoning its traditional values.

Deep Inside The Day, despite its largely sophomoric content, had one positive feature. While it didn't stand out for its writing, it highlighted the good reporting skills that existed on the newspaper. Whoever prepared the publication had access to confidential salary information, for the publication accurately stated Smith's starting salary of $45,000. The authors also had access to a confidential document circulated among the directors detailing estimates of the costs of new positions at the newspaper. They also had unusually detailed insights into management activities that had not been extensively discussed in the open, including the study on whether *The Day* should become a morning newspaper. The whole newsroom was caught up in the juicy intrigue.

Smith's personal conduct played into the hands of the effort to drive him out of his job. Disgruntled reporters and editors for the most part avoided confronting MacCluggage with their concerns, but instead brought their complaints to the board, in particular to Evan Hill and Deane Avery. These two directors were best known and most accessible to the staff. The board was already worked up over what a few of the directors perceived as a bald example of hubris. Hill was particularly upset. He now was convinced MacCluggage was getting too big for his britches. He was worried about Avery's feelings over all the assaults on his work. Avery's presence on the board was awkward. He had considered stepping down as a director when he retired, recalling the awkwardness of having Colby remain on the board in his twilight years. But Hill and the others talked him into staying.

Hill knew Avery felt reluctant to speak up, but Hill certainly wasn't afraid to say what was on his mind. Shain, who was not as outspoken but had a longer relationship with Avery, had some of the same apprehensions. These concerns came to a head when MacCluggage reported to the board on July 17, 1985, about his first year as publisher. MacCluggage told the board that he had strengthened the management, improved employee relations, made strides in special news coverage, improved the *Day's* profile in community relations, improved the organization and appearance of the newspaper, and had undertaken new projects. He felt he had a strong management team, which included Almeida; Flath; Peterson, the production manager; Lance Johnson; Jim Smith; Dick Willis, the new controller; and Morgan McGinley, the editorial page editor. Why had he chosen to make the management changes?

> *Because our goals won't be achieved without strong leadership in each department. A year ago, we found a management group that was cautious and security minded. There were no risk-takers. The group didn't work because there was a strong resistance to accept individual responsibility. There was an absence of irreverence, fresh ideas, new approaches.*

This glowing, and, Hill felt, arrogant and disrespectful review did not square with reality for several of the directors. Hill was furious. Shain was upset. Shain wrote notes to Hill and Walter Baker. Hill called Avery and wrote a letter to Baker. They even had a meeting of their own before a regular board meeting, in which they reinforced each other's outrage over MacCluggage's impudence. Hill called it "the rump meeting."

"I have been unsettled with Reid for several months," Hill wrote Baker. "Some people solve problems by forming a committee .... Reid seems to solve problems by hiring high-priced executives." He added up the cost of new salary expenses and it came to $500,000, he claimed. That didn't include a large increase in MacCluggage's salary, then $69,000. On top of that, the newspaper spent even more money to hire a consultant to find information *The Day* already knew. "He (MacCluggage) leaves the impression he took over a newspaper in trouble and finally put it back on its feet." On the contrary, he continued, "Reid now has a company that's got the lowest morale I've heard of in years."

The turmoil over Smith's behavior reflected both the frenzied state of newsroom politics at the time and legitimate concerns that Smith's fraternization with a subordinate was disrupting the newsroom and hurting morale. Under pressure, Smith resigned on February 17, 1986. He moved to the *News-Times* of Danbury, Connecticut, as managing editor. He divorced and married Jacky Flinn and later became editor of the Meriden *Record-Journal.*

A month before Smith left, he had appointed Lance Johnson deputy managing editor. In March, Johnson became the seventh managing editor during the history of The Day Trust, following in the footsteps of George Clapp,

Deane Avery, Ken Grube, Curt Pierson, John Foley, and, briefly, James Smith. The week his appointment was announced, the New England Newspaper Association announced *The Day* had been chosen the New England Newspaper of the Year for medium-sized newspapers for its Sunday edition. In the same competition, the newspaper won honorable mention for its daily newspaper. Both Smith and Johnson could claim pieces of the credit for those honors.

The Day forged ahead after these unfortunate circumstances. The board was sufficiently convinced that equilibrium had been restored to award both a three-week Christmas bonus and bonuses of $10,000 and $5,000 for MacCluggage and Almeida that November. Walter Baker had urged more generous rewards for the two executives. "I'm finally and fully convinced that the management of the company is in good hands," he wrote the other directors on November 5, 1986, "Reid has dispelled my doubts and I think he's doing an excellent job. In a low-keyed manner, he carries on a very full agenda."

Baker pointed out that MacCluggage had plunged into community activities. He had put together a middle management team, without which *The Day* couldn't have advanced as much as it had. Baker was impressed by the way MacCluggage had handled the personnel problems of the past year. It couldn't have been easy for him to see his good friend leave under such circumstances. He had turned the idea of strategic planning into more than a mere buzzword. He had brought participatory management to the newspaper, entrusting the entire budget preparation to the department heads.

IN DECEMBER 1986, THE directors accepted MacCluggage's recommendation to make *The Day* a morning newspaper. The newspaper had started out as a morning paper in 1881, but joined the trend in that decade to become an evening newspaper in 1884, when the *Evening Telegram* was forced out of business. For decades before television, newspapers were read by families when workers arrived home in the evening. Theodore Bodenwein had built *The Day* as an evening newspaper, full of features and information that entertained and informed readers after evening meals. The newspaper was sold on the street to workers returning home. Bodenwein had tried his hand at publishing a morning newspaper when he bought the *Morning Telegraph* at the turn of the century, but gave up on it after only a few years because it was unprofitable. The experience had convinced him that New London preferred an afternoon newspaper, although he realized that tastes and circumstances might someday change this. He had left open that possibility in his will.

Habits did change, but not until much later. In New London's case, sports led the way. New London loved sports. It had its own semi-professional baseball teams. Morton Plant, who owned the *Morning Telegraph* for a brief period of time, was a patron of baseball and endowed a baseball field in New London. There was a team named after him called the Planters. Professional boxers competed at Ocean Beach. Bars across the city had their walls lined with autographed photographs of professional sports greats.

Bodenwein catered to these needs aggressively. Shortly after he took over *The Day*, he began publishing major league baseball box scores on the front page. Before long, he had developed a sports section, and some of the *Day's* most durable and memorable staff members contributed to it, including John Mallon, John DeGange, Jim Watterson, and Jack Cruise. Many of the writers came from local sports traditions, having played for Chapman Technical High School or Bulkeley School. During World Series baseball games before the age of radio, *The Day* had charted the progress from inning to inning for audiences with a mechanical contraption displayed in its front window.

But by the 1960s, *The Day* had begun to display its shortcomings for the sports fans among its readers. In particular, it couldn't provide timely news about nighttime sports competition, including the box scores and detailed information sports enthusiasts desire. This had allowed a foothold in New London for the *Day's* morning rival, the Norwich *Bulletin*. Many bought both the *Bulletin* and *The Day*, but some bought only the *Bulletin*. *The Day* could do little more than catch up and provide some fresh insights with feature stories and new angles on stale news. Despite the affection in which the *Day's* sports writers and editors were held and the strong emphasis on local and scholastic sports, the sports page had, by the 1970s, become the weak link on the newspaper. The New England Daily Newspaper Survey pointed this out bluntly.

The managing editor is unhappy with sports. Rightly so.
Too much of the department's copy consists of the traditional overnight material warmed over through the wire services for afternoon newspapers.

The advantage sports gave the *Bulletin*, and to a lesser degree, the *Hartford Courant* helped these publications compete with *The Day* in other news, as well. For example, the morning newspapers could provide the closing stock market prices and more timely news about local government, which conducted most of its public meetings at night.

The Day had withstood this competition and retained the loyalty of its readers well into the 1970s, possibly from sheer momentum. But another study done in 1985 showed that morning competition was beginning to eat into the

Day's readership. The Urban & Associates study showed that the *Day's* penetration, the percentage of households it reached in its circulation area, after peaking near ninety percent in the 1970s, had dropped to around sixty-six percent by 1984.

"The decision was made to protect the long-term security of *The Day*, and to provide opportunities for growth," MacCluggage told the employees in the letter announcing the decision on December 17, 1986.

"Going mornings" was nevertheless traumatic for the staff, the readers, and yet another group that had been part of *The Day* tradition from its inception: the young carriers. The Sunday newspaper had forced them to get up before dawn on Sunday mornings, while problems with the *Day's* rickety press often detained them into long after dark on weekdays. During one troublesome press run, the papers weren't delivered to carriers until midnight. The improved, heavier *Day* was becoming an increasing burden to carry. And the carriers were often the first to field the complaints from readers unhappy with late deliveries, forced Sunday subscriptions, and Thames East and West. And now they were confronted with getting up before dawn every day.

During the late 1970s and early 1980s, the Circulation Department tried to keep its carrier force together by various rewards, including all-day picnics at Ocean Beach Park and expense-paid trips abroad for a few. But the effort could not reverse the breakup of this proud workforce of cheap labor going back generations. Even if nothing else happened, *The Day* still had to compete with Little League, Peewee Football, and other rivals for the time of the young people. The morning newspaper was probably the last straw. As the 1980s drew to a close, *The Day* resorted more and more to motorized routes and young carriers began to go the way of the town correspondents and Linotype operators.

The change to a morning newspaper also signaled a new offensive against the Norwich *Bulletin*. On March 9, 1987, the same day *The Day* began publishing in the mornings, it opened an office in downtown Norwich with a catered reception and for the first time went head-to-head against the *Bulletin* in its own territory. The new office had three reporters led by Paul Choiniere who had been the *Bulletin's* court reporter. Choiniere was laid back, conscientious, thorough, and liked and respected by the newsmakers in the city. He quickly gained ground for *The Day* merely by being a good reporter. *The Day* also made inroads into the rural towns north of Norwich, which had been unhappy with the *Bulletin's* skimpy coverage under Gannett. Towns began to plead with *The Day* to cover them.

The Day raised its advertising rates, a move MacCluggage felt was necessary both to raise money and compete more effectively with the *Bulletin*. *The Day* had always kept its rate below normal market prices on the theory that it was a public trust and that lower rates helped local businesses. But MacCluggage felt the lower rates afforded advertisers the opportunity to divide their advertising budgets between *The Day* and the *Bulletin*. "We were giving away advertising to the *Bulletin*," he said.

The Day, flush with new advertising revenue from a new wave of economic growth, increased rates and its circulation and advertising gains in the *Bulletin's* territory, moved forward in 1987 and 1988 to carry out long-awaited plans.

The directors were grateful to MacCluggage for the progress he had made, and rewarded him in December 1987 by raising his salary to $125,000 from $98,228.

THIRTY-TWO

More Than a Business

I regret that the tribe and the casino have banned distribution of The Day *and I hope that good relations between the tribe and the newspaper will return. The newspaper holds no grudge against members of the Tribal Council or any Foxwoods executive. But* The Day *will be steadfast in its obligation to cover and uncover the news, and any attempt to use economic pressure to influence coverage will be unsuccessful.*

—Reid MacCluggage, May 6, 1996

THE *DAY'S* EDITORS DIDN'T like Ronald Reagan, the former Hollywood actor who had replaced Jimmy Carter as president in 1981. The newspaper's editorial page seized every opportunity to lambaste the president's policies, particularly the administration's trickle-down or supply side theory of economics and also its nuclear arms stance. Trickle-down was the theory that if businesses were allowed to get rich and weren't overburdened by government regulations, the wealth that was produced would result in investments that would benefit everyone. It was a newer version of the 1920s creed that what was good for business was good for America. *The Day*, pointing to the growing homelessness in America, argued that many weren't benefiting from the nation's prosperity. The newspaper documented this argument in its own territory. The *Day's* tireless anti-Reagan crusading intensified the charge that the newspaper wore liberal and Democratic blinders.

When Reagan ran for reelection in 1984, the *Day* editors believed that the election was crucial to the future of the country and produced a series of editorials that examined the major issues in depth. Each consumed an entire editorial page. To no one's surprise, they concluded that former Vice President Walter Mondale's election was essential to the future well-being of the republic.

MacCluggage, who wrote a column prefacing the series, held views that were different from the editors'. However, he didn't contest the Mondale endorsement because he didn't like Reagan either. He had expressed that view to the directors when he applied for the job. He thought Reagan was an airhead. But much of the substance of what the Republican president was attempting rang true with the publisher. Reagan had set out to dismantle the New Deal, and MacCluggage was sympathetic with that idea. His anti-government views intensified with the passage of time. The dynamics of the editorial board became more complicated as the philosophical differences among the publisher and the other editors grew more distinct. But in most cases, MacCluggage didn't force his views upon the others or upon the editorial policy of the newspaper. The exceptions came during Clinton's reelection campaign in 1996, when MacCluggage's one vote decided the newspaper would endorse Robert Dole and in congressional elections, when the publisher vetoed the other editors' views and endorsed opponents of Sam Gejdenson, the liberal congressman.

THE REAGAN ERA WAS accompanied by an intoxicating sense of comfort with materialism. The idea grew that acquisitiveness was not necessarily bad, as the liberals had professed, because it stimulated business activity and that was good for everyone. Reagan's strength reflected a disillusionment with the kind of liberalism embraced by the editorial page in the late 1960s, when Ken Grube had taken over from George Clapp. Clapp loyally had carried on the campaign against the New Deal for nearly thirty years after Bodenwein's death.

The poor were not the beneficiaries of welfare programs, the new view argued; they were the victims. The battles against poverty in the past robbed people of their dignity, and more important, their productivity. *The Day* still didn't buy this. In MacCluggage's early years on the newspaper, the editorial page adhered to the earlier ideals. Homelessness and the shortage of affordable housing frequently were revisited on the page with sympathy and concern.

But Deane Avery joked with McGinley that the policies of Reagan were at the same time filling the pockets of many Americans. The nation's phenomenal new wealth was evident in New London, where prosperity gave rise to a new attempt to jump-start the downtown New London revitalization effort. The mood of material hope radiated from Jay Levin, an energetic 32-year-old politician who became mayor the same year MacCluggage arrived in 1984. He seemed destined to follow in the footsteps of local heroes like Bryan Mahan, the city's mayor early in the century who had won backing in Hartford for the Ocean Pier. Levin had been one of the first men admitted at Connecticut College when *Day* trustee Charles E. Shain, as president of the college, oversaw its change to a school that admitted men as well as women. Levin was handsome, intelligent, and charismatic. He belonged to a liberal wing of the Democratic Party that had challenged the control of the Satti wing. Dr. C. John Satti's family and political descendants had brought what many, including *The Day*, felt was a narrowly selfish focus to the party. The insurgents thought of themselves as more progressive. Levin had been elected to the City Council in 1983, and became the chairman of the Economic Development Committee. Everyone thought he would bring a new, more positive tone to local politics. In a column February 19, 1984, Morgan McGinley welcomed Levin's arrival on the scene, stating that Levin had taken on "what could be the most controversial and troublesome job on the City Council, trying to create a sense of coordination and cooperation among the several agencies involved in New London's revitalization."

Under the city's system of government, mayors were selected every year by the City Council and had little real authority. Bodenwein and the other leaders who had produced the 1921 charter didn't want a single politician possessing as much power as strong mayors had in the past. They wanted a professional in charge, one they could influence and count on to protect the city's interests from the corrosive influences of politics. But one of the unfortunate outcomes was that city managers were largely insulated from the popular will, and what democratic leadership existed was dispersed among seven city councilors. In truth, nobody was in charge or responsible.

Levin raised the prospect of exploiting the mayor's position to promote the city's development as well as preside at ceremonial events. MacCluggage was impressed. The publisher had sized up New London, and concluded its greatest deficiency was a lack of leadership. He agreed with critics who felt there had been too much negativism in the city, including even some of the *Day's* carping criticism of the city government. During MacCluggage's first months on the job, the newspaper organized a forum to discuss the future of the downtown.

As a result, the languishing New London Development Corporation formed in 1978 to administer loans to small businesses was reactivated in June 1985 and given a more ambitious task: to find a developer at long last for downtown New London. MacCluggage became a member of the board but later resigned. Another of the leaders in this effort was Richard Creviston, president of the venerable New England Savings Bank next door to *The Day*. Banks were awash in cash and Creviston had taken a lead in financing development in the city. The bank expanded its quarters and invested funds to restore a rundown street in the city, Starr Street, turning it into an upper middle-class island in a blighted area.

The search for a downtown developer led to the Congress Group of Boston. The company proposed to transform the waterfront into a glitzy business and residential quarter with condominiums, marinas, and chic shops that would rise on the edge of the river in the area behind Union Station and along Bank Street. The newspaper was enthusiastically supportive. Neither the newspaper nor the city anticipated that the mucky river bottom wouldn't support the development, nor, in a short time, would the economy.

THE EXUBERANT TIMES IN the 1980s were reminiscent of the 1920s, when Theodore Bodenwein and several other local businessmen had developed the Garde Theater block, and when the *Day's* business was so profitable the newspaper doubled the size of its building on Main Street. The New England Savings Bank, formerly the Savings Bank of New London, accumulated more cash than it knew what to do with in compound interest from the investment boom. New grass-roots banks materialized from the explosion in real estate development. Workers streamed into the region to work on the giant Trident submarines under construction at Electric Boat. The fearsome nuclear-missile submarines were a cornerstone of America's last showdown with the Soviet Union under Reagan. Electric Boat built eighteen of them, each costing more than $2 billion, making them the most expensive weapon in the United States' arsenal. The flood of new shipyard workers created a serious shortage of affordable housing. *The Day* responded with a forum on the housing problems and a series of editorials calling for a regional effort to create affordable housing. New England Savings Bank added to its financial war chest when it decided in 1988 to issue publicly owned stock. It formed a new corporation, NESB, and encouraged the bank's depositors to invest in the bank's promising future as a major player in the region's development. Thousands of small investors purchased shares in the initial issue of stock, which soared in value and added to the euphoria in the city. Depositors, retirees, charitable foundations, some of the *Day's* editors, bought shares. Everyone was going to get rich. The young executives at NESB became local celebrities.

The Day, as much as everyone, was caught up in this giddy atmosphere. The newspaper rushed ahead with plans to modernize its plant and added some new flourishes. The $9 million capital improvement plan expanded rapidly to $20 million, causing alarm in the newspaper's business office and at the bank. The original more modest plans to install a press in the existing building grew to include a new press building. This led to a big debate on the board over whether the newspaper should move its printing plant outside the downtown, as many metropolitan newspapers had done in the 1970s, or keep it there. The board concluded Bodenwein's will demanded that the development take place in downtown New London. Otherwise, why would Bodenwein have been so explicit about building attractive structures there? The resulting new press building alone added $3 million to the escalating costs of the newspaper's plans.

The directors also went ahead with a four-story addition on Atlantic Street, originally conceived in the 1960s but delayed for more than a decade. The newspaper's original agreement with the Redevelopment Agency had called for the demolition of the garage behind *The Day* and construction of a new building on the spot to enhance that section of the city. But the company postponed the move, painting the 1928 brick façade of the old building instead. MacCluggage not only persuaded the directors to go forward with the addition, but also convinced them to add third and fourth stories. The fourth-floor was to be for executive offices, including his own. The parallels with 1920s are again striking. During the earlier era of prosperity, Bodenwein doubled the size of the *Day* building, and, in doing so, created new executive quarters for himself. Under MacCluggage, the newsroom got a modern new home on the third floor, with a state-of-the-art photo lab and more room. The fourth floor renovations, which were the last to be accomplished, created luxury offices for the publisher and other executives overlooking the Thames River. Yet another similarity would unfold, when MacCluggage and others led in restoring the derelict Garde Theater and turning it into a regional arts center in the 1990s.

The *Day's* plans also came to include a park where the newspaper's parking lot had been located, between the original building and the new press building to the south. This was where the old Bishop Studio building and Salvation Army had been located before *The Day* acquired the real estate under urban renewal. Rick Flath was in charge of that project as well. It cost $600,000. The park, with walking paths, stone benches and gardens, was dedicated to Bar Colby, who finally had vacated his seat on the board after an association of more than fifty years with *The Day*.

ALL THESE RAPID DEVELOPMENTS at the newspaper added to the jitters that MacCluggage's spending was leading the newspaper toward a devastating wreck. Capital spending wasn't the only concern, either. The newsroom swelled with new reporters and editors. The news staff rose in number from fifty to seventy-three under Lance Johnson's management. The size of the newsroom bureaucracy grew, as well, requiring the masthead—the list of editors and executives published every day on the editorial page—to be changed and enlarged regularly. Johnson came to be regarded as the villain among the other managers. MacCluggage insisted that the managers prepare the newspaper budget, and the publisher stayed clear of the fray while his subordinates battled among themselves to achieve his bottom line. The fastest growing part of the budget always was Johnson's. But what was often lost in the grumbling among the other managers was that Johnson had a mandate from MacCluggage, and MacCluggage believed he had a mandate from Bodenwein's will, to lavish money on newsgathering. To support his case before the board, as Bar Colby, Deane Avery, and Wes Hammond had done before him, MacCluggage brought out the Bodenwein will. Each director was given a copy, as well as supporting literature.

MacCluggage came to enjoy more personal influence over the board than his predecessors had. He reshaped the group. All the members were male when he arrived, and his first recommendations for replacements were women. Antoinette Dupont, then the chief judge of the Connecticut Appellate Court, became a director in February 1986. In May 1990, Lynda Blackmon Smith, a young psychologist, became the third woman to serve on the board and the first black. She replaced Charles Shain, who had retired from the board at the mandatory age of 70. Her husband, Merle Smith, had been the first black cadet to graduate from the Coast Guard Academy.

Evan Hill had retired in 1989 at the age of 70. When he stepped aside, he recommended the board extend the tenure of Walter Baker, his early adversary, who became 70 the same year. He proposed this because of Baker's business knowledge and the respect he had developed for him. Baker had been MacCluggage's strongest supporter. Hill more than anyone had been responsible for MacCluggage's hiring. But he became one of the new publisher's severest critics. He was the conscience of the board and a gadfly with

MacCluggage. When Francis McGuire had been alive, Hill had challenged the propriety of McGuire's doing the legal work for the newspaper in the costly IRS case. Nobody ever had challenged McGuire before. Hill also led the attack against MacCluggage during the controversy over managing editor Jim Smith.

MacCluggage's relations with the directors settled down. But Hill remained troubled. He felt MacCluggage manipulated the board too much and used the newspaper to promote himself. "It was always obvious to me that one of his goals was to improve his image, locally, in the state and in the nation." But Hill conceded that the newspaper improved under the publisher. When Hill retired from the board, MacCluggage gave him an affectionate farewell in a personal letter May 11, 1989:

> *You delighted in asking the "dumb" questions, the Inspector Columbo questions that no one else dared to ask. The answers, of course, got right to the essence of an issue … I will miss your love of* The Day. *You believed in the ideal, and the love led to an extraordinary dedication. You have been a careful reader of the paper and strong advocate for the reader.*

The newspaper's spending in the late 1980s caused alarm among the other managers and turnover at the top among several of MacCluggage's appointees added to the uneasiness. MacCluggage's early appointments of production, advertising, and marketing managers didn't work out and the three were replaced. But as matters turned out, the "wild spending" of those years, from 1986 until the early 1990s, did not bankrupt the newspaper. In fact, the spending turned out to have been ideally timed between the end of one recession and the start of another.

Many of these early concerns of the staff found their way to Al Almeida, the good-natured and empathic general manager, who became the father confessor for both staff and managers. Almeida, himself, had some fears, for he had to ensure there was money for the new projects and staff. Almeida had both a steadying influence on *The Day* during a turbulent period and a significant impact on the newspaper in an unlikely field that had been thrust upon him by earlier managers: technology. Bar Colby had placed him in charge of updating the newspaper's technology. And while during that time *The Day* haltingly went about replacing its old Hoe press, it moved forward with other technological innovations, including electronic editing machines and the introduction of the electronic darkroom in the photo department. *The Day* preceded many larger newspapers in these making improvements. The newspaper also introduced a fully automated mailroom, in which advertising supplements were inserted by machines. These replaced some of the newspaper's most colorful and congenial holdovers of the past: the "stuffers," a group of part-time workers, many of them elderly women, who had performed this exacting and monotonous task since the pre-printed advertising inserts were introduced in 1969.

DURING THE SAME PERIOD, two events—one in Washington and one in another part of the world—dramatically transformed southeastern Connecticut and the nature of the news *The Day* covered. The fall of the Iron Curtain in Europe and the end of the Cold War led to major cutbacks throughout the defense industry, including Electric Boat. And a succession of new federal laws helped the nearly extinct Mashantucket Pequot and the Mohegan Indian tribes to ultimately replace the defense industry as the major driver of economic growth in the region. The controversial new industry that made this possible was casino gambling.

During the 1980s, the *Day's* editors shared the alarm of many editorial writers in the country over Ronald Reagan's militant policies in Europe, including the deployment of new and more accurate nuclear missiles in Germany. The newspaper opposed the Reagan arms buildup, though it carefully carved from this policy the nuclear missile submarines that were built in Groton. *The Day* was sympathetic to the new wave of anti-nuclear protestors at the Trident launchings. It covered the activities of the Nuclear Freeze Movement, which sought to halt the growth of nuclear weapons, with increased interest and thoroughness. The fact that some of the region's most solid citizens, including retired naval officers, belonged to the movement added to its credibility with *The Day*.

The fear that Reagan's brinkmanship against "the evil empire" of the Soviet Union was driving the world toward a nuclear holocaust concerned newspaper editors. The New England Society of Newspaper Editors started an exchange program with Russian journalists earlier in the decade to defuse the alarming Cold War tensions. It was the first and only program of its kind in the country. Morgan McGinley was active in the organization, and *The Day* was a host to one of the first Russian delegations. Later, MacCluggage, McGinley, Maura Casey, former editorial page editor of the Lawrence (Massachusetts) *Eagle-Tribune* who was hired onto the *Day's* editorial page staff in 1986, and I traveled on different occasions to the Soviet Union under the exchange. Victor Gribachev, a Soviet journalist, spent a summer at *The Day* as an observer and editor. Gribachev was a proud and unrepentant communist, who believed there was a future for communism and that the two systems could coexist. But he developed a warm relationship with the editors and reporters at *The Day*, including MacCluggage, who lent him a car for the summer.

Gribachev turned out to be wrong in his faith in the future of the communist system. Soviet leader Mikhail Gorbachev's permissive policies toward political dissent, known as *glasnost*, encouraged protests across the Soviet Bloc in Eastern Europe. East Germans began boldly escaping the country through Hungary and Czechoslovakia. The exodus became a flood, and the frustrated East German government finally opened the borders to relieve the pressure. Huge crowds formed on both sides of the Berlin Wall and began tearing it down piece by piece with sledgehammers and even pieces of the wall in November 1989.

The fall of the Berlin Wall was followed by the collapse of communist regimes in the rest of Eastern Europe. Early in 1990, as the Soviet Empire was collapsing, *The Day* sent me on a trip sponsored by the National Conference of Editorial Writers through Eastern Europe, from East Berlin, through Czechoslovakia, Hungary, and Poland. That same year, Maura Casey went to the Soviet Union. MacCluggage wanted to make the newspaper thorough and complete enough in its coverage to eliminate the need of readers to buy other newspapers. He supported the coverage of international and national news from a local perspective. Bodenwein had had the same view, believing that the military community wasn't too interested in local news and wanted more world news. The *Day's* stories describing the turbulence and changes its writers witnessed firsthand in Europe after the Cold War appeared in 1990.

The fall of communism wasn't good news in southeastern Connecticut, which had prospered for nearly forty years on Cold War military spending. After the Soviet Union collapsed, President George Bush, Reagan's successor, and Congress were eager to slow down the wave of military spending, which had created an annual federal deficit and mounting national debt. They began looking at slowing down or halting work on new Cold War weapons and shutting down military bases. Targets of their cost cutting included the new Seawolf class of attack submarine under development at Electric Boat and the Submarine Base in Groton. The Seawolf was the only business the shipyard had on the horizon. The Submarine Base employed thousands in and out of the military. However, the immediate step the government took was to close down the Navy Undersea Warfare Center (NUWC), as it was then called, in New London and consolidate it with another laboratory in Newport, Rhode Island.

That closing jolted the region. The laboratory employed more than one thousand scientists and engineers and sustained dozens of small engineering companies that did contracting work for it. These contractors employed thousands of well-paid workers and rented or owned extensive real estate in New London and other communities. Much of the anger over this turn of events was focused on Sam Gejdenson, the region's liberal congressman. Defense workers felt Gejdenson had allowed this catastrophe to happen by being inattentive to military matters. The region's defense work in the past had come fairly effortlessly to the region and Gejdenson had never angled for positions on the committees that made decisions about defense procurement—the House Armed Services Committee and its Seapower Subcommittee. He hadn't needed to. While the military community chafed over Gejdenson's cavalier attitude, *The Day* was sympathetic toward him, sharing his view that the region was precariously over-reliant on defense spending and ought to follow his advice to branch into other industries.

The workers and management at Electric Boat were anxious about the possible loss of the Seawolf program that threatened to shut down the shipyard. General Dynamics had recruited an executive from its Virginia rival, Newport News & Shipbuilding Company, James E. Turner, Jr., to replace Fritz Tovar. Turner swiftly mobilized the company to protect Electric Boat's Pentagon business. General Dynamics was the nation's largest defense contractor, producing military aircraft and tanks as well as submarines. The corporation, sensing that its vital interests were in jeopardy, moved its headquarters from St. Louis, Missouri, to the Washington Beltway, in Falls Church, Virginia. Barbara Nagy, the *Day's* defense writer, began shuttling between New London and Washington to cover the story as it unfolded in Congress. Turner visited with the *Day's* editors and cultivated a good relationship with the newspaper.

The *Day's* editorial page for more than a decade had been calling upon Electric Boat to diversify into nonmilitary production. Gejdenson was among the most vociferous proponents of this approach, which Electric Boat, with all its submarine business, persistently eschewed. I had written editorials in favor of diversification and one morning, Maura Casey dropped an application on my desk for a $25,000 fellowship for an editorial writer and urged me to apply for the money to look at the conversion of the arms industries to peacetime manufacturing. The fellowship was awarded by the Society of Professional Journalists to one editorial writer each year.

I was late in submitting the application. Morgan McGinley forgot to write his recommendation for me until the last minute. To my amazement, I won with an application emphasizing that I had lived in southeastern Connecticut all my life and wanted to use the money to find ways to protect the region from an economic calamity. I had stressed how small newspapers like *The Day* needed help to cover complex and important stories in their backyards. I used the money to visit places across the United States and in Europe on both sides of the former Iron Curtain that had been dependent on Cold War spending. *The Day* paid me my salary during the months I was away and Casey and McGinley filled in for me on the editorial page. The result was a thirteen-part series called "Peace at Work," followed by several front-page editorials recommending steps southeastern Connecticut ought to take to survive in the wake of the Cold War.

Electric Boat didn't take the ideas in the series seriously and general manager Roger Tetrault, who had succeeded Turner, was outraged at the suggestion that he take a more active role in the discussions about economic restructuring. Turner, who had been transferred to General Dynamics' headquarters in Falls Church, was trying to hold on to the shipyard's submarine business. While *The Day* was recommending that the region stop wasting so much energy on defense and start looking for new industry for its skilled workforce of shipyard workers, scientists, and engineers, Turner was lobbying Congress to build several more Seawolf submarines. The Bush administration wanted to cancel the program. The craft unions at the shipyard rallied around Turner's efforts, sending bus loads of demonstrators to Washington. Arkansas Governor Bill Clinton pledged to support the additional submarines in his presidential campaign against George Bush, a promise he repeated as he campaigned in the region in the winter of 1991 and I interviewed him on a bus during a snowstorm. *The Day* endorsed Clinton, although MacCluggage had reservations about his character and values. MacCluggage, nevertheless, wrote the endorsement.

IT WAS AT THIS time that the Mashantucket Pequot tribe was on the threshold of striking it rich after centuries of poverty, isolation, and adversity. Several members of the tribe had been struggling since the 1970s to reconstitute the exiled Mashantucket Pequots. The tribal council, under the leadership of Richard A. "Skip" Hayward, a former shipyard worker, made several unsuccessful tries to make money for the tribe in various enterprises, including lettuce cultivation, before discovering a winner in 1986: high-stakes bingo.

Two years later, Congress passed the Indian Gaming Act, a law that was intended to clarify federal policy on gambling on Indian reservations. Gambling had become a promising enterprise for the impoverished Indian population.

Indian gambling was attracting interest in a nation where many forms of gambling were against the law. The Indian gaming law encouraged rather than controlled new casino development, creating virtual enterprise zones in some locales for that activity. It opened the door to gambling on Indian reservations in states where games of chance already were allowed. The Mashantuckets, flush with capital from their successful high-stakes bingo, took advantage of the law and in 1990 announced plans to open a casino.

The state government went to the federal courts to fight the tribe and lost. Governor Lowell P. Weicker worked out an agreement that conceded to the tribe a right to have slot machines in return for which Connecticut would share the profits. Weicker theorized granting this monopoly would stop the spread of gambling and assure the state a cut in the revenue. Las Vegas gambling interests were trying to enter the state and focused their attention on the economically distressed city of Bridgeport.

The Day opposed casino gambling, but praised Weicker for the deal, which soon began to pour millions of dollars of slot machine revenues into the state treasury each year. The bonanza was highly appreciated in the political community. The deal was sealed a short time after Connecticut, under Weicker's leadership, had taken the unpopular step of levying a state income tax, a cause *The Day* had supported for years. The revenue from slot machines helped ease the impact of this new levy.

It was evident by 1993 that the two seemingly unrelated events, the end of the Cold War and the arrival of Indian casino gambling, were combining to change the southeastern corner of Connecticut beyond what anyone would have imagined. Electric Boat, which at its peak had employed more than thirty thousand tradesmen, draftsmen, and engineers, shrank to a fifth of that number before the end of the decade. At the same time, the Foxwoods Resort & Casino in Ledyard and a second casino in Montville opened by the Mohegan tribe in 1995 reached a combined employment that approached that of Electric Boat at its peak. The Mashantuckets' Foxwoods casino became the largest casino in the world. Many of the unemployed shipyard workers went to work there as dealers and in other jobs. Just as the shipyard had once competed for labor with other industries, the casinos started to siphon off labor from other businesses and became the major commercial power in the region.

The Day went to work on a special project that examined the story of the Pequots from the time of the Pequot Wars in the 1630s when the English had nearly wiped out the tribe. Maria Hileman, the projects editor, supervised the work and did much of the research and writing herself. It began:

Four centuries of isolation, rural poverty and racism are wellsprings of the Pequots' casinos as surely as their much-beloved Mashantucket woods are the setting.

But *The Day* also kept an eye on the intricate and exotic business the Pequots operated, realizing that the potential existed for corruption and penetration by organized crime. *The Day* covered the casino and Pequot tribe from several perspectives. The reporters who covered the towns in the vicinity of the casino wrote stories about a growing dispute over the tribe's attempts to add land to its reservation. Tribal land was exempt from state and local regulation and taxation. The business desk covered the casino, which was run by G. Michael "Micky" Brown, a former New Jersey prosecutor and gambling regulator. David Collins, the business reporter, was named reporter of the year and Penelope Overton, the town reporter who covered the tribe, was named rookie of the year by the New England Press Association in January 1994 for their coverage of the tribe's arrival on the scene and the development of the casino.

Prior to joining forces with the Mashantucket Pequots, Brown had helped fashion the New Jersey law that regulated the gambling industry in Atlantic City. He became a middleman between the Pequot tribe and the Lims, a Malaysian family that financed the Mashantucket casino when local blanks would not. When the casino opened, Skip Hayward placed Brown in charge and Brown brought in Alfred Luciani, another former New Jersey regulator, to be chief executive officer.

Under the compact between the state and the tribe, state police helped regulate the casino. They did background checks for licensing workers and contractors doing business with Foxwoods. The state police ran afoul of Brown and the Pequots when officers broke into a trailer that contained casino records, an action police later said was part of an investigation. Hayward complained to the governor, John G. Rowland. Tensions grew with the police and soon with *The Day*, which had begun to publish embarrassing stories about the casino. Reporter David Collins wrote a series about various individuals with organized crime connections who were hired by or doing business with the Pequots. But the story that irritated Brown the most had to do with him. Collins learned about an unusual delay in processing Brown's license to work in a casino.

Collins called Brown's office for a comment. Brown wasn't there. Collins left a message with a secretary, explaining the reason for his call. Later in the day, while Collins was meeting with Lance Johnson in the managing editor's office, Johnson got a call from the advertising department. Foxwoods had just cancelled all its advertising. The Mashantuckets later restored their advertising, but banned the sale of *The Day* on the reservation. When a *Day* truck entered the reservation, the tribal police detained the driver before escorting him off the property. This began a year-and-a-half-long standoff between the tribe and the newspaper in which *The Day* refused to carry the Indians' advertising as long as newspaper was banned from the reservation. The tribe claimed *The Day* had written untrue and unfair stories about links to organized crime. It bought a full-page in the Norwich *Bulletin* blasting *The Day* and asserting it employed a "zero tolerance" policy toward organized crime.

MacCluggage, who later was spurned by Hayward, responded in a column on June 8, 1997, that listed the facts and all the people with mob connections who had been hired by the casino. "If I were Tribal Chairman Skip Hayward," MacCluggage wrote, "I'd be concerned about how easy it has been for people with organized crime ties to land jobs at Foxwoods, and I'd have some questions for Foxwoods President G. Michael Brown and other executives who do the hiring." A year passed before the tribe let *The Day* back onto the reservation and during that time, *The Day* refused all the tribe's advertising. The casino needed the advertising to promote its Las Vegas style entertainment, including major exhibition boxing events and appearances by celebrities like Frank Sinatra. The two made up in 1997. The improved relations were evident when a tribal representative took part in planning a new magazine, *Mystic Coast & Country*, to promote area tourism that was published by *The Day*. The magazine was named after a tourism organization partly financed by the tribe.

THE DAY ASSUMED A resurgent leadership position in the 1990s. It influenced the development of regional organizations to promote economic growth and cooperation among the diverse towns. Connecticut's defense industry had subsidized a political system that produced widespread waste and inefficiency and high costs. The state could no longer afford to do that, *The Day* preached in editorials. *The Day* also took aim at badly managed development. In 1996, its staff led by Maria Hileman produced a series on suburban sprawl and brought in an expert speaker to lead a forum on controlling growth by concentrating development in city downtowns and rural villages.

New London in the early 1990s suffered the downfall of one of its most staid and important institutions, the New England Savings Bank. When Theodore Bodenwein said in 1916 and again in 1938 that he wanted his newspaper to be a New London institution, he had in mind institutions like the savings bank, which had been a leader in promoting the city's development. The

New London Redevelopment Agency reverentially excluded the edifices of the bank, as well as *The Day*, from its demolition plans. One of the city's greatest scandals and tragedies in the 1930s had been the suicide of Leroy Harwood, an officer in the Mariners Savings Bank, later absorbed by the Savings Bank of New London, which was in turn absorbed by New England Savings Bank. Harwood left a note confessing his embezzlements to make up for stock losses after the Stock Market Crash in 1929.

Shortly after Richard Creviston, the bank's president, retired with a large bonus and moved to Florida in 1993, the bank collapsed from imprudent investments made in the 1980s, including the purchase of another regional bank that failed. The savings bank's collapse caused outrage among the bank's many stockholders, including some of the local foundations, who lost all their investment. The collapse demoralized New London because the savings bank had been a pillar of the city's development since the whaling era. Thousands of small investors who had purchased shares in the initial issue of stock lost all their savings. Many were retirees on limited income.

Another collapse added to New London's misfortunes. In April 1993, one side of the State Pier crumbled. Built just before World War I, the pier had cost $1 million, but in the seventy-five years that followed its construction little additional money was invested in it. Its failures were many. The refusal by New London longshoremen to work overtime killed Waldo Clarke's plans to seize from New York the trade in shipping flour. World War I ended plans to make the city a major port for European trade, including an undersea one with German submarines like the *Deutschland.* The Depression ended a scheme for four-day ocean liners from New London to Europe. Foreign navies and the United States Navy made great use of the pier and by the end of World War II, the Navy had secured control of one side. In the 1950s, the *Fulton*, a giant Navy submarine tender, pulled up to the pier and stayed there. The pier became a submarine base for nuclear attack submarines.

Waldo Clarke, the pier's original ardent supporter, was also the last for a long time. When he died, a succession of political appointees had run the pier and their lack of enthusiasm compounded problems. There was little room around the pier to store cargoes and with the military leases, little space for ships to berth and be unloaded. New London had a fine deep-water port, but it required more dredging for it to attract the latest type of shipping. The dredging problem was solved when the Navy dug a deeper channel for deep-draft submarines and at the state's request detoured to the pier. With the end of the Cold War, the Navy retired the submarine tender *Fulton*, and removed its submarines from the pier, opening the possibility of using the entire pier for ocean shipping for the first time since 1917.

A political problem arose when part of the pier collapsed. State bureaucrats saw little future in the pier. New London officials, including City Manager Richard Brown, decided that the pier was a waste of money and the land nearby ought to be devoted to industrial development, which would produce more local taxes. They lobbied against repairing the pier. Several people strongly disagreed. These included Harold E. Shear, Jr., a retired Navy admiral and former Chief of Naval Operations, who battled to rebuild the pier. His allies included the former Central Vermont Railroad, which used tracks adjacent to the pier. The railroad had recently been taken over from the Canadian government by a Texas firm. The belief in New London was that Canada had clung to a nearby railroad pier to prevent New London from becoming a rival of its port in Halifax, Nova Scotia. *The Day*, which originally had supported the pier's construction and was Waldo Clarke's most passionate supporter, embraced Shear's cause. The newspaper conducted a public forum on the pier. McGinley let loose with an editorial that lambasted the New London politicians and administrators for being so shortsighted in desiring to shut down the pier. "Who made them king?" the headline asked.

> *Countless military battles have been fought over keeping deep-water ports open. But in New London, the local pols have learned nothing from history and are trying to give away one of the city's and region's finest assets, a port of entry at State Pier.*

Governor John G. Rowland's office in Hartford was flooded with mail-in coupons *The Day* ran with its editorial urging the state to reopen the pier. The state eventually invested nearly $30 million in restoring the pier, largely on the *Day's* uninterrupted faith that someday it would work.

THIRTY-THREE

The Legacy Endures

The newspaper's role is not to boost but to ask probing questions about the role other institutions should be playing.

—Reid MacCluggage, May 26, 1996

ON THE AFTERNOON OF February 3, 1998, a procession of men and women dressed in business clothes crossed the railroad tracks and filed across a parking lot on the New London waterfront to board the *John H*, a Long Island Sound ferry boat. They crowded into the main cabin, where a platform had been set up. Television cameras were mounted on either side of the cabin and radio microphones and wires cluttered the deck. John G. Rowland was seated on the platform, but the object of everyone's attention was not the first-term Republican governor but the striking, dark-haired woman next to him. Claire Gaudiani, president of Connecticut College since 1988 and head of the revitalized New London Development Corporation, was beaming. To her other side sat George Milne, head of the Pfizer pharmaceutical company's central research division in Groton and one of the college's trustees.

When all the invited guests were aboard, the ferry moved slowly into the harbor and circled while the personages on the platform joined in announcing that Pfizer planned to build a clinical research facility on an old industrial site on New London's waterfront. The special effects were unnecessary for producing excitement in New London, where the city's sense of destiny had been aroused again. It wasn't the first time. There had been many false hopes.

But this time it seemed real. The substance of the announcement was astounding enough for New London, where no major new industrial development had taken place for more than one hundred years. Equally significant, Gaudiani, the 55-year-old academic, who had been a Connecticut College student when Charles Shain was president, had brokered the deal, and emerged as a leader not to mention a heroine unlike any New London had seen in at least forty years. The only thing that diminished the impact of the event was that everyone in the room knew the story before it was officially made public. Despite Gaudiani's attempts to keep the development quiet until it was announced, *The Day* had published a detailed account of the Pfizer plans.

GAUDIANI HAD TAKEN A place along with Reid MacCluggage as a high-profile leader in the city's revitalization and their approaches and their strong wills were beginning to clash. Shortly after he arrived, in an effort to help New London, MacCluggage had marshaled the *Day's* resources behind an effort to turn the derelict Garde Theater into a regional performing arts center. The flight to the suburbs that had drained New London of its vitality in the 1960s had turned the old theater into a decaying, empty shell. In 1995, *The Day* pledged $500,000 toward the project, half this amount in free advertising. It was the second occasion a *Day* publisher had invested in the Garde. Theodore Bodenwein was one of the businessmen who bought the land where the theater is located and developed it as a business block with a movie and vaudeville theater just before the Stock Market Crash of 1929. The Garde Arts Center that marked its reincarnation in the 1980s became the new home for the Eastern Connecticut Symphony Orchestra, which had been performing in a high school auditorium. The center fulfilled a purpose that New London had been unable to do for more than twenty years: it brought crowds back to the downtown from the suburbs. It was not long before the civic effort to restore the Garde encompassed the whole city block Bodenwein and Fred Mercer had helped redevelop from the front yard of an old whaling family's estate.

The Day was also an early booster of a plan advanced by several defense workers to develop an educational center and camp concentrating on submarines and undersea exploration. The venture was called OceanQuest and was to include a hotel and conference center. When the idea first surfaced, editorials scolded government officials for not having the imagination to appreciate the potential of that idea. The city and state eventually embraced the proposal, and furnished $2 million in loans for OceanQuest. But the poorly managed project, as had many others in the city's history, went sour and the developers defaulted on their loan in 1997, leaving the city with the site, once the location of an old linoleum factory and before that, the Babcock Printing Press factory where one of the *Day's* early presses was assembled. Much of the blame for this fiasco and for the stalled efforts to develop the downtown was aimed at the city administration, particularly Richard Brown, the city manager, and Bruce Hyde, the development director. The newspaper's editorials both mirrored and reinforced a sentiment in the community that inertia in the city's politics and government bureaucracy were holding back the city's development.

Officials, on the other hand, faulted *The Day* for the newspaper's sometimes less than flattering portrayal of developments in the city. They were particularly irritated at McGinley's scolding editorials over the city's opposition to the State Pier plans. *The Day* fell further out of official grace when the editors took issue with local politicians over the disposal of property vacated by the Navy's sonar laboratory. The newspaper and the government officials found common ground only in a plan, developed in public meetings, to build a park along the ramshackle waterfront. *The Day* enthusiastically supported the idea, which would clear away the last of the rubble left by the 1938 hurricane and reopen the waterfront to the public for the first time since the whaling era.

In May 1996, *The Day* published a series of articles entitled "New London: Image and Reality" that exposed myths many in the suburbs subscribed to about life in New London. One of the articles dealt with what New Londoners felt was the *Day's* "negative coverage." Schools superintendent Rene Racette, who had been regularly criticized on the editorial page for the schools' low mastery test scores, accused *The Day* of unfairly comparing the city to richer school districts. The *Day's* response had been that Racette and other school officials were using poverty as an excuse for schools' poor performance, and continued to demand that the superintendent be held accountable for the test scores.

Brown, the city manager, said *The Day* always portrayed the city "as the glass half empty." While the other stories pointed to active neighborhood movements that were making progress against drugs and crime, critics said the *Day's* editors were out of touch with what was going on in the city. The popular theory for why this may have been true was that most of the *Day's* news and editorial staff didn't live in the city.

THE PFIZER IDEA STARTED to form in 1996. Rowland learned that the company intended to expand and was determined to keep that investment in the state. Pfizer had developed into one of the world's biggest pharmaceutical firms since the time Waldo Clarke had helped locate its plant in Groton after World War II. But the company almost had left Connecticut in the middle of a tax crisis in the early 1990s. Rowland and economic development officials saw the expansion as a way to cash in on the nation's growing biotechnology industry as well as benefit from the expansion of the Fortune 500 company.

The governor retained Jay Levin, the former New London mayor and at the time a lobbyist in the state Capitol, to work on a strategy to snare Pfizer. Levin served as a liaison among the state, Claire Gaudiani, and George Milne in arranging a deal for Pfizer to expand in New London. Milne was a college trustee and Levin had been a trustee on the board that hired Gaudiani. It's fair to say that while Levin didn't succeed as mayor at producing a downtown project, he played a crucial role in the giant Pfizer expansion in New London. Pfizer's board of directors approved the New London plan on January 21, 1998. Different versions exist about how the deal fell together.

The most colorful, and the one of record, was told by Gaudiani. It had almost a biblical quality. She said that as she approached her tenth year at the college, she retreated to a convent to meditate on her next role. She said her meditations led her to the idea of helping New London. She consulted with "elders" in the community, former leaders then late in life. They advised her to gather together leaders from her generation and lead them in rebuilding New London. During a chance meeting with Levin and Connecticut's top economic development official, Peter Eleff, Eleff challenged her to organize a group and search for a Fortune 500 company for New London. With Levin's help, she revived the New London Redevelopment Corporation. One of the directors she selected was Milne. At first half-seriously, but later earnestly, she tried to persuade Milne to ask the company to build its facility on an old industrial site in New London, next to the sewage treatment plant. He came to share her vision and sold the idea with difficulty to Pfizer's board of directors with help from the state government.

Whatever actually transpired, the results point to Gaudiani as one of the exceptional community leaders in the city's history, despite her controversial persona. MacCluggage admired Gaudiani. As the Connecticut College president, she was a refreshing change from her low-key predecessor, physicist Oakes Ames, who succeeded Charles Shain. In a 1999 interview, she told Stan DeCoster, "I'm in the academic world where there's an expectation of seriousness and deliberation, which I obviously appreciate and admire. But the world is full of playfulness and I'm playful." The first article *The Day* wrote about her alluded to her physical beauty. When she was whisked before the press when her appointment was announced in 1988, reporter Kyn Tolson itemized her clothing in detail and described her as "porcelain skinned." The physical description outraged some in the community who said the newspaper was being sexist and demeaned the new president. Her conduct didn't become any less uninhibited. At one elite social event in 1996, she wore a tight red dress. *Day* photographer Robert Patterson took a picture that captured her gyrating on the dance floor and the editors aroused further controversy in the straitlaced community by placing the evocative picture on the front page of the next day's edition.

When Gaudiani began to assert her leadership in New London, relations between her and *The Day* cooled. The development group barred *Day* reporters from meetings. This precipitated an escalating conflict between the corporation and *The Day*. The struggle unfolded at two different levels. While Johnson and other newsroom managers jockeyed to open up the meetings to the press, *The Day* appealed to the state Freedom of Information Commission and took the offensive on its editorial page. She told the *Day's* editorial board in December that the corporation didn't have to follow the state's Freedom of Information law because it was a private group. Morgan McGinley and Gaudiani went at each other on the pages of the newspaper early the next month.

> *Dr. Claire Gaudiani made a foolish gaffe when she closed a development group meeting to the public and press Oct. 24. She had revived the New London Development Corp. assumed its chairmanship and promised teamwork with the city. Then boom: she closed the meeting.*

"Morgan McGinley missed a chance to help make progress in New London with his ready, aim, fire column of November 2," she shot back in an article that was published a week later. If she had expected *The Day* to back down, she had seriously miscalculated. For the *Day's* editors, the Freedom of Information Law was sacrosanct. Ken Grube had helped frame the legislation. Deane Avery served on the state Freedom of Information Commission after he retired. Both Reid MacCluggage and Morgan McGinley were active in the foundation that supported the cause and created an annual freedom of information award in Deane Avery's name.

Tensions between Gaudiani and *The Day* got worse when the newspaper broke the story about Pfizer's plans before they were announced. Real estate agents already had been approaching owners near the site about buying their properties for the project. Gaudiani and Pfizer officials had been spotted touring the site. As *The Day* pieced together the story, Gaudiani made several unsuccessful attempts with the newspaper to delay the publication until the announcement. Judy Benson, the *Day's* City Hall reporter, prepared a long and detailed description that appeared just days before the announcement. "Claire was really pissed. But we gave some advance warning to some very vulnerable people," Lance Johnson said.

The Day—MacCluggage and Morgan McGinley in particular—came under attack from Gaudiani's supporters for the newspaper's irreverent attitude. A New London politician wrote a letter to the editor asserting that Gaudiani had done more for New London in a couple of years than *The Day* had during its entire history. I wrote a column responding that *The Day* had played a leading role in much of the city's development, including the establishment of Connecticut College. "*The Day* needs to get back to the idealism that inspired Theodore Bodenwein," Gaudiani remarked in an interview for this book. Gaudiani said she was hurt that *The Day* had not taken a more supportive role of the Development Corporation. She felt the newspaper was grandstanding. "That's different from leading," she said. She felt the newspaper should engage more in "civic journalism," a school of thought in which newspapers took the lead in civic development. *The Day* had its roots in such causes, she said. MacCluggage had this to say:

> *The renewal of New London needs a point person. She couldn't have been a better selection. She's tireless, fearless, articulate. What she's doing is great. I just don't like the way she's doing it. I don't like the secrecy that cloaks the NLDC. The paper is also worried about boondoggles and abuse that arise when plans are made behind closed doors by the few. New London has been through a zillion failures, one flop after another. I see* The Day *as an independent check on what's happening to be sure everything is proper. That's the contribution the newspaper can make to its community.*

Although *The Day* was attacked for belaboring the open-government issue, it continued its attacks on the issue. When the New London Development Corporation appealed a finding against it, *The Day* fought the appeal. The newspaper's position reflected a major difference between Bodenwein, who boosted development projects and was an insider on many development deals, and MacCluggage, who kept a distance from private business ventures. The bitter relations between Gaudiani and the newspaper illustrated that the college was no longer a sacred cow.

Connecticut Governor John Rowland went to the newspaper's support, warning Gaudiani that the state would withhold financial support for the group until the corporation agreed to obey the state's open-government laws. The corporation acquiesced to the request. But she also shot off a letter to MacCluggage, and sent copies to other editors and reporters, in which she invited MacCluggage and others at the newspapers to participate in a meeting with William Taylor, retired publisher of the Boston *Globe* and a former trustee at Connecticut College, to discuss civic journalism:

> *I am hopeful that on behalf of the city of New London and its great past, we can move forward as fellow citizens in the new year, the new century and the new millennium.* The Day *has played a powerful role in the city's past. I am looking forward to its playing an equally powerful role in the city's future, appreciated by New London citizens as wise, insightful and aspirational for the future of the city.*

MacCluggage was out of town when the letter arrived and others received it. When he returned, he wrote back refusing the offer:

> *I wish you had consulted me before asking Bill Taylor to come to* The Day *for a discussion of civic journalism. I have the highest regard for Mr. Taylor, and you have put me in the position of turning him down. I don't like that. Had you contacted me first to ask whether I would be amenable, I would have explained that the staff and I already are very familiar with the notion of civic journalism. It is apparent you are unaware of the leadership role* The Day *played in the early discussions of the concept nearly a decade ago.*

THE DAY WAS JUST as unyielding in its coverage of nuclear safety issues when tangling with Northeast Utilities, the electric monopoly in Connecticut and operator of four aging nuclear power plants in eastern Connecticut. The newspaper's reporting on Indian gambling and nuclear safety prompted a cover story in the New York *Times* Connecticut section on December 20, 1998, that ran under a headline, "New London's Feisty Newspaper, *The Day*":

> *Over the years, everyone from blue-chip corporations to hometown officials has lambasted the newspaper's coverage. As one of the fast-shrinking group of independent daily newspapers,* The Day *prides itself on its autonomy and willingness to uncover facts, regardless of how unpopular they may prove with major advertisers or subscribers.*

Northeast Utilities had brought together a number of local utilities in southern New England and had been one of the first in the country to use the technology developed in building nuclear submarines to generate commercial electric power. The first commercial nuclear plant was built on the Connecticut River in East Haddam. Northeast built three more plants in the 1960s and 1970s on the site of an abandoned granite quarry in Waterford, the town west of New London.

Nobody, including *The Day*, worried about this. After all, the Navy's nuclear submarine program had shown that nuclear power could be safe. *The Day* had welcomed the possibilities of the peaceful use of the atom since the *Nautilus* was launched. The plants, with their taxable and expensive equipment, were embraced as a bonanza for the rural community of Waterford, which had had no tax base to speak of. Waterford's citizens were more receptive to the nuclear plants than they were to the Eugene O'Neill Theater, an innovative complex for emerging playwrights and actors. The plants brought jobs and tax dollars to the community, while all the theater brought was decadent artists, many old-timers in town felt.

By the early 1970s, the two concrete-encased nuclear plants on Niantic Bay were providing most of the electricity Connecticut used and much of New England's power supply. A third plant was under construction. The plants also provided jobs for retiring Navy officers and enlisted men who had served on nuclear submarines based in New London and Groton. And they provided Waterford with a tax bounty that was the envy of New London and other communities. It wasn't long before Waterford's volunteer fire companies were equipping themselves with state-of-the-art fire engines. By the 1980s, Waterford had the most expensive public schools in Connecticut. By the 1990s, it was purchasing Volvo police cruisers.

Lelan Sillin, the CEO of Northeast Utilities, was widely respected in the nuclear power field. As the use of nuclear power expanded, Northeast, under Sillin's stewardship, gained a reputation for excellence. It was earned. Sillin emphasized safety at any cost. The agency that regulated public utilities in Connecticut made it easy to invest in safety by agreeing to most of the rate increases the utility sought to pay for its new plants. But other developments foreshadowed problems for the utility.

The Arab oil embargo in the 1970s contributed to rising energy costs. These boosted electric rates across the country and added to a serious inflation. Connecticut Governor Ella T. Grasso responded by promising to hold the line on the rising cost of electricity. The result was the creation of a stronger regulatory agency in the state called the Department of Public Utility Control. The reforms created a consumer counsel, who was a watchdog for consumer interests.

Early in 1979, a catastrophe struck a nuclear power plant at Three Mile Island in central Pennsylvania that shattered the notion that nuclear power was the most promising way to free the country of its dependence on oil in producing electricity. On March 19, an inoperative valve released thousands of gallons of coolant from the plant's reactor. This caused thousands of nuclear fuel rods to melt and burn through the lining of the reactor chamber. Only by the grace of God did the meltdown burn its way into the ground and not release massive amounts of radioactivity into the atmosphere. The Three Mile Island disaster prompted Congress to demand stringent new safety standards for nuclear power plants. These standards further compounded the costs of a third nuclear plant that was under construction in Waterford. Such new regulations and inflation drove up the cost of the plant sixfold before it was finished in 1984, virtually obliterating the argument that nuclear power was a cheap alternative to that generated by fossil fuel. The end of the oil crisis in the 1980s finally seemed to bury this argument for nuclear power.

A third development that would change the course of Northeast Utilities occurred during the administration of Ronald Reagan. Reagan entered office on a promise to remove the burden of government regulation from business, and discussions began during his administration over deregulating utilities and opening the field of commercial electric power to competition. At the same time that Northeast confronted the rising costs of its third Millstone power plant and faced a new state regulatory agency intent on holding down rates, it looked forward to the day when it would have to compete with other companies for the sale of electricity.

Sillin retired in 1983 and later became a probate judge in Old Lyme. His successors set out to contain the utility's costs so that the company could continue to reward stockholders under its new restraints and eventually sell electricity at competitive rates in an open market. The trailblazer among these new executives was Bernard Fox, who had been in charge of the utility's nuclear operations and took over as chairman of the board in 1986. Fox's ascent signaled a dramatic change in emphasis. The company was staffed by former nuclear Navy officers who had been trained under Admiral Hyman Rickover to believe that safety was paramount at any cost. That had been the so-called "Rickover effect." More than anything, Rickover feared an accident that would jeopardize the future of the nuclear Navy. But under Fox the emphasis at Northeast changed from safety at any cost to cost-effectiveness. *The Day* realized this and reported on it long before the issue became common knowledge outside the *Day's* readership area.

Because of the complexity of nuclear power plants and because most plants were located in out-of-the-way areas, the safety of nuclear plants had not been raised as an important national issue until the Three Mile Island incident. The industry and the Nuclear Regulatory Commission were required to maintain records of its malfunctions and mishaps in local public libraries, but the voluminous technical documents were unfathomable to the casual observer.

The Day had assigned reporters to cover the Millstone plants starting in the late 1970s. In one of the newspaper's early investigations, Lance Johnson and Suzanne Trimel disclosed dangerous lapses in safety regarding the exposure of nuclear workers to radioactivity. This danger arose among workers who took part in the refueling of plants around the country, one of the most hazardous jobs in the industry. These were well-paid transient workers, and Johnson and Trimel found that the nuclear utilities were not monitoring their cumulative radioactive exposure as they moved from job to job. The newspaper stepped up its coverage after Three Mile Island. In 1982, Garrett Condon and Steve Fagin prepared a three-part series that disclosed safety lapses in the construction of the third Millstone plant.

Reporter Robert Hamilton later found in the records at the Waterford Public Library evidence that the utility was cutting corners and not operating the plants safely. The company was, among other things, racing through the risky process of replacing fuel rods to minimize the time the plants were not in operation, for it cost the company millions of dollars to buy replacement power. "Whistleblowers," employees and former employees who had called attention to safety shortcomings at the plants, began providing Maura Casey, who had joined the editorial page staff in 1985, information about careless maintenance, shortcuts being taken to economize, poor training, and recriminations against employees who brought any of this to the attention of the company. Casey, a young mother, stayed up nights after her children were put to bed reading technical documents furnished by her sources. *The Day* also took aim at the Nuclear Regulatory Commission for lax oversight over the plants.

Many of the whistleblowers had formerly served in the nuclear Navy and had become disillusioned with the company's cavalier attitude toward safety. Hamilton's reporting and Casey's editorials were clearly upsetting the company in the early 1990s. A steady stream of utility officials, including Bernard Fox, paid visits to the newspaper. On one occasion, Fox demanded to meet privately with MacCluggage. The publisher responded that he would be willing to meet with the Northeast head only if Hamilton, Casey, and the rest of the editorial board could be present. Fox called off the meeting.

The editors listened politely each time the company visited. But the Northeast officials were unable to document any inaccuracies in the *Day's* stories or editorials. These included a highly technical editorial in 1993 that detailed the sloppy and dangerous handling of a leak in a critical valve in the cooling system of one of the plants. The company banned the sale of *The Day* at the Millstone station and purchased full-page advertisements in *The Day* defending the company's performance. In the fall of 1996, *Time* magazine published a cover story detailing the utility's problems with its nuclear plants and the recriminations against the whistleblowers, including a high-ranking former engineer, George Galatis. Galatis' photograph appeared on the cover of the magazine. Although the magazine did not acknowledge the *Day's* role, most of the facts in the article already had appeared in the local newspaper. That same year, the NRC ordered the company to shut down the reactors and the first of these wasn't brought back on line until two years later. The first unit built at Millstone was shut down permanently.

THE MODERNIZATION OF THE *Day's* plant raced forward after the recession-caused delay in the early 1990s. The fourth-floor offices were completed in 1994. They cost nearly $500,000. MacCluggage, Alcino Almeida, and Dick Willis moved into suites overlooking the Thames River. MacCluggage's secretary, Donna Lloret, supervised the decorating and furnishings. The project provided luxurious quarters for the editorial page editors and the executives as well as a public auditorium for use by *The Day* and civic groups. The board moved into a new Bodenwein Room with a view of the water, elegant furniture, silver services, and recessed lighting. The room was lined with oil paintings of earlier leaders of the newspaper: Theodore Bodenwein, Orvin Andrews, Bar Colby, Wes Hammond, and Deane Avery.

When the work on the fourth floor was completed, each editorial writer had his or her own modern office with windows overlooking the downtown. *The Day* had and has three members on its editorial staff, an unusual number for a newspaper its size. A fourth position was added to process letters to the editor, which averaged more than one hundred twenty a month. The number of letters had increased tremendously after Morgan McGinley decided to fill the page next to the editorial column with them. The newsroom moved into airy, well-lighted modern quarters on the third floor. Lance Johnson's office had the same striking view of the river that MacCluggage enjoyed just overhead. The *Day's* new magazine, *Mystic Coast & Country*, occupied the old executive offices of Theodore Bodenwein on the second floor. The magazine, a glossy publication featuring the area's attractions, was a response to the increasing importance of tourism.

The Day used its unusually large news staff to enhance the depth of its local coverage. The arts news staff increased to four, including a music writer and the graphics department did most of the layout work in the arts sections. The business section had three reporters, including one who specialized in casino coverage. It had food, education, and Internet editors. In 1994, *The Day* hired Tammy-Jo Ferdula, only its fourth librarian since George Grout started a library in 1929. Each of the librarians had advanced the library from Grout's card file to Claire Peckham's clip files. Tammy-Jo Ferdula developed the newspaper's first electronic library to store stories in a computer database.

The Day had become one of New London's biggest taxpayers with a building complex that occupied three times the space it had possessed when Bodenwein died and that contained the most modern publishing machinery available. The newspaper had a new Goss offset press and an electronic photo laboratory. It also had "pagination" computers, installed at a cost of more than $1.2 million that enabled editors to lay out pages electronically and send them completed to the composing room. The changes in technology had reduced the composing room, once a bustling and noisy scene of activity, to a quiet handfull of technicians. This change also added to the editors' burden. They now were engaged in production as well as writing and editing tasks. Copy editors seated at electronic paginating machines now did what the composing room had done: setting type and photographs on pages. An event that marked the end of the printers' era at the newspaper occurred in March 1997. Editors were given the go-ahead to send, by the click of a computer mouse button, finished pages directly to a machine in the composing room to be engraved onto printing plates for the press. Out of old habits, the few printers left behind still kept an eye out for mistakes and let the editors upstairs know when they found any. Once there had been more than fifty printers. Now there were fewer than ten.

The staff in the newsroom numbered seventy, whereas the Norwich *Bulletin* had a news staff of fewer than fifty and other newspapers the *Day's* size averaged between forty and fifty. *The Day* had a deputy managing editor, and five assistant managing editors, eight photographers, a four-member graphics department, an eight-member sports staff. It had a projects editor, Maria Hileman, who had special reporting projects underway continuously. Some of the subjects examined were life at the new casinos, which operated round the clock; problem gambling; controversial plans by Amtrak, the national

Above, The Mashantucket Pequot tribe became a major economic force and *The Day's* biggest story when it built the world's largest casino in rural southeastern Connecticut in the early 1990s.
Sean D. Elliot, The Day

Above, Theodore Bodenwein was one of the original investors when the Garde Theater was built, and Reid MacCluggage and *The Day* were leaders in its revival as the Garde Arts Center 60 years later.
The Day

Above, Connecticut fell in love with the University of Connecticut's championship women's basketball team in the 1990s and *The Day* followed its every move. *Sean D. Elliot, The Day*

Left, Connecticut College President Claire Gaudiani stood out in conventional New London with her uninhibited style. *The Day* ran this photo of her dancing at a celebration of New London's 350th anniversary in 1996. *Robert Patterson, The Day*

Above, The New London skyline, dominated by the Mohican hotel, left, and three church steeples, from left, First Congregational Church, Second Congregational Church, and St. James Episcopal Church.
Skip Weisenburger, The Day

Left, New London's fortunes seem to have turned around finally when Pfizer Inc., one of the world's largest pharmaceutical companies, broke ground for a major facility in the city in 1998. John Rowland, the governor of Connecticut, and Claire Gaudiani are at the center of the photo.
Skip Weisenburger, The Day

Upper right, Submarine building slowed to a trickle after the Cold War. Electric Boat workers wave as *Columbia* is launched into the Thames River in September 1994.
Robert Patterson, The Day

Lower right, This memorial in Groton to the more than 3,000 men who lost their lives in submarine service during World War II was among causes *The Day* supported.
Sean D. Elliot, The Day

Below, The village of Mystic was the scene of numerous big fires *The Day* wrote about, including this one in March 2000.
Tim Martin, The Day

bove, Shipbuilding remained a part of the scene *The Day* covered, from nuclear submarines to a replica f the 19th century schooner *Amistad*, shown here at its launching in Mystic in March 2000.
acquie Glassenberg, The Day

Left, The textile industry gradually slipped from the scene in Eastern Connecticut after World War II, but the elegant buildings it left behind remained in the news in efforts to preserve them and in their loss in fires like this one at the Ashland Mill in Jewett City in the late 1990s.
Sean D. Elliot, The Day

Left, The waterfront village of Mystic became such an attraction to tourists that its name became more familiar to outsiders than New London's.
Sean D. Elliot, The Day

Above, *The Day* entered the 21st century with a board made up entirely of members selected by Reid MacCluggage, standing at left. No chief executive of the newspaper since Theodore Bodenwein's death has enjoyed that advantage. The others are, seated from left, Maureen Croteau, Antoinette Dupont, and David Nol
The others standing, from left, are Lynda Smith, George White and Richard Willis.
Skip Weisenburger, The Day

Left, *The Day's* circulation was more than 40,000 for its daily editions and nearly 47,000 on Sundays as it entered the year 2000. The newspaper was distributed in 49 towns in three states, Connecticut, Rhode Island and New York, where Fisher's Island residents received the newspaper every day on the ferry boat.
Dana Jensen, The Day

Above, *The Day*'s news staff numbered nearly 72 as the 20th century drew to a close.
Skip Weisenburger, The Day

Left, Lance C. Johnson, managing editor, and Karen Ward, art director, discuss the design of an education page cover.
Skip Weisenburger, The Day

Above, *The Day*'s directors eschewed the idea of building outside New London and instead expanded to the south of its home on Main Street, renamed Eugene O'Neill Drive in the 1970s. The land was made available by urban renewal. The original building is at the far left. The structure at the far right was constructed for a new press in the late 1980s. Between the two are an addition built in the early 1960s and a park named in memory of Barnard L. Colby, the former publisher.
Robert Patterson, The Day

Above, The building where *The Day* started in 1881 is still standing and houses an electronics store.
Robert Patterson, The Day

passenger rail corporation, to provide high-speed electrified service through the region; the criminalization of mental health care; youth problems among the newly rich Indians; abuse in nursing homes; the fate of the Portuguese fishing community in the village of Stonington after the rich moved in; managed health care; the controversy over a proposal to build a huge theme park in the rural community of North Stonington; and conflicts of interest over development in the rural community of Griswold, in the heart of *Bulletin* territory. The *Day's* last project in 1999, completed in October, was an examination of race and its impact on the lives of the people in southeastern Connecticut, including the *Day's* successes and failures in hiring minority writers and providing a voice for minorities. The series was published in four special sections.

Hileman also was in charge of entering contests and *The Day* harvested awards in unusual abundance. Between 1986, when *The Day* won its first New England regional newspaper of the year award, and 1991, it won six such awards from the two major regional newspaper organizations, the New England Press Association and the New England Newspaper Association. The newspaper began to win national recognition. The American Society of Newspaper Editors said *The Day* was among ten Examples of Excellence in the nation, and the *Columbia Journalism Review* included the newspaper among the best one hundred in the United States, placing it in the top six percent. *The Day* also was among the ten finalists for The Associated Press Managing Editors Association public service award for a series on economic restructuring after the Cold War in 1992. Steve Slosberg won national awards for his columns. *The Day* began covering religion in a weekly section called "Beliefs," and Lisa McGinley, Morgan McGinley's wife, won a national award as a religion writer.

As the newspaper's revenues rose, the *Day* trustees increased their annual contributions to the Bodenwein Public Benevolent Foundation. In the ten years between 1987 and 1997, The Day Publishing Company's dividends added nearly \$3 million to civic causes through the foundation. After Elizabeth Miles' death in 1978, the Bodenwein Fund and the region's other largest charitable fund, the Palmer Fund, were placed in the hands of a community distribution committee. The combined funds became one of the region's largest single source of charitable funds. The combined Palmer and Bodenwein funds produced a steady stream of money for museums, hospitals, arts, and social projects unparalleled in the region's history. Some of the funds were used to preserve on microfilm the deteriorating editions of the *Morning Telegraph*, the newspaper Bodenwein helped found that later had been the *Day's* most formidable rival.

Copies of the newspaper, which included the earliest examples of Eugene O'Neill's writing, were decaying in the attic of the public library and at the New London County Historical Society.

MacCluggage and Morgan McGinley each became active in national professional organizations in the 1980s, as Bar Colby had been when he was a director of the American Newspaper Publishers Association in the 1960s. MacCluggage facilitated this activity by a liberal policy of financing travel for the staff. McGinley followed in Kenneth Grube's footsteps in the National Conference of Editorial Writers (NCEW), an organization of which Gordon Bodenwein had been a charter member in 1948. MacCluggage became a director of The Associated Press Managing Editors association in 1987. McGinley and MacCluggage rose through the ranks to lead the groups as presidents in the same year, 1998. The same year, Maura Casey was elected a director of the NCEW. Most of the officers in these groups were from much larger newspapers.

MacCluggage also remade the board of directors. The board retreated from the day-to-day details of the newspaper's operation and became engaged more in planning. He ended the practice, introduced by trustees Francis McGuire and Charles Shain, of involving the board in the newspaper's political endorsements. At the same time, he assumed a stronger hand than his predecessors had had in the endorsement of political candidates. While he did not take part in most of the local endorsements, he exerted his authority in congressional and presidential races. His philosophical and personal differences with the liberal Congressman Sam Gejdenson and his distaste for Bill Clinton rivaled Bodenwein's strong feelings against Franklin Roosevelt and the New Deal in their intensity. MacCluggage had evolved into a libertarian, and his jaundiced views toward government, which found their way into the thinking of the editorial page, disappointed and angered many of the *Day's* liberal readers who had become accustomed to the policies of Ken Grube.

Al Almeida retired in 1997 and was replaced as a director and trustee by Richard Willis. That left MacCluggage with a board made up for the first time entirely of his own appointees. No publisher other than Bodenwein had enjoyed that advantage. Three were women: Maureen Croteau, the head of the journalism department at the University of Connecticut; Lynda Blackmon Smith, a psychologist and the first black member; and Antoinette Dupont, who had been the chief judge of the state appellate court. His appointments also had included William Pedace, a former public relations director at Electric Boat and later development director at Lawrence & Memorial Hospital, who resigned in 1996. George White, the founder of the Eugene O'Neill Theater Center in Waterford, and David Nolf, a defense-company executive, became directors. The trustees as the decade ended were MacCluggage, Willis, Croteau, Smith, and Dupont.

MacCluggage and the board also changed the composition of the board from what had been established in the Bodenwein will in one important respect. In 1994 and again four years later, the trustees skirted the provision which called for a representative of the *Day's* bank, originally the National Bank of Commerce, to sit on the board. When Walter Baker retired from the board as the bank representative, the board appointed William Pedace, who had no association with the bank. When Pedace resigned four years later, he was replaced by Maureen Croteau, also with no bank credentials.

Rather than taking the risk of trying to change the will, the trustees followed the provisions of the existing will in appointing nonbank trustees, obtaining the consent of the Probate Court and the bank. The bank had changed hands three times by the time Baker retired and a fourth time when Pedace left the board. The bank, which still had the *Day's* business, was under the control of Shawmut Bank in Boston in 1994, and Fleet Bank in 1998. MacCluggage said the trustees felt the provision was meaningless since the banks were based out of the *Day's* region and could appoint trustees who were not from the community the newspaper served. This would be valid unless Bodenwein and the original trustees had intended by this provision to guard the financial interests of the foundation and look after the business of Earle Stamm's bank.

The consolidation of banks was similar to that which continued to change the character of the newspaper industry. As the end of the 20th century approached, fewer than three hundred independent and locally owned daily newspapers were left in the United States. A third *Day* competitor, the Westerly *Sun* just across the Rhode Island border from southeastern Connecticut, was purchased by the Meriden (Connecticut) *Record-Journal*, where MacCluggage's friend and former *Day* managing editor, James Smith, was editor. Now all three of the *Day's* daily newspaper competitors, the Norwich *Bulletin*, the *Hartford Courant*, and Westerly *Sun*, were owned by out-of-town companies. Along with the *Sun* went the *Mystic River Press*, a weekly based in Mystic.

The Day proceeded, in a pattern that had become familiar, to protect its territory from new competition. It set up a bureau in Pawcatuck, near the Westerly border, and hired the *Mystic River Press's* only reporter, Michael Costanza. McGinley distributed maps of Rhode Island to his staff and both the newsroom and editorial page showed more interest in the contested territory of Stonington, Mystic, and Westerly.

The Day approached another competitor with less confidence and familiarity: the Internet. Dramatic changes in technology threatened the newspaper's advertising market, circulation, and, arguably, its very future. The newspaper was sluggish and uncertain as it attempted to construct a place for itself in this mysterious new world. But, as usual, it sought guidance in Theodore Bodenwein's will. The first words it placed on its new Web site in 1997 described the history of The Day Trust and the unusual mandate under which *The Day* had operated since January 1939.

The publisher and directors knew that, at least, they could approach the future with a degree of assurance they had never felt at other turning points in the history of The Day Trust. The legal threats that had hung over the newspaper in the 1940s when Gordon Bodenwein fought his father's will, and in the 1970s and 1980s, when the Internal Revenue Service challenged the propriety of the trust, no longer posed a threat. *The Day* occupied a modern plant in the heart of New London, where old hopes and confidence had been rekindled. The financial limitations that had held it back were now a distant memory. The managers and directors who had had to contend with those obstacles had been replaced with a new group of men and women without such memories or ties to the past. *The Day* was in good financial health, although the media revolution taking place had begun to erode its advertising revenues. Automobile dealers, for example, were starting to divide their advertising budgets among cable television, the Internet, and newspapers.

THE CHARTER BODENWEIN HAD left to preserve his life's work had proven to be a remarkable plan of action for the newspaper. Each succeeding generation of managers followed it with increasing confidence and fruitfulness. Orvin Andrews and the first trustees had the task of defending it against Gordon and piloting it through the end of the Depression and the war years. Bar Colby led a battle for control of Groton and the suburbs and restored some of the leadership that had been lost when Bodenwein died. He and his successors, Deane Avery and Wesley Hammond, were assisted by Francis McGuire, the influential New London power broker, in guiding the newspaper through a period of recovery and modernization. The newspaper, with renewed confidence, pursued a course of modern and aggressive journalism that began to earn the newspaper respect outside the territory it covered. Reid

MacCluggage, the first outsider to preside over *The Day*, pried it loose from its remaining restraints and enlarged its horizons. *The Day* took on the character of a metropolitan newspaper found in much larger cities than New London. But unlike all but a few of those metropolitan dailies, *The Day* was still locally owned and operated. The dividends from its steadily rising profits were invested directly in the community rather than returned to stockholders.

After fifteen years in charge, MacCluggage began planning for his retirement scheduled for 2001. To prepare the board for the search for his successor, he instructed the members to reread Theodore Bodenwein's will, where MacCluggage and his predecessors had found most of the answers to the questions that arose in guiding the newspaper forward.

Sixty years had passed since Bodenwein, the German shoemaker's son-turned-publisher, had died, leaving control of *The Day* to the employees rather than to his family. A fourth generation was preparing to pass on his legacy to the next generation. Bodenwein's instructions prepared during the summer and fall of 1938 were still the guiding force. The only things that could possibly subvert their continued fulfillment were, as Patrick Mullarkey, the lawyer who had presented the IRS case against *The Day*, suggested, the shortcomings of the men and women entrusted to carry them out.

The government's lawyer in the IRS case accurately had pointed to the vulnerabilities of the Bodenwein trust. The stewards of the trust could, and actually did at times, take advantage of the arrangement to reward themselves. Executives could take care of relatives and feather their own nests unfettered by the usual restraints of a stockholding corporation. Watchdogs occasionally appeared nevertheless to check some of these impulses. Edna Bodenwein, the widow, and trustee Evan Hill called attention to abuses of power by the trustees and managers. Francis McGuire kept an eye on the Avery and Colby families, even while he also looked after his own interests. Walter Baker looked out for the Bodenwein Foundation as the bank's representative on the board. But *The Day* entered the 21st century without a bank representative, an annoying heir, or a gadfly quite as vocal as Evan Hill. The importance of guarding against abuses from self-interest presents one of the greatest tests to the future generations of trustees, directors, and managers. Yet the Bodenwein will at least still provides a clear direction, and enjoys the force of law for any member of the public, employee, or member of the board to invoke, in the Probate Court if necessary. Mullarkey assumed the worst of the trustees, but succeeding generations of *Day* trustees, despite their individual shortcomings, have been indoctrinated in the will and attempted to follow its intent. It is remarkable, considering the temptations a profitable newspaper without stockholders posed, how close Theodore Bodenwein's successors remained faithful to his wishes.

ONE OF THE REMARKABLE things about Theodore Bodenwein's will is its brevity. In its published form, it's only fourteen pages long on small pages with large type. Yet in that brief space, it took care of the immediate problem of who would run the newspaper for an indefinite future, made provisions for his family, and charted the course of *The Day* for the rest of the century and beyond.

The trustees looked after themselves in many ways, including hiring relatives onto the *Day* payroll. But they also did everything Bodenwein told them to do. They tried to pay the employees liberally, took care of the plant, added onto it, bought the latest equipment, and tried to run a newspaper that was more than just another business.

The Day was a profitable business. Like any good newspaper, it confronted and subdued competitors that entered its territory. Unlike ordinary businesses, it plowed more of its profits than normal back into the business and shared its dividends with civic causes.

The will is like a time capsule. Bodenwein's values as a newspaperman, ingrained in him from the time he was a printer's apprentice in New London in 1881, are spelled out in crisp English in the 1938 document. They remained in the consciences of successive generations of managers and trustees, in some more than others. Though *The Day* grew in sophistication and the breadth of its interests, it remained true to the cause of developing the port of New London and promoting the region's material progress in other ways, as he had set out to do. Trustees and some of the employees can recite passages of the will from memory. They may argue about its meaning, but basically, they have been guided by it. Not many publishers can say with any confidence that the values they consider most important will be on the tips of the tongue and foremost in the minds of their successors generations later.

The will also has protected the newspaper from the threat of chain ownership, an eventuality Bodenwein began to fear as early as 1916. Frank Munsey struck fear in the heart of the young publisher from the time the newspaper's landlord almost evicted *The Day* in the 1890s. Bodenwein feared that outside interests wouldn't care about the parochial causes of New London and the men and women who worked for him. *The Day* cannot be sold unless it becomes unprofitable, something that still seems highly unlikely. Nobody but the

Bodenwein Foundation can benefit from its sale, and the foundation technically no longer has a vote. The last threat to this arrangement was removed when *The Day* won its case against the Internal Revenue Service in 1984.

Finally, Bodenwein dealt with the problem of stockholders. Edna and Gordon were the closest the newspaper came to having watchful stockholders after Theodore's death. And they were little more than an annoyance. There are virtually no stockholders other than the trust. Nobody other than the newspaper and the charitable foundation can benefit from holding down costs. This has given the *Day's* managers a freedom to concentrate the revenue of the newspaper on making a better newspaper, highly unusual in today's free marketplace of newspaper publishing.

Acknowledgments

I am indebted to Reid MacCluggage, editor and publisher of *The Day*, and the *Day's* directors for the opportunity to write this book and to my editors, Neild Oldham and Susan Munger, for their help and encouragement. I relied largely on original sources. The most important of these was *The Day* itself, from its first edition July 2, 1881, until the present. Theodore Bodenwein left a large body of historical and autobiographical material on the pages of his newspaper, particularly in his "Tattler" columns. Anniversary and special editions, especially the one marking the 25th anniversary of Bodenwein's purchase of *The Day* on September 13, 1916; the 40th anniversary edition on October 30, 1921; and the monumental one marking the newspaper's 50th year in July 6, 1931, during the onset of the Great Depression, were rich sources of history from Bodenwein's and the newspaper's perspective.

In the navigating through back editions of the newspaper over many years, I benefited from the systematic and painstaking work of the *Day's* librarians of the past: George Grout, Phyllis Bankel and Claire Peckham. In addition, Elisabeth Bohlen, in research financed by a Bodenwein grant, produced a detailed index of the newspaper from 1881-1896. Grout created an indexing system in 1929 that was continued by Bankel. Peckham developed a clipping file morgue, ending the loose index-card system in 1977. Tammy-Jo Ferdula, the *Day's* current librarian, has developed an electronic library. She was a great help in directing me to materials, as well as in keeping the newspaper's finicky microfilm machine operating.

Other early New London newspapers provided important pieces of the story, principally the *Daily Star*, the *Morning Chronicle*, the *Evening Telegram* and the *Morning Telegraph*. I made extensive use of a handwritten index of stories in these newspapers, as well as others, laboriously compiled in longhand by the late Harold R. Cone, president of the New London County Historical Society, Inc., from 1974 to 1979 (and a high school classmate of Gordon Bodenwein). The index is on file in the Custom House maritime museum in New London. The *Star*, *Chronicle*, *Telegram* and *Telegraph* are preserved in their original state at the historical society's headquarters, the Shaw-Perkins Mansion in New London, and in the New London Public Library archives.

Local historians Lucille Showalter, Dale Plummer, Carol Kimball, Sally Ryan, and Alma Wies contributed invaluable information and insight and helped fill gaps left by the absence of a detailed, coherent written record of the area's history.

The New London Public Library, Groton Public Library, Connecticut State Library, New Jersey State Library, Trenton, New Jersey, Public Library, G. W. Blunt White Library at Mystic Seaport and Charles E. Shain Library at Connecticut College had many of the materials and documents used in this book. I am particularly grateful to Marcia E. Stuart, head of adult services at the New London Public Library; Brian Rogers, the special collections librarian at the Shain Library, Lucille Showalter, president of the New London Maritime Society and director of the Custom House museum; Groton reference librarian Elisabeth Bohlen; Charles Webster, the local history librarian at the Trenton public library; Barry Moreno, a National Park Service librarian at the Ellis Island Immigration Museum; and Alice Sheriff, curator and director of the New London County Historical Society.

Donald B. Mitchell, of Waterford, Connecticut, provided me with a wealth of information in the form of the personal papers of Edna Bodenwein preserved from her estate. His mother, Josephine Mitchell, a close friend of Edna's, had been the executor. These materials included extensive and candid correspondence between the publisher's wife and directors at *The Day* and valuable estate and financial records pertaining to *The Day* as well as personal correspondence and records related to her divorce from Victor Heimbucher and her relationship with Bodenwein. Other fruitful sources were the personal papers of Lieutenant Governor Ernest E. Rogers, a Bodenwein contemporary and friend, preserved among the Shain Library's special collections, files of *Day* trustee Thomas E. Troland, which were provided to me to me by his nephew, John A. Troland, and extensive materials about the life of Waldo Clarke gathered and assembled by Alma Wies, his daughter. Jack DeGange, son of John DeGange, was a great help in furnishing access to his late father's voluminous papers.

I used public records at the New London City Hall, Groton Town Hall, and the New London-Waterford Probate Court. I used city directories, census records, and local land records extensively to trace the lives of some of the early characters in the book. Genealogical material about the Bodenwein family came from the family research archives of Church of Jesus Christ Latter Day Saints. I am indebted to Robert Albert, Jr., of Bakersfield, California, a genealogical researcher, for assisting me with this. Mathew H. Greene, the judge of probate in New London, helped me with my research into the Bodenwein estate and Day Trust, among other subjects. New London City Clerk Clark van der Lyke was extremely helpful. Attorney Robert W. Marrion, of New London, made available records from the estate of Gordon Bodenwein.

Attorney Mark Kravitz, a partner, and others in the New Haven law firm of Wiggin & Dana greatly assisted in securing court documents related to the Internal Revenue Service case against *The Day*. I also received assistance in researching the case from attorney James C. McGuire, of New London.

I found many clues about the lives of the Bodenweins in cemeteries. Theresa Suanno, special services counselor for the Greenwood Cemetery Association in Trenton, New Jersey, provided me extensive useful information about Edna Bodenwein's working-class family, including pictures of grave sites and records. Edna J. McCraw, secretary for the Cedar Grove Cemetery Association. in New London, led me to a wealth of facts from the cemetery's files about the Bodenwein and Muir families.

The Day provided me with whatever I requested of financial records, minutes of board meetings, and assorted artifacts, photographs, and documents. I am particularly grateful to Richard A. Willis, the chief financial officer and employee trustee of the newspaper, and Donna Lloret, special assistant to Publisher Reid MacCluggage, for their time and help and to Reid MacCluggage and the directors of the newspaper for giving me the run of the *Day's* archives to do my research.

I interviewed more than three hundred people, a few with memories reaching as far back as the 1920s. I am grateful for their time and insight.

Several secondary sources were particularly helpful to me. I am indebted to the late Louis Sheaffer and to Arthur and Barbara Gelb for their excellent descriptions of life in New London in the early part of the century in their respective biographies of Eugene O'Neill: *O'Neill, Son and Playwright* and *Eugene O'Neill*. Other books that helped furnish historical perspective were *The Century*, by Peter Jennings and Todd Brewster, *The Rickover Effect*, by Theodore Rockwell, *Brotherhood of Arms*, by Jacob Goodwin, *The Savings Bank of New London*, by Gertrude Noyes and *Forty Years, Forty Million: The Career of Frank Munsey*, by George Britt.

NOTES

CHAPTER ONE. The accounts of Theodore Bodewein's death and funeral come from the *Day's* stories beginning on January 12, 1939 and from interviews of contemporaries of Bodenwein who were there: William Brutzman, who photographed the funeral for *The Day*; Thomas Elliott, a printer at the time; Elizabeth Latham, the *Day's* switchboard operator, John DeGange and Jack Cruise. I used material from an interview with John DeGange for my 1984 master's thesis: "Newspaper Without Stockholders: The Story of The Day Trust." The Newspaper Association of America reported in January 2000 there were two hundred sixty-five daily newspapers remaining in the United States that were not "group owned."

CHAPTER TWO. Details about the Bodenwein family in Germany were obtained from the genealogical records of the Church of Jesus Christ of Latter Day Saints (Mormon). Anton's military service is referred to in his obituary in *The Day* January 30, 1917. His discharge papers June 18, 1867, are among belongings his son retained. The May 6, 1869, passenger list of the *Smidt* was obtained through the Mormon genealogical records. The information about the *Smidt* was contained in N.R.T. Bonsor's *North American Seaway*. The conditions onboard trans-Atlantic ships during the period, including the quotes, came from John Malcolm Brinin's *The Grand Salon: A Social History of the North Atlantic*. Another source was *Atlantic Highway*, by Warren Armstrong. Descriptions of Castle Garden and its history were taken from Ann Novotny's *Strangers at the Door: Ellis Island, Castle Garden and the Grand Migration to America;* an account in the East Boston *Argus Advocate* of May 28, 1887; and "A Day in Castle Garden," *Harper's New Monthly Magazine*, December 1870-May 1871. Both magazine articles were in the archives of the United States Park Service's Ellis Island Immigration Museum. The account of Dickens' experience with the local ferry is from *Dickens, His Character, Comedy and Career* by Hesketh Pearson. Dickens' passage through New London was reported in the January 8, 1868, edition of the *Star*. The story about the *Nile* was described in the May 7, 1871, edition of the *Star*. The location of the Bodenweins' residence in Groton was determined through the 1870 census and Groton land records. The quote regarding Captain William Allen and other information about the Bodenweins' prominent neighbors was contained in the April 27, 1977, report of the Groton Bank Historic District Study Committee, a copy of which is in the

Groton Public Library. Historian Carol Kimball described the social stratification of the time in an interview.

CHAPTER 3. The Bodenweins' early history in New London was traced through New London city directories. Several accounts of Bodenwein's life, including his own, refer to his early acquaintance with George E. Starr and the fact that Starr published his teenage effort, *The Thames Budget*, on his Main Street press. The *Morning Telegraph*, of which Bodenwein was one of the founders, also was published briefly in Starr's printing plant located in a building at State and Main Streets in New London. The Bolles pamphlet in 1877 was entitled, "New London, a Seaport for the North and West and Outport of New York." Harold Cone summarized the publication from the original in the New York Public Library. The quotation from the *Chronicle* on the Gold Rush appeared on January 27, 1849. John Dray's narrative about the history of newspapers in New London appeared in *The Day* on March 28, 1896. The Breckinridge endorsement appeared in the August 31, 1860, edition of the *Star*. The *Star's* attack on Henry Ward Beecher appeared December 28, 1860. The exchange between the *Chronicle* and Ruddock was printed in the *Star* February 3, 1862. The reflections on newspaper leaders of the past were contained in a history of local newspapers that appeared in *The Day* February 29, 1896. Anton's citizenship record is on file on microfilm in the Connecticut State Library. The anecdote about the visiting commission from Washington appeared in the *Star* June 23, 1871. An editorial in the first edition of the *Evening Telegram* noted that failing health was a consideration in Ruddock's decision to give up his interest in the newspaper to Shepard.

CHAPTER 4. Tibbits' editorial on the temperance debate appeared in the *Telegram* May 26, 1877. On the other hand, as editor of *The Day*, he was later accused in the Stonington *Mirror*, in September 1882, of being "a truly good, up and up, anti-whiskey cocktail prohibitionist." The remark was republished in *The Day* on September 9, 1882. The New York *Sun* story on New London's resurgence was reprinted in the *Telegram* August 1, 1877. The New York *Evening Mail* editorial was reprinted in the *Telegram* May 25, 1877. Bertie LeFranc's performance was described in the *Telegram* August 1, 1877. The story about the James O'Neill scandal appeared in the *Telegram* on September 13, 1877. John Turner's disappearance was reported in the *Telegram* on November 9, 1878. Judge John G. Crump took over the job as editor of the *Telegram* and was the likely author of the opening editorial under the new editorship. The *Telegram* published a notice on May 30, 1878, that mentioned Walter Fitzmaurice was a member of the staff. Bodenwein described John McGinley's qualities as a journalist in the 25th anniversary edition on September 13, 1916, and his affection for him in a personal tribute in *The Day* after his death on October 2, 1915. The story of *The Day* was told in anniversary editions, on September 13, 1916, October 30, 1921, and July 1, 1931, among other places. The stories are of questionable accuracy. For example, in the 50th anniversary edition, among other places, *The Day* stated that an account of the assassination attempt on President Garfield wasn't reported in *The Day* until the following Tuesday, when actually a thorough account appeared on Monday, July 4. One of Bodenwein's versions is contained in the 1922 edition of *A Modern History of New London County, Connecticut* edited by Benjamin T. Marshall, the president of Connecticut College. Charlotte Holloway's role as editor is mentioned in Holloway's obituary in *The Day* on February 8, 1939. A biography of Thomas Waller is contained in Marshall's *A Modern History of New London County*. Bodenwein described Augustus Brandegee's revenge against the *Telegram* in the 25th anniversary edition.

CHAPTER 5. Bodenwein described Fitzmaurice's struggle with alcohol in "The Tattler" September 4, 1926. The background on the Muir family was obtained from the 1870 New London census, New London vital records, and records at Cedar Grove Cemetery in New London. Bodenwein related that he persuaded the others to join him in starting the *Telegraph* on a budget of $35, using George Starr's printing plant. However, city directories show Sturdy and Fitzmaurice running the newspaper briefly while Bodenwein was still a printer at *The Day*. Accounts of Ezra Whittlesey's death appeared in *The Day* on August 9, 1887, and the *Morning Telegraph* published its account, including the interview with Frederick Perry, the following day. The *Telegraph's* editorial on the incident appeared August 10 and its story on the funeral August 11. The story on the Republican celebration of the Harrison victory appeared in *The Day* on November 15, 1888. Anton's role in the fraternal organization is listed in the 1890 New London City Directory in a section on such organizations. Bodenwein mentioned temperamental differences between himself and others on the staff of the *Telegraph* in the 25th anniversary edition. Tibbits' letter on Holloway is quoted in her obituary. Holloway's book, entitled *Nathan Hale*, was published in 1902. Tibbits' cause of death was reported on his death certificate. Bodenwein's account of the sale of the *Telegraph* and deal with the Chappells over the purchase of *The Day* is contained in his history of *The Day* in the 50th anniversary edition. Theodore R. Bodenwein died on October 7, 1890, of exhaustion from cholera, according to his death certificate on file in New London.

CHAPTER 6. Bodenwein described his takeover of *The Day* in 25th, 40th and 50th anniversary editions. The *Telegraph's* political declaration was quoted in Arthur and Barbara Gelb's *O'Neill;* the Gelbs identify young Eugene O'Neill as the socialist and anarchist on the staff. The legal agreement with the Chappells, which included Bodenwein's assurance that it would remain a Republican newspaper, was recorded in the New London land records on September 5, 1891. The *Day's* emblem at first had no logo. Tibbits added a simple rising sun, and replaced that with the more stylistic river scene. Bodenwein published his statement of purpose in an advertisement in the 1892 edition of the New London City Directory. Bodenwein's observation on the value of homegrown reporters is contained in his reflections in the 40th anniversary edition. The special editions for the gathering of the Grand Army of the Republic appeared in June 18-19, 1895. The editorial on the beautiful baby calendar ran on January 4, 1897. Bodenwein's tribute to Alfred H. Chappell was included in Chappell's obituary on August 4, 1912. Bodenwein's first columns were entitled: "Told by the Tattler: Things Pertinent and Impertinent as He Sees Them in the Passing Show." The column on the park commissioners ran June 17, 1910. The one on the hotel clerk appeared on July 12, 1901. John Crump's suicide was described in *The Day* on June 20, 1894. An editorial about his death appeared in the same day's edition. The Bodenweins bought the building lot for their house at 302 Montauk Avenue in Jennie's name from Frank B. Brandegee and Thomas M. Waller in 1896. The house was completed the following year and still is standing. This information was obtained from land records and in an inventory of historic houses in New London on file with the Connecticut Historical Commission.

CHAPTER 7. Details of New London's 250th anniversary are taken from the accounts May 6, 1896, in *The Day* and the *Morning Telegraph*. The Joint Committee of the Court of Common Council for the celebration was listed in *The Day* December 30, 1895. Alfred H. Chappell was the chairman. Bodenwein and my grandfather Eben Stone were among members of a less prestigious citizens advisory committee. A story about Perry & Stone jewelry store appeared with a photo in *The Week* on December 15, 1893. Carol Kimball provided background and perspective on James Hill. The story of the *Minnesota* launching appeared on April 16, 1903. Bodenwein's purchase of the *Telegraph* took place on January 19, 1901. Stonington lawyer Herbert W. Rathbun negotiated the transaction for Bodenwein. The documents dealing with the sale are among Bodenwein's papers retained by *The Day*. The accounts of the political races of 1904 are drawn from the pages of *The Day* and the *Telegraph*, both of which Bodenwein then owned. *The Day* reported on the Republican state convention in a front-page story on September 14, 1904. The *Day's* editorial appeared the following day. *The Day* described how it intended to project the results on a "big canvass" across the street on November 5, 1904. Biographies of Bodenwein appeared both in *Men of Progress in Connecticut*, published in 1898, and *Men of Mark in Connecticut*, in 1910. Ernest E. Rogers' papers provide a running account mostly in the form of newspaper clippings of the political strife of 1907. According to a story in *The Day* May 5, 1910, the Day Minstrels included Arthur McGinley, his brother, Lawrence and Alfred Ligourie, among others. The Day Publishing Co. was incorporated August 19, 1909, with $50,000 of capital stock. The incorporators were Theodore Bodenwein, William H. Rolfe, Walter M. Slocum, Joseph

P. Chapman, and Alfred W. Newman. *The Day* reported that Jennie Bodenwein was one of the founding members of the Faire Harbour Club on January 23, 1908. By a strange coincidence, earlier that month, a *Day* editorial stated that women's clubs were a major cause for divorce. On June 18, 1910, *The Day* reported that the Faire Harbour Club staged a contata, "A Garden of Singing Flowers," for members of the Harbour Club; Elizabeth, 13, performed "Mary, Mary, Quite Contrary." Anton's residence after his wife's death was determined from city directories and from probate papers. Details of the Bodenwein's divorce were derived from the divorce decree, still on file in the Norwich, Connecticut, Superior Court, and dated April 3, 1911, and from New London land records. The changes of residence during the breakup of the marriage were gleaned from city directories.

CHAPTER 8. The agreement in which *Day* stock was put up to guarantee alimony payments to Jennie is contained among papers retained by *The Day* and in New London real estate records. Notices of Edna Winfield's and Bodenwein's wedding were published in the Trenton *Daily Star Gazette* on May 25, 1911 and the Trenton *Sunday Advertiser* on May 28. *The Day* and *Morning Telegraph* announcements appeared on May 24. All the announcements except the *Telegraph's* listed Edna's residence as Trenton. The *Telegraph* said she lived in New York. The prevailing gossip in New London was that Bodenwein met Edna during a business trip to New York. John Simpson's occupations were obtained from Trenton city directories. Edna's and Lewis Winfield's marriage license was dated April 12, 1897. Edna lied about her age. She was 14, not 18, when they were married. Winfield was 27. Winfield listed his occupation as laborer. He and Edna's brother, Philip, were friends and Philip was a witness for the wedding certificate. Other details about the Simpson family were obtained from New Jersey and Trenton vital records and Trenton city directories. Albert L. Collins' biography appears in *The Story of New Jersey*, published in 1945. The Simpsons were buried in Greenwood Cemetery, and the Greenwood Cemetery Association furnished additional biographical information about the family. Edna's relationship with her nieces is revealed in later correspondence obtained for this book from Donald Mitchell. Donald Mitchell, who knew Edna through his mother's friendship with her, described her flamboyance. Andrew Freedman related the story about his grandmother's relationship with Edna. The story in the *Telegraph* on "business patriotism" appeared on April 8, 1911. The article in the New Haven *Union* was reprinted in *The Day* July 13, 1911. Alma Wies furnished much of the information about her father, Waldo E. Clarke, and their families. The 1922 edition of *A Modern History of New London County, Connecticut* contains his biography. The editorial on the Coast Guard training school appeared February 20, 1908. Colin Buell's remarks appeared in a story June 6, 1910. The editorial on business leadership appeared September 11, 1911. During this period, Alfred

Ligourie, the city editor of *The Day*, wrote an article for *New England Magazine* entitled "The Spirit of New London: An Industrial Awakening." It was reprinted as a pamphlet to promote New London. *The Day* published an article on harbor engineering and New London's potential on September 7, 1911; it went into detail about the article in the trade publication. *The Day* reported on A.J. Campbell's address on February 10, 1908. The editorial urging businessmen to get involved in politics ran September 11, 1911.

CHAPTER 9. I relied extensively on George Britt's biography, *Forty Years, Forty Million: The Career of Frank Munsey*, and Theodore Bodenwein's written commentary and reflections on Munsey in preparing this chapter. *The Day* broke the story of Munsey's plans to publish his magazine in New London on December 16, 1895. Bodenwein related the conversation he had with A.H. Chappell over Munsey's interest in New London in a story published in *The Day* December 22, 1925, after Munsey's death. The allusion to "Munseyvilles" came from the same source. Details about the founding of the New London Typographical Union are contained in the 50th anniversary edition of *The Day*, as well as *The New London Typographical Union No. 159, the First Hundred Years*, an unpublished history. Bodenwein described his reasons for buying the *Telegraph* in the 1916 25th anniversary edition. Munsey's statement about small units being uncompetitive is quoted in Britt's book from the New York *Sun*. David Lawrence's reflections on Munsey's politics were a sidebar to the story about Munsey's funeral arrangements on the front page of *The Day* December 23, 1925. The huge impact of Munsey in New London, and upon Bodenwein, was reflected in the lavish front-page coverage of his death, tributes to him and his funeral. Frederick Latimer's column appeared on December 22, under the headline "We Admired Mr. Munsey." Latimer went to Munsey for help when he and Malcolm Mollan were attempting to keep the *Telegraph* afloat. *The Day* carried the account of its move from Bank Street to its new building on Main Street on August 13, 1907.

CHAPTER 10. *The Day* reported on Bodenwein's 50th birthday party on January 26, 1914. Agnes' death notice was published on March 12, 1898. The story stated she died suddenly. It reported she was 65, adding to a long history of apparent dissembling regarding the subject of her age. According to her birth and marriage records, she was born on April 27, 1823, and would have recently turned 75 when she died, not 65. On the passenger list of the *Smidt* in May 1869, she gave her age as 46, which was accurate. However, in the 1870 census in Groton a year later, she said she was 37, when she was actual 47. Ten years later, the census taker in New London recorded she was 46, when she was really 57. Bodenwein's role in planning his mother-in-law's funeral are recorded in the records of Cedar Grove Cemetery. Andrews' reminiscences of the day he was hired are contained in "Sentences by the Judge" column on June 30, 1956. The union's resolution on Bodenwein is recorded in the typographical union history. Bodenwein's quotations are taken from the 25th anniversary edition. Bodenwein emulated the *Telegraph's* editorial page, and Frederick Latimer largely replicated the *Telegraph* editorial pages in *The Day* when he joined *The Day*. The period marked a high-water mark in the newspaper's appearance as well as its editorial page.

CHAPTER 11. Ernest E. Rogers' papers and scrapbooks, on file in Connecticut College's special collections library, were invaluable in putting together this chapter. Details of the *Deutschland's* visit are taken mostly from the pages of *The Day* and the *Morning Telegraph*, which competed fiercely to cover the event. Bodenwein described *The Day* getting scooped by its rival in "The Tattler" on November 4, 1916. He took a poke at the reporter for not interviewing the doctors who had been aboard the submarine. Alma Wies is the source about Waldo Clarke's continued friendship with Paul Koenig. The story about Fred Swanson and the booklet about the *Deutschland's* voyage was reported in *The Day* November 13, 1918. Eugene O'Neill's presence in New London during the draft registration and brush with the law in Provincetown are mentioned in a story in *The Day* June 4, 1917. The subject of the story was a three-act play O'Neill had just completed. Gordon's military service was documented in *Service Records of Connecticut for World War I.* According to the record, he entered the Navy September 5, 1918, serving at the Philadelphia Navy Yard. He was discharged a Quartermaster Corpsman Second Class on January 21, 1919. Walter W. Conklin's letter criticizing the Chappells' coal deal with Connecticut College appeared in *The Day* on March 19, 1917. The *Day* editorial opposing the no-license law was entitled "Fighting Evil With Good" and appeared on September 20, 1917.

CHAPTER 12. Waldo Clarke was street superintendent from October 1906 until July 1907. The controversy over his performance unfolded in the spring of 1907, during a power struggle between wings of the party headed by Mayor Benjamin Armstrong and the Chappells. Bodenwein expressed his worries over the future of the military activities in the region in a "Tattler" column on November 23, 1918. The United States Grain Corp. deal and labor problems were described in successive stories in the *Morning Telegraph* in the late fall and early winter of 1919. The texts of the letters exchanged between Bodenwein and Frank Brandegee were published in *The Day* on September 3, 1919. *The Day* formally started its campaign for charter reform in an editorial entitled "Time to Revamp" on October 18, 1920. The appeal to women voters appeared on June 3, 1921. *The Day* boasted of its rising circulation on January 2, 1921. The succession of control of the *Telegraph* was traced largely through New London land records. Benjamin Armstrong acquired control on October 1, 1908; George S. Palmer and Frederick Latimer on August 26, 1910; Latimer and Malcolm Mollan on December 4, 1912;

Morton Plant, February 12, 1916, and Julian D. Moran on March 17, 1920. Moran was the last owner before the newspaper folded that year.

CHAPTER 13. The city election took place on September 26, 1921. *The Day* was profuse in its coverage in the next day's edition, in which it also ran an editorial entitled "Good government on trial." John Mallon's reputation among Democrats as a mouthpiece for the Republican Party and fixer with the police department was described by Morton Kenyon, a driver for *The Day* in the 1930s, in an interview for this book. Kenyon and Elizabeth Latham, the newspaper's telephone operator for many years, provided me extensive detail about life at *The Day* during the Depression. Gordon described his feelings toward his father and stepmother years later to Raymond Izbicki, a friend, whom I interviewed for this book. John DeGange furnished me information about Gordon's early years as a priest during a 1984 interview. Gordon was ordained in Viterbo, Italy, on August 1, 1926. The announcement was among the papers of John DeGange, provided to me by Susan Cattanach, his daughter. John R. "Jack" Cruise and Elizabeth Latham described typical encounters between Bodenwein and the staff on the stairway. I am indebted to Andrew Freedman, the current owner of the Bodenwein home and grandson of David and Miriam Elfenbein, who bought the house from Edna, for rich and detailed information about the house's history. Edna's personal records contain detailed information about the house, including an inventory of all the furniture she bought. Margaret "Marge" Bonville, a longtime friend of Edna, told me about Edna's trips to Europe to do research and buy furniture for her house. Documents and notes dealing with the Bodenweins' real estate transactions and other investments are among personal papers retained by Donald Mitchell and *The Day*. George E. MacDougall wrote a long story about the Garde for *The Day* September 1, 1926. The four-day line proposal is described, among other places, in *The Day* on May 23, 1928. The details of Frank Brandegee's death, including his note to his household help, were reported in *The Day* October 14, 1924. The same day, Bodenwein wrote a long story extolling Brandegee's virtues and importance and John Mallon described the senator's political career.

CHAPTER 14. Bodenwein's goals were summarized in the *Day's* "An Agenda for New London" printed daily on the editorial page. Andrews analyzed the Stock Market crash in his column November 2, 1929. Judge Latimer's column about the widespread participation in the Stock Market appeared October 25, 1929. Bodenwein reflected on the impact of radio November 18, 1929. Bodenwein's remarks on the 1930 economic outlook are taken from *The Day* January 7, 1930. In his remarks two years later in a January 7, 1932, story, Bodenwein recalled being optimistic the year before, but admitted he no longer saw much hope for a recovery soon. Andrews' column on the impact of the military industry in delaying the impact of the Depression appeared July 23, 1932. Gardens for the jobless were discussed in *The Day* May 7, 1932. Negotiations with the typographical union are discussed in the union history. The Local 159 history also describes the Central Labor Council's concern over the future of the *Globe*. Bodenwein's column on ticket splitting appeared November 5, 1932. The appeal for newsboys and their parents to write to Congress about child-labor restrictions appeared October 21, 1934.

CHAPTER 15. An account of Bodenwein's 70th birthday party appeared in *The Day* January 26, 1934. Edna represented New London County on the executive board of the McKinley Club. Morton Kenyon, who sometimes drove Bodenwein to the doctor, described the publisher's failing health in 1934 and identified his physician in an interview for this book. *The Day* reported September 22, 1934, that Bodenwein tripped and fell, suffering a serious head injury, as he left *The Day* building. Inga Nilsson Carlson, who was a cook for the Bodenweins from 1925 to 1935, provided some of the material about the Bodenwein marriage for this chapter. Nilsson, who emigrated from Sweden as a young woman, was living in a Groton convalescent home when I interviewed her. One of her collateral duties had been as a driver for Bodenwein. A December 30, 1936, bill to Bodenwein from attorney Charles L. Smiddy, among papers retained by *The Day*, referred to services related to the preparation of an earlier will. Thomas Elliott and Elizabeth Latham described Bodenwein's interest in "The Junior Day." Kenyon told of Edna's late-night appearances at *The Day* looking for her husband and Latham described Edna's demanding phone calls. The arrangement with Christina Rolfe is documented in correspondence with Charles Smiddy and in copies of deeds preserved by *The Day*. The story of Dr. C. John Satti's rise to power is taken, for the most part, from news and commentary in *The Day* and the Norwich *Bulletin*. William Fox was quoted in a story on the city convention August 17, 1934. The *Day's* front-page story about the Democratic state convention in Groton appeared September 5, 1934. Leroy Harwood's praise of Bodenwein is contained in an August 29, 1934, story in *The Day*. Satti and Harwood are later quoted responding to the election in a November 4, 1934, story. Bodenwein's column defending the newspaper's objectivity appeared August 18, 1934. Edna's jewelry in my father's appraisal January 23, 1937, included an $800 diamond and saphire pin, a $600 brooch, $250 diamond hat pin and $2,000 diamond watch pendant and chain. Bodenwein's election to represent the 18th senatorial district was reported in *The Day* on November 16, 1935. The *Day* story on Bodenwein's speech to the Young Republicans appeared on December 10, 1935. The story on the Chamber of Commerce 20th anniversary meeting and tribute to Bodenwein was published on May 16, 1935.

CHAPTER 16. John DeGange's recollection of Gordon's return to New London is from a 1984 interview. *The Day* chronicled the progress of the Little Slam bridge club that summer on its Women's Page. The course of deliberations over Bodenwein's will during the summer of 1938 is drawn from *Day* and Norwich *Bulletin* accounts of the legal proceedings. Brutzman described his activities on the day of the hurricane in an interview for this book. Bar Colby's perspective on the storm comes from a 1984 interview and story after the storm. The quote is from a story Colby wrote for the September 22, 1938, edition, the day after the hurricane struck. Thomas Elliott described the scene inside the newspaper during the storm in an interview for this book. Thomas DiMaggio, of Waterford, described the tidal wave in a presentation to the New London Maritime Society in September 1998. Brutzman described the fire and difficulty getting around the city in an interview. The September 21 edition was printed but never distributed. Much of the information about the early history of Ocean Beach, including Waller's role, comes from the plan to redevelop the beach, "Restoration, Expansion and Development of Ocean Beach," prepared by the engineering firm of Andrews and Morgan after the storm. *The Day* retained Andrews' copy of the report, with his notes. Andrews' power of attorney was discussed in a New London Probate Court hearing October 30, 1939.

CHAPTER 17. Margaret "Marge" Bonville, Edna's friend, stated in an interview a Roman Catholic priest was at Bodenwein's deathbed. Smiddy's fees are listed in the executors' account filed with the New London Probate Court on March 23, 1944. Information regarding Joseph Pulitzer's will was taken from records of the Surrogate's Court, New York County, February 26, 1931, and *American Journalism* by Frank Luther Mott. Two copies of Edna's divorce papers were found in her safe deposit box at the National Bank of Commerce after she died, according to a September 27, 1950, inventory filed for her estate. The agreement that settled the case was reached October 6, 1941, and went into effect January 10, 1942. *The Day* ran a two-paragraph story on the settlement on January 10, 1942, without any of the details except that Gordon would be a trustee. The deliberations over the monument for Bodenwein's grave were detailed in correspondence between the Rock of Ages Memorials Corporation and Orvin Andrews and Edna Bodenwein. The letters were among Edna's papers. Edna received a $1,200 bill for the completed monument dated May 15, 1940. Orvin Andrews discussed the impact of the settlement of the estate on the newspaper's surplus in a letter to Edna dated January 17, 1951. The direct expenses listed in the executors' account on February 29, 1944, were $92,259. These included the state succession tax of $6,088, a federal estate tax of $22,604, executor fees of $4,000 each for Smiddy, Andrews, Stamm, and Grout, the $26,000 settlement with Gordon and his lawyers, payments to Edna of $20,531 for her widow's allowance and $970 for the funeral. The executors had to borrow $100,000 from the *Day's* surplus to pay these expenses. Gordon contested this payment, but unsuccessfully. Thomas E. Troland's papers were extremely helpful in reconstructing the story of Ocean Beach Park. The Bridgeport *Herald* described the patronage war on August 6, 1939. Along with Andrews, the Ocean Beach subcommittee of the City Restoration Committee included Frank Valentine Chappell, Lucius Whiton, Joseph C. Keefe and Earle Stamm.

CHAPTER 18. The section about Gordon's relations at *The Day* after the settlement is drawn from interviews with Elizabeth Latham, Thomas Elliott, Raymond Izbicki, and from correspondence between Edna and the directors. Helen McGuire, Francis McGuire's widow, furnished information and insights about Elizabeth Miles in interviews. The McGuires were close friends of Elizabeth. Edna's trip and welcome home by her bridge club were recounted in *The Day* April 24, 1941. The controversy with the Navy over Alfred Holter's plan is described in a June 9, 1943, and subsequent stories in *The Day*. The stories on the opening of Ocean Beach Park appeared on July 1, 1940. Lucille Showalter is the source of some of the colorful detail about the park when it was new. The *Day's* struggle to produce a newspaper under wartime conditions is chronicled in the minutes of the board of directors. The dinner for Jack Cruise's is described in an April 16, 1942, story in *The Day*. Gordon's editorial was among several that were reprinted in the *Connecticut Circle* article. Edna's account of Victor's proposal to her and her version of other events in their marriage are contained in the draft of a letter to Victor prepared by a professional writer, Carol O. Hopper, in March 1950. The draft was among her papers. Edna's hospitality in Florida is documented in personal correspondence retained by Donald Mitchell from her estate and described by him in an interview. The "Big Blow" editorial appeared on September 15, 1944.

CHAPTER 19. Alma Wies described her father Waldo Clarke's role in Pfizer's decision to locate in Groton. Pfizer's real estate consultant, Charles Buermann & Company, looked at eighty sites along the Atlantic seaboard. They ranged from undeveloped land to developed sites, including several in Connecticut. Clarke, a member of the Connecticut Development Commission, helped gather material to support a site in the state, among which he favored the Victory Yard. Pfizer announced its plans to purchase the twenty-eight-acre Groton site from the War Assets Administration for $911,999 on December 18, 1946. Clarke's undated notes about the future of southeastern Connecticut after the war were preserved by Alma Wies. They appear to have been written in 1945. Clarke's defense of his role with the State Pier is contained in an April 13, 1947, *Day* article. Alfred Ligourie's newsroom demeanor and the story about reporters returning from Hammy's were described by Elizabeth Latham. David Carlson told of Jim Watterson's rivalry with Bar Colby in an interview for this book. The arguments in the divorce case are contained in copies of court documents and correspondence retained by Edna and preserved by Donald Mitchell. I interviewed both

Duncan Fraser and Joseph G. Ryan, who were retired and living in Florida, for background on *The Day* in the 1950s. In addition, Duncan Fraser furnished me a section of his unpublished autobiography dealing with the time he worked at *The Day*. In 1950, Edna's dividend income from *The Day* was $35,917, with Elizabeth and Gordon each receiving $17,958. In a letter March 10, 1951, Orvin Andrews explained to Edna that *The Day* declared a dividend of $127,000 on the surplus from the estate to pay back money the trustees had borrowed to pay estate and legal expenses, and pay federal taxes.

CHAPTER 20. The various actions by the directors to follow the will are chronicled in the board minutes and a history kept by *The Day*. Gordon's early role in the National Conference of Editorial Writers is documented in that organization's archives. The series on Mexico began on April 18, 1949. Gordon attended the political conventions during the summer of 1948. Gordon established a residence in Santa Maria de Guido, Michoacan, Mexico in 1945, while he continued working for *The Day*. He quit his job at *The Day* in May 1950, a fact noted in the board of directors' minutes of May 20. While Gordon was no longer a director, he remained a trustee until his death in 1967. In an interview, Joseph Ryan furnished me with much of the information about the editorial page in the early 1950s when he worked for the newspaper. Bar Colby's column on the survey appeared on October 31, 1953. The initial front-page editorial on the proposed charter change appeared on April 18, 1955. The Groton "streamer" was introduced in June 1952. The directors discussed whether to change the name of the newspaper to the *New London Evening Day and Groton News* at its April 16, 1955 meeting.

CHAPTER 21. The story about Rickover and O.B. Robinson is quoted from a company history by Jeffrey L. Rondegen, *The Legend of Electric Boat*. The history of New London Ship & Engine Company is contained in the *Day's* 40th anniversary edition. It was necessary to develop a diesel engine for the submarine because of the danger of using gasoline. Joyce Olson Resnikoff, daughter of Martin Olson, furnished many of the details about her father's work. Colby's remarks on the use of the Bodenwein will to promote change with the directors are taken from a 1984 interview. Max Foley was taken off the city hall beat because of "bad chemistry" with Henkle, according to Duncan Fraser. Foley was replaced by Deane Avery, who had been working in Groton. The newsroom changes were announced at the February 12, 1958, board meeting. Andrew's retrospective column appeared on June 30, 1956.

CHAPTER 22. David Carlson and John Foley provided me with much of the information about *The Day* newsroom in the early 1960s. Robert Donovan, Thomas Elliott, and Paul Libera furnished me with details about the printing and technology of the era and the atmosphere at the newspaper. A December 24, 1949, letter from John

DeGange to the Burroughs Adding Machine Company offering to sell the company the use of his "shear bar" was found among his papers. There is no indication what the company's response was. The story about John Blotsky's rampage in the courthouse appeared September 29, 1960. The story about Annie Sadd appeared February 22, 1955. Sally Ryan, who worked as a social worker in New London in the 1960s, described social conditions in New London in an interview for this book. Michael Bagwell was the source of the story about Steve Downey and Palmerlee Tilton.

CHAPTER 23. This chapter drew upon interviews with, among others, F. Jerome Silverstein, C. Francis Driscoll, Angelo Santaniello, Sally Ryan, Morgan McGinley, and John Foley. Henkle stated concerns about New London's future in a message to the City Council on March 9, 1960. The *Day's* editorial on the opening of the new highway appeared on January 2, 1958. The editorial on the Heyman shopping center proposal appeared on May 21, 1955. The editorial favoring extending public water to Waterford appeared on April 3, 1957. *The Day* discussed what it would cost to move in an editorial on April 1, 1962. The $2 million was to build a new building and purchase a new press. The newspaper said it would take another $100,000 to move its other equipment. The editorial stated redevelopment was "desperately needed." *The Day* announced the agreement with the Redevelopment Agency in its December 19, 1964, edition. Dwight Lyman's estimate that probably not more than a dozen buildings were suitable for preservation appeared in a September 28, 1961, story in *The Day*.

CHAPTER 24. Hammond became controller in December 1962. The story of the Hoe press comes from *Day* board minutes and interviews with Alcino Almeida, Robert Donovan, and Thomas Elliott. Charles E. Shain, in an interview for this book, said he and McGuire felt the board should have a strong role in deciding not only business but editorial policy. He felt this should apply not only to political endorsements, but other issues. "After all, the board was the legal head." Shain also said that McGuire had the greatest influence of all the board members. Francis Driscoll's story about the Redevelopment Agency's meeting with the McGuires was related in an interview. Bar Colby was elected publisher on May 25, 1964. Almeida described the early problems with the new Hoe press in an interview. Ken Grube's editorial on endorsements appeared in *The Day* October 26, 1972. The board endorsed Richard Nixon on October 26, 1968. David Carlson related the story of Jim Watterson's outburst at the *Day* meeting in an interview. Morgan McGinley's column on Jim Watterson appeared in *The Day* on March 24, 1975. Details about Bob Craigue's and Gina Muzzi's disappearance were noted in the minutes of *The Day* board of directors.

CHAPTER 25. Linwood Bland described Alfred Garvin's style and role in controversies with *The Day* in interviews. An account of the NAACP picketing against the F.W. Woolworth department store in New London appeared in *The Day* June 1, 1963. Gordon Bodenwein's change of his will and other details of his last years are documented in legal files retained by Attorney Robert Marrion. Marrion corresponded with Raymond Cote, who informed the lawyer that Gordon was prevented by Mexican law from owning property in that country. Morgan McGinley made his remarks about David Anderson in an interview. David Carlson described the advances in photography in an interview. The editorial on the assassination of The Rev. Dr. Martin Luther King, Jr., "True Compassion and Dr. King," appeared on April 10, 1968. Norman Soderberg's five-part series, "The Negro and the City," was published the week of October 15, 1968. The editorial appeared on October 16. Soderberg's seven-part series on redevelopment began on August 22, 1968. Soderberg, as special affairs reporter, attended a two-week seminar at the American Press Institute in New York in the fall of 1969.

Chapter 26. Deane Avery told about his confrontation with David Anderson in the composing room in an interview for this book. Extensive background for this chapter came from interviews with Morgan McGinley, John Foley, and David Carlson. Soderberg's two-part series on the Coast Guard Academy ran on June 27 and 28, 1969. William Mitchell related the story of his firing over the Coast Guard assignment in an interview for this book. He also furnished copies of his letter to *The Day*, Ken Grube's response August 14, 1969, and a copy of his pink slip, dated July 31, 1969. Colby's hurt feelings over the guild movement were related in an interview with Almeida. Morgan McGinley described the deeper issues behind the union movement in an interview. Charles E. Shain said in an interview for this book that he had gotten to know Deane Avery and Bar Colby well and telegraphed to them his interest in working with *The Day*. "I almost invited myself," he said. Helen McGuire described her husband's interest in Shain's appointment to the board. Shain was elected a trustee on August 28, 1969. The challenge of Robert Colby's vote in the guild election was noted in the *Day's* official chronology. Robert Flanagan told the story about covering for Avery at City Hall meetings in an interview. David Carlson and John Foley related the story about the Ukraine murder and Joe DeBona. McGinley described refusing the job offer from the Norwich *Bulletin* in an interview. Almeida and Robert Donovan described the job security assurances connected with new technology in interviews. Almeida described the steps toward cold type and other technological advances in interviews. *Evaluating the Press: The New England Daily Newspaper Survey* was published in December 1973.

Chapter 27. C. Francis Driscoll told the story of his tongue-lashing by Ken Grube in an interview for this book. Stan DeCoster described the state Capitol beat in the early 1970s in an interview. Michael Bagwell gave his recollections about the exhilarated mood in the newsroom in an interview. Morgan McGinley and John

Peterson, in interviews, described the newsroom reaction to changes, including David Heckerman's promotion. A story describing Curt Pierson's going-away party appeared in *The Day* on September 29, 1973. L. Patrick Gray's newsroom interview appeared on May 8, 1972. In a story the following day, he clarified that he was not transported about in a bullet-proof Cadillac, as he had implied in the interview. Gray's interview was conducted by Michael Bagwell, Stan DeCoster, and me. Ken Grube and L. Patrick Gray were close friends, and Grube defended him throughout the Watergate controversy. Gray and Grube later were members together of the First Wednesday Club, a gathering of cronies who also included former Governor John N. Dempsey. A brief story on June 14, 1978, chronicled the closing of the Mohican Bar. Morgan McGinley's column on the train station, "Wanted: Imagination," appeared on November 18, 1972. The special section commemorating the rededication of the station was published July 29, 1976. The front page story on A.A. Constantine's background ran on March 7, 1977. I spent two days going through federal court records in a depository in Jersey City, New Jersey, to prepare the story. The story about Veliotis and the raft race ran on September 4, 1979.

CHAPTER 28. The series "Electric Boat: Boom or Bust?" ran the week of October 25, 1977. John Foley wrote about *The Day* rushing into print with the Electric Boat story in *Inside The Day*, the newspaper's employee newsletter. Joan Poro also described the reporting effort in an interview for this book. Morgan McGinley described the newsroom's understanding of Rickover's conversation with Poro. Electric Boat's criticism of *The Day* quoted here appeared in the January 6, 1978 edition of "EB Topics," the shipyard newsletter. Electric Boat's news blackout of *The Day* began March 18, 1978, but didn't become public until nearly a year later in February 1979 when Veliotis granted interviews to other local newspapers but not *The Day*. *The Day* ran a page-one story describing the problem on February 2, and an editorial February 5. Isaacs' and Arthur's reactions to the decision by the National News Council not to take a stronger stance against Electric Boat were reported in *The Day* June 12, 1979. *The Day* reprinted the Danbury *News-Times* editorial on June 27, 1979. Dick Polman, a former *Day* reporter who later was editor of the Hartford *Advocate*, an alternative weekly newspaper, described the blackout controversy in a September 26, 1979, story. Polman mentioned the newspaper's down-home flavor, but went on to describe its efforts to cover the most important business in its territory. He pointed out this wasn't always true. In the 1950s, he said, the newspaper relied on news releases. But Polman said the controversy showed how the newspaper had changed. Deane Avery recalled the dinner meeting with Veliotis in an interview for this book. Steve Fagin related the story of the Elks Club strippers in an interview for this book. His story ran on November 16, 1977. The *Day's* story on the lobbying surrounding the "bottle bill" appeared February 23, 1978. The editorial, "Don't let the industry sidetrack the bottle bill," ran on March 26,

1978. I interviewed John Peterson, among others, for background on the Showalter case. *The Day* attacked Dannehy's findings as unfair to Mallove in an editorial on March 3, 1978. Helen McGuire related the story of Elizabeth Miles' return after her husband's death in an interview.

CHAPTER 29. Details about Elizabeth Bodenwein Miles' estate came from records of the New London-Waterford Probate Court. Most of the background and developments in the Internal Revenue Service came from court records, interviews with attorney Mark Kravitz and my own familiarity with the case, having reported on it throughout. Charles E. Shain described the board's response to the case in an interview. The newspaper's preparations for the case and progress were chronicled in the board minutes. The anecdote about the belief that the employees would cash in on the Bodenwein Fund after the last heir died came from Alcino Almeida.

CHAPTER 30. Deane Avery expressed his concern at the October 17, 1979, board meeting that four reporters had left in a short period of time. These included me; I left to work for the Associated Press from October 1979 until February 1980. The Bank Street stories appeared on March 17, 1980. The controversial part was contained in a short paragraph in the 25th paragraph of the lead story. The *Day's* retraction and apology ran March 27, 1980. Reid MacCluggage described the developments and conditions at *The Hartford Courant* after its purchase in an interview for this book. The debate between Evan Hill and Walter Baker was described in interviews with the two former directors. The attacks by Massad and Brennan occurred in September 1979. The editorial on the Custom House, "Living Legacy: Let the Custom House Tell New London's Story," ran on March 6, 1983. *The Day* furnished the services of its lawyer, Frank L. McGuire, and paid the incorporation costs for the New London Maritime Society. The minutes of the October 17, 1979, board meeting note a delay in starting the Sunday newspaper because *The Day* couldn't get assurances of an adequate newsprint supply. Worsening economic conditions were discussed at the June 16, 1982, meeting and again August 18, when the directors voted not to sponsor a regional spelling bee because of the recession. Sunday circulation surpassed daily circulation for the first time on October 17, 1984. Steve Slosberg's column on Judge Seymour L. Hendel ran on August 9, 1988; the case was heard by the Judicial Review Council on February 23, 1989. The council decided that Hendel had not committed any misconduct. Jack Sauer and Ann Baldelli described details of Sauer's plane accident and its aftermath in interviews. The directors asked the managers to get bids on a new press at the March 16, 1983, board meeting. The appeal of flexography came up at the May 25 and July 20 meetings. Almeida, Shain, and Walter Baker described the problems associated with having two publishers in interviews. Interviews with Maureen Croteau, Shain, Baker and

MacCluggage contributed to the section on MacCluggage's hiring by *The Day*. The fact the board was leaning toward Ungaro was contained in a December 27, 1983, note from Evan Hill to Deane Avery. Avery referred to Hill's reservations about Ungaro in a letter to the directors on January 4,1984.

CHAPTER 31. MacCluggage's critique is among his papers he furnished for this book as were the notes he prepared for his address to the new staff. Walter Baker described his favorable impressions of MacCluggage in an interview. MacCluggage's remarks at the celebration of the IRS victory were recorded in the June 1965 edition of *Inside The Day*. Evan Hill described his feelings about Richard Flath in an interview for this book. Lance Johnson acknowledged his interest in the managing editor's job in an interview. Steve Slosberg's full-time job was as a columnist, while John Foley presumably had other duties as an assistant to MacCluggage. The *Day's* coverage of the Electric Boat story was described in interviews with Marcelle Dufresne, Jacky Flinn, Maria Hileman, and James Smith. Hill's concerns over MacCluggage's early months on the job were expressed in an interview and in a July 24, 1985, letter to Walter Baker, in which Hill takes the liberty of describing the sentiments of Avery and Shain, as well. The exchanges of notes and phone calls after MacCluggage's first-year report are described in Hill's July 24, 1985, letter to Walter Baker, and in an interview with Hill. Walter Baker's defense of MacCluggage and recommendations for bonuses for MacCluggage and Almeida appear in a note to the directors dated November 5, 1986. The lesser bonuses were approved at the November 19 meeting. The directors voted unanimously to make *The Day* a morning newspaper on December 17, 1986. The report by Urban & Associates Inc. of Sharon, Massachusetts, is dated September 11, 1985. The midnight deliveries because of press problems occurred on October 18, 1984. Salary details came from board minutes and directors' documents.

CHAPTER 32. Reid MacCluggage described the reasoning behind constructing the new production plant next to the *Day's* downtown building in an interview. The *Day's* forum on New London development occurred in August 1984. An account and edited transcript appeared in *The Day* August 5, 1984. This meeting led to the formation of an advisory group, which revived the New London Development Corporation. Bruce Hyde, a planner from Burlington, Vermont, was hired to be its director. The forum was part of a series initiated under MacCluggage called The Day Forum. A forum on *The Day* itself took place in December 1984. The forum on housing was March 23, 1986. Evan Hill and Walter Baker each described Hill's recommendation that Baker stay on the board beyond his 70th birthday. Baker described Almeida as a "father confessor" in an interview. The government decided to consolidate the Navy laboratory in Newport, Rhode Island, and give up the laboratory's historic site in New London in 1991. The stories on the collapse of communism, "Eastern Europe: the Morning After the Revolution," appeared from June 10-14, 1990. My paid leave of absence extended from January to June 1992. David Collins described his coverage of Indian gambling in an interview. The series on the Pequot tribe, "Rebirth of a Nation," appeared the week of December 12, 1993. The series on development sprawl ran May 18-23, 1997. In connection with it, *The Day* sponsored a community forum, paying Thomas Hylton, a Pulitzer prize winning editorial writer from Pennsylvania, to be the main speaker. New London City Manager Richard Brown echoed the sentiments of earlier city administrators and politicians against the 1915 pier. At a forum on the pier sponsored by *The Day* on March 7, 1996, he raised the question: "I still come back to what does this do for New London." Earlier in the year, Brown said that if the pier were to remain a regional shipping port facility, the region should pay New London for its lost taxes. The editorial "Who made them king" appeared on February 2, 1996, after work had halted on repairing the pier. On February 23, in a press conference on the pier, Governor John G. Rowland announced that the project would be completed.

CHAPTER 33. The article on the *Day's* "negative coverage" of New London ran May 26, 1996. Claire Gaudiani related the story of how the Pfizer deal came about in an interview for this book. DeCoster interviewed Gaudiani for a profile that appeared on the front page on June 6, 1999, entitled, "An Apostle Charges Ahead." Kyn Tolson described covering Gaudiani's arrival in New London in 1988. McGinley's column criticizing Gaudiani for closing the development corporation's meeting ran November 24, 1997. Robert Hamilton and Maura Casey provided background for the *Day's* coverage of the Millstone nuclear power plants. The *Time* magazine cover piece on safety at the Millstone nuclear power stations appeared on March 4, 1996. Editors first began sending pages directly to cameras in the composing room in July 1998. That was when new electronic editing machines, known as paginators, were installed and placed in operation. The appointments of William Pedace and Maureen Croteau are recorded in New London-Waterford Probate Court on November 17, 1994, and January 5, 1998, respectively.

Theodore Bodenwein, Last Will and Testament

I, THEODORE BODENWEIN, OF NEW LONDON, Connecticut, do make, publish, and declare the following to be my last will and testament.

ARTICLE FIRST. I have devoted nearly all my life to building up a newspaper in New London which should become a recognized institution in the community, a leading factor in the growth, development, and improvement of the city and vicinity and the happiness and prosperity of the people. I believe a newspaper should be more than a business enterprise. It should also be the champion and protector of the public interest and defender of the people's rights. I am not unmindful that I owe the success of The Day in large degree to the confidence and support of the people of Eastern Connecticut, and I believe the profits of the large business I have created with their help should, except for the provisions I have made for my dear wife and for my children, be returned to the community for the purposes hereinafter provided. For this reason I have created the following trusts. It is my hope that there will be a substantial increase in the profits of the Day Trust by reason of the increase in the size of its field and that through this means large sums will be available to the Foundation hereinafter described. Much of my success in operating The Day Publishing Company has been due to the loyalty and assistance of its employees. Much of any future success is equally dependent upon those employed. I authorize liberal compensation and various forms of assistance and rewards, such as insurance, bonuses and pensions, be established by the Day Trustees, hereinafter described, so far as they in their discretion consider that wise management permits.

ARTICLE SECOND. All debts, expenses, cost of administration, and taxes are to be paid; first, from property other than my stock in The Day Publishing Company owned by me at the date of my death; second, from dividends declared on stock of The Day Publishing Company out of surplus of that Company existing at the time of my death; and, third, out of income received in the remainder of the year of my death and the year following, including dividends declared during said time on stock of The Day Publishing Company out of its earnings during that period. I desire to avoid, if possible, a pledge or sale of any of The Day Publishing Company stock.

ARTICLE THIRD. I charge my executors with distributing to the Foundation, as hereinafter defined, in lieu of any statutory allowance, such sums as will permit said Foundation Trustee to pay to my wife one thousand dollars ($1,000.00) each month during the administration of my estate. I authorize my executors to cause the necessary dividends to be declared on The Day Publishing Company stock to effect this purpose. This provision is subordinate to the provisions of Article Second.

ARTICLE FOURTH. I give and bequeath all of my stock in The Day Publishing Company, including all my interest as the same now is or may hereafter be in the six hundred (600) shares of The Day Publishing Company stock in which my wife, Edna S. Bodenwein, by reason of a trust created by me, has an interest, to the trustees hereinafter named, and their successors, in trust (to be known as the Day Trust and said trustees to be known as the Day Trustees), however, for the following uses and purposes:

A. To hold said stock; to manage and operate by means thereof a newspaper to be published in New London, Connecticut, hereinafter referred to as "The Day", and morning or Sunday newspapers, or both, should the growth in the field or competition warrant it: to so manage said newspaper or newspapers as to provide liberal compensation and various forms of assistance and rewards, such as insurance, bonuses, and pensions, to its employees; to pay sufficient salaries to assure a high type of executives and skilled writers and workmen; to make provision for providing in the course of time a new building to house the paper and such other tenants as they consider it desirable to provide space for, such building to be distinctive in character, a credit to the City architecturally, and an evidence of a farsighted policy; to constantly improve and maintain the mechanical plant used for publishing the paper; to maintain reasonable reserves for all of the above and for unforeseen contingencies, including taxes; said provisions as to compensation, assistance, and rewards to employees, salaries to executives, the erection of a building, and the maintenance of reserves are to be in every respect at the discretion of said trustees, and said trustees to be mindful always, in making such expenditures or reserves therefor, of my desire that the Foundation receive sufficient funds to pay the sums hereinafter provided for my wife and children: to annually determine the net income from said business over and above all expenditures and reserves: to pay out of said net income all taxes and expenses in connection with the trust, and pay all remaining net income to The National Bank of Commerce, as Trustee, as hereinafter set forth, of The Bodenwein Public Benevolent Foundation.

B. In the event that the Trustees of the Day Trust shall cease to publish a newspaper in New London, Connecticut, or fail to pay to said Bank, as said Trustee, in each of any two successive calendar years following the year after the year of my death the sum of twenty-five thousand dollars ($25,000.00), then said trust shall terminate as soon thereafter as said trustees can, in their reasonable discretion, sell said stock or the property held in lieu thereof, the terms of said sale to be approved by the Probate Court, and said trustees shall then forthwith thereafter pay all sums properly payable for taxes and expenses connected with the administration of said trust and pay over all of the principal and income remaining to said The National Bank of Commerce, as said Trustee of The Bodenwein Public Benevolent Foundation, hereinafter called the Foundation.

C. Until the termination of the Day Trust, the Trustees of the Day Trust shall consist of five trustees, one and only one of whom shall be a director of The National Bank of Commerce, two (but not more than two) of whom must be exclusively employed in publishing the newspaper published by said Day Trust. Vacancies may be filled, if done within sixty (60) days, by majority vote of the survivors, except that said Bank shall fill any vacancy as to the Bank Trustee. In event of the failure by said Bank or said trustees to fill such vacancy within sixty (60) days then such vacancy shall be filled by the Probate Court of the State of Connecticut having jurisdiction of the trusts herein created, observing, however, the intentions of this instrument in reference thereto. That trustee who is a Director of The National Bank of Commerce, or is an employee trustee, shall cease to be such upon ceasing to be such director or employee. Those acting as Directors of The Day Publishing Company at the time of my death shall be the original trustees. If at such time there are less than five, any vacancy shall be filled as aforesaid. The agreement of a majority of the trustees shall determine all matters, except that while there is any vacancy, the approval of all shall be required. Successor trustees shall have the same power as original trustees. The Trustees of the Day Trust shall hold a meeting at least once a month at such time as they determine, and each trustee shall receive for each such meeting attended by him the sum of one hundred dollars ($100.00) for a total of not more than twelve (12) meetings in any calendar year, and the sum of twelve hundred dollars ($1200.00) in any calendar year received in respect to such meetings shall be the maximum amount which any trustee shall receive for all of his services performed during such calendar year, except that in any year when the Day Trustees pay to the Trustee of The Bodenwein Public Benevolent Foundation one hundred thousand dollars ($100,000.00), then each of them shall be entitled to additional reasonable compensation. Employee trustees shall be entitled to compensation as trustees in addition to such sums as they are properly entitled to for their services as employees without regard to duplication of services. My son, Gordon Bodenwein, is now employed by The Day Publishing Company. Although I give full discretion to my trustees, I trust and believe that at some future date his services may justify his being employed as publisher and being made a trustee.

ARTICLE FIFTH. I give, devise, and bequeath any sums or other property paid over or transferred to said The National Bank of Commerce by my Trustees of the Day Trust in trust (to be known as The Bodenwein Public Benevolent Foundation), however, for the following uses and purposes:

A. To hold, manage, invest, and reinvest said trust estate, receiving the issues, profits, and income thereof; and after paying all taxes, disbursements, charges, and expenses incident to such trust and trust estate properly chargeable against the principal and income, to thereafter expend the income and principal of said trust in the following manner, exhausting available income, however, before disbursing principal:

B. To pay nine-tenths (9/10) of the same to my wife, Edna S. Bodenwein, and to my children, Gordon Bodenwein and Elizabeth B. Miles, so long as all of them are living, said sums to be paid annually or more often, one-half of the same to be paid my wife, the other one-half to be divided equally between my two children. Upon the death of my son, during the period thereafter that he is survived by my wife and my daughter, said sum shall be divided equally between them. The same shall be true as to my son and my wife if my daughter dies leaving them surviving. Upon the death of my wife said sum shall then be divided equally between my children so long as they are both living. During any time when only my wife or my son or my daughter is living, then all of said sum shall be paid to such survivor during his or her life. The trusts created in this paragraph shall terminate upon the death of the last survivor of my wife and my said children.

C. After making payments as aforesaid then all remaining net income and principal shall be paid or expended as follows: Said Trustee, by a vote of a majority of its Board of Directors, shall determine upon a use within the limitations hereinafter provided, and shall determine the amount to be utilized for such purpose, and the manner in which it shall be made available. The uses to which said Trustee is restricted are the following:

(a) Payments may be made to the Town or City of New London, the Town of Groton, the Town of Waterford, or any town contiguous to any of the same, or any town or city in the State of Connecticut in which any newspaper published by the Day Trustees has a substantial circulation, providing said payment is made for a purpose exclusively public; or said Trustee may expend said sum for any exclusively public purpose in respect to any of said towns or cities:

(b) Payments may be made to any corporation organized under the laws of the State of Connecticut, providing said corporation is engaged solely in religious, charitable, scientific, or educational purposes, and providing that the sums so paid are restricted to the use exclusively for one or more of such purposes within one or more of the towns or cities above described; or said trustees may expend any sum for such purposes. No such trustee or corporation shall be engaged in carrying on propaganda or influencing legislation, nor shall the earnings of any such corporation inure to the benefit of any stockholder or individual. Said Trustee should not make a large accumulation before providing funds for any of the above purposes but should utilize small sums at the same time that it may accumulate amounts for objects requiring large sums.

D. In the event of the termination of the Day Trust then, although paragraphs C, (a), and (b) shall still be applicable, the distributions provided for by said paragraphs shall thereafter be made out of income and not out of principal.

E. Said Bank, in the investment of trust funds, shall be limited to those investments which are legal for the investment of trust funds under the laws of the State of Connecticut as such laws exist at the time of making any such investment as to seventy-five per cent (75%) of said trust funds but may invest the remaining twenty-five per cent (25%) irrespective of any statutory limitation. If at any time more than twenty-five per cent (25%) of said trust funds are invested in investments other than those legal for the investment of trust funds under the laws of the State of Connecticut, said Bank shall have a reasonable time in which to dispose of said excess. Said percentages shall be so construed as to apply to the trust funds as the same exist from time to time.

ARTICLE SIXTH. All the rest, residue, and remainder of my property I give to my wife, Edna S. Bodenwein.

ARTICLE SEVENTH. No bond shall be required of any executor or of any trustee named hereunder, or of any successor trustee to any trustee named hereunder, except that a reasonable bond shall be procured by the Day Trustees, at the expense of said Trust, as to any of said Trustees holding funds or negotiable securities of the Day Trust.

ARTICLE EIGHTH. In the event that, in the opinion of the Day Trustees, there is a substantial, justifiable saving, at any time, from the standpoint of taxes, by having The Day Publishing Company dissolved and its assets held by the Day Trustees, or in having the sums hereinabove to be paid by The Bodenwein Public Benevolent Foundation to my wife and children paid to them by the Day Trust, then in that event the trusts hereinabove created shall be so construed as to permit the Day Trustees to hold directly the assets of The Day Publishing Company rather than to hold the stock of The Day Publishing Company and to permit them to make the distributions to my wife and children which otherwise will be made by The Bodenwein Public Benevolent Foundation.

ARTICLE NINTH. I appoint those who at the time of my death are qualified to act as the Trustees of the Day Trust the executors of this will.

ARTICLE TENTH. I hereby revoke all wills heretofore made by me.

IN WITNESS WHEREOF I have hereunto set my hand and seal this 24 day of October, 1938.

THEODORE BODENWEIN [SEAL]

Signer, sealed, and declared to be his last will and testament by the above named testator, Theodore Bodenwein, in the presence of us, who, in his presence and at his request and in the presence of each other, have hereunto subscribed our names as witnesses.

JAMES M. SHAY DDS
GEORGE E. CLAPP
JOSEPHINE L. GOMES

State of Connecticut
SS. New London, Oct. 24, 1938.
County of New London

The undersigned, James M. Shay DDS George E. Clapp, and Josephine L. Gomes, being duly sworn, depose and say that they witnessed the within will of the within named testator, Theodore Bodenwein, and subscribed the same in his presence and at his request and in the presence of each other; that the said Theodore Bodenwein, at the time of the execution of said will, appeared to them to be of full age and of sound mind and memory; and that he signed said will and declared the same to be his last will and testament in their presence; and that they make this affidavit at the request of said testator.

JAMES M. SHAY DDS
GEORGE E. CLAPP
JOSEPHINE L. GOMES

Subscribed and sworn to, at the request of the within named testator, Theodore Bodenwein, the day and year above written, before me,

ERNEST L. WHITON
Notary Public

INDEX

B

C

D

G

H

I

J

K

L

Mc

M

N

Q

R

S

T

U

Y

Z